TRANSITRÄUME
TRANSIT SPACES

EDITION BAUHAUS BAND 19 HERAUSGEGEBEN VON DER STIFTUNG BAUHAUS DESSAU

BAUHAUS KOLLEG V

Teilnehmer Participants: Zeigam Azizov, Ariel Barbosa, Maja Ciric, Martin Cagno, Ruben Reis Dias, Anne Deschka, Wael Fahmy, Slava Filimonau, Leonardo Finotti, Jacek Gadecki, Nina Gribat, Ivana Jaksic, Samuel G. R. Johnston, Angela Harutyunyan, Tanya Keskevich, Kathleen Lane, Vanja Larberg, Kate Nelson, Linda Hilfing Nielsen, Akari Nishii, Vladan Paunovic, Diane Pfeiffer, Ana Maria Pradilla Posada, Maximiliano Piperno, Anastassia Rejepp, Joanne Richardson, Carolin Schröder, Olga Shchukina, Oleksandr Svetlov, Barbara Sterk, Elena Trubina, Vadim Vetrov, Vania Valkova, Marcena Zajaczkowska ▪ Leiter Advisers: Regina Bittner, Wilfried Hackenbroich, Kai Vöckler ▪ Wissenschaftliche Mitarbeiter Research collaborators: Silke Steets, Bastian Lange ▪ Management: Ina Goegel

 ▪ Übersetzung Translation Echoo Konferenzdolmetschen, www.echoo.de ▪ Buchgestaltung Book design Sven Schrape ▪ Lithographie Lithography Galrev Druck- und Verlagsgesellschaft, Berlin ▪ Druck und Bindung Printing and binding bookwise, München ▪ Gedruckt auf säurefreiem und chlorfrei gebleichtem Papier Printed on acid-free and non-chlorine bleached paper ▪ ISBN 3-936314-80-2

HERAUSGEGEBEN VON EDITED BY
REGINA BITTNER / WILFRIED HACKENBROICH / KAI VÖCKLER

TRANSITRÄUME
TRANSIT SPACES

FRANKFURT/ODER-POZNAN // WARSCHAU // BREST // MINSK // SMOLENSK // MOSKAU
FRANKFURT/ODER-POZNAN // WARSAW // BREST // MINSK // SMOLENSK // MOSCOW

JOVIS

INHALT CONTENTS

VORWORT

OMAR AKBAR

„Transiträume" – mit diesem Begriff werden zumeist Orte des Durchgangs wie Flughäfen, Raststätten und Bahnhöfe assoziiert. Es sind Zwischenstationen auf dem Weg von A nach B. Das Bauhaus Kolleg V wählte nicht ohne Grund diesen Begriff für ein postgraduales Programm aus, das sich mit dem Wandel der Städte im östlichen Europa auseinander setzte – Städte, die Fallbeispiele für einen spezifischen, radikalen Strukturwandel des urbanen Raumes zu Beginn des 21. Jahrhunderts sind. Hier treffen globale Transformationsprozesse auf gesellschaftspolitische Umbrüche, die im Zusammenhang mit dem Ende der sozialistischen Ostblockstaaten vor rund 15 Jahren stehen. Der Begriff „Transiträume" ist daher eine Metapher für den Übergang, in dem sich die osteuropäischen Regionen zur Zeit befinden.
Konkretes Untersuchungsfeld des Kollegs waren ausgesuchte Orte entlang des Korridors Berlin – Moskau. Als geographische Figur stellt dieser Korridor selbst einen Transitraum dar: Er durchzieht zurückgebliebene Agrarräume genauso wie militärisch abgeriegelte Grenzgebiete, postsozialistische Stadträume und Freihandelszonen; er kreuzt die Wege der Pendler, Arbeitsmigranten und Geschäftsleute. Verkehrskorridore wie dieser bestimmen über Zugehörigkeit oder Abkopplung von aktuellen urbanen Entwicklungen und damit über Lebenschancen. Sie stehen für eine selektive Integration in das Neue Europa.
Das Programm „Transiträume" bildete den Auftakt einer über drei Jahre gehenden Themensequenz, die sich mit neuen Relationen zwischen Stadt und Raum, Ort und Identität im Kontext globalen Strukturwandels auseinander setzt. Das Bauhaus Kolleg ist ein internationales „Urban-Studies-Programm" für Architekten, Planer, Künstler und Kulturwissenschaftler. Es bietet einen besonderen Arbeitsrahmen an. Die hier versammelten Disziplinen und Kulturen erlauben einen transdisziplinären und transnationalen Zugang zum Thema Stadt.
Was der vorliegende Band vereint, sind Momentaufnahmen, Untersuchungen und Reflexionen. Sie bieten wesentliche Einblicke in die urbanen Dynamiken und räumlichen Veränderungen osteuropäischer Städte zwischen sozialistischem Erbe und globalem Kapitalismus – eine Anthropologie postsozialistischer Stadtentwicklung.

PREFACE

OMAR AKBAR

"Transit spaces" are mostly associated with airports, motorway service areas and railway stations. They are stopovers somewhere on the way from A to B. It was no accident that the Bauhaus Kolleg V should have chosen this heading for a post-graduate programme to examine the changes taking place in eastern Europe cities that serve as case studies of a specific form of radical urban structural change in the early 21st century. In these cities, global transformation processes are running head-on into the social upheavals brought about by the collapse of the socialist Eastern bloc states some 15 years ago. The term "transit spaces" is thus a metaphor for the transitional phase the eastern European regions are currently undergoing.

The Kolleg studied a selection of places along the corridor connecting Berlin with Moscow. As a geographical figure, this corridor itself constitutes a transit space. It passes through backward agricultural areas as well as border areas cordoned off by the military, post-socialist urban areas and free-trade zones; it also crosses the routes taken by commuters, migrant labourers and businessmen. Transport corridors of this kind determine whether people and places are linked into urban developments or separated from them, thus deciding on their prospects for the future. They stand for integration into the New Europe on a selective basis.

The "Transit Spaces" programme marked the start of a three-year series of topics examining new relationships between city, space, place and identity against the backdrop of global structural change. The Bauhaus Kolleg is an international urban studies programme for architects, planners, artists and cultural scientists. The framework provided for its studies is special in that the disciplines and cultures it brings together pave the way for a trans-disciplinary and trans-national approach to city-related issues.

This volume combines snapshots, investigations and reflections that offer telling insights into the urban dynamics and spatial changes affecting eastern European cities that are grappling both with their socialist heritage and global capitalism. It thus constitutes an anthropology of post-socialist urban development.

TRANSITRÄUME – TERRAINS OF UNCERTAINTY

REGINA BITTNER

Wer im Herbst 2003 die Grenze zwischen Frankfurt/Oder und Slubice überqueren wollte, musste mit langen Warteschlangen von Lkws rechnen. Oft kalkulierten die Fahrer, die den Warenaustausch zwischen Ost und West gewährleisteten, bis zu 48 Stunden Wartezeit ein, ehe sie die Grenzposten passieren konnten. Hatten sie es geschafft, warteten auf der anderen Seite unzählige Dienstleister: kleine Hotels, Nachtbars und Tankstellen, Bistros und Grillbuden, Gartenzwergläden und Prostituierte. Die E30 zwischen Frankfurt/Oder, Slubice und Warschau war ein Paradies für Kleinunternehmer jeder Art. Hier im EU-Erwartungsland im Westteil Polens ist die Straße der eigentliche Agglomerationsraum. Vom Waren-, Arbeitsmigranten- und Kapitalstrom, der auf dieser Strecke fließt, leben die anliegenden Orte und Gemeinden. Die Landstraße hat hier den Kapitalismus angekurbelt. Wenn die EU-finanzierte Autobahn die alte Landstraße ersetzt, hat das Ringen um einen Platz an der Ausfahrt längst stattgefunden. In Warschau ist die Orientierung nach dem Zentrum schwieriger, verliert doch der Kulturpalast inmitten der neuen Banken, Versicherungs- und Hotelriesen seine vertikale Dominanz. Aus der monumentalen Stadt wird ein postindustrielles Downtown. Im Westteil, Richtung Weißrussland, ist die E30 nahezu verkehrsfrei. Weder Servicestationen noch postindustrielle Containerlandschaften säumen den Straßenrand: Ostpolen gehört mittlerweile zu den ärmsten Regionen des neuen Europa. An dessen Grenze wird aufgerüstet. Brest liegt dahinter und hat, wie der Vizebürgermeister uns versichert, die besondere Aufgabe, Grenzpolizei zu spielen. EU-Gelder fließen in die neue/alte Festungsstadt, um zwischen dem neuen Europa und dem Osten eine sichere Grenze zu garantieren. In den Räumen der Stadtverwaltung regiert noch immer die Nomenklatura, während viele Straßen Brests am Abend in Dunkelheit liegen. Am Denkmal für die gefallenen Soldaten bietet einer der wenigen Kleinunternehmer Familienfotos an – Jugendliche mit adidas-Shirts, Hochzeitspaare, Veteranen. Aus der E30 wird die M1, und zum ersten Mal taucht auf dem Straßenschild Moskau auf; noch mehr als 1 000 Kilometer. Minsk, die Hauptstadt Weißrusslands, erinnert an Gemälde des sozialistischen Realismus. Eher bruchlos wird die monumentale Stadt des Sozialismus im Zentrum fortgebaut. Scharen von vor allem weiblichen Arbeitskräften sorgen rund um die Uhr für Sauberkeit und Ordnung. Die abendliche Illumination verstärkt diese Inszenierung. Die Studenten amüsieren sich über die jüngsten Neubauten entlang der Skarina-Avenue, der Prachtstraße, und bevorzugen die Inseln westlichen Lebensstils. In der Auseinandersetzung um die symbolische Repräsentation der postsozialistischen Metropole haben schon mehrere städtische Architekten ihren Posten

TRANSIT SPACES – TERRAINS OF UNCERTAINTY

REGINA BITTNER

Anyone wanting to cross the border from Frankfurt/Oder to Slubice in autumn 2003 had to reckon with long queues of trucks. The drivers who assure the exchange of goods between East and West often had to allow for a wait of up to 48 hours before they could pass the border checkpoints. Once they had done so, countless service providers – small hotels, all-night bars, filling stations, bistros, grills, shops selling garden gnomes, prostitutes – awaited them on the other side. The E30 between Frankfurt/Oder, Slubice and Warsaw was a paradise for small traders of every kind. Here in the western part of EU applicant Poland the road is the actual agglomeration area. The adjacent localities and communities make their living from the stream of goods, migrant workers and capital that flows along this route. Here it is the road that has given capitalism its boost. By the time the EU-financed motorway replaces the old road the struggle for a place at the exit will have long been over. In Warsaw it is harder to take one's bearings from the centre, as the Palace of Culture has lost its vertical dominance amid the new high-rise buildings of banks, insurance companies and hotels. The monumental city is becoming a post-industrial downtown area. In the eastern part, in the direction of Belarus, the E30 is almost free of traffic. Neither service stations nor post-industrial container landscapes line the edge of the road. Eastern Poland is now one of the poorest regions of the new Europe. At its border new installations are under construction. Brest lies beyond and has, the deputy mayor assures us, the special task of playing the frontier guard. EU funding is flowing into the new/old fortress city in order to guarantee a secure border between the new Europe and the East. In the offices at City Hall the nomenklatura still rules, whereas in the evening many of Brest's streets are plunged in darkness. At the war memorial one of the few small traders offers to take people's photos – young people in adidas shirts, newlyweds, veterans. The E30 becomes the M1, and we see the first signpost to mention Moscow, which is still more than 1,000 kilometres off. Minsk, the capital of Belarus, is reminiscent of a Socialist Realist painting. In the centre of this monumental socialist city building continues apace. Hosts of mainly female workers ensure round-the-clock tidiness. The evening illumination reinforces the theatrical effect. The students make fun of the latest buildings along Skarina Avenue, the central boulevard, and prefer to patronise the islands of Western lifestyle. In the disputes over the symbolic representation of a post-socialist metropolis several urban architects have already lost their jobs, and at our meeting with the municipal authorities the interpreter was suddenly replaced for not striking the right official note.

verloren, und auch bei unserem Treffen mit der Stadtverwaltung wurde die Übersetzerin plötzlich ausgewechselt, weil sie den offiziellen Ton nicht traf.
Erneut passieren wir die Grenze, diesmal nach Russland. Auf dem Weg nach Smolensk liegt Katyn: Erst Anfang der 1990er Jahre wurde auf Druck der polnischen Regierung zum Andenken an die Massenexekutionen an Polen und Russen in dem Kiefernwald eine Gedenkstätte errichtet. Auf Kupfertafeln sind die Namen der erschossenen Polen genau dokumentiert, während für die russischen Opfer nur eine Zahl steht. Hier, so schildert eine unserer russischen Mitreisenden, trafen die zwei totalitären Regimes des 20. Jahrhunderts zusammen, in diesem „Totenwald" jenseits der M1. Im Smolensker Mikrorayon Papovka/Kiseljowka zerstiebt der kollektive Traum gleicher Lebensverhältnisse, die maroden, aber privatisierten Plattenbauten und die zu Kiosken umfunktionierten Garagen zeugen davon. Dazwischen verkaufen Rentnerinnen aus den umliegenden Datschas ihr selbst angebautes Gemüse. Früher hätte sich wohl keiner der ehemaligen Arbeiter, Lehrer und Ingenieure, die in den 1970er Jahren in die modernen Wohnungen des Mikrorayons eingezogen waren, vorstellen können, an der Ecke zu stehen und Sachen zu verkaufen. Die Transition vom Sozialismus in den Kapitalismus hatten sie sich anders gedacht.
Schon 100 Kilometer vor Moskau bekommt die Straße eine andere Dynamik: Tankstellen, Märkte, suburbane Villensiedlungen, umgeben von hohen Zäunen. Mega-Shopping-Malls wie IKEA, Dienstleistungs- und Logistikareale, riesige Wohngebiete bilden die Ringe, die man durchfährt, um ins Zentrum zu gelangen.
Am nächsten Morgen ist der U-Bahnhof verstopft von Menschenmassen, Ismailowski-Park, in den 1980er Jahren das Herzstück des Olympiadorfs, zu einer Zeit, als Moskau noch Hauptstadt einer Supermacht war; er ist umgeben von scheinbar endlosen Kioskmärkten. Hierher kommen die Moskauer am Wochenende zum Einkaufen, denn die neuen Luxusboutiquen im Zentrum wenden sich nur an einen kleinen Kundenkreis. Die Waren stammen zumeist aus China und der Türkei. Moskau ist eine Drehscheibe des transnationalen Pendlerhandels: Hier treffen aus allen Regionen Russlands Busse mit Händlern ein, die Waren in großer Stückzahl erwerben wollen, um sie dann auf ihren heimischen Märkten weiterzuverkaufen. Moskau sei eher eine asiatische Stadt, meint der Architekt Andrej Bokov. Das betrifft die ungeheure Dynamik, mit der die Stadt immer wieder umgeordnet wird. Nach Stalins Monumentalbauten ist heute ein neuer Ring gigantischer Hochhäuser in Planung: Zumindest stilistisch teilen sie vieles mit ihren historischen Vorläufern. Nicht umsonst spricht Bart Goldhoorn hier von kapitalistischem Realismus.[1]
Die Notizen stammen aus einem Reisetagebuch. Sie umreißen knapp die Stationen entlang des Korridors zwischen Berlin und Moskau. Es sind Eindrücke von einer der Forschungsreisen, die das Postgraduiertenkolleg „Transiträume" der Stiftung „Bauhaus Dessau" – eine internationale Gruppe von Architekten, Künstlern, Soziologen und Planern – zwischen Sommer 2003 und Frühjahr 2004 unternommen hatte. Die Eintragungen beziehen sich auf die sieben Orte und Themen, die entlang des Korridors zwischen Berlin und Moskau ausgewählt worden sind: die Transformation des deutsch-polnischen Grenzraumes zwischen Frankfurt/Oder und Slubice, neue städtische Szenen in Warschau, der Umbau von Brest zur Grenzstadt im erweiterten Europa, der Wandel des öffentlichen Raumes in Minsk, die Zukunft des sozialistischen

Again we cross a frontier, this time into Russia. On the road to Smolensk lies Katyn. Not until the early 1990s, under pressure from the Polish government, was a memorial set up in the pine forest in memory of the Poles and Russians shot there in mass executions. The names of the murdered Poles are precisely documented on copper plaques, whereas for the Russian victims there is only a number. Here, one of our Russian fellow travellers tells us, the two totalitarian regimes of the 20th century met in this "forest of death" beyond the M1. In the Smolensk microrayon of Papovka/ Kiselyovka the collective dream of equal living conditions for all has dissipated, as the dilapidated (but privatised) concrete blocks and the garages doing duty for kiosks testify. In between old women from the surrounding dachas sell their home-grown vegetable produce. Probably none of the former workers, teachers, and engineers who had moved into the modern flats of the microrayon in the 1970s ever dreamed that one day they would stand at the street corner peddling their wares. They never thought the transition from socialism to capitalism would be like this.

When we are still 100 kilometres from Moscow the road acquires another dynamic: filling stations, markets, and residential suburbs surrounded by high fences. Mega shopping malls like IKEA, service and storage areas, and sprawling housing estates form the rings you have to pass through to get to the centre.

The next morning the metro station is crammed with people, while Ismailovski Park, the heart of the Olympic Village in the 1980s when Moscow was still the capital of a superpower, is surrounded by a seemingly endless series of open-air markets. This is where Muscovites come to shop at the weekends, for the new luxury boutiques in the centre cater to a very small clientele. The goods on sale here mainly come from China and Turkey. Moscow is a hub of the cross-border shuttle trade: buses arrive here from all regions of Russia, filled with traders seeking to buy up goods in bulk for resale in their domestic markets. Moscow is more of an Asian city, the architect Andrei Bokov tells us. He is referring to the enormous dynamism with which the city is constantly being reordered. After Stalin's monumental buildings a new ring of huge high-rise buildings is currently being planned. They have a lot in common with their historical predecessors, at least in a stylistic sense. It is not for nothing that Bart Goldhoorn talks of capitalist realism in this context.[1]

Notes from a travel diary sketching the way stations along the corridor between Berlin and Moscow record impressions of one of the study trips undertaken as part of the post-graduate course on "Transit spaces" held by the Bauhaus Dessau Foundation – an international group of architects, artists, sociologists, and planners – between summer 2003 and spring 2004. The entries refer to the seven places and topics selected along the corridor between Berlin and Moscow: the transformation of the German Polish-border area between Frankfurt/Oder and Slubice, new urban scenes in Warsaw, the conversion of Brest into a frontier town in an enlarged Europe, the transformation of the public space in Minsk, the future of the socialist urban model of the "microrayon" in Smolensk, the role of kiosks in Russia's capitalism, and the change in Moscow's urban culture.

We were just as mindful of the historical significance of this route – it is essentially that taken by Napoleon's Grande Armée and later by the German Army Group Centre in the Second World War – and of its new symbolic and political importance in

Stadtmodells „Mikrorayon" in Smolensk, die Rolle der Kioske in Russlands Kapitalismus sowie die Veränderung der urbanen Kultur in Moskau.
Das historische Gewicht der Achse war uns dabei ebenso bewusst – es ist in etwa der Weg der Napoleonischen Armee und stimmt mit der Route der Heeresgruppe Mitte im Zweiten Weltkrieg nahezu überein – wie deren neue symbolische und raumpolitische Bedeutung im Kontext der EU-Osterweiterung. Zudem trieb uns der Zweifel darüber an, ob die evolutionistische Perspektive der Transition, im Sinne eines klar gezeichneten Weges des Übergangs vom Sozialismus zum Kapitalismus, mit der Alltagsrealität der zu untersuchenden Städte in Deckung zu bringen ist. Oder ob nicht andere Denkfiguren, Metaphern und Begriffe, die außerhalb der gewohnten kulturellen Kartierung in West und Ost liegen, angemessener wären? Über die Bestimmung von Korridoren wird heute eine Vision zukünftiger Entwicklung im europäischen Raum formuliert. Mobilität wird auf diese Weise entlang von und hin zu Räumen potentiellen Wachstums gesteuert. Zugangs-, Anschluss- und Ausschlussbedingungen für Regionen und Räume sind definiert, neue Beziehungen zwischen Nachbarschaften, Regionen, lokalen Märkten, Unternehmen und Aktivitäten entstehen.
Die vier Freiheiten, die als Kernpunkte der europäischen Integrationsvereinbarungen formuliert sind, basieren auf der Bewegung von Menschen, Gütern, Kapital und Dienstleistungen. Die Entscheidung, wer mit wem im neuen europäischen Raum verbunden wird, ist auch eine Entscheidung darüber, wie in Zukunft gearbeitet, gelebt und gereist wird. Dabei entwickeln sich neue Relationen zwischen Mobilität und urbanem Raum. Insofern ist der Korridor zugleich Metapher für ein neues Raumregime: „Er ist ein Raum verdichteter Bewegung, mit Staus und Knotenpunkten. Er ist ein beeindruckender Transitraum mit Kontakthöfen und Relaisstationen (...). Die Städte, die am *metropolitan corridor* liegen, haben mehr miteinander zu tun als mit den Provinzen, die sie umgeben. (...) Während durch den Korridor die zivile Armada der Trucks rollt, leuchtet in der Dunkelheit, die jenseits des Korridors herrscht, der Mond. (...) In den Korridoren wächst das urbane Europa zusammen, aber an seinen Rändern staut sich der Neid und die Wut der Zurückgebliebenen und Zu-kurz-Gekommenen. Diese Ungleichzeitigkeit der Zeit ist bedrohlicher als der ‚*clash of civilisations*'."[2]
Zwei gegensätzliche Tendenzen sind es, die in der heutigen Realität ökonomischer Globalisierung die Zukunft des Postsozialismus bestimmen werden: Fragmentierung und Integration. Während ausgewählte Orte durch Verbindungen zu den Zentren des Kapitals in die globale Ökonomie inkorporiert sind, geraten andere in den Zustand der Bedeutungslosigkeit. Welche räumliche Gestalt gewinnt dieses neue Europa, in dem sich der Übergang vom Sozialismus zum Kapitalismus unter den Bedingungen einer globalisierten Ökonomie vollzieht? Ist der Korridor ein Fallbeispiel für eine Entwicklung, bei der unter dem Druck des globalen Finanzkapitalismus eine neue Phase des Zentrum-Peripherie-Widerspruchs in der sozialen Geographie der Kapitalakkumulation zu beobachten ist?
Das Programm „Transiträume" hat nach generativen Mustern räumlicher Agglomeration gesucht, die in Reaktion auf die Mobilisierung und Fragmentierung der postsozialistischen Landschaft entstanden sind. Es beschäftigte sich mit den Effekten der transnationalen Durchzugsterritorien auf lokaler Ebene, im Hinblick auf neue Raummuster und Relationen, auf Netzwerke und Mechanismen der sozialen Integration.

the context of the EU eastern enlargement. We were also driven by doubts as to whether the evolutionary aspect of the transition, in the sense of a clearly marked path from socialism to capitalism, could be brought into line with the everyday reality of the cities to be studied. Or whether other intellectual constructs, metaphors and concepts lying outside of the usual cultural division into West and East might not be more appropriate?

A vision of Europe's future spatial development is now being formulated in terms of corridors. In this way mobility is guided along and towards areas of potential growth. Conditions for accessing, connecting and excluding regions and spaces are defined, while new contacts are established between neighbourhoods, regions, local markets, enterprises and activities.

The four freedoms enshrined in the European integration agreements concern the movement of people, goods, capital and services. The decision as to who is to be linked with whom in the new European space is also a decision about how we are going to work, live and travel in future. New relations will develop between mobility and urban space. In this sense the corridor is also a metaphor for a new spatial regime: "It is an area of compressed movement, with traffic jams and nodal points. It is an impressive transit space with contact zones and relay stations ... The cities lying along the metropolitan corridor have more to do with one another than with the provinces that surround them. ... While the civilian armada of trucks rolls through the corridor, in the brooding darkness beyond the moon is shining ... In the corridors urban Europe is growing together, but at its fringes the pent-up envy and fury of the left behind and the empty-handed is mounting. This temporal imbalance is a greater threat than the 'clash of civilisations'."[2] There are two opposing tendencies that will determine the future of post-socialism in the present realities created by economic globalisation: fragmentation and integration. While some places are incorporated in the global economy through their links to the centres of capital, others have declined into a state of insignificance. What spatial form will be assumed by this new Europe, in which the transition from socialism to capitalism is taking place under the conditions of a globalized economy? Is the corridor a sample case of a development in which, under the pressure of global finance capitalism, a new phase of the centre-periphery contradiction is to be observed in the social geography of capital accumulation?

The "Transit spaces" programme sought for generative models of spatial agglomeration which have arisen as a reaction to the mobilisation and fragmentation of the post-socialist landscape. It dealt with the effects of the cross-border transit territories at local level, with regard to new spatial patterns and relations, to networks and mechanisms of social integration. It focused particularly on the relationship between city and space, place and identity in post-socialist cities. These are urban spaces in which transition means above all two things: insecurity and uncertainty.

TRANSITION

"Through the flow of foreign capital, open foreign exchange markets and domestic economic liberalisation most socialist countries are increasingly integrated into the global political economy. For most of them the decade of transition was a rollercoaster ride. Moscow has earned a reputation of the second most expensive city in

Es hat sich insbesondere mit dem Verhältnis zwischen Stadt und Raum, Ort und Identität in postsozialistischen Städten auseinander gesetzt. Das sind urbane Räume, in denen Transition vor allem eines bedeutet: Unsicherheit und Ungewissheit.

TRANSITION

„Through the flow of foreign capital, open foreign exchange markets and domestic economic liberalization most socialist countries are increasingly integrated into the global political economy. For most of them the decade of transition was a roller-coaster ride. Moscow has earned a reputation of the second most expensive city in the world whereas thousands of Russians where paid in irons and frying pans for their work. Prague and Budapest have turned into the new Meccas of Eastern Europe luring tourists and businessmen with low costs and reasonable service, whereas neighbours are killing each other in former Yugoslavia."[3]

„Transiträume" steht in Relation zu Transition, jenem Begriff, um den die osteuropäischen Transformationsdebatten der letzten 15 Jahre kreisten und mit dem der Prozess des Übergangs ehemaliger Länder des Ostblocks nach dem Fall des Eisernen Vorhangs vom Sozialismus zum Kapitalismus beschrieben wird. Hauptprinzipien des Paradigmas der Transition waren die möglichst rasche Privatisierung, Liberalisierung und Demokratisierung. Dahinter verbarg sich die Vorstellung, dass sich die ost- bzw. mittelosteuropäischen Transformationsländer auf einer Art Nachholweg befinden würden. Zwar seien die Ausgangsbedingungen sehr unterschiedlich, aber die Richtung des Veränderungsprozesses sowie die Beschaffenheit des Ziels der Transformation seien weitgehend bekannt, da es sich ja um Spielarten gesellschaftlicher Modernisierung handelte. Das Theorem der „nachholenden Modernisierung", wie Wolfgang Zapf es benennt, ist in diesem Kontext lange Zeit richtungsweisend gewesen. „Transformation und Transition", schreibt er, „sind Modernisierungsprozesse, die sich von offenen Modernisierungsprozessen dadurch unterscheiden, dass ihr Ziel bekannt ist: die Übernahme, Errichtung und Inkorporation von modernen demokratischen und marktwirtschaftlichen Strukturen."[4]

Nach 15 Jahren Transformationsforschung wird heute zu Recht die Frage gestellt, ob es zulässig war, die Verfassung der westlichen Gesellschaften als Ziel der Transition zu erheben. Und um welches Modell von Kapitalismus handelte es sich, das als Zielgröße formuliert wurde? Anders als zu den Konstitutionsbedingungen westlicher nationalstaatlich verfasster Marktwirtschaften im 19. Jahrhundert waren osteuropäische Gesellschaften mit einem doppelten Strukturwandel konfrontiert: Der Übergang von der Plan- zur Marktwirtschaft verlief unter den Bedingungen einer Globalisierung von Wirtschaft und Finanzkapital. Diese wiederum zog eine Schwächung nationalstaatlicher Regulationsfähigkeit nach sich. Der Nationalstaat wird immer unfähiger, Finanzströme in und aus seinem Territorium zu kontrollieren, bzw. gibt bewusst die Kontrolle in bestimmten ökonomischen Bereichen auf. Osteuropäische Reformpolitik hat sich vor allem unter der Anleitung internationaler Akteure wie dem IWF auf die radikale Liberalisierung der Wirtschaft bezogen. Dabei ging es um die Privatisierung staatlicher Betriebe, die Liberalisierung der Preise sowie des Kapitalverkehrs, um ausländische Investitionen und das nötige Know-how ins Land zu holen. Der Staat sollte lediglich durch Subventionsabbau und Rückzug aus der Geldpolitik zur Haushaltskonsolidie-

the world whereas thousands of Russians were paid in irons and frying pans for their work. Prague and Budapest have turned into the new meccas of Eastern Europe luring tourists and businessmen with low costs and reasonable service, whereas neighbours are killing each other in former Yugoslavia."[3]

"Transit spaces" is related to the concept of transition around which the East European transformation debate of the last fifteen years has revolved and which is used to describe the process of transition from socialism to capitalism in the former countries of the Eastern bloc after the fall of the Iron Curtain. The main principles of the transition paradigm were privatisation, liberalisation and democratisation, to be implemented as fast as possible. The thinking behind this was that the Eastern or Central and East European transformation countries would find themselves with some catching up to do. The starting conditions might be very different, but the direction of the transformation process and the nature of its goal were largely known, since it was just a question of varieties of social modernisation. The theory of "modernising to catch up" (Wolfgang Zapf) for a long time held unquestioned sway in this context. "Transformation and transition," writes Wolfgang Zapf, "are modernisation processes which differ from open modernisation processes in that their goal is known: adoption, erection and incorporation of the modern democratic and market economy structures."[4]

Today, after fifteen years of research into this transformation, the question is rightly being asked as to whether it was right to set up the constitutional model of Western societies as the goal of the transition. And what model of capitalism was it that was supposed to be the goal? Unlike the market economies constitutionally regulated by Western nations in the 19th century, East European societies were confronted with a double structural change. Their transition from a planned to a market economy took place while the economy and finance capital were undergoing globalisation. This weakened the ability of national governments to engage in regulation. National governments are less and less capable of controlling the flow of capital into and out of their territory, or they deliberately surrender control in certain economic sectors. East European reform policy has mainly focused on the radical liberalisation of the economy under the guidance of international actors like the IMF. This meant privatizing state enterprises and liberalising prices and capital movements in order to attract foreign investment and needed know-how into the country. The state was merely to contribute to budget consolidation by reducing subsidies and ceasing to have a monetary policy. "Primacy was given to a free-market policy because such a policy induced, according to the liberal credo, complementary changes in other social fields."[5] These tendencies were later described as shock therapy. Transition here meant no more than the deregulation of the private sector. This excessive faith in market forces went hand in hand with a blindness to non-economic conditions without which reforms cannot be successful. This is why Klaus Müller speaks of a gamble, when state and socially integrative institutions are discredited and government is assigned the negative role of "organising the withdrawal of the state from society, instead of redefining the tasks of politics."[6] This free-market policy brought about almost the opposite of what was intended. In Russia, for example, the liberalisation of capital movements without a sufficient institutional framework led to a massive flight

rung beitragen. „Der Politik des Marktes wurde auch deshalb das Primat eingeräumt, weil sie dem liberalistischen Credo gemäß komplementäre Veränderungen in anderen gesellschaftlichen Bereichen induziert."[5] Diese Tendenzen wurden später auch als Schocktherapie bezeichnet. Transition meinte hier also nicht mehr als die Deregulierung des privaten Sektors. Dieses Übervertrauen in die Kräfte des Marktes ging einher mit einer Blindheit gegenüber den außerökonomischen Bedingungen, ohne die erfolgreiche Reformen nicht zu haben sind. Klaus Müller spricht deshalb von einem Hasardspiel, wenn staatliche und sozialintegrative Institutionen diskreditiert werden und der Politik nur noch eine negative Rolle zugedacht wird: „nämlich den Rückzug des Staates aus der Gesellschaft zu organisieren, anstelle die Aufgaben der Politik neu zu bestimmen."[6] Als Resultat dieser Politik des Marktes sind nahezu gegenteilige Tendenzen zu beobachten: Die Liberalisierung des Kapitalverkehrs ohne ausreichende institutionelle Einbettung hat zum Beispiel in Russland zu einer massiven Kapitalflucht geführt. Anstelle der Ausdifferenzierung von Staat und Wirtschaft sind undurchsichtige Eigentumsverhältnisse bzw. Mischwirtschaften entstanden. Können die Unterschiede in den Transformationspfaden zwischen Mittel- und Osteuropa deshalb vor allem auf das vorhandene bzw. nicht vorhandene institutionelle Rahmenwerk zurückgeführt werden?

Was die ost- und mittelosteuropäischen Länder zunächst gemeinsam haben, ist das Layout der Neukonstitution demokratischer Verhältnisse. Denn aus der Perspektive der Marktliberalen war die Konsolidierung demokratischer Regierungen weniger an die Existenz staatlicher Institutionen als vielmehr einer Zivilgesellschaft gebunden. „Zivilgesellschaft" spielte in den osteuropäischen Revolutionen eine herausragende Rolle und inspirierte dann auch in den 1990er Jahren westliche Gesellschaftskonzepte. Die unterschiedlichen Vorstellungen, die mit diesem Begriff assoziiert wurden, geben Hinweise auf die Verschiedenheit, ja Gegensätzlichkeit der Kontexte, in denen sie Bedeutung erlangten. War „Zivilgesellschaft" ursprünglich das Credo des aufkommenden städtischen Bürgertums in Europa gewesen, mit dem es sich gegen die Aristokratie wehrte, so versetzte der Begriff in den 90er Jahren des 20. Jahrhunderts „nicht nur in Osteuropa, sondern global aufkommende politische und intellektuelle Eliten in schiere Begeisterung". War deren Aktualität in den 1980er Jahren einer Legitimationskrise der sozialistischen Ideen geschuldet, so gab der Fall der Berliner Mauer nach 1989 neuen transnationalen Koalitionen osteuropäischer Eliten neuen Auftrieb. Zudem „steuerte dieses Konzept die Erarbeitung der gesamten institutionellen Gestaltung der postsozialistischen Gesellschaft". Wenn dennoch Ethnologen wie Don Kalb von einem hohen Maß an „Unzivilisiertheit" sprechen, das in den postsozialistischen Staaten zu beobachten ist, so fragt man nach den Gründen. Liegt es an der Tatsache, dass ein westliches Konzept auf nicht-westliche Regionen angewandt wurde? Liegt es an der völlig anderen sozialen Konstellation in den postsozialistischen Gesellschaften, zum Beispiel im Hinblick auf die Existenz einer bürgerlichen Klasse? Es ist wohl nicht so sehr das Dilemma einer willkürlichen Oktroyierung, denn zumindest in Osteuropa existierten eigene zivilgesellschaftliche Traditionen. Vielmehr wurde im mittelosteuropäischen Diskurs „der Begriff zunehmend mit der Fähigkeit assoziiert, den Druck des Marktes zu verinnerlichen und sich diesem anzupassen". Über den Weg der Märkte sollte die Bevölkerung ziviles Verhalten lernen, und gerade priva-

of capital. Instead of clearly defined spheres for the state and the economy, murky forms of ownership and mixed economies came into being.

Can the differences in the transformation courses followed by the Central and East European countries therefore be traced back to the existing or non-existent institutional framework?

What the Eastern or Central and East European countries have in common is the reconstitution of democratic norms. From the point of view of the market liberals the consolidation of democratic governments was linked less to the existence of state institutions than to the existence of civil society. In the East European revolutions "civil society" played an outstanding role and afterwards inspired the Western social concepts of the 1990s. The different ideas that were associated with this concept indicate the differences, indeed the contrasts between the contexts in which they acquired their significance. If "civil society" had originally been the credo of the rising urban bourgeoisie in Europe, who had used it as a defence against the aristocracy, in the 1990s the concept had filled "political and intellectual elites with heady enthusiasm not just in Eastern Europe, but other emerging elites all over the world." If its topicality in the 1980s was due to the crisis of legitimacy experienced by socialist ideas, the fall of the Berlin Wall in 1989 gave new impetus to transnational coalitions of East European elites. Furthermore "this concept guided the overall institutional design of post-socialist society." If ethnologists like Don Kalb speak of the high degree of uncivilised behaviour to be observed in the post-socialist states, we have to ask what the reasons are. Is it because of the fact that a Western concept was applied in non-Western regions? Is it because of the completely different social constellation in the post-socialist societies, for example with regard to the existence of a bourgeois class? It is probably not so much a case of arbitrary imposition, for Eastern Europe at least had its own civil society traditions. It is rather because in Central and East European discourse "the concept was increasingly associated with the ability to internalize the pressure of the market and adapt to it." The markets were to teach the population civil behaviour, and the right to private ownership was considered a universal formula. This meant that civil society as a concept was much more linked with monetarism, so that "the East European revolutions saw themselves mainly as alliances of the market and civil society against the state."[7]

Against the background of this negative view of state regulation and institutionalisation it is not surprising that another assumption concerning the goals of the transition must be critically reviewed. In view of the re-emergence of authoritarian regimes – for example in Belarus – or "feckless pluralism" in a number of post-communist countries, it has proved erroneous to declare liberal democracy the only valid political system. Political scientists like Thomas Carothers therefore speak of the end of the transition paradigm. In contrast to the disappointed attitude of Western observers faced with the failure of democratic reforms in post-socialist states, he proposes a change of perspective. The question of how the democratic transition is proceeding should be replaced by a more open formulation that seeks to find out: "what is happening politically."[8]

So does the key problem of transition today consist in the constitution of institutional orders which could facilitate the coherent development of these disintegrated so-

tes Eigentumsrecht galt als Universalformel. Das heißt, Zivilgesellschaft als Konzept war hier viel stärker mit dem Monetarismus verknüpft, so wie „die osteuropäischen Revolutionen sich vor allem als Bündnisse des Marktes und der Zivilgesellschaft gegen den Staat" verstanden.[7]

Vor dem Hintergrund dieser negativen Fassung staatlicher Regulation und Institutionalisierung muss es nicht verwundern, dass auch eine weitere Vorannahme in Bezug auf die Zielgrößen der Transition kritisch überprüft werden muss: Angesichts des Wiederaufkommens von autoritären Regimes – zum Beispiel in Weißrussland – oder von „feckless pluralism" in einer Reihe von postkommunistischen Ländern hat es sich als Irrtum erwiesen, die liberale Demokratie zur einzig relevanten Politikform zu erklären. Politikwissenschaftler wie Thomas Carothers sprechen deshalb vom Ende des Transition-Paradigmas. Im Gegenzug zu der enttäuschten Haltung westlicher Beobachter angesichts des Scheiterns demokratischer Reformen in postsozialistischen Staaten schlägt er einen Perspektivwechsel vor: Anstelle der Frage, wie die demokratische Transition vorangehe, sollte eine offenere Formulierung treten, die danach sucht: „what is happening politically".[8]

Besteht also heute das zentrale Problem der Transition in der Konstitution institutioneller Ordnungen, die eine kohärente Entwicklung dieser desintegrierten Gesellschaften ermöglichen könnten? Und warum scheinen gerade die Länder Mittelosteuropas erfolgreicher im Hinblick auf die Stabilisierung von Wirtschaft und Demokratie?

DAS NEUE EUROPA

„Back to Europe" ist eine Formel, in der jenseits der politischen und ökonomischen Integrationstendenzen im Rahmen der EU-Osterweiterung noch eine besondere symbolische Bedeutungsebene mitschwingt: Transition wird auch mit Normalisierung gleichgesetzt, und diejenigen Länder, die diesen Prozess am erfolgreichsten vorangetrieben haben, sind nun „normale europäische Länder".

Der pejorative Unterton, der hier anklingt, ist vielfach kritisiert worden, passt er doch in das „Western patronizing cliché according to which the Eastern European post-communist countries are a kind of retarded poor cousins who will be admitted back into the family if they will behave properly".[9] Dennoch hatte die Rückkehr nach Europa für die mittelosteuropäischen Länder nach 1989 eine eigene Legitimität. Denn für sie bedeutete die Zugehörigkeit zum Sowjet-Block eher die gewaltsame Unterbrechung eines europäischen Lebensmodells; die postkommunistische Periode in diesen Ländern wurde auch ein Stück weit als Wiederentdeckung der normalen Zeiten interpretiert. „Hence, the transition to western institutions and values came as a relative success not because westernisation and modernization are universally one and the same, but because the history and the traditions of the CEEC's (Central Eastern European Countries) have always been those of European peoples. For them history has not ended with the fall of communism, it has been resumed after a half century interruption."[10]

„Europäisierung", so Klaus Müller, sei als kulturelle Kodierung der osteuropäischen Transformation aufzufassen. „Rückkehr nach Europa" habe zweifellos den Umbruch von 1989 vorangetrieben, nicht nur als historische Idee, sondern auch als stabilisierendes politisches Umfeld der Transformation. Müller betont jedoch, dass Europäisie-

cieties? And why do the countries of Eastern and Central Europe seem more successful at achieving economic stability and democracy?

THE NEW EUROPE

"Back to Europe" is a formula which contains a certain symbolic level of meaning over and above the processes of political and economic integration involved in the EU's eastern enlargement. Transition is also equated with normalisation, and those countries which have been most successful in pushing this process forward are now "normal European countries."

The pejorative undertone that can be detected here has often been criticised, as it fits in with the "Western patronising cliché according to which the Eastern European post-communist countries are a kind of retarded poor cousins who will be admitted back into the family if they will behave properly."[9] Nevertheless the return to Europe had its own legitimacy for the Central and East European countries after 1989, since they had tended to see membership of the Soviet bloc as a violent interruption of their national lives which had been based on European models, and the post-communist period was interpreted in these countries as a return to normality. "Hence, the transition to western institutions and values came as a relative success not because westernisation and modernisation are universally one and the same, but because the history and the traditions of the CEEC's (Central Eastern European Countries) have always been those of European peoples. For them history has not ended with the fall of communism, it has been resumed after a half century interruption."[10] "Europeanisation," according to Klaus Müller, is to be seen as a cultural code for East European transformation. "Back to Europe" had undoubtedly fuelled the upheavals of 1989, not just as a historical idea, but also as a stabilising political context for the transformation. Müller emphasises, however, that Europeanisation – becoming part of the political geography of the European Union – did not actually mean a return, but, first and foremost, a breach with nationalistic ideologies. And, secondly, Europeanisation is not a question of mentality or culture; for the new members the EU enlargement entailed adapting to a complex institutional, legal and economic framework. But this integration process gained legitimacy for yet another reason. The European social model also acted as a link between the existing egalitarian value structure and the social system, a legacy of socialist modernisation in these countries.[11] Still it remains to be asked, first, whether the underlying explanation of the Europeanisation code and the successes of the Central and East European countries should not be sought mainly in their geographical proximity to Western Europe; and, secondly, what kind of integration are we dealing with in the case of the new member states?

Researchers into development paths often emphasize the differences between the Central and East European countries as determining their post-socialist economic cultures. It is argued that the ex-Soviet economy was organised on monopolistic lines, whereas in Poland and Hungary a number of attempts to decentralize the economy had already been taken even before 1989, so that their existing fragmented economies had better starting conditions for the transition to a market economy. Sociologists also stress the relative strength of civil society and other constellations of actors and elites in these countries as compared to Russia.[12]

rung – das Eintreten in die politische Geographie der Europäischen Union – gerade keine Rückkehr bedeutete, sondern, erstens, einen Bruch mit nationalistischen Ideologien. Und zweitens ist Europäisierung keine Frage der Mentalität oder Kultur; die EU-Erweiterung zog für die neuen Mitglieder die Anpassung an ein komplexes institutionelles, rechtliches und ökonomisches Regelwerk nach sich. Dieser Integrationsprozess gewann aber noch durch ein weiteres Motiv seine Legitimation. Das europäische Gesellschaftsmodell vermittelte auch zwischen der vorhandenen egalitären Wertstruktur und dem Sozialsystem, einem Erbe sozialistischer Modernisierung in diesen Ländern.[11] Dennoch bleibt zu fragen, erstens: ob nicht als dahinter liegender Begründungszusammenhang des Codes der Europäisierung und der Erfolge der mittelosteuropäischen Länder vor allem deren geographische Nähe zu Westeuropa anzuführen wäre. Und zweitens: um welche Art von Integration es sich bei den neuen Mitgliedsstaaten handelt.

Oft heben Forschungen zur Pfadabhängigkeit vor allem die Differenzen zwischen den mittel- und osteuropäischen Ländern hinsichtlich der postsozialistischen Wirtschaftskulturen hervor. So wird argumentiert, dass die Ex-Sowjet-Ökonomie monopolistischer organisiert gewesen sei, während in Polen und Ungarn bereits vor 1989 eine Reihe von Versuchen zur Dezentralisierung der Wirtschaft unternommen worden waren und die vorhandene fragmentierte Ökonomie bessere Startbedingungen für den Übergang zur Marktwirtschaft besaß. Soziologen betonen zudem die relative Stärke einer Zivilgesellschaft in diesen Ländern und andere Akteurs- und Elitenkonstellationen als in Russland.[12]

Aber mehr als alle anderen Begründungszusammenhänge sei Russlands Scheitern, so behauptet zumindest Don Kalb, „a failure of space".[13] Diese Behauptung wird nur dann nachvollziehbar, wenn man sich der zweiten Frage, nach dem Modus der Integration, etwas genauer zuwendet. Denn es scheint, als würden trotz beeindruckender Investitionen transnationaler Firmen in Polen, Ungarn oder Tschechien nur bestimmte, geopolitisch interessante Räume, wie zum Beispiel der Korridor zwischen Berlin und Warschau, in den globalen Markt integriert, während andere Regionen wie der Osten Polens schlichtweg in Vergessenheit geraten. Don Kalb spricht von drei Tendenzen globaler Restrukturierung des postsozialistischen Raumes: erstens, die Erosion der Strukturen und der Kohärenz des Nationalstaates; zweitens, die Verschärfung sozialer Differenzen und Ungleichheiten zwischen Zentrum und Peripherien sowie zwischen und innerhalb der Nationalstaaten; und, drittens, Globale Kapital-, Finanz-, Informations- und Menschenströme fließen höchst ungleich in die jeweiligen Empfänger-Territorien.[14] Diese globalen Kräfte operieren in zwei Richtungen: als Fragmentierung und Integration. Fragmentierung findet außerhalb der Zonen von Kapitalakkumulation statt, entlang von ethnischen, regionalen oder sozialen Grenzziehungen. Periphere Gebiete sind weniger kontrollierbar, und anstelle lokaler Politiken treten mafiaähnliche Gruppen auf, um die Grenzen zwischen diesen Territorien und der EU zu kontrollieren. Eine Mischung aus ökonomischer Ungleichheit und Ohnmacht, schwacher lokaler Autorität und ethnischen Grenzziehungen ist Voraussetzung für Konflikte, wie sie im Kaukasus oder auf dem Balkan stattgefunden haben.

Integration ereignet sich in solchen Zonen, die in den Zirkel der Kapitalakkumulation und zentraler politischer Aufmerksamkeit gehören. „The urban areas of Central Euro-

But more than all the other reasons for Russia's failure, according to Don Kalb at least, was "a failure of space."[13] This assertion only becomes comprehensible when one looks more closely into the second question, concerning the mode of integration. For it seems that, despite impressive investments by transnational companies in Poland, Hungary or the Czech Republic, only certain areas of geopolitical interest – like the corridor between Berlin and Warsaw, for example – have been integrated into the global market, while other regions, like eastern Poland, have simply been allowed to fall into oblivion. Don Kalb speaks of three tendencies in the global restructuring of the post-socialist space: first, the erosion of the structures and coherence of the nation state; secondly, the aggravation of social differences and inequalities between centre and periphery as well as between and within the nation states; and, thirdly, global capital, finance, information and people flow in very unequal measure into the various recipient territories.[14] These global forces operate in two directions: fragmentation and integration. Fragmentation takes place outside the zones of capital accumulation, along ethnic, regional or social boundaries. Peripheral territories are less controllable, and instead of local political elites mafia-like groups emerge to control the frontiers between these territories and the EU. A mixture of economic inequality and powerlessness, weak local authorities and ethnic divisions pave the way for conflicts of the kind we have seen in the Caucasus and the Balkans.

Integration takes place in zones that belong to the circle of capital accumulation and are at the centre of political attention. "The urban areas of Central Europe are in this zone, as are those where there has been considerable Western investment in new enterprises or humanitarian aid. The integrated areas are those where the telephones work, where an internet café is close by, where the roads are well-paved, where young people have not all emigrated."[15]

This process of selective integration has been the subject of studies, taking as examples the separation of the Baltic states from the former USSR or the role of Slovenia in the break-up of the former Yugoslavia. In order to create conditions for a selective integration, a separation from the less favoured neighbour was absolutely essential. Burbah et al. speak of "Kuwaitisation" in this connection.[16]

INVOLUTION OF CAPITALISM

And Russia? If belonging to "Europe" was used for a long time by the Central and East European countries as a formula for distancing themselves from the Soviet Union, it is used all the more now. Even if the President of the European Commission officially recognized Russia's status as a market economy on 29 May 2002, the country continues to face deep-rooted structural and institutional problems: barter and unpaid work in the industrial sector, an immense flow of capital abroad, lack of investment, social polarisation, great differences in income, and corruption at all levels.

In an essay entitled "Transition without Transformation" Michael Burawoy used the concept of "involution" instead of evolution to describe the emergence of a new system in Russia. Drawing on Karl Polanyi's book *The Great Transformation* he analyses the differences between England in the 19th and Russia in the 20th century. There are three special features that lead him to the assertion that a "great involution" has taken place in Russia. First, there was no economic expansion that would have ne-

pe are in this zone, as are those where there has been considerable Western investment in new enterprises or humanitarian aid. The integrated areas are those where the telephones work, where an internet café is closed by, where the roads are well-paved, where young people have not all emigrated."[15]

Diesen Prozess der selektiven Integration haben Studien am Beispiel der Herauslösung der baltischen Staaten aus der ehemaligen UdSSR bzw. am Fall von Slowenien im Zuge des Zusammenbruchs des ehemaligen Jugoslawien untersucht. Zur Schaffung passender Bedingungen für eine selektive Integration war die Absetzung von den weniger begünstigten Nachbarn nachgerade notwendig. Burbah et al. sprechen in diesem Zusammenhang von „Kuwaitisation".[16]

INVOLUTION OF CAPITALISM

Und Russland? War die Zugehörigkeit zu „Europa" seit langem eine Distanzierungsformel mittelosteuropäischer Länder von der Sowjetunion, so gilt das heute umso mehr. Auch wenn am 29. Mai 2002 der Präsident der Europäischen Kommission offiziell Russlands Status als Marktwirtschaft anerkannt hat, ist das Land nach wie vor mit tiefliegenden strukturellen und institutionellen Problemen konfrontiert: Tauschhandel und unbezahlte Arbeit im industriellen Sektor, immenser Kapitalfluss ins Ausland, Mangel an Investitionen, soziale Polarisierung, große Einkommensunterschiede und Korruption auf allen Ebenen.

Michael Burawoy hat in seinem Aufsatz „Transition without transformation" anstelle der Evolution eines neuen Systems in Russland den Begriff „Involution" verwendet. In Anlehnung an Karl Polanyis Buch *The Great Transformation* analysiert er die Unterschiede zwischen England im 19. und Russland im 20. Jahrhundert. Drei Besonderheiten sind es, die ihn zu der Behauptung führen, in Russland hätte eine „great involution" stattgefunden. Zum einen: Es gab keine ökonomische Expansion, die im selben Atemzug Regulation und Institutionalisierung notwenig gemacht hätte. Zweitens, die Expansion des Marktes in England ging einher mit der Entfaltung einer dynamischen Gesellschaft, während Russlands erodierende Gesellschaft in einer Welt von sozialen Netzwerken und informellen Beziehungen aufging. Und drittens: Die große Transformation war mit dem Aufstieg eines souveränen Staates verbunden, während Russland mit dem Zerfall der ehemaligen Sowjetunion in autonome Regionen konfrontiert war. Was vonstatten ging, war eine Transition in die Marktwirtschaft ohne einen effektiven Nationalstaat, der zum Beispiel die Finanzkonsolidierung hätte unterstützen und schützen können. Das heutige Russland ist insofern durch die Abwesenheit von drei wesentlichen Eigenheiten der „great transformation" gekennzeichnet: die Transformation der Produktion, der Gesellschaft und des Staates. „The economy undergoes neither a neoliberal revolution nor an institutional evolution but rather an economic involution, a market that sucks resources out of production, sending it into a spiralling contraction."[17]

Die Abwesenheit marktwirtschaftlicher Mechanismen in der Arbeitssphäre ist dafür ein interessantes Beispiel: So sind Arbeiter immer noch in den Staatsbetrieben angestellt, erhalten aber keinen Lohn, sondern stattdessen nicht-geldliche Ressourcen. Das führt unter anderem dazu, dass der Arbeitsplatz lediglich dazu dient, die Sozialabgaben bezahlt zu bekommen und informelle Kontakte zu pflegen, die bei der Suche

cessitated simultaneous regulation and institutionalisation. Secondly, the expansion of the market in England went hand in hand with the development of a dynamic society, whereas Russia's eroding society became submerged in a world of social networks and informal contacts. And thirdly, the great transformation was connected with the rise of a sovereign state, whereas Russia was confronted with the disintegration of the former Soviet Union into autonomous regions. What happened was a transition to a market economy without an effective nation state that could have supported and protected the financial consolidation, for example. In this sense today's Russia is characterised by the absence of three essential features of the "great transformation": the transformation of production, of society, and of the state. "The economy undergoes neither a neoliberal revolution nor an institutional evolution but rather an economic involution, a market that sucks resources out of production, sending it into a spiralling contraction."[17]

Examples like the decommodification of labour highlight the dilemma. Workers continue to be on the payrolls of the state enterprises, but they receive no pay. Instead they are given non-cash resources. This means that the job merely lets them have their social security contributions paid while they cultivate informal contacts of the kind that are helpful when looking for a second job. While enterprises act as informal welfare agencies, working-class families find ways of supporting themselves outside the production process.

Katherine Verdery has taken the involution argument a step further, taking as an example privatisation in Russia, where state property found its way into private hands by a different route. On the one hand there was the difficulty of estimating the value of state enterprises. In addition, many former company executives deliberately tried to force their enterprises into bankruptcy so as to buy or sell them later at favourable prices long before there were any legal regulations. At the same time there were massive efforts, despite the deliberate selling out of state assets, to maintain the power of the state for the sake of subsidies and resources. These moves towards renationalisation followed the familiar logic of Soviet times when the state was seen as a provider of handouts.[18] But what does the thesis that Russia is not going through a "great transformation" so much as a "great involution" have to do with world economic conditions? For that, it might be said, is the crucial difference from 19th century England. As a result, Michael Burawoy asserts, Russia is polarised into two worlds: "the hypermodern world of currency exchange and international commodity flows and the pre-modern world of barter, trade, petty commodity production, and peasant subsistence. As the centre is integrating into the most advanced circuits of the global information society, the hinterland is hurtling in the other direction toward a neo-feudalism."[19] The same argument is put forward by Katherine Verdery, who maintains that Russia is not so much moving from socialism to capitalism as from socialism to feudalism. She is less concerned with identifying distinct elements of the Russian transformation societies with a view to comparing them with those of feudal systems, than with using the feudalism metaphor to switch to a perspective that is not burdened with the concepts of liberal capitalism. "The feudalism argument points us in directions which are at least as fruitful for recognising what is happening in the former Eastern bloc as images of a transition with its big bangs,

nach einem zweiten Job hilfreich sind. Während Unternehmen als informelle Wohlfahrtsagenturen agieren, sichern sich Arbeiterklassefamilien die Mittel zum Lebensunterhalt außerhalb der Produktion.
Katherine Verdery hat am Beispiel der Privatisierung in Russland das Argument der Involution weitergeführt: Staatseigentum ist hier auf unterschiedliche Weise in private Hände gelangt. Zum einen bestand die Schwierigkeit, den Wert der Staatsbetriebe zu schätzen. Zudem versuchten viele ehemalige Firmenmanager, einen Bankrott der Betriebe absichtlich voranzutreiben, um die Firmen dann günstig zu erwerben oder zu verkaufen, lange bevor es gesetzliche Regelungen gab. Zugleich gab es massive Bestrebungen, trotz absichtlichen Ausverkaufs des Staates am Erhalt des staatlichen Einflusses festzuhalten, vor allem der Subventionen und Ressourcen wegen. Diese Ansätze zur Wiederverstaatlichung bewegten sich zudem in der Logik des vertrauten Allokationsstaates der Sowjetzeit.[18] Wie aber verhält sich nun die These, Russland durchmesse weniger eine „great transformation" denn eine „great involution", zu den Bedingungen einer Weltökonomie? Denn das, so möchte man meinen, sei doch im Vergleich mit dem England des 19. Jahrhunderts der entscheidende Unterschied. Als Ergebnis, so Michael Burawoy, ist Russland in zwei Welten gespalten: „the hypermodern world of currency exchange and international commodity flows and the pre-modern world of barter, trade, petty commodity production, and peasant subsistence. As the center is integrating into the most advanced circuits of the global information society, the hinterland is hurtling in the other direction toward a neo-feudalism."[19]
Mit diesem Begriff argumentiert auch Katherine Verdery: Sie behauptet für Russland anstelle der Bewegung vom Sozialismus zum Kapitalismus eher eine Tendenz vom Sozialismus zum Feudalismus. Es geht ihr dabei weniger um die Herausarbeitung distinkter Elemente der russischen Transformationsgesellschaften, um sie mit denen feudaler Ordnungen zu vergleichen, als vielmehr um die Nutzung der Feudalismusmetapher für einen Perspektivwechsel, der nicht mit den Konzepten des liberalen Kapitalismus befrachtet ist.
„Das Argument des Feudalismus weist uns in Richtungen, die für die Erkennung dessen, was im früheren Ostblock geschieht, mindestens ebenso fruchtbar sind wie Bilder eines Übergangs mit seinen Big Bangs, Märkten, Schocktherapie und Privateigentum. Sie alle beleuchten nicht die gegenwärtige Entwicklung, sondern die Erwartung, einen Telos. (...) Teleologisches Denken hat die Region jahrzehntelang gequält; vielleicht sollten wir es aufgeben. Auf das zu achten, was vor sich geht, statt nach dem Aussicht zu halten, was geschehen müsste, wäre fairer, bescheidener, vernünftiger."[20]

GAMEKEEPER STATES

Für das Ende der Transition als Diskursfigur und als Realität lassen sich eine Reihe von Gründen anführen. 15 Jahre nach dem Zerfall des Ostblocks, meint Steven Sampson, sei es angemessener, von Post-Postsozialismus zu reden, denn die Transitionsperiode, die wir Postsozialismus nannten, sei vorbei. Die Leute haben sich eingerichtet, hinter drei Schichten Gardinen in den Wohnzimmern im Mikrorayon Kiseljowka, in den Servicestationen entlang der E30, sie haben sich an das Pendeln zwischen Siemeaticze und Brüssel gewöhnt. Post-Postsozialismus, so Sampson, ist eine Zeit, „in

markets, shock therapy and private property. What they illuminate is not the present development, but the expectation, a *telos*. ... Teleological thinking has tormented the region for decades; perhaps we should give it up. Paying attention to what is happening instead of keeping a lookout for what ought to happen would be fairer, humbler, more sensible."[20]

GAMEKEEPER STATES

A number of reasons might be cited for seeing the end of the transition as part of the discourse and as a reality. Steven Sampson argues that fifteen years after the disintegration of the Eastern bloc it is more appropriate to talk of post-post-socialism, since the transition period, which we called post-socialism, is over. People have settled down, whether behind three layers of curtains in the living rooms of the Kiselyovka microrayon or in the service stations along the E30. They have got used to shuttling back and forward between Siemiatycze and Brussels. Post-post-socialism, in Steven Sampson's view, is a period "in which the shock of the new is a spent force ... People in the post-post-socialist world are no longer so confused as they were. They have become consumers or political nationalists. They are angry or depressed or just weary."[21] The main feature of this new period, however, is that the West is no longer on the other side, but has now become an integral part of everyday life.

Does the talk of "the end of the transition" and the beginning of a new era stand for the arrival of a horizon of expectation and for the abandonment of that teleological rhetoric which was bound up with the transition discourse?

The problem of the normative nature of the transition discourse has already been discussed elsewhere. This is based on theoretical notions of modernisation which assume a uniform, universally apprehended time frame based on a division into those who are "advanced," those who have been "left behind," and those who are "catching up." As an alternative to this unilinear version Dieter Goetze proposes a co-evolutionary perspective based on a conflict-ridden reciprocal relationship between various social contexts, which follow different political, economic or cultural parameters and create links between different time horizons. The simultaneity, the combination of quite different time modes, leads to the emergence of development options which have little to do with a fixed target and are more concerned with the dynamic intertwining of quite different time modes.

When applied to the transformation societies, this means that up to the fall of the Iron Curtain the East European societies found themselves in a state of competition with the West European industrial social model, and that both East and West were operating on a comparable time frame. [22] What was also common to both social models was a concept that John Urry has described with the metaphor of the "gardening state": the "container society" based on the coincidence of a territorialised social frame of reference and organised socialisation. If one takes this co-evolutionary perspective seriously and looks more for points in common and interdependences, as the advocates of post-cold war studies do,[23] the legacies of socialism appear in a different light. Janos Matyas Kovacs maintains that "the communist era was not just a period of rapid modernisation, it was also, albeit in a perverse way, a school of capitalism ... Communism conserved or reproduced a kind of capitalist ethos which has

der der Schock des Neuen seine Wucht verloren hat. (...) Die Menschen in der post-postsozialistischen Welt sind nicht mehr so verwirrt, wie sie es einmal waren. Sie werden zu Konsumenten oder zu Nationalisten politisiert. Sie sind zornig und niedergeschlagen oder einfach nur müde."[21] Diese neue Periode sei aber vor allem dadurch geprägt, dass der Westen nicht mehr auf der anderen Seite, sondern inzwischen integraler Bestandteil des Alltags geworden ist. Steht das Reden vom „Jenseits der Transition" und dem Beginn einer neuen Ära nun für den Einzug des Erwartungshorizonts und für die Aufgabe jener teleologischen Rhetorik, mit der der Transitionsdiskurs verbunden war?

Über die Problematik insbesondere der Normativität des Transitionsdiskurses ist an anderer Stelle schon diskutiert worden. Dahinter stehen modernisierungstheoretische Vorstellungen, die von einem einheitlichen, universell gefassten Zeitrahmen ausgehen, der von der Anordnung von „Fortschrittlichen", „Zurückgebliebenen" und „Nachholenden" ausgeht. Dieter Goetze schlägt gegenüber dieser einseitigen Lesart eine ko-evolutionäre Perspektive vor, die von einem konfliktreichen Wechselverhältnis verschiedener gesellschaftlicher Kontexte ausgeht, die unterschiedlichen politischen, ökonomischen oder kulturellen Parametern folgen. Darüber werden jeweils unterschiedliche Zeithorizonte miteinander verknüpft. Die Gleichzeitigkeit, die Kombination ganz unterschiedlicher Zeitmodi führen zur Entstehung von Entwicklungsoptionen, die wenig mit einer fixierten Zielgröße von Entwicklung zu tun haben, als vielmehr aus der dynamischen Verflechtung ganz unterschiedlicher Zeitlichkeiten erwachsen.

Auf die Ebene der Transformationsgesellschaften angewandt, heißt das, dass bis zum Fall des Eisernen Vorhangs für die osteuropäischen Gesellschaften noch eine Konkurrenzsituation mit dem westeuropäischen Industriegesellschaftsmodell bestand, Ost wie West auf einer vergleichbaren Zeitschiene ablief.[22] Was beide Gesellschaftsmodelle ebenfalls teilten, war ein Konzept, das John Urry mit der Metapher des „gardening state" umschrieben hat: die „Container-Gesellschaft", die auf der Koinzidenz von territorialisierten gesellschaftlichen Referenzrahmen und organisierter Vergesellschaftung beruht. Nimmt man diese ko-evolutionäre Perspektive ernst und zieht eher die Verflechtungen und Interdependenzen in den Blick, wie das Befürworter von Post-Cold-War-Studies tun[23], dann erscheinen auch die Hinterlassenschaften des Sozialismus in einem anderen Licht. Janos Matyas Kovacs behauptet, „die Ära des Kommunismus war nicht nur eine Periode rapider Modernisierung, sie war auch, wenngleich auf verquere Weise, eine Schule des Kapitalismus. (...) Der Kommunismus hat eine Art von kapitalistischem Ethos konserviert bzw. reproduziert, das im Westen inzwischen weitgehend erodiert ist – gekennzeichnet durch starke Präferenz für Vertrauen gegenüber formalen Regeln, für direkte interpersonelle gegenüber institutionellen Transaktionen, für kleine gegenüber großen Organisationen."[24]

Mit dem Fall des Eisernen Vorhangs wird jedoch dieser gemeinsame Referenzrahmen obsolet: Das westeuropäische Modell, konfrontiert mit den Konditionen der Globalisierung, wird zunehmend labiler hinsichtlich seiner sozialstaatlichen Steuerungskapazität. Dieter Goetze behauptet, während Westeuropa mit der Neuregulierung, Demontage oder auch Umorientierung des „gardening state"-Modells beschäftigt ist, würde sich Osteuropa eher an Regulationen und Orientierungen internationaler Vereinigungen und Organisationen, wie der WTO, dem IWF oder der EU ausrichten. Es

now largely eroded in the West – an ethos characterised by a strong preference for trust as against formal rules, for direct transactions between persons rather than institutions, for small rather than large organisations."[24]

With the fall of the Iron Curtain, however, this common frame of reference became obsolete: The West European model, confronted with the conditions of globalisation, is becoming increasingly feeble with regard to its capacity to control the welfare state. Dieter Goetze believes that while Western Europe is occupied with the re-regulation, dismantling or reorientation of the "gardening state" model, Eastern Europe is bowing to the regulations and guidelines of international associations and organisations like the WTO, IMF or EU. These are the actors and institutions of a global capitalism, which is largely based on networks, informality, flexible and decentralised generation of knowledge, etc. Given this development, could the East European virtues of Manchester capitalism described above not give these countries a comparative advantage?

This represents a reversion to a model which Urry has described as the "gamekeeper state": "[The gamekeeper] is mainly interested in tending the hunting grounds which he tries to keep attractive so that the game (in this case large corporations and conglomerates, which provide jobs and a share of their profits in the form of tax revenues) roams through his territory and can be made use of as necessary."[25] This gives rise to a multitude of open ramification situations and development options of which actors can make flexible use by a combination of different social spaces. And East European economic cultures with their preferences for social networks, decentralised bargaining processes and flexible solution strategies seem to be particularly suited to this.

What seems to make this argument so interesting for the case of the E30, the beginning of our excursion through the transit spaces, is the fact that this process gives rise to new social spaces with different time modes. The territorial spaces enclosed within state borders dissolve to give way to new, ramified space-time combinations arising from networks and flows of information. The erosion of the "gardening state" leads to new forms of social mobility which can scarcely be kept within the boundaries of the nation state. But it also results in a reordering of the territory in the shape of the coexistence of very different spaces.[26] The E30 is a classic example of "gamekeeping" – it assures the exchange of goods, capital, services and labour for the locations that are attractive to investors and large corporations. But the hinterland of the transit territories of global actors seems to belong to another time.

If one accepts Urry's argumentation, the obvious question is, are the Central and East European countries better suited to meeting the conditions of a new global order? And would it not be appropriate in this case to change our vantage point and ask: Can the West learn something from the East that goes beyond – to use Urry's terminology – the familiar rules of tending one's own garden? Whatever the answer may be, the past fifteen years have witnessed the emergence of another reality in the post-socialist cities which no longer corresponds to the yardsticks and assessment criteria with which we are used to categorizing the world into East and West. It was to reach this insight that we travelled the 2,500 kilometres to Moscow.

handelt sich um Akteure und Institutionen eines globalen Kapitalismus, der in hohem Maße auf Netzwerken, Informalität, Flexibilität dezentralisierter Wissensproduktion etc. beruht. Könnten nicht angesichts dieser Entwicklung die oben beschriebenen osteuropäischen Tugenden des Gründerzeitkapitalismus diesen Ländern eine komparativen Vorteil verschaffen?
Hier findet die Umsteuerung auf ein Modell statt, das Urry als „gamekeeper state" beschrieben hat: „Dieser ist vor allem an der Pflege der Jagdgründe interessiert, die er attraktiv zu gestalten sucht, damit das Wild (sprich Großunternehmen und Konzerne, die Arbeitsplätze und Gewinnanteile in Form von Steueraufkommen zur Verfügung stellen) durch sein Territorium zieht und fallweise daraus Nutzen gezogen werden kann."[25] Was dabei entsteht, sind vielfältige offene Verzweigungssituationen, Entwicklungsoptionen, die Akteure flexibel durch die Kombination unterschiedlicher sozialer Räume nutzen können. Und osteuropäische Wirtschaftskulturen mit ihren Präferenzen für soziale Netzwerke, dezentrale Aushandlungsprozesse und flexible Lösungsstrategien scheinen dafür besonders passfähig zu sein.
Was an dieser Argumentation für den Fall der E30, den Beginn unserer Transiträume-Exkursion, so interessant scheint, ist die Tatsache, dass aus diesem Prozess neue Sozialräume mit unterschiedlichen Zeitlichkeiten erwachsen. Die staatlich umgrenzten und territorial geschlossenen Räume lösen sich auf, neue weitverzweigte Raum-Zeit-Kombinationen entstehen aus Netzwerken und Informationsströmen. Die Erosion des „gardening state" hat neue Formen von sozialer Mobilität zur Folge, die in den Grenzen des Nationalstaates kaum noch zu erfassen sind. Aber daraus resultiert auch eine Neuordnung des Territoriums in Gestalt des Nebeneinanders sehr unterschiedlicher Räume.[26] Die E30 ist geradezu ein Paradebeispiel für „game-keeping" – sie sichert den Austausch von Waren, Kapital, Dienstleistungen und Arbeitskräften für die Orte, die für Investoren und Großunternehmen attraktiv sind. Aber das Hinterland des Durchzugsterritoriums globaler Akteure scheint einer anderen Zeit anzugehören.
Folgt man Urrys Argumentation, so liegt die Frage nahe: Sind die mittel- und osteuropäischen Länder besser geeignet, den Konditionen einer neuen globalen Ordnung zu begegnen? Und wäre in diesem Fall nicht die Blickrichtung einmal zu tauschen und zu fragen: Kann der Westen vom Osten etwas erfahren, das die bekannten Regeln der Pflege des eigenen Gartens – um in Urrys Terminologien zu bleiben – überschreitet? Wie immer die Antwort auch ausfällt, seit 15 Jahren ist in den postsozialistischen Städten eine andere Realität entstanden, die den Maßstäben und Beurteilungskriterien, mit denen wir gewohnt sind, die Welt in Ost und West zu kategorisieren, nicht mehr entspricht. Um zu dieser Einsicht zu gelangen, macht man sich auf die Reise, 2500 Kilometer Richtung Moskau.

ANMERKUNGEN

1 Siehe den Beitrag „Stadtplanung nach dem Ende des Kommunismus" von Bart Goldhoorn in diesem Band.
2 Schlögel, Karl: *Promenade in Jalta und andere Städtebilder.* München 2001, S. 19
3 Nesvetailova, Anastasia: From Transition to Dependent Development. The new Periphery in Global Financial Capitalism. http://www.shef.ac.uk/perc/dev/papers/nesvetailovna.pdf

NOTES

1 See the article "Urban Planning after Communism" by Bart Goldhoorn in this volume.

2 Schlögel, Karl: *Promenade in Jalta und andere Städtebilder.* Munich 2001, p. 19

3 Nesvetailova, Anastasia: From Transition to Dependent Development. The New Periphery in Global Financial Capitalism. http://www.shef.ac.uk/perc/dev/papers/nesvetailovna.pdf

4 Zapf, Wolfgang: *Modernisierung, Wohlfahrtsentwicklung und Transformation.* Berlin 1994, p. 138

5 Müller, Klaus: "Countries in Transition – Entwicklungspfade osteuropäischer Transformation". In: *Osteuropa.* Heft 10, 2001, p. 1150

6 Ibid., p. 1156

7 Kalb, Don: "Nachwort. Globalismus und postsozialistische Perspektiven". In: Hann, Christopher (ed.): *Postsozialismus, Transformationsprozesse in Europa und Asien aus ethnologischer Perspektive.* Frankfurt am Main 2002, p. 455 et seq.

8 Carothers, Thomas: "The End of the Transition Paradigm". In: *Journal of Democracy.* Vol. 13 (1), 2002, p. 18

9 Zizek, Slavoj: "Was will Europa?" In: Hlavajova, Maria/Winder, Jill (eds.): *Who if not we ...?* Amsterdam, 2004, p. 188

10 Gray, John: *False Dawn. The Delusions of Global Capitalism.* London 1998, p. ???

11 Müller, Klaus, loc. cit., p. 1163

12 Cf. Eyal, Gil/Szelenyi, Ivan/Townsley, Eleanor: *Making Capitalism without Capitalists, The New Ruling Elites in Eastern Europe.* London 2000, p. 30

13 Kalb, Don: "Afterword. Globalism and Postsocialist Prospects". In: Hann, Christopher (ed.): *Ideas, Ideologies and Practices in Eurasia.* New York 2002, p. 328

14 Cf. ibid., p. 318

15 Nesvetailova, Anastasia, loc. cit.

16 Cf. Burbah, R./Kagarlitsky, Boris/Or, Nunez: *Globalisation and its Discontents.* London 1997

17 Burawoy, Michael: Transition Without Transformation: Russia's Involutionary Road to Capitalism. http://www.sociology.berkeley.edu/faculty/BURAWOY/burawoy_pdf/transition.pdf

18 Cf. Verdery, Katherine: "Vom Sozialismus zum Feudalismus". In Oswalt, Philipp: *Schrumpfende Städte,* Vol. 1, Ostfildern-Ruit 2004, p. 107

19 Burawoy, Michael, loc. cit.

20 Verdery, Katherine: "Vom Sozialismus zum Feudalismus". In Oswalt, Philipp, loc. cit., p. 110

21 Sampson, Steven: "Jenseits der Transition". In: Hann, Christopher (ed.): *Postsozialismus. Transformationsprozesse in Europa und Asien aus ethnologischer Perspektive.* Frankfurt am Main 2002, p. 426

22 Cf. Goetze, Dieter: "Forschungsperspektiven Transformation, Transition, Entwicklungsoptionen". In: *Berliner Debatte,* Heft 15, 2004/3, p. 19

23 Cf. Verdery, Katherine: "Wohin mit dem Postsozialismus". In: Hann, Christopher (ed.): *Postsozialismus. Transformationsprozesse in Europa und Asien aus ethnologischer Perspektive.* Frankfurt am Main 2002, p. 34

24 Kovacs, Janos Matyas: "Vergangenheit oder Vorvergangenheit? Kultur und Wirtschaftsentwicklung in Osteuropa nach 1989". In: *Berliner Debatte.* Heft 15, 2004, p. 30

25 Urry, John: *Sociology Beyond Societies. Mobilities for the 21Th Century.* London 2000, p. 189

26 Cf. Goetze, Dieter, loc. cit.

4 Zapf, Wolfgang: *Modernisierung, Wohlfahrtsentwicklung und Transformation.* Berlin 1994, S. 138

5 Müller, Klaus: „Countries in Transition – Entwicklungspfade osteuropäischer Transformation". In: *Osteuropa.* Heft 10, 2001, S. 1150

6 Ebd., S. 1156

7 Kalb, Don: „Nachwort. Globalismus und postsozialistische Perspektiven". In: Hann, Christopher (Hg.): *Postsozialismus. Transformationsprozesse in Europa und Asien aus ethnologischer Perspektive.* Frankfurt/Main 2002, S. 455 ff.

8 Carothers, Thomas: „The End of the Transition Paradigm". In: *Journal of Democracy.* Heft 13.1, 2002, S. 18

9 Zizek, Slavoj: „Was will Europa?". In: Hlavajova, Maria/Winder, Jill (Hg.): *Who if not we ...?* Amsterdam 2004, S. 188

10 Gray, John: *False Down. The Delusions of Global Capitalism.* London 1998,

11 Müller, Klaus, a.a.O., S. 1163

12 Vgl. Eyal, Gil/Szelenyi, Ivan/Townsley, Eleanor: *Making Capitalism without Capitalists. The new ruling Elites in Eastern Europe.* London 2000, S. 30

13 Kalb, Don: „Afterword. Globalism and Postsocialist Prospects". In: Hann, Christopher (Hg.): *Ideas, Ideologies and Practises in Eurasia.* New York 2002, S. 328

14 Vgl. ebd., S. 318

15 Nesvetailova, Anastasia, a.a.O.

16 Vgl. Burbah, R./Kagarlitsky, Boris/Or, Nunez: *Globalisation and its Discontents.* London 1997

17 Burawoy, Michael: Transition without transformation: Russia's Involutionary Road to capitalism. http://www.sociology.berkeley.edu/faculty/BURAWOY/burawoy_pdf/transition.pdf

18 Vgl. Verdery, Katherine: „Vom Sozialismus zum Feudalismus". In: Oswalt, Philipp (Hg.): *Schrumpfende Städte.* Bd. 1, Ostfildern-Ruit 2004, S. 107

19 Burawoy, Michael, a.a.O.

20 Verdery, Katherine: „Vom Sozialismus zum Feudalismus". In: Oswalt, Philipp, a.a.O., S. 110

21 Sampson, Steven: „Jenseits der Transition". In: Hann, Christopher (Hg.): *Postsozialismus. Transformationsprozesse in Europa und Asien aus ethnologischer Perspektive.* Frankfurt/Main 2002, S. 426

22 Vgl. Goetze, Dieter: „Forschungsperspektiven Transformation, Transition, Entwicklungsoptionen". In: *Berliner Debatte.* Heft 15 (3) 2004, S. 19

23 Vgl. Verdery, Katherine: „Wohin mit dem Postsozialismus". In: Hann, Christopher (Hg.): a. a. o., S.34

24 Kovacs, Janos Matyas: „Vergangenheit oder Vorvergangenheit? Kultur und Wirtschaftsentwicklung in Osteuropa nach 1989". In: *Berliner Debatte.* Heft 15, 2004, S. 30

25 Urry, John: *Sociology beyond societies. Mobilities for the 21st century.* London 2000, S. 189

26 Vgl. Goetze, Dieter, a.a.O.

BERLIN – MOSKAU

BERLIN – MOSCOW

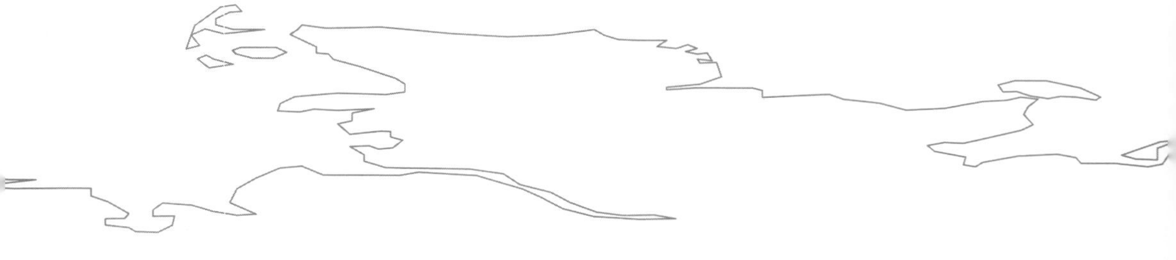

GERMANY

	357.023 skm
	82.333.000
	68 %
www users	30 .800.000

IM	522,062 BILLION E
EX	648.306 BILLION E
	+126.244 BILLION E

GDP 2001	1.939.581 MIO. $
REAL GROWTH 1990 - 2001	1,5%
UNEMPLOYMENT RATE 2002	9,8%
INFLATION 1990 - 2001	1,8%

DIRECT FLIGHTS FROM ALL BERLIN AIRPORTS

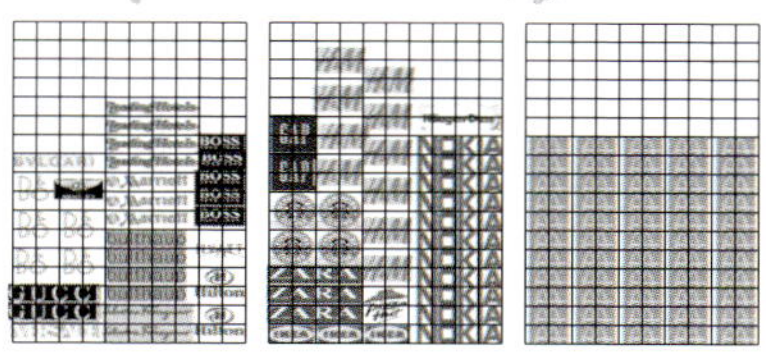

LUXURY BRANDS 65 % | EVERYDAY BRANDS 82 % | MC DONALDS 65 %

BERLIN

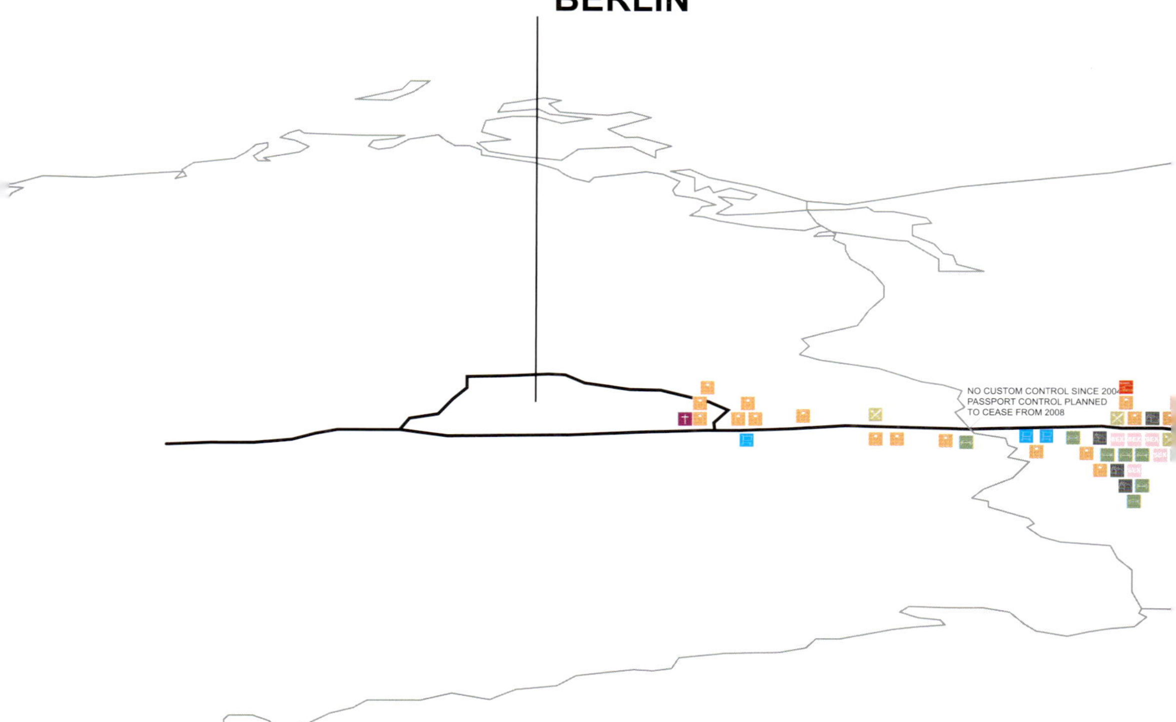

LEGEND CORRIDOR BERLIN - MOSCOW

TRUCK STOP | GAS STATION | AUTO GAZ | HOTEL, MOTEL | RESTAURANT, CAFE, BAR | NIGHT CLUB | BIG SHOP | SMALL SHOP | SOUVRNIR SHOP | POLITICAL MONUMENT | CHURCH, CEMENTARY | BILLBOARD | VILLAGE, TOWN, CITY

INFRASTRUCTURE & SETTLEMENT
ALONG THE TRANSEUROPEAN CORRIDOR II BERLIN-MOSCOW

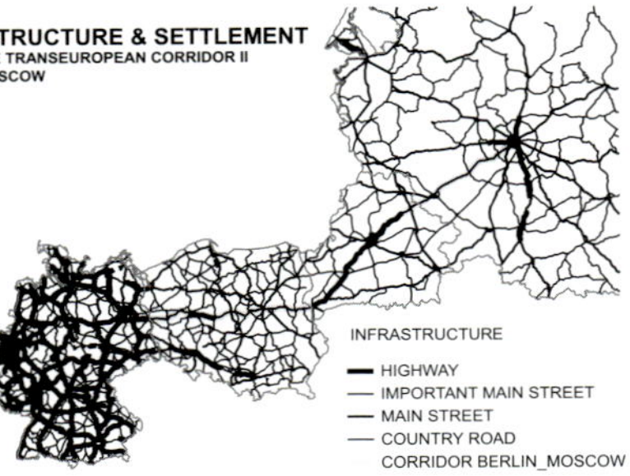

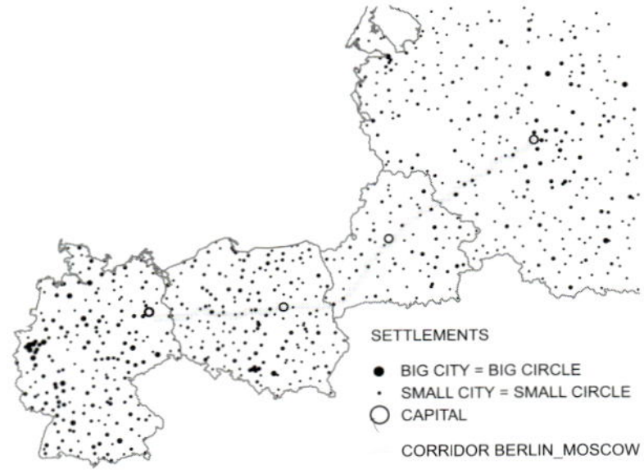

9 PAN-EUROPEAN CORRIDORS
TRAFFIC CONFERENCE IN KRETA, 1994

1_TALLINN - RIGA - WARZAWA

2_BERLIN - WARZAWA - MINSK - MOSKVA - NISHNIJ NOWGOROD

3_BERLIN/DRESDEN - WROCLAW - KATOWICE - KRAKOW - LWOW - KYJIV

4_DRESDEN/NUERNBERG - PRAHA - WIEN/BRATISLAVA - BUDAPEST - ARAD - CONSTANTA/ SOFIJA - THESSALONIKI/PLOVDIV - ISTANBUL

5_TRIEST - LJUBLJANA - BUDAPEST - BRATISLAVA - UTZGOROD - LWOW

6_GDANSK - WARZAWA - ZILINA

7_INLAND WATERSTREET_ DONAU

8_DURRES - TIRANA - SKOPJE - SOFIJA - VARNA

9_HELSINKI - KYJIV/MOSKVA - ODESA/CHISINAU/BUCURESTI - PLOVDIV

ALL PAN-EUROPEAN CORRIDORS ARE CONCEPTUALIZED TO BE MULTIMODAL, THAT MEANS THEY ARE FOR ROADS, RAILWAY AND WATERWAYS.

FLOW OF GOODS

MOBILE PHONE ACCESS
ALONG THE CORRIDOR BERLIN - MOSCOW

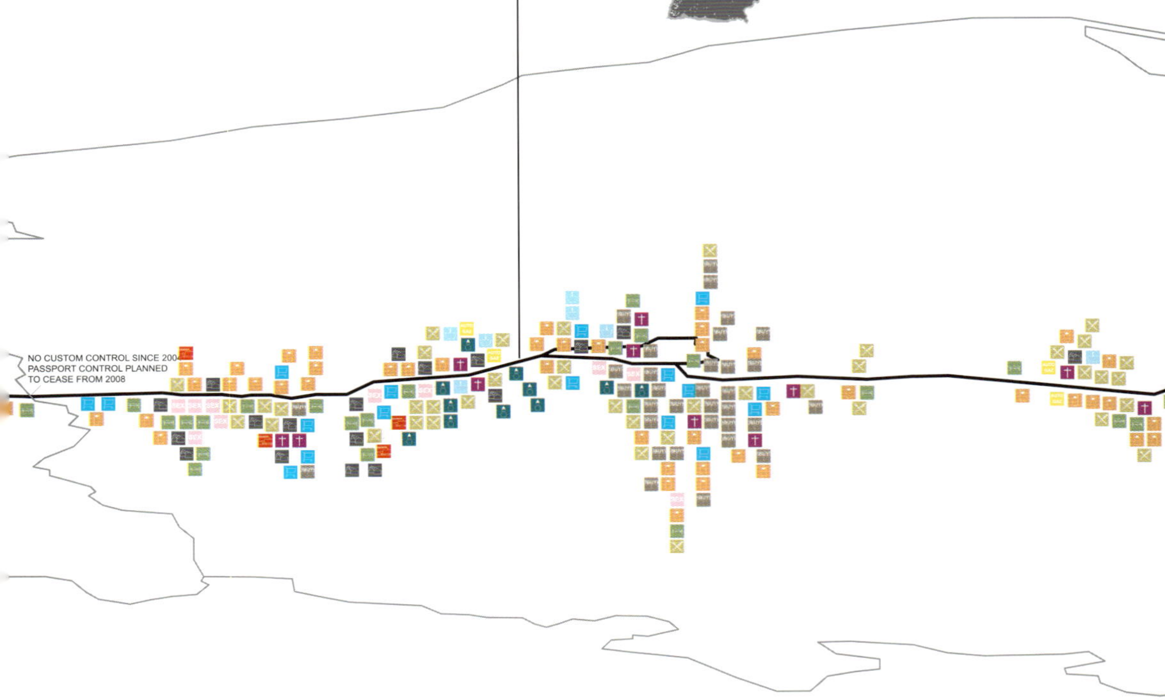

DEVELOPMENT OF THE EUROPEAN UNION

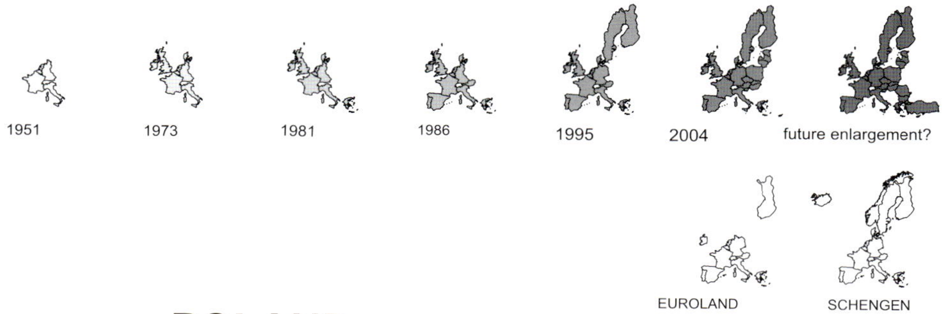

POLAND

312.685 skm	IM	55,113 BILLION $	GDP 2001	176.256 MIO. $
38.641.000	EX	41,010 BILLION $	REAL GROWTH 1990 - 2001	4,5%
26 %		-14,103 BILLION $	SHARE OF PRIVATE SECTOR 2001	62,9%
www users 3.800.000	DEPTH	- 62.393 MIO $	UNEMPLOYMENT RATE 2002	18,1%
			INFLATION 1990 - 2001	21,3%

DIRECT FLIGHTS FROM WARSAW FREDERIC CHOPIN AIRPORT

WARSAW

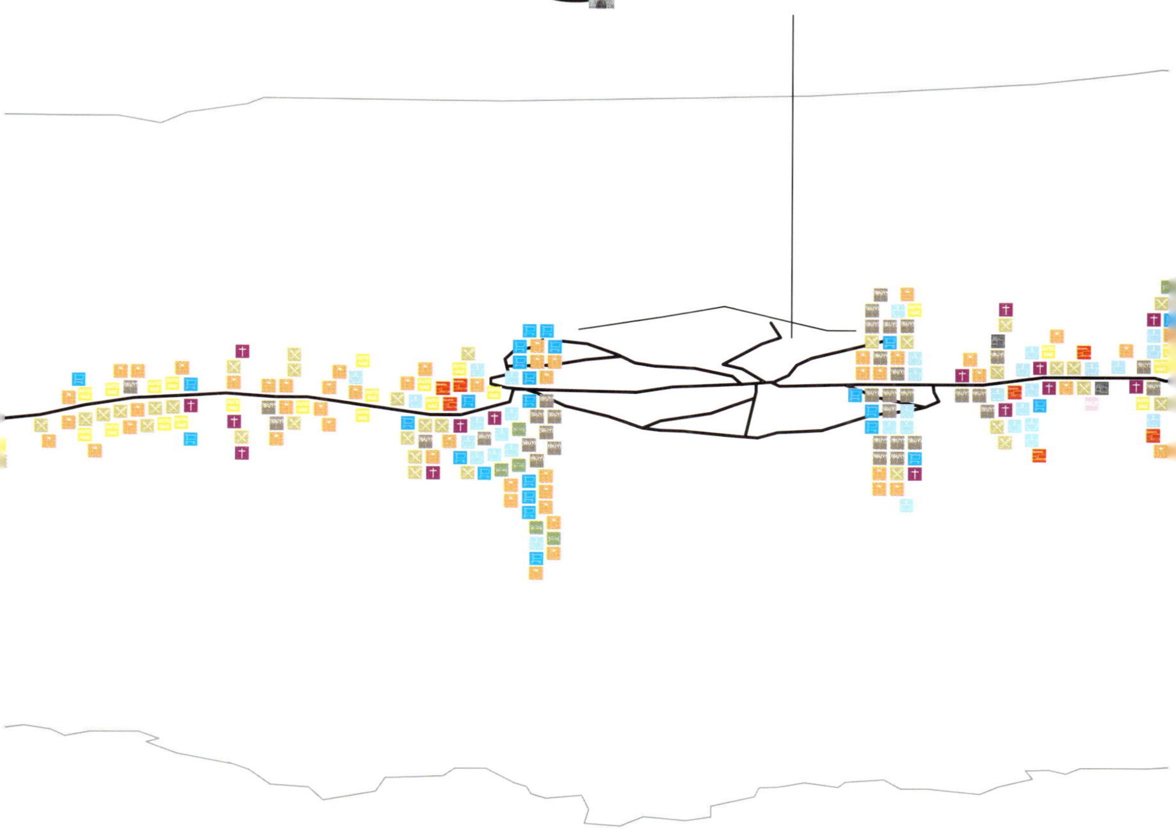

VISA REGULATIONS

FEDERAL REPUBLIC OF GERMANY

- ■_visa required
- □_visa not required
- ▩_federal republic of germany

POLAND

1 9 9 7 27th of July, Polish government declares intention of implementing harmonised EU visa politics before date of accession.

2 0 0 0 Poland imposes visa requirements on Azerbaijan, Georgia, Kyrgyzstan, Tajikistan and Turkmenistan.

2 0 0 1 - 0 2 Poland does not renew expiring visa-free agreements with 54 states.

2 0 0 3 1st of October, Poland imposes visa requirements on Russian Federation, Belarus and Ukraine.

- ■_visa required _ airport transit visa required
- ■_visa required
- ■_visa required _ fast-track procedure for multiple and long-time visa.
- □_visa not required < 14 days
- □_visa not required < 30 days
- □_visa not required < 90 days
- □_visa not required < 6 months
- ▩_poland

BELARUS

- ■_visa required
- ■_visa required_to be obtained on arrival
- ▩_visa required_except holders of diplomatic or service or special passports
- ▩_visa required_except holders of diplomatic or service passports or in case of group tourism
- □_visa not required
- ▩_belarus

RUSSIAN FEDERATION

- ■_visa required
- □_visa not required
- ▩_russian federation

DIRECT FLIGHTS FROM BREST INTERNATIONAL AIRPORT

BREST

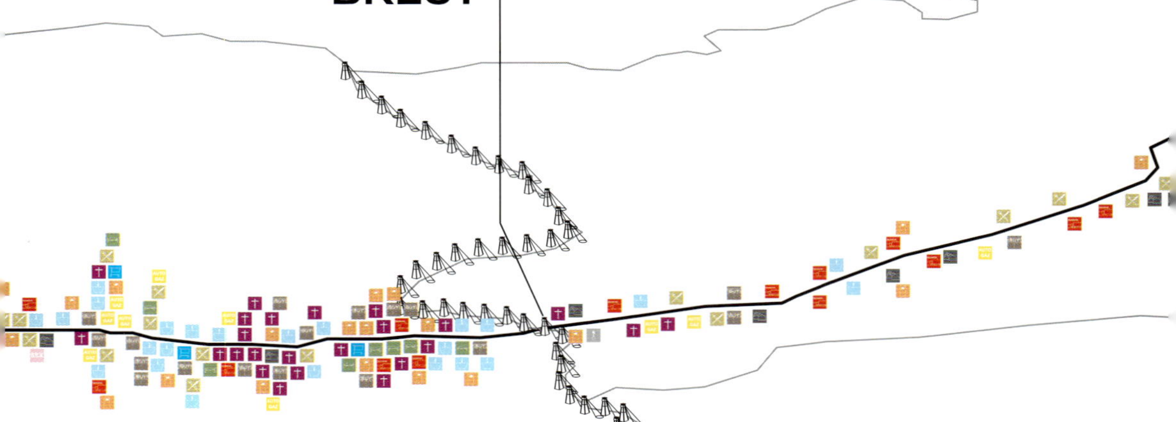

ESTABLISHMENT OF
EXTERNAL EU-BORDER

- TO BE COMPLETED UNTIL 2008

FORTIFIED WATCHTOWWER PLANNED TO BE BUILD EVERY 15-20 KM AT THE 1 143 KM LONG BORDER

5 UNITS FOR AERIAL RECONNAISSANCE

60 MOBILE HAND HELD SURVEILLANCE DEVICES

236 MOBILE HEAT SENSITIVE CAMERAS

BORDERGUARDS, TODAY 5 300 - FUTURE PLANS INCREASE TO MORE THAN DOUBLE

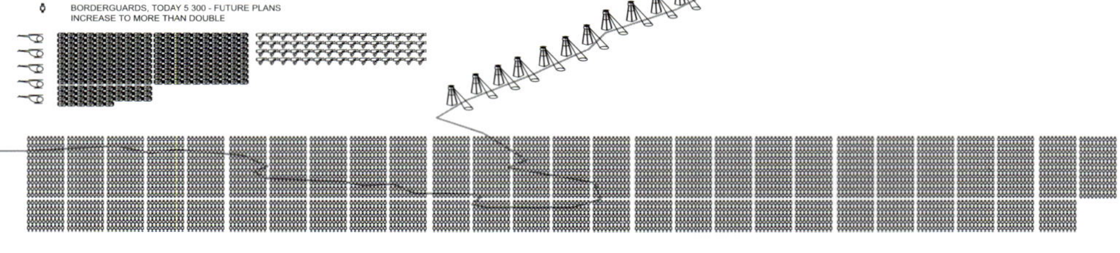

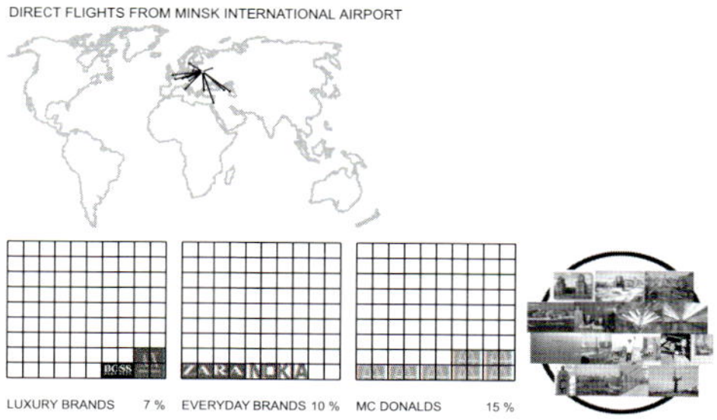

MINSK

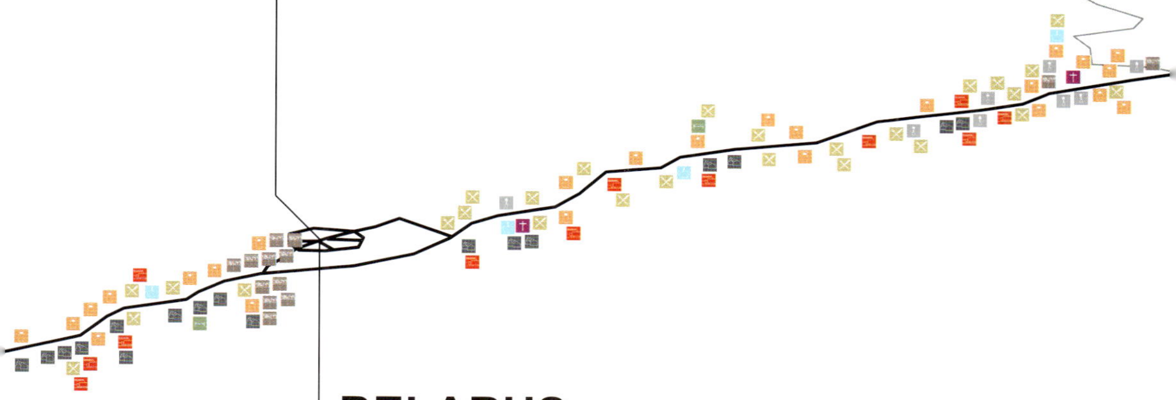

BELARUS

	207.595 skm	IM	8,960 BILLION $	GDP 2001	12.219 MIO. $
	9.970.000	EX	8,098 BILLION $	REAL GROWTH 1990 - 2001	-0,8%
	1,3 %	=	-0,862 BILLION $	SHARE OF PRIVATE SECTOR 2001	20%
www.users	422.200	DEPTH	- 869 MIO $	UNEMPLOYMENT RATE 2002	3%
				INFLATION 1990 - 2001	318%

POLITICAL UNIONS

COMECON

Council for Mutual Economic Assistance

- 25.01.1949 FOUNDATION OF THE COMECON by UDSSR, Poland, Czecheslovakia, Hungary, Rumania and Bulgaria
- 1950 GDR JOINS THE COMECON
- 1950 China, North-Corea, Vietnam are joining the COMECON AS OBSERVERS
- 1950 Albania joins the COMECON, but is 1962 excluded
- 1962 Mongolia, Cuba, 1964 Federal Republic of Yougoslavia are joining the COMECON
- 1973 COOPERATION CONTRACT WITH Finnland
- 1983 Afghanistan, Angola, Ethiopia, Jemen, Laos, Mocambique and Nicaragua are joining the COMECON AS OBSERVERS

WARSAW - PACT

CIS

- 08.12.1991, AGREEMENT OF MINSK: Russia, Belarus and Ukraine found the CIS
- 21.12.1991, AGREEMENT OF ALMA-ATA: Armenia, Azerbaijania, Kazakhstan, Uzbekistan, Tadzhikistan, Kyrgyzstan and Turkmenistan join the CIS
- 23.10.1993, Georgia joins the CIS

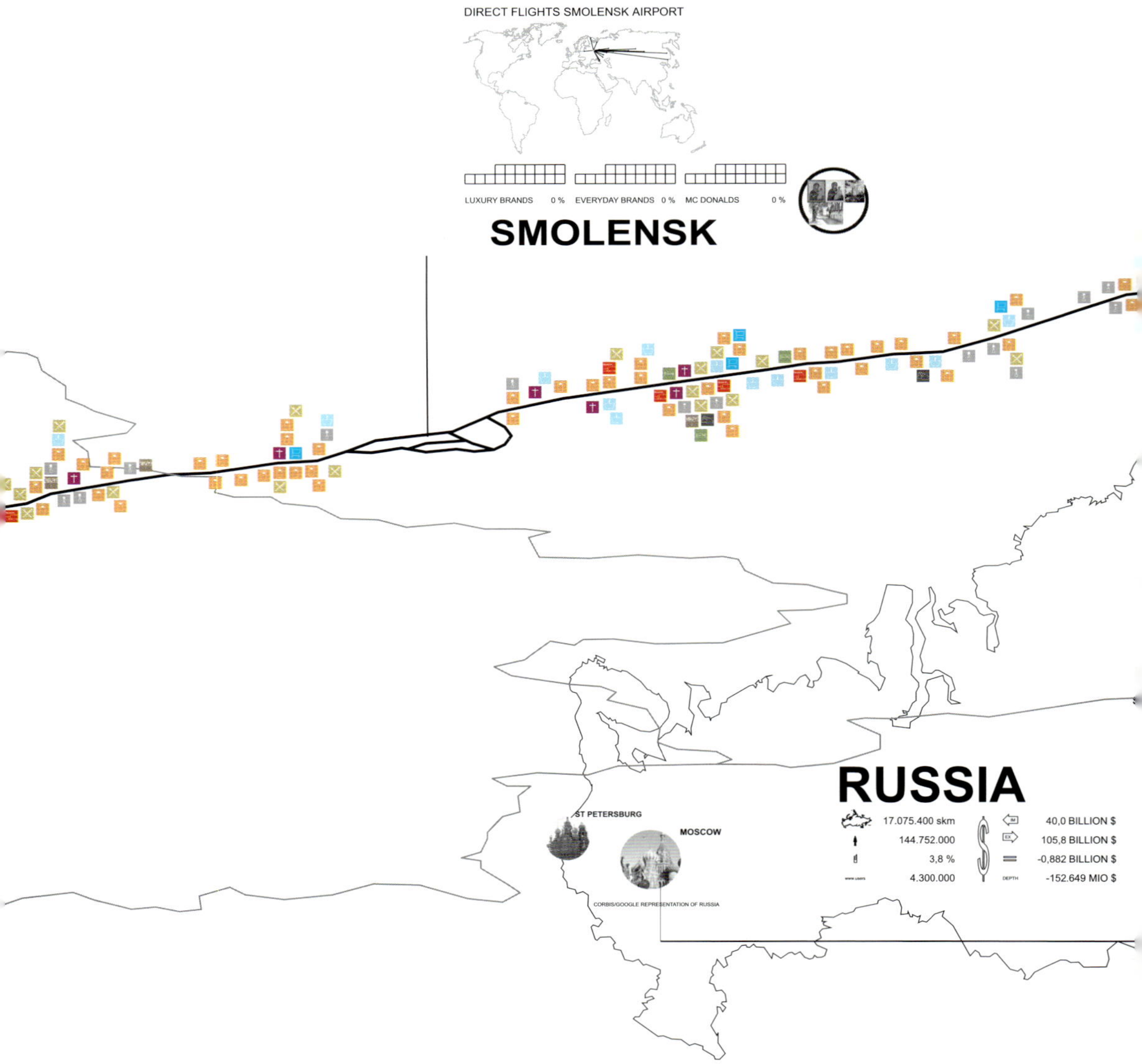
DIRECT FLIGHTS SMOLENSK AIRPORT
LUXURY BRANDS 0 %
EVERYDAY BRANDS 0 %
MC DONALDS 0 %
SMOLENSK
RUSSIA
17.075.400 skm
144.752.000
3,8 %
www.users
4.300.000
IM
40,0 BILLION $
EX
105,8 BILLION $
-0,882 BILLION $
DEPTH
-152.649 MIO $
ST PETERSBURG
MOSCOW
CORBIS/GOOGLE REPRESENTATION OF RUSSIA

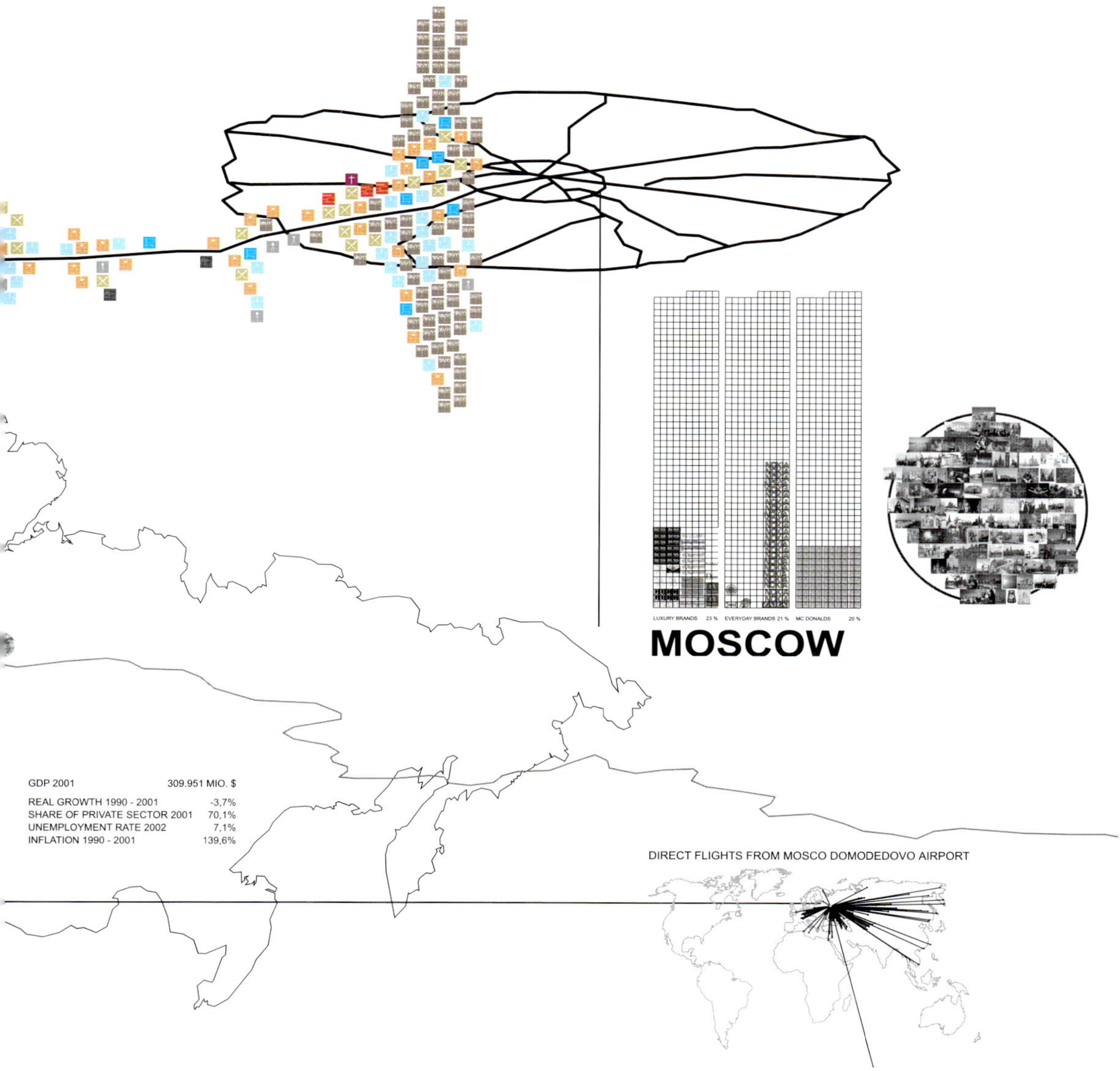

KARTE BERLIN – MOSKAU

MAP BERLIN – MOSCOW

Martin Cagno and Nina Gribat

City information flow by Martin Cagno / City information Google by Anastassia Rejepp / City information direct flights by Nina Gribat / Country information by Nina Gribat / Country information illustration by Linda Hilfing Nielsen

Flow of goods by Nina Gribat and Linda Hilfing Nielsen / 9 Pan European corridors by Nina Gribat / EU development by Nina Gribat / Visa regulation by Linda Hilfing Nielsen / Establishment of external EU border by Linda Hilfing Nielsen / Warsaw pact, Comecon and CIS by Nina Gribat

Quellen: Website of mentioned companies / www.google.com, websites of airports / www.worldbank.com / Fischer Weltalmanach 2004 / Falkplan Europa 1:4.500.000, / Interview mit Logistikfirmen / *The New Border Regime at the Bug*, by Helmut Dietrich

GRENZGEOGRAPHIEN

BORDER GEOGRAPHIES

► GRENZLAND ► BORDERLAND

SWITCH TO ERA MOBILE
era
Get more

BRACIA LUDWIŃSCY
TEL.-(091)4644 855
DREWNO KLEJONE
Szczecin ul. Struga 63
OKULARY

RYBY
100 m
BAR
SŁONECZKO
BAR
SŁONECZKO

► BREST

БЕЛАРУСЬ
Coca-Cola

EUROPÄISCHE RÄUME SCHAFFEN – NEUE WEGE IN OSTEUROPA

MAKING EUROPEAN SPACE – NEW CORRIDORS IN EASTERN EUROPE

GRENZRAUM

BORDER SPACE

E 30 TRANSIT/STASIS

E 30 TRANSIT/STASIS

DIE GRENZREGION: EIN LAND DER MÖGLICHKEITEN

BORDER REGION: LAND OF OPPORTUNITIES

GRENZSTADT BREST

BORDER CITY BREST

EUROPÄISCHE RÄUME SCHAFFEN – NEUE WEGE IN OSTEUROPA

TIM RICHARDSON

EINLEITUNG

Die umfassende Erweiterung der Europäischen Union im Jahre 2004 stellt die EU vor neue Herausforderungen, insbesondere in Bezug auf die Ausdehnung des Projekts zur Schaffung eines Europäischen Raumes auf das Gebiet einer Gruppe von relativ kleinen und (nach EU-Standards) unterentwickelten Ländern. Im Zusammenhang mit ihrem EU-Beitritt haben die zehn neuen Mitglieder aus Mittel- und Osteuropa sowohl einzeln als auch gemeinsam eine weitreichende Umorientierung ihrer Raumplanung begonnen, was umfassende Auswirkungen auf ihre künftige Entwicklung haben wird. Ein entscheidendes Ergebnis hierbei ist eine grundsätzliche Auseinandersetzung mit den Kategorien des Territoriums, wozu das Anlegen veränderter Maßstäbe ebenso gehört wie eine Beteiligung an transnationalen Verkehrsnetzen und -strömen. Dieses grundsätzliche Überdenken führte zu einer Neuorientierung im strategischen Denken von einflussreichen Akteuren in Mittel- und Osteuropa. In diesem Kapitel werde ich diese Neuorientierung untersuchen und den Versuch unternehmen, einige der einleuchtenden und überzeugenden Argumente zu den damit verbundenen Risiken und Chancen zu hinterfragen. Ich werde zeigen, dass der von den Regierungen der europäischen Länder rasch aufgegriffene neue politische Diskurs über europäisierte Räume über offensichtlich recht überzeugende Argumente verfügt. Ich werde anschließend darauf eingehen, dass sich eine gewisse Unsicherheit durchgehend bemerkbar macht, die auf die Risiken und Gefahren einer europäisierten Raumpolitik hinweist.
Diese Themen finden sich in Plänen zur Schaffung internationaler Korridore wieder, die Europa von West nach Ost verbinden und den auf dem Ideal einer reibungslosen Mobilität beruhenden neuen Beziehungen zwischen den europäischen Regionen sowohl symbolisch als auch real eine konkrete Form geben. Der Einfluss dieser gesamteuropäischen Korridore auf die täglichen Infrastrukturen wie Straßen und Bahnlinien ist das zentrale Thema dieses Kapitels. Es behandelt die Auswirkungen dieser Zeugnisse europäischer Integration auf die Regionen, die Lebensorte und die Bevölkerung der neuen Mitgliedsländer.

EIN EUROPÄISCHES RAUMPROJEKT

Angesichts der ökonomischen Bedeutung des europäischen Einigungsprozesses ist es nicht verwunderlich, dass der doppelte Diskurs über die europäische Integration und den einheitlichen Binnenmarkt einen starken Einfluss auf die Politik in Europa hat. Man muss hierbei die Gegebenheiten der europäischen Wirtschaft berücksich-

MAKING EUROPEAN SPACES – NEW CORRIDORS IN EASTERN EUROPE

TIM RICHARDSON

INTRODUCTION

The dramatic enlargement of the EU in 2004 raised challenging questions about the extension of the European spatial project into the territories of a relatively small and (by EU standards) underdeveloped group of nations. As part of their accession to the EU, the ten new members in central and eastern Europe have begun a far reaching spatial re-orientation, both individually and collectively, which has dramatic implications for their future development. A critical outcome has been a fundamental rethinking of territory which includes a scale-shift, and an engagement with transnational networks and flows, leading to a realignment in the strategic thinking of powerful actors across central and eastern Europe. In this chapter I will examine this realignment, and attempt to interrogate some of the evidence and persuasive rhetoric about the associated risks and benefits. I will suggest that a new policy discourse of Europeanised spatiality, spreading rapidly across the governments of Europe, presents a seemingly persuasive case. I then argue that a continuous thread of uncertainty runs through the new spatial tapestry, which points to the risks and dangers of a Europeanised spatiality. These issues are starkly revealed in plans for international corridors reaching across European territory from west to east, symbolically and materially concreting the new relations between European regions, grounded in an ideal of frictionless mobility. The arguments and evidence about the impacts of these pan-European corridors of everyday infrastructures – such as roads and railways – are the central concern of this chapter. It considers the implications of these material instruments of European integration to regions, places, citizens across the new member states.

A EUROPEAN SPATIAL PROJECT

Given the significance of the economic dimensions of the European project, it is not surprising that the twin discourses of European integration and the single market together have a strong effect in shaping EU policy making. Here we need to consider the nature of the European economy: a fragmented economy which translates the regional dichotomies of many of its constituent nations onto a continental scale. A prosperous core stands in stark contrast with its periphery, meaning that further concentration is an inevitable tendency, and redistribution of the benefits of the single market, and "balance" between regions are, not surprisingly, key policy aims. The effects of globalisation, and the political action of creating a single European economic bloc has many implications: for the capacity of cities, regions and nations to restruc-

tigen: Es handelt sich um eine fragmentierte Wirtschaft, welche die regionalen Dichotomien vieler ihrer Mitgliedsstaaten auf eine europäische Ebene überträgt. Ein prosperierendes Zentrum steht in starkem Kontrast zu den Randzonen, was unvermeidlich eine Tendenz zu weiterer Konzentration zur Folge haben wird. Es ist daher nicht überraschend, dass die Verteilung der Gewinne des europäischen Binnenmarktes und der Ausgleich zwischen den Regionen zentrale politische Ziele sind. Die Folgen der Globalisierung und der Politik zur Schaffung eines gemeinsamen europäischen Wirtschaftsraums sind in vielen Bereichen spürbar. Sie wirken sich aus auf die Fähigkeit von Städten, Regionen und Staaten, ihre Wirtschaft angesichts des Zusammenbruchs traditioneller Industriezweige umzustrukturieren; auf die Entscheidungen der Wirtschaft zu Standorten und Organisation ihrer Aktivitäten und damit einhergehend auf die Arbeitsmärkte; auf die Organisation städtischer Räume und die Planung neuer Landnutzungen; auf die Mobilität und die Anforderungen an die Infrastruktur und notwendigerweise auf die Umwelt. Diese politischen und ökonomischen Aspekte der europäischen Integration stellen sehr spezifische Anforderungen an die Mobilität; für ihre Durchsetzung bedarf es einer Diskussion über ein Europa der Ströme, wie Maarten Hajer in Übereinstimmung mit Castells schrieb.[1] Die Situation ist durch einen steigenden Bedarf an persönlicher Mobilität und durch die Entwicklung von Techniken wie der Just-in-Time-Logistik gekennzeichnet, die auf den schnellen und kostengünstigen Gütertransport über die Straße setzen und damit den Zugang zu ökonomischer Entwicklung unabhängig vom Standort erleichtern.
Wenn wir davon ausgehen, dass die europäische Vereinigung auch ein räumlicher Prozess ist, können auch die diesem Prozess zugrunde liegenden Prinzipien als inhärent räumlich betrachtet werden. Ob man an die Bedeutung der Friedenssicherung, die Schaffung neuer Mobilitätskorridore und global wettbewerbsfähiger Wirtschaftzonen oder gar an europäische Werte und Identität denkt – stets hat man eine räumliche Einheit mit dem Namen Europa vor Augen. Mit der Erweiterung hat dieses Thema sogar noch an Bedeutung gewonnen, da neue Mitglieder und Anwärter ihre räumliche Logik in den Kontext der Europäischen Union einbringen. Die verschiedenen politischen Bestrebungen, die auf die Schaffung eines europäischen Raums mit freiem Verkehr für Menschen, Waren und Ideen abzielen, verkörpern so die räumliche Umsetzung der europäischen Einigung als eine „Gesellschaft ohne jegliche Reibung".[2] Die Vorstellung eines reibungslosen Raums europäischer Verkehrsströme kann als Agenda für die Schaffung eines europäischen „Monotopias" verstanden werden, womit ein eindimensionaler (Mono-)Diskurs über Raum und Territorium (topia/topos) gemeint ist.[3] Darunter kann eine Reihe raumordnender Ideen verstanden werden, die das Territorium der EU in einer übergreifenden Überlegung als einen zu schaffenden einheitlichen Raum („one space") auffassen. Dieser Raum besteht aus nahtlosen Netzen und einer reibungslosen Mobilität und ist „unlösbar verknüpft mit einer Regierbarkeit Europas, die durch den Willen zur Ordnung des Raums und zur Schaffung eines nahtlosen und integrierten Raums im Kontext des europäischen Einigungsprozesses zum Ausdruck kommt".[4] Obwohl sich das Wort „Monotopia" in keinem europäischen Plan, in keinem politischen Dokument und in keiner politischen Rede findet, bestimmt diese Idee eines monotopischen Europas doch die Neudefinition des europäischen Territoriums. Das Weißbuch der EU zur Verkehrspolitik[5] beschreibt die

ture their economies in the face of the collapse of traditional industries; for the decisions made by businesses locating and organising their activities; as a result for labour markets; for the organisation of urban space and the location of new land uses; for mobility and the requirements for infrastructure provision; and consequently for the environment. These political and economic discourses of European integration create very specific demands on mobility, necessitating what Maarten Hajer, following Castells, has described as a discourse of a Europe of flows.[1] This discourse is characterised by an increasing demand for personal mobility, and by the development of technologies such as Just in Time logistics, which have enabled a more footloose approach to economic development, reliant on the fast, low cost movement of goods by road. If we accept the spatial character of the European Project it can also be argued that its grounding principles are also inherently spatial. Whether one stresses the importance of securing peace, creating the new mobility corridors and economic zones of global competitiveness or even the notion of European values and identity, the spatial entity called Europe is imagined. In the context of enlargement this issue is even more evident as new and aspirant member states reconfigure their spatial logic into an EU context. The multiple policies aiming at producing an EU territory with free flows of people, goods, ideas, and capital embody the spatialisation of the European project as a "zero-friction society".[2] Thinking about such a smooth space of European flows can be understood as an agenda for producing a Europe of "Monotopia". By this is meant the idea of a one-dimensional (mono) discourse of space and territory (topia/topos).[3] This can be understood as an organising set of ideas that looks upon the EU territory within a single overarching rationality of making a "one space", made possible by seamless networks enabling frictionless mobility which is "inextricably linked with a governmentality of Europe, expressed in a will to order space, to create a seamless and integrated space within the context of the European project."[4] Though the word "monotopia" will not be found in any European plan, policy document or political speech, this idea of monotopic Europe lies at the heart of the reframing of European territory. The EU White Paper on Transport[5] frames the alternative in dramatic terms: "During the 1990s, Europe began to suffer from congestion in certain areas and on certain routes. The problem is now beginning to threaten economic competitiveness. Paradoxically, congestion in the centre goes hand in hand with excessive isolation of the outlying regions, where there is a real need to improve links with central markets so as to ensure regional cohesion within the EU. To paraphrase a famous saying on centralisation, it could be said that the European Union is threatened with apoplexy at the centre and paralysis at the extremities."[6]

THE POLICY IDEA: PAN EUROPEAN CORRIDORS

Connectivity, then, has become a critical concern. The poor quality cross border links across what was once the iron curtain are now framed as mobility bottlenecks in the enlarged EU space. But these friction points – where trucks queue for many hours at border crossings – are only the most obvious signs of transport systems that, from an EU perspective, are simply inadequate to enable the growth of regional economies that will contribute to the European single market. One of the big European spatial policy ideas is the trans-European transport network (TEN-T), a project which realizes

Alternativen in dramatischen Worten: „In den neunziger Jahren ist das Problem der Überlastung in bestimmten Regionen und auf bestimmten Achsen Europas erstmals aufgetreten. Inzwischen bedroht es die Wettbewerbsfähigkeit der Wirtschaft. Paradoxerweise geht die Überlastung im Zentrum mit einer zu starken Isolierung der Randregionen einher, die nach wie vor auf eine bessere Anbindung an die zentralen Märkte warten, so dass der territoriale Zusammenhang der Europäischen Union gewährleistet werden kann. In Anlehnung an eine bekannte Aussage über die Zentralisierung kann man sagen, dass der Europäischen Union ‚der Infarkt im Zentrum und die Lähmung an den Extremitäten' droht."[6]

EINE POLITISCHE IDEE: GESAMTEUROPÄISCHE KORRIDORE

Erreichbar zu sein wurde nun zu einem wichtigen Anliegen. Die schlecht ausgebauten Verbindungswege über die frühere Ostgrenze hinweg bilden nun wahre Engpässe für die Mobilität im erweiterten EU-Raum. Doch diese Reibungspunkte, an denen Lkws viele Stunden lang auf den Grenzübertritt warten, sind nur die sichtbarsten Zeichen eines Verkehrssystems, das aus Sicht der EU das Wachstum der zum europäischen Binnenmarkt beitragenden regionalen Ökonomien einfach nicht gewährleisten kann. Eine der großen Ideen europäischer Raumordnungspolitik ist das Transeuropäische Verkehrsnetz (TEN-V). Dieses Projekt beinhaltet die Ambitionen der Industrie- und Infrastrukturlobby, es verkörpert die Vision Jacques Delors', der sich selbst als Architekt Europas sah. Das TEN-V stellte eine der bedeutendsten praktischen und symbolischen Initiativen zur Integration des europäischen Raums dar. Verglichen mit früheren Karten transeuropäischer Straßen- und Bahnnetze, setzt das neue Konzept auf eine stärkere Integration und weist eine Reihe von vorrangigen Korridoren aus. Das TEN-V bildet einen Meilenstein in der Entwicklung der europäischen Raumpolitik.[7] Mitte der 1990er Jahre beschloss die EU die Leitlinien für den Aufbau eines Verkehrsnetzes, über das jeder Punkt Europas erreichbar sein sollte und das sich über die EU-Außengrenzen hinweg in die nördlichen, südlichen und östlichen Regionen erstreckt. Das Transeuropäische Verkehrsnetz verfolgt eine wahrhaft globale Vision: Ein integriertes Netz moderner Schnellstraßen, Bahnverbindungen und anderer Infrastrukturen sollte den europäischen Kontinent durchziehen, die bislang fehlenden Verbindungen zwischen den nationalen Verkehrssystemen sollten geschaffen und modernste Informationstechnologien für das Funktionieren des Netzes verwendet werden. Steigende Wettbewerbsfähigkeit, stärkerer Zusammenhalt und größeres Wirtschaftswachstum, Schaffung von Arbeitsplätzen und Reduzierung der Randständigkeit – das sind die Vorteile, die man sich für diese Schlüsselregionen im Ergebnis des 1992 eingeleiteten Prozesses erhoffte. Mit der Erweiterung erreicht das TEN-V über den Weg der gesamteuropäischen Verkehrskorridore nun auch die neuen Mitgliedsstaaten und darüber hinaus weitere Regionen. Schon als das TEN-V in die Maastrichter Verträge aufgenommen wurde, diskutierte man auf der ersten Gesamteuropäischen Verkehrskonferenz in Prag 1991 über seine östliche Erweiterung und nahm das Konzept der gesamteuropäischen Korridore an. Auf der zweiten Konferenz auf Kreta 1994 wurden neun multimodale Korridore ausgewiesen, zu denen 1997 auf der Konferenz in Helsinki ein zehnter hinzugefügt wurde. Diese Korridore sollten eine Reihe von Städten zu einer Kette verbinden. Ein Beispiel: Korridor 2 sollte Berlin über Moskau mit

the ambitions of European industrial and infrastructure lobbies, and articulates the vision of Jacques Delors, who saw himself as an architect of Europe. The TEN-T became one of the major early practical and symbolic initiatives of European spatial integration. From early maps of trans-European road and rail networks, the concept has become more integrated, a series of priority corridors have been identified, and it stands as an important milestone in the development of European spatial policy.[7] In the mid 1990s agreement was reached by the EU on Guidelines for the development of a transport network which would reach into every corner of Europe, extending its physical contact across EU external borders into regions to the north, south and east. The TEN-T vision was truly global: an integrated network of modern high speed roads, railways, and other infrastructure crossing the European continent, filling the missing links between national transport systems, and applying state of the art information technology to the operation of the network. Increasing competitiveness, cohesion, and economic growth, creating jobs and reducing peripherality: benefits were expected to flow in these key areas of the 1992 process. With enlargement, the TEN-T is now beginning to reach into the new member states and beyond, through pan-European transport corridors. Even as the TEN-T was being written into the Maastricht Treaty, its eastern extension was already being debated at the first Pan-European Transport Conference, held in Prague in 1991, where the concept of pan-European corridors was adopted. In 1994, at the second Conference in Crete, nine multi-modal corridors were identified, to which a tenth was added at the Helsinki Conference in 1997.

These corridors would connect strings of cities. For example: Corridor 2 would link Berlin via Moscow to Niznij Novgorod with 2,313 km of rail and 2,200 of road infrastructure; Corridor 5 would link Venice, Trieste/Koper, Ljubljana, Budapest and Kiev; Corridor 10 would link Salzburg, Ljubljana, Zagreb, Belgrade and Thessalonike. In all, the corridors comprise 48,000 km of infrastructure, of which 25,000 km were rail network and 23,000 km were road network. In addition, airports, sea- and river ports and major terminals were identified as key nodes.[8] The adoption of these corridors at conferences of transport ministers from across the wider Europe does not indicate any legal status or political decision to build them. However they are aspirational, and can be seen to play a part in new spatial visions and development strategies emerging across the Eastern half of the European continent.In parallel with this pan-European intergovernmental process, the EU was making more formal preparations for extending the trans-European networks into central Europe.[9] In 1997 a high level group was formed with representatives from the EU member state governments and those of the accession countries. Under the aegis of this group, the Commission initiated the 'Transport Infrastructure Needs Assessment' (TINA) programme. TINA focused on infrastructure plans in the CEE countries, and in particular on financing arrangements. The initial report[10] mirroring the early work on TENs, set out the need for a dramatic increase in infrastructure development in the accession countries. It identified an existing core network of 13,430 km of railway and 11,890 km of road – and recommended new projects which would extend the road network to 18,030 km, and the rail network to 20,290 km.

Perhaps not surprisingly, EU financial support for its new members is biased towards infrastructure spending. The key corridors proposed for development required some

Nishni Nowgorod über 2313 km Schienenweg und 2200 km Straße verbinden; Korridor 5 sollte Venedig, Triest/Koper, Ljubljana, Budapest und Kiew, Korridor 10 Salzburg, Ljubljana, Zagreb, Belgrad und Thessaloniki miteinander verbinden. Insgesamt umfassen die Korridore 48000 km Verkehrswege, davon sind 25000 km Bahnstrecken und 23000 km Straße. Zusätzlich wurden Flughäfen, See- und Binnenhäfen und wichtige Terminals als Knotenpunkte festgelegt.[8] Die Festlegung dieser Korridore auf den verschiedenen Konferenzen der europäischen Verkehrsminister gibt ihnen keinerlei rechtlichen Status bzw. stellt keine politische Entscheidung über deren Einrichtung dar, sie drückt jedoch einen Anspruch aus und kann eine Rolle in den neuen Raumvorstellungen und Entwicklungsstrategien spielen, die in der Osthälfte des europäischen Kontinents entstehen. Parallel zu diesem gesamteuropäischen zwischenstaatlichen Prozess unternahm die Europäische Union konkrete Anstrengungen, um das Transeuropäische Netz nach Mitteleuropa auszudehnen.[9] 1997 wurde eine hochrangige Gruppe aus Regierungsvertretern der Mitgliedsländer und der Anwärterstaaten der Europäischen Union gebildet. Unter Leitung dieser Gruppe initiierte die Kommission das Verkehrsinfrastrukturprogramm TINA (Transport Infrastructure Needs Assessment). TINA konzentrierte sich auf die Infrastrukturpläne der Staaten Mittel- und Osteuropas und befasste sich im Besonderen mit Finanzierungsfragen. Der erste Bericht[10], der die erste Phase der Arbeit für die Transeuropäischen Netze beschrieb, unterstrich die Notwendigkeit einer deutlichen Intensivierung der Infrastrukturentwicklung in den Beitrittsländern. Er ermittelte ein bestehendes Hauptnetz von 13430 km Bahnstrecke und 11890 km Straße und empfahl neue Projekte zur Erweiterung des Straßennetzes auf 18030 km und des Bahnnetzes auf 20290 km.
Es ist wohl kaum überraschend, dass die finanzielle Unterstützung der EU überproportional in Infrastrukturprojekte geht. Die für den Ausbau vorgeschlagenen Korridore erfordern eine Neuinvestition von rund 87 Milliarden EUR, von denen über 36 Milliarden EUR in das Schienen- und über 45 Milliarden EUR in das Straßennetz fließen sollen. Allein in Polen sind die vorgeschlagenen Investitionen enorm hoch und belaufen sich auf 24 Milliarden EUR, davon zehn Milliarden EUR für den Ausbau des nationalen Straßennetzes und neun Milliarden EUR für die Schiene.[11]
Schon in den 1990er Jahren flossen die Investitionen der EU in den Beitrittsländern im Rahmen des PHARE-Programms (das Programm unterstützt den Prozess der Anpassung der Beitrittskandidaten) zunehmend in Infrastrukturmaßnahmen (1,488 Milliarden EUR bei einem Gesamtbetrag von 6,6 Milliarden EUR in der Zeit zwischen 1990 und 1996). Nach dem Jahr 2000 trug das neue strukturpolitische Instrument zur Vorbereitung auf den Beitritt (Instrument for Pre-accession Aid – ISPA) zur weiteren Förderung der Verkehrsinfrastrukturentwicklung bei. Seit der Erweiterung sind im Ergebnis der Reform der Strukturfonds höhere Ausgaben für die Infrastruktur in den neuen Mitgliedsstaaten zu erwarten. Wie in den alten EU-Staaten bedingt die notwendige Anbindung der neuen internationalen Korridore einen damit verbundenen starken Ausbau der regionalen Infrastruktur. Das TINA-Netz hat jedoch im Gegensatz zu den zwischenstaatlich festgelegten gesamteuropäischen Korridoren keinen offiziellen Status und bringt Probleme bezüglich seiner demokratischen Legitimierung mit sich, da es „weder Gegenstand einer offenen Debatte noch einer parlamentarischen Prüfung war und aus diesem Grunde vor allem durch Nichtregierungsorgani-

87 billion EUR of new investment, of which over 36 billion EUR would go to rail and over 45 billion EUR to road. In Poland alone, the scale of proposed investment proposed was enormous, some 24 billion EUR: of this 10 billion EUR for developing the national road network and 9 billion EUR for rail.[11]

Through the 1990s, then, EU investment in the accession countries through the PHARE programme became increasingly biased towards infrastructure investment (1.488 billion EUR of 6.6 billion EUR total in the period 1990–1996). After 2000, a new Instrument for Pre-accession Aid (ISPA) contributed further support for transport infrastructure development. Since enlargement, the reform of the structural funds promises more significant spending on infrastructure in the new member states. As in the existing member states, the need for accessibility to new international corridors suggests the prospect of a correspondingly dramatic increase in regional infrastructure development. However, unlike the pan-European corridors which have been agreed through an intergovernmental process, the TINA network has no official status, and raises problems of democratic legitimacy, since it has "not been subject to open debate or parliamentary scrutiny, and for this reason it has been criticised, particularly by NGOs, as an inadequate basis for major transport funding decisions."[12] The development of TENs policy in Central Europe, through TINA, is complicated by the longstanding TEMs programme (TEM – Trans-European North-South Motorway Network). This quite separate plan for a predominantly north-south oriented transport corridor originated behind the iron curtain, and does not mesh seamlessly with the new east-west agenda of TENs, posing a political dilemma of whether to prioritise the Central European consolidation symbolised by TEM, or the EU integration symbolised by TEN. In the 1990s the Czech transport network, for example, was being planned within these twin policy frameworks.[13] Once again the political symbolism of the alignment of corridors can be seen. Comparing the spatial orientation of these different networks, it is clear that the pan-European corridors prioritise east-west connectivity, perhaps at the expense of connectivity within Central Europe: "... when the network [of pan-European corridors] was devised all regional aspects which did *not* support the extension of previously developed TEN corridors played a role of secondary importance."[14]

POST ENLARGEMENT TALKS

Following enlargement to EU25, a High Level Group was established to integrate the Trans-European Transport Network and the Pan-European Corridors by identifying a "set of major transnational transport axes and priority projects on these axes".[15] Questions at the heart of this consultation process are: "Which are the major axes? Which investments, and how? How to ensure seamless and efficient use of the axes?"[16] A rarefied debate of geopolitical significance is currently taking place which has major consequences for the future development of central Europe, and for the place of the new members within the EU spatial order.

CORRIDORS IN A SPATIAL CONTEXT: EUROPEAN AND NATIONAL

But how do these transport networks and corridors relate to the overall vision for European space? Here we need to refer to the European Spatial Development Perspective[17], in which desired spatial interventions are set out in concrete terms: a chapter

sationen kritisiert wurde, die es nicht als angemessene Basis für grundlegende Verkehrsentscheidungen ansehen".[12] Die Politik zur Schaffung Transeuropäischer Netze in Mitteleuropa mit Hilfe von TINA wird durch die langfristigen TEM-Programme (TEM – Trans-European North-South Motorway Network) erschwert. Dieser weitgehend eigenständige Plan eines vorrangig nord-südlich ausgerichteten Verkehrskorridors wurde in Osteuropa vor dem Fall des Eisernen Vorhangs entwickelt und lässt sich nicht nahtlos mit der neuen Ost-West-Agenda der Transeuropäischen Netze verknüpfen. Daraus ergibt sich das politische Dilemma, entweder der mitteleuropäischen Konsolidierung in Form der TEM oder der EU-Integration in Gestalt des TEN-V den Vorrang zu geben. In den 1990er Jahren wurde zum Beispiel das tschechische Verkehrssystem innerhalb dieses doppelten politischen Rahmens geplant.[13] Dabei wird in der Ausrichtung der Korridore auch die politische Orientierung sichtbar. Vergleicht man die räumliche Ausrichtung der verschiedenen Netze, ist die Bevorzugung der Ost-West-Verbindungen in den gesamteuropäischen Korridoren klar erkennbar. Dies geschieht vielleicht um den Preis einer guten Anbindung innerhalb Mitteleuropas: „(...) als das Netz [der gesamteuropäischen Korridore] entwickelt wurde, spielten alle regionalen Aspekte, die die Erweiterung der zuvor entwickelten TEN-Korridore *nicht* unterstützten, eine zweitrangige Rolle."[14]

GESPRÄCHE NACH DER ERWEITERUNG

Nach der Erweiterung der Europäischen Union auf 25 Mitgliedsstaaten wurde eine hochrangige Gruppe eingesetzt, um eine Integration des Transeuropäischen Verkehrsnetzes und der gesamteuropäischen Korridore durch die Festlegung einer „bestimmten Anzahl transnationaler Hauptverkehrsachsen und vorrangiger Projekte entlang dieser Achsen"[15] herbeizuführen. Folgende Fragen stehen im Zentrum des Konsultationsprozesses: „Was sind die Hauptachsen? Welche Investitionen sind nötig, und wie sind sie zu realisieren? Wie lässt sich eine nahtlose und effiziente Nutzung der Achsen gewährleisten?"[16] Gegenwärtig findet eine geopolitisch wichtige Debatte im engeren Kreis statt, die weitreichende Konsequenzen für die künftige Entwicklung Mitteleuropas haben wird und die den Platz, den die neuen Mitglieder innerhalb der räumlichen Ordnung der Europäischen Union einnehmen werden, in starkem Maße mitbestimmen wird.

KORRIDORE IM EUROPÄISCHEN UND NATIONALEN RAUMKONTEXT

In welchem Verhältnis stehen diese Verkehrsnetze und Korridore mit der übergreifenden Vision eines europäischen Raums? Zur Beantwortung dieser Frage muss man sich auf das Europäische Raumentwicklungskonzept (EUREK) beziehen[17], in dem die angestrebten Eingriffe in den Raum konkret formuliert werden: Ein Kapitel ist der Bedeutung des TEN-V für die Beseitigung von Kommunikationshindernissen und die Herbeiführung von wirtschaftlicher Konvergenz und Wettbewerb gewidmet. Das Herzstück der EUREK-Vision in Bezug auf den europäischen Raum – Schaffung eines polyzentrischen urbanen Netzes und „dynamischer wirtschaftlicher Integrationszonen" – hängt entscheidend von der Infrastrukturentwicklung ab. Daher sollten sich gemäß EUREK EU-Investitionen, einschließlich der Strukturfonds, auf die Schaffung einer „hocheffizienten Infrastruktur auf transnationaler, nationaler und regionaler Ebene" konzentrie-

is devoted to the significance of TEN-T in removing barriers to communication and in facilitating economic convergence and competition. The core elements of the ESDP's spatial vision – the creation of a polycentric urban network and "dynamic zones of economic integration" – are crucially dependent on this infrastructure development. It states that EU investment, including the Structural Funds, should focus on providing a "highly efficient infrastructure at transnational, national and regional level".[18] Significantly, the ESDP states that prioritisation of development of the major arteries and corridors of TEN-T will not suffice. It is necessary to upgrade the regional transport networks which will feed into TEN-T, if economic benefits are to be secured. The mobility implications of transnational corridors also need to be thought about in the context of the specific conditions in the new member states, summarised as: "growth in road traffic; increasing congestion and air quality problems in urban areas; a decline in the modal shares of rail and public transport; and generally rather undeveloped policies towards walking and cycle use for short journeys."[19] The dramatic changes in transport conditions are such that, for example, the volume of freight traffic on Estonian roads grew by more than 240 per cent between 1993 and 1998, while rail traffic in many central European countries declined by around 50 per cent. Infrastructure development renewal are already major challenges for governments across central Europe, and there is an emphasis on road projects, with consequent threats to biodiversity.[20]

BEING ON THE MAP: REALIGNING SPATIAL STRATEGIES

The countries of Central and Eastern Europe (CEE) are undergoing dramatic institutional and cultural changes, accompanied by more concrete changes as national infrastructure networks become part of a European whole. Infrastructure links with the EU are clearly not just about getting people and goods from Arhus to Budapest. They symbolise a political east-west realignment, which has turned the pattern of trade movements on its head. Poor quality infrastructure links with western Europe are being placed under increasingly heavy pressure as trade flows re-orient westwards. For these geo-political and economic reasons, there is a strong political will for improvements to transport infrastructure. A feature of the cultural change is the strong support for European (and generally westwards) linkages to be forged, and an acceptance of market driven policy, as part of a restructuring of national transport systems. The pan-European corridors are critical in this realignment, and this significance is not lost on new and aspirant EU members, who perceive the corridors as a key element of a political, economic and territorial project: "The concept for construction of Pan-European Transport Corridors should be viewed as a specific form of implementing EU policy on infrastructural development of Central and South Eastern European countries. It is an essential constituent part of a large-scale work on establishment of a unified economic and political space on the territory of the continent."[21]

Back in the 1990s, in the long march towards EU membership, the political and economic importance of the TEN-T was already being articulated in national policy documents across the Central European countries. The Czech Republic, for example, articulated its crossroads location in a wider European space (rather than a peripheral location on the edge of the EU). Its importance for transit traffic was frequently men-

ren.[18] Bemerkenswert ist, dass nach Auffassung EUREKs eine vorrangige Entwicklung der Hauptstrecken und der wichtigsten Korridore im Rahmen des TEN-V nicht ausreicht. Die in das Transeuropäische Verkehrsnetz mündenden regionalen Verkehrsnetze müssen stärker entwickelt werden, wenn wirtschaftliche Vorteile gesichert werden sollen. Die Auswirkungen der Mobilität in den transnationalen Korridoren müssen auch im Kontext der spezifischen Bedingungen der neuen Mitgliedsstaaten gesehen werden. Sie lassen sich wie folgt zusammenfassen: „Anwachsen des Straßenverkehrs; Zunahme von Verkehrsstaus und Luftverschmutzungsproblemen in städtischen Regionen; rückläufige Nutzung der Schienenwege und der öffentlichen Verkehrsmittel; eine allgemein geringe Förderung des Fußgänger- oder Fahrradverkehrs auf kurzen Strecken".[19] Die tiefgreifenden Veränderungen der Verkehrsbedingungen haben zum Beispiel zu einer Zunahme des Güterverkehrs auf den Straßen Estlands zwischen 1993 und 1998 um mehr als 240 Prozent geführt, während der Bahnverkehr in vielen mitteleuropäischen Ländern um rund 50 Prozent abgenommen hat. Die Erneuerung der Infrastruktur ist eine der wesentlichen Herausforderungen für die Regierungen in Mitteleuropa. Dabei werden Straßenprojekte bevorzugt, die eine Bedrohung der Biodiversität zur Folge haben.[20]

DAZU GEHÖREN IST ALLES: NEUAUSRICHTUNG VON RAUMSTRATEGIEN

Die Länder Mittel- und Osteuropas durchlaufen tiefgreifende institutionelle und kulturelle Umwälzungen, die von ganz konkreten Veränderungen, wie der Eingliederung des nationalen Infrastrukturnetzes in das europäische Gesamtnetz, begleitet werden. Infrastrukturverbindungen mit der Europäischen Union bedeuten natürlich nicht nur, Menschen von Arhus nach Budapest zu transportieren, sondern sie verkörpern politisch eine Ost-West-Ausrichtung, die die hergebrachten Muster der Güter- und Handelsströme auf den Kopf stellt. Die schlechten Infrastrukturverbindungen mit Westeuropa geraten mit der Neuausrichtung der Warenströme nach Westen unter erheblichen Druck. Aus diesen geopolitischen und wirtschaftlichen Gründen heraus entstand ein starker politischer Wille zur Verbesserung der Verkehrsinfrastruktur. Ein Merkmal des kulturellen Wandels liegt in der starken Unterstützung europäischer (und im allgemeinen westwärts gerichteter) Verbindungen und in der Akzeptanz einer marktorientierten Politik als Teil der Umstrukturierung der nationalen Verkehrsysteme. Die gesamteuropäischen Korridore spielen in dieser Neuausrichtung eine entscheidende Rolle; die neuen Mitglieder oder Beitrittskandidaten der EU sind sich dessen sehr bewusst und sehen die Korridore daher als Schlüsselelemente eines politischen, wirtschaftlichen und territorialen Projektes an: „Das Konzept der gesamteuropäischen Verkehrskorridore sollte als eine spezifische Form der Anwendung der EU-Politik auf die Infrastrukturentwicklung der mittel- und südosteuropäischen Länder gesehen werden. Es ist ein wesentlicher Bestandteil von umfassenden Maßnahmen zur Schaffung eines einheitlichen wirtschaftlichen und politischen Raums auf unserem Kontinent."[21]
In den 1990er Jahren, als sich die mitteleuropäischen Staaten auf dem langen Weg zur EU-Mitgliedschaft befanden, wurde die politische und wirtschaftliche Bedeutung des TEN-V schon in ihren nationalen politischen Dokumenten formuliert. Die Tschechische Republik beispielsweise definierte ihre Lage als Kreuzungszone in einem größeren europäischen Raum und nicht etwa als Randlage an der EU-Peripherie. Ihre

20=40
złotych*
minut
SIEMENS MC60
99 zł

Bedeutung für den Transitverkehr wurde dabei häufig unterstrichen. Die symbolische politische Bedeutung des TEN-V als Ausdruck einer Neuorientierung auf den Westen war unumstritten, doch seine wirtschaftliche Bedeutung wurde heruntergespielt. Klarer ausgesprochen wurde dagegen der Investitionsbedarf, um Staus zu verhindern und die Qualität der Infrastruktur zu verbessern. Den Verkehrskorridoren, die Prag mit Deutschland und Österreich verbinden, galt das besondere Interesse der Tschechischen Regierung, da diese besonders stauanfällig und von schlechter Qualität waren. Bei all dem gab es nur wenige Überlegungen zu den räumlichen und wirtschaftlichen Auswirkungen des Transeuropäischen Netzes auf das Territorium der Tschechischen Republik. Der Aspekt von ungleichmäßiger Entwicklung als Folge des Transeuropäischen Verkehrsnetzes wurde nicht angesprochen. Doch die tschechische Regierung war nicht die einzige, die ihr Territorium als europäischen Transitraum betrachtete. Zahlreiche Regierungen der neuen Mitgliedsstaaten stellten ihre Staatsgebiete als strategische Kreuzungen im neu geordneten europäischen Raum dar. Die slowenische Regierung beispielsweise formulierte es folgendermaßen: „Lange Zeit war Slowenien ein Kreuzungspunkt von Handelsstraßen und verband den Osten mit dem Westen, den Norden mit dem Süden; dieser geographische Vorteil gibt dem Land eine besondere Stellung im gegenwärtigen europäischen Integrationsprozess wie auch im Prozess des wirtschaftlichen Wiederaufbaus der mittel- und osteuropäischen Länder."[22] Weiter östlich versuchen bulgarische Politiker, dasselbe zu tun: „Gegenwärtig durchqueren fünf der zehn bei den Treffen der Verkehrsminister der europäischen Länder auf Kreta und in Helsinki festgelegten gesamteuropäischen Korridore das Gebiet der Republik Bulgarien: die Korridore 4, 7/Wasser/, 8, 9 und 10. Diese Festlegung verdeutlicht die besondere Stellung unseres Landes als eine bedeutende Drehscheibe für die Verbindungen zwischen den Regionen Europas und ihren natürlichen Verlängerungen nach Asien und in den Nahen Osten."[23]

In all diesen Fällen sind transnationale Verkehrsströme innerhalb der EU und über deren Grenzen hinweg das bestimmende Merkmal einer neuen Sicht auf das Territorium als transnationalen Transitraum. Diese Sicht geht einher mit der Erwartung von Vorteilen, die daraus resultieren, dass man innerhalb anstatt außerhalb einer europäisierten Karte steht.

Es lohnt sich, die genannten Beispiele aus Slowenien und Bulgarien genauer zu betrachten, um zu sehen, wie diese Europäisierung die nationale Verkehrspolitik beeinflusst. Im Falle Sloweniens ist klar ersichtlich, dass die nationale Verkehrspolitik die europäische Dimension vollständig aufgenommen hat: „Dem Ministerium für Verkehr und Kommunikation Sloweniens zufolge sollte die Integration des slowenischen Verkehrsystems in das der EU bei der Umsetzung der Verkehrspolitik berücksichtigt werden. (...) Slowenien wird bis zum 1. Januar 2005 jährlich rund 152,2 Milliarden Tolar für den Verkehr ausgeben. (...) In Übereinstimmung mit den EU-Regelungen im Verkehrsbereich wird der Großteil der Summe für die Anbindung an das gesamteuropäische Straßennetz verwendet werden."[24]

In Bulgarien ist eine Europäisierung der Verkehrspolitik ebenfalls offensichtlich: „Eines der Hauptziele der nationalen Politik zur Entwicklung und Erneuerung der Straßennetze in Bulgarien ist der Autobahnbau in Richtung der Hauptachsen sowie der Straßen, die zu den gesamteuropäischen Verkehrskorridoren gehören und durch un-

tioned. The political symbolism of the TEN-T in terms of reorientation to the west was undisputed, but its economic significance was played down. What was more clearly argued was the need for investment to alleviate congestion and improve infrastructure quality. Transport corridors linking Prague with Germany and Austria were singled out by the Czech Government for special attention, being congested and of poor quality. In all of this, there has been little consideration of the spatial or economic impact of TENs within Czech territory. The redistributive impacts of TEN-T were not addressed. But the Czech government has not been alone in branding its territory as a European transit space. Many of the new member state governments locate their territories, distinctively, as a strategic crossroads in the reconfigured European space. The Slovenian Government, for example, puts it like this: "For a long time, Slovenia has been the crossroads for trade routes, linking the East with the West and the North with the South; this geographical advantage gives the country a special position in current European integration processes as well as in the economic reconstruction of the Central and Eastern Europe countries."[22]

Further east, Bulgarian politicians seek to do the same: "At present, the territory of the Republic of Bulgaria is crossed by the road routes of five out of ten Pan-European Corridors – 4, 7/water/, 8, 9 and 10, defined at the Crete and Helsinki Meeting of the Transport Ministers of the European countries. Their definition determines the special position of our country as an important centre of the connections between the regions of the continent and their natural extension into Asia and the Near East."[23]

In each of these cases, transnational flows within the EU and beyond it are the defining features of a new articulation of territory as transnational transit space, which carried with it expectations of benefits of being on, rather than off, the Europeanised map.

It is worth looking further into these examples of Slovenia and Bulgaria, to see how this Europeanisation is affecting national transport policies. In the Slovenian case, it is clear that national transport policy has fully embraced a European dimension: "According to the Slovene Ministry of Transport and Communications, the integration of Slovenia's transport system into that of the EU should be taken into account in implementing the transport policy ... Slovenia will allocate around 152.2 billion Slovene tolars for transport per year until 1st January 2005 ... In line with EU transport regulations the majority of the sum will be used to establish links with the pan-European road network."[24]

In Bulgaria, too, Europeanisation of transport policy is evident: "One of the chief aims of the national policy on the road network development and modernization in Bulgaria addresses the motorway construction in the direction of the main road routes and those belonging to the Pan-European Transport Corridors crossing the territory of the country. ...The further improvement of the ten transport corridors can be viewed as a process of construction of a more perfect and compact transport network in the context of our country's aspiration for integration into the EU political and economic processes."[25]

ser Land verlaufen. (...) Der weitere Ausbau der zehn Verkehrskorridore dient dazu, ein besseres und dichteres Verkehrsnetz zu schaffen und entspricht somit dem Streben unseres Landes nach Integration in die politischen und wirtschaftlichen Prozesse der Europäischen Union."[25]

RISIKEN UND CHANCEN TRANSNATIONALER MOBILITÄTSKORRIDORE

Gegenwärtig findet offensichtlich eine Neuorientierung statt, bei der die Idee transnationaler Mobilitätskorridore eine wesentliche Rolle spielt. Welche Folgen können diese Korridore haben? Welche Auswirkungen hat ein vernetzter europäischer Raum auf die Wirtschaft, die Gesellschaft und die Umwelt der Gebiete, über die er sich erstreckt? Die Entwicklung von transnationalen Korridoren geht mit Unsicherheiten einher, die politischen Analysten bekannt sind, auch wenn sie in der geglätteten Sprache politischer Reden und Dokumente nicht erwähnt werden. Im Zentrum steht das Problem, dass der Bau von Infrastrukturen ungewollte und ungewünschte Auswirkungen haben kann. Das können sowohl schwere Eingriffe in die Umwelt als auch negative Einflüsse auf regionale Ökonomien sein, wobei zwischen Gewinnern und Verlierern neue räumliche Grenzen gezogen werden, da die Netze und Korridore ihr Augenmerk auf neue Zentren, Knotenpunkte und Wachstumszonen lenken. Hier praktiziert EUREK die gleiche Verschleierungspolitik wie frühere Kommissionspapiere.[26] Im Papier „Europe 2000+"[27] wurde das TEN-V ins Zentrum eines gesamteuropäischen Raumplanungsrahmens gestellt und dessen problematische Doppelrolle benannt, nämlich einerseits bei der Errichtung eines Binnenmarktes zu helfen und andererseits gleichzeitig die Gemeinschaft als Ganzes ausgleichend zu entwickeln. Es wurde durchaus gesehen, dass das TEN-V zu Spannungen zwischen diesen Kernzielen der Raumpolitik führt. Während globale Wettbewerbsfähigkeit nach einer „Fortsetzung und sogar Beschleunigung der Umsetzung der großräumigen TEN" verlangt, wird dies von der Gefahr „sich vertiefender Ungleichheiten in der Union" begleitet, die durch die „Stärkung des Zentrums zum Nachteil der Peripherie" (neben anderen Faktoren) hervorgerufen wird.[28] Die Frage einer harmonischen, ausgeglichenen Entwicklung hängt mit der Frage der Wettbewerbsfähigkeit zusammen. Die Wettbewerbsfähigkeit der Regionen der EU untereinander zu sichern heißt, zwischen diesen Gebieten „die inakzeptablen Risiken und Kosten einer sich vergrößernden Disparität zu vermeiden."[29] Es wird davon ausgegangen, dass eine ausgewogene Entwicklung durch einen Abbau der Wettbewerbsnachteile in den peripheren Regionen herbeigeführt werden kann. Diese beiden Ziele können nur erreicht werden, wenn die mit dem TEN-V verbundenen Zentralisierungseffekte verhindert werden. Es wird also klar erkannt, dass das TEN-V einen Keil zwischen die europäische globale und die innere räumliche Wettbewerbsfähigkeit zu treiben droht. Diese starke Spannung scheint sich durch die ganze Raumpolitik der EU zu ziehen. Während EUREK die Sorgen über „Pumpeffekte" (bei denen durch neue Hochgeschwindigkeits-Infrastrukturen Ressourcen aus strukturschwachen und peripheren Regionen abgezogen werden) und „Tunneleffekte" (bei denen Regionen zwar durchquert, aber nicht miteinander verbunden werden) wiederholt[30], wird in allen bestehenden politischen Optionen das allgemeine Ziel einer verbesserten Erreichbarkeit als eine unproblematische Lösung präsentiert. Neuere Studien haben die räumlichen Auswirkungen eines europäischen Verkehrsnetzes um-

RISKS AND BENEFITS OF TRANSNATIONAL MOBILITY CORRIDORS

It is clear that a rescaling and reorientation is taking place, which embraces the idea of transnational mobility corridors. The next issue to consider is what might be the effects of these corridors. What might be the impacts of a networked European space on the economies, societies and environments of the territories within it? The development of transnational corridors is fraught with uncertainties that are familiar to policy analysts even though they may not be mentioned in the smooth language of political speeches and policy documents. At the heart of this is the problem that building infrastructure can have unintended and undesirable consequences. As well as harmful environmental impacts, there can be negative impacts on regional economies, and a redrawing of the spatial boundaries between winners and losers as networks and corridors focus attention on new centres of gravity, nodes and growth zones. Here the ESDP repeats the blurring of earlier Commission policy documents.[26] "Europe 2000+"[27], placing TEN-T at the centre of a pan-European spatial planning framework, identified the problematic double role of assisting the creation of the single market whilst enabling balanced development of the Community as a whole. Significantly, it was recognised that TEN-T creates a tension between these core territorial issues. While global competitiveness requires "continuation, even acceleration of the implementation of large-scale TENs", this is accompanied by the risk "of an increase in the imbalances in the Union", stemming from the "strengthening of the centre to the detriment of the periphery"[28] (among other factors). The question of harmonious, or balanced, development is linked with competitiveness. Ensuring spatial competitiveness between regions within the Union depends on "avoiding the unacceptable risks and costs of widening disparities"[29] between regions. Balanced development, in turn, is seen as reliant upon decreasing the competitive disadvantage of peripheral regions. Achieving both of these objectives relies on avoiding the centralising impacts associated with TEN-T. So, TEN-T is clearly identified as threatening to drive a wedge between European global competitiveness and internal spatial competitiveness. It appears that there is a strong tension here, which runs throughout the EU's spatial policy. So, whilst the ESDP repeats these concerns about "pump" effects (where new high speed infrastructure removes resources from structurally weaker and peripheral regions) and "tunnel" effects (where such areas are crossed without being connected)[30], all of the policy options identified pursue the general aim of improving accessibility as an unproblematic generic response.

Recent research has investigated the spatial impacts of the development of a European transport network more fully. The difficulty of sustaining a persuasive spatial narrative is particularly forcefully revealed by examining the way that recent ESPON analysis has attempted to understand the spatial impacts of the trans-European transport network.[31]

This work identifies threats to territorial cohesion, and worsening long term congestion as a consequence of building the network – clearly an undesirable outcome. The detailed research findings are somewhat problematic, and reveal the uncertainty surrounding the actual benefits of constructing transnational infrastructure corridors. The research highlights the problem that "not one accession country has a transport node of European significance"[32] and suggests that the completion of the

fassender untersucht. Die Schwierigkeiten einer überzeugenden Darstellung räumlicher Entwicklungen werden besonders in dem bei der ESPON-Analyse (ESPON – Forschungsnetzwerk zur Beobachtung der europäischen Raumentwicklung) gewählten Ansatz zur Untersuchung von räumlichen Auswirkungen des Transeuropäischen Verkehrsnetzes deutlich.[31]
Die Studie kommt zu dem Schluss, dass als Konsequenz der Netzbildung die territoriale Kohäsion gefährdet wird und es langfristig zu mehr Verkehrsstaus kommen wird, was natürlich ein unerwünschtes Resultat darstellt. Die detaillierten Forschungsergebnisse sind ziemlich besorgniserregend und offenbaren die Unsicherheit in Bezug auf die tatsächlichen Vorteile, die die Einrichtung transnationaler Infrastrukturkorridore mit sich bringen. Die Untersuchung hebt das Problem hervor, dass „kein einziges Beitrittsland einen Verkehrsknoten von europäischer Bedeutung besitzt"[32], und stellt fest, dass mit dem Ausbau des europäischen Verkehrsnetzes das Gebiet Wien-Bratislava zur wichtigsten Kreuzung für Verkehrsströme zwischen Nordwest- und Südost-Europa werden kann. Damit ginge das Risiko einer Belastung der Straßen an der Kapazitätsgrenze einher. Interessanterweise wird dieses Gebiet als grenzübergreifende Wachstumsregion CENTROPE stark gefördert: „Im Herzen des ‚Neuen Europa' (...) liegt die CENTROPE-Region mit ihrer strategischen Lage; sie ist eine der dynamischsten Wirtschaftsregionen des Kontinents. Im Gegensatz zu den gesättigten Märkten Westeuropas eröffnet Osteuropa mit einem prognostizierten jährlichen Wirtschaftswachstum von durchschnittlich 5 Prozent in den nächsten Jahren enorme Wachstumsmöglichkeiten."[33]
Die ESPON-Forschungsergebnisse lassen auch erkennen, dass der weitere Ausbau der Infrastruktur in den europäischen Kernregionen kaum neue Impulse für das wirtschaftliche Wachstum geben wird. Andererseits haben die Regionen an der Peripherie Europas und in den Beitrittsländern viel zu gewinnen, aber auch viel zu verlieren: „Eine bessere Anbindung durch eine neue Autobahn oder Eisenbahnstrecke kann einen deutlichen Fortschritt in der wirtschaftlichen Entwicklung mit sich bringen. Doch auch das Gegenteil kann eintreten, wenn diese neue Verbindung eine vormals isolierte Region dem Wettbewerb mit effizienteren oder billigeren Anbietern aus anderen Regionen aussetzt."[34] Insgesamt könnte die gegenwärtig verfolgte EU-Verkehrspolitik die Unterschiede im BIP (Bruttoinlandsprodukt) zwischen den prosperierenden Kernregionen Europas und seiner Peripherie durchaus vergrößern. Der Forschungsbericht stellt weiter fest, dass die Schaffung der transnationalen Mobilitätskorridore zu einer Vertiefung der Ungleichheiten innerhalb der mitteleuropäischen Länder führen kann, indem ausgewählte Städte und ihre Umgebung die Vorteile der neuen Wachstumsmöglichkeiten wahrnehmen, während die peripheren Regionen im Schatten dieser Entwicklung bleiben. „Einige Indikatoren deuten darauf hin, dass die räumlichen Ungleichheiten innerhalb der Beitrittsländer durch die TEN- und TINA-Projekte verstärkt wurden. (...) Es besteht in diesen Ländern, in denen die Probleme der räumlichen Ungleichheit in den nächsten Jahrzehnten sehr deutlich in Erscheinung treten werden, zumindest das Risiko, dass die Infrastrukturentwicklung die Tendenz einer polarisierten wirtschaftlichen Entwicklung eher verstärken als mildern wird. (...) Diese Projekte tendieren dazu, innerhalb der Beitrittsländer die Mobilität in Ballungsgebieten mit relativ hohem Einkommen stärker zu erhöhen als in den Randgebieten."[35]

European transport network could result in the Vienna/Bratislava area becoming a major crossroads for flows between north west and south east Europe, with the accompanying risk of the saturation of roads. It is interesting to note that this space is being strongly promoted as a crossborder growth region, CENTROPE: "In the heart of the 'NEW EUROPE' ... The CENTROPE region, strategically located in the heart of the "New Europe", is one of the continent's most dynamic economic regions. In contrast to Western Europe's saturated markets, Eastern Europe offers enormous growth opportunities, with an economic expansion rate of up to five percent anticipated over the next few years."[33]

The ESPON research findings also suggest that further development of infrastructure in the core European regions will create few additional incentives for economic growth. Conversely, for regions at the European periphery and in the accession countries there is more to gain, and more to lose: "A gain in accessibility through a new motorway or rail line may bring significant progress in economic development. But also the opposite may happen if the new connection opens a formerly isolated region to the competition of more efficient or cheaper suppliers in other regions."[34] Overall, it is possible that pursuing EU transport policies may actually worsen the GDP difference between Europe's prosperous core regions and its periphery. More specifically, the research suggests that the construction of these transnational mobility corridors may lead to the deepening of inequalities within central European countries, as key cities and conurbations take advantage of new growth opportunities, becoming important nodes in the emerging European city network, leaving more peripheral regions in the shadows: "Some indicators point to spatial inequality within accession countries [being] enhanced by the TEN and TINA projects ... there is at least a risk that in these countries, where spatial inequality problems will be most pronounced during the decades to come, infrastructure development reinforces rather than mitigates a tendency of polarised economic development. ... these projects tend to improve accessibility in the agglomerations with relatively high income more than in the periphery within the accession countries."[35]

The implication is that creating more cohesive infrastructures for mobility at the European scale directly worsens cohesion at a national and local scale. What should be done? Does this mean that corridors are a bad thing? Here the researchers conclude, perhaps controversially, that the challenge is to build more infrastructure within the new member states so that international routes become more accessible, "allowing their peripheries to gain from the spread effects of more rapid growth in the centers".[36] There are difficult unresolved issues here, and the key challenge is how to develop corridors in a way that can open up new opportunities for the regional economies across central Europe in a way which doesn't simply create new sharp distinctions between winners and losers.

CONCLUSION

There is no doubt that, through a complex interweaving of Commission policy analysis and intergovernmental negotiating across and beyond the EU, a new vision of European space is emerging, made concrete through the development of a network of transnational mobility corridors. The implications for eastern Europe are dramat-

Die Auswirkungen einer kohärenteren Verkehrsinfrastruktur auf europäischer Ebene haben einen direkten negativen Einfluss auf die Kohäsion auf nationaler und lokaler Ebene. Was kann dagegen getan werden? Heißt das, dass die Korridore schlecht sind? Die Studie kommt zu dem nicht unumstrittenen Schluss, dass diese Herausforderung durch mehr Infrastruktur innerhalb der neuen Mitgliedsländer gelöst werden kann, denn durch die bessere Erreichbarkeit internationaler Verkehrswege könnten „die Randzonen von dem Streueffekt eines rascheren Wachstums in den Zentren profitieren".[36] Es gibt hier schwierige und ungelöste Probleme, und die zentrale Frage ist die Art der Entwicklung der Korridore, damit sie neue Möglichkeiten für die regionalen Ökonomien in Mitteleuropa schaffen, ohne dabei neue scharfe Trennlinien zwischen Gewinnern und Verlierern zu ziehen.

SCHLUSSFOLGERUNG

Es gibt keinen Zweifel, dass durch eine komplexe Verflechtung der politischen Analysen der Kommission und der Regierungsverhandlungen innerhalb und außerhalb der EU eine neue Vision des europäischen Raums entsteht, die in der Entwicklung eines Netzes transnationaler Mobilitätskorridore konkrete Form annimmt. Die Auswirkungen für Osteuropa sind von größter Bedeutung. Die Umstrukturierung, die nach dem Fall des Eisernen Vorhangs einsetzte, setzt sich nunmehr im Rahmen einer Transeuropäischen Agenda fort. Internationale Verkehrsströme schaffen neue Möglichkeiten und Risiken und führen zu einer Neuorientierung, Neupositionierung und Neuordnung nationaler Raumentwicklungsstrategien. Es liegt allerdings auf der Hand, dass das neue Raumprogramm auf der Basis transnationaler Korridore rasch voranschreitet, ungeachtet der großen Unsicherheiten bezüglich möglicher Auswirkungen auf die Wirtschaft, die Umwelt, die Gesellschaft und die Mobilität. Hier bedarf es einer engagierten Debatte in den an den vorgeschlagenen Korridoren gelegenen mitteleuropäischen Ländern, die im Zusammenhang mit der neuen transnationalen Agenda geführt werden sollte. Die sich verändernde räumliche Ordnung wirft schwierige Fragen für die Umwelt, die Politik und die Demokratie auf. Zu den gesamteuropäischen Korridoren hat es noch keine tiefer gehende öffentliche Debatte gegeben. Darin spiegelt sich eine tiefere Krise der Demokratie in der EU wider. Das allgemeine Problem mangelnder demokratischer Legitimität europäischer Entscheidungsprozesse wird reproduziert und durch den informellen, innerstaatlichen Charakter vieler Entscheidungen in der Raumpolitik sowie den nichtkonstitutionellen Status vieler der neuen grenzüberschreitenden und Transeuropäischen Institutionen sogar noch verstärkt. Damit wird dieses Problem zu einer der wichtigsten Herausforderungen in der zukünftigen Entwicklung der Korridore: Wie kann ihre Entwicklung ein hohes Niveau an Legitimität, Transparenz und Verantwortlichkeit erreichen? Wenn diese Fragen gelöst werden, könnten die transnationalen Korridore zur Herausbildung des gegenwärtig fehlenden staatsbürgerlichen Bewusstseins beitragen. Sie könnten durch die Schaffung neuer transnational vernetzter Gemeinschaften einen Ausgleich schaffen für das Fehlen des „Volkes", von dem eine demokratische Legitimität ausgehen kann.[37] Es ist sicherlich die Rolle der Zivilgesellschaften, die Logik der Korridore zu hinterfragen, indem alternative Mobilitätsgrundsätze formuliert werden und die Frage nach dem Nutzen der neuen Raumstrategien für die zentralen und die randständigen Gemeinschaften Osteuropas ge-

ic. The restructuring which followed the collapse of the iron curtain now responds to a trans-European agenda. International flows create new opportunities and risks, resulting in a reorientation, rescaling and reframing of national spatial development strategies. However it seems clear that the new spatial programme, with transnational corridors at its heart, is moving rapidly forwards in the face of grave uncertainties about what the impacts on economies, environments, societies and mobilities might be. This suggests the need for vigorous debate in the central European countries, along the proposed corridors, which engages with the new transnational agenda. The changing spatial order clearly raises difficult questions for development, politics and democracy. The creation of pan-European corridors has not so far benefited from deep public deliberation. This reflects the wider crisis of democracy in the EU. The general problem of the lack of democratic legitimacy of EU decision making is reproduced and even amplified in the informal, infranational nature of much of the work of spatial policy making, and the non-constitutional nature of many of the new cross-border and trans-European institutions that have been established. This, then, is one of the most important questions for the future development of the corridors: how can their development attain high standards of legitimacy, transparency and accountability? If this could be achieved, it is possible to imagine that transnational corridors could play a part in addressing the vacuum of citizenship, and making up for the absence of a "people" from which democratic legitimacy can flow, by creating new transnational networked communities.[37] There is surely a role here for civil society to question the logic of the corridors by articulating alternative mobility rationales and seeking to clarify how new spatial strategies might benefit the reconfigured central and peripheral communities of eastern Europe. These are questions of spatial inequality and justice, which prefigure a new battle over European space: a battle over meanings of territory and over the practices of spatial development. It follows that we need to maintain a critical vigilance on how stories about European policy ideas like the corridors are created to work for particular audiences and within particular contexts, and also how norms are mobilised within them. In this chapter I have argued that very particular stories are being told about the necessity of the corridors as part of a political, economic and spatial reconfiguration, and that attempts are being made to make these stories more persuasive in the face of new risks. But this is an incomplete task, and the fragility of the exercise of persuasion suggests many opportunities exist to debate, critique, challenge and subvert the meaning and practice of the corridors – and this is a necessary and inevitable dimension of productive spatial development.

This article benefits from a longstanding research collaboration with Professor Ole B. Jensen of Aalborg University, Denmark.

stellt werden. Diese Fragen nach Ungleichheit und Gerechtigkeit in der Raumpolitik gehen einer neuen Auseinandersetzung um den europäischen Raum voraus, in dem es um die Bedeutung des Territoriums und um die Praxis räumlicher Entwicklung gehen wird. Wir müssen uns daher eine kritische Wachsamkeit bewahren, um zu erkennen, wie die Diskurse über die europäische Politik – zum Beispiel die über die Schaffung der Transeuropäischen Korridore – für bestimmte Gruppen und innerhalb eines besonderen Kontextes wirken und welche Normen dabei gelten. In diesem Kapitel habe ich aufgezeigt, dass es über die Notwendigkeit der Korridore als Teil einer politischen, wirtschaftlichen und räumlichen Neuausrichtung ganz spezielle Diskurse gibt und dass Versuche unternommen werden, diesen Diskursen trotz der neuen Risiken noch mehr Nachdruck zu verleihen. Doch noch sind diese Prozesse nicht abgeschlossen, und die Tatsache, dass diese Überzeugung ungefestigt ist, deutet darauf hin, dass es noch viele Möglichkeiten gibt, die Idee und die Umsetzung der Korridore zu diskutieren, zu kritisieren, herauszufordern oder abzulehnen – was eine notwendige und unabdingbare Dimension einer produktiven Raumentwicklung ist.

Dieser Artikel ist ein Ergebnis der langjährigen Zusammenarbeit mit Professor Ole B. Jensen, Universität Aalberg, Dänemark.

ANMERKUNGEN

1 Vgl. Hajer, M.: „Transnational networks as transnational policy discourse. Some observations on the politics of spatial development in Europe". In: Faludi, A./Salet, W. (Hg.): *The revival of strategic planning.* Dordrecht 2000

2 Hajer, M./Kesselring, S.: „Democracy in risk society? Learning from the new politics of mobility in Munich". In: *Environmental Politics.* Heft 8 (3), 1999, S. 1–23; vgl. auch Flyvbjerg, B./Bruzelius, N./Rothengatter, W.: *Megaprojects and risk. An anatomy of power.* Cambridge 2003

3 Vgl. Jensen, O. B./Richardson, T.: *Making European Space: Mobility, power and territorial identity.* London 2004

4 Ebd., S. 3

5 Europäische Kommission: *Weißbuch. Die europäische Verkehrspolitik bis 2010. Weichenstellungen für die Zukunft.* Luxemburg 2001

6 Ebd., S. 11

7 Vgl. Giannakourou, G.: „Towards a European spatial planning policy. Theoretical dilemmas and institutional implications." In: *European Planning Studies.* Heft 4 (5), 1996, S. 595–613

8 Vgl. TINA-Sekretariat und Generaldirektion Energie und Transport: *Status of the Pan-European transport corridors and transport areas. Developments and activities in 2000 and 2001.* Abschlussbericht. Wien 2002[9], Kommission der Europäischen Gemeinschaften (KEG): *Pressemitteilung der Kommission IP/96/401, 8.5.96.* Brüssel 1996

10 Transport Infrastructure Needs Assessment (TINA) – Verkehrsinfrastrukturanalyse-Sekretariat: *Identification of the network components for a future Trans-European Transport Network in the candidate countries for accession*, Entwurf des ersten TINA-Arbeitsberichts. 1998

11 Kommission der Europäischen Gemeinschaften (KEG): *Pressemitteilung der Kommission IP/98/565, 24.6.98.* Brüssel 1998

12 Skinner, I./Fergusson, M.: Background for the integration of environmental concerns into transport policy in the accession candidate countries. Abschlussbericht an die Generaldirektion Umwelt der Kommission der Europäischen Gemeinschaften. Teil I des Gesamtberichtes. Institut für Europäische Umweltpolitik. http://www.europa.eu.int/comm/environment/trans/ceec/index.htm, 2001

13 Vgl. Machart, M.: *Das Straßen- und Autobahnnetz der Tschechischen Republik im gesamteuropäischen Kontext.* Konferenzbeitrag, Verkehrsminister der Tschechischen Republik, 1995

14 Fleischer, T.: Infrastrukturnetze in Mitteleuropa und die EU-Erweiterung. Vorlage für den polnisch-ungarischen Workshop der Wissenschaftsakademien beider Länder in Warschau. http://www.vki.hu/~tfleisch/PDF/pdf02/INFNET-CE_021008en.pdf, 7./8.10.2002

NOTES

1 Cf. Hajer, M.: "Transnational networks as transnational policy discourse: some observations on the politics of spatial development in Europe." In: Faludi, A./Salet, W. (eds.): *The revival of strategic planning.* Dordrecht 2000

2 Hajer, M./Kesselring, S.: "Democracy in risk society? Learning from the new politics of mobility in Munich". In: *Environmental Politics.* Issue 8 (3), 1999, S. 1–23; cf. Flyvbjerg, B./Bruzelius, N./Rothengatter, W.: *Megaprojects and risk: an anatomy of power.* Cambridge 2003

3 Cf. Jensen, O. B./Richardson, T.: *Making European Space: mobility, power and territorial identity.* London 2004

4 Ibid., p. 3

5 European Commission: *White Paper. European Transport Policy for 2010: time to decide.* Luxembourg 2001

6 Ibid., p. 11

7 Cf. Giannakourou, G.: "Towards a European spatial planning policy: theoretical dilemmas and institutional implications". In: *European Planning Studies.* Issue 4 (5), 1996, p. 595–613

8 Cf. TINA Secretariat and DG Energy and Transport: *Status of the Pan-European transport corridors and transport areas. Developments and activities in 2000 and 2001.* Final report. Vienna 2002

9 Commission of the European Communities (CEC):) *Commission Press Release,* IP/96/401, 8.5.96. Brussels 1996

10 Transport Infrastructure Needs Assessment (TINA) Secretariat: *Identification of the network components for a future Trans-European Transport Network in the candidate countries for accession,* Draft First TINA Progress Report, 1998

11 Commission of the European Communities (CEC): *Commission Press Release* IP/98/565, 24.6.98. Brussels 1998

12 Skinner, I./Fergusson, M: *Background for the integration of environmental concerns into transport policy in the accession candidate countries.* Final report to DG Environment. Part 1 Full Report. Institute for European Environmental Policy. http://europa.eu.int/comm/environment/trans/ceec/index.htm

13 Cf. Machart, M.: *Road and motorway network of the Czech Republic in pan-European context.* Conference speech, Ministry of Transport of the Czech Republic, 1995

14 Fleischer, T: "Infrastructure networks in Central Europe and the EU enlargement." Paper prepared for the Polish-Hungarian Workshop organised by the Academies of Sciences of the two countries in Warsaw, on October 7–8, 2002. Available at http://www.vki.hu/~tfleisch/PDF/pdf02/INFNET-CE_021008en.pdf

15 DG Energy and Transport (TREN)(2005): *Public consultation: Questions to the stakeholders.* http://europa.eu.int/comm/ten/transport/2005_03_31_tent_consultation/doc/public_consultation_tent.pdf

16 Ibid.

17 Committee for Spatial Development (CSD): *European Spatial Development Perspective – Towards Balanced and Sustainable Development of the Territory of the EU.* Presented at the Informal Meeting of Ministers Responsible for Spatial Planning of the Member States of the European Union, Potsdam May 10/11 1999. Committee for Spatial Development 1999

18 Ibid.

19 Skinner/Fergusson, loc cit.

20 Ibid.

21 Cerovski, V., Bulgarian Minister for Regional Development and Public Works (2004): *Pan-European transport corridors passing through the territory of Bulgaria.* Speech to the Business Consultative Council for South Eastern Europe Bulgarian Chamber of Industry Business Meeting. *Sheraton Hotel, Sofia, 11 February 2004.* (full text available at http://unpan1.un.org/intradoc/groups/public/documents/UNTC/UNPAN016221.pdf, accessed 10/06/2005)

22 Slovenian Government (2005): *Slovenia, a Country at the Crossroads of Transport Links.* http://www.uvi.si/eng/slovenia/background-information/transport/, accessed 10 June 2005

23 Cerovski, loc cit.

24 Slovenian Government, loc cit.

25 Cerovski, loc cit.

26 Richardson, T.: "Trans-European Networks: good news or bad for peripheral regions?" In: *Proceedings of seminar A, pan-European transport issues.* Warwick 1995, pp. 99–110

27 Commission of the European Communities (CEC): *Europe 2000+: co-operation for European territorial development.* Luxembourg 1994, Office for Official Publications of the European Communities

28 Ibid.

29 Ibid.

15 Generaldirektion Energie und Verkehr: Öffentliche Anhörung: Fragen an die Interessenvertreter. http://www.europa.eu.int/comm/ten/transport/2005_03_31_tent_consultation/doc/public_consultation_tent_de.pdf

16 Ebd.

17 Ausschuss für Raumentwicklung (CSD): *Für eine ausgewogene und nachhaltige Entwicklung des Territoriums der EU. Der Beitrag der Raumentwicklungspolitik,* vorgestellt auf dem Informellen Rat der für die Raumordnung zuständigen Ministerinnen und Minister der Europäischen Union in Potsdam am 10./11. Mai 1999

18 Ebd.

19 Skinner/Fergusson, a.a.O.

20 Ebd.

21 Cerovski, V., Minister für regionale Entwicklung und öffentliche Arbeiten in Bulgarien: „Die Bulgarien durchquerenden europäischen Verkehrskorridore." Rede vor dem Wirtschaftsrat für Südosteuropa und der Bulgarischen Industriekammer. Sofia, 11. Februar 2004 http://www.unpan1.un.org/intradoc/groups/public/documents/UNTC/UNPAN016221.pdf

22 Slowenische Regierung: Slovenia, a Country at the Crossroads of Transport Links. http://www.uvi.si/eng/slovenia/background-information/transport/, 10.06.2005

23 Cerovski, a.a.O.

24 Slowenische Regierung, a.a.O.

25 Cerovski, a.a.O.

26 Richardson, T.: „Trans-European Networks: good news or bad for peripheral regions?" In: *Proceedings of seminar A, pan-European transport issues.* Warwick 1995, S. 99–110

27 Kommission der Europäischen Gemeinschaften (KEG): *Europa 2000+. Europäische Zusammenarbeit bei der Raumentwicklung.* Luxemburg 1994

28 Ebd.

29 Ebd.

30 Ausschuss für Raumentwicklung (CSD), a.a.O.

31 ESPON-Projekte 1.2.1. *Verkehrsleistungen und -netze: Territoriale Tendenzen und infrastrukturelle Grundversorgung für eine territoriale Kohäsion,* und 2.1.1: *Territoriale Auswirkungen der EU-Verkehrs- und TEN-Politik,* verfügbar unter http://www.espon.lu

32 ESPON 2004, ebd., S. 18

33 http://www.centrope.com

34 ESPON 2004, ebd., S. 18

35 Ebd.

36 Ebd.

37 Vgl. Morley, D./Robins, K.: *Spaces of identity. Global media, electronic landscapes and cultural boundaries.* London 1995; Weiler, J. H. H.: *The constitution of Europe. "Do the new clothes have an Emperor?" and other essays on European integration.* Cambridge 1999

30 Committee for Spatial Development (CSD), loc cit.

31 ESPON Projects 1.2.1. *Transport services and networks: territorial trends and basic supply of infrastructure for territorial cohesion* and 2.1.1 *Territorial impacts of EU Transport and TEN policies*, available at www.espon.lu

32 ESPON 2004, ibid., p. 18

33 http://www.centrope.com

34 ESPON 2004, ibid., p. 18

35 Ibid.

36 Ibid.

37 Cf. Morley, D./Robins, K.: *Spaces of identity: global media, electronic landscapes and cultural boundaries.* London 1995; Weiler, J. H. H.: *The constitution of Europe: "do the new clothes have an Emperor?" and other essays on European integration.* Cambridge 1999

GRENZRAUM

WILFRIED HACKENBROICH

In den letzten 300 Jahren war der Korridor zwischen Berlin und Moskau in geostrategischer Hinsicht eine der sensibelsten Regionen Europas. Er ist Symbol für zahlreiche, von verschiedenen Diktatoren geführte, verheerende Kriege und trennte die Menschen über Generationen hinweg, während er gleichzeitig auch eine überaus wichtige Kultur- und Handelsachse ist. Mit der Überwindung der Trennung in Blöcke, das Verschwinden der Grenzen und der Fall der Mauern beginnt eine Zeit, wo der Raum, der für die Mehrzahl seiner Bewohner jahrhundertelang als unüberwindlich galt, offen für eine bequeme Durchreise zu sein scheint.
Seit Anfang der 1990er Jahre ist der Korridor von neuen räumlichen Hierarchien und Ungleichheiten geprägt. Die Hoffnung auf ein Paradies am anderen Ende der Straße sowie die Aussicht auf Arbeit, Wohlstand und soziale Sicherheit für jedermann zerschlug sich schon bald. Komplexe Faktoren wie die Versorgungsinfrastruktur, nationale und europaweite Arbeitsmigration sowie die strengen Richtlinien und Bedingungen, die von der EU zur Voraussetzung für eine strukturelle Unterstützung gemacht werden, schaffen heute neue – und bisher weitgehend unscharfe – räumliche Grenzen. Durch die Verschiebung der EU-Grenze in Richtung Osten entstehen Transitökonomien und neue, vielschichtige Zuteilungsrichtlinien – und damit neue räumliche Strukturen und Differenzierungen. Grenzüberschreitend wurden so neue räumliche Barrieren und Grenzen geschaffen, die zwar unsichtbar, aber sehr effektiv sind.
Bei näherer Untersuchung des Korridors machten wir schon bald die Feststellung, dass wir ein reines Gedankenkonstrukt vor uns haben. Die physische Beschaffenheit dieses Transitraums ist so heterogen wie die politischen, sozialen und kulturellen Bedingungen, die in ihm herrschen. Der Korridor ist über seine Länge von 2500 km hinweg fragmentiert und differenziert. Mit Hilfe verschiedener Karten haben wir das Kraftfeld der einzelnen Abschnitte dieses Korridors verdeutlicht. (siehe S. 32–40) Dieses Kartenmaterial umfasst Bestandskartierungen der Dienstleistungen und Infrastruktur, Daten, die wir auf unserer Reise von Berlin nach Moskau gesammelt haben, ferner Karten von Straßennetzen, Ansiedlungen, Mobilfunknetzen und Flugverkehrsstrecken sowie kartierte politische Allianzen wie EU, OSZE, RGW und Warschauer Pakt, die auf veröffentlichten Quellen sowie „mentalen" Karten als Ergebnis einer Google-Bildsuche basieren. Dieses Material quantifiziert und qualifiziert die visuelle Präsenz die Städte und Länder in der internationalen Web-Gemeinschaft. Ergänzt durch Berichte, Interviews und Videos, gaben uns diese unterschiedlichen Karten einen tieferen Einblick in die Mechanismen und Entwicklungen im Gebiet zwischen Berlin und Moskau.

BORDER SPACE

WILFRIED HACKENBROICH

For the past 300 years the corridor between Berlin and Moscow has been one of Europe's most sensitive geo-strategic areas. It is a symbol of numerous devastating wars waged by several dictators and it has divided generations, yet at the same time it is an extremely important culture and trade axis. The overcoming of block divisions, of borders and walls initiates a time where the space, which for centuries was regarded as insurmountable for most of the inhabitants, is seemingly open for convenient transit.
From the beginning of the 1990s, the corridor has been subject to new hierarchies and disparities of space. The hope for a paradise at the other end of the road and the prospect of jobs, wealth and social security for everybody lasted for only a short time. Complex factors like supply infrastructure, national and European work migration, the EU's tough policies and conditions for structural support are leading to new – and so far largely blurred – boundaries of space. Transit economies and new, multilayered allocation policies are emerging from the EU's shift to the east, bringing with them new spatial structures and differentiations. Beyond the national borders, new invisible but effective spatial barriers and frontiers have emerged.
In investigating the corridor we soon discovered that it is a mental construction. The physical condition of this transit space is as diverse as the political, social and cultural conditions within it. The corridor is fragmented and differentiated throughout its 2,500 kilometres. Through various maps we have unrolled the force field of the sections of this corridor. (see page 32–40) These maps include inventory mapping of services and infrastructure, data we collected during our journey from Berlin to Moscow, also maps of road networks, settlements, mobile phone networks and air routes and maps of political unions such as the EU, OSCE, COMECON and Warsaw Pact based on published sources as well as "mental" maps through an image search via Google that quantifies and qualifies which visual presence the cities and countries have in the international web community. These different maps, accompanied by reports, interviews and videos have given us a deeper insight into the mechanisms and developments from Berlin to Moscow.

CORRIDOR CONDITIONS

It takes 36 hours to travel by coach from Berlin to Moscow. Brief stops along the broad and differently developed roads and border controls interrupt the passengers' sleep. As they get closer to home, their experience of life and work in Western Europe becomes transfigured and turns to dust. They pass new premium spaces, crossing cit-

BEDINGUNGEN IM KORRIDOR

Eine Busfahrt von Berlin nach Moskau dauert 36 Stunden. Kurze Halts an den breiten und unterschiedlich gut ausgebauten Straßen und Grenzkontrollen unterbrechen den Schlaf der Fahrgäste. Je näher das Zuhause rückt, desto weiter weg rücken Erlebnisse vom Leben und Arbeiten in Westeuropa; übrig bleibt nur Staub. Der Reisende durchquert infrastrukturell hoch entwickelte Gebiete, aber auch Städte, in denen die Zeit stillzustehen scheint. Russen mit einem guten Job in Berlin können sich einen Flug leisten. Für sie dauert die Reise nach Moskau nur wenige Stunden. Die Reise im Bus ist billig und damit für viele die einzige Möglichkeit der Rückkehr.

Der physisch heterogene Transitkorridor zwischen Berlin und Moskau durchquert Gebiete mit heterogenen politischen und ökonomischen Bedingungen (siehe dazu auch die einleitenden Abbildungen). Die Region zwischen Berlin und der deutsch-polnischen Grenze ist hoch entwickelt. Neue Infrastruktur entstand, und das frühere politische und wirtschaftliche System der Deutschen Demokratischen Republik erfuhr eine Angleichung an westdeutsche Verhältnisse. Seit 1991 flossen 35 Milliarden EUR in 17 Infrastrukturprojekte und etwa 550 km gut ausgebaute Straßen.[1] Weitere Investitionen sollten das Wirtschaftswachstum in Ostdeutschland fördern; 2004 stellte man den Sinn und Zweck dieser Investitionen im Rahmen einer politischen Diskussion in Deutschland in Frage. Der in diesem Bereich liegende 60 km lange Abschnitt des Korridors verfügt augenscheinlich über die beste Infrastruktur, rangiert aber hinsichtlich seiner Wirtschaftskraft weit hinter Westdeutschland. Die Bevölkerung in den Städten nimmt ab, die Arbeitslosenraten sind enorm hoch, und die Höchst- und Durchschnittslöhne liegen unter dem Landesmittel. Im Vergleich mit dem östlichen Teil des Korridors weist der deutsche Abschnitt dennoch den höchsten Lebensstandard auf (soziale Sicherheit, gesellschaftlicher Wohlstand, Bildung), auch wenn von dynamischem Wachstum und positiver Entwicklung keine Rede sein kann.

Die deutsch-polnische Grenze befindet sich in einer Übergangssituation. Während unserer Untersuchungen in den Jahren 2003/2004 war sie bereits in Auflösung begriffen. Im Mai 2004 verschwanden im Zuge des Beitritts Polens zur EU weitgehend die Zollkontrollen. Eine Einreisekontrolle findet weiterhin statt, aber bis 2008 wird auch diese verschwinden. Zu Zeiten, zu denen beide Länder demselben politischen System (RGW, bis 1991 Warschauer Pakt) angehörten, war diese Grenze prinzipiell offen. In den 13 Jahren nach 1991 hatte die Grenze die Funktion als Trennlinie zwischen zwei Welten, als ein Nadelöhr für die Ein- und Ausreise, für offiziellen und inoffiziellen Handel, als eine Sicherheitslinie für die EU und ein 30-Stunden-Wartebereich für Lkw-Fahrer. Zwischen 1991 und 2000 wurden die Kontrollpunkte nach EU-Standards aus- und umgebaut; 2008, wenn die Passkontrollen enden, verschwindet die Grenze nahezu ganz.

Im westlichen Teil des polnischen Korridors stieß die deutsch-polnische Grenze eine außergewöhnliche Entwicklung an. Beflügelt von der Nähe zur Europäischen Union beschleunigte sich die wirtschaftliche Entwicklung im Gebiet um Poznan bis nach Warschau enorm. Die polnische Industrie profitiert von den Unterschieden zwischen der EU und Polen. Niedrigere Löhne und weniger strenge Auflagen für die Produktion sowie einfacher Zugang zu den Verbrauchern in der EU ließen ausländisches Kapital nach Polen strömen. Im Gegensatz zu Warschau, wo eine Zunahme des internationalen Dienstleistungssektors (Banken, Hauptsitze, Verwaltung) zu verzeichnen

ies where time has come to a standstill. It takes just a few hours by plane for Russians successful holding a job in Berlin to get to Moscow. Travelling by coach is the cheap and, for many, the only way of returning.

The physically diverse transit corridor between Berlin and Moscow cuts through heterogeneous political and economic conditions (see also the introductory corridor illustrations). The area between Berlin and the German-Polish border is highly developed. New infrastructure has been built and the former political and economic system of the German Democratic Republic (East Germany) has been transformed to the West German set-up. Since 1991 some 35 billion EUR has been spent on 17 infrastructure projects and around 550 km of high-quality motorways.[1] More investments have been called for to stimulate economic growth in eastern Germany; in 2004, a political discussion in Germany raised questions about the validity of these investments. Looking at the 60 km section of the corridor, it obviously has the best infrastructure, but in economic terms this part of the country lags behind western Germany. Urban populations are shrinking, unemployment rates are exceptionally high and average incomes are below the national standard. Yet compared to the eastern part of the corridor, the German section has the highest living standard (social security, social welfare, education) even though it is far from enjoying dynamic growth and a positive development.

The German-Polish border is in a transitory situation. During our investigation in 2003/2004 the border was in the process of dissolution. In May 2004, customs controls were largely removed as a result of Poland joining the EU. There is still immigration control which will also disappear by 2008. This border used to be open when both countries were part of the same political system (COMECON, Warsaw Pact up to 1991). For 13 years after that the border was a dividing line between two worlds, a bottleneck for migration, formal and informal trade, a security line for the EU and a 30-hour-waiting-area for lorry drivers. Between 1991 and 2000 the control points were extended and rebuilt to comply with EU standards; in 2008, when passport controls cease, the border here will disappear almost completely.

The German-Polish border has given rise to an exceptional development in the western part of the Polish corridor. Stimulated by proximity to the European Union, economic development around Poznan up to Warsaw has been boosted considerably. Polish industries have taken advantage of the disparity between the EU and Poland, while lower wages and standards for production in Poland and easy access to consumers in the EU have increased international investment. In contrast to Warsaw, where international services have increased (banking, headquarters, administration) the area around Poznan has attracted production, which has benefited from the tradition of the city's trade fair and the presence of production industries. This economic development has triggered a chain reaction along the corridor; more traffic is moving between Berlin and Poznan, and small country road has been activated by these global flows of goods. Consequently small, informal businesses have been established to cater to the needs of mobility, firstly in informal developments and latterly in a more formalized manner with global service providers to the fore. Meanwhile the country road is still in use, while the new motorway is slowly being built.

In the east of Poland the corridor is vanishing, the road is small and the services are minimal. The east of Poland, which has traditionally been an underprivileged area, is

ist, zog die Gegend um Poznan das produzierende Gewerbe an. Förderlich für diesen Prozess waren die bekannte Handelsmesse und die bereits bestehende Industrieinfrastruktur der Stadt. Diese wirtschaftliche Entwicklung löste im gesamten Korridor eine Kettenreaktion aus; zwischen Berlin und Poznan wuchs das Verkehrsaufkommen, und eine schmale Landstraße wurde durch den globalen Güterfluss zur wichtigen Verkehrsader. Im Zuge dessen entstanden kleine inoffizielle Gewerbe, die den Bedürfnissen der Mobilität Rechnung tragen, zunächst im Rahmen einer informellen Entwicklung, in letzter Zeit mit stärker offiziellem Charakter und globalen Dienstleistern in der ersten Reihe. Die Landstraße wird immer noch genutzt, parallel dazu entsteht aber langsam eine neue Autobahn.

Im Osten Polens verschwindet der Korridor nahezu, die Straße ist schmal und das Dienstleistungsgewerbe ist unterentwickelt. Der polnische Osten – von jeher eine strukturschwache Region – ist nach wie vor von der Landwirtschaft, verlassenen Industriebauten, geringem Wirtschaftswachstum und hohen Arbeitslosenzahlen geprägt. In dieser Region besuchten wir Siemiatycze, eine Kleinstadt mit 15 000 Einwohnern. Ein Viertel der Bevölkerung verdient seinen Lebensunterhalt im Ausland – mit Jobs, die sich in reichen europäischen Ländern nicht mit Einheimischen besetzen lassen. Die Mehrzahl arbeitet in Brüssel und pendelt mit dem Bus hin und zurück. Diese Arbeitsmobilität ist in Polen durchaus normal und sorgt entlang des Korridors in Richtung Europa für zusätzliches Verkehrsaufkommen.

In Richtung polnisch-weißrussischer Grenze nehmen die Aktivitäten entlang des Korridors an den Grenzkontrollpunkten in Terespol plötzlich zu. Hier warten Reisende in langen Schlangen auf den Grenzübertritt. Ähnlich wie die deutsch-polnische Grenze erlebte diese Demarkationslinie große Veränderungen; bis 1991 war sie eine schwach gesicherte Grenze zwischen „Bruderstaaten" der Sowjetunion. Nach der Geburt der GUS (Gemeinschaft unabhängiger Staaten) im Jahre 1991 wurde sie zur Trennlinie zwischen den mit Russland verbündeten Staaten und den der NATO angehörigen Ländern (seit 1999 ist Polen Mitglied der NATO). 2004, im Jahr des Beitritts Polens zur EU, wurden die Grenzsicherungsmaßnahmen an der neuen Trennlinie zwischen Europa und der GUS verschärft.

In der Grenzstadt Brest manifestieren sich die Auswirkungen großer politischer und wirtschaftlicher Veränderungen. Für den Transitkorridor in Weißrussland sind diese Auswirkungen in geringerem Maße spürbar; er besteht hier aus einer größtenteils vierspurigen Schnellstraße unterbrochen von Dörfern. Die Zahl der Raststätten entlang dieser Schnellstraße, nimmt ab; sie haben einen offizielleren Charakter und sind meist an Tankstellen angegliedert. Als neue Elemente tauchen entlang der Straße Polizeikontrollpunkte und Denkmäler auf, die an Schlachten während der Kriege der zurückliegenden Jahrhunderte erinnern. Im Vergleich zu Polen ist der weißrussische Teil des Transitkorridors organisierter und kontrollierter, lokales Gewerbe ist aber weniger verbreitet. Es stehen nur wenige Menschen an der Straße, um Obst und Gemüse zu verkaufen.

Die weißrussisch-russische Grenze ist mittelstark gesichert. Beide Länder gehören derselben politischen und ökonomischen Allianz (GUS) an und haben gemeinsame Visa- und Zollregelungen. Kontrollen an der Grenze sind weiterhin erforderlich, aber die Wartezeiten sind kurz und die Kontrollen weniger penibel. Hinter der Grenze, auf der russischen Seite, steigt die Anzahl der inoffiziellen Dienstleistungen, Ansammlun-

still dominated by agriculture, abandoned industrial buildings, little economic growth and a high unemployment rate. In this area we looked at Siemiatycze, a small town with 15,000 inhabitants. One quarter of the population travels abroad to work in jobs other Europeans do not want, most of them being employed in Brussels and commuting back and forth by bus. This labour mobility is not uncommon in Poland and creates additional traffic along the corridor towards Europe.

Towards the Polish-Belarusian border, activities along the corridor suddenly increase at the border control points in Terespol where travellers wait in long queues to cross. This border has undergone changes similar to those at the German-Polish border; up to 1991 it was a soft border between "fraternal" countries of the Soviet Union and, following the birth of the Commonwealth of Independent States (CIS) in 1991, it became a dividing line between the states affiliated to Russia and the states attracted to the North Atlantic Treaty Organization (NATO, Poland joined in 1999). In 2004, when Poland joined the EU, the border was transformed into a hard border, separating Europe and the CIS.

The border city of Brest shows the effects of large-scale politics and economic development. For the transit corridor in Belarus these effects are less visible; it consists of a mostly four-lane motorway, interrupted by villages. Along this motorway there is a drop in the number of service stations; they are more formal and combined with petrol stations. New components along the road are the police control points and the monuments built in recollection of the battles fought in various wars here in recent centuries. In comparison to Poland, the Belarus part of the transit corridor is more organised and controlled, but there are fewer local businesses, just a few people stood at the roadside selling fruit and vegetables.

The Belarus-Russian border is a semi-soft border. Both countries are part of the same political and economical alliance (CIS) and both have common visa and customs regulations. The control at the border is still needed, but waiting times are short and controls are less meticulous. Behind the border, on the Russian side, the number of informal services, service agglomerations, monuments and billboards increase, while the infrastructure decreases and the road has mostly two lanes. The closer you get to Moscow, the more the traffic increases and there is a correspondingly larger number of services, petrol stations and billboards, the latter fencing in the high-rise apartment buildings that populate the outskirts of Moscow.

E30 FROM THE GERMAN BORDER TO POZNAN

Along the two-lane transit road from the German-Polish border to Poznan there is a dense sequence of service stations, 24-hour bars, nightclubs, restaurants and hotels. Service station complexes have been built and placed – like pearls on a chain – along new goods traffic axes with so far undeveloped territories. They are nodes in the network of a global flow of goods, information and products of daily use. The increasing traffic generated by the exchange between eastern Europe and the European Union has brought about this transit space. The transformation of a country road into a transit road shows the spatial impact of border regulations, economic factors, different salaries and the flows of goods. The borderline between the European Union and eastern Europe has been transformed into a border space, a 200-km-long tenta-

gen von Dienstleistern, Denkmälern und Plakatwänden. Die Infrastruktur nimmt hingegen ab, und die Straße ist fast durchgehend zweispurig. Je näher Moskau rückt, desto stärker nimmt der Verkehr zu, die Dichte an Raststätten, Geschäften, Tankstellen, Werkstätten und Werbetafeln steigt. Die Wohnhochhäuser in den Außenbezirken Moskaus werden von diesen Werbetafeln geradezu eingerahmt.

E30 VON DER DEUTSCHEN GRENZE NACH POZNAN

Entlang der zweispurigen Transittrasse von der deutsch-polnischen Grenze nach Poznan finden sich in schneller Abfolge Tankstellen, 24-Stunden-Bars, Nachtclubs, Restaurants und Hotels. Die Tank- und Raststättenkomplexe reihen sich wie Perlen an einer Schnur entlang der neuen Güterverkehrsachsen bisher strukturschwacher Gebiete auf. Sie sind Knoten in einem Netz eines globalen Flusses von Waren, Informationen und Produkten des täglichen Gebrauchs. Die vom Austausch zwischen Osteuropa und der EU hervorgebrachte Zunahme des Verkehrs hat diesen Transitraum entstehen lassen. Die Umwandlung einer Landstraße in eine Transittrasse zeigt die räumliche Auswirkung von Grenzregelungen, wirtschaftlichen Faktoren, Lohngefällen und des Warenflusses. Die Grenzlinie zwischen der Europäischen Union und Osteuropa wurde zu einem Grenzraum, einem in Polen hineinwachsenden Tentakel von 200 km Länge. Eine gesamte Region wurde auf die Erfordernisse des internationalen Wandels und die Teilhabe am Fluss von Waren und Kapital ausgerichtet.

Aus einer kleinmaßstäblichen dörflichen Struktur erwachsen Cluster von Service-Punkten, die neuen Regeln gehorchen. Die Tankstellen und Raststätten bilden ein expansives Regime, das den lokalen Räumen neue Konturen verleiht. Diese neuen Orte geben erstens ganzen Regionen einen Impuls; zweitens sind sie Schnittstellen von Netzen. Von diesen Punkten aus erfolgt die Speisung, Lenkung und Leitung der neuen, von Global Playern geschaffenen Netze. Diese überlagern bestehende ältere Netze. Eine neue Geographie, differenziert durch die Service-Strukturen, ist im Entstehen. Bei unserer Untersuchungen haben wir uns die „Gewinner" und „Verlierer" des Rennens um Teilhabe an diesem Kapitalismus des Übergangs angeschaut.

Auslöser der zunehmenden Aktivitäten im westlichen Teil des polnischen Transitkorridors sind die neuen Fabriken, die Zunahme der Warenmengen, die nach Osteuropa[2] transportiert werden, die steigende Zahl der Arbeitspendler zwischen Russland, Polen und Osteuropa sowie die wachsende Zahl der Transithändler.

Im westlichen Teil Polens fanden wir drei wichtige Gebiete mit Fertigungsstätten (siehe dazu auch die Untersuchung von Martin Cagno): Die Sonderwirtschaftszonen (SWZ)[3], von denen die erste 1996 entstand, waren mäßig erfolgreich; unter den 13 SWZ in Polen rangieren sie auf Platz 5. Die zweite Form von Produktionsstätten bilden die Fabriken, die sich aus Geschäftsbeziehungen aus der Zeit vor 1991 entwickelten. Prominentestes Beispiel dafür ist Ikea. Die zum Konzern gehörende Swedwood-Group im Gebiet von Zbaszynek wurde 1991 gegründet; 1999 entstanden neue Fabriken.[4] Der dritte und erfolgreichste Typ von Produktionsstätten findet sich im Gebiet von Tarnowo Podgorne (14 000 Einwohner) in der Nähe von Poznan; hier haben sich 1800 Firmen angesiedelt, 32 davon entlang des Korridors Berlin–Moskau.[5] Dank der Deregulierung und einer kooperativen Stadtverwaltung weist dieses Gebiet das größte Wirtschaftswachstum in ganz Polen auf.[6]

cle reaching into Poland. An entire region has been adapted to the needs of international transition in order to participate in the flow of goods and capital.
Clusters of service points are emerging from a small-scale village structure and obeying new rules. The service stations are an expansive regime, adding new outlines to local spaces. These new places firstly provide an impulse for entire regions; secondly, these premium spaces are interfaces of networks. New networks created by global players are fed, directed and steered from the service stations. They overlap existing older networks. A new geography, differentiated by the service structures, is building up. In our research we looked at the "winners" and the "losers" of the race to participate in this capitalism of transition.
The triggers for the increased activities along the western part of the Polish transit corridor are the new factories, the increase in the amount of goods being transported to eastern Europe[2], the rise in the numbers of labour commuters between Russia, Poland and eastern Europe and the increase in informal traders.
In the western part of Poland we found three main areas with production facilities (see also the research by Martin Cagno); the Special Economic Zones (SEZ)[3], the first of which were established in 1996, have been marginally successful; they rank fifth out 13 SEZ locations in Poland. The second form of production facilities are the factories developed out of business relations before 1991. Ikea is one such example; the Swedwood Group it owns in the area of Zbaszynek was founded in 1991 and new factories were built in 1999.[4] The third and most successful type of production facility is the area of Tarnowo Podgorne (pop. 14,000) near Poznan; it has attracted 1,800 companies, 32 of which are located along the Berlin–Moscow corridor[5]. Thanks to deregulation and a supportive city administration, this area has the fastest rate of economic growth in the whole of Poland[6].
The growth in services has been mapped along the 150 kilometres between the German-Polish border to Broje (see also the research by Nina Gribat and Linda Hilfling). The inventory shows a population of approximately 10,000 inhabitants, 16 petrol stations, 13 hotels, 12 restaurants, 12 retail outlets, 11 cafés, 10 settlements, 9 truck washes, 7 brothels, 6 bureaux de change, 6 filling stations for cars, 5 truck stops, 4 repair garages, 2 souvenir shops, 2 radio stations and 2 toilets. If we compare these figures with Berlin and the ratio per inhabitant, we get following figures[7]: one restaurant or café for 700 inhabitants in Berlin and for 434 inhabitants on the 150-km Polish corridor; one hotel for 4.000 inhabitants in Berlin and for 770 inhabitants on the corridor; one petrol station for 12,600 inhabitants in Berlin and for 625 inhabitants on the corridor. This comparison illustrates the urban density along the Polish corridor; bearing in mind that all these restaurants, cafés, bars and hotels work 24 hours a day, it is justifiable to speak of a metropolitan activation.
This service agglomeration is currently undergoing its third wave of transformation. The first wave after 1991 was the transition of a country road into a service line with informal, individual services in underdeveloped typologies. The second wave started around 2000 and involved transformation into formal, legal and developed services with adequate typologies. The success of these new transit service typologies is presently triggering more individual investment to participate in these global flows. The third wave is the globalisation of the service market. This transformation began

Die Zunahme an Dienstleistungen wurde in den 150 km zwischen der deutsch-polnischen Grenze bis Broje genau kartiert (siehe dazu die Untersuchung von Nina Gribat und Linda Hilfling). In diesem Gebiet mit circa 10000 Einwohnern befinden sich 16 Tankstellen, 13 Hotels, 12 Restaurants, 12 Geschäfte, 11 Cafés, 10 Siedlungen, 9 Waschanlagen für Lkw, 7 Bordelle, 6 Wechselstuben, 6 Befüllanlagen für Fahrzeuge, 5 Lkw-Raststätten, 4 Werkstätten, 2 Souvenirläden, 2 Radiosender und 2 öffentliche WC. Wenn wir diese Zahlen mit Berlin und dem Pro-Kopf-Verhältnis vergleichen, kommen wir auf folgende Werte[7]: ein Restaurant oder Café auf 700 Einwohner in Berlin und auf 434 Einwohner im 150-km-Abschnitt des Korridors in Polen; ein Hotel auf 4000 Einwohner in Berlin und auf 770 Einwohner im Korridor; eine Tankstelle auf 12600 Einwohner in Berlin und auf 625 Einwohner im Korridor. Dieser Vergleich veranschaulicht die urbane Dichte entlang des polnischen Korridors; wenn man dabei berücksichtigt, dass all diese Restaurants, Cafés, Bars und Hotels rund um die Uhr geöffnet haben, kann man von Bedingungen sprechen, wie sie in einer Metropole herrschen.
Diese Ansammlung von Dienstleistungen durchläuft gegenwärtig eine dritte Welle des Wandels. Im Verlauf der ersten Welle nach 1991 erfolgte der Wandel von einer Landstraße zu einer Service-Linie mit inoffiziellen, einzelnen Dienstleistungsangeboten in unterentwickelten Typologien. Die zweite Welle begann um das Jahr 2000 herum. In ihrem Verlauf erfolgte die Umwandlung in offizielle, legale und entwickelte Dienstleistungen mit adäquaten Typologien. Der Erfolg dieser neuen Transitservice-Typologien löst gegenwärtig in stärkerem Maße Einzelinvestitionen zur Teilhabe an den globalen Flüssen aus. Die dritte Welle besteht in der Globalisierung des Dienstleistungsmarktes. Dieser Wandel begann Mitte der 1990er Jahre, als Tankstellen von global agierenden Marken aufgekauft wurden. Heute geht der Trend dahin, komplette Dienstleistungszentren zu erwerben und diese dann zu einer für den globalen Verbrauch optimierten Umgebung umzugestalten. Die nächste Welle des Wandels wird im Bau der Autobahn bestehen, die Polen von West nach Ost durchquert. Bisher wurden weniger als 100 der geplanten 700 km realisiert. Polen ist nicht in der Lage, die 50 bis 70 Prozent Eigenfinanzierung aufzubringen, um die Bezuschussung als EU-Projekt zu erhalten. Der Bau der Autobahn hat sich deshalb verzögert, wird aber auf jeden Fall abgeschlossen. Für den Westteil des polnischen Korridors bedeutet dies einen extremen Wandel. Die bisher bestehende E30 ist eine langsame Landstraße; sie führt durch Dörfer und Siedlungen, bietet aber auch Zugang zu den globalen Warenströmen. Mit der Autobahn wird sich die Reisegeschwindigkeit erhöhen. Dadurch lassen sich die großen Städte unter Umgehung der Dörfer schneller erreichen. Die einzige Chance zur Erhaltung der bestehenden Dienstleistungsangebote bietet sich an den Autobahnausfahrten; die lautlose Schlacht um den Zugang zu dieser Infrastruktur hat bereits begonnen. Die Investitionen in die Dienstleistungsbranche haben nicht aufgehört. Lokale Investoren verlassen sich dabei auf Folgendes: Die Ausfahrt liegt in der Nähe ihres Gewerbestandortes; für die Nutzung der Autobahn wird eine Maut erhoben; die Nutzung der bestehenden E30 wird deshalb nicht abnehmen; bzw. der Bau der Autobahn wird sich noch viele Jahre hinziehen. Unseren Untersuchungen zufolge stehen die Standorte der meisten Ausfahrten bereits fest. Wir erhielten jedoch keine Auskunft über einen endgültigen Realisierungstermin, weil die Frage der Finanzierung nicht geklärt ist.

ALASKA
EXCHANGE
24 h
WC
200 m

FALLSTUDIEN: E30 VON DER DEUTSCHEN GRENZE NACH POZNAN

Als Fallstudien möchte ich drei typologische Situationen nennen: die neue, umfassende Dienstleistungstypologie am Fall von „Las Vegas" (siehe dazu auch die Untersuchung von Nina Gribat, Linda Hilfling); die Verflechtung von globalen Dienstleistungsgebieten mit der lokalen Dorfstruktur am Fall von Torzym (siehe dazu auch die Untersuchung von Nina Gribat, Linda Hilfling); sowie die Umwandlung durch globale Marken, die in die Dienstleistungszentren investieren, am Fall von Orlen (siehe dazu die Untersuchung von Nina Gribat, Linda Hilfling).

Das „Las Vegas"-Forschungsprojekt untersucht die neue Typologie, die aus den inoffiziellen 24-Stunden-Dienstleistungszentren hervorgegangen ist. Die „künstliche Stadt" Las Vegas ist in das sie umgebende Dorf Mostki in Westpolen eingebettet, aber dennoch getrennt von ihm; Las Vegas ist eine in sich geschlossene Einheit, in der Transitreisende ihren kompletten Bedarf an Waren und Dienstleistungen decken können. Das 24-Stunden-Programm umfasst einen Supermarkt, ein Motel, eine Tankstelle, eine Lkw-Waschanlage, ein Restaurant, eine Bar, eine Wechselstube, einen öffentlichen Fernsprecher, Lkw-Parkplätze, einen bewachten Wagenpark und Prostitution. Lkw-Fahrer (75 Prozent) verbringen hier bis zu elf Stunden, Kfz-Fahrer eineinhalb Stunden (15 Prozent). In Las Vegas befinden sich bis zu 60 oder 70 Lkws gleichzeitig, gelegentlich auch nur 20 bis 30. Von Montag bis Donnerstag halten sich russische Lkw-Fahrer in Las Vegas auf, am Wochenende sind es hauptsächlich polnische Fahrer. Die Einrichtungen bieten circa 70 Personen aus dem Umland Arbeit.[8] Diese künstliche Stadt funktioniert wie eine Mini-Stadt, in der die Trucker alle Dienstleistungen und Annehmlichkeiten vorfinden, die sie in ihren Lkws nicht haben. Die Fahrerkabinen der Lkws sind gut ausgestattet. Meist verfügen die Fahrer über eine mobile Wohneinheit mit Radio, Fernsehgerät, Kühlschrank, Bett, kleiner Küche und Familienfotos, die an der Service-Station Las Vegas andocken und die Mini-Stadt komplettieren.

Die in Torzym durchgeführte Untersuchung zeigt die Entwicklung des Servicebereichs in einem kleinen Dorf auf. Entlang der E30 ist eine Vielzahl von Transitaktivitäten angesiedelt, während nur wenige Meter entfernt die typischen Dörfer zu finden sind. Das ganze Dorf ist auf die Teilhabe am globalen Waren- und Menschenstrom ausgerichtet; der starke Verkehr im Dorf wird ignoriert, zwischen globalen und lokalen Interessen ist eine für beide Seiten vorteilhafte Balance entstanden. In wirtschaftlicher Hinsicht erwies sich der Verkehr auf der Transitstrecke als vorteilhaft; der Bürgermeister des Dorfes plant daher den Bau öffentlicher Einrichtungen – eine Turnhalle, ein Schwimmbad sowie andere Sport- und Freizeiteinrichtungen.

Der Fall des Maier's Western Grill ist das Ergebnis der Untersuchung der Mineralölgesellschaft PKN Orlen. Er zeigt in kleinem Maßstab, wie ein global agierendes Unternehmen kleine lokale Dienstanbieter vom Markt drängen kann.

GRENZGEBIET – ZUSAMMENFASSUNG

Die Bedingungen entlang des Transitkorridors zwischen Berlin und Moskau sind äußerst heterogen. In Deutschland gibt es eine gut entwickelte Infrastruktur bei stagnierender wirtschaftlicher Entwicklung; in Polen treffen wir bei einem Minimum an Infrastruktur auf eine prosperierende Wirtschaft; in Weißrussland ist die Infrastruktur gut

in the mid-1990s with petrol stations being bought by global brands. The trend today, however, is to buy into complete service agglomerations and reshape them to form an environment optimised for global consumption. The next wave of transformation will be the implementation of the motorway running from west to east through Poland. Less than 100 of the some 700 planned kilometres of motorway have been realised so far. EU funds have been provided to build more kilometres of this motorway, but Poland is unable to afford the 50 per cent to 70 per cent of national financing. The construction of the motorway has thus been slowed down, but it is sure to come. For the western part of the Polish corridor this has meant an extreme transformation. Today the E30 country road is slow; it runs through villages and settlements but it also provides direct access to the global stream of goods. The motorway will increase the speed of travel, resulting in faster connections between the bigger cities and the bypassing of small villages. The only chance to maintain existing services in the future is a motorway exit; the silent battle for this infrastructure access is well under way. Investments in the service industries have not stopped. Local investors tend to believe one of several things: that the exit will be close to their business; that the use of the highway will not be toll free; that the existing E30 will therefore be used to the same degree it is now; or that the building of the motorway will take many more years to complete. From our research we know that most of the positions of the exits have been decided, but we could not get a definite realisation date; the financing is too uncertain.

CASE STUDIES: E30 FROM THE GERMAN BORDER TO POZNAN

As case studies I would like to mention three typological situations; the new emerging all-in-one-service typology in the case of "Las Vegas" (see also the research by Nina Gribat, Linda Hilfling); the interweaving of global service areas and the local village structure in the case of Torzym (see also the research by Nina Gribat, Linda Hilfling); and the transformation by global brands investing in the service agglomerations in the case of Orlen (see also the research by Nina Gribat, Linda Hilfling).

The "Las Vegas" research investigates the new typology that has arisen from the 24-hour informal service agglomeration. The "instant city" of Las Vegas is embedded in, but disconnected from, the surrounding village of Mostki in western Poland; Las Vegas is a singular entity providing everything transit travellers need. The 24-hour programme includes a supermarket, motel, petrol station, truck wash, restaurant, bar, bureau de change, telephone, truck parking area, a guarded car park and prostitution. The time spent by truck drivers (75 per cent) can be up to 11 hours, for car drivers (15 per cent) one-and-a-half hours. The amount of trucks at any one time varies from 60 to 70 and occasionally only 20 to 30. The Russian truck drivers are at Las Vegas from Monday to Thursday and the Polish truck drivers at the weekend. The place employs approximately 70 people from nearby towns.[8] This instant city acts like a mini-city, where the truck drivers find all the services and amenities they do not have in their trucks. The truck drivers' cabins are well equipped and provide a mobile living unit with radio, TV, refrigerator, bed, small kitchen and family pictures that plug into the service station Las Vegas and complete the mini-city.

ausgebildet, die Wirtschaft jedoch schwach entwickelt; und in Russland ist entlang des Korridors eine geringe wirtschaftliche Aktivität und elementare Infrastruktur anzutreffen. Diese Bedingungen hängen weniger von der Infrastruktur ab, als Planer glauben mögen. Die meisten Entwicklungen sind vielmehr mit politischen und globalen wirtschaftlichen Faktoren verknüpft. Während in Deutschland nationale Investitionen primär in die Entwicklung der Infrastruktur fließen, wird die Ökonomie in Polen von der Mitgliedschaft in der EU und der Deregulierung stimuliert. In Weißrussland entwickelt sich die Wirtschaft trotz der guten Infrastruktur aufgrund der politischen Isolation nur langsam. Das heißt aber trotzdem nicht, dass die Infrastruktur keine Rolle spielt; es müssen einfach grundlegende Bedingungen erfüllt sein, damit die Infrastruktur überhaupt zum Tragen kommt. Im globalen Wettbewerb um Standorte für Fabriken zieht Polen häufiger den Kürzeren. Im März 2004 entschied sich beispielsweise die Hyundai Motor Group aufgrund der besseren Infrastruktur für die Slowakei. Nach dem schnellen Wachstum im Westen Polens hat das Land einen Punkt erreicht, an dem sich weiteres Wachstum nur durch eine Entwicklung der Infrastruktur erreichen lässt. In Deutschland wollte man mit Investitionen den Weg zu lokalem Wachstum ebnen, das – flankiert von Deregulierungsmaßnahmen – vorhandenes Potenzial erschließen und so mittels infrastruktureller Entwicklungen Wachstum bringen sollte.

Für die Länder entlang des Korridors könnte die Zukunft eine Verschiebung mit sich bringen. Durch den höheren Lebensstandard in Polen und steigende Produktionsstandards, wie sie von der EU gefordert werden, steigen auch in Polen die Fertigungskosten. Die entstehende Autobahn in Polen lässt Weißrussland näher an den europäischen Markt rücken. Niedrige Arbeitskosten und Produktionsstandards in den Sonderwirtschaftszonen um Brest können durchaus eine Verlagerung von Fertigungsstätten nach Weißrussland zur Folge haben, sofern die politische Situation eine sichere Investition verspricht.

Auf lokaler Ebene führt die Fertigstellung der Autobahn möglicherweise zum wirtschaftlichen Niedergang der bisherigen Standorte an der E30. Statt vorteilhafter Teilhabe an den globalen Warenströmen wird dann entlang des Korridors der massenhafte Verlust von Arbeitsplätzen zu beobachten sein – ein Prozess, in dessen Verlauf die Dörfer zu Vororten von Berlin, Poznan und Warschau werden. Für Planer stellt sich die Frage, wie sich entlang des Korridors eine globale Geschwindigkeit realisieren und damit eine Teilhabe für die lokale Wirtschaft erreichen lässt. Auf der Basis der vorhandenen Dienstleistungstypologien müssen neue Typologien entwickelt werden, die globalen Standards und Erfordernissen Rechnung tragen.

The research carried out in Torzym reveals the service developments within a small village. There are many transit programs along the E30 transit road, while only a few metres away the typical small village programmes appear. The entire village has adjusted so as to participate in the global streams of goods and people; ignoring the heavy traffic cutting through the village, they have worked out a beneficial balance between global and local needs. In economic terms the traffic on the transit road has proved beneficial; consequently the village mayor is planning public amenities like a gym, a pool and other sports and leisure facilities.
The case of Maier´s Western Grill is the product of research into the PKN Orlen petrol company that shows on a small scale how a globally active company can push local small service providers out of business.

BORDERLAND CONCLUSION

Conditions along the transit corridor between Berlin and Moscow are very diverse. In Germany, there is very good infrastructure and no economic development; in Poland there is minimal infrastructure and prosperous business; in Belarus there is good infrastructure and minimal business; and in Russia there is basic infrastructure and a little business along the corridor. These conditions depend less on infrastructure than planners might think, most of the developments being linked to political and global economic factors. While national investment in Germany goes primarily into infrastructure development, in Poland the economy is being stimulated by membership of the EU and deregulation. In Belarus economic development is slow, despite the good infrastructure, because of political exclusion. Yet the argument is not that infrastructure is irrelevant; it is just that basic conditions need to be fulfilled for the infrastructure to have an effect. Poland is losing out more often in the global competition for factories. In March 2004, for instance, the Hyundai Motor Group decided to go to Slovakia because of the better infrastructure there. After the rapid growth in the west of Poland the country has reached a point at which further growth can only be stimulated by infrastructure development. In Germany, investments have been designed to stimulate and pave the way to local growth which – in combination with de-regulation – should tap potential and consequently enhance growth by means of infrastructure developments.
Future prospects for the countries along the corridor might entail a shift. Higher living standards in Poland and the rising production standards called for by the EU will increase production costs in Poland. The future motorway in Poland will bring Belarus closer to the European market. Low labour costs and production standards in the Free Economic Zones around Brest may well attract business to Belarus if the political situation promises a secure investment.
At the local level, developments might include the bypassing of villages by the motorway. Advantageous participation in the global flows might then turn into a drop in employment along the corridor, turning the villages into suburbs of Berlin, Poznan and Warsaw. The question for planners is how global speed along the corridor can be provided, thus enabling local businesses to participate. New service typologies need to be developed, based on the existing ones, but extended to integrate global standards and needs.

AMERKUNGEN

1 „Multiplicity, The doubling of the highway, Interview mit Hans Jörg Klofat, USE". In: *Uncertain States of Europe*. Italien 2003, S. 114–117

2 Transportunternehmen wählen wegen der strengeren Zollbestimmungen in Weißrussland zunehmend die nördliche Route nach Moskau über Litauen und Lettland.

3 Bartosz Begej, Vertriebsmanager SWZ, Kostrzyn-Slubice, in einem Interview im März 2004 mit Martin Cagno und Wilfried Hackenbroich; Standorte von Sonderwirtschaftszonen in Kostrzyn seit 1996, 246 ha, 23 Unternehmen; Gorzow Wlkp, seit 2001, 62 ha, 2 Unternehmen; Slubice seit 1996, 101 ha, 23 Unternehmen, Nowa Sol seit 2001, 48 ha, 1 Unternehmen

4 Robert Gdula, Produktionsleiter bei der Swedwood Group im Gebiet Zbaszynek, in einem Interview mit Martin Cagno, März 2004

5 14 deutsche, 7 polnische und 11 westeuropäische Unternehmen

6 Waldy Dzikowsk, Distriktverwalter Tarnowo Podgorne, in einem Interview mit Martin Cagno, März 2004

7 Untersuchung der Zahlen und Standorte für Berlin: http://www.berlin.de/branchenbuch/_bin/index.php; Berlin hat 3,4 Millionen Einwohner, 270 Tankstellen, 4 860 Restaurants und Cafés, 840 Hotels und Pensionen.

8 Manager von „Las Vegas", in einem Interview mit Maximiliano Piperno, März 2004

NOTES

1 Multiplicity, The doubling of the highway, Interview with Hans Jörg Klofat USE. In: Uncertain States of Europe, Skira Editore S.p.A., Italy 2003, pp. 114-117

2 Transport companies are increasingly opting for the northern route to Moscow via Lithuania and Latvia because of the more stringent customs regulations in Belarus.

3 Bartosz Begej, marketing manager SEZ, Kostrzyn-Slubice, in an interview in March 2004 with Martin Cagno and Wilfried Hackenbroich; Special Economic Zones locations in: Kostrzyn since 1996, 246 ha, 23 companies; Gorzow Wlkp, since 2001, 62 ha, 2 companies; Slubice since 1996, 101 ha, 23 companies, Nowa Sol since 2001, 48 ha, 1 company

4 Robert Gdula, production manager with the Swedwood Group in the Zbaszynek area, interviewed in March 2004 by Martin Cagno

5 14 from Germany, 7 from Poland and 11 from other western European countries

6 Waldy Dzikowsk, district administrator, Tarnowo Podgorne, interviewed in March 2004 by Martin Cagno

7 Research of quantities and locations for Berlin: http://www.berlin.de/branchenbuch/_bin/index.php Berlin has 3.4 million inhabitants, 270 petrol stations, 4,860 restaurants and cafés, 840 hotels and guest houses.

8 Manager of "Las Vegas" interviewed in March 2004 by Maximiliano Piperno

E30 TRANSIT / STASIS

NINA GRIBAT / LINDA HILFLING NIELSEN

ES IST EINE LÄNDLICHE GEGEND, SIE BESTEHT ZU 95 PROZENT AUS WALD UND BAUERNHÖFEN. ABER SIE IST AUCH MIT EINER STRASSE GESEGNET – DER TRANSITSTRASSE ZWISCHEN BERLIN UND MOSKAU. JEDEN TAG FAHREN HIER 10000 LKWS ENTLANG.[1]

Kurz hinter der deutsch-polnischen Grenze in Polen ändert sich die Typologie grundlegend. Nach zehn Kilometern wird aus der vierspurigen, deutschen Autobahnen ähnlichen E30 eine idyllische zweispurige Landstraße. Dieser Teil der E30 führt durch Wälder, Felder und kleine Dörfer und wird sogar von Fahrradfahrern und Fußgängern benutzt. Die E30 ist Teil des stark befahrenen Korridors zwischen Berlin und Moskau, ihre meist ländliche Umgebung liegt demzufolge am Rande eines intensiven Güterflusses.

Entlang der Straße ist eine vielfältige Servicelandschaft entstanden – hervorgegangen aus den umliegenden kleinen Dörfern und verwoben mit ihnen. Als lokale Konglomerate für einen globalen Handelsmarkt sind diese Orte „glokale" Interaktionspunkte, wo sich verschiedene Ebenen der Realität, globaler Transit und lokale Stasis, verbinden und überlagern – zum Beispiel als Bar in einem Truck Stop, in der die einheimischen Teenager freitags nachts abhängen, oder als ein Supermarkt, an dem die Vorbeifahrenden halten, um einzukaufen.

Mitgerissen von der E30, wird die polnische Landschaft in Bewegung versetzt und bildet die semi-urbane Vision eines fiktiven Konsumentenhimmels. So ist eine hybride Form urbaner Kultur in einer sonst ländlichen Umgebung entstanden. Die Gemeinden entlang der E30 haben die wirtschaftlichen Flüsse auf unerwartete Weise ihren eigenen Bedürfnissen angepasst, woraus ein – wie wir es hier nennen möchten – aktiver ländlicher Urbanismus hervorgegangen ist, im Gegensatz zu dem für solche Gebiete sonst typischen passiven Suburbanismus.

Die Gestaltung eines neuen Europa hat Auswirkungen auf das polnische Grenzgebiet.[2] Parallel zur E30 ist eine Autobahn geplant; sie soll die existierende, eher unterentwickelte Infrastruktur der Landstraße ersetzen. Dieses Vorhaben ist Teil einer globalen Tendenz, wichtige Zentren so effektiv wie möglich zu stärken und miteinander zu verbinden. Die neue Autobahn wird im Grenzland mit nur drei Serviceeinheiten auf jeder Seite ausgestattet sein, im Gegensatz zu den mehr als 130 Services der heutigen E30. Darüber hinaus sind in diesem Bereich nur zwei Abfahrten geplant, wodurch das Grenzland höchstwahrscheinlich vom Zugang zu eigenständigem Wirtschaften abgeschnitten und in ein Schlafgebiet für die nächstgelegenen größeren Zentren Berlin und Poznan verwandelt werden wird, möglicherweise sogar in ein schwarzes Loch der neuen polnischen Hochgeschwindigkeitsgesellschaft.

Dieser Beitrag untersucht die Servicelandschaft im polnischen Grenzgebiet und entwirft Szenarien für eine Entwicklung der Gegend. Statt dabei eine Strategie zu verfolgen, die auf Zurückweisung und Ausgrenzung beruht, geht er vom Bestehenden aus und legt dessen Prinzipien einer möglichen Entwicklung zugrunde.

HINTERGRUND

IHR SOHN LEISTET IHR BEI DER ARBEIT GESELLSCHAFT. ER IST ZEHN JAHRE ALT UND SIEHT GERNE FERN, WÄHREND SIE VERSICHERUNGEN AN LKW-FAHRER VERKAUFT; SEIN VATER IST AUCH LKW-FAHRER. SIE LEBEN EINIGE KILOMETER ENTFERNT IN RZEPIN. ALS SIE EIN KIND WAR, KAM SIE MIT IHRER OMA AN DIESEN ORT, UM PILZE ZU SAMMELN. SIE SAGT, DASS ES JETZT KEINE PILZE MEHR GIBT, SIE STATTDESSEN ABER EINEN JOB HAT.[3]

Mit dem Zusammenbruch des sozialistischen Systems (und der deutschen Wiedervereinigung) ver-

E30 TRANSIT / STASIS

NINA GRIBAT / LINDA HILFLING NIELSEN

95 PER CENT CONSISTS OF FARMS AND FOREST. IT IS AN AGRICULTURAL AREA. BUT THE AREA IS ALSO BLESSED WITH A ROAD – THE TRANSIT ROAD BETWEEN BERLIN AND MOSCOW – EVERY DAY 10,000 TRUCKS ARE PASSING BY.[1]

Soon after passing the German-Polish border and entering Poland the typology changes dramatically. After 10 km the four lanes German-like highway E30 turns into a two lanes idyllic country road. This part of E30 runs through forests, fields and small villages and it is even used by cyclists and pedestrians. The route of E30 is part of the highly trafficked corridor from Berlin to Moscow and its surrounding, mostly countryside, landscape is thus situated in the midst of an intense flow of goods carried by trucks.

Along the road a diverse landscape of services has emerged. These services are interweaving with and springing from the small towns along the road. As local conglomerations for a global trade market, these spots are "glocal" interaction points where different layers of reality, of global transit and local stasis, exchange and interfere. For instance as a bar in a truck stop where local teens are hanging out a Friday night or as a local supermarket where people in transit stop in order to do their shopping. Swept through by the E30, the Polish countryside is set in motion, reforming into a semi-urban vision of a fictive consumer heaven. In this way a hybrid form of urban culture has emerged in otherwise rural settings. The community along E30 has in unexpected ways appropriated these economical flows to its own needs, giving birth to what we here would like to call a form of active rural urbanism, as opposed to a more typical and passive sub-urbanism.

A new Europe with new borders is now affecting the Polish borderland.[2] Parallel to E30, a new highway is planned to substitute the existing, rather underdeveloped infrastructure of the country road. This development is a natural part of a global tendency where capital nodes are strengthened and inter-connected as effectively as possible. The new highway will provide the borderland with three service units on each of its sides, compared to the more than 130 services of today's E30 in Poland. Moreover, with only two highway exits planned in this area, the borderland is most likely to become cut off and turn into a sleeping area of the closest capital centres, the city of Berlin and the city of Poznan, or turn into a black hole of a new Polish high-speed society. This article examines the past and future of the service-landscape and proposes scenarios for a development of the area with the aim of implementing the principia of the existing rather than a development built on rejection and exclusion.

BACKGROUND

HER SON KEEPS HER COMPANY AT WORK. HE IS 10 YEARS OLD AND LIKES TO WATCH TELEVISION WHILE SHE IS SELLING INSURANCES TO TRUCK DRIVERS. HIS DAD IS A TRUCK DRIVER, TOO. THEY LIVE IN RZEPIN A

schob sich die Grenze zwischen Ost- und Westeuropa zunächst von der deutsch-deutschen Grenze zur deutsch-polnischen Grenze. Weil die Lkws, die die Grenze zu Polen überqueren wollten, bis zu 46 Stunden auf der Autobahn warten mussten, wurde 1994 auf der deutschen Seite ein offizieller Truck Stop eröffnet.[4] Er sollte die Wartezeiten der Lkw-Fahrer organisieren helfen, die der Engpass bei der Zollabfertigung verursachte. Der Truck Stop A12 wurde mit 960 Parkplätzen für Lkws, einem Geschäft, einem Supermarkt, einem Reifenladen, einer Cafeteria und sanitären Einrichtungen ausgestattet. Die Lkw-Fahrer konnten nun mit ihren Wagen die Straße verlassen, am neuen Truck Stop parken und eine Pause machen. Die Wartezeiten auf der polnischen Seite waren natürlich ebenso lang, nur wurde hier kein offizieller Halt organisiert. Der Zusammenbruch des sozialistischen Systems ermutigte dort aber eine neue Generation von Pionieren des Kapitalismus: Das Grenzland und die Möglichkeiten, aus seinem Verkehrsfluss wirtschaftlichen Vorteil zu ziehen, lockten viele hoffnungsvolle Unternehmer an. So entstand seit Beginn der 1990er Jahre eine blühende Servicelandschaft entlang der polnischen Landstraße.

Die meisten dieser neuen Services sind kleinmaßstäblich und wirken improvisiert, haben aber fast alle rund um die Uhr geöffnet. Die Fahrer der Transportunternehmen sind ihre Hauptkunden. Alles ist für Lkws und Lkw-Fahrer ausgelegt: Es gibt riesige Lastwagenparkplätze, Lkw-Waschanlagen in fast jedem Dorf, und ein standardisiertes Menü, das auf den kulinarischen Geschmack des prototypischen Lkw-Fahrers zugeschnitten ist, wird überall angeboten.

Ein Vergleich zwischen 60 Kilometern der E30 auf deutscher und 60 Kilometern auf polnischer Seite macht die extrem unterschiedlichen Bedingungen deutlich: Auf deutscher Seite gibt es in diesem Bereich neun Zufahrtsstraßen und keine Geschwindigkeitsbegrenzung, wogegen die polnische Seite 27 Zufahrtsstraßen aufweist und Geschwindigkeitsbegrenzungen von 90 km/h für Autos und 70 km/h für Lkws gelten – innerhalb von Ortschaften sogar 60 km/h. Auf den letzten 60 Kilometern in Deutschland gibt es nur eine Rast- und Serviceeinheit und ein paar Parkplätze mit einfachen Sanitäreinrichtungen, auf der polnischen Seite dagegen eine große Auswahl von ca. 130 Serviceeinrichtungen aller Art.

Während die Services in Polen aus den lokalen Gemeinden entstanden oder zumindest mit ihnen verbunden sind, gilt auf deutscher Seite das Gegenteil. Hier werden fast alle Serviceeinrichtungen von großen, global agierenden Unternehmen betrieben, die Tankstellen von Shell, BP, DEA und anderen, die Restaurants von Mövenpick und McDonald's. Informeller Service findet an den deutschen Hochgeschwindigkeitsstraßen nicht statt. Die Serviceunternehmen gehen hier nicht aus den umliegenden Gemeinden hervor und haben kaum eine Verbindung zu ihnen, obwohl sie mehr als bereit sind, sie auszunutzen.

TYPOLOGIEN DER E30

ER WAR EIGENTLICH MEHR AN AUDIOSYSTEMEN FÜR AUTOS INTERESSIERT, ABER NUN BETREIBT ER ZUSAMMEN MIT EINEM FREUND EINEN CBS-REPARATURSERVICE. ES WAR DIE IDEE SEINES FREUNDES, UND WEIL ER NICHTS ANDERES ZU TUN HATTE, MACHTE ER MIT.[5]

Entlang der E30 sind die Bedingungen für individuelle Unternehmer gut. Jeder Haus- oder Landbesitzer, der sein Geschäftstalent beweisen möchte, hat direkten Zugang zu einer Vielzahl möglicher Kunden. Die formale Einrichtung der Services erfolgt durch die jeweilige Gemeindeverwaltung, die Richtlinien für Werbung, Zufahrten etc. vorgibt. Diese Regelungen werden jedoch von vielen informellen Unternehmern übergangen, die Erfrischungen, billige Zigaretten, Wodka oder sogar Gartenzwerge an die Vorbeifahrenden verkaufen. Einige stellen einfach ein Bed-and-Breakfast-Schild auf und vermieten ein Zimmer ihres Hauses an die Reisenden. Aber es gibt auch andere, ausgefeiltere Konzepte, aus der Grenze und dem Verkehr Nutzen zu ziehen: etwa das des Secondhand-Möbelladens Lamus, dessen Besitzer Sperrmüllmöbel in Deutschland sammelt und sie dann an Kunden aus ganz Polen weiterverkauft, oder, vergleichbar, das des Autokiosks, bei dem verschrottete Autos billig in Deutschland eingekauft, über die Grenze transportiert, repariert und teuer wiederverkauft werden. Jeder dieser Services kann als *single purpose service* (Einzweckservice) kategorisiert werden, ebenso wie Bars, Motels oder Prostituierte, die im Wald auf Kunden warten. Alle diese Unternehmen sind lokal, auch wenn sie oft versuchen, mögliche Kunden durch Namen zu verführen, die die heimische Umgebung vergessen machen sollen – wie Motels namens Paradise und Oaza oder eine Bar mit Namen Heaven.

Mit der Zeit haben sich aus den *single purpose services* kleine Enklaven entwickelt und Serviceagglomerationen sind entstanden. Meistens be-

FEW KILOMETRES AWAY. WHEN SHE WAS A CHILD SHE USED TO COME TO THIS PLACE WITH HER GRANDMOTHER IN ORDER TO PICK MUSHROOMS. SHE SAYS THAT NOW THERE ARE NO MUSHROOMS BUT INSTEAD SHE HAS A JOB.[3]

As the socialist system broke down, the border between Eastern and Western Europe moved from the West German-East German border to the German-Polish border. At the German side of this border an official truck stop, Truck stop A12, was established next to the autobahn in 1994 when the trucks wanting to cross the border to Poland had to spend up to 46 hours queuing on the highway.[4] The main task of this rather special service facility was to organize the waiting time of the truck-drivers caused by the actual bottle neck-situation at the border. The trucks that were waiting at the highway would now get off the road and park at Truck Stop A12 and the drivers would be able to get a rest there. Truck stop A12 was set-up with basic parking facilities for up to 960 trucks, a shop, a supermarket, a tire store, a cafeteria and sanitary facilities. Truck-drivers had to wait here until they were allowed to pass the border and enter Poland. On the Polish side, the waiting hours were the same of course, but here no official stop was organized, and as the breakdown of the political system encouraged a new generation of pioneer capitalism, many hopeful entrepreneurs got attracted to the borderland and its possibility of taking advantage of the flow of traffic. Since the beginning of the 1990's, a flourishing landscape of services has started to emerge along the polish country road.

Most of the services are rather small scale and have an improvised style, but almost all of them are offering a 24hour service. The services are generated by the border traffic and the flows of goods between the East and the West. The carriers of goods – truck-drivers – are the main customers for the service facilities along the road. Everything is laid out for trucks and truck-drivers: there are huge parking lots for the trucks, truck washings in almost every village and a standardized menu that seems to be tailored to the culinary taste of the prototypical truck driver is offered everywhere.

A short comparison between 60 km of E30 on the German side and 60 km on the Polish side, effectively reveals the extreme difference of conditions on each side of the border. There are 9 access roads and no speed limits on the last 60 km in Germany. Whereas the Polish side has 27 access roads and runs through 8 villages at a speed limit of 90 km/h for cars and 70 km/h for trucks – in towns or villages the speed limit even decreases to 60 km/h. On the last 60 km of the German side, there is only one rest and service unit and a few parking lots with sanitary facilities in contrast to the Polish side where there is a wide range of about 130 services of all kinds.

While the services in Polish borderland are mostly springing from the local communities or are at least connected to the locality, the opposite is true of the services along the German Autobahn. Here, almost all service facilities are provided by big global co-operations, gas stations by Shell, BP, DEA and others and restaurants such as Mövenpick and McDonalds. Informal service is not taking place along the German high-speed-way. The services there aren't emerging from local communities and hardly have any connection to it, even though they are more than ready to exploit them.

TYPOLOGIES OF E30

HE USED TO BE MORE INTERESTED IN AUDIO SYSTEMS FOR CARS, BUT NOW HE RUNS A CBS-REPAIR SERVICE TOGETHER WITH A FRIEND. IT WAS HIS FRIEND'S IDEA AND HE DIDN'T HAVE ANYTHING ELSE TO DO, SO HE WENT WITH IT.[5]

The conditions for the individual entrepreneur along E30 are good. Any house or landowner wanting to test their business talent has direct access to the stream of customers. The formal set-up of businesses goes through the local city council where guidelines are given according to advertisements, entrances etc. But many informal businesses are going beyond the regulations; selling refreshments, cheap cigarettes, vodka or even garden dwarfs to people passing by. Some are simply

stehen sie aus einer Tankstelle und einem Restaurant, manchmal kombiniert mit einer Auto- und Lkw-Waschanlage, oder aus einer Lkw-Werkstatt mit Waschanlage und Restaurant. Mitunter findet man zusätzlich Versicherungskioske oder CBS-Reparatur-Services. Der Kunde spart Zeit. Er muss nur einmal halten, um seinen Tank zu füllen, ein Restaurant zu besuchen, einzukaufen und vielleicht sogar neue Versicherungen abzuschließen, bevor er wieder auf die Straße zurückkehrt. Die einzelnen Unternehmen in den Serviceagglomerationen haben normalerweise unterschiedliche Besitzer und sind nicht in einen übergeordneten Rahmen eingebunden. Sie stehen nicht miteinander im Wettbewerb, haben aber gemerkt, dass sie durch die Ergänzung ihres jeweiligen Angebots mehr Profit aus dem Transitverkehr ziehen können.

All-in-one service units (Alles-in-einem-Serviceeinheiten) vergrößern den Maßstab. Ihre Grundlage ist ein riesiger Lkw-Parkplatz, umgeben von Einrichtungen für Lkw-Fahrer – hier kann alles, was man während der Reise brauchen könnte, gekauft werden. Die *all-in-one service unit* besteht aus einer Kombination von Restaurant, Bar, Tankstelle, Lkw-Werkstatt, Lkw-Waschanlage und bietet unter anderem Geldwechselstube, Duschmöglichkeiten, Supermarkt, Motel und manchmal sogar einen Friseur. Die mehr oder weniger zufälligen Anordnungen von Serviceagglomerationen, die sich im Laufe der Zeit entwickelt hatten, wurden upgedatet – sie wurden Stück für Stück zu einer Einheit. Die riesigen *all-in-one service units* gehören in der Regel nur einer Person. Fast alle benutzen ein spezielles Logo oder eine themenparkähnliche Aufmachung als Rahmen für die verschiedenen Services, die sie anbieten, wie etwa Las Vegas, Nevada oder Port 2000.

Für *all-in-one service units* genügt es jedenfalls nicht mehr, bloß Paradise genannt zu werden – jetzt muss der Truck Stop selbst paradiesisch sein. Die großen Services werden zu exotischen Traumlandschaften, die ihre Kunden einladen, der Straße zu entfliehen und in eine andere Welt einzutauchen – in ihre Welt exotisierter globaler Kultur, wo aus Transit temporär Stasis wird, während die Realität des Konsums einen umfängt. Große *all-in-one service units* staffieren ihre Gehwege mit künstlichen Palmen und mexikanischen Lampen aus und heißen ihre Kunden mit einem großen Schild willkommen, das verkündet, dass sie nun wirklich in Las Vegas angekommen seien.

AKTIVER RURALER URBANISMUS

TORZYM HAT 2 700 EINWOHNER UND NEBEN DEM MOTEL PIZZERIA SIEBEN ANDERE MOTELS: EIN BURG-MOTEL, EIN GESCHÄFTS-MOTEL, EIN MOTEL, DAS EINEM EHEMALIGEN TAXIFAHRER GEHÖRT, EIN BED-AND-BREAKFAST, EIN MOTEL PARADISE, AN DEM RUSSISCHE TOURISTEN AUF IHREM WEG NACH PARIS ODER ARBEITSMIGRANTEN AUF IHREM WEG ZUR ARBEIT HALTEN, UM EINE PAUSE ZU MACHEN, EIN MOTEL MIT ZWEI BESITZERN – UND EIN 24-STUNDEN-ZIMMER, DESSEN BESITZERIN GERNE SCHLIESSEN MÖCHTE. ABER DAS SCHILD VOR DEM HAUS HAT EIN SOLIDES FUNDAMENT, DAS SIE NICHT ENTFERNEN KANN.

Bis zu einem gewissen Grad ist durch den Service-Korridor in der ländlichen Umgebung eine hybride Form von Urbanität entstanden. Neben seinen acht Motels verfügt Torzym über vier Tankstellen, drei Supermärkte, ein Modegeschäft und eine gute Kiosk-Infrastruktur. Während einige großmaßstäbliche Services entlang der E30 in einem Gewerbegebiet am Ortsrand angesiedelt sind, entstanden die meisten direkt im Ortskern. Wohnhäuser neben der Straße wurden zu Motels, Baulücken wurden mit einem Supermarkt oder einer Reihe von Kiosken gefüllt.

Es ist wichtig zu betonen, dass der Begriff „hybride Urbanität" nicht einfach im Sinne städtischer Dichte zu verstehen ist. Torzym ist nicht urban, weil es acht Motels hat – normalerweise der Standard für viel größere Städte. Urbanität bedeutet hier vielmehr die Möglichkeit des Austauschs und der Interaktion zwischen lokalen und globalen Realitäten – eine „Glokalität", bei der das Lokale mit seinen informellen und/oder familiengeführten Unternehmen mehr ist als nur von den globalen Flüssen abhängig und diese Flüsse nährend.

Im Gegenteil, die örtlichen Bewohner nutzen die Transitservices auch. Services, die entstanden sind, um dem Verkehrsfluss zu dienen, wurden lokal integriert und zum Bestandteil des alltäglichen Lebens der Bewohner. So zum Beispiel eines der Motels in Torzym, das Motel Paradise. Das Paradise liegt am Rand von Torzym – ein großes Haus, das schon einige Male erweitert wurde, mit Wintergärten zum Drinsitzen und einer eher eleganten Erscheinung. Das rote Neonschild an dem türkisfarbenen Gebäude ist weithin sichtbar, da das Motel auf einem Hügel liegt. Es wurde für die Transitreisenden eingerichtet, hat sich aber zu einem Ort entwickelt, der von verschiedenen Gruppen genutzt wird. Auf der einen Seite ist es ein Stopp

putting up a sign with 'bed and breakfast' and then hiring out an extra room of the house to travellers. Other more advanced ways of taking advantage of the border are concepts like the second-hand furniture store Lamus, where the owner is collecting scraped furniture in Germany and then selling it to customers from all over Poland or – quite similar to this – a "car-kiosk", where broken and scraped cars are bought cheaply in Germany and then taken over the border, where they are repaired and resold expensively. Each of these services can be categorized as *single purpose services* along with bars, motels or prostitutes waiting in the forest. All of these enterprises are local, though their names often try to seduce possible costumers and make them forget their present surroundings and give into their domain, such as motels with names like Paradise and Oaza or a bar named Heaven.

Over time, *single purpose services* have evolved into small enclaves creating service agglomerations. They most often appear as a combination of a gas station and a restaurant, sometimes with a car and truck wash, or a truck service with a truck wash and a restaurant. Additional variations are insurance kiosks or cbs-repair-services. The customer saves time by only having to make a single stop where he can combine the filling of gas with eating, shopping and maybe even renewing his insurances before taking off again. The services in the service agglomeration have usually got different owners and are not bound in an overall framework. They are not competing with each other but have realized that by complementing each other's services they are better equipped to make profit of the transit-traffic.

All-in-one service units increase the scale. The basis of these units is a huge truck parking lot surrounded by facilities for the truck-driver – here it is possible to get hold of everything you ever thought needed during travelling. The *all-in-one service units* consist of a combination of a restaurant, a bar, a gas station, a truck service, a truck wash, a money exchange, shower facilities, a supermarket, a motel and some times even hairdressers. The more or less accidental formations of service agglomerations that developed during time have become up-dated – they have gradually become one entity. The huge infrastructure service units are owned by one person (or company) and most of them use a special sign or a theme-like style as a framework to the different services they offer, like Las Vegas, Nevada or Port 2000. However, for *all-in-one service units* it is no longer enough to be called Paradise – now the whole truck stop itself has to *be* a paradise. The big services transform themselves into exotic dreamscapes, making customers capable of escaping the road and enter into another world – into their world of exoticised global culture where transit temporarily becomes stasis as you suck into consumer reality. In that way, big *all-in-one service units* such as Las Vegas are equipping their pavement with artificial Palms and Mexican lamps, while welcoming customers with a big sign announcing that now they are truly entering Las Vegas.

ACTIVE RURAL URBANISM

THERE ARE 2,700 INHABITANTS IN TORZYM AND SEVEN OTHER MOTELS BESIDES MOTEL PIZZERIA: A CASTLE MOTEL, A BUSINESS MOTEL, A MOTEL OWNED BY A FORMER TAXI DRIVER, A BED AND BREAKFAST, A MOTEL PARADISE WHERE RUSSIAN TOURISTS ON THEIR WAY TO PARIS OR SHUTTLE MIGRANTS ON THEIR WAY TO WORK, STOP TO HAVE A BREAK, A MOTEL WITH TWO OWNERS AND A 24H ROOM – THE OWNER WANTS TO CLOSE THE PLACE, BUT THE SIGN IN FRONT OF THE HOUSE IS GROUNDED IN A SOLID CONCRETE FOUNDATION AND SHE CANNOT REMOVE IT.

To a certain point the corridor of services has created a hybrid form of urbanity in the rural settings. Besides its eight Motels, Torzym is also the home of four gas stations, three supermarkets, a fashion store and a good kiosk infrastructure. While some of the big scale services are located in an industrial area next to the road at the edge of the city most of the others are springing directly from the local fabric. Houses next to the road are transformed into motels and gaps are filled with a supermarket or a range of kiosks.

für Touristen auf der Reise nach Paris oder Berlin und für Arbeitsmigranten aus dem Osten auf ihrem Weg in den Westen. Auf der anderen Seite ist das Motel aber auch *das* gute Restaurant der Gegend. Offizielle Abendessen der Gemeindeverwaltung finden hier statt, und an den Wochenenden kommen die Bewohner der Gegend auf ein Stück Kuchen oder ein feines Diner ins Paradise.

Andere Beispiele für die lokale Einbindung der Transitservices sind der Truck Stop „Las Vegas" in Mostki oder die Tankstelle V12 in Boczów. Das Las Vegas ist, wie schon erwähnt, eine große *all-in-one service unit* mit einem Supermarkt, zwei Bars und Restaurants, einer Lkw-Werkstatt und -Waschanlage, einem riesigen Lkw-Parkplatz, einer Tankstelle und einem Motel. Es besteht hauptsächlich aus Containern, die dem Thema der Wüstenstadt entsprechend gestaltet sind: Dekoriert mit künstlichen Palmen, unter Verwendung von Western-Schrift und mit einer rustikalen Einrichtung, wurde das Las Vegas offensichtlich für Lkw-Fahrer und ihre Bedürfnisse geschaffen. Weil es aber in der Gegend keine Disko oder andere Vergnügungsstätten für Teenager gibt, wurde dieser Ort zum beliebten Treffpunkt der einheimischen Jugendlichen. Am Wochenende hängen sie beim Las Vegas ab, wetteifern darum, wer die lauteste Auto-Hi-Fi-Anlage hat, oder konsumieren im 24-Stunden-Supermarkt.

Die Tankstelle V12 befindet sich am Ortsausgang von Boczów. Sie gehört nicht zu einem globalen Unternehmen, hat aber trotzdem eine professionelle *corporate identity* und große Pläne für die Zukunft: Sie soll um ein Hotel und einen Truck Stop erweitert werden. Neben der V12 befinden sich eine eher improvisierte Autogas-Tankstelle, die Containerruine eines Bar-Imbisses, ein Postamt und, auf der anderen Straßenseite, der Dorffriedhof. Die V12-Tankstelle ist deutlich für den Transitverkehr ausgelegt, aber ihr Sortiment umfasst auch zwei ganze Regalreihen mit Grabutensilien und Friedhofskerzen.

Kurzum, die V12 hat das Angebot ihrer spezifischen Lage neben einem Friedhof angepasst und ist demzufolge nicht mit jeder anderen beliebigen Tankstelle zu vergleichen. Das Las Vegas ist ein cooler Ort zum Abhängen, obwohl oder gerade weil es ein 24-Stunden-„Themen"-Truck-Stop ist. Das Motel Paradise ist mehr als ein reines Touristenhotel, da es durch seine außerordentliche Qualität zu *dem* guten Restaurant der Gegend geworden ist. Und schließlich: Torzym, wo sich die Häuser entlang der Straße fast in einen Service-Strip verwandelt haben, nennt sich selbst „TIR-City"![6] Fast unnötig, zu erwähnen, dass die starke Verbindung zum Transitverkehr die lokale Gemeinschaft bis zu einem gewissen Grad beeinflusst: Die Bevölkerung von Torzym hat 24 Stunden am Tag Zugang zu Shopping, Restaurants, Bars und Unterhaltung, ein Angebot, das normalerweise nur mit dem metropolitanen Lebensstil in Verbindung gebracht wird.

Im polnischen Grenzland der E30 verweben sich die Realitäten von Lokalem (Pionierkapitalismus) und Globalem (Transitverkehr). Die daraus entstehende sehr spezifische Form ländlicher Urbanität stellt nicht nur für die Dörfler, sondern auch für die Lkw-Fahrer eine ungewohnte Umgebung dar. Die entscheidende Qualität der E30 ist ihr aktiver ländlicher Urbanismus, der aus dem vagen, undefinierten Status des Gebiets, nicht zuletzt hinsichtlich der Planung, entstanden ist, im Gegensatz zu den beschränkten Möglichkeiten der Autobahn und den passiven Suburbs in deren Umgebung.

NEUES EUROPA – NEUES GRENZLAND

SIE KAM ZUFÄLLIG ZU DIESEM TRUCK STOP, WOLLTE EIGENTLICH NUR IN DIE STRASSE NAHE DER GRENZE INVESTIEREN UND FUHR HIER VORBEI. SIE SAGT, DASS ES WÄHREND DES SOZIALISMUS NORMALERWEISE SCHWER WAR, VIEL GELD ZU VERDIENEN. ABER MIT DER RICHTIGEN LIZENZ WAR ES DOCH MÖGLICH, WEIL MAN KAUM KONKURRENZ HATTE. SIE SCHAFFTE ES, EINE LIZENZ ZUM BLUMENVERKAUF FÜR EINEN DER WICHTIGSTEN POLNISCHEN FEIERTAGE ZU BEKOMMEN. JETZT SIND DIE ZEITEN VIEL HÄRTER. DER TRUCK STOP LOHNT SICH NICHT RICHTIG. SEIT DER EU-ERWEITERUNG HAT DER VERKEHR ZWAR SEHR ZUGENOMMEN, ABER GLEICHZEITIG KOMMEN IMMER WENIGER LEUTE HIERHER. SIE IST SCHLIESSLICH NICHT EINMAL SICHER, OB SIE DIESEN TRUCK-SERVICE BEHALTEN WILL.[7]

It is important, though, to emphasize that the notion of "hybrid urbanism" shall not entirely be understood as a calculation of density and comparison of statistics between city and rural areas – Torzym is not urban because it contains eight motels, an amount that usually is the standard for a city of much larger scale. What is much more crucial is the understanding of this urbanism as a possibility of exchange and interaction between local and global realities – a "glocality", where the local with its informal and/or family run businesses are more than just fed by or feeding the global flows.

What is happening is that the locals are also using the transit services. Services created to serve the flow of traffic have become integrated locally as resources of the area and are a part of the inhabitants' everyday life. An example is one of the Motels of Torzym – Motel Paradise. Motel Paradise is situated on the edge of Torzym in a giant house that has been extended several times with winter gardens to sit in and a rather elegant appearance. The red neon sign on top of the turquoise building is visible from far away since the Motel is situated on top of a hill. Motel Paradise is designed to serve the people in transit, but it has developed to a place where a mixed variety of agents interweave. On one hand it is the stop for tourists on their way to Paris or Berlin and for shuttle migrants from the east on their way to work in the west, but on the other hand the hotel has also come to be considered as the nice restaurant of the area. Official dinners of the local government take place here and during the weekends the local people come for a piece of cake or a fine dinner if a special occasion has to be celebrated.

Other examples of local involvement in the transit services are the Las Vegas truck stop in Motski, or the gas station V12 in Boczow. Las Vegas is as earlier mentioned a large scale *all-in-one service unit* with a supermarket, two bars and restaurants, a truck service and truck wash, a huge parking lot, a gas station and a motel. It mainly consists of container boxes that are bound in the theme of the desert city: decorated with artificial palm trees, using western front and rustic interior. Las Vegas is layed out for truck drivers and their needs but because the area is not supplied with a disco or other entertainment facilities for youngsters, the place has become a popular site among the local teens. During the weekends they enjoy hanging out at Las Vegas competing with their car hi-fi equipment or just consuming at the 24-hour supermarket.

V12 Gas Station is located at the edge of Boczow. It is not a global enterprise but nevertheless the station has a professional corporate appearance and big future plans for extending with a hotel and a truck stop. Next to it is a rather improvised auto gaz station, a container-ruin of a bar-imbiss, a post office and situated on the opposite side of the street is the village cemetery. V12 is clearly designed to attract the bypassing transit traffic but among the range of goods they offer, two full rows of shelves filled with funeral relics and cemetery candles have been included.

V12 adapts its offers to the specific location next to a cemetery and is therefore not just the same like any other gas station. Las Vegas is a cool spot to hang out although – or perhaps *because* it is a themed 24h truck stop. Motel Paradise becomes more than a tourist hotel and a working place, it also takes its place within the local community and becomes *the* nice restaurant of the whole area by providing an outstanding quality. And finally, Torzym, where the houses along the E30 almost turn into a service strip, calls itself a "TIR-city"![6] Needless to say, the strong connection to the traffic is shaping the local identity to a certain extent. To such an extent that the services are serving the people of the area too: With non-stop activity the local inhabitants have got access to shopping, eating, drinking and entertainment 24h a day, something which is usually only related to a metropolitan lifestyle.

In the E30 Polish borderland the interweaving of local (pioneer capitalism) and global (transit traffic) realities and its specific form of rural urbanism forms not only an unusual setting for the villagers but also for the truck-drivers. The main quality of the E30 is the active rural urbanism that has emerged out of its vague and indefinite state, at least in planning terms, as opposed to the determined setting of a highway and the passive suburbs around it.

NEW EUROPE – NEW BORDERLAND

SHE GOT THIS TRUCK STOP BY CHANCE, WANTING TO INVEST IN THE ROAD CLOSE TO THE BORDER AND JUST DROVE BY. SHE SAYS THAT DURING SOCIALIST TIMES IT WAS GENERALLY HARD TO MAKE MONEY. BUT HAVING THE RIGHT LICENSE YOU COULD EARN A LOT, BECAUSE YOU HARDLY HAD ANY COMPETITION. SHE MANAGED TO GET A LICENSE TO SELL FLOWERS AT ONE OF THE MAIN POLISH HOLIDAYS. NOW TIMES ARE MUCH HARD-

Am 1. Mai 2004 ist Polen der EU beigetreten; die Grenzsituation zwischen Polen und Deutschland hat sich damit geändert. Obwohl die eigentliche Grenzkontrolle bis 2006 oder 2008 bestehen bleibt – je nachdem, wann Polens Ostgrenzen die Schengen-Standards erfüllen –, hat die Zollkontrolle an der deutsch-polnischen Grenze ihren Betrieb seit dem 1. Mai 2004 eingestellt.[8] Damit sind die langen Lkw-Warteschlangen verschwunden; sie haben sich nun, zusammen mit der Zollkontrolle, an die neue EU-Außengrenze zwischen Polen und Weißrussland verlagert. Seit die Lkw-Fahrer wählen können, auf welcher Seite der Grenze sie ihre obligatorische Wartezeit[9] verbringen, hat der Truck Stop A12 in Deutschland fast alle seine Kunden verloren und wird wohl bald schließen. Die Fahrer ziehen es vor, im polnischen Grenzland zu rasten, wo der Service „besser und billiger"[10] sei.

Seit Polens EU-Beitritt und den damit verbundenen Veränderungen der Grenzpraxis hat der Verkehr auf der Strecke um mindestens 50 Prozent zugenommen. Trotzdem wird es für die Services schwieriger, die Aufmerksamkeit auf sich zu lenken. Der Wettbewerb nimmt zu. Große Serviceunternehmen werden größer, und die Kleinen kämpfen ums Überleben. Darüber hinaus unterstreichen große Serviceeinrichtungen ihre Professionalität, indem sie sich von den informellen abzuheben versuchen. Sie setzen unterschiedliche Mittel ein, um die kleineren informellen Services unter Kontrolle zu bekommen, zum Beispiel indem sie diese in ihre eigene Struktur einbinden – wie im Fall des Gartenzwerg-Ladens Asterix.

Asterix war bis vor kurzem in einem kleinen, containerähnlichen Kiosk direkt neben der E30 untergebracht. Der Laden hatte Gartenzwerge, billige Zigaretten und Wodka für deutsche Touristen im Angebot. Als aber Nevada, eine große *all-in-one service unit*, einige Meter weiter öffnete, wurde der Kiosk geschlossen und in den neuen Komplex integriert. Asterix ist jetzt nicht mehr von der Straße aus sichtbar.

Im Gegensatz zu Nevadas Strategie, unerwünschte Wettbewerber einfach zu absorbieren, steht der Fall Orlen.[11] Hier wurden aggressivere Mittel eingesetzt, um das Umfeld der Tankstelle so zu säubern, dass ihr Image oder ihre Marke nicht vom improvisierten Erscheinungsbild des benachbarten informellen Service angegriffen und „infiziert" würde. Die erste und letzte Tankstelle in Polen, 1 200 Meter vor der polnisch-deutschen Grenze, war einmal eine echte Serviceagglomeration, bestehend aus einem Diner – Bar Venus –, einem informellen Geldwechselkiosk, einem informellen Imbiss – Maier's Western Grill – und ebenjener Tankstelle. 2003 hat Orlen diese Tankstelle gekauft. Nur einige Monate später, im Februar 2004, entschied sich das Unternehmen, eine Mauer zu errichten, die jeden direkten Zugang zu Maier's Western Grill von der Straße verhindert. Damit wurden die Angestellten des Grills ein-, die Kunden aber ausgeschlossen. In Maier's Western Grill reduzierte sich die Zahl der Kunden von ca. 1 000 am Tag auf 100 im Monat! Überflüssig, hier noch zu erwähnen, dass der Grill kurz darauf geschlossen wurde. Zeitgleich mit diesen kleinen Geschichten, individuellen Beispielen der Transformation im Grenzland, finden große infrastrukturelle Veränderungen entlang der gesamten Route statt.

DIESE MASCHINE IST NAGELNEU. ER HAT MIT IHR ERST ZWEI WOCHEN GEARBEITET. SIE KANN EINEN HEKTAR ZWEIGE AM TAG ZERKLEINERN. SIE WURDE VON PHARE GEFÖRDERT – DEM EU-FONDS, DER DIE BEITRITTSLÄNDER DABEI UNTERSTÜTZT, DIE EU-STANDARDS ZU ERREICHEN.[12]

Waldarbeiter bereiten die Strecke für die neue Autobahn vor, parallel zur E30; sie holzen den Wald neben der Straße ab. Die neue Autobahn ist Teil des Korridors 2 von Berlin nach Moskau im Transeuropäischen Netzwerk (TEN) der Europäischen Union. TEN wird damit beworben, ungleiche Wettbewerbsbedingungen innerhalb der EU auszugleichen, schafft aber in erster Linie den Zugang zu den wichtigsten wirtschaftlichen Zentren Osteuropas. Bis heute gibt es fast keine Autobahnen in Polen – das ganze Land wird von Landstraßen wie der E30 erschlossen.

Das Fehlen eines angemessenen Straßennetzes erscheint heutzutage als eine kritische Barriere für die Entwicklung des Landes, da die Potentiale, die die Wettbewerbsvorteile der polnischen Wirtschaft wie geographische Lage und Größe des Marktes eröffnen, nicht genutzt werden. Der Zustand von Polens Straßen behindert den internationalen Handel mit der EU und anderen Nachbarländern und hat einen negativen Einfluss auf ausländische Direktinvestitionen und die Mobilität der Arbeitskräfte. Diese negativen Faktoren führen zu einer verminderten Wettbewerbsfähigkeit der polnischen Wirtschaft und behindern die Entwicklung und innovative Prozesse in Polen. Transportministerium Polen, Warschau[13]

ER. THE TRUCK STOP DOESN'T PAY OFF SO WELL. SINCE THE EU ENLARGEMENT THE TRAFFIC HAS INCREASED A LOT, BUT AT THE SAME TIME LESS AND LESS PEOPLE ARE COMING HERE. FINALLY SHE IS NOT EVEN SURE THAT SHE WILL STAY WITH THIS TRUCK SERVICE.[7]

The 1st of May 2004 Poland entered the EU and in connection to this, changes appeared in the border situation between Poland and Germany. Although an actual border control will continue to exist until 2006–2008, when the Polish East border has reached Schengen standards, the custom control ceased to exist at the German-Polish border from May 1st.[8] This abolished the long waiting line of trucks which along with the custom control moved eastwards to the new external EU border between Poland and Belarus. Since the truck drivers can choose on which side of the border they spend their obligatory waiting time[9], Truck Stop A12 has lost almost all of its customers and will probably close down soon. The truck drivers prefer to rest in Polish borderland where they get "better and cheaper"[10] services.

Since Poland's accession to the EU and the transformation of the border practice connected to it, the traffic has increased by at least 50 per cent. But at the same time it is getting harder for the services to catch any attention from the heavy flow of traffic. Competition is increasing. Big services are getting bigger while the medium sized and small ones are fighting to survive. Moreover successful big service facilities are underlining their professionalism by trying to distinguish themselves from the informal services. They use different means in order to get the smaller informal services under control, for instance by implementing the informal services into their own structures, as it is the case with the dwarf-shop Asterix.

Asterix was until recently located in a small container-like kiosk just off the E30-road providing German tourists with garden dwarfs, cheap cigarettes and vodka, but after Nevada opened a big theme-park-like *all-in-one-service unit* some hundred meters away, the kiosk was closed down and implemented within the new complex. Asterix is no longer visible from the street.

In contrast to Nevada's strategy of absorbing unwanted competition stands the case of Orlen.[11] Here more aggressive means are used to clean up their surroundings so that their image or brand is not affected or rather infected by the improvised style of the informal services.

The first and last gas station in Poland 1,200 m before the Polish-German border used to be a true service agglomeration consisting of a diner – Bar Venus, an informal money exchange kiosk, an informal imbiss – Meier's Westerngrill and a gas station. In 2003, Orlen bought the gas station in question. Just a few month later – in Febuary 2004 – Orlen decided to erect a wall prohibiting any direct access to Meier's Western Grill from the road. As a consequence, the employees of the Grill where effectively walled in while the customers were walled out. This resulted in a decrease of costumers at the Grill from approximately 1,000 a day to 100 – a month! Needless to say, the Grill was closed down soon after. Simultaneous to these small stories as individual examples of the borderland transformation, bigger infrastructural changes are taking place along the whole route, to pave way for new flows.

THIS MACHINE IS BRAND NEW. HE WORKED WITH IT FOR ONLY 2 WEEKS. IT CAN DEMOLISH ONE HECTARE OF BRANCHES IN ONE DAY. IT IS SPONSORED BY PHARE – THE EU FUND ASSISTING ACCESSION COUNTRIES IN REACHING EU STANDARDS.[12]

Workers are now preparing the route for a new highway running parallel to E30. They are tearing down the forest next to E30. The new highway is a part of Corridor II from Berlin to Moscow in the Trans-European Network (TEN) of the European Union. TEN is promoted to equalise competition in the EU but in first line it provides access to the main economic centres of Eastern Europe. Until now there are almost no highways in Poland – the whole country is moreover opened up by country roads like E30.

The lack of road network of adequate standard, appears nowadays as the critical barrier to the country development, limiting the potential of Polish

Nach den Plänen bis 2015 sollen in Polen zwei Autobahnen von West nach Ost und eine von Nord nach Süd gebaut werden. Die von uns untersuchte Gegend – das polnische Grenzland an der E30 – liegt im Abschnitt zwischen Swiecko, der Stadt neben der deutsch-polnischen Grenze, und Nowy Tomysl. Dieser Abschnitt soll 2010 fertig gestellt sein. Der Bau erfolgt in zwei Abschnitten, wobei der erste – bis 2007 – die Öffnung der Strecke für den Verkehr einschließt.

DER BÜRGERMEISTER VON TORZYM ERZÄHLT, DASS ES PLÄNE FÜR EINE AUTOBAHN GIBT, DIE DIE EXISTIERENDE E30 ERSETZEN SOLL. DIE NEUE AUTOBAHN WIRD NICHT DIE DÖRFER DURCHQUEREN, DAFÜR ABER DEN WALD PARALLEL ZUR HEUTIGEN STRECKE. SIE WIRD IN ZWEI ABSCHNITTEN GEBAUT. TORZYM MUSS BIS ZUM ZWEITEN BAUABSCHNITT WARTEN, UM EINE AUSFAHRT ZU BEKOMMEN.
GESTERN HATTEN SIE EIN MEETING IN DER STADTVERWALTUNG. SIE HABEN BESCHLOSSEN, EINE AUSFAHRT FÜR TORZYM SCHON IM ERSTEN BAUABSCHNITT ZU FORDERN.[14]

Die 154 Kilometer Autobahn von Swiecko nach Nowy Tomysl sollen im ersten Bauabschnitt vier Abfahrten bekommen und 2007 fertig gestellt werden. Die Abfahrten sind in Swiecko, Rzepin, Jordanowo und Nowy Tomysl vorgesehen. Im zweiten Bauabschnitt, der für 2010 geplant ist, soll eine Abfahrt für Torzym enthalten sein.[15]
Die Anzahl der Raststätten ist sogar noch niedriger. Nur drei auf jeder Seite sind geplant. Verglichen mit der Servicelandschaft entlang der E30 scheint das sehr wenig, es entspricht jedoch der Dichte von Raststätten entlang westlichen Autobahnen.
Die neue Autobahn wird nach einem Konzessionsmodell ausschließlich von privaten Investoren finanziert und gebaut. Autostrada Wielkopolska SA (AWSA) ist Kreditnehmer und Besitzer der 40 Jahre geltenden BOT-Konzession (BOT steht für: built, operate, transfer – bauen, unterhalten, übergeben). 77 Prozent der investierten 875 Millionen Euro kommen aus Polen, 23 Prozent von internationalen Geldgebern. Als Gebühren-Autobahn mit Bezahlstationen an jeder Abfahrt soll sich die Straße innerhalb von 40 Jahren, der Dauer der vergebenen Konzession, selbst refinanzieren.

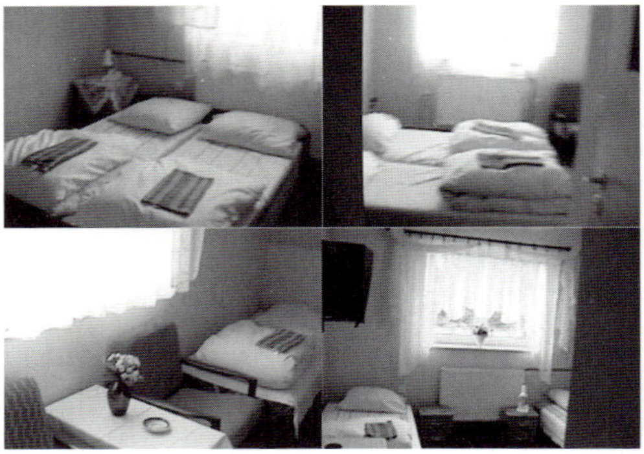

ER ZEIGT UNS DIE ZIMMER SEINES MOTELS. ES GIBT 30 BETTEN IM ALTEN UND 50 BETTEN IM NEUEN TEIL – 80 BETTEN ZUSAMMEN. ABER JETZT SIND NUR FÜNF BETTEN BELEGT. NORMALERWEISE WIRD ES AM WOCHENENDE ETWAS BESSER.[16]

„Die Ausfahrten werden in Torzym, in Rzepin und Jordanowo sein (…) ich weiß aber nicht, inwieweit das mein Geschäft beeinflussen wird." (Besitzerin des Motels Paradise)
Bei der Recherche über alle Services im polnischen Grenzland war die Besitzerin des Motels Paradise die Einzige, die tatsächlich über die geplanten Ausfahrten der neuen Autobahn informiert war. Die Besitzer kleinerer Serviceunternehmen waren skeptisch, ob ein solch großes Projekt in Polen überhaupt jemals fertig gestellt würde, und wenn ja, wann. Einige waren auch überzeugt, dass viele Leute die Autobahn wegen der hohen Kosten nicht benutzen würden.
Nichtsdestotrotz verlieren kleinere Services schon heute durch den ansteigenden Verkehr und die sich erhöhende Geschwindigkeit derart viel Kundschaft, dass es mehr als fraglich ist, ob sie die kommende Autobahn überhaupt erleben werden. Einige der größeren Services hoffen, dass sie – als bekannte und etablierte Einrichtungen – weiterhin für Lkw-Fahrer attraktiv sein werden, die ihren Gewohnheiten treu bleiben. Diese Hoffnung scheint angesichts der eingeschränkten Möglichkeiten, aus dem Transitverkehr einer Autobahn Nutzen zu ziehen, vergeblich. Eine dieser Möglichkeiten ist die *rest and service area* (Rast- und Servicestätte) an der Autobahn selbst, die andere der *highway multi complex* (Autobahn-Multi-Komplex), ein Gewerbegebiet in Sichtweite neben der Autobahn. Für kleine Serviceunternehmen ist der Zugang zu beiden begrenzt.

economy competitive advantages such as geographical position and market size. The condition of Poland's roads hampers the international trade with EU and the other neighbouring countries, and has a negative impact on foreign direct investments and mobility of labour force. Those negative factors result in decreasing Polish economy competitiveness and create a barrier to the development and innovative processes in Poland. Ministry of Transport, Warzawa[13]

The plans until 2015 are to build two highways from West to East and one from North to South. The E30 Polish borderland area lies in the section of Swiecko (the town next to the German-Polish border-crossing) to Nowy Tomysl. It is planned to be finished in 2010. The construction will be carried out in two stages whereas the first – until 2007 – includes the opening for the traffic on this section.

HE IS THE MAYOR OF TORZYM. HE TELLS THAT THERE ARE PLANS FOR A HIGHWAY TO SUBSTITUTE THE EXISTING E30 ROAD. THE NEW HIGHWAY WILL NOT RUN THROUGH VILLAGES BUT THROUGH THE FOREST PARALLEL TO THE CURRENT ROAD. IT WILL BE BUILT IN TWO STAGES. TORZYM HAS TO WAIT UNTIL THE SECOND STAGE TO GET AN EXIT.

YESTERDAY THEY HAD A MEETING IN THE CITY COUNCIL. THEY DECIDED TO DEMAND AN EXIT FOR TORZYM IN THE FIRST STAGE.[14]

The 154 km from Swiecko to Nowy Tomysl will have four exits in the first stage and will be completed in 2007. These exits are in Swiecko, Rzepin, Jordanowo and Nowy Tomysl. There is a second stage planned for 2010. It will include an exit for Torzym.[15]

The number of service areas is even smaller: only three on each side – compared to the service landscape along the E30 that seems to be very little but matches the usual distance of service areas along western highways.

The highway will be completely financed and built by private investors in a concessionary model. Autostrada Wielkopolska SA (AWSA) is the borrower and the owner of the 40-year BOT[16] (build-operate-transfer) concession. 77 per cent of the investment of 875 Million Euro is Polish, 23 per cent international. As a tolled highway with cash stations at each exit, the highway itself will refinance the investment within the 40 years period of the concession.

TYPOLOGIES OF THE HIGHWAY

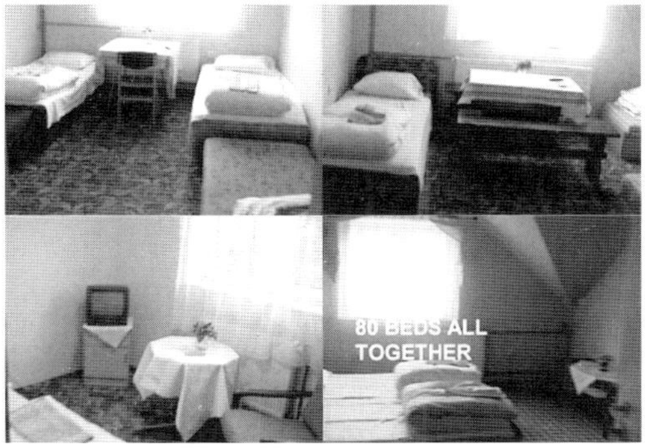

HE SHOWS THE ROOMS OF HIS MOTEL. THERE ARE 30 BEDS IN THE OLD PART AND 50 BEDS IN THE NEW PART – 80 BEDS ALTOGETHER. BUT NOW THERE ARE ONLY 5 BEDS IN USE. USUALLY IT GETS A BIT BETTER ON THE WEEKENDS.[17]

"The exits will be here in Torzym, in Rzepin and in Jordanowo ... but I don´t know how this will effect my business." (Owner of Motel Paradise).

Doing research at all of the services in the Polish borderland the owner of Motel Paradise was the only one who was actually informed of the exits of the new highway. Owners of smaller enterprises were either sceptical if such a big project would ever be completed in Poland or when this would actually happen and some were also sure that a rather big share of people would not use it because of the costs.

Nevertheless smaller services are already facing the decrease in customers since the traffic got bigger and faster, so that it is more than questionable that they will survive the coming highway. Some of the bigger services hope that they – as well-known and established services – will still be attractive to truck-drivers sticking to their old habits. This hope

Die *rest and service areas* an deutschen Autobahnen gehören in der Regel großen globalen Unternehmen. Sie sind durchgeplant, nicht nur um die Standards der firmeneigenen *corporate identities* zu erfüllen, sondern auch wegen der Sicherheitsanforderungen, die mit der hohen Geschwindigkeit zusammenhängen. Sie benötigen eine eigene Fahrspur als Einfahrt und sind von ihrer Umgebung klar abgegrenzt. Das heißt, sie haben keinerlei Verbindung zu den Orten im Umkreis, zu einer lokalen Gemeinschaft, da sie direkt an der Autobahn liegen – sie sind ein Teil der Autobahn. Informeller Service oder lokale Beteiligung finden in diesem beschränkten Rahmen nicht statt.

Highway multi complexes liegen in Sichtweite der Autobahn an einer Autobahnzufahrt. Man kann sie als den Versuch lokaler Gemeinschaften betrachten, einen Nutzen aus der Autobahn zu ziehen. Diese Komplexe haben eine höhere Attraktivität für großmaßstäbliche Unternehmen, da sie in der Lage sind, allein durch ihre Größe die Aufmerksamkeit der Vorbeifahrenden auf sich zu ziehen. Die „TIR-City" Torzym versucht ihre verkehrsbezogene Zukunft zu sichern, indem sie schon jetzt Zeitungsanzeigen schaltet, in denen 30 Hektar Land neben der Autobahn angeboten werden.

Die Autobahn ist eine monofunktionale Struktur, die nur als Verbindung zwischen A und B dem schnellen Verkehr dient. Anhalten, Auffahren und Abfahren sind durch Geschwindigkeits- und Sicherheitsvorschriften strikt geregelt. Als geschlossenes System hat die Autobahn kaum einen Bezug zur Umgebung. Im Gegensatz dazu wird die Landstraße E30 für verschiedenste Zwecke genutzt, und es besteht die Möglichkeit zufälliger Begegnungen: Ein Bauer aus der Gegend trifft einen Lkw-Fahrer aus der Ukraine, eine Frau, die mit ihrem Hund Gassi geht, einen Bus mit Schulkindern oder ein Paar, das vom Lebensmittelgeschäft heimradelt. Die E30 ist die Hauptstraße der Gegend, mit der neuen Autobahn jedoch wird diese Hauptstraße ihre Bevölkerung verlieren. Der Transitverkehr wird völlig andere Auswirkungen auf das polnische Grenzland haben.

SCHLUSSFOLGERUNG: PASSIVER SUBURBANISMUS VS. AKTIVER LÄNDLICHER URBANISMUS

Entlang der hier vorgestellten Route ist ein ländlicher Urbanismus mit einem alternativen Netzwerk entstanden – einem Netzwerk, in dem lokale Akteure die globalen Strukturen nutzen und einen eigenen Platz in ihnen beanspruchen. So hat sich eine sonst ländliche Gegend in eine aktive multifunktionale Gegend verwandelt, charakterisiert durch Einkaufs- und Unterhaltungsmöglichkeiten rund um die Uhr.

Die neue Autobahn im polnischen Grenzland wird durch eine Beschleunigung des Verkehrs die nächstgrößeren Knotenpunkte stärken, aber den tatsächlichen Zugang in der Fläche limitieren. Die Möglichkeiten der lokalen Gemeinschaft, sich in die globalen Flüsse einzumischen, werden damit eingeschränkt, wenn nicht sogar aufgehoben. Der Transitverkehr, der bis jetzt eine spezifische Servicelandschaft und eine einzigartige Form des Urbanismus hervorgebracht hat, wird die Landstraße meiden und das Gebiet auf der Autobahn umfahren – die im Ergebnis vergleichbar ist mit einer Mauer –, und es ist sehr wahrscheinlich, dass der Servicekorridor von heute verschwindet.

Die oben zitierte Auffassung des polnischen Verkehrsministeriums deutet klar in diese Richtung. Sie ist im Kontext jenes globalen Entwicklungstrends zu betrachten, nach dem Regionen um neue Investitionen konkurrieren. Entsprechend sollen die Finanzzentren gestärkt und in eine hochentwickelte Infrastruktur eingebunden werden. Auf diesen Knotenpunkten liegt das Hauptinteresse, und die Verbindung zwischen ihnen bilden Korridore, die von schwarzen Löchern umgeben sind – und deren einzige Existenzberechtigung im Transit besteht. Dies führt zu regionaler Zentralisierung; periphere Gegenden werden umgangen, ländliche Gegenden schrumpfen. Dieser Trend vollzieht sich natürlich auch in anderen Teilen der Welt, nicht zuletzt in Europa (zum Beispiel in Deutschland); wir sehen es aber als besonders unglücklich an, dass Polen dem wohl recht unkritisch folgen wird.

Die neue Autobahn wird die Gemeinden an den Autobahnabfahrten mit einem direkten Zugang zu hochprofilierten Wirtschaftszentren à la Poznan versorgen. Sie könnten sich so in eine ländliche Schlafgegend für die in der Stadt arbeitenden Leute verwandeln. Für die ganze Gegend würde sich daraus eine eher monofunktionale Zukunft ergeben. Dieser passive Suburbanismus mit seiner segregierten Landschaft findet überall statt – gibt es aber Wege für die lokale Gemeinschaft, sich den Zugang zu den globalen Flüssen zu bewahren?

Wenn man die Typologien der untersuchten Gegend betrachtet, so könnte die Serviceagglomeration ein alternatives Entwicklungsmodell darstellen, mit dem versucht würde, die Gegend einzubinden, anstatt sie zu umfahren. Wie schon erwähnt haben sich über eine gewisse Zeit Ser-

seems to be pointless, since there are only two ways of benefiting from the transit-traffic of a highway: one is the *service and resting areas* on the highway itself and the other is the *highway multi complex* – an economic area within view distance next to the highway. The access of informal or small services to both of these areas is limited.

The *resting and service facilities* on the German Autobahn are provided by big global corporations. They are planned and designed through, not only to fulfil the standards of the companies' corporate identities, but also to meet the safety regulations connected to the high speed. Therefore they need to have an own line for the traffic to slow down and have clearly defined borders to their surroundings. They are not connected to any local community since they exist within the highway – they are a part of the highway. Informal service or local engagement is not taking place in this determined setup.

Highway multi complexes lie within view distance next to the highway and are connected to a highway access. They can be seen as the attempt of the local communities to benefit from the highway. These areas are more attractive to big scale enterprises to catch the attention of the passing traffic. "TIR-city" Torzym tries to save its traffic related future by advertising the 30 hectares of land next to the highway in the newspaper.

The highway is a mono-functional structure as it only serves as a connector for fast traffic. Stopping, entering and exiting the highway is strictly regulated due to the high speed and safety regulations connected to it. It is a closed system and does hardly interfere with its surroundings. In contrast to this, the E30 country road is used for many purposes and its travellers are prone to chance meetings: a local farmer meets an Ukrainian truck driver, a lady walking her dog, a bus full of schoolchildren or a couple biking home from the grocery. E30 is the main road of the area but with the new highway this main road will loose its population. With this process of change, the Polish borderland will be introduced to completely new forms of spatial effects of transit traffic.

CONCLUSION: PASSIVE SUBURBANISM VS. ACTIVE RURAL URBANISM

Along the specific route here in consideration, a rural urbanism with an alternative network has occurred – a network where local agents use the global structures and claim places *of their own*. The otherwise rural area has thereby turned into an active multifunctional area characterized by 24h shopping and entertainment facilities.

With the introduction of the highway in the Polish borderland the speed will strengthen the main destination points, but also limit the actual access, moreover it will make it less possible (if not entirely impossible) for the local community to interfere with the global flows. The transit traffic that so far has generated the specific landscape of services and the unique form of urbanism will bypass the country road via the new highway – like a wall, and it is most likely that the current corridor of services will disappear.

The standpoint taken by the Polish Ministry of Transport, as quoted earlier, is clearly pointing towards this direction and should be understood in the context of a global development trend, where regions are competing for investments of new capital. The focus is on strengthening financial centres – capital nodes – by integrating them within a highly developed and effective infrastructure. In other words the nodes are the fields of interest and the infrastructure become corridors surrounded by black holes – existing only as landscapes necessary to pass through. This is leading to regional centralization, peripheral parts are bypassed and the rural areas are shrinking. We can see this trend already happening in other parts of the world, not the least in Europe (for example in Germany) and it is unlucky that Poland will now uncritically follow suite.

The new highway will provide the communities located at the highway exits with direct access to more high-profile economic centres à la Poznan. These communities might transform into a countryside sleeping area for people working in the city. Resulting in a rather mono-functional future for the whole area. Passive sub-urbanism with its segregated landscape is taking place everywhere, but are there any possible ways to let the local community maintain an access to profiting from the global flows?

Looking at the typologies provided by the area itself – the service agglomeration might be a possible model for an alternative future development trying to implement the area rather than by-passing it. As mentioned earlier, service agglomerations are formations developed over time, where different owners are complementing rather than competing with each other in order to benefit and take advantage of the transit traffic. What will happen if

viceagglomerationen entwickelt, bei denen mehrere Kleinunternehmer nicht miteinander konkurrieren, sondern ihr Angebot gegenseitig ergänzen, um aus dem Transitverkehr Nutzen zu ziehen. Was würde passieren, wenn die lokalen Gemeinden die Chance bekämen, mit den großen Services an der kommenden Autobahn zusammenzuarbeiten?
Es ist nicht unsere Absicht, die lokalen und informellen Services an der E30 zu romantisieren – viel eher wollen wir auf die Gefahr des passiven Suburbanismus hinweisen. Wir möchten eine Diskussion darüber eröffnen, wie die bestehende Tradition aufgegriffen und upgedatet werden kann – auch mit dem Ziel, Brüche in die Zukunftsplanung für diese Gegend zu implementieren. Schließlich hat Maier's Western Grill nur einen Monat mit einer Mauer ohne Brüche überlebt.

ANMERKUNGEN

1 Interview mit R. Stanulewicz, Bürgermeister von Torzym, April 2004

2 Unsere Untersuchung bezieht sich auf die ersten 60 Kilometer der E30 in Polen von Swiecko bis Mostki. Der Text basiert auf Recherchen vom Oktober 2003, April 2004 und Juli 2004.

3 Interview mit M. Susko, die im Versicherungskiosk in Rzepin arbeitet, April 2004

4 Interview mit S. Gosemann, Leiterin des Truck Stop A12 in Frankfurt/Oder, 15. März 2004

5 Interview mit Patrick, Besitzer des CBS-Reparaturservice bei Nevada, Juli 2004

6 TIR = Transport Internationaux Routiers, wie in der UNECE-TIR-Konvention definiert, http://www.iru.org

7 Interview mit M. Bozena, Besitzerin des Truck-Service E30 in Boczów, April 2004

8 In der EU werden Zollkontrollen dezentral durchgeführt, zum Beispiel direkt dort, wo die Ware produziert wird.

9 Nach bis zu vier Stunden Fahrt müssen die Fahrer mindestens 45 Minuten rasten; sie dürfen am Tag bis zu neun Stunden fahren.

10 Z. Jagodzinski, Besitzer von Duo Trans, einem Transportunternehmen. Jagodzinski fuhr selbst, als wir ihn bei seiner obligatorischen Pause, die er beim Truck Stop Nevada verbrachte, trafen.

11 PKN ORLEN ist der größte Veredler und Verkäufer von Erdöl, hochwertigem Petroleum und ähnlichen Produkten in Polen. Orlen unterhält ein Netzwerk von ca. 2000 Tankstellen in Polen und 494 in Deutschland. http://www.orlen.pl

12 Interview mit einem Waldarbeiter beim Fällen des Waldes neben der E30 nahe Rzepin, Juli 2004

13 Ministry of Transport: *Strategy of Transport Infrastructure Development in 2004–2006 and the following years (summary), draft translation*, Warschau 2003, S. 1; Übersetzung: Nina Gribat

14 Bezogen auf ein Treffen in der Stadtverwaltung in Torzym im Juli 2004

15 Der Bürgermeister von Torzym, R. Stanulewicz, hat diese Ausfahrt erwähnt, obwohl sie auf der Website der Firma, die die Autobahn baut, nicht auftaucht. http://www.a2-autostrada.pl

16 Interview mit A. A. Sucheccy, Besitzer des Motels Olka in Boczów, Juli 2004

local communities get a chance to agglomerate to the big services along the coming highway?
Our mission is not to romanticize any specific authenticity according to the local and informal services along this corridor, but rather to point out the danger of passive sub-urbanism. We wish to open up a discussion on the possibility of updating the existing tradition of informal service, as a way of implementing cracks in the future plans for the area – after all Meier's Western Grill lasted only one month with a wall without any cracks.

NOTES

1 R. Stanulewicz, the mayor of Torzym.

2 The E30 Polish borderland as mentioned in this text stands for the area we did research in, the first 60km of the E30 in Poland, from Swiecko to Mostki. The text is based on research done in October 2003, April 2004 and July 2004.

3 M. Susko, working in the insurance kiosk in Rzepin.

4 Interview with S. Gosemann head of the Truck Stop A12 in Frankfurt/Oder the 15th of March 2004.

5 Patrick, one of the owners of the CBS repair service at Nevada.

6 TIR=Transport Internationaux Routiers, as defined in the UNECE TIR Convention.

7 M. Bozena, owner of Truck Service E30 in Boczow.

8 Within the EU the custom control is carried out decentrally e.g. directly where the goods are produced.

9 After up to 4 1/2 hours of driving a truck driver has to rest at least 45 minutes. Truck drivers are allowed to drive up to 9 hours a day.

10 Z. Jagodzinski, owner of Duo Trans, a trucking company. Z. was driving himself, as we met him at his obligatory break that he spent at Nevada.

11 PKN ORLEN is Poland's and Central Europe's largest refiner of crude oil and marketer of world-class petroleum and related products. It operates a network of approximately 1,900 petrol stations in Poland and around 500 outlets in Germany. www.orlen.pl

12 Worker tearing down the forest next to the E30 close to Rzepin interviewed in July 2004.

13 Ministry of Transport, Strategy of Transport Infrastructure Development in 2004–2006 and the following years (summary), draft translation, Warzawa, 2003

14 Refering ro a meeting held in the City Council of Torzym, July 2004

15 The mayor of Torzym was mentioning this exit although it is not to be found on the website of the company who builds the highway. www.a2-autostrada.pl

16 BOT-model means: The highway is built and then operated by private investors. Operated means mostly the maintainance of the highway and the receiving of the tolls which should in return cover the prior investment. After a fixed period of time (here it is 40 years) the highway is transferred to the Polish state.

17 A.A. Sucheccy, owner of Motel Olka in Boczow

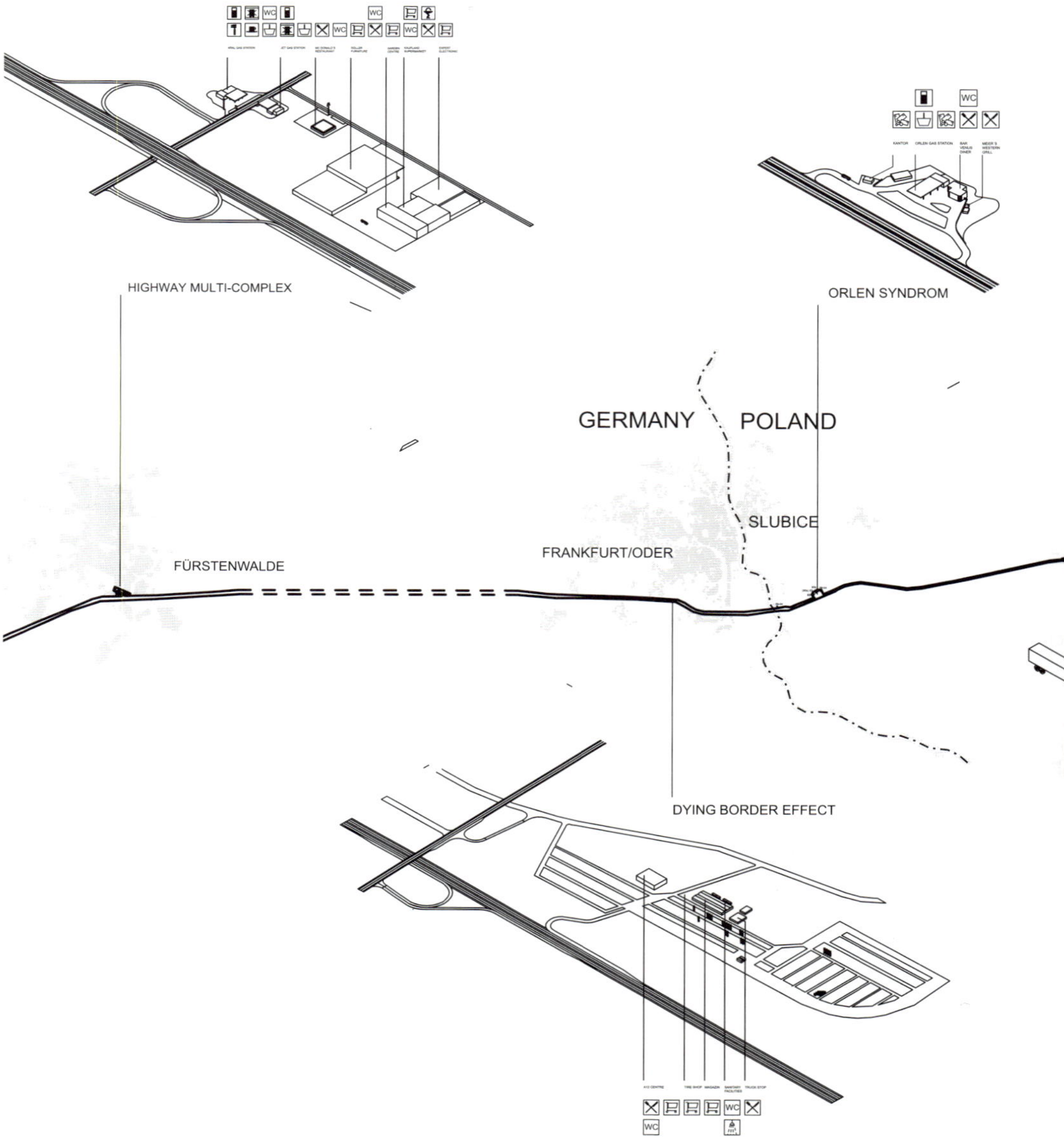

KARTIERUNG ENTLANG DER E30 IM WESTEN VON POLEN
INVENTORY ALONG THE E30 IN WEST POLAND
Karte Map: Nina Gribat/Linda Hilfing Nielsen

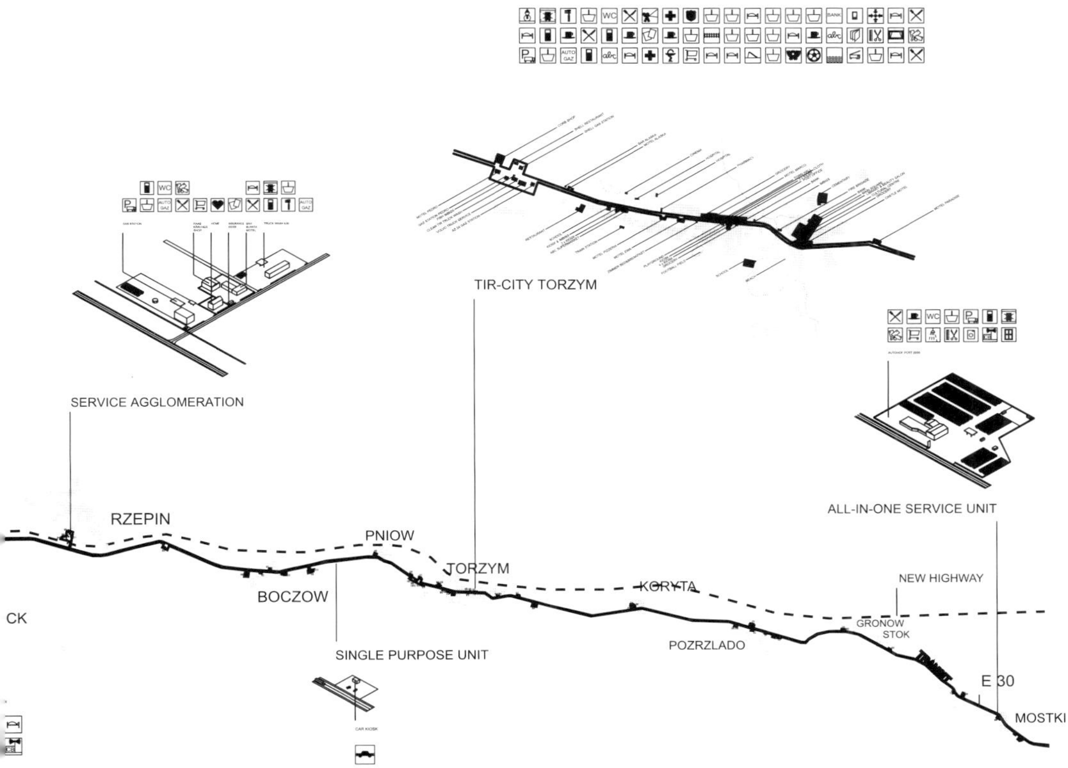

TIR-CITY TORZYM
SERVICE AGGLOMERATION
ALL-IN-ONE SERVICE UNIT
RZEPIN
PNIOW
TORZYM
KORYTA
NEW HIGHWAY
CK
BOCZOW
SINGLE PURPOSE UNIT
POZRZLADO
GRONOW
STOK
E 30
MOSTKI

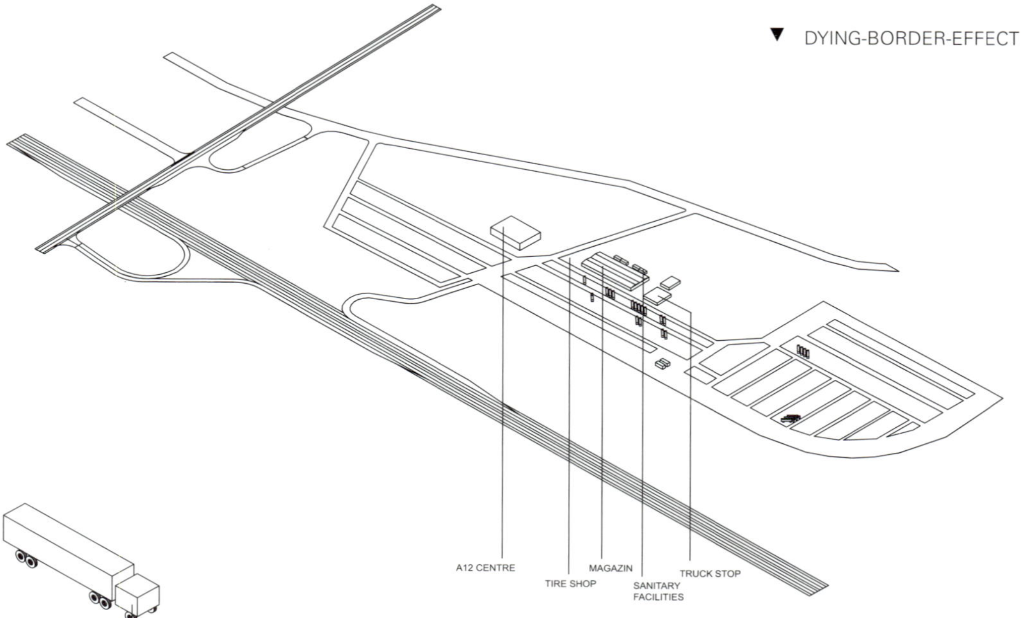

▼ DYING-BORDER-EFFECT

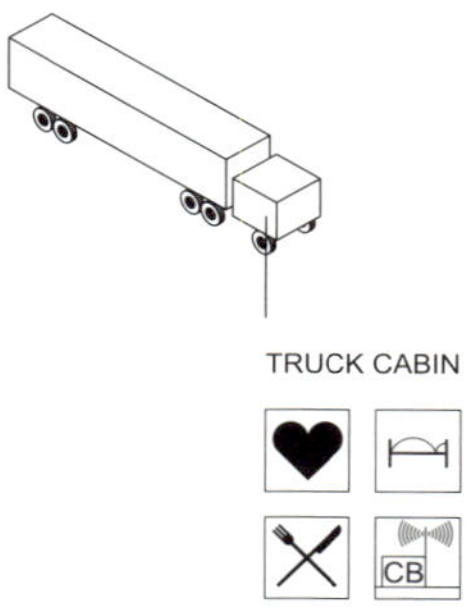

▲ TRUCK

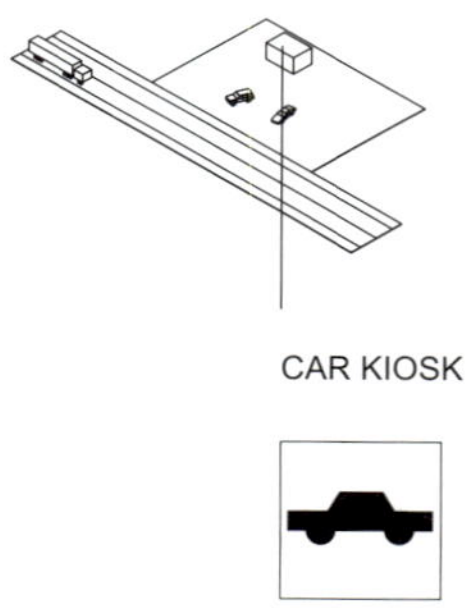

▲ SINGLE PURPOSE UNIT

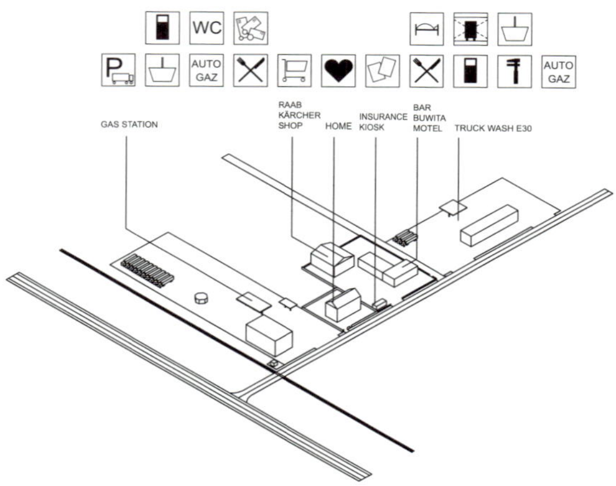

▲ SERVICE AGGLOMERATION

TYPOLOGIEN ENTLANG DER E30 IM WESTEN VON POLEN
TYPOLOGIES ALONG THE E30 IN WEST POLAND
Karte Map: Nina Gribat/Linda Hilfing Nielsen

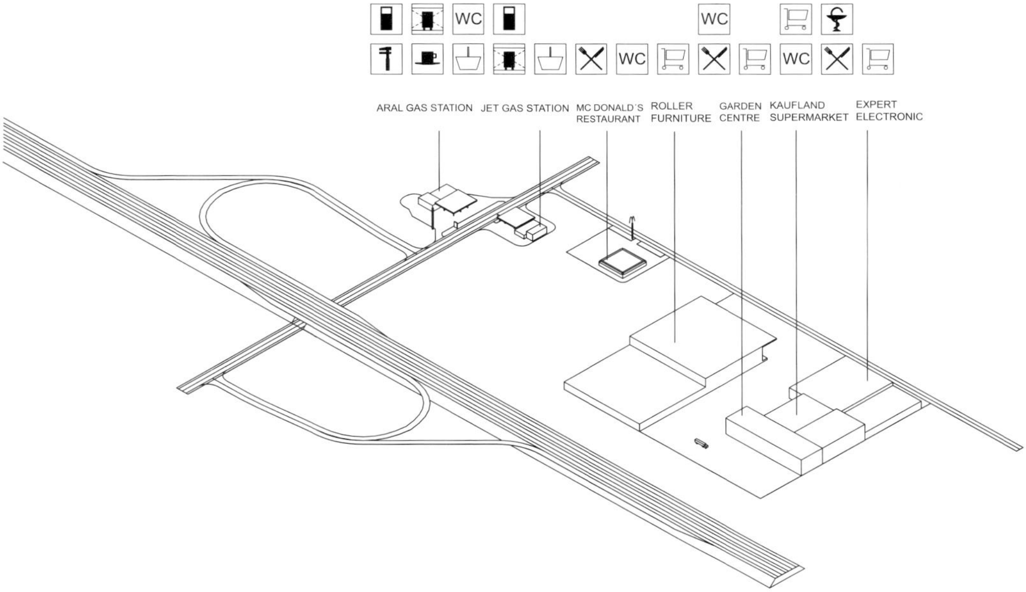

▲ HIGHWAY-MULTI-KOMPLEX

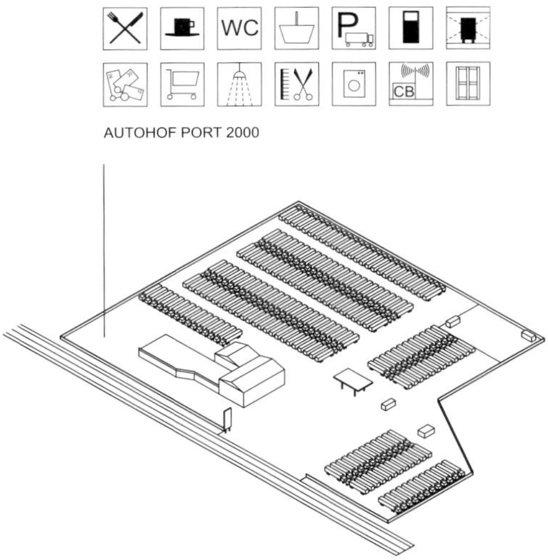

▲ ALL-IN-ONE SERVICE UNIT

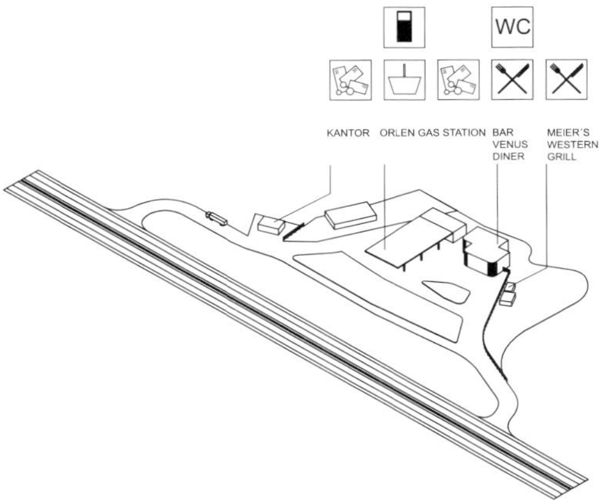

▲ ORLEN SYNDROM

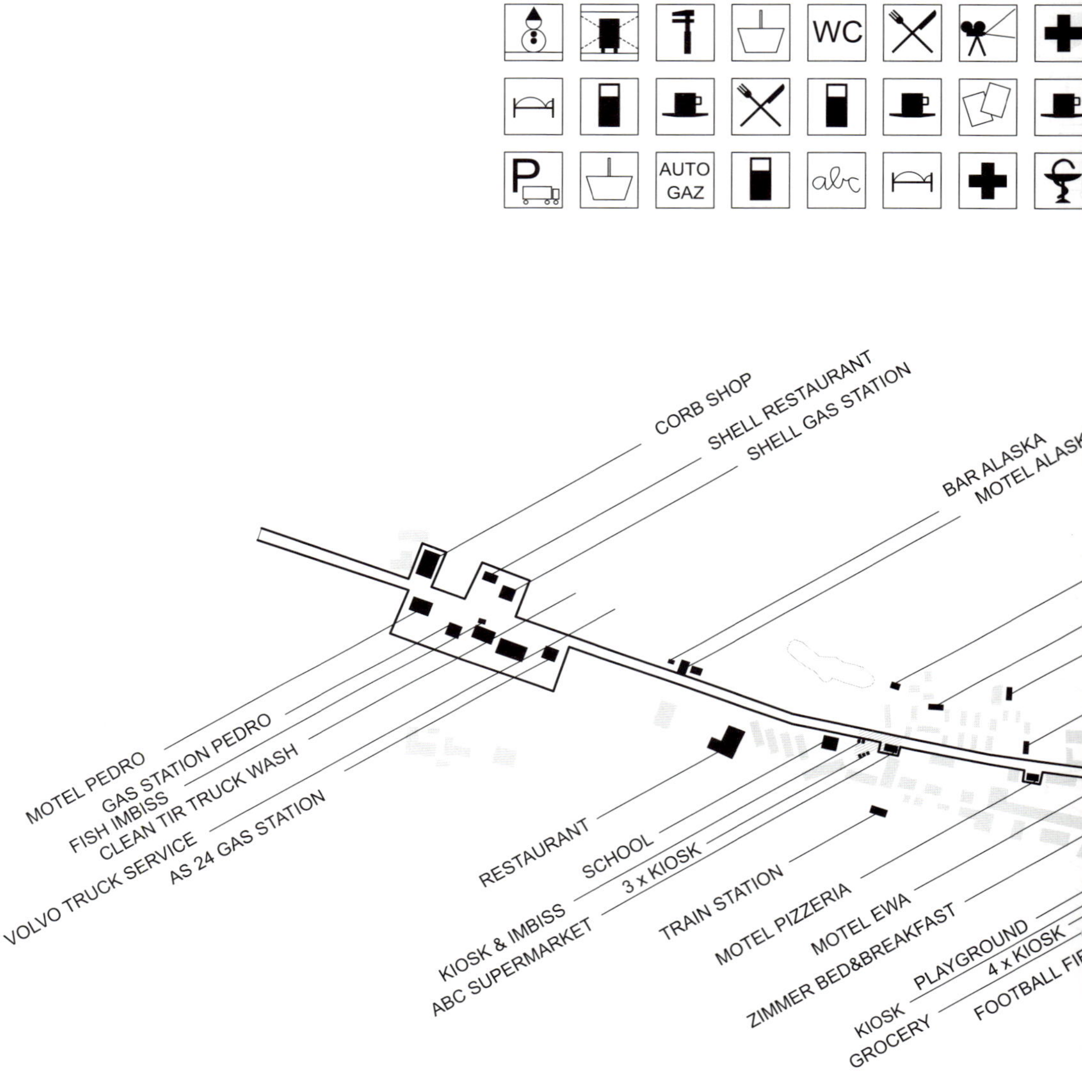

KARTIERUNG DER STADT TORZYM AN DER E30 IM WESTEN VON POLEN

INVENTORY OF THE CITY OF TORZYM AT THE E30 IN WEST POLAND

Karte Map: Nina Gribat / Linda Hilfing Nielsen

BANK
abc

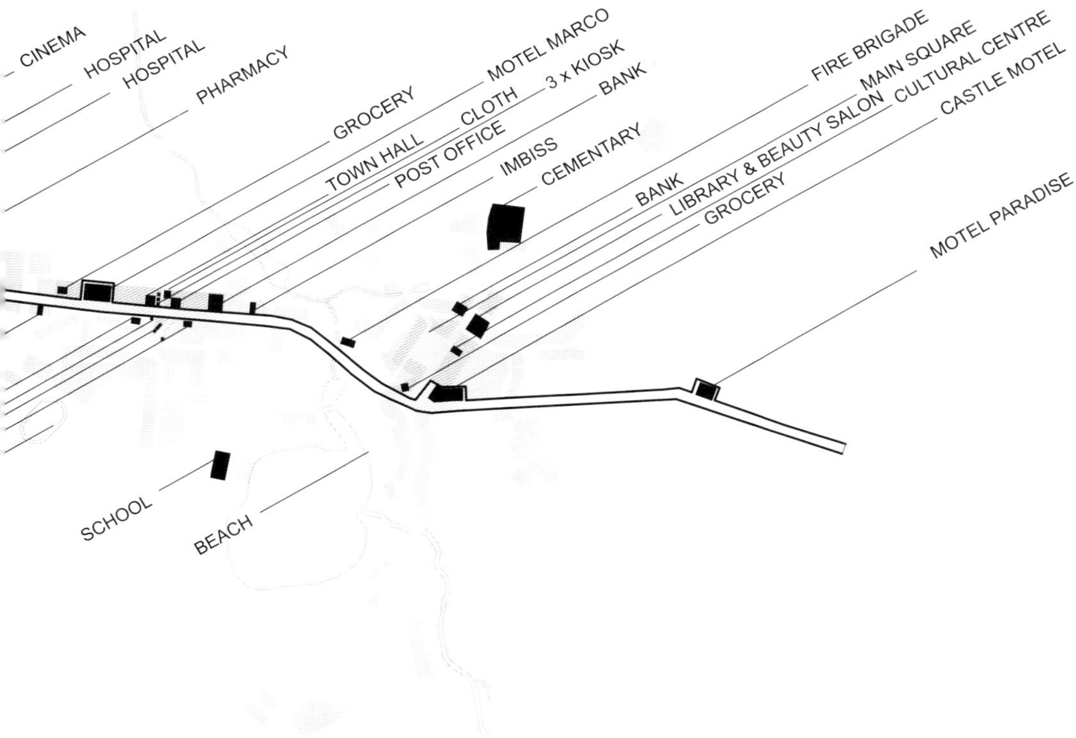
CINEMA
HOSPITAL
HOSPITAL
PHARMACY
GROCERY
MOTEL MARCO
TOWN HALL
CLOTH
3 x KIOSK
POST OFFICE
BANK
IMBISS
CEMENTARY
FIRE BRIGADE
MAIN SQUARE
CULTURAL CENTRE
BANK
LIBRARY & BEAUTY SALON
CASTLE MOTEL
GROCERY
MOTEL PARADISE
SCHOOL
BEACH

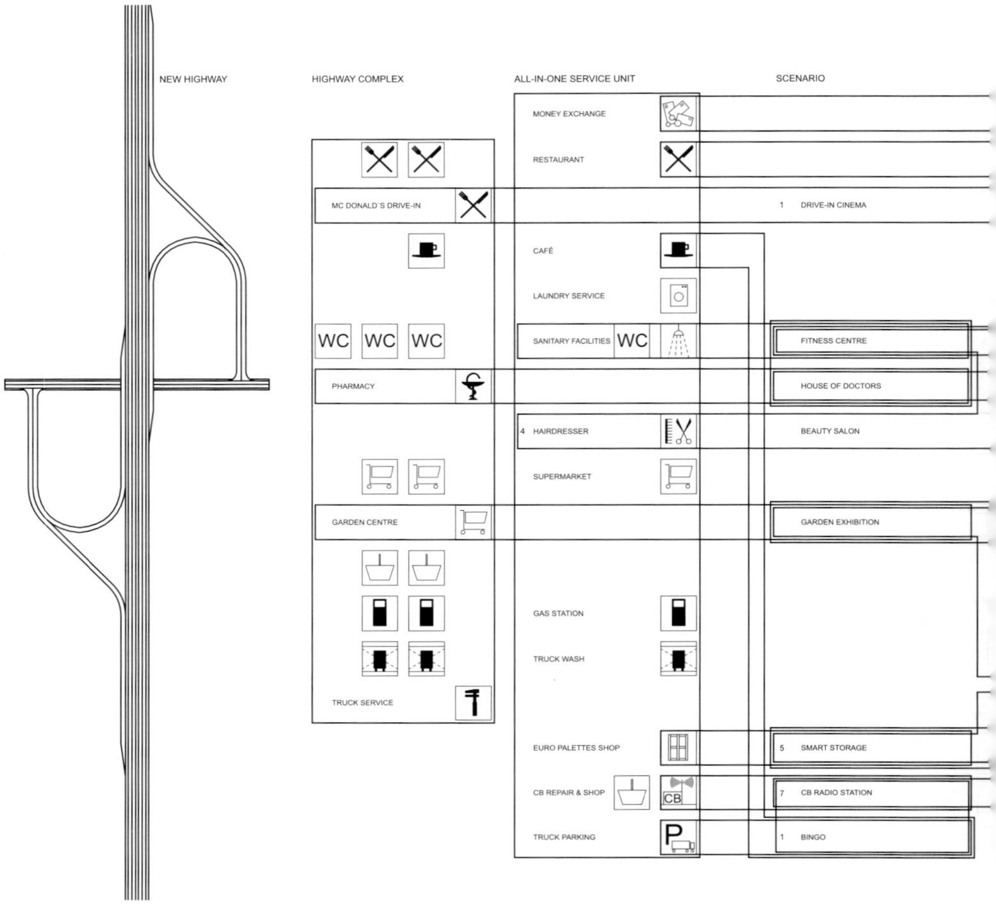

SZENARIO TORZYM

SCENARIO TORZYM

Karte Map: Nina Gribat / Linda Hilfing Nielsen

1 Marcena, 85 walks with her friends to the highway exit of Torzym every thursday afternoon. It is bingo time in the nice café next to the CB radio station. Bingo is transmitted by the CB station and it was Marcena´s daughter who started to do the show as an advertisement for her trucking centre located nearby. Initially it was planned to be a show for truckdrivers but soon Marcena got engaged in it, too. She just loves bingo and so do her friends. Soon they found a meeting place café CB where they could receive the show and play with the truck drivers.

2 Someone got the idea to open a drive-in cinema next to the drive-in Mc Donalds.

3 The sanitary facilities of the truck service Torzym were no longer sufficient to serve the growing demands of the truckdrivers who realised that they were the most important target group of the services along the highway. The simple showers were therefore soon integrated in a fitness club with an extensive sauna world. Soon after the fitness club started a cooperation with the school to raise money for a swimming hall. The commuters coming form Poznan and Berlin were happy to take a swim after work as well as the truckdrivers and school-children or Torzym.

4 A truckdriver, while having his obligatory break, goes to the hairdresser next to his favorite truckstop at the highway exit of Torzym. The man sitting next to him just bought some flowers in the garden centre to which is connected a local flower farm. The man is a little insecure if he really picked nice ones. „They are much more beautiful than the ones from Holland which I am going to deliver to Poznan tomorrow," the truckdriver assures him.

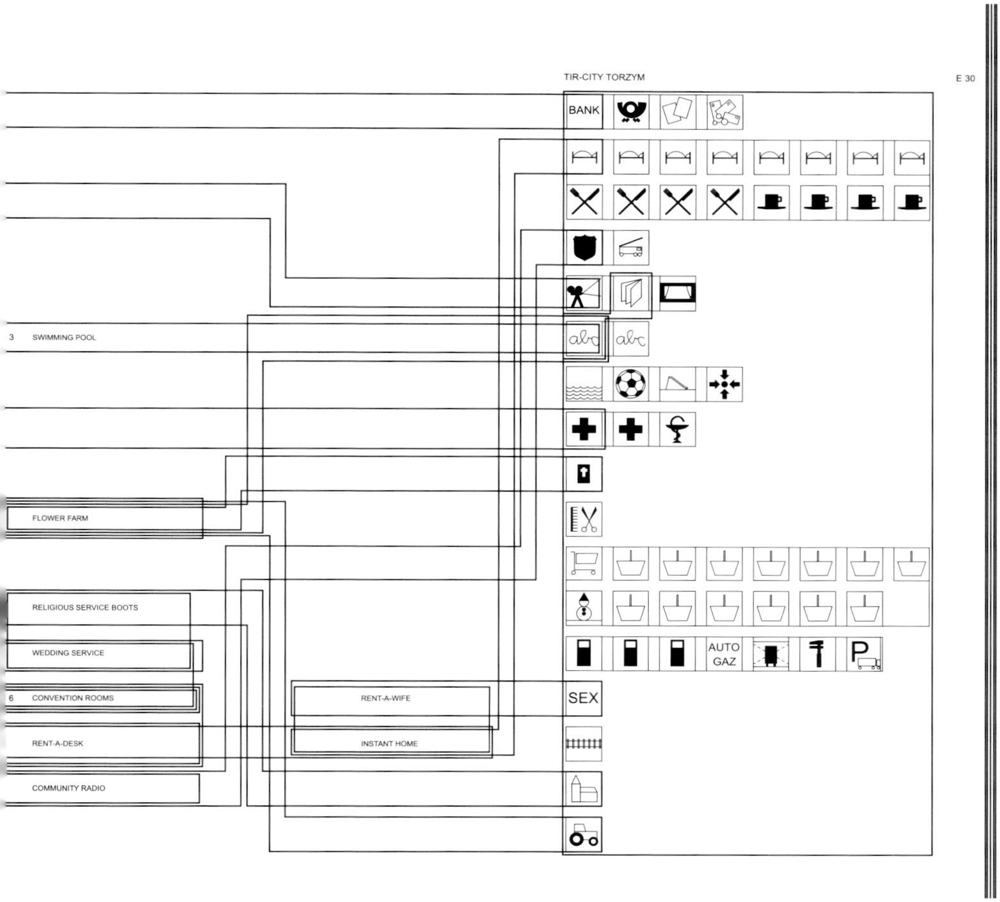

5 Most of the space at Torzym exit was used for smart storage. Smart storage connects a huge storage space with an office hotel. Different logistic companies share the same facilities and have like this a slim administration.

6 The weekly meeting at the logistic companies being engaged in smart storage has to end at five today. They are using the convention centre which is connected to the office rent a desk where all of them arev rented in. The chairman of the meeting this time exceptionally knows why. It is his daughter who is celebrating her 40th birthday here. She really likes this place situated on top of the storage with a nice view on the highway since her best friend got married here last month. It was a really modern wedding, the priest blessed them at the little pavillion in the exhibition space of the garden centre and the whole wedding society had a wild party on the roof. The food they served from the hotel next to was delicious.

7 „CB radio channel 7 proudly presents truckers karaoke: Sing your meal at truckstop Torzym. Everybody who sings his favourite song will get a free meal. Those who are voted to be the best singers win a one hour massage and 3 times sauna in the wellness centre next to." What started out as a last desperate idea of a business man became a big success. Soon bingo was established and some riddle games. Besides the man target group and the truckdrivers soon the local people started to take part, too, CB radio became a forum for the city of Torzym. Even now the mayor opened a special channel to get engaged in the cities development everybody can take part in.

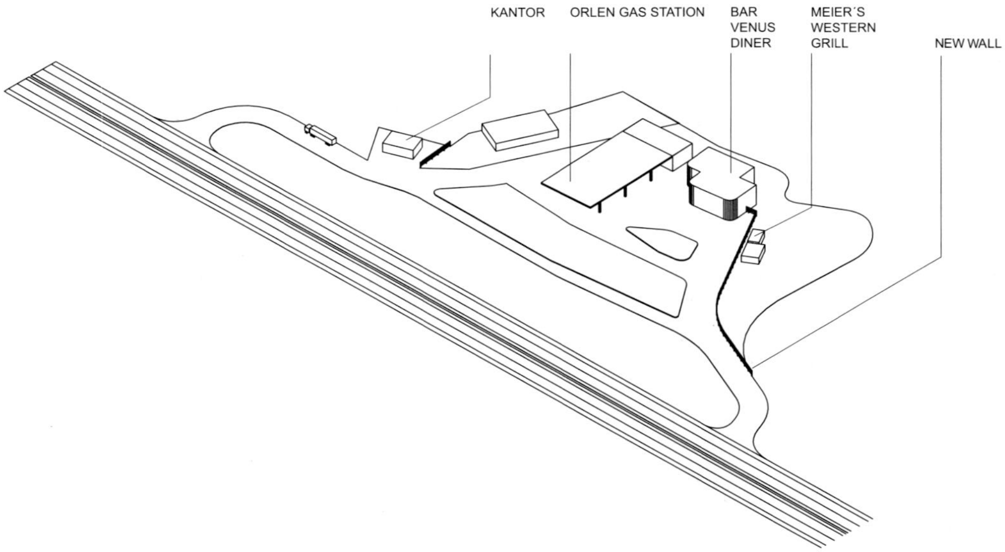

To the Gascompany Orlen 5th of April 2004

We write to you in concern of the Orlen Gasstation at E30 - the first and last gas station in Poland, 1200 m before the Polish-German border, which we visited on the 23rd of March this year. It is not that we want to file a formal complaint - there was good service at the station - however we both have a background in the field of architecture and did found the specific architectural layout of your stations site to be most peculiar and would appreciate an explanation.

Our main concern is the relationship between the gas station, Venus Bar, the Exchange Kiosk and last but not the least Meiers Western Grill. We have supplemented this letter with detailed sketches that illustrate our observations. On these you can clearly see how the recently erected wall prohibits any direct access to Meiers Western Grill. The result is that the employees at the Grill are effectively walled in while the customers are walled out.

According to the people working there, the Grill is 3 years old and was upgraded last year by demand of Venus Bar. Before the wall, Meiers Western Grill had four employees and around 1000 visitors a day - it was after all located along a densely trafficked road. However, after the wall was built, access from the road was cut off and the number of visitors understandably shrunk to less than 100, a month! Needless to say, the Grill had to close down and its employees lost their jobs.

We are wondering why anyone would make such a fatal design and ask you kindly to enlighten us with the story behind this wall - Why was it built? Was it all by mistake and why doesn't it have any doors?

Best regards,

Nina Gribat and Linda Hilfling

Nina Gribat
Muskauer Str. 19
D-10997 Berlin

Linda Hilfling
Enghave Plads 17, 2.tv
DK-1670 Copenhagen V

www.architough.com

Dear Orlen Gas Company, 21th of April 2004

In a letter directed to you the 5th of April 2004 concerning the architectural layout of the Orlen gas station at E30, we hoped to get your help in the enlightening of the story behind the wall erected between Orlen gas station, Venus Bar and the recently closed down Maier's Western Grill.

To our disappointment we still haven't received any comment from you. We assume that this must rely entirely on your company being occupied with more important matters, but we are still waiting in anticipation and hope that you'll soon get the time to return to us.

Meanwhile we have taken the opportunity to make some suggestions on how you can alter and re-design the wall. Our designs vary in range an expense from big luxurious versions to simple almost no-budget solutions. However, we must underline that any of the suggestions - without regard to their actual cost - will enable you to improve upon the spatial mistakes due to the fatal design of your wall.

All suggestions have been enclosed in this letter together with a detailed budget. Costs for removing pieces of the wall and attaching the doors are not included. Between 1.000 and 10.000 euro for the construction-site have to be added to the netto prices of the doors.

We are looking very much forward to hear your comments to our suggestions. Please don't hesitate to contact us with any questions related to the suggested alterations.

Yours sincerely,

Nina Gribat & Linda Hilfling

Nina Gribat
Muskauer Str. 19
D-10997 Berlin

Linda Hilfling
Enghave Plads 17, 2.tv
DK-1670 Copenhagen V

www.architough.com

ORLEN GEGEN MAIER'S-WESTERN-GRILL,
ORLEN VERSUS MAIER'S-WESTERN-GRILL
Nina Gribat / Linda Hilfing Nielsen

BUDGET CLIMBER
79 EURO

BELVEDRE
9.500 EURO

GENEROUS ELEVATION
500.000 EURO

MODERN WHITE
500 EURO

AUTOMATIQUE COMFORT
8.000 EURO

PRACTIC TWINS
8.500 EURO

A TOUCH OF TUNIS
20.000 EURO

SAFE&SECURE
950 EURO

DIE GRENZREGION: EIN LAND DER MÖGLICHKEITEN

MARTIN CAGNO

„Der Raum der Ströme drückt die Auflösung von ortsgebundenen Gesellschaften und Kulturen aus. In letzter Konsequenz werden selbst Demokratien machtlos gegenüber der Fähigkeit des Kapitals, global zu zirkulieren, der Information, geheim übertragen zu werden, der Märkte, erobert oder vernachlässigt zu werden. (...) Die Ströme von Macht erzeugen Strömungskräfte, deren materielle Realität sich wie ein Naturphänomen durchsetzt, das weder kontrolliert noch vorhergesagt, sondern lediglich akzeptiert und gesteuert werden kann. (...) Funktionale Ströme und historisch determinierte Orte können als zwei getrennte Bereiche menschlicher Erfahrung betrachtet werden. Menschen leben an Orten, die Macht zeigt sich in den Strömen." (Manuel Castells)

Auch wenn hier noch wesentlich mehr als dieses binäre Kräftespiel zwischen Bewegung und Ort hineinwirkt, gibt Castells Beschreibung doch eine zutreffende Kurzcharakteristik des Korridors Berlin–Poznan. Die Übergangsphase, die diese Region erlebt, konfrontiert die vorrückende globalisierte Wirtschaft mit einer Landschaft aus veralteten Staatsfabriken, kleinen Dörfern und bäuerlichen Betrieben, die durch eine mangelhafte Infrastruktur aus engen und verfallenen Straßen miteinander verbunden werden. Bei genauerer Untersuchung kann man feststellen, dass sich kombinierte und globalisierte Handlungsformen entwickeln, die abstrakte Ströme und konkrete Orte miteinander verbinden und damit neue Räume für eine Gegenbewegung auf verschiedenen Ebenen schaffen. Während die Zeit des Sozialismus für die Konsolidierung einer rigiden und starken Regierung, für die Entwicklung staatlicher Betriebe nach dem Modell der Ford'schen Massenproduktion und für einflussreiche Gewerkschaften steht, entspricht die neue polnische Realität eher Bennett Harrisons Beobachtung darüber, wie die heutige Wirtschaft die früheren Großbetriebe, die rigide Regierung und die einflussreichen Gewerkschaften schlank und klein werden lässt. In dieser Ära der postfordistischen Wirtschaft, in der Flexibilität als Schlüssel für die Ansiedlung von Industrieunternehmen und für das weitere Wachstum der Wirtschaft gesehen wird, vollzieht sich in dieser polnischen Region am Rande der Europäischen Union eine stürmische wirtschaftliche und politische Veränderung. Sie könnte damit als ein idealer Ort für internationale Investitionen betrachtet werden. Dennoch gibt es entlang des Korridors Berlin–Poznan viele verschiedene Gebiete, die versuchen, Teil dieser globalisierten Wirtschaft zu sein, und nicht alle sind dabei erfolgreich. Die osteuropäischen Staaten arbeiten gegenwärtig mit ihrer neuen neoliberalen Politik an der Schaffung einer neuen Synthese, die den Globalisierungsprozess und die zunehmend globale Ausrichtung von Industrieproduktion und Handel unterstützt.

Einige dieser Übergangsprozesse haben die Ansiedlung globaler Produktionen erleichtert: die zunehmende Privatisierung des öffentlichen Sektors, die Beseitigung von Handelsbarrieren, der freie Kapitalfluss, die billigen Arbeitskräfte und die Bemühungen, den Wohlfahrtsstaat abzubauen und den Einfluss der Gewerkschaften zurückzudrängen. Dieser Prozess, der in den letzten zehn Jahren stattgefunden hat (und in der polnischen Grenzregion besonders deutlich zu Tage getreten ist), wird in diesem Artikel an drei Fallstudien dargestellt, die verschiedene Aspekte dieses Übergangs widerspiegeln. In der Rolle des Generaldirektors eines multinationalen Konzerns auf der Suche nach Standorten in der Region, die von der deutsch-polnischen Grenze bis nach Poznan reicht, sollte ich die Gründe herausfinden, die für eine eventuelle Standortwahl durch einen Investor sprachen. Die drei Fälle beschreiben die Situation nach einer

BORDER REGION: LAND OF OPPORTUNITIES

MARTIN CAGNO

"The space of flows expresses the disarticulation of place-based societies and cultures. In the end, even democracies become powerless confronted with the ability of capital to circulate globally, of information to be transferred secretly, of markets to be penetrated or neglected ... The flows of power generate the power of flows, whose material reality imposes itself as a natural phenomenon that cannot be controlled and predicted, only accepted and managed ... functional flows and historically determined places can be seen as two disjointed fields of the human experience. People live in places, power rules through flows." (Manuel Castells)

Although there is much more than this binary power-play between flows and places, Castells' description fits as a quick conceptualization of what can be perceived along the corridor between Berlin and Poznan. The transition that is taking place in this area confronts the penetration of the globalised economy with a landscape of obsolete state-owned factories, small villages and domestic farms, all connected by a deficient infrastructure of narrow and deteriorating roads. Through deeper research it can be observed that hybridised and globalised movements and practices are developing, combining abstract flows and concrete places, opening up new spatialities of resistance on multiple levels.

If socialist times implied the consolidation of rigid and powerful governments, the development of state-owned factories under a model of Fordist mass production and the strong presence of labor unions, the new Polish reality corresponds more with Bennett Harrison's observation on how economies should operate nowadays with big business, big government and big labor all drastically downsized to become lean and mean. In this age of post-Fordist economy when flexibility is seen as the key ingredient in the propulsive expansion and multiplication of industrial regions, this Polish border area undergoing a hectic political and economic transition at the edge of the European Union could have been considered an ideal opportunity for international investment. Yet there are many different areas along this corridor trying to be part of this globalised economy and not all of them are having success.

The new neoliberal politics of Eastern European countries are forging a new synthesis that promotes the globalization process and the increasingly global nature of industrial production and commercial trade.

Certain processes that have been taking place in their transition have facilitated the location of global production: the increasing privatisation of the public sphere, the breakdown of barriers to trade, the free flow of capital, cheap labor and the efforts to diminish the weight of the welfare state and labor unions. The process that has been taking place over the past 10 years (and more specifically in the Polish border area) is illustrated in this article by three case studies that respond to different aspects of this transitional stage. Playing the role of chief executive of a multinational company considering locations from the German-Polish border to the city of Poznan, the aim has been to look for the reasons why investors should choose these locations. The three cases are described after on-site observations and interviews, analysing their benefits and drawbacks in a global context, their recent past and their possible future. The attempted consolidation of a special economic zone in the border city of Slubice and its surroundings, the installation of the IKEA group in the towns of Szbasyn and Babimost and the fast industrial development of the district of Tarnowo Podgorne on the outskirts of Poznan are three scenes of post-

Ortsbesichtigung und nach Gesprächen, in denen die Vor- und Nachteile der drei Orte im globalen Kontext, ihre jüngste Vergangenheit und ihre mögliche Zukunft analysiert wurden. Der Versuch der Einrichtung einer Sonderwirtschaftszone in und um die Grenzstadt Slubice, die Niederlassung der IKEA-Gruppe in Szbasyn und Babimost und die schnelle industrielle Entwicklung der Gemeinde Tarnowo Podgorne am Stadtrand von Poznan sind drei Szenarien postsozialistischer Entwicklungen, mit ihren Gewinnern und Verlierern, ihren sozialen Polarisierungen und den sich vergrößernden wirtschaftlichen Ungleichheiten.

WIRTSCHAFTSINSELN

Die Sonderwirtschaftszone von Kostrzyn Slubice besteht aus einer Reihe in sich geschlossener Gebiete, die verstreut in der polnischen Grenzregion in der Nähe der deutschen Stadt Frankfurt/Oder liegen. Diese Gebiete sind für Investoren besonders interessant: Befreiung von der Körperschaftssteuer, dank der Universitäten und Hochschulen von Szczecin, Gorzow und Zielona Gora gut qualifizierte Arbeitskräfte und nicht zuletzt Arbeitslöhne, die nur einen Bruchteil der Löhne in den alten EU-Mitgliedsstaaten betragen.
Ihre Verteilung auf die einzelnen Standorte entspricht der Vielfalt der Interessen und Bedürfnisse der Investoren. Wer eine möglichst grenznahe Lage bevorzugt, kann zwischen Slubice und Kostrzyn wählen, wer dagegen die Nähe größerer Städte braucht, um mehr qualifizierte Arbeitskräfte zur Verfügung zu haben, kann sich für die Standorte Gorzow oder Zielona Gora entscheiden. Alle Gebiete haben Wasser-, Gas-, Strom- und Abwasseranschluss, in einige führt sogar eine Eisenbahnlinie. Die nächsten Flughäfen liegen in Berlin und für Inlandsflüge in Babimost. Der große Nachteil dieser Sonderwirtschaftzone ist jedoch der schlechte Zustand der Straßen, die die Gebiete untereinander und mit den Vertriebszentren verbinden.
Das Gebiet Slubice liegt östlich von Frankfurt/Oder auf der anderen Seite der Oder am Korridor Berlin–Moskau. Seine Chancen stehen besonderes gut, weil es an die Autobahn, die Berlin mit Poznan und weiter mit Warschau verbinden soll, angeschlossen wird. Darüber hinaus gibt es eine direkte Anbindung an ein Wasserstraßennetz, das bis in den weniger als 80 km entfernt liegenden Berliner Hafen führt. Hier lassen sich vorwiegend kleine Firmen nieder, die ihre Erzeugnisse an die EU-Mitgliedsstaaten verkaufen; doch bis zum Jahre 2004 verlief die Ansiedlung eher langsam und blieb hinter den Prognosen zurück. In der Sonderwirtschaftszone wird jedoch nach der EU-Erweiterung ein Anstieg der Investitionen erwartet. Seit 2004 gibt es für Investitionen aus Westeuropa keine Hindernisse mehr, da die Lohnkosten sehr viel niedriger sind und in den nächsten zehn Jahren kaum Veränderungen erwartet werden. Selbst wenn die Lohnkosten schrittweise steigen, ist der Unterschied doch so groß, dass es viele Jahre dauern wird, bis polnische Löhne denen in den alten Mitgliedsstaaten der EU entsprechen werden. Bartosz Begej, der Marketingchef der Sonderwirtschaftszone, sieht in dem schlechten Zustand der polnischen Infrastruktur das Hauptproblem für die Entwicklung des Gebietes. Er vergleicht die polnische Situation mit der in anderen osteuropäischen Staaten wie der Slowakei, in denen umfangreiche Mittel in den Bau von Autobahnen investiert wurden. Polen hat mit der Verbesserung seiner Infrastruktur gerade erst angefangen und könnte daher schon ins Hintertreffen geraten sein.
Das zeigt sich an dem bekannten Beispiel der Errichtung einer Hyundai-Fabrik im Jahr 2004 für die Versorgung des europäischen Marktes. Polen verlor dabei gegen die Slowakei wegen der schlechten Anbindung an die Standorte, die von der polnischen Regierung vorgeschlagen wurden. Hinzu kamen die niedrigeren Steuern und Löhne in der Slowakei sowie die schwächeren Gewerkschaften. Bartosz Begej gibt der mangelnden Entschlossenheit der polnischen Verwaltung die Schuld am Scheitern dieses Geschäfts. Während die Slowakei noch zu sozialistischen Zeiten seine Infrastruktur ausgebaut und auch in den letzten Jahren eine neue Infrastruktur geschaffen hatte, waren in Polen nur einige Autobahnabschnitte gebaut worden.

VOM GENOSSENSCHAFTSWESEN ZUR GLOBALEN PRODUKTION

Eine weitere Fallstudie aus der Region des Korridors untersuchte die Auswirkungen, die die Errichtung einer Fabrik des IKEA-Konzerns auf die drei kleinen polnischen Dörfer Zbansyn, Chastawa und Babimost hatte. Swedwood, ein hundertprozentiges IKEA-Unternehmen, produziert Möbel ausschließlich für IKEA-Warenhäuser und ist der weltweit größte Produzent von Möbeln im Rahmenbauverfahren. Die Zusammenarbeit zwischen IKEA und Polen begann in den 1960er Jahren. In Schweden hatte IKEA starke Konkurrenten im Bereich preiswerter Möbel. Nach dem Boykott durch

socialist geographies, a landscape of winners and losers where social polarisation and widening economic inequalities are taking place.

ECONOMIC ISLANDS

The special economic zone of Kostrzyn Slubice is formed by a group of closed areas scattered around the Polish border region next to Frankfurt/Oder (Germany). These closed areas offer special attractions for investment: exemption from corporate taxes, well-qualified human resources thanks to the presence of universities and engineering schools in Szczecin, Gorzow and Zielona Gora and, last but not least, labor costs that are several times lower than in the older member states of the EU.
Their distribution in different locations responds to the variety of interests and needs of the investors. For those investors who prioritise a location nearest the border, they can choose between Slubice and Kostrzyn, while those that need to be in bigger cities in order to attract more qualified workers can choose the locations in Gorzow or Zielona Gora. All the areas have water, gas, electricity and sewage services, and some of them offer railway sidings. The two nearest airports that serve the region are those in Berlin and the domestic airport of Babimost. Yet the big drawback of this special economic zone is the deficient condition of the roads that connect the areas with one another and with the distribution centers.
The area of Slubice, situated to the east of Frankfurt on the other side of the River Oder and along the Berlin–Moscow corridor, has a special potential since it will be well connected to the highway that will link Berlin to Poznan and thence to Warsaw. In addition, the area offers a close connection to a river network that links up with the river port of Berlin which is less than 80 km from Slubice. It is often preferred by small companies that sell products to EU members, but up to 2004 the establishment of companies was rather slow and lagged behind estimates. However, the FEZ expects more investments after EU enlargement. Since 2004, there have been no obstacles for Western European investment because labor costs are much lower and expected to remain unchanged for at least 10 years. The cost of labor might increase gradually, but the difference is so great that it will take many years for salaries in Poland to equal those in the older members of the EU.
According to Bartosz Begej, marketing manager of the special economic zone, the major problem for the development of the area is the condition of Polish infrastructure. He compares the Polish situation with that in other Eastern European countries such as Slovakia, where major investments have been made in the construction of highways. Meanwhile, Poland is just starting to develop its infrastructure and might be running late.
A well-known case in 2004 was the location of a Hyundai factory to serve the European market. Poland lost out to Slovakia because there was poor access to the location that the Polish government offered. In addition, the tax rates and the labor costs are lower in Slovakia and there is less presence of labor unions. Bartosz Begej put the blame on the lack of resolve of the Polish administration. While Slovakia had developed its infrastructure during socialist times and has also constructed new infrastructure in the past few years, only certain stretches of highway have been built in Poland.

FROM COOPERATIVISM TO GLOBAL PRODUCTION

Another case study carried out within this corridor examines the location of a factory for the IKEA Group and its effect on three Polish small villages: Zbansyn, Chastawa and Babimost. Swedwood, a company wholly owned by the IKEA Group, produces furniture exclusively for the IKEA stores. Swedwood is the biggest producer of board-frame furniture worldwide. Cooperation between IKEA and Poland started in the 1960s. IKEA had strong competition in Sweden in the sale of inexpensive furniture. Once boycotted by its suppliers in Sweden, it started a search to produce furniture outside Scandinavia.
Although during socialist times Polish furniture production was problematic, because the products usually did not meet the quality standards of Western countries, IKEA started to subcontract some of its furniture production to the woodworkers in Poland. In the 1990s, IKEA decided to sell only its own exclusive furniture. The Swedwood group was bought and started developing production, mainly in Poland, Slovakia and other Eastern European countries.
The main reason that Swedwood invested in this area was because existing factories in Zbansyn and Babimost were already producing furniture that was being sold to IKEA. Because of the dramatic changes in Poland in the 1990s, the factories were running out of capital and the poor machinery

seine schwedischen Zulieferer begann IKEA, nach Möglichkeiten für eine Möbelproduktion außerhalb Skandinaviens zu suchen.
Auch wenn zu sozialistischen Zeiten die polnische Möbelproduktion nicht den Qualitätsstandards der westlichen Länder entsprach, begann IKEA, einige Bereiche seiner Möbelproduktion an Subunternehmer in Polen abzugeben. In den 1990er Jahren beschloss IKEA, nur noch die ausschließlich in Eigenproduktion hergestellten Möbel zu vertreiben. Es kaufte die Swedwood-Gruppe und baute die Produktion vor allem in Polen, in der Slowakei und in anderen osteuropäischen Ländern nach und nach aus.
Den Hauptgrund für Investitionen in der Region bildeten für Swedwood die schon bestehenden Fabriken in Zbansyn und Babimost, die schon früher für IKEA Möbel hergestellt hatten. Durch die dramatischen Veränderungen in Polen in den 1990er Jahren ging den Betrieben das Kapital aus, und der veraltete Maschinenpark war der Nachfrage des Marktes nicht gewachsen. Swedwood entschloss sich zum Kauf und zur Modernisierung der Fabriken. Die Arbeiter, die Mitglieder der Genossenschaft waren, beschlossen einstimmig, ihre Betriebe an die Swedwood-Gruppe zu verkaufen. Dank dieser Entscheidung wuchs die hier ansässige Bevölkerung in den letzten Jahren, ganz im Gegensatz zu anderen Kleinstädten in Polen. Heute gibt es aufgrund der harten Marktbedingungen, die Anfang der 1990er Jahre herrschten, nur noch sehr wenige Unternehmen, die noch aus sozialistischen Zeiten stammen. Die Genossenschaften dagegen überlebten, da sie ihre Betriebe in den Jahren 1991 und 1992 verkauften.
Der Standort dieser Unternehmensgruppe wurde nicht durch die Infrastruktur, sondern durch die Nähe zu einem Waldgebiet bestimmt, da diese Lage schon fast eine Garantie für Traditionsbewusstsein und Fachwissen in der Möbelproduktion darstellte. Jedoch wird Rohholz für im Rahmenbau hergestellte Möbel nicht mehr verwendet. Holzchips für Hartfaserplatten und andere Materialien werden daher von polnischen und ausländischen Zulieferern gekauft.
Das Rohmaterial für die Produktion wird mit Lkws angeliefert. Der Transport auf der Schiene ist geplant, doch dafür bedarf es einer erheblichen Verbesserung des Schienennetzes und der Verwendung geeigneter Waggons für einen beschädigungsfreien Materialtransport. Eine auf drei Fabriken verteilte Produktion schafft logistische und transporttechnische Probleme. Die in Babimost und Zbansyn hergestellten Artikel werden direkt auf Lkws verladen und nach Chastawa transportiert, wo sich das Logistikzentrum befindet. Die Straße, die diese drei Städte miteinander verbindet, genügt den Anforderungen nicht und muss umfassend ausgebaut werden.
Der Korridor Berlin–Moskau hat nach den Worten Robert Gdulas, Produktionsleiter der Swedwood-Gruppe, keine besondere Relevanz für die Swedwood-Betriebe. Mit den künftigen Verbesserungen der Infrastruktur gewinne er jedoch an Bedeutung für die Suche neuer Zulieferer in der Nähe von Poznan, zwischen Berlin und Warschau, und auch nahe der Tschechischen Republik und der Slowakei. Die meisten der 1 700 Arbeitnehmer, selbst die des Managements, kommen aus der Region, da die Strategie von IKEA auf die Nutzung lokaler Ressourcen zielt. Die Arbeiter stammen aus der näheren Umgebung, doch wird man mit dem künftigen Wachstum auf der Suche nach Arbeitskräften bis in das Gebiet um Gorzow gehen müssen, und Mitarbeiter mit Hochschulbildung dürften dann als Pendler mitunter sogar aus den Universitätszentren Zielona Gora, Poznan und Szczecin kommen.
Die Swedwood-Gruppe denkt nach dem Beitritt Polens zur Europäischen Union nicht an einen Umzug in ein anderes Land. Sweedwood hat sich an diesem Standort mit seinen Zulieferern für die Möbelproduktion, für Beschläge, Holzkomponenten usw. gut eingerichtet. Hinzu kommt, dass die polnische Forstpolitik zu den besten Europas zählt. Selbst zu sozialistischen Zeiten gab es ein sehr strenges Bewirtschaftungssystem, so dass die polnischen Maßstäbe der Forstbewirtschaftung den weltweit höchsten Ansprüchen genügen. Das ist das Resultat guter, in der Vergangenheit geltender Bewirtschaftungsregeln, einer langjährigen guten Waldpflege und der gegenwärtig engen Zusammenarbeit mit dem Minister für Forstwirtschaft. Obwohl auch am Aufbau weiter östlich gelegener Produktionsstätten Interesse besteht, gibt es zur Zeit lediglich eine Fabrik in der Ukraine; eine weitere beginnt in Russland gerade mit der Produktion. Nach Robert Gdulas Meinung ist jedoch die Holzqualität in diesen Ländern schlechter, und Vorschriften zu ihrer Verbesserung blieben wirkungslos. Der Hauptnachteil indes seien die Arbeiter, die nicht vertrauenswürdig sind oder Alkoholprobleme haben. Um diese Situation zu ändern, brauche es wohl noch eine Generation.

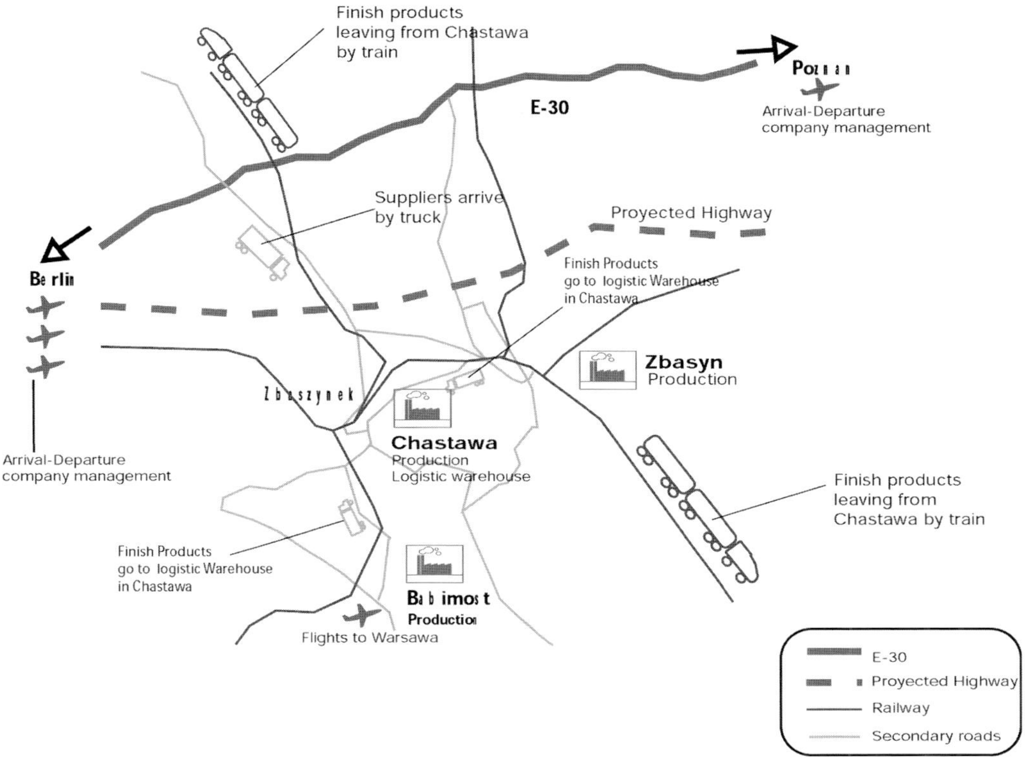

SWEDWOOD GROUP LOGISTIK UND INFRASTRUKTUR
SWEDWOOD GROUP LOGISTICS AND INFRASTRUCTURE
Martin Cagno

could not cope with market demands. Swedwood decided to buy the factories and update them. Formerly members of cooperative communities, the workers unanimously decided to sell their companies to the Swedwood Group. Thanks to this decision, the whole community has been growing in recent years, unlike other small towns in Poland. Nowadays, very few companies from the socialist past are still in existence because of the demanding market conditions at the beginning of the 1990s, but these cooperatives survived by selling their companies in 1991/92.

The location of these groups of factories was not determined by infrastructure but by their proximity to a forest area, which all but guaranteed a tradition of, and expertise in, wood furniture production. However, raw wood is not used any more in framed board production. Hardboard chips and other types of material are bought from suppliers in Poland and from abroad.

The raw materials for production come by truck. Transportation by rail is planned but a significant improvement in the railways and the use of proper rail cars are needed to ensure that materials arrive undamaged. Production divided among three factories creates logistics and transportation problems. The articles produced in Babimost and Zbaszyn are loaded directly onto trucks and sent to Chastawa, where the logistical warehouse is located. The road connecting these three cities is deficient and needs to be drastically improved.

According to Robert Gdula, production manager of the Swedwood Group, the Berlin–Moscow corridor does not have any special relevance to the operations of the Swedwood factories, although with the future improvements in infrastructure it will be very important in the search for new suppliers to be located near Poznan, between Berlin and Warsaw and also near the Czech Republic and Slovakia.

DIE CHANCEN NUTZEN

Zu sozialistischen Zeiten war Poznan eines der akademischen Schlüsselzentren. Die Stadt gehörte zu den sich wirtschaftlich am stärksten entwickelnden Regionen Polens und besaß viele gut ausgebildete Arbeitskräfte. In den letzten Jahren haben viele deutsche Hersteller aufgrund der hohen Produktionskosten Deutschland den Rücken gekehrt, und das Gebiet um Poznan entwickelte sich zum ersten größeren Handelszentrum im Osten.

Die geographische Lage der Stadt im Herzen Europas nahe an der polnisch-deutschen Grenze trug entscheidend zu ihrer gegenwärtigen Entwicklung bei. Die schlechte Verkehrsanbindung beeinträchtigt jedoch die Wettbewerbsfähigkeit. Die Autobahn, die in Zukunft den Osten und den Westen verbinden wird, ist noch in Bau, und die Bahnverbindungen müssen ebenfalls modernisiert werden. Ein Konsortium staatlicher und privater Firmen baut die Autobahn Warschau–Poznan, doch das ist ein langfristiges Projekt, dessen Fertigstellung zeitlich unbestimmt ist.

Die Stadtverwaltung Poznans bemühte sich, die Vorteile der Stadt für ausländische Investoren herauszustellen, doch stand die Stadt nach der politischen Wende ohne einen Stadtentwicklungsplan da. Viele Baugenehmigungen stecken fest, Investitionen sind blockiert. Diese Situation führte unter anderem dazu, dass die industrielle Entwicklung in Satellitensiedlungen außerhalb Poznans wie z. B. in Tarnowo Podgorne stattfand.

Der Distrikt Tarnowo Podgorne wird durch Poznan und die A2 begrenzt, die als internationale Autobahn Ost- und Westeuropa verbindet. Er umfasst eine Fläche von 113 km^2 und zählt 14 000 Einwohner. In den letzten fünf Jahren hatte der Distrikt nicht nur das höchste Wirtschaftswachstum der gesamten Region um Poznan aufzuweisen, sondern er zählt heute zu den Regionen mit dem höchsten Wachstum in Polen. Waldly Dzokowski, der für die Verwaltung des Distrikts verantwortlich ist, sagt, dass viele Investoren Tarnowo wegen des Engagements der lokalen Verwaltung und der geringen Entfernung nach Deutschland wählten. Die gesamte Gegend entwickelt sich zu einem neuen regionalen Zentrum, was der Fähigkeit der Distriktverwaltung zu verdanken ist, die finanzielle Unabhängigkeit gegenüber dem Staat zu wahren und sich so eigene Einkommensquellen zu erschließen.

Das Entwicklungsprogramm begann 1994 mit grundlegenden Investitionen. Von 1994 bis 1998 wurden zwei Abwasserleitungen verlegt, eine Gasleitung für die zwölf Gemeindebezirke gebaut und eine moderne, 15 Hektar große Mülldeponie mit maschineller Sortierung und Wiederverwertung errichtet. Schließlich wurden ein städtisches Verkehrsunternehmen gegründet und bessere Telefonverbindungen geschaffen. Diesen Investitionen und flexiblen, fortschrittlichen Vorschriften war es zu verdanken, dass potenzielle Investoren nach Tarnowo kamen. Im Jahr 2004 waren 1 800 Firmen registriert, darunter 300 Kapitalgesellschaften, die zusammen mit Investitionen vor Ort mehr als 350 Millionen Dollar auf sich vereinen.

EIN FLEXIBLER ÜBERGANG

Edward Soja zufolge „gründet sich die auf der so genannten flexiblen Akkumulation aufbauende neue Wirtschaft auf neu organisierten Produktionsprozessen und -technologien und ermöglicht die Bildung von Clustern kleiner und mittlerer Unternehmen, die nicht mehr an die alten Ford'schen urbanen Agglomerationen gebunden sind. Das schlägt sich räumlich in weit verstreut liegenden Produktionsstandorten außerhalb der großen städtischen Zentren nieder und erzeugt Innovationen, die selbst von kleinen städtischen Siedlungen ausgehen können." Dieses globale wirtschaftliche Phänomen trat auch in unserem Untersuchungsgebiet auf, in dem der politische und wirtschaftliche Übergang und die spezifische grenznahe Lage eine einmalige Möglichkeit für internationale Investitionen geschaffen hatten. Trotzdem war es, wie unsere Fallstudien zeigen, nicht überall gelungen, Kapital anzuziehen. Es stellt sich damit die Frage: Warum entwickeln sich einige Standorte besser als andere?

Allen Scott vermied es in seinem Buch *Regions and the World Economy*, eine allgemeine Theorie der Standortwahl in Abhängigkeit von den Transportkosten und von anderen Kostenkriterien aufzustellen. Stattdessen verwies er auf die unvorhersagbaren lokalen Konvergenzen von Ereignissen, Personen und Institutionen. Auf die klassische Frage, warum sich Betriebe an einem bestimmten Ort ansiedeln, antwortet Scott mit einem Ansatz zu einer ganz anderen Standorttheorie, die sich auf weichere Kriterien wie lokale Vereinbarungen, Reflexivität[1], Lernfähigkeit und Synekismus[2] stützt.

Scott beschreibt zwei Wachstumszyklen eines Industriekomplexes: Der erste oder originäre Zyklus beginnt mit einer „chaotischen Serie initiierender Ereignisse und einer Abfolge von Zufälligkeiten,

Since IKEA's strategy is focused on the use of local resources, most of the 1,700 employees working in these factories, even at management level, live in the area. Blue-collar workers are mainly local, but with the future growth of the company there might be a need to look for workers in the Gorzow area. Qualified workers with a university education might commute from academic centers like Zielona Gora, Poznan and Szczecin.

The Swedwood Group is not considering shifting to another country after the union of Poland and the EU. Swedwood is now settled in this location with good suppliers for furniture production, fittings, wooden components, etc. In addition, Polish forest policies are considered to be among the best in Europe. Even during socialist times there was a very strict operating structure, so Polish forest standards today are set according to the highest world requirements. This has to do with good habits from the past and good care of the forests over time plus good contemporary cooperation with the Ministry of Forestry.

Although there is interest in developing production further to the east, so far there is only one factory in Ukraine and one set to start operating in Russia. According to Robert Gdula, the quality of wood in those countries is inferior and regulations do not help, but the main drawback is the workers, who might be untrustworthy or have alcohol problems. Any change in this situation might take another generation.

CATCHING THE FLOW

During socialist times, Poznan was one of the key academic centers. It belonged to the most economically flourishing region of Poland and had a strong, well-educated work force. In recent years, the high cost of production in Germany has been driving many producers away, and the Poznan area appears as the first important trade center in the East.

The geographical location of Poznan in the heart of Europe and near the Polish-German border has stimulated the recent development of the city. However, problems of accessibility are diminishing its competitiveness. The highway that will connect east and west is still under construction and the railways also need to be modernised. A consortium of state and private investors is developing the Warsaw–Poznan highway, but this is a long-term enterprise and it is uncertain when it will be finished.

The Poznan government has been making efforts to promote the benefits of the city with a view to foreign investment, but the political transition has left the city without a master plan. As a result, many building permits get bogged down, thus blocking investment. This situation, among other things, has resulted in industrial development taking place in satellite villages outside of Poznan like Tarnowo Podgorne.

The Tarnowo Podgorne district borders Poznan and the A2, the international highway running from Eastern to Western Europe. The district comprises an area of 113 sq km and has a population of 14,000 residents. The district has not only experienced the fastest rate of economic growth in the whole Poznan region during the past five years but is now also among the districts with the biggest growth in Poland. Waldly Dzokowski, the district administrator, says that many investors have chosen Tarnowo because of the dynamism of the local government and the shorter distance to Germany. The whole area is developing as a new regional center, thanks to the district's ability to achieve financial independence from the state, thereby creating its own sources of income.

The development program began in 1994 with basic investment. Two sewer lines were built in 1994–1998 and a gas line for the 12 communities of the municipality was constructed, as was a modern 15-hectare landfill equipped with machinery for sorting and recycling. Finally, a municipal transport company was founded and a better telephone service has been provided. These investments framed by flexible and dynamic regulations were what persuaded potential investors to choose Tarnowo. By 2004, 1,800 companies had been registered, including 300 corporations that combined with local investments to total more than 350 million US dollar.

FLEXIBLE TRANSITION

According to Edward Soja, "the new economy built on what is called flexible accumulation is based on reorganized production processes and technologies and allows clusters of small and middle-sized companies no longer bound to old Fordist urban agglomerations. This spatially condenses in a wide scattering of production sites outside the largest urban centers, producing innovation that can arise in even small urban agglomerations."

This global economic phenomenon has landed in our specific area of study, where the political and

die in der Regel von lokalen Vorreitern in der Industrie ausgelöst werden und auf spezifische räumliche und lokale Umstände zurückzuführen sind. Die nachfolgenden Phasen dienen der Festigung und dem Ausbau der eingeleiteten Entwicklung."
Scott betont die große Bedeutung von Netzwerken lokaler Entscheidungsträger und ihrer Fähigkeit, die entscheidenden Ressourcen und Energien zur Förderung des lokalen Wirtschaftswachstums zu mobilisieren. Im Falle der polnischen Grenzregion, die in den drei Fallstudien betrachtet wurde, zeigt sich, dass die Ansiedlung von Betrieben und Logistikzentren trotz schlechter infrastruktureller Voraussetzungen erfolgte. Die chaotischen Veränderungen, die diese Region in der Übergangsphase erlebte und die das Ergebnis von drastischen Privatisierungen und Gesetzeslücken waren, erwiesen sich für manche lokal agierenden Gruppen, Behörden und ausländische Investoren als vorteilhaft. Wer zuerst kam, mahlte zuerst. Heute nun stellt man fest, dass es infolge dieser unausgewogenen Situation sowohl stagnierende als auch sich stürmisch entwickelnde Gebiete gibt, die dringend angemessene Infrastrukturen brauchen. In Ostdeutschland hatte der umgekehrte Prozess stattgefunden. Die deutsche Regierung traf nach der Wiedervereinigung zentral die Entscheidung, umfassende Investitionen zu tätigen und eine angemessene Infrastruktur mit Autobahnen im ganzen Land zu schaffen, doch kam die globale Produktion nicht wie erwartet.
Jetzt, da Polen in die EU aufgenommen wurde, steht die polnische Grenzregion vor der Herausforderung, eine Formalisierung und Verbesserung der Lage durch den Bau ihres Abschnittes der Autobahn Berlin–Moskau zu erreichen, ohne die Flexibilität zu verlieren, die ihre Entwicklung in der postsozialistischen Ära ermöglicht hat. Das beständige Ziel von nun an muss es sein, weiterhin Kapital anzuziehen, das sich auch andere osteuropäische Länder mit besserer Infrastruktur oder noch weiter östlich gelegene Regionen mit weniger Vorschriften und Regelungen aussuchen könnte. Wie Castells schon sagte, setzt sich die materielle Gewalt der Ströme wie ein Naturphänomen durch, das nicht vorhergesagt, sondern lediglich akzeptiert und gesteuert werden kann.

ANMERKUNGEN

1 „Reflexivität umfasst die komplexen und unbeständigen Beziehungen zwischen Organisationen, zwischen einzelnen Teilen komplexer Organisationen, zwischen Personen und zwischen Personen und Organisationen, für die räumliche Nähe aufgrund der substanziellen Komplexität und Unbeständigkeit dieser Beziehungen wichtig ist. Das interaktive Netz urbaner Aktivitäten ist konventionell und beziehungsabhängig, und es ist urban, weil bestimmte Konventionen und Beziehungen nur im Kontext räumlicher Nähe funktionieren." (Michael Storper)

2 Synekismus beschreibt den spezifisch räumlichen Kontext von sozialer Organisation, Innovation, Entwicklung, Veränderung und sozialem Wachstum. Er kann mit dem Impuls zu urbaner Agglomeration verbunden sein. (Edward Soja)

LITERATUR

Castells, Manuel: *The Rise of the Network Society.* Berkeley 2000

Chung, Chuihua Judy (Hg.): *Great Leap Forward – Harvard Design School Projects on the City.* Harvard 2002

Douglas, Mike/Friedman, John: *Cities for Citizens: Planning and the Rise of Civil Society in a Global Age.* Chichester 1998

Harrison, Bennett. *Lean and Mean. The Changing Landscape of Corporate Power in the Age of Flexibility.* New York 1994

Sassen, Saskia. *Cities in a World Economy.* Chicago 2000

Scott, Allen. *Regions and the World Economy: The Coming Shape of Global Production, Competition and Political Order.* Oxford 1998

Soja, Edward. *Postmetropolis: Critical Studies of Cities and Regions.* Oxford 2000

Storper, Michael/Salais, Robert: *Worlds of Production. The Action Framework of the Economy.* New York 1997

economical transition and the specific position in a border area have created a unique opportunity for international investments. Even so, not all our case studies could be regarded as being able to achieve their aims of attracting capital. The challenging question is: Why do some locations develop more than others?

Allen Scott in his book *Regions and the World Economy* avoids creating a general theory of locations based on transportation and other cost criteria. He points instead to unpredictable local convergences of events, individuals and institutions. Answering the classic questions of why industries locate where they do, Scott provides an opening for a very different location theory based on softer factors such as the role of local conventions, reflexivity[1], learning and synekism.[2]

Scott describes two cycles of growth of an industrial complex: the first or original cycle begins with a "chaotic series of initiating events and set of fortuitous circumstances usually involving local industrial pioneers and spatially specific local circumstances. Subsequent phases deal with what makes initial development stick and grow." Scott notes the importance of the network of activities created by local power brokers and the ability to mobilize critical resources and energies in support of local economic growth. The general case of the Polish border area looked at through the three case studies shows that the establishment of factories and logistical warehouses has taken place despite infrastructural conditions. The chaotic changes that the region has been experiencing in this transition stage, due to drastic privatisation and legal voids, have been profitable for some local groups, authorities and foreign investors. The faster ones were able to catch the flow first. Suddenly today the uneven situation shows areas that are dying and areas of explosive growth that urgently need to be supplied with appropriate infrastructure. The opposite process has happened in the former East Germany. The post-unification German government made the top-down decision to make a huge investment and construct the appropriate infrastructure of highways for the whole nation, but global production has not arrived as expected.

The challenge for the Polish border region in the coming years, now that it is part of the European Union, might be to formalise and improve the situation through the construction of the stretch of the Berlin–Moscow highway without losing the flexibility that allowed its recent development in the post-socialist era. The permanent mandate from now on is to keep attracting capital that could choose other Eastern European countries with better infrastructure or that could head even further east to more unregulated territories. As Castells states, the material power of flows imposes itself as a natural phenomenon that cannot be predicted, only accepted and managed.

NOTES

1 "Reflexivity involves complex and uncertain relationships between organisations, between the parts of complex organisations, between individuals and between individuals and organisations, in which proximity is important because of the substantive complexity and uncertainty of this relationships. The transactional tissue of urban activities is of conventional/relational nature and it is urban because certain conventions and relations only work in a context of proximity." (Michael Storper)

2 Synekism describes the spatially specific context for social formation, innovation, development, growth and change. It can be associated with the stimulus of urban agglomeration. (Edward Soja)

LITERATURE

Castells, Manuel: *The Rise of the Network Society*. Berkeley 2000

Chung, Chuihua Judy (ed.): *Great Leap Forward – Harvard Design School Projects on the City*. Harvard 2002

Douglas, Mike/Friedman, John: *Cities for Citizens: Planning and the Rise of Civil Society in a Global Age*. Chichester 1998

Harrison, Bennett: *Lean and Mean: The Changing Landscape of Corporate Power in the Age of Flexibility*. New York 1994

Sassen, Saskia: *Cities in a World Economy*. Chicago 2000

Scott, Allen: *Regions and the World Economy: The Coming Shape of Global Production, Competition and Political Order*. Oxford 1998

Soja, Edward: *Postmetropolis. Critical Studies of Cities and Regions*. Oxford 2000

Storper, Michael/Salais, Robert: *Worlds of Production: The Action Framework of the Economy*. New York 1997

TARNOWO PODGORNE IM VERGLEICH ZU POZNAN

TARNOWO PODGORNE VERSUS POZNAN

Martin Cagno

LIDL

one of europe's leading grocery retailers
GERMANY

Stollwerck Alpia Alprose

chocolate company.
GERMANY - U.K.

tobacco company.
GERMANY - U.K.

IVECO

shipping company;car sale and service
ITALY/FRANCE/GERMANY

BALMA

furniture making factory
POLAND

VERHOEVEN

logistics services within central europe
HOLLAND

Remmers

building renovation and protection equipment
GERMANY

decor printers, supplies decors for wood products
GERMANY

DEMOCO

general contracting and projects; design services
BELGIUM

JAKON

constructing, installations and finishing work
POLAND

KOMPLET

bakery products
GERMANY

euro druk

web offset printing company
GERMANY

Jowat

glue producer for furniture, car and nutritive trades
POLAND

POZNAN PACK+DISPLAY

products: packaging, display
GERMANY

SHOPPING PLAZA

shopping center
BELGIUM

Auchan

hipermarket
FRANCE

INDUSTRIEGEBIET VON TARNOWO PODGORNE

INDUSTRIAL DISTRICT OF TARNOWO PODGORNE

Martin Cagno

GRENZSTADT BREST

WILFRIED HACKENBROICH

ZUR SITUATION VON GRENZSTÄDTEN

Grenzstädte müssen anpassungsfähig sein. Während ein natürlicher oder künstlich geschaffener Hafen das Wachstum einer Hafenstadt stimuliert, existierten zum Zeitpunkt der Gründung der meisten heutigen Grenzstädte die Grenzen noch nicht. Daher lässt sich das Wachstum der meisten Grenzstädte nicht ursprünglich auf die Grenzsituation zurückführen. Grenzstädte müssen sich an jeweils neue Bedingungen anpassen; ist die Wirtschaftskraft auf beiden Seiten der Grenze unterschiedlich, profitiert die schwächer entwickelte Seite von diesem Gefälle. Die Stadt Shentsen in China ist ein solches Beispiel, die Kluft zwischen der blühenden Wirtschaft Hongkongs und dem schwächer entwickelten chinesischen Hinterland kommt ihr zugute. In den meisten Fällen liegen Grenzstädte in den Randzonen national ausgerichteter Produktionssysteme. Im Gegensatz zu Hafenstädten sind sie weder Reiseziele noch Orte von Handel und Wandel. Grenzstädte fungieren als Durchgangsstationen, die von Menschen und Gütern passiert werden. Gibt es keine extremen Unterschiede in der Wirtschaftskraft zwischen beiden Seiten der Grenze, werden sie zu Verwaltungszentren. Heute haben viele traditionelle Grenzstädte aufgrund transnationaler Regelungen ihren Einfluss verloren: Der Personen- und Gütertransport erfolgt weltweit oft per Flugzeug, und die Grenzstädte werden einfach umgangen.

DIE GESCHICHTE VON BREST

In unserer Studie über den Korridor Berlin–Moskau beschäftigten wir uns auch mit der Grenzstadt Brest. Im Laufe ihrer fast tausendjährigen Geschichte erlebte diese Stadt viele territoriale Veränderungen. Sie liegt auf einer Landzunge, die durch das rechte Ufer des Bug und den linken Flussarm des Muchavet begrenzt wird, und befindet sich an der Kreuzung wichtiger Handelstraßen, die durch Polen, die baltischen Staaten und Europa verlaufen. Diese Lage hat sie häufig zum Objekt verschiedener Besitzansprüche und zur Ursache opferreicher Konflikte werden lassen. Brest gehörte mal zu Polen, mal zu Russland oder Litauen, es wurde von Schweden und Deutschland besetzt.
Brests Bedeutung als Handelsstadt änderte sich erstmals im 18. Jahrhundert, als das Russische Reich mit der Befestigung seiner westlichen Grenze begann. Brest wurde zur Grenzstadt und verlor in dieser neuen Funktion während der Zugehörigkeit zu Polen (1921–1941) einen Teil seiner Bedeutung. Im Zweiten Weltkrieg gehörte die Stadt zu den ersten Opfern des Überfalls Deutschlands auf die Sowjetunion. Nach dem Kriegsende lag Brest bis 1991 an der wenig befestigten Grenze zwischen den „Bruderstaa-

BORDER CITY BREST

WILFRIED HACKENBROICH

SITUATION OF BORDER CITIES

Border cities have to be adaptable. While a port or natural harbour usually stimulates the growth of a port city, the borders in most of today's border cities didn't even exist at the time the city came into being. Consequently, developments in most border cities were not initially related to a border situation. Border cities had to adapt to the new circumstances; if the economic capacity on the respective sides of the border varied, the city on the less developed side would gain from the economic discrepancy. One such city is Shenzen in China, which exploits the gap between the thriving economy of Hong Kong and the less developed Chinese hinterland. In most cases, border cities are at the fringes of national economic production. Unlike port cities, border cities are not a destination, nor are they centres of exchange and trade. Border cities act as gateways, enabling flows of goods and people to pass through them; they are administrative nodes, unless there is an extreme difference in economic power on each side of the border. Today, many traditional border cities have lost their influence as a result of trans-national regulations: people and goods travelling the world by plane simply pass them by.

HISTORY OF BREST

Our study of the corridor between Berlin and Moscow took us to the border city of Brest. In the course of its almost 1,000-year history, Brest has undergone many territorial changes. Situated on a cape formed by the right bank of the River Bug and the left arm of the River Mukhavets on the crossroads of important commercial routes through Poland, the Baltic countries and Europe, the city was frequently the focus of different territorial claims and the cause of internecine struggle. Brest belonged to various regimes in Poland, Russia and Lithuania and was occupied by Sweden and Germany.
Brest's main role as a trading city first changed in the 18th century, when the Russian Empire began fortifying its western limits. Its new function as a border city diminished in importance during the time when Brest belonged to Poland (1921–1941). The city was one of the first victims when Germany launched its assault on the USSR during the Second World War. After the war was over, and up to 1991, Brest was part of a soft border between the "fraternal" countries of the Soviet Union. With the emergence of the Commonwealth of the Independent States (CIS) in 1991 the border between Poland and Belarus became a dividing line between the states affiliated

ten" der Sowjetunion. 1991 wurde mit der Gründung der GUS die Grenze zwischen Polen und Weißrussland zur Trennlinie zwischen den Russland zugewandten Staaten und den auf die NATO orientierten Ländern (Polen trat dem Bündnis 1999 bei). Mit dem Beitritt Polens zur Europäischen Union im Jahre 2004 wurde aus der „weichen" eine „harte" Grenze, die Europa und die GUS voneinander trennte und Brest von neuem zu einer Grenzstadt am westlichen Rand der GUS machte.

WEISSRUSSLAND HEUTE

„Vereint mit Russland nach Europa"[1] ist heute ein sehr populärer politischer Slogan in Weißrussland. Er vereint die Gruppe der Befürworter einer Zusammenarbeit mit Russland mit denen, die eine europäische Ausrichtung favorisieren. Dabei handelt es sich bei diesem Slogan natürlich nur um eine politische Formel und nicht um ein realistisches Konzept. Russland kooperiert zwar mit Europa, doch eine russische Mitgliedschaft in der EU ist höchst unwahrscheinlich, wodurch auch der weißrussische Weg nach Europa mit einem Fragezeichen versehen wird. Weißrussland ist anders als andere postsozialistische Länder wie Polen, Ungarn, die Tschechische Republik oder die Slowakei, die kulturell und wirtschaftlich Westeuropa sehr nahe stehen.[2] Diese Länder orientieren sich an den wirtschaftlichen und politischen Standards Europas, während die Entwicklung in Weißrussland auf Russland und die Vergangenheit gerichtet ist.
Die gegenwärtige wirtschaftliche Situation in Weißrussland wird auch von externen Faktoren wie der globalen Finanzkrise, dem harten internationalen Wettbewerb und der Einführung diskriminierender Maßnahmen für Nicht-Mitglieder der Welthandelsorganisation bestimmt. Hinzu kommen andere, interne Hindernisse wie die makroökonomische Instabilität, die ineffektive Steuer- und Währungspolitik, die veralteten und abgewirtschafteten Exportunternehmen, der Einsatz veralteter Technologien, die den heutigen Qualitätsstandards nicht mehr gerecht werden, der Mangel an Investitionen für Entwicklung und Modernisierung der Produktion und schließlich die schwach entwickelte Außenhandelsstruktur.[3] Einer der Hauptgründe für diese internen Nachteile ist die Wiedereinführung der staatlichen Kontrolle. Der in den ersten Jahren des Transformationsprozesses von 1991 eingeleitete Abbau staatlicher Kontroll- und Interventionsrechte kehrte sich ab 1995 wieder um. Die heutigen staatlichen Kontroll- und Interventionsmechanismen sind extrem marktfeindlich.[4] Der Einfluss des Staates auf den Handel, die Privatisierung und die Währungspolitik zeigt sich deutlich in den vom Präsidenten erlassenen Gesetzen, wie zum Beispiel in der Entscheidung, die „Goldene Aktie" in Unternehmen mit staatlicher Beteiligung einzuführen und somit dem Staat zu ermöglichen, Unternehmensentscheidungen auch als Minderheitseigner zu treffen (das entsprechende Dekret wurde im Januar 1998 erlassen). Die staatliche Kontrolle von Unternehmen ist nach wie vor stark und erstreckt sich auch auf ausländische Firmen. Sie wird immer mehr ausgebaut, selbst die Koordination der Zentralbank (Dekret Nr. 152, März 1998), die entschädigungslose Enteignung juristischer oder natürlicher Personen (Dekret Nr. 40) und die Preisbindung für alle in Weißrussland hergestellten Waren (Dekret Nr. 285, Mai 1999) sind davon betroffen.[5] Durch diese Gesetze entfernt sich das Land von den Funktionsmechanismen des freien Marktes, werden Handelsmöglichkeiten mit der Europäischen Union eingeschränkt und kann das für ausländische Investitionen notwendige Vertrauen nicht entstehen.

to Russia and those attracted to the North Atlantic Treaty Organisation (Poland joined in 1999). In 2004, when Poland was admitted to the EU, the soft border was transformed into a hard border, separating Europe and the CIS, making Brest once more a border city defining the western limits of the CIS.

BELARUS TODAY

"Together with Russia to Europe"[1] is today a very popular political slogan in Belarus. It unites the group that prioritises cooperation with Russia and the group that favours a development towards Europe. But it is clear that this is a political formula and not a realistic concept. Russia is cooperating with Europe, but its membership of the Union is very unlikely and that puts a question mark against the road to Europe for Belarus. Belarus is different from other transforming post-socialist countries like Poland, Hungary, the Czech Republic and Slovakia with their cultural and economic proximity to Western Europe.[2] These countries are shaping up to the economic and political standards of Europe, while Belarus is developing towards Russia and the past.
Today, the economic situation of Belarus is also influenced by such external factors as the global financial crisis, tough competition from international partners and the introduction of discriminating measures for non-members of the World Trade Organization. Other disadvantageous internal factors are macroeconomic instability; ineffective fiscal and currency policy; the old and run-down capital stock of export companies; the use of outdated technology which fails to meet quality standards; a lack of investment in the development and modernisation of production; and the underdeveloped external trade structure.[3] A major reason for these internal disadvantages is the re-installation of state control. The reduction of state control and state intervention during the initial years of transformation after 1991 has been reversed since 1995; today state control and interventions are extremely hostile to the market.[4] State influence on trade, privatisation and currency policy is illustrated by the laws which the president has brought in; for example the option to introduce "golden stock" for companies with state participation, allowing the state to implement decisions even if it has only minority ownership (Decree promulgated in January 1998). State control of companies remains extensive and extends to foreign-owned companies. It is expanding and covers even the coordination of the central bank (Decree No. 152, March 1998), the expropriation of legal and physical persons without compensation (Decree No. 40) and the limitation of prices for all products manufactured in Belarus (Decree No. 285, Mai 1999).[5] These laws move Belarus further away from free market regulations, limit trade opportunities with the European Union and reduce the trust needed for foreign investment.

BREST TODAY

Situated next to the border with Poland and the Ukraine, Brest has a population of about 296,300 and covers an area of 8,758 hectares, making it the second largest city in Belarus. The city is located at the crossroads of various east-west and north-south infrastructure routes. Brest is connected to the rest of Belarus and neighbouring countries by 20 local and 70 long-distance trains, 100 local and international buses, motorways along the transit corridor between Berlin and Moscow, and various waterways. The city's airport is greatly underused, providing only one flight a week to

BREST HEUTE

An der Grenze zu Polen und der Ukraine gelegen, zählt Brest heute ca. 296 300 Einwohner und erstreckt sich über eine Fläche von 8 758 Hektar. Damit ist sie die zweitgrößte Stadt in Weißrussland. Sie liegt im Schnittpunkt verschiedener von Ost nach West und von Nord nach Süd verlaufender Infrastrukturachsen. Brest ist mit den anderen Regionen des Landes und mit den Nachbarstaaten über 20 Regional- und 70 Fernzugverbindungen, 100 lokale und internationale Buslinien, durch die entlang dem Korridor Berlin-Moskau verlaufende Autobahn und zahlreiche Wasserstraßen verbunden. Der städtische Flughafen ist nur wenig ausgelastet, von hier geht nur einmal pro Woche ein Flug nach Kaliningrad. Die Grenze zu Polen, vormals eine „weiche" Grenze zwischen verbündeten Staaten, trennt jetzt zwei verschiedene politische und wirtschaftliche Systeme voneinander.

Diese Grenze ist gegenwärtig die Trennlinie zwischen der Europäischen Union und Osteuropa. Brest bereitet sich auf die künftigen Veränderungen mit dem Ausbau seiner Infrastruktur als Grenzstadt, der Schaffung von Freien Wirtschaftszonen und der Erstellung eines Stadtentwicklungsplans für die Zukunft der Stadt vor. Doch obwohl die Stadt im Zentrum verschiedener Verkehrswege liegt, scheint sie von Waren- und Personenströmen unberührt zu bleiben. Unsere Untersuchung hatte das Ziel, den Einfluss der Grenze und der gut ausgebauten Infrastruktur auf Brest verständlich zu machen und die Aussichten für eine Stadt zwischen zwei Welten zu beleuchten. Kann Brest in naher Zukunft die Rolle übernehmen, die Polens Grenzregionen heute innehaben? Können Brest und das westliche Weißrussland von Westpolen lernen? Wie funktionieren die Freien Wirtschaftszonen in diesem postsozialistischen Umfeld, verglichen mit dem westlichen Wirtschaftssystem? Wird das Angebot billiger Arbeitskräfte in den nächsten Jahren für Brest von Vorteil sein? Wie beeinflussen die verschiedenen Branchen gegenwärtig die Stadtentwicklung? Welche Potentiale hat diese Stadt, und welche Probleme werden in Zukunft auf sie zukommen?

DIE GRENZANLAGEN

Es gibt drei Grenzübergänge, einen für Pkws und Fußgänger zwischen Terespol und Brest, einen nördlich gelegenen und die Stadt umgehenden Übergang für Lkws und eine ebenfalls nördlich von Brest liegende Grenzstation für Züge. 2001 waren die meisten der bei Brest die Grenze überquerenden Personen Transitreisende. Der Prozentsatz lag für Reisende aus Weißrussland bei 82 Prozent, aus Russland bei 92 Prozent, aus Kasachstan bei 96 Prozent und aus Deutschland und der Tschechischen Republik bei 100 Prozent.[6]

Der Bus-, Pkw- und Fußgängerübergang an der Warschauer Brücke zwischen Terespol und Brest wird täglich von 2 700 Fahrzeugen passiert. Er ist damit der meistgenutzte Grenzübergang zwischen der GUS und der EU. Reisende von Polen nach Weißrussland werden auf polnischer, Reisende von Weißrussland nach Polen auf weißrussischer Seite kontrolliert. Hier gibt es an der Grenzstation ein Postamt, eine Tankstelle, Läden, ein Café, Versicherungsagenturen und eine Erste-Hilfe-Station sowie 100 Parkplätze für Pkws und Reisebusse. Der Bau eines Einkaufszentrums ist geplant.

Der Eisenbahnübergang liegt nördlich von Brest. Hier erfolgt die Zollkontrolle; außerdem muss das Fahrgestell der Züge gewechselt werden, um auf dem russischen

Kaliningrad. The border with Poland, previously a "soft" border with an affiliated country, is now a border between different political and economic strategies.
The border is currently the dividing line between the European Union and eastern Europe. The city of Brest is preparing for future changes by extending its border infrastructure, establishing free economic zones and creating a master plan for the city's future. Yet, while it is at the heart of various flows, the city seems unaffected by the streams of goods and people. Our research was designed to help us understand the impact of the border on Brest, the effect of the extensive infrastructure and the prospects for a city between two worlds. Can Brest assume the role in the near future that Poland's border space has today? Can Brest and western Belarus learn from western Poland? How do the free economic zones in this post-socialist environment function compared with the Western economic system? Will the cheap labour market be advantageous for Brest over the next years? How are the individual trades currently affecting the city's development? What potential will the city have and what problems will it face in the future?

BORDER INSTALLATIONS

There are three border crossing points, one for cars and pedestrians between Terespol and Brest, one for lorries in the north, bypassing the city of Brest, and one for trains, which is also in the north of Brest. In 2001, most travellers crossing the border in Brest were in transit. 82 per cent of the travellers from Belarus, 92 per cent of those from Russia, 96 per cent from Kazakhstan and 100 per cent from Germany and the Czech Republic were only passing through Brest.[6]
The car, bus and pedestrian crossing point at Warsaw Bridge between Terespol and Brest is passed by 2,700 cars per day, making it the most frequented border crossing point between the CIS and the EU. Travellers from Poland to Belarus are controlled on the Polish side, while travellers from Belarus to Poland are controlled on the Belarusian side. The border point on the Belarusian side provides services such as a post office, a petrol station, shops, a café, insurance companies and a first aid point as well as 100 parking spaces for cars and coaches; the construction of a supermarket is planned.
The border crossing point for trains is in the north of Brest. In addition to the customs control the trains also have to change their wheels here to be able to run on the Russian track, which have a wider gauge. The hall for this exchange is to the west of Brest railway station. During the eastward journey the border controls are carried out during the changing of the train wheels. After the controls are over, passengers can spend one hour outside the train. However, the immediate surroundings are not attractive and the main train station is two kilometres away, so most passengers stay on the train. For the westward journey from Brest, the customs controls are performed in Brest railway station. Here the situation is similar to that at an airport; there is a duty-free area with passport control and customs control. The train platform is already "outside" of Belarus and so, once the trains have been fitted with European-gauge wheels, travellers can continue their journey uninterrupted up to the Polish-German border. The border train station in Brest is also the crossing point for the local electric trains, which are used by shuttle traders from Brest. The tickets cost about 4 US dollar in Belarusian roubles, and the trains depart on time from Brest at 7:50, 9:54, 11:20,

Schienennetz mit seiner größeren Spurweite fahren zu können. Die Halle, in der dieser Wechsel erfolgt, liegt westlich des Brester Bahnhofs. Bei Fahrten in Richtung Osten finden die Grenzkontrollen während des Fahrgestellwechsels statt. Nach Beendigung der Kontrollen können die Fahrgäste eine Stunde außerhalb des Zuges verbringen, doch ist die unmittelbare Umgebung nicht sonderlich attraktiv, und der eigentliche Bahnhof liegt in zwei Kilometer Entfernung. So bleiben die meisten Reisenden im Zug. Bei Fahrten in Richtung Westen finden die Zollkontrollen im Bahnhof von Brest statt. Die Einrichtung gleicht der in einem Flughafen: Es gibt einen Duty-free-Bereich mit Pass- und Zollkontrolle. Der Bahnsteig liegt bereits „außerhalb" von Weißrussland, so dass die Reisenden, sobald die Züge mit Fahrgestellen europäischer Spurweite ausgestattet sind, ihre Reise ohne Unterbrechung bis an die polnisch-deutsche Grenze fortsetzen können. Der Grenzbahnhof von Brest ist auch der Knotenpunkt der elektrisch betriebenen Regionalzüge, die von Transithändlern im Pendelverkehr genutzt werden. Die Fahrkarten kosten ca. vier US-Dollar in weißrussischen Rubeln, und die Züge fahren in Brest um 7:50, 9:54, 11:20, 16:50 und 19:47 Uhr ab. Die Ankunftszeit im drei Kilometer entfernt liegenden polnischen Terespol hängt stark von den Zollformalitäten ab: Eine kurze Fahrt dauert wenigstens zwei Stunden.

Die Straße, die zum Lkw-Kontrollpunkt nördlich von Brest führt, zweigt vom Korridor E30 ab und umgeht die Stadt, um nach den Grenzkontrollen östlich von Brest wieder in die E30 zu münden. Die Lkws, die aus Weißrussland Richtung Polen fahren, verlassen die Autobahn Moskau–Minsk–Berlin bei Vestavto, das nordöstlich von Brest liegt (Brest-Sadwartzy), um zum weißrussischen Kontrollpunkt zu gelangen; dessen Grenzübergang für den Güterverkehr liegt in Kukuryki-Koslovichi. Hier wird also auf beiden Seiten der Grenze kontrolliert, die passierenden Fahrzeuge müssen zweimal halten.[7]

Die Zollkontrollen für Gütertransporte nach Westeuropa wurden bereits in Weißrussland oder in Russland durchgeführt, so dass die Kontrollen am Grenzübergang Brest eher oberflächlich sind.[8] Der Kontrollpunkt hat eine Kapazität von 1 000 Lkws pro Tag und wird von durchschnittlich 500 Fahrzeugen pro Tag genutzt.

FESTUNG EUROPA

Polen hat im Rahmen der PHARE-Programme 2001 und 2002 (Teil I) bisher 450 Millionen EUR erhalten. 77 Millionen EUR waren dabei für Justiz und Inneres und damit auch für den Zoll bestimmt. Davon wurden 31 Millionen EUR für Grenzkontrollen ausgegeben. In Übereinstimmung mit der von der EU verfolgten Linie, die diese Maßnahmen im engen Zusammenhang mit dem Kampf gegen Kriminalität sieht, wurde der größte Teil des Geldes in moderne Grenzkontrolltechnik investiert, wie z. B. Computer, Software und Glasfaserkabel für die Datenübertragung. Es handelt sich dabei um die größten Einzelprojekte in der Geschichte des PHARE-Programms.[9]

Mit der Umsetzung der EU-Pläne zur Sicherung ihrer Außengrenzen bis 2008 wird es in Zukunft noch rigidere Kontrollen geben. So sollen entlang der 1143 km langen Grenze Wachtürme im Abstand von 15 bis 20 km errichtet werden. Zusätzlich werden fünf Aufklärungsflugzeuge, 60 tragbare Überwachungsgeräte und 236 mobile Wärmekameras und die doppelte Zahl von Wachpersonal (mehr als 5 300 Personen) im Einsatz sein.[10] Brest ist sich seiner neuen Aufgabe bewusst, „unerwünschte Elemente" an der Einreise nach Europa zu hindern.[11]

16:50 and 19:47 hours. The time of arrival in Terespol, Poland, which is three kilometres away, varies a great deal depending on the customs formalities: a short journey takes at least two hours.
The road leading to the truck border control point in the north of Brest splits off the E30 corridor and bypasses the city proper to rejoin the E30 after the border control east of Brest. The trucks leaving Belarus for Poland turn off from the Moscow–Minsk–Berlin motorway to the Belarus checkpoint at Vestavto which is north-east of Brest (Brest-Sadwartzy). This border crossing point for goods traffic in Kukuryki-Koslovichi is a two-stop border, which means controls are conducted on both sides of it.[7] The customs control for cargo transports to western Europe has been carried out inside Belarus or in Russia, so the controls at the border crossing point in Brest are more casual.[8] The cargo control point has a capacity of 1,000 trucks per day and is used by an average of 500 trucks per day.

FORTRESS EUROPE

Poland has so far received 450 million EUR as part of PHARE 2001 and 2002 (Part I). 77 million EUR has been allocated to justice and home affairs as well as customs. 31 million EUR has gone on border controls and, in line with EU logic, the closely related fight against crime, most of this money having been spent on high-technology equipment for border controls as well as for computers, software and fibre optics for data transfer. These are the largest individual projects in the history of the PHARE programme.[9]
The future will produce an even more rigid border following implementation by the EU of its plans to upgrade it by 2008. There will then be watchtowers every 15 to 20 kilometres along the 1,143 kilometre-long border, five aerial reconnaissance units, 60 mobile hand-held surveillance devices, 236 mobile heat-sensitive cameras and a doubling of the border guards to over 5,300[10]. The city of Brest is aware of its new duty to keep "undesirable elements" out of Europe.[11]
The new terminal will process up to 2,000 trucks per day in 2007, which is twice its current capacity. The construction cost of 16 million EUR for the customs clearance building will be covered in full by the European Union's TACIS programme. The terminal will comprise three parts: customs clearance, a commercial section and a 27,000 square-metre storage area. The storage building will accommodate facilities for customs storage and confiscated goods and provide covered parking and loading areas. The commercial part will have a hotel, restaurant, two car/truck washes, a petrol station, a duty-free shop, several insurance agencies and parking spaces.[12]

BORDER PERFORATION – EU FUNDING

While building up the new European border, the protagonists on both sides are seeking to perforate it. The European Union is exerting influence on the development of neighbouring countries in the form of programmes such as PHARE CBC and TACIS CBC. The government of Belarus is trying to establish a link with the European market by setting up six free economic zones, while people living in Brest succeed in penetrating the border in the form of small-scale shuttle trade. A closer investigation of these perforations reveals the driving forces behind these developments and the impact they have on the border city of Brest.

Der neue Lkw-Terminal von Brest wird bis zu 2000 Fahrzeuge pro Tag abfertigen können, was einer Verdopplung seiner derzeitigen Kapazität entspricht. Die 16 Millionen EUR Baukosten, die für das Gebäude der Zollabfertigung ausgegeben wurden, werden vollständig von der Europäischen Union über das TACIS-Programm übernommen. Der Terminal wird drei Teile umfassen: die Zollabfertigung, einen kommerziellen Bereich und ein 27 000 Quadratmeter großes Lager. Im Lagergebäude werden Zollwaren und beschlagnahmte Güter gelagert werden können, und es wird über überdachte Park- und Ladeflächen verfügen. Im kommerziellen Bereich werden sich ein Hotel, ein Restaurant, zwei Auto- und Lkw-Waschanlagen, eine Tankstelle, ein Duty-free-Shop, mehrere Versicherungsagenturen und Parkplätze befinden.[12]

DIE UNTERSTÜTZUNG DER EU FÜR DURCHLÄSSIGE GRENZEN

Während die neuen europäischen Außengrenzen befestigt werden, sind beide Seiten bemüht, sie durchlässig zu gestalten. Die Europäische Union nimmt dabei über Programme wie PHARE CBC und TACIS CBC Einfluss auf die Entwicklung in den benachbarten Ländern. Die weißrussische Regierung versucht ihrerseits, über die Einrichtung von sechs Freien Wirtschaftszonen eine Verbindung zum europäischen Markt zu schaffen. Einige Einwohner Brests überqueren die Grenze immer wieder als Transithändler. Eine nähere Untersuchung dieser undichten Stellen in der Grenze zeigt die treibenden Kräfte hinter diesen Entwicklungen und ihre Auswirkungen auf die Grenzstadt Brest.

Die von der Europäischen Union zwischen 1991 und 2005 an Weißrussland geleistete Beihilfe beläuft sich auf 222,1 Millionen EUR.[13] Die Durchlässigkeit ihrer Außengrenze wurde von der INTERREG-Gemeinschaftsinitiative gefördert, die die grenzüberschreitende und transnationale Kooperation zwischen EU-Mitgliedsstaaten und ihren Nachbarn fördert. Nur die EU-Mitglieder erhalten Finanzmittel; das PHARE-CBC-Programm gibt Unterstützung und Finanzhilfen für grenzüberschreitende Kooperationen zwischen EU-Mitgliedern und Beitrittskandidaten, während das TACIS-CBC-Programm entsprechende Beihilfen für die Zusammenarbeit der westlichen Grenzregionen Russlands, Weißrusslands, der Ukraine und Moldawiens mit den EU-Mitgliedern leistet.[14]

Überdies hat Brest das TRIC-Programm (Grenzüberschreitende Informations- und Kontaktplattform) entwickelt, das Teil des europäischen TACIS-Programms ist. Das TRIC-Programm fördert den Austausch zwischen der Region Brest und Biala Podlaska in Polen. Mit dem geplanten „EU-Nachbarschaftsprogramm"[15] soll eine bessere Koordination der grenzüberschreitenden Zusammenarbeit erreicht werden. Ziel dieses Programms ist es, mehr Wohlstand und Stabilität auf beiden Seiten der EU-Außengrenze zu erreichen. Damit ermöglicht es den Nichtmitgliedsstaaten, an der wirtschaftlichen Entwicklung der EU teilzuhaben, ohne dass politische Verpflichtungen eingegangen werden müssen – sozusagen eine EU-Mitgliedschaft „light".

Der Gesamtbetrag von 222,1 Millionen EUR, der zwischen 1991 und 2005 an Weißrussland aus EU-Mitteln gezahlt wurde, verteilt sich wie folgt: 76,55 Millionen EUR für das TACIS-Länderprogramm; 6,5 Millionen EUR für das TACIS-Nuklearsicherheitsprogramm; 36,5 Millionen EUR für das TACIS-CBC-Programm; 2,74 Millionen EUR für das CBC-SPF-Programm; 55,6 Millionen EUR für das TACIS-Regionalprogramm; 9,19 Millionen EUR für das ECHO-Programm; 5,02 Millionen EUR für das INTAS-Programm und 30 Millionen EUR als makrofinanzielle Unterstützung.[16]

The assistance provided to Belarus by the European Union from 1991 to 2005 amounted to 222.1 million EUR.[13] The resulting puncturing of the EU border by the EU has been stimulated by the INTERREG Community Initiative which supports cross-border and trans-national cooperation among member states and neighbouring countries. Funds are only for EU members; the PHARE CBC provides support and funding for cross-border cooperation between EU members and candidate states, while the TACIS CBC gives support and funding for cross-border cooperation between the western border region of Russia, Belarus, Ukraine and Moldavia and the EU member states.[14]

Furthermore, Brest has developed the TRIC (Transborder Information and Contact platform) that is part of the EU's TACIS programme. The TRIC programme stimulates exchange between the Brest region and Biala Podlaska in Poland. The EU's forthcoming "neighbourhood programme"[15] should provide for better coordination of cross-border cooperation and is intended to increase prosperity and stability on both sides of the EU border, thus allowing the non-member states to participate in the economic development of the EU without having any political commitments – EU membership 'light', as it were.

The distribution of the total financial support for Belarus between 1991 and 2005 amounting to 222.1 million breaks down as follows: TACIS National Programme 76.55 million EUR; TACIS Nuclear Safety 6.5 million EUR; TACIS CBC 36.5 million EUR; CBC SPF 2.74 million EUR; TACIS Regional Programme 55.6 million EUR; ECHO 9.19 million EUR; INTAS 5.02 million EUR; macro-financial assistance 30 million EUR.[16]

"EU technical assistance, in line with 1997 EU Council of Ministers' Conclusions, was previously limited" to humanitarian or regional projects or those which directly support the democratisation process." Between 1991 and 2004, a total of 221 million EUR was provided specifically to Belarus. Since 1997, two TACIS National Programmes for Belarus have been launched for 2000/2001 and 2002/2003, both worth 5 million EUR and focusing on the development of civil society. Under the programme endorsed by Belarus in 1999, a further 5 million EUR was allocated in 2003, this being targeted at civil society and activities related to the effects of Chernobyl. At the same time, Belarus received 16 million EUR between 2001 and 2003 from the CBC (cross-border cooperation), Interstate/Regional and Nuclear Safety Programmes. In addition to TACIS resources, Belarus was given 3.2 million EUR in food aid from 1998 to 2001. ECHO provided 6.7 million EUR to Belarus for humanitarian assistance linked to the effects of the Chernobyl accident. The CORE programme (Cooperation for Rehabilitation), in which the EU is participating, was established with the objective of improving the living conditions of the inhabitants of selected districts by reaching out to the people themselves, helping them to get involved in the development and execution of specific projects. The model emphasizes a participatory approach and active involvement on the part of those affected by the Chernobyl accident. National and international partners as well as governmental and non-governmental actors operate under the CORE programme. Through the European Initiative for Democracy and Human Rights (EIDHR) the EU has provided assistance to the European Humanities University, in cooperation with the OSCE. Support from the EIDHR to Belarus has also been granted in the form of a project in 2003 with the Lithuanian Union of Journalists."[17]

„Die technische Unterstützung der EU beschränkte sich in Übereinstimmung mit den 1997 gefassten Beschlüssen des EU-Ministerrates auf ‚humanitäre oder regionale Projekte oder solche, die den Demokratisierungsprozess direkt unterstützen'. Zwischen 1991 und 2004 wurden 221 Millionen EUR speziell für Weißrussland bereitgestellt. Seit 1997 wurden zwei TACIS-Länderprogramme für 2000/2001 und 2002/2003 in Weißrussland aufgelegt, die beide je fünf Millionen EUR umfassten und zur Entwicklung der Zivilgesellschaft beitragen sollten. Unter den 1999 von Weißrussland in Anspruch genommenen Programmen war eine weitere Zuwendung von fünf Millionen EUR für das Jahr 2003 enthalten, die ebenfalls für die Stärkung der Zivilgesellschaft und für Aktivitäten zur Bekämpfung der Folgen des Tschernobyl-Unglücks bestimmt waren. Gleichzeitig erhielt das Land zwischen 2001 und 2003 über das CBC (Programm zur grenzüberschreitenden Kooperation), das Interstate/Regional-Programm und das Nuklearsicherheitsprogramm 16 Millionen EUR. Zusätzlich zu den TACIS-Mitteln erhielt Weißrussland zwischen 1998 und 2001 3,2 Millionen EUR für Lebensmittelhilfen. Das ECHO-Programm stellte 6,7 Millionen EUR für humanitäre Hilfe im Zusammenhang mit den Folgen des Tschernobyl-Unglücks zur Verfügung. Das CORE-Programm (Cooperation for Rehabilitation), an dem die EU beteiligt ist, verfolgt das Ziel, die Lebensbedingungen für Einwohner ausgewählter Distrikte zu verbessern. Dabei sollen die Menschen direkt erreicht werden, indem ihnen Hilfe bei der Entwicklung und Durchführung konkreter Projekte gegeben wird. Das Programm verfolgt einen partizipatorischen Ansatz und setzt auf die aktive Einbeziehung der Betroffenen des Tschernobyl-Unfalls. Im CORE-Programm arbeiten nationale und internationale Partner aus Regierungs- und Nichtregierungsorganisationen zusammen. Mit Hilfe der Europäischen Initiative für Demokratie und Menschenrechte (EIDM) unterstützte die EU in Zusammenarbeit mit der OSZE die Europäische Humanistische Universität. Eine Unterstützung der EIDM für Weißrussland erfolgte auch in Form eines 2003 realisierten Projektes mit dem Litauischen Journalistenverband."[17]
Die EU beschreibt ihre Außenbeziehungen mit Nicht-EU-Mitgliedern in ihrer Veröffentlichung „Die Beziehungen der EU mit Weißrussland"[18] und erklärt ihre gegenwärtige und zukünftige Unterstützung für Weißrussland folgendermaßen:
„Das TACIS-Programm der EU, das für Weißrussland 10 Millionen Euro für den Zeitraum 2005/2006 bereitstellt, zielt auf die Bedürfnisse der Bevölkerung. Die Öffentlichkeitsarbeit mit Informationen über die EU und ihre Nachbarschaftspolitik wird verstärkt. Das Tempus-Programm wird die Finanzierung von Auslandsaufenthalten junger weißrussischer Studenten, die Lehrplangestaltung von Europastudiengängen und den Kapazitätsausbau der Universitäten fortführen. Weißrussland ist in die neuen Nachbarschaftsprogramme für grenzüberschreitende Kooperationen (Lettland-Litauen-Weißrussland, Ukraine-Polen-Weißrussland sowie das Ostseeprogramm) einbezogen und wird ab 2007 auch von den Instrumenten der Europäischen Nachbarschaftspolitik profitieren. Die Europäische Initiative für Demokratie und Menschenrechte (EIDM) will in den nächsten Jahren in Weißrussland eine aktivere Rolle spielen. Es sind spezifische Mittel für Mikroprojekte vorgesehen (2005 werden insgesamt 450 000 Euro durch mehrere Aufrufe zur Projekteinreichung bereitgestellt), Weißrussland ist jedoch auch zur Einreichung großer Projekte berechtigt. Im Zeitraum 2005/2006 können weißrussische Antragssteller Unterstützung für Projekte in den beiden Bereichen „Förderung,

A-76

der Kultur der Menschenrechte" und „Unterstützung des Demokratisierungsprozesses" beantragen. Das Land hat auch Anspruch auf Fördermittel aus dem dezentralen Kooperationsbudget, im Jahr 2005 werden insgesamt 1,7 Millionen Euro in mehreren Tranchen bereitgestellt. Die vorgesehenen Projekte werden einen Bereich enthalten, der über die Rolle der Nichtregierungsorganisationen bei der Unterstützung gefährdeter Gruppen, der kulturellen Entwicklung und der Hilfe zum Bürgerengagement informiert.

Im ersten Quartal 2005 wurde ein Aufruf zur Projektvorlage veröffentlicht, durch den neben anderen Bereichen auch die Entwicklung eines sozialen Dialogs zwischen lokaler Verwaltung und der Zivilgesellschaft gefördert werden soll."[19]

Wenn man bedenkt, dass zur gleichen Zeit 31 Millionen EUR für den Ausbau der Grenzen sowie für die Kontrolle von Nicht-EU-Bürgern an den Grenzen und die Verhinderung von deren Einreise ausgegeben werden, so wird klar, dass die Europäische Union gleichzeitig in zwei entgegengesetzte Richtungen arbeitet. Sie betrachtet ihr Territorium als Entität und will es schützen; hier liegen die Interessen der EU klar auf der Hand. Gleichzeitig will die Europäische Union den Handel mit ihren Nachbarn weiter entwickeln, wobei es ihr darum geht, den unkontrollierten Strom von Migranten und Gütern zu unterbinden. Ob diese Politik Erfolg haben wird, hängt wesentlich vom Wohlwollen der Nachbarstaaten ab. Für die EU kommt es dabei auf politische Stabilität und Freiheit in den Nachbarstaaten an, während die EU-Nachbarländer nach Handelsvorteilen suchen.

Die EU-Investitionen sind strategischer Natur, sie sind Ausdruck des Wertesystems der Gemeinschaft; sie fördern die Demokratie, die Menschenrechte, die Bildung und den Handel. Die scheinbar uneigennützigen Investitionen der EU werden größtenteils zu ihrem eigenen Vorteil getätigt; eine bedingungslose Hilfe und Teilhabe am Wohlstand der Europäischen Union ist für deren Nachbarn nicht möglich. Die EU verfolgt eine Politik der gewaltlosen Lenkung und Kontrolle ihrer Nachbarn durch wirtschaftliche Anreize.

ZUR DURCHLÄSSIGKEIT DER GRENZE – DIE BRESTER FWZ

Zusätzlich zu den Bemühungen der EU um Durchlässigkeit der Grenze versucht Brest seinerseits mit der ersten von insgesamt sechs Freien Wirtschaftszonen (FWZ) die Grenze zu überwinden. Die zwei Produktionsstandorte dieser FWZ haben gegenwärtig einen extraterritorialen Status. Die Zollkontrollen der importierenden Länder wurden in die Freie Wirtschaftszone verlagert, die FWZ profitiert von niedrigeren Steuersätzen, und auch die Produktionsstandards und die Löhne liegen unter denen in der Europäischen Union.

Von den beiden Standorten der Brester FWZ liegt der eine mit einer Fläche von 5800 Hektar in Kozlovichi nordwestlich der Stadt und der andere in der Nähe des Flughafens auf einem Gelände von 330 Hektar Größe. Beide gelten als vorrangige Entwicklungsgebiete. Angesichts der Gesamtfläche Brests von 8758 Hektar ist die geplante Ausdehnung der FWZ gigantisch, eine volle Auslastung scheint in weiter Ferne zu liegen: Die derzeit genutzte FWZ-Fläche beträgt nur ca. 200 Hektar.[20] Offizielle Darstellungen der FWZ sprechen von 97 Unternehmen aus 19 Staaten, die 2004 in der Zone produzierten. Die Investitionen von insgesamt 130 Millionen US-Dollar vertei-

The EU describes its external relations with non-EU countries in the publication "The EU's relations with Belarus"[18] and explains the present and future support for Belarus as follows:

"The EU TACIS programme (10 million EUR in 2005/06) in Belarus will focus on addressing the needs of the population. Information dissemination to the public on the EU and the European Neighbourhood Policy will be strengthened. The Tempus programme will continue to finance exchanges of young Belarusian university students abroad, curriculum development on European studies and capacity building in local universities. Belarus is eligible under the new Neighbourhood Programmes for cross-border cooperation (Latvia-Lithuania-Belarus; Ukraine-Poland-Belarus; Baltic Sea Programme) and it will benefit from the European Neighbourhood Policy Instrument (as of 2007). The European Initiative for Democracy and Human Rights (EIDHR) plans a more active role in Belarus in the coming years. There is a specific allocation for Belarus for micro-projects (in total 450,000 EUR will be made available through several calls for proposals in 2005)". Belarus is also eligible under the calls for proposals for macro-projects. In 2005/06, Belarusian applicants will be able to apply for support under two campaigns, notably "Fostering a culture of human rights" and "Promoting democratic process". Belarus is eligible under the Decentralised Cooperation budget line (in total 1.7 million EUR will be made available through several calls for proposals in 2005). Envisaged projects will include an information component regarding the role of NGOs in assistance to vulnerable groups, social and cultural development and community mobilisation. A call for proposals focusing among other areas on development of social dialogue between local governments and civil society was launched in the first quarter of 2005.[19]

If we bear in mind that 31 million EUR is being spent simultaneously to strengthen the border as well as to exclude and control other country members, it becomes clear that the EU is working at opposite poles at the same time. The EU territory is an entity that has to be protected, and the EU's interests are very clear; the EU appreciates trade with its neighbours but wants to stop an uncontrolled flow of migrants and goods. The sympathy of the neighbouring countries is an essential feature for the success of the EU. Political balance and freedom in the neighbouring countries are important for the EU while its neighbours seek trade benefits.

EU investments are strategic in nature and convey the value system of the EU; they promote democracy, human rights, education and trade. These seemingly unselfish investments are mainly for the benefit of the EU; unconditional help and participation in the prosperity of the European Union is not possible for its neighbours. The EU follows a policy of the non-violent steering and control of its neighbours by means of economic benefits.

BORDER PERFORATION – FEZ IN BREST

In addition to this puncturing of the border by the EU, Brest is perforating the border itself in the form of the first of six free economic zones (FEZs) with two production areas that are actually exterritorial. The customs control of the importing countries is carried out in this free economic zone, taxes are reduced, and production standards and wages are lower than in the European Union.

len sich wie folgt: 27 Prozent aus Weißrussland, 25 Prozent aus Deutschland, 15 Prozent aus Russland, 10 Prozent aus Polen, 10 Prozent aus der Tschechischen Republik und 13 Prozent aus anderen Staaten. Das erfolgreichste Unternehmen ist der Fischverpackungshersteller Santa Bremor, ein weißrussisch-deutsches Joint Venture, das bisher 25 Millionen US-Dollar investierte.

Obwohl die Brester Freie Wirtschaftszone erfolgreicher ist als die fünf anderen weißrussischen FWZ, wird sie nur teilweise genutzt. Die Organisatoren und Stadtplaner haben gute Rahmenbedingungen geschaffen, und doch ist der Erfolg weit von dem einer chinesischen FWZ entfernt, die als Modell diente. Die Gründe dafür legte der Geschäftsführer, Herr Kriwelkij, während einer Präsentation in der Stadt dar: „Meiner Meinung nach sind die Bedingungen für ausländische Investitionen hier sehr vorteilhaft, das Haupthindernis ist jedoch die Haltung der westlichen Massenmedien gegenüber unserem Land. Daher glauben westliche Investoren nicht, dass ihr Geld hier sicher angelegt ist."

Der geringe Erfolg der FWZ liegt nicht an zu geringen Gewinnaussichten: In den ersten fünf Jahren zahlen Unternehmen keine Steuern, danach entrichten sie, wenn ihre Produktion zu mindestens 70 Prozent für den Export bestimmt ist, lediglich den halben für Investoren der FWZ festgelegten Steuersatz (7,5 Prozent).[21] Verglichen mit dem durchschnittlichen Mindeststeuersatz innerhalb der EU von 24,3 Prozent und der Körperschaftssteuer von 19 Prozent bis 40 Prozent in Polen und 15 Prozent bis 42 Prozent in Deutschland werden die großen Steuervorteile der Brester FWZ deutlich. Hinzu kommt, dass die Produktionsstandards weit unter denen der Europäischen Union liegen und der Mindestlohn in Weißrussland ca. 19 Euro pro Monat beträgt, was im Vergleich zu Großbritannien (1083 EUR), Spanien (537 EUR) und selbst Polen (177 EUR) extrem wenig ist.[22]

Die sechs weißrussischen Freien Wirtschaftszonen liegen wie Inseln im Land; sie sind durchaus konkurrenzfähig und wollen mit der EU kooperieren. Diese extraterritorialen Inseln weisen einerseits ein westliches Wirtschaftssystem auf, während sie andererseits von EU-Produktionsrichtlinien, Zöllen, Sozialabgaben und Steuern zumindest teilweise ausgenommen sind. Die Freien Wirtschaftszonen inmitten einer postsozialistischen Umgebung erleichtern eine wirtschaftliche Liberalisierung ohne eine Beeinträchtigung der nationalen Betriebe und ohne Öffnung der lokalen Märkte für importierte Waren. Es handelt sich dabei um den Versuch, am kapitalistischen Wirtschaftssystem der EU zu partizipieren, ohne die wirtschaftliche Kontrolle der weißrussischen Betriebe in ausländische Hände zu geben.

In Brest verbindet man die Freie Wirtschaftszone mit der Hoffnung auf Arbeitsplätze, obwohl die Zone außerhalb der Stadt liegt und sich kaum aktivierend auf die Stadt auswirken kann. Alle notwendigen Voraussetzungen wurden zwar geschaffen, doch die Wahrnehmung im Ausland ist negativ, und die Investoren zögern. Brest ist auf Europa vorbereitet, doch Europa nimmt dieses Angebot nicht wirklich an.

ZUR DURCHLÄSSIGKEIT DER GRENZE – DIE TRANSITHÄNDLER

Zu den Bemühungen der Europäischen Union und der Brester Freien Wirtschaftszone um die Schaffung einer durchlässigen Grenze kommt hinzu, dass die wirtschaftliche Situation in der Region zur Herausbildung einer aktiven informellen Wirtschaft geführt

The FEZ in Brest has two sites, one in Kozlovichi north-west of the city covering an area of 5,800 hectares and one next to the airport covering an area of 330 hectares, both of which function as priority development areas. Considering that the entire urban area of Brest is 8,758 hectares, the planned area for the FEZ is gigantic and far from being fully used; the FEZ area used today is about 200 hectares.[20] Official figures put out by the Brest FEZ indicate that some 97 companies from 19 countries were producing there in 2004. Investments in the FEZ amounting to 130 million US dollar broke down as follows: 27 per cent Belarus, 25 per cent Germany, 15 per cent Russia, 10 per cent Poland, 10 per cent Czech Republic and 13 per cent others. The most successful company is the fish packaging company, Santa Bremor, a German-Belarusian joint venture with an investment of 25 million US dollar.

Despite the fact that this FEZ is more successful than the other five in Belarus, its capacity is only partially used. The organizers and city planers have provided a framework that is well developed, but the success of the FEZ is far from matching that in China, on which it is modelled. The reasons for this development were explained by Mr. Kriwelkij, Chief Executive Officer of the Brest FEZ, during a presentation in the city: "In my opinion the rules of the game for foreign investments are very favourable but the main obstacle is the attitude of mass media in the west to our country. Because of this western investors don't believe their money will be safe here."

The reason for the minimal success of the FEZ are not the benefits: after a five-year, tax-free period Brest FEZ occupants providing not less than 70 per cent of the production in Brest FEZ for export purposes pay 50 per cent from an established FEZ occupants tax rate (7.5 per cent).[21] Compared to the average effective marginal tax rate in the EU of 24.3 per cent and the corporate income tax of between 19 per cent and 40 per cent in Poland and 15 per cent to 42 per cent in Germany, it is clear that the tax advantages are huge in the Brest FEZ. Additionally, production standards are far below those in the European Union; moreover, the minimum wage of about 19 EUR per month in Belarus is extremely low compared to that in the United Kingdom (1,083 EUR), Spain (537 EUR) and Poland even (177 EUR).[22]

The six FEZs in Belarus are islands in the country, which are able to compete with and participate in the European Union. These exterritorial islands provide a western economic system with liberation from EU production laws, customs, social demands and tax – in part at least. The free economic zones in this post-socialist environment facilitate a liberation and acceleration of the economy without contaminating national industries and opening the local market to foreign products. It is an attempt to participate in the capitalist system of the EU without passing economic control of businesses in Belarus to foreign owners.

In Brest the FEZ provides hope for the creation of jobs, but structurally the areas are outside of the city and have no potential to activate it. All the requisite features have been installed, but the perception from foreign countries is negative and investors are hesitant. Brest seems to be prepared for Europe but lacks access.

BORDER PERFORATION – SHUTTLE TRADERS

In addition to the perforation of the border by the European Union and the Brest FEZ, the local economic situation has stimulated an active informal economy. Shuttle trad-

hat: Transithändler, oft ehemalige Manager, Lehrer oder Ingenieure, überqueren die polnisch-weißrussische Grenze in beide Richtungen und verkaufen Wodka und Zigaretten aus Weißrussland in Polen und billige polnische Waren in Brest. Dieser „Ameisenhandel" wird von den wechselnden Visavorschriften direkt beeinflusst, und die informellen Händler müssen sehr erfindungsreich mit ihnen umgehen.

Die Tour beginnt 30–40 Minuten vor der Zugabfahrt. Man muss sich mit all den anderen Händlern durch die enge Tür der Zollkontrolle drängeln. Jeder muss in zwei Exemplaren eine Zollerklärung ausfüllen, die er bei sich trägt, wenn er durch ein Drehkreuz des Grenzübergangs geht. Ganz in der Nähe der Drehkreuze befindet sich ein Duty-free-Shop, in dem die Händler aus Brest die Waren kaufen, die sie nach Polen einführen dürfen: ein Liter Wodka und anderthalb Stangen Zigaretten (weitere Waren werden geschickt versteckt und über die Grenze geschmuggelt). Der „Ameisenhandel" ist schwer zu kontrollieren, da die Mitnahme einiger Waren für den persönlichen Gebrauch erlaubt ist.

Wir konnten einen besonders anschaulichen Fall des „Ameisenhandels" im Wartesaal des Bahnhofs von Brest beobachten: Eine Frau verteilte Nike-Sweatshirts und Adidas-Trainingsanzüge an 20 bis 30 Personen. Dabei wurde kein Geld ausgetauscht, sondern die Frau notierte etwas in einem kleinen Buch. Viele schienen sich untereinander zu kennen, die meisten von ihnen waren Frauen im Alter von 40, 50 oder 60 Jahren, die anderen waren ältere Männer oder jüngere Frauen. Einige öffneten die Plastikverpackungen und zogen die Kleidungsstücke über die eigenen Sachen. Bald schon war der Brester Bahnhof mit älteren Frauen und Männern in schwarz-roten Trainingsanzügen und blauen Sweatshirts bevölkert.

Nachdem sich die elektrischen Zügen in Bewegung gesetzt hatten, kamen die Kontrolleure. Während der ersten Kontrolle verlangte der Grenzbeamte, das mitgeführte Bargeld zu sehen. Es ist dabei ratsam, wenigstens 30 Dollar je angegebenen Aufenthaltstag mit sich zu führen. Danach fragte der Zollbeamte nach der Menge des mitgeführten Wodkas und nach Zigaretten. Nach der Zollkontrolle konnten sich die Händler entspannen und erst einmal tief durchatmen. ... Terespol. Die Trainingsanzüge und Sweatshirts wurden auf der gegenüberliegenden Bahnhofsseite einer anderen Frau übergeben, die anderen verkauften ihre Zigaretten und den Wodka.

Eine Stunde später stand ein halbes Dutzend der Frauen aus dem Zug am Grenzübergang an der E30. Sie waren die drei Kilometer gelaufen, trugen Plastiktüten mit in Polen gekauften Waren bei sich und fragten die in der Schlange wartenden Autofahrer nach einer Mitfahrmöglichkeit über die Grenze. Viele liefen um die Schlange wartender Autos herum; manche Autos fuhren kurz vor der Grenzkontrolle auf einen Parkplatz und wurden dort neu bepackt. Viele der Autos waren schwer beladen, sie transportierten Geschirrspüler, verpackte Fernseher, Autowracks und Baumaterialien. Einige der Waren wurden ausgepackt und auf mehrere Fahrzeuge verteilt. Der Zoll erlaubt die Einfuhr von 50 Kilogramm Waren pro Person bei einer Einreise von Polen nach Weißrussland. Deshalb suchen sich die Fahrer die „Ameisenhändler", um das zulässige Einfuhrgewicht zu erhöhen. Fünf Dollar werden für diese „Arbeit" bezahlt. Zurück in Brest gehen die Händler erneut auf Tour.

Wie anfällig und dabei doch auch wichtig diese Art des Handels ist, zeigt die Entwicklung der polnischen Visabestimmungen für Bürger aus Weißrussland seit 2004. Die

ers cross the Polish-Belarusian border, some of them former managers, teachers or engineers, who sell Belarus vodka and cigarettes in Poland and cheap Polish products in Brest. This "ant" (or *mruvki*) trade is directly affected by the changing visa regulations, and informal traders have to be inventive to handle the changes.

The journey starts 30–40 minutes before departure, and those involved have to squeeze through the narrow doors of the customs inspection hall with a crowd of other "shuttle traders." Everybody has to fill in the declaration forms in duplicate and take them through the boundary turnstiles. Close to the turnstiles there is a "duty-free" shop where inhabitants of Brest buy the goods they are allowed to import into Poland; one litre of vodka and 1.5 blocks of cigarettes (additional goods are cleverly concealed and carried over the border by the ants). The ant trade is difficult to control, since the carrying of a few goods for personal use is permitted.

We saw a special case of ant trade in the waiting room at Brest railway station; a woman was handing out Nike sweat suits and Adidas trainers to 20–30 people. There was no money exchanged and instead she wrote notes in a little book. Many of these people seemed to know each other; most of them were women in their 40s, 50s or 60s together with a few older men and younger women. Some of them opened the plastic packages they were receiving and began putting on the new clothes on top of their own. Soon black-and-red versions of the same trainers and blue Nike sweat suits were being worn by the middle-aged women and men populating the train station.

The journey began and the control took place on board the electric train. During the first control the border guards asked the travellers to show them the currency they were carrying. It is advisable to carry a minimum of 30 US dollars for each declared day of stay. Customs officers then asked how much vodka and cigarettes were being carried. After the inspection by the customs officers the travellers were able to change carriages and take a deep breath ... Terespol. The people with the trainers and sweat suits returned the clothes to another woman in front of Terespol railway station; others sold their cigarettes and vodka.

An hour later, half a dozen women from the train were at the vehicle crossing point on the E30 highway. They walked the three kilometres from the station and were carrying other plastic bags with new goods. They asked car drivers, who were waiting in the queue, one by one, for a ride across the border. Many walked around the queue; cars pulled off the road into the car park just before the checkpoint and reloaded their cargo. Dishwashers, televisions in boxes, wrecked cars and construction materials – many of the vehicles were hauling large items. Some of the cargo was dismantled and redistributed to different cars. The customs regulations allow 50 kilos of goods per person to be brought into Belarus from Poland. Consequently, the drivers were looking for "ants", to expand the possible weight of goods they could take to Brest, 5 US dollars being the fee for the "job". When they arrived in Brest, the journey for the ants began all over again.

How vulnerable and yet how precious these shuttle trades are is indicated by the development of visa regulations for Belarusians travelling to Poland since 2004. The experts of the countries' foreign ministries planned that a one-off visa to Poland for Belarusians would cost 10 EUR, while a multiple-entry visa would cost 50 EUR. In fact, Belarusians are required to pay 6 US dollar for a single-entry Polish visa,

Experten des Außenministeriums sahen für ein einmaliges Einreisevisum einen Betrag von 10 EUR und für ein mehrfach gültiges Visum einen Betrag von 50 EUR vor. Tatsächlich bezahlen Einreisende aus Weißrussland sechs Dollar für eine einmalige, zwölf Dollar für eine zweimalige und 30 Dollar für eine mehrfache Einreise.
Die Visabestimmungen für weißrussische Reisende nach Polen sind also noch immer unbefriedigend. Rund 300 000 Menschen aus Weißrussland reisten 2004 nach Polen, während gerade mal 46 000 Polen nach Weißrussland fuhren. Der Vergleich der beiden Werte zeigt, wie viele Menschen von den Visabestimmungen betroffen sind. Während des diplomatischen Konflikts zwischen Polen und Weißrussland im Jahre 2005 wurde nicht nur einzelnen Diplomaten ihr Visum entzogen, sondern es wurde auch über eine generelle Visapflicht verhandelt. Der Direktor der Konsularabteilung der polnischen Botschaft in Minsk, Andrzej Buczak, zitierte den Vertreter des polnischen Außenministeriums, Herrn Checko, mit den Worten, die Ausweisung des polnischen Diplomaten Andrzej Buczak bliebe „nicht ohne Auswirkungen auf die Effizienz der Visaerteilung und der Einreiseerleichterungen nach Polen".[23] Später im Juli 2005 suchte Herr Checko nach einem Kompromiss, um bessere Beziehungen zu Minsk herzustellen: „Aus diesem Grund plant Polen, in naher Zukunft niedrigere Visagebühren für weißrussische Bürger einzuführen und sich für Programme zur grenzüberschreitenden Kooperation, zur Entwicklung der Handelsbeziehungen und des wissenschaftlichen und kulturellen Austauschs einzusetzen."[24]
Die wichtigste Grundlage der informellen Wirtschaft von Brest, die Möglichkeit der Einreise nach Polen, bleibt damit weiterhin in der politischen Diskussion, und viele Händler fürchten um ihre wirtschaftliche Existenz. Beiden Staaten ist die Bedeutung dieser Einreisemöglichkeit für die Menschen der Grenzregion bewusst, doch die geopolitische Situation wird eine neue Trennung mit sich bringen. Künftige Verhandlungen werden also einen Ausgleich zwischen den lokalen Bedürfnissen und der europäischen Politik zu finden haben.

GRENZLAND VERSUS GRENZSTADT: BRESTS ZUKUNFT

Um die Aussichten und die mögliche Zukunft Brests als Grenzstadt zu verstehen, kann man sie mit der Westgrenze Polens vergleichen, die ebenfalls vormals eine EU-Außengrenze war. Polen hat sich in den letzten zehn Jahren wirtschaftlich positiv entwickelt, und Brest möchte es den Polen in manchem gleichtun. Es gibt zwar einige Unterschiede in den Voraussetzungen zwischen Polen und Weißrussland, doch es gibt auch einige Gemeinsamkeiten: In beiden Ländern, in Polen in den 1990er Jahren und in Weißrussland heute, waren die Löhne, die Produktionsstandards und die Steuersätze niedriger als im betreffenden EU-Nachbarland, beide Staaten erhielten von der EU finanzielle Unterstützung, Polen als Anwärter auf eine EU-Mitgliedschaft und Weißrussland als Nachbarstaat.
Die polnische Grenzregion zwischen Poznan und der deutsch-polnischen Grenze beteiligte sich direkt am Austausch mit der EU. Das Hauptwachstumsgebiet in Westpolen ist das Areal um Tarnowo Podgorne bei Poznan, in dem es keinen anderen Standortvorteil als ein dereguliertes Industriegebiet und die Nähe zu einer attraktiven Stadt gab. Selbst die Infrastrukturverbindungen nach Deutschland waren unzureichend, doch kompensierte die gut ausgebaute Autobahn auf deutscher Seite diesen Nach-

12 US dollars for a double-entry visa and 30 US dollars for a multiple-entry visa. The visa regulations for Belarusians travelling to Poland remain unsatisfactory. About 300,000 Belarusians visited Poland in 2004, while Belarus had 46,000 visitors from Poland, this balance making it clear how many people are affected in Belarus by the regulations. During the diplomatic conflict in 2005 between Poland and Belarus, not only were visas for individual diplomats withdrawn, the negotiations on a general visa were also addressed. In July 2005, Andrzej Buczak, director of the consular department of the Polish Embassy in Minsk, said that Mr. Checko of the Polish Foreign Ministry had explained that the expulsion of Mr. Buczak, a Polish diplomat in Minsk, "cannot remain without influence on the efficiency of visa services and facilitations in travelling to Poland" for Belarusians.[23] Later, in July 2005, Mr. Checko was willing to seek a compromise and better relations with Minsk. "For this reason, Poland foresees, in the near future, lower visa fees for Belarusian citizens and also programmes aimed at developing cross-border cooperation, as well as commercial, scientific and cultural exchange."[24] The most important basis for the informal economy around Brest – and access to Poland – remains a tool for political debate; at the same time many shuttle traders are fearful of losing their economic basis. Both countries are aware that this access is important to the people in the border region, but the geopolitical circumstances will force a new division, and future negotiations will have to strike a balance between the local needs and European politics.

BORDERLAND VS. BORDER CITY: THE FUTURE OF BREST

To understand the prospects and possible future for Brest as a border city, it can be compared to the western border of Poland which was previously the border with the EU. Poland has undergone a positive economic development over the past 10 years – something Brest would like to experience as well. Some differences exist concerning the different points of departure for Poland and Belarus, but there are also some similarities. Both countries, Poland in the 1990s and Brest today, have lower wages, production standards and tax rates than in the respective neighbouring EU country; both countries have been the recipients of financial support from EU funds, Poland as a candidate country and Belarus as neighbouring country.

The Polish region that has directly participated in links with the EU is the border region between Poznan and German-Polish border. The main area of growth in western Poland is Tarnowo Podgorne near Poznan, which has nothing except a deregulated industrial area and the proximity of an attractive city. Even the infrastructure connection with Germany is insufficient, but the well-built motorways on the German side compensate for that, providing quick access to other European countries. The industrial boom of the past 15 years is exceptional and far better than the SEZs, the special economic zones in Poland. It is interesting that Poland has not developed its infrastructure in the very frequented area between the German-Polish border and Poznan. The small country road carries a huge amount of traffic and, as a result, a large number of micro-businesses have sprung up along the road providing transit services. Prosperity for the entire border region stems from these small businesses. What can be learned from Poland is that deregulation, the encouragement of micro-businesses and political stability stimulate economic development.

teil und ermöglichte die schnelle Erreichbarkeit anderer europäischer Länder. Der industrielle Aufschwung war in den vergangenen 15 Jahren außergewöhnlich stark und überstieg bei weitem den der SWZ, der polnischen Sonderwirtschaftszonen. Interessanterweise hat Polen in der stark frequentierten Region zwischen Poznan und der deutsch-polnischen Grenze seine Infrastruktur nicht ausgebaut. Die schmalen Landstraßen sind stark befahren, und entlang der Strecke entstanden viele Kleinstunternehmen, die Serviceleistungen für die Fahrer anbieten. Diese Kleinstunternehmen brachten der gesamten Grenzregion einen gewissen Wohlstand. Von Polen kann also gelernt werden, dass Deregulierung, Förderung von Kleinstunternehmen und politische Stabilität wirtschaftliches Wachstum fördern.

Ob die Aussichten auch für Brest positiv sein werden, hängt von der geplanten Autobahn ab. Wenn Polen die Autobahn von der deutsch-polnischen bis zur polnisch-weißrussischen Grenze führt, würde eine schnelle Verbindung zwischen Weißrussland und dem Zentrum der EU entstehen. Für Polen kann dies jedoch dazu führen, dass es in derselben Art und Weise übersprungen würde, wie Ostdeutschland in den 1990er Jahren auf dem Weg nach Polen übersprungen wurde. Dank der europäischen Zollkontrollen in den Freien Wirtschaftszonen müssten die Lkws noch nicht einmal an der polnisch-weißrussischen Grenze warten, Europa läge für Brest in nur wenigen Kilometern Entfernung. Wenn in Polen die Preise und Produktionsstandards steigen, könnten das hohe Bildungsniveau und die niedrigen Arbeitskosten in Weißrussland weitere Investitionen ins Land holen. Die Transithändler würden sich zu Kleinunternehmern entwickeln und hätten so die Möglichkeit, legal Handel zu treiben, was den gleichen regionalen Effekt hätte wie der der Kleinstunternehmer entlang der Strecke zwischen der deutsch-polnischen Grenze und dem polnischen Poznan. Der letzte Anstoß zum wirtschaftlichen Aufschwung müsste allerdings von der Herstellung politischer Beziehungen mit der Europäischen Union und vertrauensvoller Verbindungen zwischen Weißrussland und der EU gegeben werden.

ANMERKUNGEN

1 Ulachovi , Uladzimir: „David ohne Goliath". In: *Konturen und Kontraste, Belarus sucht sein Gesicht. Osteuropa. Heft 2,* 2004; S. 212

2 Neumann, Frank: „Der Transformationsverlauf in Belarus und Perspektiven". In: *Belarus. Zwischenbilanz einer stornierten Transformation. Osnabrücker Studien. Heft18.* 2001; S. 264

3 Medvedev, Vitalij: „Aktuelle Wirtschaftslage". In: *Belarus, Zwischenbilanz einer stornierten Transformation. Osnabrücker Studien Heft18.* 2001; S. 215

4 Neumann, Frank: „Der Transformationsverlauf in Belarus und Perspektiven". In: *Belarus, Zwischenbilanz einer stornierten Transformation. Osnabrücker Studien Band 18.* Osnabrück 2001, S. 268

5 Neumann, Frank: „Der Transformationsverlauf in Belarus und Perspektiven". In: *Belarus, Zwischenbilanz einer stornierten Transformation. Osnabrücker Studien Band 18.* Osnabrück 2001, S. 279

6 Straz Graniczna Rzeczypospolitej (Border Control of the Polish Republic)

7 Krzysztof Kolanowski: *Wartezeitenanalyse bei der Abfertigung am Grenzübergang Kukuryki – Koslowitschi.* Frankfurt (Oder), November 2002, S. 4

8 Krzysztof Kolanowski: a. a. o., S. 10

9 Helmut Dietrich: „The New Border Regime at Bug River, FFM". In: *Statewatch Bulletin Vol. 13,* Januar–Februar 2003

10 Helmut Dietrich: „The New Border Regime at Bug River, FFM". In: *Statewatch Bulletin Vol. 13,* Januar–Februar 2003

11 Alexander Sergej, stellvertretender Bürgermeister von Brest, bei einem Treffen in Brest, Oktober 2003

12 Krzysztof Kolanowski: a. a. o., S. 20

13 Derzeitige und zukünftige Hilfe für Weißrussland, http://europa.eu.int/comm/external_relations/belarus/intro/

The most optimistic outlook for Brest depends on the motorway through Poland. If Poland completes this motorway from the German-Polish to the Polish-Belarusian border, a rapid link with the centre of the EU would be a possible outcome. That could lead to Poland being bypassed in the same way that east Germany was bypassed by Poland in the 1990s. With the European custom checks being carried out in the FEZs, the lorries would not even have to wait at the Polish-Belarusian border; Europe would be just a few kilometres from Brest. If prices and production standards rise in Poland, the high level of education and low labour costs could stimulate further investment. If shuttle traders turn into small entrepreneurs they would have the chance to develop into legal traders, which could then have a regional effect similar to the transit services along the road between the German-Polish border and Poznan in Poland. The ultimate economic stimulus would be political links with the European Union and relations between Belarus and the European Union that are based on trust.

NOTES

1 Ulachovi , Uladzimir: "David ohne Goliath" In: *Konturen und Kontraste, Belarus sucht sein Gesicht. Osteuropa, Volume, No. 2,* 2004 p. 212

2 Neumann, Frank: "Der Transformationsverlauf in Belarus und Perspektiven". In: *Belarus, Zwischenbilanz einer stornierten Transformation. Osnabrücker Studien Volume 18.* Osnabrück 2001, p. 264

3 Medvedev, Vitalij: "Aktuelle Wirtschaftslage". In: *Belarus, Zwischenbilanz einer stornierten Transformation. Osnabrücker Studien Volume 18.* Osnabrück 2001, p. 215

4 Neumann, Frank: "Der Transformationsverlauf in Belarus und Perspektiven". In: *Belarus, Zwischenbilanz einer stornierten Transformation. Osnabrücker Studien Volume 18.* Osnabrück 2001, p. 268

5 Neumann, Frank: "Der Transformationsverlauf in Belarus und Perspektiven". In: *Belarus, Zwischenbilanz einer stornierten Transformation. Osnabrücker Studien Volume 18.* Osnabrück 2001, p. 279

6 Straz Graniczna Rzeczypospolitej (Border Control of the Polish Republic)

7 Krzysztof Kolanowski: *Wartezeitenanalyse bei der Abfertigung am Grenzübergang Kukuryki – Koslowitschi,* Europa-Universität Viadrina, Frankfurt (Oder), November, 2002, p. 4

8 Krzysztof Kolanowski: *Wartezeitenanalyse bei der Abfertigung am Grenzübergang Kukuryki – Koslowitschi,* Europa-Universität Viadrina, Frankfurt (Oder), November, 2002, p. 10

9 Helmut Dietrich: „The New Border Regime at Bug River, FFM". In: *Statewatch Bulletin Vol. 13,* Januar–Februar 2003

10 Helmut Dietrich: „The New Border Regime at Bug River, FFM". In: *Statewatch Bulletin Vol. 13,* Januar–Februar 2003

11 Alexander Sergej, Deputy Mayor of Brest, at a meeting in Brest, October 2003

12 Krzysztof Kolanowski, *Wartezeitenanalyse bei der Abfertigung am Grenzübergang Kukuryki – Koslowitschi,* Europa-Universität Viadrina, Frankfurt (Oder), November, 2002, p. 20

13 Current and future technical assistance to Belarus, http://europa.eu.int/comm/external_relations/belarus/intro/

14 Related links by the European Union: http://www.europa.eu.int/comm/world/enp/document_en.htm http://www.europa.eu.int/comm/enlargement/index_en.html, http://www.europa.eu.int/comm/external_relations/index.htm

15 Wider Europe: Commission to strengthen cross-border cooperation with new neighbours, press release by the EU, DN:IP/03/922 Date: 01/07/2003, Brussels, July, 2003, http://europa.eu.int/comm/enlargement/docs/news.htm

16 Current and future technical assistance to Belarus, http://europa.eu.int/comm/external_relations/belarus/intro/

17 The EU's relations with Belarus, http://europa.eu.int/comm/external_relations/belarus/intro/

18 The EU's relations with Belarus, http://europa.eu.int/comm/external_relations/belarus/intro/

19 The EU's relations with Belarus, http://europa.eu.int/comm/external_relations/belarus/intro/

20 http://www.fez.brest.by/place/brest.html,en,

21 Peculiarities of taxation of free economic zones for residents of the Republic of Belarus. Minister of Foreign Affairs of the Republic of Belarus

14 Verwandte Links auf den Webseiten der Europäischen Union: http://www.europa.eu.int/comm/world/enp/document_en.htm
http://www.europa.eu.int/comm/enlargement/index_en.html, http://www.europa.eu.int/comm/external_relations/index.htm

15 Wider Europe: Commission to strengthen cross-border cooperation with new neighbours, Presseerklärung der EU, DN:IP/03/922 vom: 01/07/2003, Brüssel, Juli 2003, http://europa.eu.int/comm/enlargement/docs/news.htm

16 Derzeitige und zukünftige Hilfe für Weißrussland, http://europa.eu.int/comm/external_relations/belarus/intro/

17 Die Beziehungen der EU zu Weißrussland, http://europa.eu.int/comm/external_relations/belarus/intro/

18 Die Beziehungen der EU zu Weißrussland, http://europa.eu.int/comm/external_relations/belarus/intro/

19 Die Beziehungen der EU zu Weißrussland, http://europa.eu.int/comm/external_relations/belarus/intro/

20 http://www.fez.brest.by/place/brest.html,en,

21 Peculiarities of taxation of free economic zones for residents of the Republic of Belarus. Außenministerium der Republik Weißrussland

22 Minimum Wages. EU Member States and Candidate Countries, Januar 2003, Katalognr. KS-NK-03-010-EN-C, www.europa.eu.int/comm/eurostat

23 Poland's Row With Belarus To Affect Visa Policy, 21/07/2005, RFE/RL, http://www.charter97.org/eng/news/2005/06/13/czech

24 David Ferguson, Minsk & Warsaw fight, 27/07/2005, Euro-reporters, http://www.charter97.org/eng/news/2005/06/13/czech

22 Minimum Wages – EU Member States and Candidate Countries, January 2003, Catalogue No KS-NK-03-010-EN-C, www.europa.eu.int/comm/eurostat

23 Poland's Row With Belarus To Affect Visa Policy, 21/07/2005, RFE/RL, http://www.charter97.org/eng/news/2005/06/13/czech

24 David Ferguson, Minsk & Warsaw fight, 27/07/2005, Euro-reporters, http://www.charter97.org/eng/news/2005/06/13/czech

EUROPEAN UNION

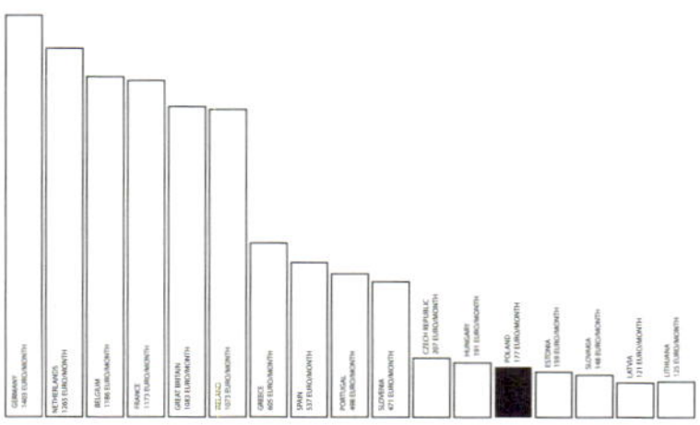

MINIMUM WAGES IN THE EU 2004

POLAND 177 EURO/MONTH

CORPORATE TAX:

POLAND 19-40%
GERMANY 15-42%

AVERAGE EFFECTIVE MARGINAL TAX RATE IN THE EU

EU AVERAGE MARGINAL TAX 24.30%

Karte Map: Tatsiana Keskevich, Martin Cagno
Graphische Überarbeitung Graphical revision: Rainer Mühr

FEZ BREST

OPERATION START: 1997 INVESTMENT: APPROX. 130 MILLION DOLLARS

19 COUNTRIES INVESTING

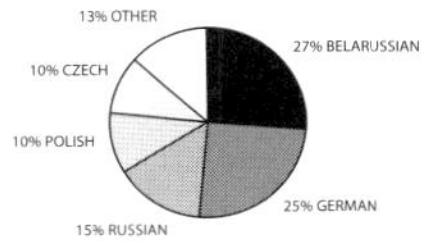

FEZ MINIMUM TAX 7.5%

AFTER A FIVE-YEAR-DUTY-FREE PERIOD FEZ "BREST" RESIDENTS THAT PROVIDE NOT LESS THAN 70% OF PRODUCTION MANUFACTURED IN FEZ "BREST" FOR EXPORT PURPOSES PAY 50% FROM AN ESTABLISHED FOR FEZ RESIDENTS TAX RATE (7.5 %).

MINIMUM WAGE 2003:

BELARUS 19 EURO/MONTH

CORPORATE TAX:

BELARUS 30%

EXISTING FEZ RESIDENTS

92 COMPANIES

FE AG MAR BEL: CABINET FURNITURE, FE ADA: HOUSEHOLD, SANITARY AND TOILET ACCESSORIES, FE ANNA-2002: MEAT PRODUCTS, JV ANREX: LAMINATED BOARDS FE ARMITA: CDS AND CD BOXES, FE ASE GROUP: LUMBER, FE ASTERISK: WOOD GLUED BARS, FE BALSAM SPORT: DESIGNING AND SEWING OF SPORTS WEAR JV BAHPOL: PET FILM AND FLEXOGRAPHICAL PRINTING, JV BELBARD: CHOCOLATES WITH FRUIT STUFFING, FE BELDENSAN: MEAT HALF-PREPARED FOODS, FE BELZA: HYGIENIC ARTICLES, FE BELKA-CARGO TRUCK TRANSPORTATION, BELARUSIAN COFFEE COMPANY LTD.: CHOCOLATE, FE BELPLANK: WOOD WORKING, JV BELROSPRODUCT: MEAT PRODUCTS, FE BELS: OFFICE FURNITURE, JV BELTRANSOIL: PETROLEUM PROCESSING, JV BELEXPOMOS: SMOKED AND HALF-PREPARED MEATS, JV BLACK RED WHITE: FURNITURE, FE SHARDO: DRY GRAPE VINES AND SUGAR SYROPS, FE BREST PHARMA INTERNATIONAL CO.: SALES OF MEDICINS AND COSMETICS, PC BREST OPTIMAL FEZ: POSTFORMING AND WOOD PARTICLES BOARDS, BRESTFEZINVEST: BANKING SERVICES, PC VARIANT PLUS: PRINTING AND PUBLISHING, FE VASTEGA: PRESERVING VEGETABLES AND MUSHROOMS IN TINS AND CANS, VEGAS LTD.: MATTRASSES, FE VECTOR: EQUIPMENT FOR RAILWAY CARS, PC VIESTA: FURNITURE, FE VOGAZ: GAZ CONSUMPRION METERS AND FITTINGS FOR INDUSTRIAL USE, JV VOX: SIDING, JV VESKOBEL: LIGHTING APPLIANCES FOR INDUSTRIAL USE, FE GALA: PLUSH FABRIC, JV GALANA: REFRIGERATING EQUIPMENT, PC GEFEST-KVARTS: WORKED GLASS, PC GEFEST-TECHNIKA: HOUSEHOLD EQUIPMENT AND KITCHEN AIR PURIFYERS, JV DELFA-BUG: INTERIOR ARTICLES, FE JOFRE LABORTECHNIC: ELECTRONIC INSTRUMENTS AND EQUIPMENT, FE DINGO ROSS: ARTICLES FOR PETS, JV DISKOM: VARNISHES, PAINTS AND ENAMELS, ROAD CONSTRUCTION UNIT DSPMK-27: ASPHALT, JV EURO TRADE BREST: FISH PROCESSING PRODUCTION FACILITIES, FE EUROBYKE: MANUFACTURE OF BYKES, JV EUROSTEKLO: GLASS BULBS AND TUBES FOR ELECTRIC LAMPS, JV INVOLUX: FURNITURE, FE INCO: MEAT PRODUCTS, FE INCO FOOD: MANUFACTURE AND WHOLESALE TRADING IN MEATS, PC INTERMEBEL: CABINET FURNITURE, JV KANTAL SOYUZ: ARTICLES IN PVC, FE [illegible]: FOOD CONCENTRATED MIXTURES, JV MORFISH: FISH PROCESSING, FE CONDOR: VARNISHES AND PAINTS, FE KONSANT: MEAT PRODUCTS, KORDEL LTD.: FLUORESCENT LIGHTING APPLIANCES, JV MEBELUX BREST: OFFICE FURNITURE, JV MZEP-[illegible]: ELECTRIC METERS, MICROSPHERA LTD.: PROCESSING OF BROKEN GLASS AND GLASS BALLS, JV MLECH: POTATOES HALF-PREPARED PRODUCTS, NIKOR LTD.: DOORS, WINDOWS, CARPENTER'S WORK, JV OKNEST: WINDOW BLOCKS, OLGA-1 LTD.: REPAIR AND RESTORATION OF TRUCK TYRES, PC OMEGA-PAK: PLASTIC ARTICLES, FE PASTER[illegible]: PLASTIC GOODS (BRUSHES, BROOMS), PC [illegible] EUROMEBEL: COVERS FOR UPHOLSTERED FURNITURE, JV PLASTOIL: PLASTIC PACKAGING, AGRICULTURAL UNIT POGRANICHNIK: AGRICULTURAL PRODUCTS, FE PROMTECHNIKA: MANUFACTURING OF REFRIGERATING EQUIPMENT FOR DAIRY FARMS, FE [illegible]: CLOSING, FE SABRINA: HOSIERY (TIGHTS IN LYCRA), JV SANTA BREMOR: FISH PROCESSING, FE SANTIBEL: LADIES CLOSING, JV SILECT: SYSTEMS OF ELECTRIC MOTOR PERFOMANCE CONTROL, JV SKIN: WOOD WORKING (DOORS AND DOOR BLOCKS), SOFTLINE LTD.: DEVELOPING AND PUTTING IN OPERATION INFORMATION SYSTEMS, SOYUZPROMLEASING: FINANCIAL LEASING, JV SPOL BREST: DROPPERS, FE SPUTNIK: TOILET PAPER, FE STARFOOD: MEATS, COCOA AND CHOCOLATE, STIM LTD.: EQUIPMENT AND MACHINERY FOR ROAD TRAFFIC MARKING, JV BRESTEURORAPS: PRODUCTION OF BIODIESEL, JV TALAN: CABINET FURNITURE AND CONSUMER GOODS, JV TREPLAST: FLUORESCENT LIGHTING APPLIANCES FOR INDUSTRIAL AND PUBLIC USE, JV UNIBEL: MACARONI, FE UNIVERSAL LUX: BISCUITS AND CRACKERS, UNIVERSAL SYSTEM LTD.: WALL AND ROOF SANDWICH BOARDS, JV FA-UN: PHARMACEUTICALS, JV FORMULA PLUS: PHARMACEUTICALS, FE FOODLINE: CRISPS, JV KHAMELEON: DETERGENTS, CLEANING AND POLISHING SUBSTANCES, FE HARVEST: SEWING OF BEDDING, FE TCHORNY KRASNY BELY: LAMINATED BOARDS AND FURNITURE, JV SHATTOYS: PUBLICITY ITEMS AND TOYS IN LATEX, EDEM LTD.: LADIES CLOSING, JV YUREX: SPEAKERS CASES AND COMPONENTS, FE YAROCHIN STYL: OFFICE FURNITURE

EU-INVESTITION IN DIE FESTUNG EUROPA – HERSTELLUNG DER GRENZE
EU INVESTMENT IN THE FORTRESS EUROPE – BUILDING THE BORDER

31 MILLION

Stärkung der EU-Grenze seit 2002:
Das PHARE 2001- und 2002-Programm (Teil I) für Polen umfasst 450 Millionen Euro. 77 Millionen davon sind für die Justiz, Innere Sicherheit und den Zoll vorgesehen. Die Grenzkontrollen und der Kampf gegen Kriminalität erhalten 31 Millionen Euro für hochentwickelte Technologie zur Grenzkontrolle, sowie Computer und Glasfaser zum Datentransfer. Das sind die größten individuellen Programme in der Geschichte der PHARE-Programme.

Strengthening the EU border from 2002
PHARE 2001 and 2002 (Part I) for Poland encompass 450 million Euro. 77 million of those are allocated to Justice and Home affairs as well as customs. Border control and fight against crime receive 31 million Euro, for equipment like high technology for border control as well as computers, software and fibre optics for data transfer. These are the largest individual projects in the history of the PHARE programme.

EU-INVESTITIONEN IN DIE PERFORATION DER GRENZE
EU INVESTMENT IN THE PERFORATION OF THE BORDER

45 MILLION

Nachbarschaftsprogramm mit Weißrussland 2001–2005:
Tacis Nationale Programme: 15 Millionen, Tacis Nukleare Sicherheit: 3 Millionen, Tacis CBC: 17,2 Millionen, CBC SPF: 0,64 Millionen, Tacis Regionale Programme: 9,6 Millionen

Neighbourhood Programs with Belarus 2001–2005:
Tacis National Programme: 15 million, Tacis Nuclear Safety: 3 million, Tacis CBC: 17,2 million, CBC SPF: 0,64 million, Tacis Regional Programme: 9,6 million

„AMEISENHANDEL" BREST
"ANT TRADE" BREST

BREST TRAIN STATION.

WAITING ROOM OF THE TR
STATION. PEOPLE MOVE
A WOMAN WITH A BIG B

PEOPLE OPEN THE PLASTIC PACKAGES AND PUT ON THE CLOTHING FROM IT.

"DUTY FREE". HERE THEY BUY 1 LITRE OF VODKA AND 1,5 BLOCKS OF CIGARETTES.

FROM THE SHOP THEY
INTO THE TRAIN

THEY ARE HIDING VODKA AND CIGARETTES FROM THE CUSTOMS INSPECTORS.

ALL OF THEM GET PLASTIC PACKAGES. THE WOMAN IS WRITING NOTES IN A LITTLE BOOK.

FROM THE WAITING
ROOM THEY
ARE GOING TO THE
BREST
PASSPORT CONTROL.

IN THE TRAIN THEY ARE NOT SITTING, BUT MOVE AND TALK WITH EACH OTHER.

TERESPOL… PEOPLE GET OUT
AND COME TO ANOTHER WOMAN
AND GIVE HER THE PACKAGES.

THEN THEY ARE GOING TO SELL
VODKA AND CIGARETTES…

… IT IS POSSIBLE TO CROSS THE
BORDER WITH A MAXIMUM OF 50 KG
OF GOODS PER PERSON… PEOPLE SEARCH
"PODSADKA".

THEY GET A FREE RIDE ACR
THE BORDER WHILE THE DRIV
ARE ALLOWED TO CA
SOME EXTRA KG OF GOO

AND WHAT THEN?

PLE WALK THE 3 KM FROM
TRAIN STATION TO VEHICLE
SSING POINT …

IN THE TWO QUEUES IN FRONT OF THE BORDER ARE SEVERAL CARS FROM BREST.

CARS CROSSING THE
BORDER
PASSPORT CONTROL.
THEY ARE
MOVING BACK … TO
BREST.

WE GUESS THAT THEY GO BACK TO THE TRAIN STATION TO MAKE THIS CIRCLE AGAIN!

Olag Shchukina and Diane Pfeifer

URBANE KULTUR IM POSTKOMMUNISMUS

POST-COMMUNIST URBAN CULTURE

► WARSCHAU ► WARZAW

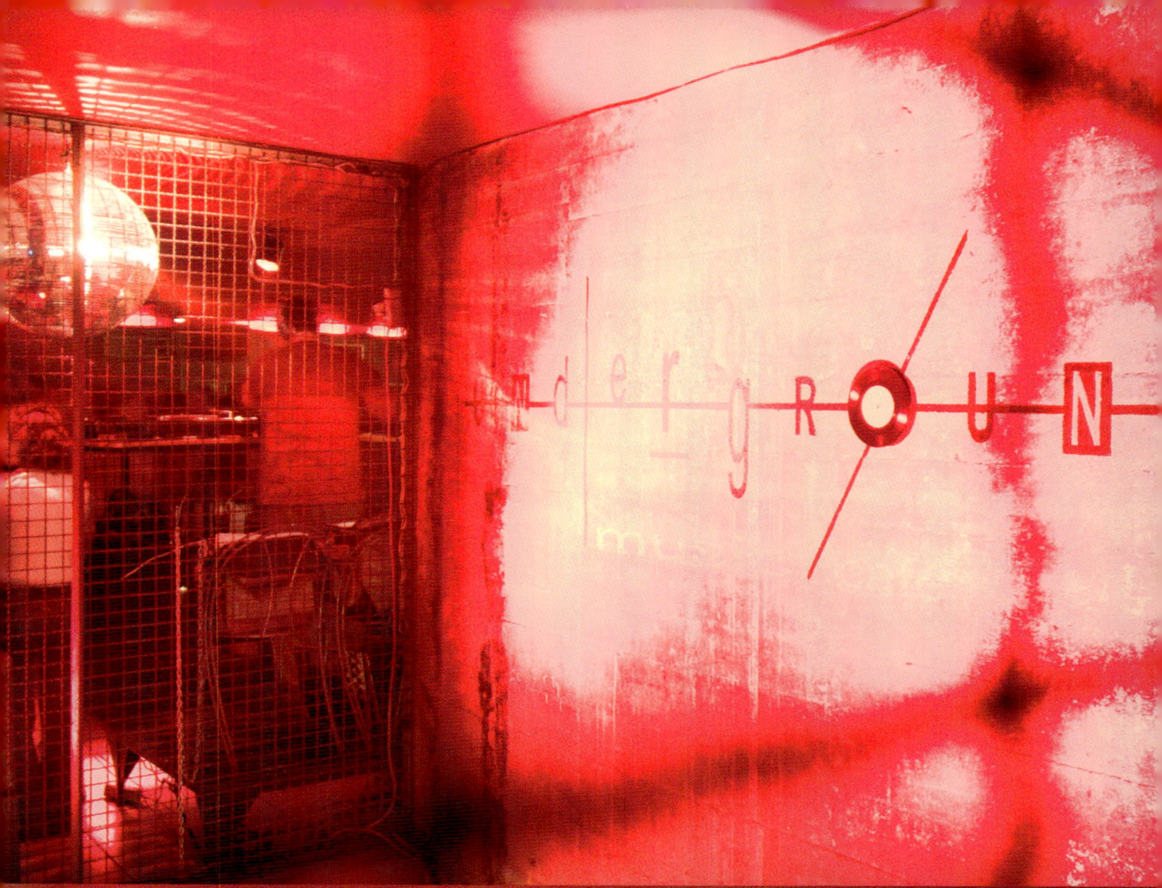

Koneser
WARSZAWSKA WYTWÓRNIA WÓDEK

FUNDACJA ARTBARBAKAN

SKLEP

▸ MOSKAU ▸ MOSCOW

ТЫ SУПЕРМОДЕЛЬ
СМОТРИ СТС

20-22 МАРТА
ЭТАП КУБКА МИРА
«МОСКОВСКАЯ САБЛЯ»
СЕВЕРНОЕ ЧЕРТАНОВО, кор. 806
ФИНАЛ - 21 МАРТА В 17.00
КИНОЗАЛ ГОСТИНИЦЫ «КОСМОС»
ПРОСПЕКТ МИРА, 150 (м. ВДНХ)
СПОРТ
NOKIA
50 000$
Panasonic ideas for life

www.fcdinamo.ru

URBANE KULTUREN IN DER POSTSOWJETISCHEN EPOCHE – SYMBOLISCHE PRODUKTIONEN UND DIE DYNAMIK DER MACHT

POST-SOVIET URBAN CULTURES: SYMBOLIC PRODUCTIONS, DYNAMICS OF POWER

GENERATION WARSCHAU

WARSAW GENERATION

GENTRIFIZIERUNG IN PRAGA – WARSCHAU ENTDECKT SEINE ANDERE SEITE

GENTRIFICATION IN PRAGA – WARSAW DISCOVERS ITS OTHER SIDE

DIE RUSSEN KOMMEN! ÜBER DIE GLOBALISIERUNG DES „PRINZIPS ABRAMOWITSCH“

THE RUSSIANS ARE COMING! ON THE GLOBALISATION OF THE „ABRAMOVICH PRINCIPLE“

URBANE KULTUREN IN DER POSTSOWJETISCHEN EPOCHE – SYMBOLISCHE PRODUKTIONEN UND DIE DYNAMIK DER MACHT

ELENA TRUBINA

EINLEITUNG

Die Analyse des städtischen Raums beschäftigt sich mit den komplexen Beziehungen zwischen Gesellschaft, Gemeinschaft und Kultur. In meinem Beitrag möchte ich zeigen, wie auf unterschiedliche Weise urbane Kulturen, so wie sie von den betroffenen Bürgern wahrgenommen und von Wissenschaftlern beschrieben werden, gesellschaftliche Veränderungen erklären können. Gesellschaftliche Veränderungen im postsowjetischen Raum weisen in unterschiedlichste Richtungen – von hoffnungsvoll bis verstörend. Dieser Raum besteht aus den „Systemen der Städte"[1] und den „Verkehrskorridoren"[2], die diese Städte verbinden. Abgesehen davon, dass die Städte vielen neuen Bürgern eine Heimstatt bieten und einen raschen Wandel durchlaufen, der alle Bürger betrifft, sind sie in eine neue Phase eines intensiven Wettbewerbs untereinander eingetreten. Dieser Wettbewerb findet auf nationaler Ebene (wie beispielsweise zwischen den beiden russischen Städten St. Petersburg und Moskau) und auf internationaler Ebene statt und schließt auch neue Ansätze der Stadtverwaltungen zur Bewältigung der Herausforderungen des postindustriellen Zeitalters mit ein.
Im Prozess der laufenden Umgestaltung der Städte verknüpfen sich neue soziale und räumliche Strukturen. Die Umgestaltung der Welt durch die Globalisierung hatte nicht nur einen Wandel in der Ökonomie, sondern auch in der Kultur zur Folge. So wie das System der Städte die komplexe Wechselwirkung verschiedener politischer, ökonomischer und kultureller Kräfte produziert und reproduziert, so findet in diesem System auch die wichtigste kulturelle Entwicklung statt, und zwar die Kommerzialisierung der Kultur. Die Kulturen der postsowjetischen Städte reflektieren zwar ganz offensichtlich die beiden Extreme materieller Wohlstand und soziale Ausgrenzung, stellen aber den vorhandenen analytischen Rahmen in Frage, da sie zunehmend von international vernetzten sozialen Prozessen beeinflusst werden. Was in der Literatur als „Intensivierung des Bewusstseins der Welt als Ganzes"[3] bezeichnet wird und vielleicht Verkehr von Träumen und Wünschen, Ambitionen und verlorenen Hoffnungen genannt werden könnte, manifestiert sich in neuen Gebäuden, auf den Straßen, bei Kulturveranstaltungen, in der Lokalpolitik und im Denken der Stadtbewohner. Während sich viele Städte rasch in Konsumzentren verwandeln, verfolgen sie unterschiedliche Strategien, um Teil des Orbis terrarum und in gewisser Weise global konsumiert zu werden. Die Marketingbemühungen der Städte spiegeln die Konfigurationen kultureller Beziehungen und die Zirkulation der Macht in den Städten wider, die den Erfolg oder Misserfolg dieser Maßnahmen bestimmen. Die Konzeptualisierung der „ur-

POST-SOVIET URBAN CULTURES – SYMBOLIC PRODUCTIONS, DYNAMICS OF POWER

ELENA TRUBINA

INTRODUCTION

Urban analysis concerns itself with the complex relationships between society, community, and culture. In this essay I show, how, in different ways, urban cultures, as they are perceived by locals and described by scholars, allow accounting for social change. Social change on the post-Soviet space takes many directions, from hopeful to disturbing ones. This space is comprised from "the systems of cities"[1] and "the transport corridors"[2] that are stretched between those cities. Except the fact that the cities provide a home for many new citizens and rapidly change for all their citizens, they've entered a new phase of intense inter-city competition. This competition takes place nationally (as between two Russian capitals, St. Petersburg and Moscow) and internationally which involves new approaches undertaken by city governments in order to cope with the challenges of post-industrial era.

In the process of cities on-going reshaping, new social and spatial structures become intertwined. The transformation of the world due to globalisation involved a change not only in economic circuits but in cultural ones as well. As the system of cities produces and reproduces the complex interaction of different political, economical and cultural forces, it is within it that the most important cultural tendency now takes place, namely, the commercialisation of culture. The cultures of the post-Soviet cities, while obviously reflecting the extremes of material prosperity and social exclusion, challenge the existing analytical frames by being affected by the increasingly interconnected world-wide social processes. What is referred to in the literature as "the intensification of the consciousness of the world as a whole"[3] and might be called the traffic of dreams and desires, ambitions and lost hopes – becomes embodied in new buildings, on city streets, in cultural events, local politics, and city dwellers' mindsets. While rapidly transforming themselves into spaces of consumption, many cities implement different strategies in order to become part of global orbit and, in a sense, to be consumed globally. The city-marketing efforts mirror the configurations of cultural relations and the circulation of power in the cities, determining success or failure of these efforts. Conceptualising "urban cultures" along with city-marketing efforts necessitates a level of analysis informed but not exhausted by reference to arts, subcultures, or pop culture. This allows, I believe, to grasp a complex dialectic of controlled and uncontrolled tendencies at play as new attitudes and practices of elites and broad public continue emerging. What I, in particular, mean is that, regardless of the "hard" economic necessities and local politics, the cities and the ties

banen Kulturen" zusammen mit städtischen Vermarktungsbemühungen erfordert ein analytisches Niveau, das auf Kunst, Subkulturen oder Pop-Kultur Bezug nimmt, sich jedoch nicht darin erschöpft. Damit lässt sich meiner Meinung nach eine komplexe Dialektik kontrollierter und unkontrollierter Tendenzen im Gefüge erfassen, während sich weiterhin neue Haltungen und Praktiken der Eliten und der breiten Öffentlichkeit herausbilden. Mir geht es dabei insbesondere darum, dass unabhängig von „harten" ökonomischen Zwängen und lokaler Politik die Städte und die Bindungen zwischen ihnen zunehmend von der neuen urbanen Imagination[4] erfasst werden. Mit anderen Worten: Die imaginären Bindungen zwischen den Städten sowie die imaginären Investitionen von Politikern, Unternehmern und Bewohnern in Vergangenheit und Gegenwart gewinnen an Bedeutung und beeinflussen das gesamte Spektrum der Lebensstile, Gewohnheiten und Sitten der sozialen Gruppen. In theoretischer Hinsicht ist mein Vorschlag in einer Tradition zu orten, die im Werk von Henri Lefebvre[5] verankert ist, jedoch auch in hohem Maße die Theorie des Konsums sowie Cornelius Castoriadis[6] und Pierre Bourdieu[7] einbezieht, wo Imagination sowohl sozial konstruiert als auch sich der sozialen Logik entziehend gesehen wird. In dieser Tradition umfassen die Symbole politischer Herrschaft, kultureller Utopien und Phantasien sowie Wünsche und Vergnügungen von Individuen „Produkte der Imagination", wie Lefebvre sie nennt,[8] die die Beziehungen zwischen den Stadtbewohnern und den Städten untereinander bestimmen.

Meine Analyse konzentriert sich zwar auf die urbanen Kulturen Moskaus, doch sollten für diesen Beitrag auch eine Reihe von Schlüsselthemen der allgemeinen Entwicklung postsowjetischer Urbanität herausgearbeitet werden, auch wenn eine gründliche Diskussion hier nicht möglich ist: Nach der EU-Erweiterung sind die postsowjetischen Städte Teil eines komplizierten Beziehungsgeflechts geworden und werden von verschiedenen Kräften angetrieben, jedoch hängt der Einfluss, den die Globalisierung auf sie hat, größtenteils von den spezifischen Bedingungen und der konkreten Geschichte einer Stadt ab. Das offenkundige Kennzeichen der neuen Zeiten in den meisten Städten ist die neue Ungleichheit (auf die oberen fünf bis zehn Prozent der Haushalte entfallen etwa die Hälfte der Konsumausgaben einer Region); obwohl die meisten der in den letzten Jahren von den Regierungen in Osteuropa getroffenen politischen Entscheidungen die zentrifugalen Tendenzen zwischen den Ländern fördern (in einigen Fällen ist das der Wettbewerb um EU-Mittel, in anderen geht es um das Versagen der Regierungen bei der Neuausrichtung überkommener Beziehungsprinzipien vor dem Hintergrund der neuen internationalen Gegebenheiten) und infolgedessen Länderbeziehungen einen geringen Stellenwert haben, demonstrieren die Städte beim Durchlaufen ähnlicher Transformationsprozesse nachdrücklich die Gemeinsamkeit ihrer Erfolge und Probleme.

MOSKAU ALS MÖCHTEGERN-METROPOLE

Am 6. Juli 2005 transportierten Busse Massen von vermeintlich begeisterten Unterstützern der Bewerbung Moskaus um die nächsten Olympischen Spiele auf den Roten Platz. Die Organisatoren wollten offensichtlich die Gelegenheit nicht ungenutzt lassen, die Präsenz von zahlreichen Moskauern zu einem solch besonderen Anlass zu inszenieren. Immer dann, wenn der Enthusiasmus von Massen vorzuführen ist, mobi-

that unite them become increasingly affected by the new urban imagination.[4] Put differently, the imaginary ties between the cities as well as imaginary investments in the past and present made by politicians, businessmen and city residents become important, affecting the entire spectrum of lifeways, customs, and mores of the social groups. Theoretically, my suggestion locates itself in a tradition, anchored in the work of Henri Lefebvre[5] but which includes much theory of consumption as well as Cornelius Castoriadis[6] and Pierre Bourdieu[7], which sees imagination as both socially constructed and escaping the social logic. According to this tradition, the symbols of political domination, cultural utopias and fantasies, individuals' desires and pleasures comprise "products of imagination", as Lefebre calls them[8], that govern the relationships of city dwellers and cities to themselves and others.

While the main focus of my analysis is Moscow's urban cultures, for the purposes of this essay a number of key themes concerning the general development of the post-Soviet urbanity should be stressed, although they can not be discussed here in depth: after the EU enlargement, the post-Soviet cities have entered the complex network of relations and are driven by various forces, yet the impact globalisation has on each of them depends largely on particular conditions and particular history of a city in question; the obvious sign of the new times in most cities is the new inequality (the top 5-10 per cent of households are responsible for about a half the region's consumer spending); although the vast majority of the policies implemented in recent years by the East-European governments facilitate the centrifugal tendencies between the countries (in some cases it is the competition for the EU recourses, while in some it is the governments' failure to re-think the old principles of relationships in light of the new international realities), and, as a result, inter-country relations remain low, the cities as they undergo very similar transformations powerfully demonstrate the commoness of their achievements and predicaments.

MOSCOW AS WANNABEE CITY

On July 6th, 2005, the buses have brought to Krasnaya Ploschad what were supposed to be the crowds of enthusiastic supporters of Moscow's winning the right to be a city of the next Olympics. The organisers apparently didn't want to miss the opportunity to create a moment of intense co-presence of great many Muscovites during a very special event. When there is a need to demonstrate enthusiasm of the masses, the college and high school students are usually mobilised by authorities in Russia. But it's summer, the college students are all gone and the high school graduates are busy preparing to their enrollment exams. The authorities obviously had a hard time finding enough "supporters" among those who work in the state-financed institutions and among the stuff of the municipal maintenance offices. The architectural treasures of the Red Square were minutes away, the Kremlin, too, was close enough, and the huge plasma screen was broadcasting the beginning of the ceremony of voting from Singapore. The city's expected victory over New York, Paris, Madrid and London was supposed to both prompt people's identification with their nation and their city and to place them within the global context. Then, when Moscow has lost during the first round of voting, the organisers simply shot down the direct translation from Singapore to prevent people from knowing the truth. The gathering in Moscow

lisieren die russischen Behörden gern Schüler und Studenten. Aber es war Sommer, die Studenten waren weg, und die Abiturienten bereiteten sich auf ihre Hochschulaufnahmeprüfungen vor. Den Behörden fiel es offenkundig schwer, genügend „Unterstützer" unter den Angestellten der staatlichen Einrichtungen und der städtischen Verwaltung zu finden. Die architektonischen Sehenswürdigkeiten des Roten Platzes und der Kreml sind nur wenige Schritte entfernt. Auf einem Plasmagroßbildschirm wurde der Beginn der Abstimmung in Singapur übertragen. Moskaus erwarteter Sieg über New York, Paris, Madrid und London sollte sowohl die Identifikation einer breiten Öffentlichkeit mit der Nation und der Stadt fördern als auch ihren Platz im globalen Kontext zeigen. Als Moskau dann in der ersten Abstimmungsrunde ausschied, unterbrachen die Organisatoren einfach die Liveübertragung aus Singapur, weil niemand etwas mitbekommen sollte. Die Veranstaltung in Moskau ging weiter, und zwei Stunden lang wurde die Hoffnung genährt, den Wettbewerb noch zu gewinnen, bevor dann bekannt wurde, dass für Moskau alles vorbei war. Am Wassiljewski Spusk, da wo Paul McCartney und andere Weltstars Konzerte gegeben hatten, war eine Bühne aufgebaut, die in den Farben der russischen Flagge weiß-rot-blau dekoriert war, und von dort rief der Animateur in regelmäßigen Abständen: „Unsere Stadt ist die beste der Welt!" und „Wollt ihr, dass Moskau Gastgeber der Olympischen Spiele wird?!"[9] Diese Frage, die ein angeheuerter Showstar an teilnahmeverpflichtete Bürger richtete, steht beispielhaft für die Art und Weise, in der Bürgerbeteiligung in postsowjetischen Städten betrieben wird.

Nun könnte man sagen, dass abgesehen von dem beispiellosen Zynismus des Umgangs mit Menschen diese „Aktion" eine der vielen, durchaus üblichen Kampagnen zur Stimmungsmache war. Es ist ja doch nichts Ungewöhnliches daran, dass ein paar politische Parteien versuchen, die Aufmerksamkeit der Medien auf sich zu ziehen, indem sie ihre Mitglieder auf dem Roten Platz antreten lassen. Ich behaupte jedoch, dass diese Art, sich in den globalen Strömungen der Gegenwart auszudrücken, für dieses Volk und für diese Stadt charakteristisch und aus Sowjetzeiten überkommen ist. Die Organisation breitester und begeisterter Zustimmung der Öffentlichkeit, egal wofür, war ein wichtiger Bestandteil der politischen Kultur der Sowjetzeit. Die Legenden vom „besten Land der Welt", dem „Leuchtturm der Freiheit" und „der einzigen Hoffnung aller werktätigen Menschen" waren in der Sowjetzeit allgegenwärtig. Es reichte nicht, das zu wissen, sie mussten auch bei besonderen Anlässen, bei öffentlichen sowjetischen Feiern, vor- und aufgeführt werden. Obwohl sie in der Regel von den Behörden initiiert wurden, sind sie im Gedächtnis der Menschen fest verankert und haben recht starke öffentliche Emotionen freigesetzt. Sie hatten auch damit zu tun, dass die Behörden die Bevölkerung sowohl emotional mobilisieren als auch die Grundwerte des Regimes respektieren lehren wollten. So waren die Feierlichkeiten in den Städten, die ihren Ursprung in vorrevolutionären Zeiten hatten, eine effektive Möglichkeit, lokale und regionale Identitäten mit einer nationalen Identität zu verschmelzen. Infolgedessen sind Feierlichkeiten und Feiern definitiv zum Bestandteil der nationalen Kultur geworden. In der Sowjetzeit wurde Moskau allmählich zu einem Symbol für die Sowjetunion als Ganzes und das sozialistische politische Regime – wobei das Zentrum zahlreiche politische Vertreterrollen zu erfüllen hatte. So entstand als beherrschende politische Legende die Funktion Moskaus als Schaufens-

went on, the hopes to win the competition continued to be expressed for about two hours since it became known that the competition for Moscow is over. On Vassilyevski Spusk (a place where the most famous concerts given by Paul McCartney and other world stars took place), the stage was set, decorated in white, red and blue (the colors of the Russian tricolor flag), from which the animator periodically shouted: "Our city is the best on earth!" and "Do you want Moscow to host the Olympic games?!"[9] There is a sense in which this question, addressed by a hired showman to the citizens who were made to participate in the gathering, comprises the predominant way of citizen participation characteristic for post-Soviet cities.

One might say that, apart from the unprecedented cynicism with which it was handled, this "action" could be counted among numerous traditional booster campaigns. After all, is there something unusual about a couple of political parties wish to get media coverage by bringing their members to the Red Square? However, it is my contention that what one witnesses here is characteristic for this nation and for this city's ways of expressing themselves within contemporary global flows, inherited from the Soviet times. The organisation of wide and enthusiastic people's support (of whatever) comprises an important part of the Soviet-era political culture. The narratives about "the best country in the world", the "beacon of freedom" and "the only hope of all the working people" were prevalent in the Soviet times. It was not enough to know about them, they had to be performed, or enacted through special events, the Soviet public celebrations. Although they were, as a rule, initiated by authorities, they have made their way into people's memories and managed to generate quite powerful public emotions. They also had to do with the authorities' desire both mobilise people emotionally and to educate them with respect to the basic values of the regime. Similarly, the celebrations of the cities that originated in the pre-Revolutionary times were an efficient way to fuse local and regional identities with national identity. As a result, the celebrations and the festivals have definitely become a part of the national culture. During the Soviet times, Moscow has come to symbolise the whole Soviet Union as a country and the socialist political regime and on its center numerous political representations were inscribed. This Moscow's functioning as the country's showcase was the dominant political narrative that was engendered. It was, in a spirit of a medieval world picture, organised around the idea of "center": the Soviet Union was thought to be a center of the world with Moscow being in the center of a center. And just as in Soviet times, for which orientation towards future was characteristic, a desired state of things was very often represented as already having been achieved, we currently see the same political logic at work. The contingency (who was to win was unknown) was out of place in this logic, so it had to be tamed, even if by switching off the TV screens. Being accustomed to the one-directional broadcasting so prevalent in recent times, the one that is implemented by the Kremlin-depended TV channels, the organisers of this show didn't seem to care of what really took place back there in Singapore. The more significant the alienation between the current Kremlin administration and people is getting, the more "staged" the public sphere becomes and the more indifferent the masters of political show-business grow to what people really think and feel. It seems that the crowd-handlers a part of whose rationale this seemingly absurd event comprised were simply expanding the

ter des Landes. Es war dem Geiste nach ein mittelalterliches Weltbild, das sich um die Idee eines „Zentrums" gruppierte: Die Sowjetunion erschien als das Zentrum der Welt und Moskau als das Zentrum des Zentrums. Und wie schon in der Sowjetzeit, für die eine Zukunftsorientierung typisch war, wurde ein wünschenswerter Zustand sehr oft als bereits erreicht dargestellt – wir erleben derzeit die gleiche politische Logik. Unvorhergesehene Ereignisse oder Ergebnisse (es war ja nicht bekannt, wer siegen würde) hatten keinen Platz in dieser Logik, also mussten die Ereignisse gezähmt werden, und sei es dadurch, dass die Bildschirme abgeschaltet wurden. Nach all der Gewöhnung an die in der Gegenwart so dominierende einseitige Fernsehberichterstattung, die von kremlabhängigen Fernsehsendern praktiziert wird, war es den Organisatoren der Show offensichtlich gleichgültig, was wirklich in Singapur passierte. Je größer die Entfremdung zwischen der derzeitigen Kreml-Administration und den Menschen wird, desto „inszenierter" wird der öffentliche Raum und desto gleichgültiger werden die Meister des politischen Showbusiness gegenüber dem, was die Menschen wirklich denken und fühlen. Man hat den Eindruck, dass die Massendompteure, deren Denkungsart dieses offensichtlich absurde Ereignis ermöglichte, für das Mega-Event der Bewerbung um die Olympischen Spiele einfach alle Verfahren und Techniken anwendeten, die ihnen vom Umgang mit internen politischen Ereignissen bereits vertraut waren.

Dieser peinlichen Zurschaustellung öffentlicher Unterstützung ging die Präsentation Moskaus als Austragungsort der Olympischen Spiele, produziert von erfahrenen Regisseuren für die Vorführung in Singapur, voraus. Darin kamen zahlreiche Fakten und kulturelle Ikonen vor, die für Moskau sprachen, wie z. B. das Konzept des Flusses Moskwa als Achse für alle künftigen kompakt stattfindenden Veranstaltungen, das in sehr überzeugender Weise dargestellt wurde. Das half aber auch nicht. Am Ende wurde London zum Gastgeber der Olympischen Spiele 2012 gewählt.[10] New York, Paris und Madrid müssen weiterhin auf ihre Chance warten. Es ist offenkundig, dass einer der Gründe für Moskaus Ausscheiden die unterentwickelte städtische Infrastruktur war. Verkehrsstaus sind ein unvermeidlicher Bestandteil des Alltags hier. Jeder kann sich noch an den Stromausfall im Mai 2005 erinnern. Es gibt praktisch keine erschwinglichen Hotels. Und übrigens sehen die meisten Flächen entlang der Moskwa überhaupt nicht attraktiv aus: Dort befinden sich vor allem Relikte des Industriezeitalters und Brachland.

In gewisser Weise haben diese und viele andere Mängel in Moskaus jüngster Entwicklung mit den vom neuen ökonomischen und politischen Kontext Russlands diktierten Verantwortlichkeiten und den oft verworrenen Beziehungen zwischen der Föderationsregierung und der Moskauer Stadtverwaltung zu tun, besonders wenn es um transnationale Aktivitäten geht. Wurden diese in der Vergangenheit einzig und allein von der Zentralregierung durchgeführt, so schicken Moskau und andere Großstädte heute oft ihre eigenen Vertreter ins Ausland, unterhalten direkte Kontakte mit vielen Regional- und Nationalregierungen und kämpfen um Wirtschaftsunternehmen und Investoren. Moskau kann ohne weiteres zu den „Stadtstaaten" gezählt werden, die um Finanzinvestitionen und eine Gelegenheit zum globalen Auftritt konkurrieren. Die Moskauer Verwaltung muss offensichtlich entscheiden, welche lokalen Gegebenheiten genutzt werden können, um ausländische Investoren zu werben. Eigenstän-

ways they've developed for handling the internal political events to the mega-event of bidding for Olympics.

This awkward performance of people's support was preceded by the presentation of Moscow as prospective home of Olympics that was prepared by skillful directors and shown in Singapore. In it, among many things and cultural icons speaking on favor of Moscow, a concept of Moskva-river as an axis along which all the prospective events would take place in a compact manner was shown in the most favorable light. But that one didn't help either. London has won right to host 2012 Olympics.[10] New York, Paris, Madrid will have to wait for their next chance. One can easily see that one of the reasons why Moscow didn't win was a lack of developed city infrastructure. Traffic jams are, indeed, the unavoidable part of everyday existence there. Everybody remembers the May 2005 blackout. Affordable hotels are impossible to find. And, by the way, most areas along Moskva-rivers don't look very attractive: they are comprised from the relics of the industrial era and empty zones.

To some extent, these and many other flaws of Moscow's recent development have to do with enhanced responsibilities by the new economic and political context Russia now exists in, as well as with, very often confused, relationships between the federal and Moscow government, especially when it comes to transnational activity. If in earlier times it was conducted solely by the federal government, today Moscow and other larger cities often send their own representatives to foreign countries, have direct contacts with a number of regional and national governments, and struggle to attract business and investment. Moscow may well be counted among the "city states" that find themselves in competition for financial investment and for a chance to be seen globally. The challenge for the Moscow government seems to be to decide which of the local conditions should be put to use to attract foreign investment. The independent entrepreneurial activities are too often cut off because of some limitations posed by the federal and municipal governments. Perhaps, this is one of the reasons why the cultural policies in Moscow remain integrated not only with economic development measures but with politics. Better to say, the new economic realities co-exist there (as well as elsewhere) with the growing nationalist sentiments which, as I hinted in my description of the event, very often are shamelessly simulated. What makes Moscow therefore a truly interesting phenomenon is that it is not only an economic necessity but the political needs that lead to a continually simulatable "toughness", "bestness in the world". I would argue that the need to enter the global competition stands in stark contrast to traditional forms of positioning itself as the old capital of empire when the powerfulness of the city, sustained and defended for centuries, went unquestioned and was accepted "by default" both internally and internationally. Since for centuries Moscow has been referred to as the only "city" in the stable Russian urban hierarchy, and since, however reluctant sometimes, the international acceptance of Moscow was, in a sense, inevitable, those who presently try to position it globally seem to be affected by the old political imagery of one reigning city from which power emanates and where all recourses get concentrated. These particular modalities of thinking and imagining don't take into consideration that if there could be one capital of empire, there is "no such entity as a single global city ... : the category global city only makes sense as a component of a global network of strategic sites".[11]

dige unternehmerische Aktivitäten werden nur allzu oft verhindert, weil die Förderationsregierung oder die Kommunalverwaltungen irgendwelche Auflagen verhängen. Vielleicht ist das einer der Gründe, warum die Kulturpolitik in Moskau weiterhin nicht nur in Maßnahmen der Wirtschaftsentwicklung, sondern auch in die Politik selbst eingebunden bleibt. Oder, besser gesagt, die neuen wirtschaftlichen Gegebenheiten gehen einher, so wie überall, mit wachsenden nationalistischen Stimmungen, die oft, wie ich in der Beschreibung der Veranstaltung bereits andeutete, schamlos simuliert werden. Was Moskau deshalb wirklich interessant macht, ist nicht nur eine ökonomische, sondern auch die politische Notwendigkeit, die zu einer ständig simulierbaren „Härte" und „Weltspitzenposition" führt. Ich bin sogar der Meinung, dass die Notwendigkeit der Teilnahme am globalen Wettbewerb im krassen Gegensatz zur traditionellen Positionierung als alter Hauptstadt des Russischen Reiches steht, als Stadt, die ihre Stärke über die Jahrhunderte hinweg aufgebaut und verteidigt hat und deren dominierende Stellung im In- und Ausland völlig fraglos und sozusagen automatisch hingenommen wurde. Da Moskau seit Jahrhunderten als die einzige „Stadt" in der stabilen urbanen Hierarchie Russlands gilt und da, wenn auch gelegentlich mit Widerstreben, die internationale Akzeptanz Moskaus in gewisser Weise unvermeidlich war, stehen diejenigen, die Moskau heute global positionieren wollen, offenbar unter dem Einfluss der alten politischen Bildersprache einer dominierenden Stadt, von der die Macht ausgeht und wo sich alles konzentriert. Dieser spezielle Denkansatz berücksichtigt nicht, dass die Existenz einer Reichshauptstadt bedeutet, dass es „so etwas wie eine einzelne globale Stadt nicht gibt (...). Die Kategorie globale Stadt ist nur als Bestandteil eines globalen Netzwerks strategischer Orte sinnvoll".[11]

John Rennie Short führt Moskau zwar nicht in seiner Liste von „Möchtegern-Metropolen" auf, aber dort (bei Paris, Los Angeles, Chicago, Mailand, Frankfurt, Melbourne und Toronto) kann es sicher angefügt werden. Seiner Meinung nach zählt zu den Kriterien dafür genau die Frage, ob sich eine Stadt um die Austragung der Olympischen Spiele beworben hat oder nicht oder sie in jüngster Vergangenheit sogar ausgerichtet hat. Der Drang einer Stadt ins mediale Scheinwerferlicht, ihr Wunsch nach einer globalen Präsenz und das Bedürfnis der Selbstvermarktung bedeutet: „man hat Metropolenambitionen, auch wenn man es noch nicht ganz geschafft hat".[12] Was die Dinge bei diesem Kriterium etwas kompliziert, ist die Tatsache, dass der Sieger des jüngsten Wettbewerbs, London, es offenkundig schon in die Liga der Weltstädte geschafft hat. Das Problem hier scheint nicht nur etwas mit der Konkurrenz der Städte um wirtschaftliche und symbolische Vorteile zu tun zu haben, die ein solcher Sieg bringt, sondern mit einer nachdrücklicheren und allgemeineren Art der Selbstpositionierung einer Stadt in der Welthierarchie.

Einerseits gibt es bereits ein Netzwerk globaler Städte.[13] Diese Städte sind die Hauptschnittpunkte in funktionierenden Netzwerken globaler Hauptstädte. Andererseits gibt es welche, die Saskia Sassen als bestenfalls mit „globalen Stadtfunktionen ausgestattet", Bob Jessop als „unternehmerische Städte"[14] und Stephen Ward als „globalisierte Städte"[15] beschreiben. Diese aufstrebenden Städte müssen sich nicht nur mit der bestehenden Welthierarchie der Metropolen auseinander setzen, sondern auch mit der Tatsache, dass sie zwar aktiv auf den verschärften Wettbewerb in der Weltwirtschaft reagieren und angestrengt versuchen, ihre Platzierung im Weltsystem zu

John Rennie Short doesn't list Moscow among "wannabee world cities", but it surely can be added to the list he provides (Paris, Los Angeles, Chicago, Milan, Frankfurt, Melbourne, and Toronto). He states that the criteria for it might be exactly whether or not a city applies to host the Olympics or has hosted the games in recent years. A city's need for media coverage, a strong desire to be shown globally, an urge to market itself means "you have world city pretensions, even if you're not quite there".[12] What makes things a bit complicated about this criterion is that the winner of the recent competition – London – is obviously already there, among the world cities. But the problem here seems to be not only related to the competition among city boosters for economic benefits and symbolic gains that a victory of this sort promises to bring but a larger, general way of a city's positioning itself in the world hierarchy.

On the one hand, there is an already existing network of global cities.[13] These cities are the main nods in the functioning networks of global capitals. On the other hand, there are those that Saskia Sassen describes as at best "having global city functions", Bob Jessop as "entrepreneurial cities"[14], and Stephen Ward as "globalized cities"[15]. These aspiring cities have to deal not only with the existing world hierarchy of cities but with the fact that, however actively they try to respond to heightened competition in world economy, however hard they try to modify their placement within the world system, it is not always possible. The obstacles specific for Russia range from "the nomenklatura's passive revolution"[16] which resulted in the development of a largely authoritarian regime which is increasingly growing hostile towards the western investors to the influence of quasi-economic forces that engage in liminal activities in the name of profit. The abundance of casinos in Moscow, in my mind, exemplifies the latter. Those who think that Moscow has already become a "world city" (politicians, cultural entrepreneurs and researchers) usually refer to its great concentration of all economic and financial activity with more than a half of the Russian banks based there, more than a fifth of the Russian retail trade, over one third of its wholesale trade.[17] However, the predominant evaluation that one finds in the literature is that Moscow in its current state is far from being there. In an impressive analysis of comparative data including stock exchange business, headquarters of major banks and headquarters of major corporations that John Short et al. have done, Moscow isn't even mentioned (while Berlin, for instance, is posed as a candidate as a European world city).[18]

Characteristic for globalized cities is "massive upgrading and expansion of certain urban areas, even as large portions of these cities fall into deeper poverty and infrastructural decay".[19] What merits our attention here is how the very functioning of city culture becomes means of expression for world city pretensions when the most "juicy" parts of it are being promoted while those not valuable enough in the eyes of city's or federal officials are left to crumble or to be used differently (mostly, as a space for lease). In this sense, among those portions of the city that are left to decay, may well be counted some former sites of the cultural industry or parts of the city's cultural heritage. To amplify Moscow's competitiveness, the federal government invests significant sums into the restoration of the sites that serve as cultural emblems of the city. In recent years, 500 million dollar were invested into the restoration of the Christ the Savior Cathedral, 320 million dollar to the one of the Big Kremlin Palace. Just recent-

verändern, aber dabei nicht immer Erfolg haben. Die für Russland typischen Hindernisse reichen von der „passiven Revolution der Nomenklatur"[16], die zur Herausbildung eines im Wesentlichen autoritären Regimes führte, das gegenüber westlichen Investoren zunehmend feindselig auftritt, bis zum Einfluss quasi-ökonomischer Kräfte, die im Namen des Profits in kriminelle Machenschaften verwickelt sind. Die in Moskau anzutreffende Fülle von Kasinos macht das meiner Meinung nach deutlich. Wer meint, dass Moskau bereits eine „Weltstadt" geworden ist, wie es beispielsweise der Ansicht von Politikern, Kulturveranstaltern und Wissenschaftlern entspricht, verweist im Allgemeinen auf die große Konzentration ökonomischer und finanzieller Aktivitäten und darauf, dass mehr als die Hälfte aller russischen Banken, mehr als ein Fünftel des russischen Einzelhandels und über ein Drittel des Großhandels hier beheimatet sind.[17] Allerdings überwiegt in der Literatur die Einschätzung, dass Moskau in seiner jetzigen Form weit davon entfernt ist, eine Weltstadt zu sein. In einer eindrucksvollen Analyse von Vergleichsdaten unter Berücksichtigung des Börsenhandels, der Zentralen von Großbanken und Großunternehmen, die John Short u. a. durchgeführt haben, wird Moskau nicht einmal erwähnt (während z. B. Berlin als Kandidat für eine europäische Weltstadt bezeichnet wird).[18]

Charakteristisch für globalisierte Städte ist „die massive Aufwertung und Ausdehnung bestimmter urbaner Räume, selbst dann, wenn große Teile dieser Städte verarmen und die Infrastruktur verfällt".[19] Was unsere Aufmerksamkeit verdient, ist die Art und Weise, wie das Funktionieren der städtischen Kultur zu einem Ausdrucksmittel für den Anspruch wird, Weltstadt zu sein, wenn die „spannendsten" Teile gefördert werden und alles, was in den Augen der Stadtväter oder der Zentralverwaltung nicht attraktiv genug ist, entweder dem Verfall preisgegeben oder umgenutzt wird (meist in Form von Mietflächen). In diesem Sinne gehören zu solchen dem Verfall preisgegebenen Flächen gegebenenfalls auch ehemalige Kulturinstitutionen oder Teile des städtischen Kulturerbes. Zur Verbesserung der Wettbewerbsfähigkeit Moskaus investiert die Föderationsregierung beträchtliche Summen in die Restaurierung von Stätten, die als kulturelle Aushängeschilde der Stadt dienen. In den letzten Jahren wurden z. B. 500 Millionen Dollar in die Wiederherstellung der Christ-Erlöser-Kathedrale und 320 Millionen Dollar in die des Großen Kreml-Palasts investiert. Erst kürzlich wurde mitgeteilt, dass ca. 700 Millionen Dollar für die Restaurierung des Bolschoi-Theaters bereitgestellt werden.[20] Um zu erklären, warum diese Maßnahmen ein Vielfaches der Restaurierung z. B. von Covent Garden (dort war es eine Summe von 360 Millionen Dollar) kosten, verwies ein Journalist einer liberalen russischen Tageszeitung nicht nur darauf, dass das Gebäude heruntergewirtschaftet ist und dass ein Großteil der Arbeiten in unterirdischen Bereichen durchgeführt werden muss, sondern auch auf den berüchtigten Charakterzug der russischen Psyche, immer nur „das Beste in der Welt" haben zu wollen („Wir müssen das Beste haben, was es in der Welt gibt!").[21] Das Bolschoi-Theater ist und bleibt sicherlich eine Stätte der Musik, die für Moskaus globalen Status von Bedeutung ist, und nach seiner Restaurierung wird es weiterhin ein wichtiger Teil der Kulturindustrie der Stadt sein[22], aber trotzdem stellt sich die Frage: Wäre es nicht vernünftiger, etwas bescheidener an die Sache heranzugehen?

Was ich meine, lässt sich vielleicht besser anhand einer Reihe anderer Probleme erklären, vor denen Moskau derzeit im Zusammenhang mit Restaurierungen steht. In

ly it was announced that about 700 million dollar will go to the restoration of Bolschoi Theater.[20] Trying to explain to the readers why it would be so much more expensive to restore Bolshoi than, say, Covent Garden (which cost 360 million dollar), the journalist of the liberal newspaper refers not only to the fact that the building is totally worn out, that the considerable amount of work has to be done underground but to the notorious Russian psychological trait, namely, "bestness in the world" ("We have to have the best things in the world!").[21] Surely, Bolshoi is (and will remain) a musical venue significant for Moscow's global status and, when restored, continue comprising a significant part of the city's cultural economy[22], but the question remains: didn't it make sense to come up with a more modest calculation?

What I imply here can be better explained by reference to a number of other restoration-related predicaments Moscow currently faces. In the letter written by the cultural activists affiliated with the Schusev State Museum of Architecture and posted on the museum's web-site[23], eight political subjects were addressed. The list itself gives a clear idea of a highly hierarchical ordering of management of culture in Moscow. It starts with President Putin, continues with the Government of the Russian Federation, the State Duma of the Russian Federation, the Ministry of Culture of the Russian Federation, the Government of Moscow, the Committee of Culture of the Government of Moscow, and ends with the Committee of Architecture and Urban Planning of the Government of Moscow and the Union of the Russian architects. The authors of the letter consider as "cultural catastrophe" the on-going process of the restructuring of Moscow's city center which resulted in the destruction or loss of a great many historical buildings. Their list is very long, ranging from some buildings located in the Kremlin district through the world-famous constructivist architecture (including the structures designed by Konstantin Melnikov) to the most impressive metro station, Mayakovskaya. What is named in the letter "a total erasure of Moscow splendor" is explained by the continuing processes of pursuing economic profit and redistribution of property. The authors even hint that the recent fire that destroyed the exhibition hall Great Manege was not occasional.

The letter is signed by "Moscow public" which brings us back to the issue of citizens' participation that I briefly mentioned in the beginning of this subchapter. From enthusiastic masses in times of social upheaval to well-groomed indifferent pedestrians skilfully navigating crowded sidewalks, the urban publics, however tangible and visible they might seem, resist conceptualisation. Jeff Weintraub, however, usefully delineates four ways in which the distinctions between "public" and "private" are present in social discourse: (1) the liberal economist model, which distinguishes between state administration as public and the market economy as private; (2) the republican-virtue approach, which sees the political community and citizenship as a primarily "public" realm, as juxtaposed to both state administration and market economy; (3) the approach that sees the "public" as existing in the fluid and polymorphous social relations of a society; and (4) the approach that sees the market economy as "public" and the family as "private".[24] This variety of understandings explains why "the familiar rhetoric that seems to inflame its hearers against a perceived loss or diminution of the public is so potent and profitable. To some, the call to restore the territory of the public will seem as an appeal for a stronger state power. To oth-

einem Brief von Kulturverantwortlichen am Staatlichen Schtschussew-Museum für Architektur, der auf der Website des Museums veröffentlicht wurde[23], werden acht politische Fragen thematisiert. Diese Liste vermittelt einen klaren Eindruck von der hierarchischen Ordnung des Kulturmanagements in Moskau. Es beginnt bei Präsident Putin, geht weiter mit der Regierung der Russischen Föderation, der Staatsduma der Russischen Föderation, dem Ministerium für Kultur der Russischen Föderation, der Moskauer Stadtverwaltung, dem Kulturausschuss der Moskauer Stadtverwaltung und endet beim Komitee für Architektur und Städteplanung der Moskauer Stadtverwaltung und dem Verband russischer Architekten. Die Verfasser des Briefes betrachten den anhaltenden Prozess der Umstrukturierung des Moskauer Stadtzentrums als „kulturelle Katastrophe", die bereits zur Zerstörung und zum Verlust zahlreicher historischer Gebäude geführt hat. Ihre Liste ist sehr lang und reicht von einigen Gebäuden im Kreml-Bezirk über weltberühmte Beispiele der Architektur des Konstruktivismus (darunter auch Bauten nach Plänen von Konstantin Melnikow) bis hin zur eindrucksvollen Metrostation Majakowskaja. Das „totale Auslöschen Moskauer Pracht", so das Schreiben, wird erklärt durch die anhaltenden Prozesse wirtschaftlichen Profitstrebens und der Umverteilung des Eigentums. Die Verfasser deuten sogar an, dass der Brand, der jüngst zur Zerstörung der Ausstellungshalle Große Manege führte, kein Zufall war.
Unterzeichnet ist der Brief mit „Die Öffentlichkeit Moskaus", was uns zu der Frage der bereits am Anfang erwähnten Bürgerbeteiligung zurückführt. Die Öffentlichkeit einer Großstadt, ob sie nun greifbar und sichtbar ist oder nicht, von den begeisterten Massen in den Zeiten des sozialen Umbruchs bis hin zu gepflegt-gleichgültigen Fußgängern, die sich geschickt überfüllte Bürgersteige entlangmanövrieren, entzieht sich der Konzeptualisierung. Jeff Weintraub beschreibt jedoch vier Unterscheidungen zwischen „öffentlich" und „privat" im aktuellen gesellschaftliche Diskurs: erstens, das liberal-ökonomistische Modell, das zwischen der staatlichen Verwaltung als „öffentlich" und der Marktwirtschaft als „privat" unterscheidet, zweitens, das Konzept der republikanischen Tugenden, bei dem die politische Gemeinschaft und die Bürgerschaft als primär „öffentliche" Sphäre, im Gegensatz zur staatlichen Verwaltung und zur Marktwirtschaft, gesehen wird, drittens, die Einordnung der „Öffentlichkeit" als Teil der fließenden und polymorphen sozialen Beziehungen in der Gesellschaft, und, viertens, die Kategorisierung der Marktwirtschaft als „öffentlich" und der Familie als „privat".[24] Diese Vielfalt der Sichtweisen erklärt, warum „das übliche Reden, das die Zuhörer gegen einen empfundenen Verlust oder eine Verminderung der Öffentlichkeit aufzubringen versucht, sowohl wirkungsträchtig als auch profitabel ist. Manchen klingt der Ruf nach der Wiederherstellung des Territoriums der Öffentlichkeit wie der Ruf nach einer stärkeren Staatsmacht. Andere wiederum verstehen ihn als Forderung nach mehr Diskussion (selbst gelegentlich auf Kosten der Exekutive) oder als Forderung nach Stärkung des Marktes auf Kosten des Staates".[25] Hier ließe sich noch auf die Unschärfe im Gebrauch des Wortes „öffentlich" in Sowjetzeiten verweisen (besonders die Verwechslung von „Volkseigentum" und „Staatseigentum"), wobei heute noch viele eine gespaltene Haltung zur Privatisierung und ihren Folgen haben. Das erklärt auch besser, warum viele Versuche fehlschlagen, den Begriff des öffentlichen Raums (Punkt zwei auf Weintraubs Liste) zu verwenden, um die Fähigkeit der Bürger zu beschreiben, eine gemeinsame Basis zu finden, sich an Debatten zu beteili-

ers, it will be heard to call for greater debate (even at some cost to executive power) or even as a call to emphasise the market at the expense of state".[25] One might add to this the confusion of the use of the word "public" during Soviet times (especially the slippage of "public-owned" and "state-owned"), a mixed attitude many people still have towards privatisation and its outcomes, and it will become clearer why many attempts to use the concept of the public sphere (the second in Weintraub's list) to describe the ability of citizens to find common ground, engage in deliberation, and reach consensus fail. The reason is not only that civil society is weak in postsocialist space, but that public consensus-building seems to be in jeopardy almost everywhere. Conservative ideology and political toughness too often hide behind the rhetoric of principled commitments to consensus. Creative impulses and pluralism have been displaced from the sphere of public deliberation to economics (public in the fourth sense) and to depoliticised social and cultural life (public in the third sense outlined by Weintraub).

How high are the Moscow's citizens' stakes in having their interests taken into consideration? Very often, when developers and city officials come up with the decisions regarding destroying old or building new, it equals to non-participation. Moreover, the growing professional and status proliferation of the educated part of the public (to which the authors of the letter obviously belong) has led to the fact that a significant number of architects, having joined the circles of planners and bureaucrats, do actually participate in on-going destruction. It would be, of course, pointless to moralize here. What, however, is worth mentioning, is that the whole new strata of cultural practitioners has found its home in Moscow. The energy of aspirations and ambitions that this city attracts leads to the fact that every young wanna-bee ends up there, in Moscow. Many of these people who aspire to belong to dominant classes will be the last ones to question the workings of power, at least openly. What I think differentiates this part of cultural industry workers from their counterparts elsewhere is that they seem to be happily embracing and expressing in their activities the middle class values without showing any desire to question the current political regime. The public sphere thus gets increasingly de-politicised.

When it comes to the much discussed issue of public space, what seems to be the dominant tendency is its increasing privatisation, especially in the city centres. As a result, what used to be sites of public provision (with "public" understood in a first sense outlined by Weintraub), namely, state-provided housing and street lighting, public baths and "palaces of culture," parks and "houses of young pioneers," libraries and squares, hospitals and sanatoriums, movie theaters and museums – all of it either subject to privatisation or, if they remain nationally or locally state-owned (thus owned by the "public" again, in the first sense) have been rather poorly maintained. If in the libraries and museums, things, as a rule, are allowed to run down, the supermarkets and other fashionable establishments are new and sleek, luring the visitors to their enclosed spaces. The tendency, first described with regard to the US, that nowadays it is the shopping malls that function as public spaces, can be definitely traced in Russia.[26] The average Muscovite is a frequent visitor to IKEA, Ashan, and similar supermarkets and warehouse shopping malls.

gen und sich zu einigen. Der Grund dafür ist nicht allein, dass die Zivilgesellschaft im Postsozialismus schwach ist, sondern dass der Prozess der öffentlichen Konsensbildung fast überall bedroht ist. Hinter dem Gerede von prinzipiellem Engagement und Konsens verbergen sich nur allzu oft konservative Ideologie und politische Härte. Kreative Impulse und Pluralismus sind aus der Sphäre öffentlicher Diskussion in die Ökonomie (öffentlich im vierten Sinne) und ins entpolitisierte soziale und kulturelle Leben (öffentlich im dritten Sinne nach Weintraub) abgedrängt worden.
Wie groß sind nun die Chancen der Bürger Moskaus, dass ihre Interessen berücksichtigt werden? Sehr häufig, wenn Entwickler und Kommunalbeamte Entscheidungen über den Abriss alter oder den Bau neuer Gebäude treffen, läuft es auf Ausgrenzung hinaus. Außerdem hat die wachsende Professionalisierung und Statusausweitung des gebildeten Teils der Öffentlichkeit (zu der offensichtlich auch die Verfasser des erwähnten Briefes gehören) dazu geführt, dass zahlreiche Architekten, die jetzt als Planer und Bürokraten tätig sind, selbst an der anhaltenden Zerstörung teilnehmen. Es wäre natürlich sinnlos, hier zu moralisieren. Erwähnenswert ist jedoch, dass eine ganz neue Schicht von Kulturverantwortlichen in Moskau eine Heimstatt gefunden hat. Diese Stadt zieht alle an, die Ambition und Ehrgeiz haben, was dazu führt, dass alle jungen „Möchtegerns" nach Moskau kommen. Viele, die zu den herrschenden Klassen gehören wollen, wären die letzten, die die Funktionsweisen der Macht in Frage stellen würden, zumindest öffentlich. Was meiner Meinung nach diese Beschäftigten der Kulturindustrie von ihren Kollegen anderswo unterscheidet, ist, dass sie offensichtlich ganz zufrieden damit sind, in ihrer Arbeit kleinbürgerliche Werte zu akzeptieren und umzusetzen und keinerlei Wunsch verspüren, das aktuelle politische Regime in Zweifel zu ziehen. So wird der öffentliche Raum zunehmend entpolitisiert.
Wenn man sich den viel diskutierten öffentlichen Raum ansieht, scheint es hier vor allem die Tendenz zu geben, dass er zunehmend privatisiert wird, insbesondere in den Stadtzentren. Stätten, die einmal der Öffentlichkeit zur Verfügung standen („Öffentlichkeit" hier zu verstehen in der ersten Bedeutung von Weintraub) – vom Staat bereitgestellte Wohnungen und Straßenbeleuchtung, öffentliche Badeanstalten und „Kulturpaläste", Parks und „Häuser der Jungen Pioniere", Bibliotheken und Plätze, Krankenhäuser und Sanatorien, Kinos und Museen – wurden entweder privatisiert oder, wenn sie im nationalen oder kommunalen Eigentum verblieben (und somit wiederum „öffentlich" in der ersten Bedeutung wurden), nur unzureichend instand gehalten. Wenn Bibliotheken und Museen jedoch in der Regel einen heruntergewirtschafteten Eindruck machen, Supermärkte und andere moderne Einrichtungen neu und schick wirken, dann gehen die Bürger eben dorthin. Die zuerst in den USA beobachtete Tendenz, dass heutzutage Einkaufszentren als öffentliche Plätze fungieren, lässt sich definitiv auch in Russland nachweisen.[26] Der typische Moskauer ist ein häufiger Besucher von IKEA, Auchan und ähnlichen Supermärkten und Einkaufszentren.

GEWANDELTE KONSUMMUSTER – VOM BITTSTELLER ZUM EXPERTEN

„Es war einmal ein Mann, der lebte im Mangel. Nach vielen Abenteuern und einer langen Reise in die Wirtschaftswissenschaft begegnete er der Überflussgesellschaft. Sie heirateten und hatten viele Bedürfnisse." Diese Fabel, die den Ausgangspunkt für einen einflussreichen theoretischen Abriss über das Konsumverhalten bildet[27], be-

R&L
МЕХА

BASIC
EDITIONS

schreibt recht gut den Weg, den viele Russen in den letzten 20 Jahren zurückgelegt haben. Das Drehbuch wurde in Millionen konkreter Lebensläufe postsowjetischer Bürger kopiert. Wenn man sich mit 30- bis 40-Jährigen unterhält, bekommt man eine Menge unterschiedlicher (und dabei doch auffallend ähnlicher) Einzelheiten ein und derselben Geschichte zu hören, die ihren Anfang in dem erniedrigenden Überlebenskampf im Land des Mangels nimmt und im – wenn auch illusorischen – spannenden Leben in der Überflussgesellschaft endet. So beobachtete z. B. ein Anthropologe, dass sich die Menschen nicht etwa unterschiedliche, für sie interessante Dinge zulegen, sondern Stil mittels Quantität zum Ausdruck bringen, indem sie mehr „Statussymbole" eines begrenzten Spektrums kaufen.[28] Konsum ist damit als sichtbarstes Kennzeichen der neuen Zeiten und als markanteste Beschäftigung der Menschen in den Vordergrund gerückt, etwas, das sie mit ihren Artgenossen überall in der Welt am Anfang des 21. Jahrhunderts verbindet. Der Konsum wird überwiegend über den Markt realisiert, und wenn sich dieser auch ungleichmäßig entwickelt, so reguliert er den Konsum doch ausreichend effizient.

Die Metapher vom Markt als Schule, in die Russland nun geht, ist bei Werbefachleuten und Experten postsowjetischer Kultur populär. So heißt es vor allem, dass „Russland nun die Grundschule des Kapitalismus besucht und, ausgerüstet mit guten Lerngewohnheiten, das Warenalphabet durchlaufen und diese Erfahrung geordnet, bemerkenswert und berechenbar finden wird".[29] Man kann für diesen Bildungsweg ziemlich viele Beispiele finden. Diese reichen von der erstaunlich schnellen Umstellung des Denkens bei den gesellschaftlich aktiven Bürgern, die nun einer Mittel-zum-Zweck-Orientierung folgen, bis hin zu langen Regalreihen mit Büchern über Marketing, Verkaufsgespräche und Existenzgründungen sowie Einkaufsführern, einschließlich solcher über Wein und Schokolade, Whisky und Luxusmode. Nancy Condee und Vladimir Padunov illustrieren ihr *ABC der Konsumkultur* unter anderem mit Umschlägen von Comic-Büchern aus einer Serie der amerikanischen Federal Reserve Bank New York, die sich mit der Geschichte des Geldes, der Banken, des Sparens usw. befasst. Inzwischen existieren Kinderbücher aus dem Ausland neben solchen, die die heimische Pädagogik an die neuen Realitäten anpassen. Ein vor kurzem erschienenes Mathematiklehrbuch für jüngere Kinder mit dem Titel *Chotschu byt bankirom* (Ich möchte Banker werden) beschreibt einleitend seine Zielstellung:

Wie kann man am besten Kinder dazu erziehen, mit Geld richtig umzugehen, es vernünftig auszugeben und Einkäufe zu planen, denn schließlich brauchen sie diese Fähigkeiten später als Erwachsene? Wie lehrt man Kinder den Umgang mit den Verführungen der Reklame, die einzig und allein versucht, sie zum ständigen Kaufen zu veranlassen?[30]

Abgesehen von ihren Instruktionen für Anfänger kümmern sich die Enthusiasten der Konsumerziehung derzeit auch mit großer Sorgfalt um erwachsene Konsumenten. Das ist aus vielen Marketinglehrbüchern für Fortgeschrittene ersichtlich, in denen z. B. der russische Konsument so beschrieben wird, dass er erstens wegen wachsender Instabilität (beruflich, persönlich, wirtschaftlich, politisch usw.) ständig Unbehagen verspürt, zweitens überwältigt ist von der zunehmenden Vielfalt der Informationen und Produkte, oder, anders gesagt, von dem „Informationslärm", der Wahrnehmung und Auswahl erschwert, drittens Waren minderer Qualität unseriöser Hersteller kauft,

THE TRANSFORMING CONSUMPTION PATTERNS: FROM SUSPENSE TO EXPERTISE

"There once was a man who lived in Scarcity. After many adventures and a long voyage in the Science of Economics, he encountered the Society of Affluence. They were married and had many needs." This fable that works as a starting point for an influential theoretical outline of consumption[27] may well describe the trajectory many Russians did follow during the last twenty years. The script of the fable has been reproduced in millions of concrete biographies of the post-Soviet subjects. Talk to nearly anyone in his or her thirties or forties, and you'd hear a lot of different (and yet strikingly similar!) renderings of one and the same story that starts from humiliatingly difficult navigating from the Land of Scarcity to the excitement of living in the (however illusory) Society of Affluence. For instance, according to one anthropologist, many people, rather then diversifying a number of items of interest, express style by quantity, by means of purchasing more of a limited range of "status" things.[28] Consumption thus has come to the forefront as the most visible marker of the new times and most telling activity of people, one that unites them with their counterparts everywhere in the world at the beginning of the twenty first century. Most consumption activity is realised through the market, and however disproportionably it is developing, it regulates consumption efficiently enough.

The metaphor of market as school that Russia has entered is popular both among the advertisers and the experts in post-Soviet culture. In particular, it is said that "Russia has entered the elementary school years of capitalism and, armed with good study habits, it will progress through the alphabet of commodities, finding the experience to be orderly, remarkable and predictable".[29] One can think of very many examples of this schooling. They range from remarkably quick transformation of thinking of the socially active categories of citizens towards ends-means orientation to the long shelves of books on marketing, sales talk, business development, shopping guides, including those on vine and chocolate, whisky and vintage clothing. Nancy Condee and Valdimir Padunov illustrate their *ABC of Consumer Culture*, among many other things, with the covers of comic books adapted from the series published by the Federal Reserve Bank of New York and devoted to the history of money, banks, thrifts, etc. By now the childrens' stories borrowed from abroad co-exist with those adjusting the local pedagogic experience to new realities. The recently published math textbook for small children titled *Hotchu byt' bankirom* (I want to be a banker) starts with an abstract that says:

How can one to develop in one's small child a habit to handle money properly, spend it rationally, to plan his or her purchase given that all these habits will be indispensable in adult life? How to teach our children to react to the cunny ads that harvest their minds by inviting them to buy and buy?[30]

Except instructing the beginners, the enthusiasts of consumer education show currently a great care about adult consumers. This is seen in many advanced textbooks on marketing where, to take one of those as an example, an average Russian consumer is characterised as, first, constantly experiencing a great discomfort due to increased instability (professional, personal, economic, political, etc.), second, as being overwhelmed by the growing diversity of information and produce, in other words, from "all this informational noise" amidst of which it is difficult to discern and to se-

weil es so viele neue Firmen und Waren gibt, und viertens seinen Wunsch, wenigstens einen gewissen Einfluss auf den Gang der Dinge zu haben, stets als vergeblich erleben muss, weil die Instabilität des Marktes die Preise hochtreibt, was ein weiterer Grund für das Unbehagen am Konsum ist.[31]

Der Kern von Jean Baudrillards Fabel ist folgender: „Der Mensch" ist „ausgestattet" mit Bedürfnissen, die ihn zu Gegenständen „lenken", die ihm „Befriedigung verschaffen".[32] Die von Baudrillard großzügig verwendeten Anführungszeichen sollen Ironie andeuten: Es geht nur um Befriedigung, die unmöglich zu erreichen ist. Ein anderer Grund für Anflüge von Ironie angesichts zahlloser Konsumverführungen ist die Unsicherheit in Bezug auf die Dinge, die der Verbraucher kontrollieren kann oder nicht. Einerseits empfinden viele, dass die Manipulierung des Verbrauchers durch Marktforschung, Segmentierungspraktiken und ausgeklügelte Verführungstechniken intensiver wird. Es vergeht kaum ein Tag, an dem man nicht auf dem Bürgersteig Leuten mit Reklametafeln und Teenagern, die Werbezettel verteilen, begegnet. Was meiner Meinung nach andererseits die russischen Verbraucher von anderen unterscheidet, ist deren großer Wunsch, zumindest ein wenig Kontrolle über ihre Konsumgewohnheiten zu haben, wie ihn viele in ihrem Verhalten zum Ausdruck bringen. Ich meine damit nicht nur das endlose Preisvergleichen in verschiedenen Geschäften und Großeinkäufe in Großhandelsmärkten, sondern auch die Verbraucherschutzbewegung, die, unterstützt von erfahrenen Anwälten, als wichtigstes Ergebnis vorweisen kann, dass die Menschen zuversichtlich sind, dass zumindest *in diesem Bereich* ihre Rechte verteidigt werden können. In dem Maße, wie sich das politische Leben von den Bedürfnissen der Normalbürger immer weiter entfernt, sind diese offensichtlich auf der Suche nach sozialen Einrichtungen und Aktivitäten, die ihnen nicht nur das Gefühl geben, dass man sie schätzt, anhört, sich um sie sorgt und kümmert, sondern dass sie auch Kontrolle über ihre Taten haben und sich in das gesellschaftliche Leben einbezogen fühlen.

Theoretisch kommen wir damit zu dem schwierigen Problem der Bewertung des Konsums als vorherrschender Kulturpraxis. Die Frankfurter Schule hat die Herrschaft über den Konsumenten, dessen geringe kulturelle Bedürfnisse zur Herausbildung der Unterhaltungsgesellschaft und zum Verschwinden der Hochkultur geführt haben, eindrucksvoll beschrieben. Ganz im Gegensatz zur weitverbreiteten Darstellung der Verbraucher als kulturell Minderbemittelte haben die Anthropologen Mary Douglas und Baron Isherwood, der Soziologe Dick Hebdidge, die Kulturtheoretiker David Morley, James Twitchell und John Fiske sowie viele andere das aktivierende Potential des Konsums hervorgehoben, das dem Leben Bedeutung geben kann.[33] Was nun Russland angeht, bin ich der Meinung, dass die Umwälzungen auf dem Verbrauchermarkt nicht nur zu Veränderungen bei Menge und Auswahl der tatsächlich konsumierten Güter, sondern auch bei ihrer Bedeutung für den Alltag, für die Lebensbedingungen, für das Verständnis von Höflichkeit und einem zivilisierten Leben geführt haben, und dass dieser Bedeutungswandel eine Metamorphose der Konfiguration der kulturellen Beziehungen und des kulturvollen Umgangs unter den gesellschaftlich aktiven Bürgern Russlands reflektiert.

Das sich derzeit in den Vordergrund schiebende neue Kulturverständnis unterscheidet sich radikal von dem von Hochschullehrern, Aktivisten der „kulturellen Aufklärung" zu Sowjetzeiten oder Mitarbeitern von Museen und Philharmonien. Deren gewohnheits-

lect something, third, the abundance of new companies and new goods often leads to a purchase of poor quality items from dishonest manufacturers, fourth, to the reasons of consumer's unease, market instability should be added which causes the growth of prices, so that a consumer's desire to have at least some impact on events remains constantly frustrated.[31]

The essence of the fable Jean Baudrillard rehearses is this: "a man, "endowed" with needs which "direct" him toward objects that "give" him satisfaction."[32] The quotation marks that Baudrillard generously uses here are supposed to indicate his irony: it all seems to be about satisfaction which is impossible to achieve. Another reason for feeling ironical about numerous lures of consumption is that it consists of an uneasy balance between what the consumer can and cannot control. On the one hand, many feel the intensification of the management of consumers through marketing research and different audience's segmenting tactics, the sophisticated techniques of persuasion. On a usual day, one can hardly make his or her way through a sidewalk without running across sandwich-board men and teenagers dispensing handbills. On the other hand, what I think significantly differentiates the Russian consumers is their great wish to have at least some control over their consumer activities many people express in their behavior. I not only mean an endless comparing of prices in the different stores, making major purchases on wholesale markets, but also the consumer rights movement that, with the help of experienced lawyers, can count among its most impressive results people's confidence that their rights *in this sphere* can be defended. As the political life grows increasingly aloof to the needs of ordinary citizens, they seem to be in search of those social situations and those actions that would not only help them feeling appreciated, heard, attended, taken care of but to exercise control at what they actually do, to feel included in social life.

Theoretically, it brings us to a thorny problem of evaluating the value of consumption itself as predominant cultural practice. The Frankfurt school thinkers produced a powerful narrative about the dominated consumers whose low cultural needs have led to the appearance of entertainment society and disappearance of high culture. Opposing the wide-spread rendering of the consumers as passive cultural dopes, the anthropologists Mary Douglas and Baron Isherwood, the sociologist Dick Hebdidge, the cultural theorists David Morley, James Twitchell, and John Fiske and many others have emphasised the enabling potential of consumption and its ability to bring meaning into people's life.[33] Coming back to the Russian matters, I would argue that the transformations of the consumer market involved a change not only in the amount and variety of actually consumed goods but also in the meaning attached to everyday life, one's living conditions, one's understanding of civility and civilised life, and that this change in meaning mirrored a metamorphosis of the configurations of cultural relations and the circulation of culture among the socially active Russian citizens.

The new understanding of culture that comes presently to the fore differs radically from the one expressed by the high school or university teachers as well as by other agents of what was called in Soviet times "the cultural enlightenment" – those working in the museums and philharmonics. The notion of culture they habitually follow is, first, an idealistic one (culture as "high" and classic), and second, as promoted by specific cultural institutions (that are mostly thought of as chronically under-

mäßige Vorstellung von Kultur ist, erstens, idealistisch (Kultur wird stets als Hochkultur oder klassische Kultur gesehen) und wird, zweitens, von speziellen Kultureinrichtungen gefördert, deren chronische Unterfinanzierung auch als Grund für ihr unzulängliches Funktionieren gesehen wird. Die neuen Verantwortlichen der Kulturindustrie, wie sie sich in den 1990er Jahren bis in die jüngste Vergangenheit herausgebildet hat, also alle diejenigen, die bei privaten und staatlichen Massenmedien, Werbeagenturen, Verlagen, Mode- und Designstudios, Architektenbüros, im Showbusiness und in Marketingabteilungen arbeiten, verfolgen eine andere Vorstellung von Kultur, die eng verbunden ist mit den Begriffen Gewinn und Lifestyle.

Was das erste Element dieses neuen Kulturverständnisses angeht, gleichgültig, ob es sich um Werbung für einen neuen Roman, eine Fernsehshow, eine Reklameidee oder einen Beruf handelt, so wird alles als Ware betrachtet, die hierarchisch nach ihrer Nützlichkeit geordnet wird. Dadurch werden die Grenzen zwischen einer Kultureinrichtung und dem Markt durchlässig, die Befürworter der Hochkultur beginnen, sich mit dem Thema Gewinn zu beschäftigen, wobei die neuen Kulturpraktiker sich zunehmend (und gut dotiert) am „Verkauf von Know-how in Bezug auf die technische, gesellschaftliche oder ästhetische Eignung von Waren" beteiligen.[34] Der Gegensatz von „Kultur" und „Ökonomie", der früher dadurch erzeugt wurde, dass beide sich in unterschiedlichen physischen Sphären befanden, wird unscharf. Vorherrschend ist die kaufmännische Haltung gegenüber der eigenen Berufstätigkeit. Zur Herausarbeitung der „biographischen" Dimension dieser Umwälzungen möchte ich anmerken, dass die Praktiker der traditionellen Kultureinrichtungen und der derzeitigen „kreativen Branchen" im Allgemeinen verschiedener sozialer Herkunft sind, aus unterschiedlichen geographischen Gegenden stammen und sehr unterschiedliche Biographien aufweisen. Aus einer Reihe von detaillierten Interviews, die ich im Winter 2005 in Moskau führte, geht hervor, dass die traditionellen Kulturschaffenden in der Regel aus Moskau stammen, einen Hochschulabschluss haben und oftmals bereits seit Jahren in ihrer Bibliothek oder ihrem Museum arbeiten, während die neuen oft aus der Provinz kommen, ihr Bildungsgang zum Teil recht ungewöhnlich ist, sie häufig ihre Stelle wechseln und vor allem in einem harten Wettbewerb mit ihren Kollegen um einen bessere Arbeit stehen.[35] Überraschend ist jedoch, dass sowohl die alten als auch die neuen Kulturverantwortlichen eifrig um die Bildung der Öffentlichkeit bemüht sind und die von ihnen kollektiv vertretenen Werte Gruppen und Einzelpersonen vermitteln wollen. Wie engagiert sich Museumsführer und Bibliothekare auch immer zeigen, sie geraten im Wettbewerb um Autorität immer denen gegenüber ins Hintertreffen, die für Verlage arbeiten und für Hochglanzmagazine schreiben. Die Ratschläge, die diese Kulturunternehmer der Öffentlichkeit erteilen, klingen so autoritär und gebieterisch, als kämen sie von meiner Grundschullehrerin. Rhetorisch macht sich das in ihren Artikeln im unbefangenen Gebrauch des Wortes „richtig" bemerkbar – so z. B., wenn sie von der „richtigen Länge der Bluse" oder dem „richtigen Ort, wo man sich sehen lassen kann" sprechen. Ihre Position als Experten in der Gemeinschaft der „richtigen Käufer" wird durch ein Phänomen gestützt, das der amerikanische Anthropologe W. Lloyd Warner bereits 1950 beschrieben hat, als er betonte, dass das Streben nach dem „richtigen Auto" oder der „richtigen Wohngegend" „einen wichtigen Ausdruck der eigenen Position in der Gemeinschaft darstellt".[36] Aufgrund ihrer innovati-

financed and thus unable to function properly). The new agents of cultural industry that emerged in 1990s and 2000s, those working in the private and state-sponsored mass-media, advertising agencies, publishing houses, fashion and design agencies, architectural offices, show business, and marketing departments, have been promoting a different idea of culture, the one closely related, first, to a notion of profit, second to one of lifestyle.

As to the first constituent of this new understanding of culture, regardless of whether one tries to promote a new novel, a TV show, an advertising idea, or a profession, understood as goods, they are placed hierarchically, depending on their utility. Thus the boundaries between cultural institutions and the market-place become porous, the proponents of high culture begin to take into consideration the issue of profit, while the new cultural practitioners become increasingly involved with and (nicely paid for) "selling of expertise regarding the technical, social, or aesthetic appropriateness of commodities".[34] The opposition of "culture" and "economy", formerly engendered in the separate physic sites that these occupied, become blurred. The mercantile attitude towards one's professional preoccupations becomes prevalent. To emphasise again the "biographical" dimension of these transformations, I should say that the practitioners from traditional cultural institutions and those from the present "creative industries" do usually come from different social backgrounds, geographic regions, and possess different personal histories. Several in-depth interviews that I conducted in Moscow in winter 2005 suggest that, as a rule, the cultural practitioners of traditional professions come from Moscow, have a university degree, tend to work for decades in their library or museum, while the new cultural workers often come from the provinces, their educational histories can be the most unusual ones, they change jobs very often and, most importantly, they find themselves in intense struggle with their counterparts for better jobs.[35] Surprisingly though, the old and new cultural workers seem to be eager to educate the public, to transmit their collectively held values to groups and individuals. However devoted to this mission the museum guides and librarians are, they definitely lose in the competition for authority to those who work in publishing houses and write for fancy magazines. The advice that these cultural entrepreneurs give to the public often sounds as authoritative and imperative as the voice of my elementary school teacher. Rhetorically it expresses itself in the ease with which the word "right" figures in their reviews, as in the "right length of a blouse", or the "right place for a girl to be seen at". Their position as experts in the community of "right shoppers" is thus sustained by phenomena described already in 1950s by an American anthropologist W. Lloyd Warner who emphasised that striving for the "right car" or the "right area to live in" comprises the important expression of one's status position in the community.[36] However, by virtue of being involved in innovative activities, they are free from being associated with "a torture by culture": this is how, sarcastically, all those numerous excursions to the museums and dusty opera performances have been now called in the high schools. In this sense, my argument comes closer to Barbara Hernstein Smith's insights about a certain inevitability with which the conflict takes place between, on the one hand, conservative "practices of the relevant community" and, on the other, "destabilising practices" of those "who stand to gain from a reclassification, circulation, and re-

von Tätigkeiten werden sie jedoch nicht mit der „Folter durch Kultur" assoziiert, wie mittlerweile Museumsbesuche oder verstaubte Opernaufführungen sarkastisch an den Hochschulen genannt werden. In dieser Hinsicht gehe ich eher konform mit den Erkenntnissen von Barbara Hernstein Smith bezüglich einer gewissen Unvermeidbarkeit, mit der der Konflikt ausgetragen wird, und zwar zwischen den konservativen „Praktiken der entsprechenden Gemeinschaft" einerseits und den „destabilisierenden Praktiken derjenigen, die von der Neuordnung, Zirkulation und Umverteilung von Waren und kulturellen Gütern profitieren können, einschließlich des Gewinns und der Macht, die sich allein aus dem *Vermitteln* dieser Zirkulation ergeben"[37], andererseits. Diese „neuen Mittelsmänner der Kultur", um einen Begriff von Mike Featherstone[38] zu verwenden, helfen Verbrauchern auf der Reise durch die verwirrende Welt der Waren und Dienstleistungen, bei der Verbesserung ihres Geschmacks und sicherlich auch bei der Umsetzung von Produzentenbedürfnissen auf dem Verbrauchermarkt. Die Signifikanz und auch das Prestige ihrer Aktivitäten haben mit dem zweiten Bestandteil des neuen Kulturverständnisses zu tun, dem Lifestyle. Man braucht sich nur einmal, wenn auch flüchtig, die Menschenmengen im Zentrum Moskaus anzusehen und wird feststellen, wie stark sich die einzelnen in ihrer Erscheinung voneinander unterscheiden – von respektabel bis nachlässig, von zurückhaltend bis demonstrativ protzig, von unauffällig bis schreiend kitschig. Die sozialen und kulturellen Unterschiede im Konsumverhalten haben nicht direkt etwas mit Klassen- oder Statuszugehörigkeit zu tun; sie bringen vielmehr innovative Formen einer persönlichen oder Gruppenidentität sowie neue Wege der sozialen Erfahrung zum Ausdruck.

James Twitchell schrieb dazu Folgendes: Lifestyles sind säkulare Religionen, kohärente Muster hochgeschätzter Dinge. Lifestyle hat nichts damit zu tun, womit man seinen Lebensunterhalt verdient, sondern was man kauft. Wir streben unter anderem danach, dass wir uns gern denen zugehörig fühlen, mit denen wir dieselben Dinge gemeinsam haben. Die „Shopping-Kultur" hat auch deshalb eine so starke Wirkung, weil sie uns aus den Strukturen der Klassenzugehörigkeit befreit. Das Ergebnis unseres materiellen Lebens wird nicht mehr vorherbestimmt durch ein Wappen, den Platz auf der Kirchenbank oder einen Treuhandfonds. Das Leben entfaltet sich stattdessen als immerwährender Wechsel der Entscheidungen des Einzelnen. Niemand will mehr zur Mittelklasse gehören. Man will viel lieber cool sein, hip, trendy oder in.[39]

Wenn hier auch einzuschränken ist, dass für viele Russen die Zugehörigkeit zur Mittelklasse ein wichtiges Element des „Cool-Seins" darstellt[40], erklärt diese Beobachtung die wachsende Popularität der erwähnten Kulturunternehmer und ihrer Sachkenntnis – mit Hilfe von Beratungsdiensten, Sonderausgaben und Zeitschriften allgemeiner Art. Menschen fühlen sich zunehmend nicht wegen ihres Konsumverhaltens an sich geschätzt, sondern dafür, wie clever und bewusst sie dieses zur Geltung bringen können.

„Die Kunst des Konsumierens, Ausgebens und Genießens", um mit Pierre Bourdieu zu sprechen[41], organisiert den städtischen Raum. Es ist inzwischen normal, die Kakophonie von Reklame und Werbetafeln in den Stadtzentren als Symbole des Wandels und des Konsumrauschs zu bezeichnen. Trotzdem hat diese Kakophonie ihre Logik: Die visuelle Landschaft des städtischen Raums spiegelt die Prozesse der Herausbildung gesellschaftlicher Schichten wider und hebt in einigen Fällen mittels Reklame

distribution of commodities and cultural goods and, thereby, of social power – including the profit and power to be had just from *mediating* their circulation".[37] These "new cultural intermediaries", to borrow the expression of Mike Featherstone[38], help consumers to traverse the confused realm of goods and services, strive to improve their taste and, surely, translate the producers' need into the consumer market. The significance and even prestige their activities achieve have to do with the second constituent of a new understanding of culture, namely, a lifestyle. It is enough to take even a brief, passing look at the crowd in Moscow's center to become struck by the variety of appearances, from "respectable" to bohemian, from low-key to conspicuously ostentatious, from unassertive to shoutingly kitschy ones. The social and cultural differences in the patterns of consumption are there, but, rather than being related directly to one's class or status, they express innovative forms of personal and group identity, new kinds of social experiences.

As James Twitchell pointed out, Lifestyles are secular religions, coherent patterns of valued things. Your lifestyle is not related to what you do for a living but to what you buy. One of the chide aims of the way we live now is the enjoyment of affiliating with those who share the same clusters of objects as we do. Mallcondo culture is so powerful in part because it frees us from the structures of social class. The outcome of material life is no longer preordained by coat of arms, pew seat, or trust fund. Instead, it evolves as never-ending shifting of individual choice. No one wants to be middle class, for instance. You want to be cool, hip, with it, with the "in" crowd, instead.[39]

With the only reservation that, apparently, for many Russians, to define themselves as belonging to the middle class comprises an important component of "coolness"[40], this observation explains the growing popularity of the expertise the above mentioned cultural entrepreneurs offer – through consulting, specialised editions and generaly used magazines. One is increasingly valued not on the basis of his or her consumption per se, but how clever and knowingly one does it.

"The art of consuming, spending and enjoying", to quote Pierre Bourdieu[41], organises city space. It has become a commonplace to refer to the cacophonies of advertisements and billboards in the urban centers as the emblems of change and consumption frenzy. Nevertheless, there is some logic to this cacophony: the visual landscape of the city space reflects the processes of social stratification, emphasising, through advertisement, in some cases, the sort of goods and services whose survival depends on low overheads, while offering "Sushi 24 hours a day" or "Your personal sommelier" to the inhabitants of the large comfortable mansions in the residential neighborhoods located along Uspenskoye shosse. The cosmopolitan pretensions of educated classes and elite find their expression in the proliferation of ethnic restaurants. Worldwide consumerist culture is visible in the presence of all major world brands. Health and fitness clubs, spa saloons are also becoming important parts of city life. Surely, it is the appearance of high-earners whose ambitions and spending habits seem to have been the major driving force in the development of many cities, the stimulus and hope behind building more and more shopping malls and similar venues. Yet, as Sharon Zukin argued, "in the fronts of the restaurants or stores, at least, consumers are strolling, eating, drinking, sometimes speaking English and sometimes not" in the manner that all this becomes "sites of visual delectation ...where everyone

die Waren und Dienstleistungen hervor, deren Überleben von niedrigen Betriebskosten abhängt, während sich gleichzeitig Angebote wie „Sushi rund um die Uhr" und „Ihr persönlicher Sommelier" an die Bewohner der geräumigen, komfortablen Luxusvillen in den Wohngebieten entlang der Uspenskoje Schosse richten. Die kosmopolitischen Ambitionen der gebildeten Klassen und Eliten finden ihren Ausdruck in einer Fülle von Nationalitätenrestaurants. Die Konsumkultur manifestiert sich weltweit in der Präsenz aller großen Marken. Erholungs- und Fitnessclubs sowie Wellness-Oasen werden zu wichtigen Elementen städtischen Lebens. Das Auftauchen von Besserverdienern mit ihren Ambitionen und Einkaufsgewohnheiten ist unbestritten eine wichtige Triebkraft bei der Entwicklung vieler Städte, die den Bau von immer neuen Einkaufszentren und ähnlichen Objekten fördern und stimulieren. Wie Sharon Zukin zeigt, „gehen Verbraucher vor den Fenstern von Restaurants oder Geschäften spazieren, essen, trinken, sprechen mitunter auch Englisch", so dass es sich hier um „Stätten des visuellen Vergnügens handelt, (...) wo jeder zur Mittelklasse zu gehören *scheint*".[42] Der Appetit der Verbraucher, der sich im Sozialismus zu entwickeln begann und nie gestillt wurde, hat regelrecht zu einer intimen Einstellung gegenüber den Dingen geführt, die nicht nur als notwendig zur Befriedigung der Grundbedürfnisse gesehen werden, sondern auch als etwas, das einen ästhetischen Traum erfüllt. Der Nase bieten sich neue Aromen, die Zunge schmeckt neue Köstlichkeiten, aber vor allem lassen sich die Dinge nun unaufhörlich ansehen, anfassen, kosten und anprobieren. Die Konsumgewohnheiten der Mittelklasse sind verinnerlicht worden und lassen sich dank Modezeitschriften, Reklame und Eintauchen in die Welt der Markenprodukte imitieren. Ich möchte jedoch betonen, dass der Konsum von Waren, ob nun erworben oder erträumt, es den Menschen nicht nur ermöglicht, sich mit den populären Schichten, „denen, die Geld haben", zu identifizieren, sondern auch ihr eigenes Leben als anhaltende Legende zu gestalten, in der man sich Genuss durch die Investition von Phantasie in den Kaufakt und die nachfolgende Kombination der Waren verschafft. Die Phantasievorstellungen von der „Überflussgesellschaft", die die Menschen so lange mit sich herumtrugen, spornen weiterhin die Erregung bei fast jedem Besuch eines Supermarkts an.

Nehmen wir ein anschauliches Beispiel. Es existiert eine seltsame Art der Befriedigung und des Genießens, die vielleicht nur die empfinden, die sich noch an die Zeit der Mangelwirtschaft erinnern, als man sich stundenlang in langen Schlangen nach dem Allernotwendigsten anstellen musste. Schon allein die Vielfalt der erhältlichen Waren schafft Befriedigung. In dem Film *Staryje kljatschi* (Alte Schachteln) des russischen Regisseurs Eldar Rjasanow, der den Kontrast zwischen den neuen und den alten Zeiten zum Thema hat, versuchen die Freundinnen der Filmheldin, einer älteren Frau, sie gegenüber ihrem argwöhnischen Vater zu entschuldigen, als sie sich bei einer Familienfeier verspätet: „Sie ist sehr beschäftigt, sie steht nach Mayonnaise an." Vielen Russen gilt diese Formulierung heute nicht nur als Symbol der Zeiten des Mangels; sie bezieht sich auch darauf, dass alles, was mit Konsum zu tun hatte, eine ernste Angelegenheit war, dass die Menschen mit verkniffenen Gesichtern und düsteren Mienen stets auf der Suche nach etwas waren. Man kann sich zwar nur schwer vorstellen, dass lange Reihen von Mayonnaisegläsern im Supermarkt Hochstimmung verbreiten, aber zweifellos bewirken sie tatsächlich ein Gefühl der Freiheit.

appears to be middle class".[42] The consumer appetites, the ones that started accumulating under socialism and remained ever unfulfilled, have led to rather intimate consumers' attitudes towards things that are perceived as not only goods capable of satisfying basic needs but everything one can have dreamt of aesthetically. Nostrils crave new scents, tongues devour new tastes but, most importantly, new things are something that can be endlessly viewed, touched, tasted and tried on. Middle class consumption styles have been absorbed and imitated through fashion magazines, advertising, and the very practice of leisurely strolling amidst brand names. I want to emphasise though that the consumption of goods, both purchased and dreamed of, enables people not only to identify with the most popular strata, "those who have money.", but to enact the on-going narratives of their lives which take their form from and secure their enjoyment through the investments of imagination to the acts of purchase and the following combining of things. The fantasies of the mythic "Society of Affluence" that people cherished for so long keep fueling the excitement characteristic for nearly every visit to the supermarket.

To take the most obvious example, there's a peculiar kind of satisfaction and pleasure available perhaps only to those who still remember the times of the deficit economy when for hours they were lining for basics around the blocks. It is the satisfaction that the very variety of the items available promises. In the Russian film director Eldar Ryasanov's movie, called *Stariye Klyachi* (Worn-out Horses), where the contrasts between the new and old times are put in play, the friends of the middle-aged woman, trying to defend her against a suspicious father when she is late for some family event, say to him: "Or, she is very busy, she is queuing for a mayonnaise." To many Russians this phrase works now not only as an emblem of the times of scarcity but refers to the times when everything about consumption was very serious, when, with their wrinkled brows and gloomy faces, people were endlessly looking for goods. It is, of course, difficult to imagine how exactly the variety of mayonnaise jars on the supermarket shelves may induce one's playfulness, but it undoubtedly can add to one's feeling of freedom.

The juxtaposition of old and new consumer's opportunities is characteristic for the style in which the rubrics "Style", "Things", "Shopping" are written in the numerous magazines. In one of them, titled *Bolshoi Gorod* (A Big City), a poetic description of the opening of Zara store next to a formerly popular shopper's destination, the shop "Podarki" (The Gifts) on Tverskaya includes a reference to former times when generic designations of goods were predominant in the names of stores. If the shops having such names "Shoes", "Clothing", "Fruit and Vegetable" were designed for satisfying mundane needs, the ones named "Podarki" were supposed to provide some items for indulgencies. Along with the endless crystal vases, kitschy wooden figures or stone incrustations, one could find there French perfume or Chinese Thermoses. "In fact", – the author rightly observes,

The Soviet shop "Podarki" was a shop for buying the meaningless bribes – something that one thinks one needs to give to one's doctor if giving money is out of question or to one's boss before he or she retires ... Now, in the stores like Zara, they buy in a contemporary sense: first, one buys for herself, for herself, for herself, and the gifts to somebody else may go to hell; second, one buys practically every day, not waiting

Die Gegenüberstellung von alten und neuen Konsummöglichkeiten ist ein typisches Stilmittel in zahlreichen Zeitschriften mit Rubriken, wie „Stil", „Waren" oder "Einkaufen". In einer Zeitschrift mit dem Titel *Bolschoi Gorod* (Großstadt) gibt es in einer poetischen Beschreibung der Eröffnung eines Geschäfts der Kette Zara neben dem ehemals populären Laden „Podarki" (Geschenke) in der Twerskaja-Straße eine Anspielung auf die Vergangenheit, als die Namen von Geschäften lediglich Oberbegriffe von Waren trugen. Läden, wie z. B. „Schuhe", „Konfektion" oder „Obst und Gemüse" erfüllten Alltagsbedürfnisse, während die mit dem Namen „Geschenke" auf so etwas wie Luxusgüter anspielten. Neben großen Mengen an Kristallvasen, kitschigen Holzfiguren oder Steineinlegearbeiten gab es hier gegebenenfalls auch französisches Parfüm oder chinesische Thermosbehälter. Der Autor stellt fest:

Die sowjetischen Geschäfte namens „Podarki" boten nichtssagende Objekte für Bestechungszwecke an – Dinge, die man meinte, seinem Arzt schenken zu müssen, wenn Geld nicht in Frage kam, oder seinem Chef vor der Pensionierung (...), In Geschäften wie Zara wird hingegen modern eingekauft: Erstens kauft man für sich selbst, und nur für sich selbst, und zum Teufel mit Geschenken für irgendjemand anders. Zweitens kann man jeden Tag etwas kaufen und muss nicht auf einen besonderen Anlass warten. Drittens ist es auch in Ordnung, wenn das, was wir kaufen, hübsch anzusehen ist, aber nur bis zur ersten Wäsche – wir sind nicht mehr besessen vom Gedanken an eine in Kristall oder Stein gemeißelte Ewigkeit.[43]

Die gleiche Gegenüberstellung der alten und der neuen Zeit findet sich im Vorwort des beliebten Einkaufsführers „Geschäfte in Moskau", der seine Leser folgendermaßen warnt:

Es ist nicht leicht, etwas in Moskau zu finden. Zwar ist es längst nicht mehr so spannend wie in den alten Zeiten, als man entweder Beziehungen benötigte oder einem geschlossenen Warenverbund angehören musste, zu dem Leute gehörten, die etwas aus dem Ausland mitbrachten. Aber auch jetzt muss, wer einkaufen geht, beharrlich und aufmerksam sein und an seinen guten Stern glauben. Früher musste man etwas erwischen, jetzt kommt es darauf an, das Gewünschte aufzutreiben. In unglaublichem Tempo vermehren sich Kioske und Pavillons, Salons und Einkaufszentren, werden größer und immer schöner. Und in einem davon versteckt sich der erträumte beigefarbene Pullover, der spitzenbesetzte Schirm, eine Flasche seltenen Ports oder eine Schlafzimmereinrichtung. Alles, was man noch tun muss, ist, genau herauszufinden wo.[44]

In einer Hinsicht hat Konsum einen wirklich kulturellen Inhalt, wenn man nämlich das Land des Mangels hinter sich lässt, um noch einmal Baudrillard zu zitieren, wenn man einkaufen kann oder eben auch nicht, weil der Kühlschrank nie völlig leer ist, wenn man sich im Alltag so sicher fühlt, dass man Freude daran empfindet, nach Luxuskleidung, Vinylschallplatten oder einer Bluse, die sonst niemand hat, Ausschau zu halten. Diese Art des Einkaufens erfüllt keinen Zweck, es ist sich selbst Zweck genug. Auch wenn hier Experten gefragt sind, die „sich auskennen", so bleibt es doch eine angeblich zweckfreie Tätigkeit, die etwas mit dem eigenen Stil, mitunter auch mit Widerstand gegen den allgegenwärtigen Glamour oder auch mit Intelligenz zu tun hat.

Unter den berühmten Moskauer Einkaufsadressen verdient das GUM eine Erwähnung. Mit seinen von Glaskuppeln überwölbten eleganten und gepflegten Galerien

for some special occasion. Third, it's OK that the stuff we buy wears nicely but only before the first wash: we are not obsessed any longer with eternity that is embodied in crystal or in stone.[43]

The same juxtaposition of old and new times is at work in the introduction of the popular guide "Shops of Moscow" that warns its readers that

It is not an easy task to find something in Moscow. Surely, shopping nowadays lacks suspense characteristic for the old times when one either had to have connections or to deal with closed distributions of goods, with those who'd bring goods from abroad. But even now, in order to shop, one has to be persistent, attentive and to have faith in his or her lucky star. In the old times one had to obtain, what is needed now is to find. The kiosks and pavilions, salons and shopping centers keep multiplying, growing, and getting prettier unbelievably fast; it is in one of them that much a needed beige sweater, or a lace umbrella, or a bottle of rare port, or a bedroom set are hiding. What remains to do is to find out where exactly they are.[44]

There is a sense in which consumption comes to have a truly cultural content only when one leaves the land of Scarcity behind, to recall again the fable Baudrillard tells, when one is free to shop or not because one's fridge is never totally empty, when one feels secure enough in his or her everyday life to indulge in looking for vintage clothing, vinyl disks, or a blouse nobody else has. This kind of shopping does not serve any purpose, but is an end in itself. Although it, too, presupposes its experts who "know the places", it remains an ostensibly purposeless activity, it has to do with one's style, sometimes with one's opposition to ever-present glamour, sometimes with one's intelligence.

Among the famous Moscow shopping places, GUM is worthy of mentioning. Reminiscent of the glass-roofed nineteenth century gallerias of Milan and Naples, elegant and sleek, it was built before World War I and remained a popular shoppers' destination during the Soviet Era. One feels lost there as well as in the TSUM department store, the Smolenski and the Petrovski Passage, in the underground arcade on Manezhnaya Square, so expensive are the goods offered, so arrogant the personnel seems. So it is a relief for an average shopper that to those traditional and new places a lot of shopping centers are now added. Their spread was facilitated by numerous foreign companies which came to Russia since the early 1990s. The democratising impact of globalisation is particularly seen in the appearance of the "MegaMalls", like the one, operated by the Swedish chain Ikea, that was opened in 2003 in the southwestern suburbs of the city. With 25,000 people shopping there on workdays and 80,000 on weekends (along with those tens of thousands who come to this area specifically to visit Ikea and Auchan stores), surrounded on one side by a 10, 000 parking lot, with sixty-five cash registers along the front, it comprises the largest shopping area in the Eastern Europe .[45] Built next to a highway, although certainly designed for car-owners, it seems to be equally popular with carless people for whom free buses are provided leaving from and too the closest metro stations. Filled with affordable goods, this space is heaven for frugal shoppers. The inflation grows, the pension reform doesn't promise a bright future, a much-cited uncertainty is in the air. This means that strategic long-time planning doesn't make a lot of sense. This only makes more important the short-time calculations people conduct daily (with regard to what to buy when and where) because it gives them a sense of control over their lives.

erinnert es an Mailand und Neapel. Erbaut vor dem Ersten Weltkrieg blieb es auch in der Sowjetzeit eine beliebte Einkaufsadresse. Hier fühlt man sich verloren, genauso wie im Warenhaus ZUM, in der Smolenski- und der Petrowski-Passage oder in den unterirdischen Arkaden des Manegenplatzes, so teuer sind die ausgestellten Waren und so arrogant das Personal. Für den durchschnittlichen Verbraucher ist es deshalb eine Erleichterung, dass jetzt viele neue Einkaufszentren zu diesen traditionellen und neuen Adressen hinzukommen. Sie konnten sich entwickeln, da seit Beginn der 1990er Jahre zahlreiche ausländische Unternehmen nach Russland drängten. Der demokratisierende Einfluss der Globalisierung zeigt sich besonders im Aussehen der Mega-Malls, wie z. B. des von der schwedischen Kette IKEA seit 2003 im Südwesten der Stadt betriebenen Zentrums. Wochentags zieht es 25000 Menschen, an Wochenenden 80000 zum Einkaufen hierher (sowie Zehntausende, die extra herkommen, um IKEA oder Auchan zu besichtigen). Auf der einen Seite befindet sich ein Parkplatz mit 10000 Stellplätzen, an der Frontseite des Gebäudes sind 65 Kassen aufgereiht, und von allen Einkaufszentren in Osteuropa hat es die größte Verkaufsfläche.[45] In der Nähe verläuft eine Autobahn; zwar ist das Zentrum für Autofahrer entworfen worden, aber auch bei Leuten ohne Auto ist es beliebt, da kostenlose Busse zu den nächstgelegenen Metrostationen pendeln. Bis an den Rand gefüllt mit erschwinglichen Waren, ist es ein Paradies für sparsame Käufer. Die Inflation zieht an, die Rentenreform verspricht nichts Gutes, es ist viel von Unsicherheit die Rede. All das bedeutet, dass langfristiges Planen nicht viel Sinn hat. Damit werden die kurzfristigen Kalkulationen, die jeder jeden Tag anstellt, was er wo und wann kauft, so bedeutsam, denn dadurch hat man das Gefühl, sein Leben irgendwie unter Kontrolle zu haben.
Was Moskauer Einkaufsadressen von anderen in Europa und den USA unterscheidet, ist die Beliebtheit von Großmärkten unter freiem Himmel für die ganze Familie. Sie befinden sich meist in der Nähe von Metrostationen und haben eine Vielzahl von Ständen, an denen alles Mögliche, von Fleisch bis Bedarfsgütern, in der Regel aus China importiert, verkauft wird. Soziale Unterschiede zeigen sich häufig darin, wo man einkaufen geht: Wer über genügend Einkommen verfügt, leistet sich schicke Boutiquen und teure Warenhäuser, während Leute mit bescheideneren Mitteln die stets vollen „Märkte der tausend Dinge" *(weschtschewyje rynki)* ansteuern.
Da viele daran gewöhnt sind, sich materiell einzuschränken, erzwungen durch das frühere niedrige Konsumniveau, haben sie sich einen regelrechten „Habitus" zugelegt, der diktiert wird von der Priorität, mit diesen Einschränkungen umgehen zu können.[46] Daher rührt der Hang zum „Praktischen" und „Preiswerten", zur Langlebigkeit und Funktionalität von Dingen, den viele beim Einkaufen demonstrieren. Die Zeiten, in denen viele der heutigen Verbraucher groß geworden sind, haben ihre Spuren in Geschmack und Konsumgewohnheiten der Menschen hinterlassen.

ZUSAMMENFASSUNG

Ein populärer Trend in der Globalisierungstheorie ist die Analyse dessen, wie Prozesse in der Wirtschaft zu Kulturerscheinungen führen, die sich nur schwer unter Zuhilfenahme vereinfachter Vorstellungen von ökonomischen Kausalzusammenhängen erklären lassen. Wie die Bewerbung Moskaus um die Ausrichtung der Olympischen Spiele beweist, enthüllt der Eintritt des postsowjetischen Russlands in die Weltwirt-

What makes the configuration of the Moscow's shopping places different in comparison to the European and American cities is the popularity of the open-air wholesale markets for family shopping. Found around most subway stations, they host plenty of individual stalls selling everything (from meet to everyday goods, imported, as a rule, from China). The social differences very often show themselves in the places where people go shopping: those with a lot of disposable income can afford attending smart boutiques and expensive department stores while those with modest means opt for the crowed "things markets" (*veschevyye rynki*).
Being accustomed to deal with material constrains caused by a formerly low level of consumption, many people seem to have developed a peculiar "habitus" based on a priority that is given to one's ability to manage those constrains.[46] Hence the "practicality", "frugality", a taste towards durability and functionality of things that people repeatedly show as they go shopping. The times in which many were raised have left their traces on people's tastes and consumption habits.

CONCLUSION

A popular current in theory of globalisation is to analyse the way in which processes brought about in the economic sphere lead to cultural phenomena which are difficult to explain relying on simplistic notions of economic causality. As the case of Moscow's bidding for the Olympics, the post-Soviet Russia's entry into global economy has made apparent the mechanisms by which urban space embodies not only new life-forms and preferences of globally oriented elite classes but consciously implemented cultural productions expressing local xenophobias, imperial ambitions, nationalist and isolationist sentiments. Moscow, while becoming an independent political and economic agent, has to mediate between the global cities' network and the national political configurations. Since the growing alienation of the citizens from the governmental policies is characteristic for the latter, the federal and city's government increasingly rely on the staged events and heavily manipulated media. This complicates the development of the citizen's political mobilisation, of the horizontal forms of governance, and renders problematic the existence of un-manipulated public space. The co-presence of the global flows and the residues of traditional local politics in material and immaterial spaces of the city channels social energy of the residents, predominantly, into cultural practices of consumption.
A substantial strata of new cultural intermediaries that finds its home in Moscow has expanded the role of profit-oriented cultural activities. These intermediaries position themselves as experts in lifestyle and consumption, as popularisers of novel cultural products, as the legitimators of the "right tastes". As a result, in Moscow as well as in many of Russia's urban centers, hybrid patterns of consumption cultures emerged in which the habits developed in the times of scarcity are combined with new opportunities and preferences (often outlined and pointed out by the new cultural workers). The radically improved consumer skills and attitudes resulted in the appearance of a very many good shoppers. The people who may well be counted among such shoppers come from very different social classes, ranging from well-off to hardly scrapping by. What unites them is both their love for shopping and a lot of knowledge that they put into this process. This knowledge necessarily includes

schaft die Mechanismen, mit deren Hilfe der urbane Raum nicht nur neue Lebensformern und Präferenzen der global orientierten Eliten zum Ausdruck bringt, sondern auch bewusst realisierte kulturelle Produktionen, die gekennzeichnet sind von lokalen Xenophobien, imperialen Ambitionen sowie nationalistischen und isolationistischen Meinungen. Moskau, auf dem Weg zu einem unabhängigen politischen und wirtschaftlichen Faktor, muss gleichzeitig zwischen dem Netzwerk der Großstädte und den nationalen politischen Gruppierungen vermitteln. Charakteristisch für Letztere ist die wachsende Entfremdung der Bürger von der Regierungspolitik, während die Föderationsregierung und die Stadtverwaltung sich zunehmend auf inszenierte Ereignisse und massiv manipulierte Medien stützen. Das erschwert die politische Mobilisierung der Bürger und die Entwicklung horizontaler Partizipationsformen und macht die Existenz manipulationsfreier öffentlicher Räume zum Problem. Die gemeinsame Präsenz von globalen Strömen und Resten traditioneller Lokalpolitik in materiellen und nichtmateriellen städtischen Räumen leitet die soziale Energie der Bewohner vor allem in kulturelle Konsumpraktiken.

Die neuen in Moskau beheimateten Mittelsmänner der Kultur haben in großer Zahl die Rolle gewinnorientierter kultureller Aktivitäten gestärkt. Diese Vermittler präsentieren sich als Experten für Lifestyle und Konsum, die neuen Kulturprodukten zum Durchbruch verhelfen und den „richtigen Geschmack" legitimieren. Dadurch haben sich sowohl in Moskau als auch in vielen anderen russischen Stadtzentren hybride Konsumkulturen herausgebildet, bei denen sich die aus der Zeit der Mangelwirtschaft herrührenden Gewohnheiten mit den neuen Möglichkeiten und Präferenzen verbinden (worauf die neuen Kulturverantwortlichen oft und gern Bezug nehmen). Die radikal verbesserten Konsumfertigkeiten und -haltungen führen dazu, dass sehr viele die neuen Einkaufsmöglichkeiten immer besser nutzen. Sie kommen aus sehr unterschiedlichen sozialen Schichten, aus solchen, denen es gut geht, bis hin zu anderen, die gerade so über die Runden kommen. Was sie verbindet, ist die Freude am Einkaufen und ein beträchtliches Wissen, das sie dabei investieren. Dazu gehört natürlich auch, dass sie wissen, was es wo gibt. Schnäppchenjagden, Flohmarktbesuche, Schaufensterbummel, entspannte Einkaufstouren durch Boutiquen und Shopping-Center bis hin zu längeren Fahrten nach außerhalb – das sind nur einige der zahlreichen Aktivitäten, bei denen kühles Kalkül neben wilden Phantasien steht und finanzielle sowie zeitliche Grenzen mit Wünschen und geheimen Sehnsüchten wetteifern.

ANMERKUNGEN

1 Modelski, Georg: „Ancient World Cities 4000-1000 BC. Center/Hinterland in the World System". In: *Global Society.* Heft 13(4) 1999, S. 383–392

2 In Europa wurden auf der 2. Paneuropäischen Verkehrskonferenz auf Kreta im März 1994 eine Reihe paneuropäischer Verkehrskorridore als „Strecken in Mittel- und Osteuropa, die in den nächsten zehn bis 15 Jahren größere Investitionen erfordern", bezeichnet. (Pan-European Corridors. Wikipedia , http://en.wikipedia.org/wiki/Pan-European_corridors). Moskau ist Teil des Ost-West-Korridors sowie des zwischen Helsinki und Odessa verlaufenden Korridors.

3 Robertson, Ronald: *Globalization. Social Theory and Global Culture.* Berkeley 1992, S. 8

4 Vgl. Donald, James: *Imagining the Modern City.* Minneapolis 1999; zur sozialen Metaphorik im postsowjetischen Kontext vgl. Oushakine, Sergei: „The Quantity of Style: Imaginary Consumption in the New Russia". In: *Theory, Culture, and Society.* Heft 17(5), 2000, S. 98–120; Shevchenko, Olga/ Schukin, Yakov: „From socialist camp to global village? Globalization and the imaginary landscapes of postsoci-

what is available where. Bargain hunting, flee market browsing, window shopping, leisurely strolling boutiques and shopping malls, shopping expeditions to the remote areas – these are only few of the numerous activities in which cold calculation co-exists with wild fantasies, and the financial and temporal constraints compete with desires and secret wishes.

NOTES

1 Modelski, Georg: "Ancient World Cities 4000–1000 BC: Center/Hinterland in the World System." In: *Global Society* 13:4 (October 1999), p. 383–392

2 In Europe, a number of Pan-European transport corridors were defined at the second Pan-European transport Conference in Crete, March 1994, "as routes in Central and Eastern Europe that required major investment over the next ten to fifteen years" ("Pan-European Corridors", see Wikipedia (http://en.wikipedia.org/wiki/Pan-European_corridors). Moscow is a part of East-West corridor as well as a part of the one that has stretched between Helsinki and Odessa.

3 Robertson, Ronald: *Globalisation. Social Theory and Global Culture.* Berkeley 1992, p. 8

4 See Donald, James: *Imagining the Modern City.* Minneapolis 1999; on the social imaginary in the post-Soviet context see Oushakine, Sergei: "The Quantity of Style: Imaginary Consumption in the New Russia". In: *Theory, Culture, and Society*, 2000, 17(5), pp. 98–120; Shevchenko, Olga/ Schukin, Yakov: "From socialist camp to global village? Globalisation and the imaginary landscapes of postsocialism". In: McCann, Leo (Ed.): *Russian Transformations. Challenging the global narrative.* London/New York 2004, pp. 89–110

5 Lefebvre, Henri: *The Production of Space.* Transl. by Donald Nicholson-Smith. Oxford 1991

6 Castoriadis, Cornelius: *The Imaginary Institution of Society.* Trans. Kathleen Blamey. Cambridge 1987

7 Bourdieu, Pierre: *Distinction: A Social Critique of Judgment of Taste*, London 2000

8 Lefebvre, Henri: *The Production of Space*, p.12

9 Jusoiti, Afsati: "Aktsiya zaderzhki". [An action of prevention]. In: *Kommersant*, no. 123, July 7, 2005, p.1, 10

10 Since the terrorist attack happened shortly after this announcement, one is struck by the inevitability with which new opportunities for contemporary cities come together with new threats.

11 Sassen, Saskia: "Introduction." In: Sassen, Saskia (Ed.): *Global Networks, Linked Cities.* New York/London (Year?)p. 36

12 These cities include Seoul, Atlanta, Barcelona, Manchester, Birmingham. See Short, John Rennie: *The Urban Order*, Oxford 1996, p. 430

13 Short, John Rennie/Kim, Yeong Hyun: *Globalisation and the City.* Essex 1999, p.11

14 Jessop, Bob: "The Entrepreneurial City: Re-Imaging Localities, Redesigning Economic Governance, or Restructuring Capital?" In: Jewson, Nick/MacGregor, Susanne (Eds.): *Transforming Cities. Contested Governance and New Spatial Divisions*, London/New York 1997, 28–41. J.R. Short e al. uses this notion as well: Short, J.R./Kim, Y.: *Globalisation and the City*, p. 117

15 Ward, Stephen: *Selling Places: The Marketing and Promotion of Towns and Cities, 1850–2000.* London 1998.

16 Bedirhanoglu, Pinar: "The nomenclatura's passive revolution in Russia in the neoliberal era". In: McCann, Leo (Ed.): *Russian Transformations. Challenging the global narrative.* London/New York 2004, pp. 19–41

17 See O'Lauphlin, Jeremy/ Kolossov, Vladimir: "Moscow as an emergent world city". In: *Eurasian Geography and Economics* 23 (3), 2002, pp. 161–270; Sakwa, Richard: "Russia and Globalisation". In: McCann, Leo (Ed.): *Russian Transformations*, p. 212

18 Short, John Rennie/Kim, Yeong Hyun et al.: "The dirty little secret of world cities research – data problems in comparative analysis". In: *International Journal of Urban and Regional Research* 20(4), 1996, pp. 697–719

19 Sassen, Saskia: "Introduction." –In: Sassen, Saskia (Ed.): *Global Networks, Linked Cities.* New York/London (year?), p. 3

20 Biryukova, Ekaterina: "Bolschoi dorozhe Kremlya" [Bolschoi is more expensive than Kremlin]. In: *Izvestia*, July 1, 2005, p. 1

21 Biryukova, Ekaterina: "Bolschoi dorozhe Kremlya", p. 8

22 At the end of May 2005 the Muscovites and tourists have spent about one million dollar only on the tickets to performance of four operas of Richard Wagner's *Der Ring des Nibelungen* performed by Mariinski theater.

alism". In: McCann, Leo (Hg.): *Russian Transformations. Challenging the global narrative.* London/New York 2004, S. 89–110

5 Lefebvre, Henri: *The Production of Space.* Übers. Donald Nicholson-Smith. Oxford 1991

6 Castoriadis, Cornelius: *The Imaginary Institution of Society.* Übers. Kathleen Blamey. Cambridge 1987

7 Bourdieu, Pierre. *Distinction: A Social Critique of Judgment of Taste.* London 2000

8 Lefebvre, Henri: *The Production of Space,* S. 12

9 Jusoiti, Afsati: „Akzija saderzhki". In: *Kommersant,* Nr. 123, 7. Juli 2005, S.1, 10

10 Der Terroranschlag geschah kurz nach der Bekanntgabe, und beeindruckend daran ist die Unvermeidbarkeit, mit der neue Chancen für moderne Städte mit neuen Bedrohungen einhergehen.

11 Sassen, Saskia: „Introduction". In: Sassen, Saskia (Hg.): *Global Networks, Linked Cities.* New York/London (2002), S. 36

12 Zu diesen Städten gehören Seoul, Atlanta, Barcelona, Manchester und Birmingham. Siehe Short, John Rennie: *The Urban Order.* Oxford 1996, S. 430

13 Short, John Rennie/Kim, Yeong Hyun: *Globalization and the City.* Essex 1999, S.11

14 Jessop, Bob: „The Entrepreneurial City. Re-Imaging Localities, Redesigning Economic Governance, or Restructuring Capital?" In: Jewson, Nick/MacGregor, Susanne (Hg.): *Transforming Cities. Contested Governance and New Spatial Divisions.* London/New York 1997, S. 28–41. J.R. Short u. a. verwendet ebenfalls diesen Begriff: Short, J.R./Kim, Y.: *Globalization and the City,* S. 117

15 Ward, Stephen. *Selling Places: The Marketing and Promotion of Towns and Cities, 1850–2000.* London 1998

16 Bedirhanoglu, Pinar: „The nomenclatura's passive revolution in Russia in the neoliberal era". In: McCann, Leo (Hg.): *Russian Transformations. Challenging the global narrative.* London/New York 2004, S. 19–41

17 Vgl. O'Lauphlin, Jeremy/Kolossov, Vladimir: „Moscow as an emergent world city". In: *Eurasian Geography and Economic.* 23 (3), 2002, S. 161–270; Sakwa, Richard: „Russia and Globalisation". In: McCann, Leo (Hg.): *Russian Transformations,* S. 212

18 Short, John Rennie/Kim, Yeong Hyun u. a.: „The dirty little secret of world cities research. Data problems in comparative analysis". In: *International Journal of Urban and Regional Research.* 20 (4), 1996, S. 697–719

19 Sassen, Saskia: a. a. O., S. 3

20 Birjukowa, Jekaterina: „Bolschoi doroshe Kremlja". In: *Iswestija,* 1. Juli 2005, S. 1

21 Birjukowa, Jekaterina: „Bolschoi doroshe Kremlja", S. 8

22 Ende Mai 2005 gaben Moskauer und Touristen ca. eine Millionen Dollar allein für Karten für die Aufführung der Tetralogie von Richard Wagners *Der Ring des Nibelungen* in der Inszenierung des Marijinski-Theaters aus.

23 http://www.muar.ru/eng/exhibitions/2004/exibit130404_e.htm

24 Weintraub, Jeff: „The Theory and Politics of the Public/Private Distinction". In: Weintraub, Jeff/Kumar, Krisnan (Hg.): *The Public/Private Distinction,* Chicago 1996, S. 12

25 Robbins, Bruce: „Introduction". In: Robbins, Bruce (Hg): *The Phantom Public Sphere.* Minneapolis 1993, S. ii

26 Vgl. Rybczynski, Witold: *City Life: Urban Expectations in a New World.* New York 1995

27 Baudrillard, Jean: „On Consumer Society". In: Poster, Mark (Hg.): *Jean Baudrillard. Selected Writings.* Stanford/Kalifornien (Jahr?), S. 33

28 Oushakine, Sergei: „The Quantity of Style. Imaginary Consumption in the New Russia". In: *Theory, Culture, and Society.* 17 (5), 2000, S. 98–120

29 Condee, Nancy/Padunov, Vladimir: „The ABC of Russian Consumer Culture: Reading, Rating, and Real Estate". In: Condee; Nancy (Hg.): *Soviet Hieroglyphics. Visual Culture in Late Twentieth-Century Russia.* Bloomington/Indianapolis 1995, S. 134, 161

30 Schalajewa, Galina: *Chotschu byt bankirom.* Moskau 2003

31 Tereshenko, V.: *Marketing-Terapia. Nowyj wsgljad na russkji marketing.* St. Petersburg 2004, S. 209

32 Ebenda, S. 34

33 Vgl. auch Douglas, Mary/Isherwood, Baron: *The World of Goods. Towards an Anthropology of Consumption.* London, 1979; Fiske, John (Hg.): „Shopping for Pleasure. Malls, Power, and Resistance". In: *Reading the Popular.* London(Jahr?), S. 132–160

34 Apparudai, Arjun: „Introduction: commodities and the politics of value". In: Apparudai, Arjun (Hg.): *The Social Life of Things: Commodities in Cultural Perspective.* Cambridge 1986, S. 3–63

35 Es fanden sechs ähnlich strukturierte Interviews mit den Kuratoren der Tretjakow-Galerie und Autoren, die für beliebte, verbraucherorientierte Zeitschriften schreiben, statt. Jedes Interview dauerte etwa eineinhalb Stunden.

36 Warner, W. Lloyd/Meeker, Marsha/Fells, Kennth: *Social Class in America. The Evaluation of Status.* New York 1949, S. 23

23 See http://www.muar.ru/eng/exhibitions/2004/exibit130404_e.htm

24 Weintraub, Jeff: "The Theory and Politics of the Public/Private Distinction". In: Weintraub, Jeff/Kumar, Krisnan (Eds.): *The Public/Private Distinction*. Chicago 1996, p.12

25 Robbins, Bruce: "Introduction." In: Robbins, Bruce (Ed): *The Phantom Public Sphere*, Minneapolis 1993, p. ii

26 See Rybczynski, Witold: *City Life: Urban Expectations in a New World*, New York 1995

27 Baudrillard, Jean: "On Consumer Society". In: Poster, Mark (Ed.): *Jean Baudrillard: Selected Writings*, ed. Stanford, Cal. (year?) p. 33

28 Oushakine, Sergei: "The Quantity of Style: Imaginary Consumption in the New Russia". In: *Theory, Culture, and Society* 17(5), 2000, pp. 98–120

29 Condee, Nancy/Padunov, Vladimir: "The ABC of Russian Consumer Culture: Reading, Rating , and Real Estate."– In: Condee, Nancy (Ed.): *Soviet Hieroglyphics: Visual Culture in Late Twentieth-Century Russia*, Bloomington/Indianapolis 1995, pp. 134, 161

30 Schalayeva, Galina: *Hotchu byt' bankirom* [*I want to be a banker*]. Moscow 2003

31 Tereshenko, V.: *Marketing-Terapia. Novy vzglyad na russki marketing* [*Marketing-Therapy. New Look at the Russian Marketing: The Problems and Perspectives]*. St. Petersburg 2004, p. 209

32 Ibid, p. 34

33 See, for example, Douglas, Mary/Isherwood, Baron: *The World of Goods: Towards an Anthropology of Consumption*. London 1979; Fiske, John: "Shopping for Pleasure: Malls, Power, and Resistance". In: *Reading the Popular*. London (year?), pp. 132–160

34 Apparudai, Arjun: "Introduction: commodities and the politics of value". In: Apparudai, Arjun (Ed.): *The Social Life of Things: Commodities in Cultural Perspective*. Cambridge 1986, pp. 3–63

35 A set of 6 semi-structured interviews was conducted with the curators of the Tretyakov Gallery and with the authors writing for popular, consumer-oriented magazines. Each interview lasted for about one and a half hour.

36 Warner, W. Lloyd/Meeker, Marsha/Fells, Kenneth: *Social Class in America: the Evaluation of Status*. New York 1949, p. 23

37 Herrnstein Smith, Barbara: *Contingencies of Value. Alternative Perspectives for Critical Theory*. Cambridge/MA 1988, p. 131

38 Featherstone, Mike: *Consumer Culture and Postmodernism*. London 1991, pp. 35–40

39 Twitchell, James: "Two Cheers for Materialism".– In: Shor, Juliet B./Holt, Douglas B. (Eds.): *The Consumer Society Reader*. New York: 2000, p. 289

40 The polls repeatedly show that the number of Russians who define themselves as belonging to the middle class significantly exceeds the number of the citizens who reasonably might claim that they are middle class, taking count of their income.

41 Bourdieu, Pierre: *Distinction*, p.311

42 Zukin, Sharon: *The Cultures of Cities*. Cambridge/MA 1995, p. 5

43 Dyogot, Ekaterina: "Economika dara" [Economy of gift]. –In: *Bolshoi Gorod*, no.11, 2005, p.7

44 *Magaziny Moskvy* [The Moscow's Stores]. Afisha Guidebook. Moscow 2004, p.5

45 Bridge, Robert: "Hyper Shopping in Moscow". In: *Moscow News*, July 10, 2005, p.3

46 Holt, Douglas B.: "Does Capital Structure American Consumption?" In: Shor, Juliet B./ Holt, Douglas B. (Eds.): *The Consumer Society Reader*. New York 2000, p. 224

37 Herrnstein Smith, Barbara: *Contingencies of Value. Alternative Perspectives for Critical Theory.* Cambridge/MA 1988, S.131

38 Featherstone, Mike: *Consumer Culture and Postmodernism.* London 1991, S. 35–40

39 Twitchell, James: „Two Cheers for Materialism". In: Shor, Juliet B./Holt, Douglas B. (Hg.): *The Consumer Society Reader.* New York 2000, S. 289

40 Umfragen haben wiederholt ergeben, dass die Zahl der Russen, die sich zur Mittelklasse zählen, signifikant die Zahl derjenigen übersteigt, die aufgrund ihres Einkommens zu Recht dorthin gehören.

41 Bourdieu, Pierre: *Distinction*, a. a. O., S. 311

42 Zukin, Sharon: *The Cultures of Cities.* Cambridge/MA 1995, S. 5

43 Djogot, Jekaterina: „Ekonomika dara". In: *Bolschoi Gorod*, Nr. 11, 2005, S.7

44 *Magasiny Moskwy.* Afisha Guidebook. Moskau 2004, S. 5

45 Bridge, Robert: „Hyper Shopping in Moscow". In: *Moscow News*, 10. Juli 2005, S. 3

46 Holt, Douglas B.: „Does Capital Structure American Consumption?" In: Shor, Juliet B./Holt, Douglas B. (Hg.): *The Consumer Society Reader.* New York 2000, S. 224

ОБУВН
ЯРМАР
ООО «КОНФИН»
БЫТОВАЯ ТЕХНИКА
ОБУВНАЯ ЯРМАРКА
ВИДЕО МАГНИТОФОНЫ
ДЖИНСЫ
ШИРОКИЙ ВЫБОР ЦВЕТОВ РАЗМЕРОВ ФИРМ
MP3 CD·MD
ИГРОВЫЕ ПРИСТАВКИ
ШИРОКИЙ выбор
DVD
120 рублей
SOFT
ИГРЫ В DVD
БОКСАХ
АУДИО
ЛУЧШАЯ
ОБУВЬ
ЖЕНСКАЯ, МУЖСКАЯ, ДЕТСКАЯ И ПОДРОСТКОВАЯ
ТАТУИРОВКА
АКСЕССУАРЫ
ИНДИВИДУАЛЬНЫЙ ДИЗАЙН

GENERATION WARSCHAU

BASTIAN LANGE

WIRKLICHKEITSBEHAUPTUNGEN EINER NEUEN GENERATION

Osteuropäische Großstädte werden aus der Distanz als extrem jung, schnell und dynamisch wahrgenommen. Eine neue Generation junger unternehmerischer Polen definiert und praktiziert Wirklichkeitsbehauptungen. Sie folgt einer praktischen Theorie des Handelns, die nicht, wie die ihrer Elterngeneration, utopiefixiert ist. Dagegen hat der Punkrocker Kuba Wandachowicz die Generation der Mittzwanziger als „Generation Nichts" beschrieben, die mit der gewonnenen Freiheit nichts anzufangen weiß: Desillusioniert, perspektivlos und konsumorientiert lebe sie den Rausch einer ewigen Party. Die hektische Betriebsamkeit in den osteuropäischen Metropolzentren spricht aber auch für eine „Generation speeded-up", die vom Leben Superlative erwartet. In kürzester Zeit haben sich hier für wenige Transformationsgewinner materieller Wohlstand, sozialer Statusgewinn und mediale Aufmerksamkeit eingestellt.
Formen des individuellen unternehmerischen Handelns sind heute aber für große Teile der polnischen Gesellschaft harte Überlebensstrategien in äußerst prekären Lebenslagen. Das gesellschaftliche Dispositiv des „unternehmerischen Selbst" wirkt als flexible Camouflage: Junge urbane Unternehmer vermitteln einerseits gesellschaftliche Rollenmodelle, während sich andererseits ein Heer von Taxifahrern, *shuttle traders*, Wanderarbeitern, Prostituierten und Saisonarbeitern in hochflexiblen Arbeitskontexten bewegt und den Kräften des neoliberalen Marktes ungeschützt ausgesetzt ist.
Gerade in den Städten Osteuropas führen sie zu extremsten sozioökonomischen Spaltungen. In der belebten Innenstadt Warschaus zeigt sich das junge, aufstrebende Polen auf der Haupteinkaufs- und Flaniermeile Marszałkowska. Bei Wodka und Elektrobeats wird im Sommer nicht weit entfernt unter der Sigismundsäule gefeiert und getanzt. Im Winter tummeln sich verschiedene experimentierfreudige Szenen bei Noise-Musik in Clubs, die in den Seitenflügeln des städtebaulich dominierenden Kulturpalasts untergebracht sind. Der offene und bezahlbare Zugang zu den Spielorten der wirtschaftlich Erfolgreichen ist dagegen beispielsweise in Moskau fast nicht mehr gegeben. Die Reichen schotten sich in Sicherheitsghettos ab und verteidigen mit Menschen, Mauern und martialischen Methoden ihre Pfründe. Die sozialräumlichen Kristallisationskerne der Erfolgreichen sind Ausdruck stetig wachsender sozioökonomischer Disparitäten. Eine kleine Klientel aufstrebender unternehmerischer Akteure beansprucht ausgewiesene Stadträume für sich als Orte des wirtschaftlichen Erfolgs.[1]
Das neue Unternehmertum bildet eine der markantesten Zäsuren zum Sozialismus. Die sich daran anschließenden, nicht vorhersehbaren Pfadentwicklungen des Postsozialismus als Modernisierungsaufforderung für das Individuum zu lesen bedeutet

WARSAW GENERATION

BASTIAN LANGE

THE SELF-ASSERTION OF A NEW GENERATION

Major Eastern European cities are perceived from a distance as extremely young, fast and dynamic. A new generation of young entrepreneurial Poles is defining and engaging in processes of self-assertion. Its members embrace a practical theory of action which, unlike that of its parents' generation, is not focused on a utopia. On the other hand, the punk rocker, Kuba Wandachowicz, has described the present generation of mid-20-year-olds as a "nothing generation", one that doesn't know what to do with its new found freedom: disillusioned, without prospects, and consumption-minded, it lives on the high of a never-ending party. However, the frantic activity found in Eastern European metropolises would also indicate that it also is a "speeded-up generation", one expecting only superlatives from life. The few individuals to profit from the political transformation very quickly found material prosperity, improved social status and media attention.

For large sections of Polish society today, however, individual entrepreneurial action is moulded by tough survival strategies in extremely precarious situations. The social declaration of intent of the "entrepreneurial self" acts like flexible camouflage: on the one hand, young urban entrepreneurs communicate social role models while, on the other hand, an army of taxi drivers, shuttle traders, migrant workers, prostitutes and seasonal workers moves in highly flexible working environments and is exposed, unprotected, to the forces of the neo-liberal market. The economically successful voice spatial demands and engage in practices of spatial appropriation, abrasively claiming various urban areas for themselves; both effects are the ambivalent result of radical cultural and systemic transformation processes.

They lead to very extreme socio-economic divisions, especially in Eastern European cities. In Warsaw's busy city centre, up-and-coming young Poles can be seen out and about on ulica Marszałkowska, the main shopping street. Not far from here, in the summer, the young party and dance to vodka and electro beats beneath Sigismund's Column. In the winter, various experimental Noise music scenes cavort in clubs housed in the wings of the Palace of Culture, which dominates the city landscape. Meanwhile, in Moscow, for example, open and affordable access to venues frequented by the economically successful is almost a thing of the past. The rich seal themselves off in high-security ghettos and defend their possessions using men, walls and warlike methods. The socio-spatial crystallisation cores of the successful are an expression of continuously increasing socio-economic disparities. A small clientele of up-and-coming entrepreneurial players claims designated urban areas for itself as places of economic success.[1]

zunächst, den sozialen und lebensweltlichen Kontext in das Verständnis neuer Unternehmerkarrieren mit einzubeziehen. Nur so kann das Verhältnis von nun möglicher unternehmerischer Individualität zur erlebten Geschichte und den milieuspezifischen Vorprägungen, die Suche nach Lösungswegen aus einer zunächst höchst problematischen Krisensituation, angemessen beschrieben werden. Vorgefertigte Lösungen standen nicht zur Verfügung; gleichwohl importierten die osteuropäischen Regierungen scheinbar zukunftstaugliche Modelle aus dem kapitalistischen Ausland und versuchten diese in Form von politisch-normativen Programmatiken zu implementieren.
Die Option „Unternehmer" ist demzufolge höchst ambivalent: Lange unterdrückt und nur unter dem Vorzeichen des Staatsmanagers toleriert, war individuelles unternehmerisches Handeln im Sozialismus offiziell nicht zugelassen. Grund und Boden, Bestand und monetäres Kapital lagen in den Händen des Staates und seines umfassenden Apparates. Die wirtschaftliche Unzulänglichkeit dieses Steuerungsapparates kam in der Mangelwirtschaft Osteuropas zum Ausdruck. Notgedrungen begegneten ihr die Bürger über Jahre mit vielschichtigen Formen des Tauschs sowie des informellen Handelns und halfen sich einfallsreich über Mangel und Missstände hinweg. Nicht zuletzt das Funktionieren dieser informellen Tausch- und Dienstleistungswirtschaft trug zu einer Stabilisierung der autoritären Regierungen bei und verlängerte deren Existenz. Kenntnis-, trick- und variationsreich „unternommen" wurde also unter anderen gesellschaftlichen Vorzeichen sehr viel.
15 Jahre nach der politischen Wende in Osteuropa kommt den wirtschaftlich erfolgreichen neuen Unternehmern gerade in den Hauptstädten eine Vorbildfunktion zu. Als Vorreiter sollen sie neue individuelle Verantwortlichkeiten, liberalistische Ansprüche und den Wert der subjektiven Verwirklichung in einem Kulturmodell vermitteln. Selbstverantwortlich muss Existenzsicherung von großen Teilen der Bevölkerung aber schon lange betrieben werden, die wohlfahrtsstaatlichen Institutionen können ihrer Aufgabe angesichts leerer Haushaltskassen, explodierender Preise und Mieten sowie aus politischen Gründen nicht mehr nachkommen.
Die in Polen als *biznismen* (Geschäftsmann), in Moskau als *biznezmeny* (Geschäftsmann), *ekaubt-menedzhery* (Account-Manager) oder *brokery* (Broker)[2] bezeichneten neuen Akteure repräsentieren visuell und habituell den Transformationsprozess. Die politische Wende hat einen neuen unternehmerischen Sozialraumtypus hervorgebracht: Die neu gewonnenen Handlungs-, Handels- und Artikulationsfreiheiten eröffneten der Nachwendegeneration neue Berufsoptionen; Selbstverwirklichung und Existenzsicherung müssen dabei zunehmend Hand in Hand gehen. Welche Handlungsstrategien entwickeln neue Unternehmer auf städtischer Ebene, wenn die staatlichen Institutionen sich aus der Verantwortung zurückziehen? Wie kann in Zeiten prekärster Existenzlagen sowie geringster bis keiner monetärer Ressourcen die Generation der nun 20- bis 35-Jährigen gesellschaftliche, kulturelle und sozioökonomische Teilhabe erlangen? Welche habituellen Modi zeigen sich bei ihren neuen unternehmerischen Praktiken, welche sozialen Orte markierten, entwickelten und transformierten sie?
In Anlehnung an Gil Eyal, Ivan Szelenyi und Eleanor Townsley, die der Frage nach der gesellschaftlichen Realisierung eines „Kapitalismus ohne Kapitalisten" in den postsozialistischen Staaten nachgehen, wäre demnach zu fragen: Welche Ausdrucksgestalt weist individuelles Unternehmertum im städtischen Polen heute auf, nachdem

New entrepreneurship represents one of the most distinctive breaks from socialism. Interpreting the associated, unforeseeable developments of post-socialism as a call for modernisation of the individual initially means including the social and environmental context in an understanding of new entrepreneurial careers. This is the only way to provide an adequate description of the relationship between the entrepreneurial individuality that is now possible, past history and milieu-specific characteristics, in other words the search for ways out of what is initially an extremely problematic crisis situation. There were no ready-made solutions available; undaunted, the Eastern European governments imported seemingly sustainable models from capitalist countries and tried to implement these in the form of standard political objectives.

As a result, the "entrepreneur" option is a highly ambivalent one. Suppressed for a long time and only tolerated under the auspices of the state manager, individual entrepreneurial action was officially not permitted under socialism. Land, stock and monetary capital were in the hands of the state and its extensive apparatus. The economic shortcomings of this management apparatus was expressed in the economy of scarcity that afflicted Eastern Europe. Of necessity, the citizens responded to this over many years by developing multi-faceted forms of bartering and informal trading, thus helping to overcome the deficiencies and deplorable state of affairs in imaginative ways. It was not least the functioning of this informal barter and service economy that contributed in part to stabilising the authoritarian governments and prolonging their existence. There were plenty of well-informed, cunning and varied "undertakings" under different social conditions.

15 years after the political transformation of Eastern Europe, new economically successful entrepreneurs have assumed the function of role models, especially in the capital cities. As pioneers they are to communicate new individual responsibilities, liberalistic claims and the value of subjective realisation in a cultural model. Needless to say, large sections of the population have long since been forced to secure their livelihoods on their own account, as welfare state institutions can no longer fulfil their duties in view of the empty coffers, exploding prices and rents, as well as for political reasons.

The new players, described in Poland as *biznismen* (businessmen), in Moscow as *biznezmeny* (businessmen), *ekaubt-menedzhery* (account managers) or *brokery* (brokers)[2], represent the transformation process in visual and habitual terms. Political transformation has created a new entrepreneurial socio-spatial type. New-found freedoms of action, trade and articulation open up new career options for the post-transformation generation; increasingly, self-realisation and the securing of livelihoods must go hand in hand. What strategies for action are new entrepreneurs developing at city level, if the state institutions are giving up their responsibility? How can the generation of now 20 to 35-year-olds achieve social, cultural and socio-economic participation in times of extremely precarious living conditions as well as very limited, or even non-existent, monetary resources? What habitual methods are demonstrated in its new entrepreneurial practices, what social places does it mark out, develop and transform?

Following Gil Eyal, Ivan Szelenyi and Eleanor Townsley, who investigate the social implementation of a "capitalism without capitalists" in the post-socialist states, it would be appropriate to ask: what form of expression does individual entrepreneurship take in

es offiziell im Sozialismus lange Zeit nicht zugelassen war und erst nach der politischen Wende durch den Staat propagiert und befördert wurde?[3] Auf welche kreativen Handlungsskripte greifen gerade jüngere Entrepreneurs zurück, wenn sie nur mit geringsten ökonomischen Kapitalbeständen ausgestattet sind? Sozialistische Vorerfahrungen und Prägungen des vormals nichtmonetären Handelns und Tauschens bekommen möglicherweise gerade in krassen postsozialistischen Transformationslagen eine unternehmerische und existenzsichernde Bedeutung für das alltägliche Überleben. Welche informellen sozialen Sicherheitsnetze stellen auf diesem Weg der beruflichen Ermöglichung neue intermediäre Institutionen dar? Und wie verfährt dabei die neue unternehmerische „Generation Warschau"?

Europäische Städte stehen seit den 1990er Jahren in einem harten Wettbewerb um kreative Talente.[4] Städtische Kultur- und Wirtschaftspolitiker attestieren jungen Kreativarbeitern wegen ihres prägenden Einflusses auf das Image der Stadt eine herausgehobene Rolle. Durch eine diversifizierte Kulturindustrie, die Herstellung von kulturell-symbolischen Gütern und die Entwicklung markanter Konsumpraktiken erhofft man sich Einkommens- und Beschäftigungseffekte für die stadtökonomische Zukunft. Kultur ist mithin zu einem städtischen Exportschlager geworden: Dependancen des österreichischen Kulturministeriums und des deutschen Goethe-Instituts in Warschau beispielsweise vermitteln in den letzten Jahren immer prägnanter das kulturelle Bild einer Stadt oder eines Landes, das letztlich durch eine junge, urbane, kulturell interessierte Unternehmerschaft repräsentiert wird. Die kulturellen Anker (Galerien, Museen, Konzerthallen etc.) generieren interkulturellen Austausch, etablieren vielfältige Wissens- und Kulturtransfers und stellen somit neben ihrer Rolle als Repräsentanten auch informelle Institutionen der Vermittlung kulturökonomischer Werte dar. Infolge dieses *Traffic of Cultures* zeigen sich in den beiden dominierenden urbanen Zentren Polens, Warschau und Krakau, erste kulturpolitische Erfolge der polnischen Nachwendegeneration. Dies ist nicht zuletzt den zahlreichen polnischen Künstlern zu verdanken, die auf europäischen Kunstausstellungen für Furore sorgen und rückwirkend in ihren Heimatstädten zu Vorbildern einer künstlerischen Club-, Galerie- und Projektszene werden.[5]

Auch in westeuropäischen Gesellschaften setzt man angesichts von Sozialstaatsabbau, leeren Kassen und der Destandardisierung beruflicher Karrieren auf individuelle Verantwortung und ein neues Unternehmertum.[6] Heinz Bude porträtierte Ende der 1990er Jahre eine „Generation Berlin", die „ganz entschieden aus unternehmerischen Wirklichkeitsmenschen" bestehe.[7] Das Leitbild des „unternehmerischen Einzelnen" ist in den vermeintlichen Wohlfahrtsstaaten Westeuropas längst von der Zukunftsvision zur gesellschaftlichen Realität geworden: Eigenverantwortlich arbeitet eine neue Generation an ihrer kulturellen und gesellschaftlich-ökonomischen Teilhabe, sie testet und entwirft Produkte, realisiert in vernetzten Projektökologien zeitlich höchst flexibel komplexe Medien-, Diskurs- und Symbolangebote.[8] Realökonomisch betrachtet befindet sich diese diskursiv gehypte Gruppe von Kreativproduzenten am Ende einer unternehmensbezogenen Kette von Dienstleistern: Sie agiert, meist mit mehreren parallelen Jobs, in fragilen Netzstrukturen am existenzgefährdeten Rand der städtischen Ökonomie – also in Ökonomien des methodischen Durchwurschtelns mit kombinierten Lebenserwartungsstrategien.

urban Poland today, after not being officially permitted under socialism for a long time and only being promoted and propagated by the state following the political transformation?[3] What creative action scripts do entrepreneurs – and especially young entrepreneurs – fall back on when they are equipped with only very limited economic capital stock? Previous experience and characteristics of formerly non-monetary trading and bartering under socialism become important for day-to-day survival in the context of entrepreneurship and the securing of livelihoods; this may be all the truer in extreme post-socialist transformation situations. What informal social safety nets do new intermediary institutions provide on this path to new career opportunities? And how will the new entrepreneurial "Warsaw generation" proceed?

There has been tough competition over creative talent between European cities since the 1990s.[4] Urban cultural and economic politicians underline the distinctive role played by young creative workers because of their shaping influence on the image of the city. It is hoped that a diversified culture industry, the manufacture of goods with a symbolic value for culture and the development of striking consumer practices will generate income and employment effects for the future of the urban economy. Culture has therefore become a top-selling urban export. Over the past few years, the Offices of the Austrian Ministry of Culture and the German Goethe Institute in Warsaw, for example, have communicated the cultural image of a city or a country that is ultimately represented by a young, urban, culturally interested entrepreneurship in an increasingly succinct manner. The cultural anchors (galleries, museums, concert halls, etc.) generate inter-cultural exchange, facilitate a multi-faceted knowledge and culture transfer, and therefore, in addition to their role as representatives, they are also informal institutions for the communication of cultural values with an economic dimension. As a result of this *traffic of cultures,* the initial cultural successes of the Polish post-transformation generation can be seen in the two dominant urban centres of Poland: Warsaw and Krakow. This is thanks not least to the numerous Polish artists who have caused a stir at European art exhibitions and have conversely become examples of an artistic club, gallery and project scene in their home cities.[5]

Individual responsibility and new entrepreneurship are coming more to the fore in Western European societies, too, in view of the dismantling of the welfare state, empty coffers and destandardisation of vocational careers.[6] At the end of the 1990s, Heinz Bude portrayed a "Berlin generation" consisting "quite distinctly of entrepreneurial realists".[7] In the supposed welfare states of Western Europe the model of the "entrepreneurial individual" has long since developed from a vision of the future into a social reality. A new generation is working on its cultural und socio-economic participation on its own account; it designs and tests products, and in networked project ecologies it realises complex media, discourse and symbol products that are highly flexible in terms of their timescales.[8] From the viewpoint of real economics, this much-hyped group of creative producers can be found at the end of a corporate-based chain of service providers: it acts, usually with several parallel jobs, in fragile network structures on the endangered fringes of the urban economy – i.e. in muddle-through economies with combined life expectation strategies.

INSTITUTIONELLE ÜBERFORMUNG ODER WIRKUNGSMÄCHTIGE PERSISTENZEN DES VERGANGENEN?

Die Neuformierung von Institutionen erfolgte in Polen auf der Basis des 1990 vorgelegten Reformschockprogramms, des so genannten Balcerowicz-Plans, umgangssprachlich auch Big-Bang-Transformation genannt.[9] Dieses Programm wurde maßgeblich durch westliche Experten wie den US-Amerikaner Jeffry Sachs mitgestaltet und umfasste folgende Kernpunkte: die Entwertung der Währung, die Einführung einer Konkurrenzdemokratie und Marktwirtschaft mit Massenkonsum, die radikale Liberalisierung der Preise und Märkte sowie – im Gegensatz zur sozial abgefederten Transformation der ehemaligen DDR – eine drastische Reduzierung des real existierenden Wohlfahrtsstaates.

Die Rolle des Unternehmertums und vor allem die der neuen Selbständigen ist zentral für jedes kapitalistische System, nicht zuletzt in Polen. An ihr kann die Bedeutung des Individuums, seine sozialen Freiheits- und ökonomischen Belastungsgrade ebenso bemessen werden wie der Stellenwert von Institutionen als soziale Akteure in gesellschaftlichen Transformationsprozessen. Der sozialistische Fall stellt eine Besonderheit dar: Es waren nicht Grund und Kapital besitzende private Akteure, die den Weg in den sich neu eröffnenden und sogleich verordneten Kapitalismus beschritten, sondern vielmehr technokratisch-intellektuelle Eliten, welche die Mechanismen der Westmärkte auf ihr Land übertrugen. Neben Top-down-Privatisierungen vormals staatlicher Wirtschaftseinheiten schufen Bottom-up-Gründungen von Unternehmen und Gewerbe eine neue privatwirtschaftliche Struktur. Der Prozess der Ablösung vom alten und der Schritt hin zu einem vorerst nur schwer zu benennenden neuen System eröffneten eine Phase der Transition.

Dem Balcerowicz-Plan lag die Idee zugrunde, das westlich-kapitalistische System auf ein vormals sozialistisches zu übertragen. Man ignorierte dabei nicht nur, dass sich das angeblich funktionierende Referenzsystem seit mehreren Jahren in einem ebenso tiefgreifenden Transformationsprozess befand, sondern auch, dass die Phase der eigentlichen Transition nur durch offene und kontextsensitive Lösungen zu bewältigen ist. Es muss zumindest partiell die Möglichkeit eingeräumt werden, eigensinnige Entwicklungen und Institutionalisierungen zu erkennen und auf sie zu reagieren.[10] Theorien der „nachholenden Modernisierung", die vorgaben, mit der Übertragung der Institutionen könnten in kurzer Zeit ähnliche Lebensbedingungen und sozioökonomische Standards wie im Westen hergestellt werden, basieren auf einem weitestgehend linear gedachten fordistischen Entwicklungsmodell. Adaption und Strukturanpassung durch Institutionentransfer sollten zum gewünschten Ziel führen. Francis Pine und Sue Bridger erkennen in dieser Auffassung der Transition als „nachholende Modernisierung" ein grundsätzliches Missverständnis zwischen Ost und West. Sie weisen darauf hin, dass der Weg zu einer freien Marktökonomie und Zivilgesellschaft seit 1989 in verschiedenen Ländern unterschiedliche Formen und Ausprägungen angenommen hat.[11] Ebenso unterschiedlich waren die Ausgangssituationen, von denen aus zum Beispiel Polen, die Ukraine oder Weißrussland in ein neues System aufbrachen. Die Laisser-faire-Haltung der polnischen Behörden zum Beispiel stand lange Zeit für eine gemäßigtere Kultur-, Arbeitsmigrations- und Reisepolitik. Das darf sicherlich nicht dazu verleiten, hier einen samtenen oder ausschließlich wohlwollenden

INSTITUTIONAL TRANSFORMATION OR PERSISTENT INFLUENCE OF THE PAST?

Institutions in Poland were reformed on the basis of the 'shock therapy' programme presented in 1990, the so-called Balcerowicz Plan, also colloquially called the 'Big Bang transformation'.[9] This programme was designed with the extensive involvement of Western experts, such as Jeffery Sachs from the USA, and it included the following key points: devaluation of the currency; introduction of a competitive democracy and a market economy with mass consumption; radical liberalisation of prices and markets as well as – in contrast to the socially cushioned transformation of the former GDR – a drastic reduction in the existing welfare state.

The role of entrepreneurship and, above all, of the new self-employed is central to every capitalist system, not least in Poland. It can be used to measure the significance of the individual, his level of social and economic freedom, as well as the status of institutions as social players in social transformation processes. The fall of socialism is a peculiar case: it was not the wealthy land-owning private players who trod the path towards the newly emerging and, at the same time, decreed capitalism, but rather technocratic-intellectual elites who transferred the mechanisms of Western markets to their country. In addition to top-down privatisations of formerly state-owned economic units, the bottom-up founding of companies and trades created a new private sector structure. The process of breaking away from the old system and stepping out towards a new one, which is at first difficult to specify, initiates a phase of transition.

The Balcerowicz Plan was based on the idea of projecting the Western capitalist system onto a previously socialist system. Not only did it ignore the fact that the supposedly properly functioning Western reference system had itself been undergoing an equally far-reaching transformation process for several years, but also that the phase of actual transition can only be overcome through open and context-sensitive solutions. The possibility of identifying and reacting to unorthodox developments and institutionalisations must be conceded, at least in part.[10] Theories of "catch-up modernisation", according to which living standards and socio-economic standards similar to those in the West can be achieved quickly by transferring institutions, are based on a Fordist development model envisaged as largely linear in character. Adaptation and structural adjustment by transferring institutions are intended to lead to the desired goal. Francis Pine and Sue Bridger detect a fundamental misunderstanding between East and West in this conception of transition as "catch-up modernisation". They point out that the path towards a free market economy and civil society has assumed various shapes and forms in the countries concerned since 1989.[11] The initial positions from which, for example, Poland, the Ukraine and Belarus started out towards a new system were equally varied. The laissez-faire attitude of the Polish authorities, for example, was synonymous for a long time with a restrained policy on culture, employment migration, and travel. This approach should not lead to the misconception that a "velvet" or exclusively benevolent socialism might be at work here. However, it highlights a significant difference from the initial positions of other states and their ongoing practices of repression, such as in Belarus. A context-based analysis rejects the idea of linear social development processes, as was still assumed in the transition from the era of Fordism to post-Fordism. For example, it regards formations of inter-

Sozialismus am Werk zu sehen. Es markiert aber eine signifikante Differenz zu den Ausgangsbedingungen anderer Staaten und deren bis heute andauernden Repressionspraktiken, wie etwa in Weißrussland. Eine kontextbezogene Analyse wendet sich von der Vorstellung linearer gesellschaftlicher Entwicklungsprozesse ab, wie man sie im Übergang von der Ära des Fordismus zum Postfordismus noch angenommen hat. Sie misst zum Beispiel intermediären Institutionsbildungen eine maßgebliche Rolle im Prozess der Transition zu.[12] In dem Moment, in dem Arbeit bzw. die Bereitstellung von Beschäftigungsoptionen als Grundlage des ökonomischen und sozialen Daseins in sozialistischen und kapitalistischen Staaten radikal transformiert wird und vielerorts nicht mehr realisierbar ist, müssen die Entwicklungspfade beider Systeme weniger gegeneinander bewertet, sondern vielmehr als interdependente Transformationsfiguren im Kontext einer fragmentierten globalen Ökonomie betrachtet werden. Transnationale Arbeitsmärkte, global zirkulierende Kultursysteme und geopolitische Verschiebungen lösen nicht nur Grenzen auf, sie implementieren ebenso durch neue Techniken und Strategien räumliche Markierungen mit lokal passfähigen Logiken und praktischen Vollzügen, aber auch mit dem Abkoppeln von Teilregionen.[13]

Aus dieser Perspektive gewinnen lokal-regionale Binnenlogiken und milieuspezifische Wissens- und Verfahrensbestände für die Analyse eine erklärungserhärtende Funktion. Komplexe, mehrschichtige Wirkungsebenen zwischen Sozialismus und Postsozialismus, lokalen und globalen Ökonomien, neuen ökonomischen Eliten vormals alter Kaderverbände und resistenten neu-alten Verwaltungsakteuren in quasi demokratisch legitimierten lokal-regionalen *Governance*-Konstellationen können somit adäquater beschrieben werden. Dies heißt nicht, dass die sozialen Geographien durch die Einbeziehung solcher Grundstrukturen komplexer werden, sondern dass sich weitaus eigenwilligere, unvorhersehbarere und überraschendere stadtregionale Entwicklungswege offenbaren. Kontextspezifische Analysen basieren nicht zuletzt auf der Grundannahme, dass postsozialistische Transformationsprozesse wesentlich stärker durch inhärente Kontingenzen und strukturelle Binnenlogiken gekennzeichnet sind als durch modernisierungstheoretisch orientierte Entwicklungsstrategien.[14] Dadurch artikuliert sich auch eine, wie Klaus Müller es bezeichnet, „prinzipielle Unsicherheit" bei der Analyse der Entwicklungswege, welche die vormals sozialistischen Staaten einschlagen werden.[15] Medial stark repräsentiert hat sich allerdings innerhalb weniger Jahre eine relativ kleine, wenngleich junge, energische und zielorientierte Gruppe von Unternehmern in den Vordergrund gedrängt; sie gilt als erfolgreich bei der Bewältigung der Krise.

POLENS BIG BANG UND DIE FOLGEN

Polens politische und ökonomische Transformation begann vor 1989 – die Gewerkschaftsbewegung Solidarnosc, erste runde Tische in den 1980er Jahren und das Balcerowicz-Programm haben die Ökonomie von Grund auf restrukturiert. Das Balcerowicz-Programm sah neben institutionellen Reformen und der drastischen Entwertung der Landeswährung um 40 Prozent eine komplette Liberalisierung und rechtliche Gleichstellung für staatlichen, gemeinschaftlichen und privaten Besitz vor. Zudem sollte durch die Freigabe der Preise und die Abschaffung der staatlichen Restriktionen sowie durch eine drastische Senkung der Steuern für ausländische Produkte das Ziel der EU-Kompatibilität bis zum Mai 2004 erreicht werden. Der dadurch verursachte Anstieg der Arbeitslo-

mediary institutions as having a significant role to play in the process of transition.[12] At the moment at which employment, or the provision of employment opportunities, as the basis of economic and social existence in socialist and capitalist states is radically transformed, and is, in many places, no longer realisable, the development paths of both systems must be assessed not so much against each other, but considered rather as interdependent figures of transformation in the context of a fragmented global economy. Trans-national labour markets, globally circulating cultural systems and geopolitical shifts not only dissolve borders; through new technologies and strategies they also introduce spatial markings with locally adaptable logics and practical executions, but also with the separation of sub-regions.[13]

From this viewpoint, local/regional internal logics and stocks of milieu-specific knowledge and procedures take on the function of reinforcing explanations when an analysis is being made. A more adequate description can therefore be provided of the complex multi-layered levels of effect between socialism and post-socialism, local and global economies, new economic elites of former cadre associations and resistant new/old administrative players in quasi democratically legitimised local/regional governance constellations. This does not mean that social geographies become more complex through the inclusion of such basic structures, but that urban and regional development paths which are much more individual, more unpredictable, and more surprising are revealed. Context-specific analyses are based not least on the fundamental assumption that post-socialist transformation processes are characterised much more strongly by inherent contingencies and structural internal logics than by development strategies based on modernisation theory.[14] This gives rise to what Klaus Müller describes as a 'fundamental uncertainty' in the analysis of development paths pursued by former socialist states.[15] However, with strong representation in the media, a relatively small, young, energetic and target-oriented group of entrepreneurs has pushed its way to the forefront within just a few years; it is regarded as successful in its attempt to come to grips with the crisis.

POLAND'S BIG BANG AND THE CONSEQUENCES

Poland's political and economic transformation began before 1989: the trade union movement Solidarnosc, the first Round Tables in the 1980s and the Balcerowicz Programme restructured the economy from the bottom up. In addition to institutional reforms and the drastic devaluation of the country's currency by 40 per cent, the Balcerowicz Programme provided for complete liberalisation and legal equality for state-owned, municipal and private property. In addition, the aim of EU compatibility was to be achieved by May 2004 by lifting controls on pricing and abolishing state restrictions as well as by drastically reducing taxes for foreign products. The resulting rise in the unemployment rate to between 20 and 25 per cent and more by the year 2004 (depending on the data source); the migration by young jobseekers, in particular, from the countryside to the Warsaw conurbation as well as to Western Poland in general (Poznan–Slubice corridor); and not least the significant increase in the number of service companies as a result of foreign direct investments of approximately 65 million dollar, of which a considerable proportion were made in the Warsaw region – all these are clear indicators of the spatial and social structural change

senquote auf 20 bis 25 Prozent und mehr bis zum Jahr 2004 (je nach Datenquelle), die Land-Stadt-Migration gerade von jüngeren Arbeitssuchenden in das Ballungszentrum Warschau sowie generell in den westlichen Bereich Polens (Korridor Poznan–Slubice) und nicht zuletzt die deutliche Zunahme von Dienstleistungsunternehmen durch ausländische Direktinvestitionen von ca. 65 Millionen US-Dollar, von denen ein umfangreicher Teil in die Region Warschau floss – all dies sind deutliche Indikatoren für den durch die Liberalisierung ausgelösten räumlichen und sozialen Strukturwandel.[16] Die im Anschluss an das Balcerowicz-Programm eingeführte staatliche Wirtschaftspolitik orientierte sich ab den frühen 1990er Jahren an der Entwicklung von „*Entrepreneurship* und Beschäftigung". Die strategischen Ziele sahen einen Anstieg der jährlichen Wachstumsrate um fünf Prozent vor, der durch erhöhte Arbeitsmigration in die Räume der globalen Investitionen, das heißt vor allem in den Westen Polens und die Hauptstadt, erreicht werden sollte. Gefördert durch finanzielle Unterstützungs- und Anpassungsprogramme der EU vor allem im Infrastrukturbereich, sollte die niedrige Beschäftigungsrate angehoben und die Hauptstadtregion sowie ausgewählte Wachstumsregionen entlang des Korridors zwischen Slubice und Poznan gestärkt werden.[17]
Die Auswirkungen der radikalen Transformation auf die sozialen Sicherheitssysteme und die Freisetzung zahlreicher Beschäftigter aus dem produzierenden Bereich lösten Anfang der 1990er Jahre eine schockartige Krise ungeahnten Ausmaßes aus. Zugleich verschärfte sich quasi über Nacht der Kampf um Beschäftigung sowie um Ausbildungs- und Studienplätze. Die Krisenerfahrungen der frühen 1990er Jahre führten zu berufs- und familienbiographischen Brüchen, erheblichen Arbeitsmigrationen und schnellen sozialen Abstiegen (für viele) und Aufstiegen (für wenige), aber auch – bei der Bewältigung der Krisensituation – zum Rückgriff auf soziale Ressourcen und Kompetenzen aus der Zeit des polnischen wie generell des osteuropäischen Sozialismus. Diese Transformationserfahrungen und die bestenfalls praktizierten Krisenlösungen im Sinne der Selbstbehauptung müssen als besonders prägend für die Generation der heute 20- bis 35-Jährigen verstanden werden.

UNTERNEHMER SEINER SELBST

Um ein „true careerist" zu werden, wie dies Alexei Yurchak für Russland für den Typus des „russischen Neoliberalen" beschreibt, braucht es mehr als nur die „technical skills of ‚doing business'. It also means learning a whole set of norms that demarcate everyday practices, dispositions, and one's relationship to the self and the world".[18] Die starke Ausprägung des Modells eines „entrepreneur of himself or herself", von Yurchak als „continuous business of living" verstanden, an den aufstrebenden Orten des neuen Warenverkehrs weise darauf hin, dass die dabei zum Tragen kommenden Normen und Werte als zentraler disziplinierender Effekt des neoliberalen westlichen Regimes die Alltagsstruktur dieser Akteure dominieren. Kurz, Yurchak schreibt das Auftauchen und den Aufstieg neureicher Russen dem neoliberalen System und seinen Wirkungsmechanismen zu.[19] Die Durchsetzung dieses Modells verlief im Postsozialismus ungleich schneller als im Westen und bot einer kleinen Gruppe von Gewinnern die Möglichkeit eines sofortigen gesellschaftlichen und ökonomischen Aufstiegs.
Das in Westeuropa diskutierte Modell des „Entrepreneurs seiner selbst", auch „Culturepreneur" genannt, hat sich dagegen langsamer und kontextspezifischer ausgebreitet.[20]

triggered by liberalisation.[16] The state economic policy introduced following the Balcerowicz Programme in the early 1990s was oriented towards the development of "*entrepreneurship* and employment". The strategic goals provided for an increase in the annual growth rate of five per cent, which was to be achieved through increased employment migration to the areas attracting global investment, i.e. mainly in western Poland and the capital. With the backing of EU financial support and adjustment programmes mainly in the area of infrastructure, the low employment rate was to be increased and the capital region, along with selected growth regions along the corridor between Slubice and Poznan, was to be strengthened.[17]

The impact of the radical transformation on the social security systems, and the redundancies of many employees from the production sector triggered a sudden crisis of unsuspected magnitude at the beginning of the 1990s. At the same time, the fight for employment as well as for places on training and study courses intensified almost overnight. The crisis experiences of the early 1990s led to break-ups in working and family lives, considerable employment migrations and rapid declines (for many) and advancements (for few) in social status, but also – in coping with the crisis situation – to the exploitation of social resources and competences from the time of Polish socialism and of Eastern European socialism in general. These experiences of transformation and the crisis solutions found in the context of self-assertion must be understood as particularly formative for the generation of today's 20 to 35-year-olds.

ENTREPRENEUR OF ONE SELF

To become a "true careerist", as Alexei Yurchak describes the "Russian neoliberal", requires more than just the "technical skills of 'doing business'. It also means learning a whole set of norms that demarcate everyday practices, dispositions, and one's relationship to the self and the world."[18] The strong development of the model of an "entrepreneur of himself or herself," construed by Yurchak as the "continuous business of living", in the up-and-coming places developing with the new movement of goods indicate that the norms and values noticeable here as the central disciplining effect of the Western neoliberal regime dominate the structure of these players' day-to-day lives. In short, Yurchak attributes the appearance and advancement of nouveau riche Russians to the neoliberal system and its effect mechanisms.[19] This model was enforced far more quickly under post-socialism than in the West and offered a small group of winners the opportunity of immediate social and economic advancement.

By contrast, the model of the "entrepreneur of himself or herself" discussed in Western Europe, also called the *culturepreneur*, has spread more slowly and in a more context-specific manner.[20] Nonetheless, in the last few years, precarisation has come about here too. The dynamics of the market economy have put creative, corporate-based service providers, in particular, under considerable pressure. Nevertheless, intelligent and international network strategies of the "new creative people" in Western and Eastern European centres illustrate their attempts to combine social and occupational networks with one another. Furthermore, the greater political influence achieved by expounding the problems of their own work structures shows that cultural entrepreneurs should be regarded not just as pioneers and forerunners of neoliberal practice.[21]

Gleichwohl ist es in den vergangenen Jahren auch hier zu einer Prekarisierung gekommen. Marktwirtschaftliche Dynamiken haben insbesondere die unternehmensbezogenen kreativen Dienstleister unter erheblichen Existenzdruck gesetzt. Dennoch, intelligente und internationale Netzwerkstrategien der „neuen Kreativen" in den west- und osteuropäischen Zentren, ihre Versuche, soziale und berufliche Netze miteinander zu verbinden, sowie nicht zuletzt die verstärkte politische Einflussnahme durch eine Problematisierung der eigenen Arbeitsstrukturen zeigen, dass die kulturellen Unternehmer nicht nur als Vorreiter und Wegbereiter einer neoliberalen Praxis anzusprechen sind.[21] Polens neue Generation der unternehmerischen Kreativen nimmt nicht nur wegen der geographischen Mittellage zwischen Russlands radikalem neostaatskapitalistischen Sonderweg und dem langsamer sich transformierenden europäischen Westen eine besondere Position ein: Die historisch und kulturell starken Beziehungen zu Frankreich, die frühen Arbeitsmigrationen in den Westen des Landes und in die angrenzenden westeuropäischen Länder (man denke etwa an die diasporaähnliche Gruppe der „Ruhrgebietspolen") sowie nicht zuletzt die im Vergleich zu anderen sozialistischen Ländern eher gewährten Freiheiten lassen die Vermutung zu, dass ein spezifischer kreativer Unternehmertypus polnischer Prägung zu identifizieren ist. Zudem wirft der frühzeitig implementierte und äußerst schonungslos vorangetriebene Transformationsprozess die Frage auf, inwiefern die derzeit in westeuropäischen Städten zu beobachtenden individualisierten Unternehmer im Vergleich zu denen in Polen ähnliche Lebenspraktiken an den Tag legen und damit möglicherweise indirekt in einem seit 2004 erweiterten Europa angekommen sind. Oder zeigt sich – auf der Grundlage der sozialistischen Vorprägung, der milieuspezifischen Transformationserfahrungen und den oftmals seit 1989 forcierten internationalen Bildungskarrieren der Akteure – ein spezifischer kultureller Unternehmer polnischer Prägung, also eine neue Generation Warschau?

SKIZZEN EINER „GENERATION WARSCHAU"

SEHNSUCHT LEBEN – FAMILIARISIERTE ARBEIT

Pusia betreibt seit zwei Jahren den Club Regeneracja. Im südlichen Übergangsraum zwischen dem repräsentativen Warschau und den mächtigen, aber tristen Mietswohnkasernen entlang einer breiten Ausfallstraße gelegen, findet man die im Dunkeln liegende Eingangstür nur nach längerem Suchen. Innen strahlen selbstgemalte paradiesisch-großflächige Wandbilder Sehnsucht und Fernweh aus. Kerzenschein und wild zusammengesuchte Sofas, Stühle und Tische vermitteln Wärme. Pusia ist die Mutter eines dreijährigen Sohnes, allein erziehend – aber was heißt hier allein? Sie wollte etwas machen, berichtet sie und lächelt dabei glücklich; gänzlich unbestimmt, sah sie vor zwei, drei Jahren kein klares Lebensziel vor Augen. Finanzielle Ressourcen waren nur begrenzt da. Zudem musste sie als alleinerziehende Mutter für ihren Sohn sorgen. Freunde waren da, kamen immer öfter und blieben länger, sie konnte ja nicht weg. Im Regeneracja scheint sie nun ihren Ort und Anker gefunden zu haben, von dem aus sie weitere Projekte entwickeln kann. Kunst wolle sie machen, findet aber partout keine Zeit dazu. Da stellt sie eben die Bilder, Skulpturen und Fotos von Freunden aus, die durch Reisen in die weite Welt der wohnlichen Enge der früheren Jahre entkommen sind – und auch ein wenig der Geschlossenheit der traditionellen Familie, ihren Erwartungen und der Kirche.

Poland's new generation of business-minded creative people not only assumes a special position because of their geographically central location between Russia's special path of radical neo-state capitalism and the more slowly transforming Western Europe. The country's strong historical and cultural relations with France, the early employment migrations to Western Poland and neighbouring Western European countries (e.g. the diaspora-like group of Poles in the industrial area of the Ruhr) as well as the freedoms available in comparison with other socialist countries, might lead one to suppose that there is an identifiable, Polish-style creative entrepreneur. In addition, the early implementation and extremely ruthless advancement of the transformation process raises the question of the extent to which the individualised entrepreneurs to be seen at present in Western European cities reveal similar practices to those in Poland and therefore, since 2004, have, perhaps indirectly, arrived in an enlarged Europe. Or is there – based on previous socialist characteristics, the milieu-specific experiences of transformation, and, often pushed since 1989, the international educational careers of the players involved – such a thing as a specific, Polish-style cultural entrepreneur, i.e. a new Warsaw generation?

SKETCHES OF A "WARSAW GENERATION"

LONGING FOR LIFE – FAMILIARISED WORK

Pusia has been running the Regeneracja club for two years. In the southern transitional area between the imposing parts of Warsaw and the mighty, but miserable blocks of rented flats built along a wide main road leading out of the city, it takes a long time to find the entrance doors that are shrouded in darkness. Inside, there are magnificent, large-scale, hand-painted wall pictures that radiate longing and wanderlust. Candlelight and a wild collection of sofas, chairs and tables convey a sense of warmth. Pusia is the mother of a three-year-old son, a single parent – but what does single mean here? She wanted to do something, she says, smiling happily; totally uncertain, she had no clear life objective in her mind's eye just two or three years ago. The financial resources available were limited. In addition, as a single parent, she had her son to look after. She had friends; they came more and more often and stayed longer and longer; she could not go out. In Regeneracja she seems to have found her refuge and anchor, a basis from which she can develop more projects. She wants to do art, but cannot find any time at all to do so. She exhibits pictures, sculptures and photos of friends who have escaped the homely narrowness of earlier years – and also a little of the closeness of the traditional family, its expectations, and the Church – by travelling in the big wide world.

Pusia orders home-made bread and dripping and pickled gherkins; electro beats of a friend living in London resound in the background; friends serve us. Clubbing with pickled gherkins and everyone feels fine. Post-modern Polish local colour.

She says that there did not use to be places like these, where one could just while away the time. They were either expensive and not very inviting, competitive, *stylish* or subject to business interests and passing fashions; they did not suit her or her friends. So they decided to do something about it. Pusia called her friends together and, in the tried and tested do-it-yourself tradition, they renovated two rooms in the immediate vicinity of her flat. She stresses that she is not the boss of this club; she

Pusia bestellt selbstgemachtes Schmalzbrot und saure Gurken, Elektrobeats eines in London lebenden Freundes rauschen im Hintergrund, Freunde bedienen uns. Clubbing mit sauren Gurken, und alle fühlen sich wohl. Postmodernes polnisches Lokalkolorit. Es gab diese Orte nicht, an denen man verweilen konnte, stellt sie fest. Entweder waren sie teuer und wenig einladend, konkurrenzbehaftet, stylish oder dem Kommerz und kurzfristigen Moden unterworfen, sie passten nicht zu ihr und ihren Freunden. Also packten sie an. Pusia rief ihre Freunde zusammen, und sie renovierten in bewährter Do-it-yourself-Tradition zwei Räume in direkter Nähe zu ihrer Wohnung. Sie sei nun nicht die Chefin dieses Clubs, betont sie, sie biete nur einen Ort an, für sich und ihre Freunde. Eine Reise hat sie unternommen, vor einigen Wochen ist sie in den Süden geflogen. Sie wollte auch einmal raus, etwas sehen, die Wärme genießen, dem Bekannten entfliehen. Es scheint also zu funktionieren, sie hat sich etwas aufgebaut.

Das Regeneracja wurde durch quasi-familiäre Selbsthilfepraktiken initiiert und anschließend auch getragen. Pusia ist formell Betreiberin einer Kneipe; informell ist der Club zudem ein leiser und temporärer Galerieraum, um den sich eine befreundete Generation gruppiert, die sich dafür verantwortlich fühlt. Es erfolgt kein gewollter Bruch mit der sozialen Identität einer nachwachsenden „Generation Warschau", vielmehr werden polnische Gurken mit Londoner Elektromusik, traditionelle Behaglichkeit mit fragwürdiger Kunst locker kombiniert. Fast alle kommen irgendwann wieder, wenigstens kurz, auch wenn sie im westlichen Europa arbeiten oder studieren. Sie bleiben ihrem Milieu gelassen treu und praktizieren damit eine vorübergehende Sesshaftigkeit in einer mobilen, transnationalen Lebensphase. Das Regeneracja wird als erweiterter Wohnraum angenommen. Für Pusia bietet er die Möglichkeit, ihre Kleinfamilie um familiarisierte Freundes- und Sozialnetze zu erweitern und sich selbst einen Entwicklungsweg zu eröffnen. Dabei betreibt sie nicht die expressive Definitionsbehauptung einer Clubbesitzerin oder eines *New Entrepreneur*, was sie beides zweifellos ist, sondern eine passfähige Machbarkeitsbehauptung.

ORTS-, ZEIT- UND SZENENWECHSEL

In den 1950er und 1960er Jahren wurde das vollständig zerstörte Warschauer Ghetto durch den Staat Polen detailgetreu wieder aufgebaut. Heute dient es als Ort der kulturellen Erinnerung für zahlreiche Touristen aus Europa und Nordamerika. Eine an die Zeit der frühen 1930er Jahre anknüpfende Einkaufs-, Gastronomie- und Kulturszenerie lässt den Ort realitätsnah erscheinen. Abends gehen die Lichter in den zweiten bis fünften Etagen aus. In einer Seitenstraße werden dann die Tore einer alten Fabrik für Le Madam entriegelt, das Wachpersonal beginnt mit der Inspektion der Eingangs- und Fluchtwege, im Inneren bauen Techniker Musikanlage und Bar auf. Hier gehen die Lichter an, ein neuer Ort für verschiedene kulturelle Szenen bereitet sich vor. Er wird zentraler und letzter Anlaufspunkt des pulsierenden Nachlebens sein.

Krystian, ein Rechtsanwalt mit multikulturellem Familienhintergrund, in Krakau aufgewachsen, betritt gelassen den langgestreckten ehemaligen Fabrikraum. Während seines Studiums wirkte er an der temporären Bereitstellung von offenen Räumen für offene Menschen mit. Queers, Schwule und Lesben, Transsexuelle und all die, denen die Praxis der Mainstreamclubs, VIPs und Großraumdiskos nur bedingt zusagte, zogen im engeren und weiteren Umfeld von Krystian durch verschiedene zeitweilige Loca-

just provides a place for herself and her friends. She has been on a journey: a few weeks ago she flew south. She too wanted to get away, see things, enjoy the sun, escape the familiar. It seems to have worked; she has set something up herself.

The Regeneracja was started up through quasi-familiar self-help practices and then supported in the same way. Formally, Pusia runs a pub; informally, the club is also a quiet and temporary gallery space around which a generation of good friends, which feels responsible for it, gathers. There is no deliberate break with the social identity of a re-emerging "Warsaw generation"; rather Polish gherkins are loosely combined with electro music from London and traditional cosiness with dubious art. Nearly everyone comes back some time, at least briefly, even when they are working or studying in Western Europe. They remain quietly faithful to their milieu and thus practise a temporary settled way of life in a mobile, trans-national phase of their lives. The Regeneracja is accepted as an extended living room. It offers Pusia the chance to expand her small family to include familiarised social networks and networks of friends and to open up a path to development for herself. She does not embody the expressive definition of a club owner or *new entrepreneur*, both of which she doubtless is, but rather an adaptable practicability.

CHANGE OF PLACE, TIME AND SCENE

In the 1950s and 1960s, the completely destroyed Warsaw Ghetto was reconstructed accurately in every detail by the Polish government. Today it serves as a place of cultural remembrance for many tourists from Europe and North America. A shopping, gastronomic and cultural scene reminiscent of the early 1930s gives the place a realistic look. In the evenings, the lights go out on the second to fifth stories. Then, in a side street, the gates of an old factory, now Le Madam, are unbolted; the security personnel start the inspection of entrances and exits, while inside the technicians set up the sound equipment and bar. The lights go on; a new place for different cultural scenes is prepared. It will be the central and last place of refuge of the city's pulsating night life.

Krystian, a lawyer from a multi-cultural family background, raised in Krakow, calmly enters the long former factory shop. While a student he got involved in the temporary provision of open spaces for open people. Gays and lesbians, transsexuals and all those to whom the practice of mainstream clubs, VIPs and large-scale discos were only partly appealing moved through various temporary locations in close and wider circles surrounding Krystian. Membership of this scene promised an attainment of social, atmospheric and spatial autonomy that continues to be vital for non-conformists in traditional Catholic Poland. Within a few years what began as a cultural refuge inevitably became an entrepreneurial project that needed to be protected economically and legally. Krystian's legal knowledge soon proved indispensable when building-related authorisations for events had to be negotiated with the local authorities and contracts entered into for the club. His modesty shows, however, that running a club for several hundred guests is only possible with the assistance of many competent friends and confidants. The scene's loose network is understood as the co-designer of the rooms, as a guarantee of openness and the desired atmosphere, but also as a social body upon which people depend for their cultural identity and to which they are also indebted.

tions. Die Zugehörigkeit zu dieser Szene versprach einen sozialen, atmosphärischen und räumlichen Autonomiegewinn, der im traditionell katholischen Polen für Andersdenkende lebensnotwendig war und ist. Was als kulturelles Refugium begann, entwickelte sich in wenigen Jahren zu einem zwangsläufig ökonomisch und rechtlich abzusichernden unternehmerischen Projekt. Krystians Rechtskenntnisse erwiesen sich schnell als unentbehrlich, wenn gebäudespezifische Genehmigungen für Veranstaltungen mit den lokalen Autoritäten ausgehandelt und Verträge für den Club abgeschlossen werden mussten. Sein Understatement zeigt jedoch, dass das Betreiben eines Clubs für mehrere hundert Gäste nur mit Hilfe vieler kompetenter Freunde und Vertrauenspersonen zu meistern ist. Das lose Netz der Szene wird als Mitgestalter der Räumlichkeiten, als Garant für Offenheit und die gewünschte Atmosphäre verstanden, aber auch als sozialer Körper, von dem man kulturell-identifikatorisch abhängig und dem man ebenso verpflichtet ist.

Demzufolge wird die Präsenz des Clubs als Ort nicht medial in der Stadt kommuniziert. Es sind keine Flyer und Mailinglisten notwendig, um dem Club Leben einzuhauchen. Er ist kein Produkt, vielmehr ist die temporäre Gemeinschaft der Körper. Spezifische Praktiken produzieren einen Ort des Geschehens, dem eine Schale, in diesem Fall eine alte Fabrikhalle, als zwischenzeitliche Behausung dient. Freundes-, Beziehungs- und Unterstützungsnetze, die ihre musikalischen, gastronomischen oder kulturell-symbolischen Projekte hier ausstellen und testen können, garantieren die Einzigartigkeit des Ortes. Eine kuratorische Leitung gibt es nicht. Bilder dürfen aufgehängt werden, und wenn sie nicht gefallen, müssen sie wieder abgehängt werden; wenn sie absolut und definitiv schlecht sind, werden sie hängen gelassen. Der jeweilige Künstler ist für alles zuständig, die Szene goutiert und reagiert. Dem Ort ist eine Aufforderung für jeden Gast eingeschrieben, sich zu zeigen, zu partizipieren und damit Vergemeinschaftungen überhaupt erst zu ermöglichen.

Die spielerische und geradezu traumwandlerische Übereinstimmung von Szenebedürfnissen und Gestaltungsoptionen an diesem Ort darf aber nicht darüber hinwegtäuschen, dass mehr als eine halbe Million Zloty in dieses Projekt investiert wurden und Krystian als Clubbetreiber ein Interesse daran hat, finanziell über die Runden zu kommen. Die einzigartige Location eröffnet ihm ungeahnte Perspektiven, wenngleich die Stadtverwaltung durch permanente Auflagen Konflikte provoziert, bei denen Krystian auf seine juristischen Fähigkeiten zurückgreifen muss. Le Madam ist kein Stachel im touristischen Tagesgeschäft des ehemaligen Warschauer Ghettos, vielmehr die letzte Anlaufstelle im Warschauer Nachtleben: Wenn andere Clubs schließen, trifft man sich im Le Madam. Die dortige Kultur- und Zeitpolitik markiert die entscheidende Differenz und sorgt auf informelle Weise für das Fortbestehen des Ortes. Er ermöglicht seinen Teilnehmern, im Rahmen verschiedener Gemeinschaften in eine andere Zeit und Identität zu wechseln und deren Emergenz mitzugestalten. Die scheinbare Privatheit des Club- und Galerieraums wird durch Aushandlungs- und Verfahrenspraktiken getragen, die Intimität und Öffentlichkeit ausbalancieren. So hält auch Krystian in seiner Person das Gleichgewicht zwischen der Praxis des Rechtsanwalts, des Clubbetreibers und des Partygängers. Seine Zukunft? Er versucht als Vertreter und Delegierter der Partei der Grünen einen Platz im Europäischen Parlament in Brüssel zu bekommen.

Accordingly, the club's presence is not advertised in the city's media. No flyers and mailing lists are needed to breathe life into the club. It is not a product; rather it is the bodies' temporary community. Specific practices produce a place of happening, for which a shell, in this case an old factory shop, serves as a temporary home. Networks of friends, contacts and supporters who can exhibit and test their musical, gastronomic or cultural-symbolic projects here guarantee the uniqueness of the place. There is no curatorial leadership. Pictures can be hung up and, if they are not appreciated, taken down again; if they are absolutely and definitively bad, they are left hanging. The particular artist is responsible for everything; the scene tastes and reacts. The place calls upon each guest to show himself, to participate and thus make socialisations possible in the first place.
However, the playful and almost somnambulistic correspondence between the scene's requirements and design options in this place should not obscure the fact that more than half a million zloty was invested in this project and that Krystian as the club owner has an interest in getting by financially. The unique location opens up undreamt-of prospects for him, even though the city administration provokes conflicts by continuously imposing conditions and, in order to counter them, Krystian is required to fall back on his legal skills. Le Madam is not a thorn in the side of the day-to-day tourism business of the former Warsaw Ghetto; rather it is the last place of refuge in Warsaw's night life. When other clubs shut for the night, people meet at Le Madam. Its policy on time and culture is its crucial difference and, in an informal way, this guarantees the continued existence of the place. It allows its participants to slip into a different time and identity and to help shape their emergence within the framework of different communities. The seeming privacy of the club and gallery space is supported by practices of negotiation and procedure that balance out intimacy and publicity. Likewise, as a person, Krystian maintains the balance between the practices of a lawyer, a club owner and party goer. What about his future? He is attempting to win a seat in the European Parliament in Brussels as a representative and delegate of the Green Party.

MULTI-TASKING – CULTURAL HYBRIDS

Zuzanna became familiar with living in expansive networks at an early age. As a child of journalist parents who left the country for the USA in the 1970s, it was important for her to establish ties with new cultural phenomena in the new world without cutting off links with the Poland she was familiar with in cultural terms. She grew up between the US techno and hip hop scene and European knowledge cultures in a Jewish environment in Chicago. A few years after the political transformation in Poland the family decided to return to Warsaw. Zuzanna's parents continue to work in their profession and have become involved in education networks for the Jewish returnee population. Thanks to her trans-cultural experience, their daughter soon found her feet professionally. In Warsaw, she became editor-in-chief of a lifestyle magazine published six times a year and a monthly city magazine for young urban players, the *Aktivist*.
One might presume that she is performing significant cultural reconstruction work for Warsaw, but that would fall wide of the mark. She thinks more highly of the natural curiosity of cultural producers in the city, their joy at experimentation and willing-

MULTITASKING – KULTURELLE HYBRIDE

Das Leben in weit gespannten Netzen hat Zuzanna schon früh kennen gelernt. Als Kind von Eltern, die als Journalisten in den 1970er Jahren das Land in Richtung USA verlassen haben, galt es auch für sie, in der Ferne Beziehungen zum kulturell Neuen zu knüpfen, ohne die Brücken zum kulturell bekannten Polen zu kappen. Im Umfeld des jüdischen Chicagoer Milieus zwischen US-amerikanischer Techno- und Hiphop-Szene und europäischen Wissenskulturen ist sie groß geworden. Einige Jahre nach der politischen Wende in Polen entschließt sich die Familie, nach Warschau zurückzukehren. Zuzannas Eltern gehen ihrem Beruf nach und engagieren sich parallel in Bildungsnetzwerken des jüdischen Rückkehrermilieus. Der Tochter gelingt es dank ihrer transkulturellen Vorprägung schnell, beruflich Fuß zu fassen. Sie leitet in Warschau binnen kurzer Zeit als Chefredakteurin ein sechsmal jährlich erscheinendes Lifestylemagazin und ein monatlich erscheinendes Stadtmagazin für jüngere urbane Aktive, den *Aktivist*.

Die Vermutung liegt nahe, dass sie maßgebliche kulturelle Aufbauarbeit für Warschau leistet. Weit gefehlt, schätzt sie doch die unbefangene Neugier der Kulturproduzenten in der Stadt, ihre Experimentierfreude und Ausdrucksbereitschaft höher ein, als dies von den vorgeblich etablierten Kulturzentren Europas propagiert wird. Mit den dort operierenden Kulturproduzenten sind die kulturellen „Ich-Unternehmer" Warschaus bestens vernetzt, oftmals getragen von EU-, Länder-, oder kulturellen Austauschprogrammen. Sprach- und Kulturkenntnisse ermöglichen es, im Heimatland an einen gut bezahlten und angesehenen Job zu gelangen. Der Statusgewinn manifestiert sich in der Person Zuzannas, die aufgrund ihrer internationalen Sozialisation einen dringend benötigen Kulturtransfer leisten kann. Kulturell hybrid, da weder einem kulturellen Herkunftsland noch einer nationalen Identität zuzuordnen, fungiert sie als vermittelnde Instanz in der strukturell offenen Kulturszene Warschaus. Da es für diese Profession noch keine ausgebildeten Institutionen gibt, verkörpert Zuzanna in ihrer Person eine intermediäre, im Werden begriffene institutionelle „Zelle".

Sie setzt Lokales und Globales, Bekanntes und Neues, Underground und Mainstream virtuos miteinander in Beziehung, in dem sie neue Trends in der Warschauer Szene erkennt und kritisch mit bereits bestehenden europäisch-amerikanischen Kulturpraktiken verbindet.. Obwohl sie auch als Angestellte in einem Verlag arbeitet, operiert sie als kultureller „Entrepreneur ihrer selbst" zwischen heterogenen Kultur-, Sprach- und Raumsphären. Die Rückkehr hat ihr einen immensen Karrieresprung und ebenso umfangreiche Aufgabenbereiche eröffnet. Aber die vorübergehend im Ausland lebende Alterskohorte der 20- bis 25-Jährigen wird nicht lange auf sich warten lassen und nach ihrer Rückkehr die kulturellen Innovationsdynamiken dieser Stadt weiter ankurbeln.

POSTMODERNES WARSCHAU?

Die unternehmerische, postsozialistische „Generation Warschau" oszilliert zwischen Party, Profit und Partizipation. Mit diese Mixtur aus zwanglosem Savoir-vivre und exzessivem Partyrausch, familiarisierten Solidarnetzen und Dienstleistungstauschringen gelingt es zahlreichen jungen Menschen, unter schwierigsten sozioökonomischen Bedingungen und bei äußerst begrenzter institutioneller Unterstützung über

ness to express themselves than she does of what is propagated by the supposedly established cultural centres of Europe. Warsaw's cultural "entrepreneurs of themselves" are extremely well networked with the cultural producers operating there, often supported by EU, national or cultural exchange programmes. Knowledge of languages and culture make it possible to get a well-paid and respected job in one's native country. The advancement in status is manifested in Zuzanna as a person; on the basis of her international socialisation she can achieve the necessary cultural transfer. Cultural hybrid, as she can be allotted neither to a cultural land of origin nor a national identity, she acts as a communication channel in Warsaw's structurally open cultural scene. As no institutions have yet been developed for this profession, Zuzanna as an individual personifies an intermediary, emerging, institutional "cell".
Multi-tasking between identifying new trends in the Warsaw scene and critically communicating existing European-American cultural practices, she relates local to global, familiar to new, underground to mainstream. Although she also works for a publishing house, she operates as a cultural "entrepreneur of herself" between heterogeneous cultural, linguistic and spatial spheres. Her return presented her with an immense career jump and equally extensive responsibilities. Her peers, 20 to 25-year-olds temporarily living abroad, will not be away long and, after their return, will boost this city's dynamics of cultural innovation.

POST-MODERN WARSAW?

The entrepreneurial, post-socialist "Warsaw generation" oscillates between party, profit and participation. With this mixture of casual savoir-vivre and excessive partying, familiarised solidarity networks and service barter rings, numerous young people have succeeded, under extremely difficult socio-economic conditions and with very limited institutional support, in finding a way out of the crisis via individual entrepreneurship. By contrast, those who can afford to do nothing (which can be understood as a response to the punk rocker, Kuba Wandachowicz, who described the generation of mid-twenty-year-olds as the "nothing generation") simply do nothing. While, from time to time, Western Europe's individualistically operating entrepreneurs fight the grim battle for shrinking possessions and increasingly difficult markets, the Warsaw generation asserts its entrepreneurial existence in the knowledge of its informal social and generational networks. These must be regarded as by far the more influential, as the socialist sounding-board in the form of support and barter systems is important for survival and life's fulfilment – alongside the Church and family, in particular.
The entrepreneurial type of a "Warsaw generation", as presented in the three case sketches, must be consciously dissociated from the Russian prototype of the "true careerist", which Alexei Yurchak construes as an expression of the neoliberal regime currently engulfing Russia. Certainly, the image of the Russian neo-mogul is characterised by just a few new billionaires, most succinctly in the figure of Roman Abramovich. The type of entrepreneur who gained access to profitable sources (of raw materials) immediately after the political transformation can be found in every Eastern European country that underwent such transformation, though the scope of his/her wealth may vary. This does not adequately describe the methods of action and ef-

den „Umweg" des individuellen Unternehmertums einen Ausweg aus der Krise zu finden. Wer es sich dagegen leisten kann, nichts zu tun – so die Antwort auf den Punkrocker Kuba Wandachowicz, der die Generation der Mittzwanziger als eine „Generation Nichts" beschrieben hat –, der kann es sich eben leisten. Während Westeuropas individualistisch operierende Unternehmer mitunter einen verbissenen Kampf um abnehmende Pfründe und schwierigere Märkte austragen, betreibt die „Generation Warschau" unternehmerische Daseinsbehauptung im Wissen um ihre informellen sozialen und generationellen Netze. Diese müssen als weitaus gestaltprägender aufgefasst werden, da der sozialistische Resonanzboden in Form von Unterstützungs- und Tauschsystemen, gerade neben Kirche und Familie, zum Überleben und Lebensvollzug bedeutsam ist.
Der in den drei Fallskizzen vorgestellte unternehmerische Typus einer „Generation Warschau" muss sich auch bewusst vom russischen Prototyp des *true careerist* distanzieren, den Alexei Yurchak als Ausdruck des gerade über Russland hereinbrechenden neoliberalen Regimes begreift. Sicherlich prägen wenige milliardenschwere Neureiche das Bild des russischen Neo-Moguls, am prägnantesten Roman Abramowitsch. Der Typus des direkt nach der Wende an die profitablen (Rohstoff-)Quellen gelangten Unternehmers ist in jedem Transformationsland Osteuropas anzutreffen; der Umfang seines Vermögens kann dabei differieren. Die Wirkungs- und Handlungsweisen junger, nachwachsender kultureller Unternehmer sind damit aber nicht hinreichend beschrieben, so stark und attraktiv das mediale Bild des erfolgreichen Unternehmers auch sein mag und so sehr sie durch dieses Bild beeinflusst sein mögen. Das Wissen um den lokalen sozialen Kontext und der Zugang zu örtlichen Ressourcen und informellen Netzwerken müssen berücksichtigt werden, um zu verstehen, wie junge Menschen in Polen sich unter prekären Lebensbedingungen kreativ und eigenwillig eine Existenzgrundlage aufbauen. Wenn sie ein unternehmerisches Risiko eingehen, haben sie, verglichen mit dem westeuropäischen Kontext, einen stärkeren Rückhalt in sozialen Solidarnetzen. Da diese Beziehungsgebilde aber gerade bei den 25- bis 35-Jährigen hochmobil und transnational sind, können sie sich der Gefahr der Abschottung und der Sklerotisierung ihrer innovativen Potentiale erwehren. Das ungezwungene und unprätentiöse Mixen von polnischen Gurken und Schmalzbrot mit Londoner Elektrobeats in Warschauer Clubs weist auf einen pfadspezifischen Weg der Herausbildung eines zukünftigen polnischen Unternehmertypus hin. Dazu gehört auch, dass die Herausbildung einer unternehmerischen Identität mit der Suche nach Wurzeln des europäischen Bürgers verbunden wird. Der Autonomiegewinn, den die Generation Warschau durch ihre spezifischen Einbettungsbedingungen zweifellos im europäischen Städtewettbewerb erzielt, könnte dadurch allerdings in Frage gestellt werden, transformiert sich diese Figur Europa doch ebenso und stellt ein zweifelhaftes Bezugsmodell dar.

ANMERKUNGEN

1 Vgl. Humphrey, Caroline: „The villas of the ‚new Russians': a sketch of consumption and identity in post-Soviet landscapes". In: Staring, Richard/Land, Marco van der/Task, Herman (eds.): *Focaal: globalization/localization: paradoxes of cultural identity*. Nr. 30–31/1998, S. 85–106

2 Vgl. Yurchak, Alexei: „Russian Neoliberal: The Entrepreneurial Ethic and the Spirit of ‚True Careerism'".

fect of young, up-and-coming cultural entrepreneurs, however strong and attractive the media image of the successful entrepreneur may be and however much they may be influenced by this image. Knowledge of the local social context and access to local resources and informal networks must be taken into account in order to understand how young people in Poland build up a basis for existence in a creative and individual manner under precarious living conditions. When they take on an entrepreneurial risk, they have stronger support in the form of social solidarity networks than is the case in the West European context. As the objects of these relationships are highly mobile and trans-national, especially with the 25 to 35-year-olds, they can fend off the risk of their innovative potential being sealed off and sclerotised. The natural and unpretentious mix of Polish gherkins and bread and dripping with London electro beats in Warsaw clubs points towards a specific development path for a Polish entrepreneurial type of the future. This also entails linking the development of an entrepreneurial identity with the search for the roots of the European citizen. However, the acquisition of autonomy, which the Warsaw generation is certainly achieving in competition with other European cities thanks to its specific embedding conditions, could be called into doubt as a result, since this European figure is also undergoing transformation and is thus a dubious reference model.

NOTES

1 Cf. Humphrey, Caroline: "The villas of the 'new Russians': a sketch of consumption and identity in post-Soviet landscapes". In: Staring, Richard/Land, Marco van der/Task, Herman (eds.): *Focaal: globalization/ localization: paradoxes of cultural identity*. No. 30-31/1998, pp. 85–106

2 Cf. Yurchak, Alexei: "Russian Neoliberal: The Entrepreneurial Ethic and the Spirit of 'True Careerism'". In: *The Russian Review*. January 2003, Volume 62, pp. 72–90, here p. 72

3 Cf. Eyal, Gil/Szelenyi, Ivan/Townsley, Eleanor: "An Introduction". In: the same (Ed.): *Making Capitalism without Capitalists. Class Formation and Elite Struggles in Post-communist Central Europe*. London 1998, pp. 1–16

4 Cf. Griffiths, Ron/Bassett, Keith, et al.: "Capitalising on culture: cities and the changing landscape of cultural policy". In: *Policy and politics*. No 2/2003, Volume 31, pp. 153–170; as well as McRobbie, Angela: "Talentbasierte Wirtschaft? Die Dynamik der Generationen auf Großbritanniens kulturellen Arbeitsmärkten". In: *Gewerkschaftliche Monatshefte*. No. 12/2002b, Volume 53, pp. 661–670

5 Cf. Altmann, Susanne/Rolke, Tadeusz: "Junge Kunst: Szene Polen. Eine Generation kämpft gegen die alten Widerstände von Kirche und Staat". In: *Art*. No. 1/2004, pp. 16–31, with information similar to that of a travel guide.

6 Cf. Lange, Bastian/Steets, Silke: "Cool Frankfurt? Verortungsstrategien von ‚New Entrepreneurs'". In: Bittner, Regina (ed.): *Die Stadt als Event. Zur Konstruktion urbaner Erlebnisräume*. Frankfurt/Main 2002, pp. 300–321; as well as Lange, Bastian: "Socio-spatial strategies of culturepreneurs. The example of Berlin and its new professional scenes". In: *Zeitschrift für Wirtschaftsgeographie. Special Issue: Ökonomie und Kultur*. No. 2/2005, Volume. 49, pp. 81-98

7 Cf. Bude, Heinz: *Generation Berlin*. Berlin 2001, pp. 8

8 Cf. Grabher, Gernot: "Learning in Projects, Remembering in Networks? Communality, Sociality, and Connectivity in Project Ecologies". In: *European urban and regional studies*. No. 2/2004, Volume 11, pp. 103-123

9 Leszek Balcerowicz was Poland's Finance Minister from the end of the 1980s to the beginning of the 1990s.

10 Cf. Thomas, Michael: "Voraussetzungsvolle Passagen Neuer Selbständiger im ostdeutschen Transformationsprozess". In: the same (Ed.): *Selbständige – Gründer – Unternehmer*. 1997, pp. 14-58; here p. 18

11 Cf. Pine, Francis/Bridger, Sue: "Introduction: transitions to post-socialism and cultures of survival". In: the same (Ed.): *Surviving post-socialism: local strategies and regional responses*. New York 1998, pp. 1–15, here p. 3 ff.

In: *The Russian Review.* Januar 2003, Jg. 62, S. 72–90, hier S. 72

3 Vgl. Eyal, Gil/Szelenyi, Ivan/Townsley, Eleanor: „An Introduction". In: dies. (Hg.): *Making Capitalism without Capitalists. Class Formation and Elite Struggles in post-communist Central Europe.* London 1998, S. 1–16

4 Vgl. Griffiths, Ron/Bassett, Keith, u. a.: „Capitalising on culture: cities and the changing landscape of cultural policy". In: *Policy and politics.* Nr 2/2003, Jg. 31, S. 153–170; sowie McRobbie, Angela: „Talentbasierte Wirtschaft? Die Dynamik der Generationen auf Großbritanniens kulturellen Arbeitsmärkten". In: *Gewerkschaftliche Monatshefte.* Nr. 12/2002b, Jg. 53, S. 661–670

5 Vgl. Altmann, Susanne/Rolke, Tadeusz: „Junge Kunst: Szene Polen. Eine Generation kämpft gegen die alten Widerstände von Kirche und Staat". In: *Art.* Nr. 1/2004, S. 16–31, mit reiseführerähnlichen Hinweisen.

6 Vgl. Lange, Bastian/Steets, Silke: „Cool Frankfurt? Verortungsstrategien von ‚New Entrepreneurs'". In: Bittner, Regina (Hg.): *Die Stadt als Event. Zur Konstruktion urbaner Erlebnisräume.* Frankfurt/Main 2002, S. 300–321; sowie Lange, Bastian: „Socio-spatial strategies of Culturepreneurs. The example of Berlin and its new professional scenes". In: *Zeitschrift für Wirtschaftsgeographie. Special Issue: Ökonomie und Kultur.* Nr. 2/2005, Jg. 49, S. 81–98

7 Vgl. Bude, Heinz: *Generation Berlin.* Berlin 2001, S. 8

8 Vgl. Grabher, Gernot: „Learning in Projects, Remembering in Networks? Communality, Sociality, and Connectivity in Project Ecologies". In: *European urban and regional studies.* Nr. 2/2004, Jg. 11, S. 103–123

9 Leszek Balcerowicz war von Ende der 1980er bis Anfang der 1990er Jahre polnischer Finanzminister.

10 Vgl. Thomas, Michael: „Voraussetzungsvolle Passagen Neuer Selbständiger im ostdeutschen Transformationsprozess". In: ders. (Hg.): *Selbständige – Gründer – Unternehmer.* Berlin 1997, S. 14–58, hier S. 18

11 Vgl. Pine, Francis/Bridger, Sue: „Introduction: transitions to post-socialism and cultures of survival". In: dies. (Hg.): *Surviving post-socialism: local strategies and regional responses.* New York 1998, S. 1–15, hier S. 3 ff.

12 Vgl. Thomas, Michael, a. a. O., S. 17–24

13 Vgl. Maresch, Rudolf/Werber, Niels: „Permanenzen des Raums". In: dies. (Hg.): *Raum – Wissen – Macht.* Frankfurt/Main 2000, S. 7–32, hier S. 7–12

14 Vgl. Müller, Klaus: „Kontingenzen der Transformation". In: *Berliner Journal für Soziologie.* Heft 4/1996, S. 449–466, hier S. 450

15 Ebd., S. 454

16 Vgl. Smetkowski, Maciey: „New Relationships between the Metropolis and the Region in Information Economy: Warsaw Metropolitan Region – A Case Study". Paper presented at the Third Euro Conference „The European City in Transition", Bauhaus-University Weimar, 14./15. November 2003

17 Vgl. Korcelli, Piotr/Nowosielska, Ewa: „The concept of spatial development policy ‚Poland 2000 plus'. The urban system of Poland". In: *EU-Interreg IIc-Projekt: Urban Systems and Urban Networking in the Baltic Sea Region, Visions and Strategies 2010 around the Baltic,* 1997–1999. Brüssel 2000; sowie Rada, Uwe: *Zwischenland: Europäische Geschichten aus dem deutsch-polnischen Grenzgebiet.* Berlin 2004

18 Vgl. Yurchak, Alexei: „Entrepreneurial Governmentality in post-socialism Russia. A cultural investigation of business practices". In: Bonell, Victoria /Gold, Thomas (Hg.): *The New Entrepreneurs of Europe and Asia.* New York 2002, S. 1–39; sowie Yurchak, Alexei: „Russian Neoliberal: The Entrepreneurial Ethic and the Spirit of ‚True Careerism'", a. a. O., S. 73

19 Vgl. Humphrey, Caroline, a. a. O., S. 85–106

20 Vgl. Lange, Bastian: „Socio-spatial strategies of Culturepreneurs. The example of Berlin and its new professional scenes", a. a. O.; Verwoert, Jan: *Die Ich-Ressource. Zur Kultur der Selbst-Verwertung.* München 2003; Rothauer, Doris: *Kreativität und Kapital. Kunst und Wirtschaft im Umbruch.* Wien 2005, für den Diskurs in der BRD und Österreich; Wießner, Frank: „Neues von der ICH-AG. Nicht jeder Abbruch ist eine Pleite". In: *IAB Kurzberichte.* Heft 2/2005, S. 1–6 für empirische Analysen im Bereich der Ich-AG; für den Diskurs in Großbritannien vgl. McRobbie, Angela: „Talentbasierte Wirtschaft? Die Dynamik der Generationen auf Großbritanniens kulturellen Arbeitsmärkten", a. a. O.; sowie McRobbie, Angela: „Clubs to Companies: Notes on the Decline of Political Culture in Speeded up Creative Worlds". In: *Cultural Studies.* Nr. 4/2002b, Jg. 16, S. 516–531; für Russland vgl. Yurchak, Alexei: „Entrepreneurial Governmentality in post-socialism Russia. A cultural investigation of business practices", a. a. O., und Yurchak, Alexei: „Russian Neoliberal: The Entrepreneurial Ethic and the Spirit of ‚True Careerism'", a. a. O.

21 Vgl. Osten, Marion von/Bismarck, Beatrice von (Hg.): *Norm der Abweichung.* Zürich 2003

12 Cf. Thomas, Michael, loc. cit., pp. 17–24

13 Cf. Maresch, Rudolf/Werber, Niels: "Permanenzen des Raums". In: the same (Ed.): *Raum – Wissen – Macht*. Frankfurt/Main 2000, pp. 7–32; here pp. 7–12

14 Cf. Müller, Klaus: "Kontingenzen der Transformation". In: *Berliner Journal für Soziologie*. Volume 4, pp. 449-466; here p. 450

15 Ibid., p. 454

16 Cf. Smetkowski, Maciey: "New Relationships between the Metropolis and the Region in Information Economy: Warsaw Metropolitan Region – A Case Study". Paper presented at the Third Euro Conference "The European City in Transition", Bauhaus-University Weimar, 14/15 November 2003

17 Cf. Korcelli, Piotr/Nowosielska, Ewa: "The concept of spatial development policy 'Poland 2000 plus'. The urban system of Poland". In: *EU Interreg IIc Project: Urban Systems and Urban Networking in the Baltic Sea Region, Visions and Strategies 2010 around the Baltic*, 1997-1999. Brussels 2000; as well as Rada, Uwe: *Zwischenland: Europäische Geschichten aus dem deutsch-polnischen Grenzgebiet*, Berlin 2004

18 Cf. Yurchak, Alexei: "Entrepreneurial Governmentality in Post-socialism Russia. A cultural investigation of business practices". In: Bonell, Victoria /Gold, Thomas (ed.): *The New Entrepreneurs of Europe and Asia*. New York 2002, pp. 1–39; as well as Yurchak, Alexei: "Russian Neoliberal: The Entrepreneurial Ethic and the Spirit of 'True Careerism'", loc. cit., p. 73

19 Cf. Humphrey, Caroline, loc. cit., pp. 85–106

20 Cf. Lange, Bastian: "Socio-spatial strategies of culturepreneurs. The example of Berlin and its new professional scenes", loc. cit.; Verwoert, Jan: *Die Ich-Ressource. Zur Kultur der Selbst-Verwertung*. Munich 2003; Rothauer, Doris: *Kreativität und Kapital. Kunst und Wirtschaft im Umbruch*. Vienna 2005 for discourse in FRG and Austria; Wießner, Frank: "Neues von der ICH-AG. Nicht jeder Abbruch ist eine Pleite". In: *IAB Kurzberichte*. Volume 2/2005, pp. 1–6 for empirical analysis in the area of self-employment in Ich-AGs; for discourse in Great Britain cf. McRobbie, Angela: "Talentbasierte Wirtschaft? Die Dynamik der Generationen auf Großbritanniens kulturellen Arbeitsmärkten", loc. cit.; as well as McRobbie, Angela: "Clubs to Companies: Notes on the Decline of Political Culture in Speeded-up Creative Worlds". In: *Cultural Studies*. No. 4/2002b, Volume. 16, pp. 516–531; for Russia cf. Yurchak, Alexei: "Entrepreneurial Governmentality in Post-socialism Russia. A cultural investigation of business practices", loc. cit. and Yurchak, Alexei: "Russian Neoliberal: The Entrepreneurial Ethic and the Spirit of 'True Careerism'", loc. cit.

21 Cf. Osten, Marion von/Bismarck, Beatrice von (Ed.): *Norm der Abweichung*. Zurich 2003

GENTRIFIZIERUNG IN PRAGA – WARSCHAU ENTDECKT SEINE ANDERE SEITE

ANNE DESCHKA

AUF ZU NEUEN UFERN

Wenn es Sommer wird in Warschau, kann man mit der WARS eine kurze Bootstour auf der Weichsel unternehmen: 40 Minuten flussaufwärts, dann wieder zurück zur Anlegestelle. Um die wechselnden Stadtansichten zu verfolgen, muss man den Kopf dabei nicht ein einziges Mal drehen. Denn obwohl der Fluss mitten durch die Stadt fließt, scheint Warschau ausschließlich auf der westlichen Uferseite zu liegen. Promenaden, Verkehrswege, Wohnviertel, die Skyline – all das zieht nur in dieser Blickrichtung vorbei.

Die gegenüberliegende Seite gleicht dagegen einem Naturreservat. Eine Vielzahl dicht bewachsener Sandbänke und kleiner Haine säumt hier das Ufer. Hin und wieder sieht man ein paar Angler und ein Boot der Wasserpolizei, sonst nichts, weder Straßen noch Passanten. Wären nicht im Hintergrund die Dächer von drei Wohnblocks zu sehen und gäbe es nicht die von Autos, Zügen und Straßenbahnen stark befahrenen Brücken, könnte man meinen, das Gebiet östlich der Weichsel sei unbesiedelt. Doch der Eindruck täuscht. Denn hinter dem unzugänglichen Ufer liegt Praga, der andere Teil der Stadt, in dem rund 100 000 Einwohner verteilt auf ca. elf Quadratkilometern leben.

Die ungleichen Flussansichten spiegeln ein Dilemma der polnischen Hauptstadt wider, das von den Stadtplanern jahrzehntelang ignoriert wurde: Während sich das Gebiet westlich der Weichsel mitsamt seinen touristischen Attraktionen, seinem Nachtleben und seinen Bürohochhäusern zu Warschaus Schokoladenseite entwickelte, wurde Praga in jeder Hinsicht vernachlässigt. Viele der meist zu Beginn des 20. Jahrhunderts entstandenen Wohnhäuser des einstigen Arbeiterviertels sind bis heute nicht ein einziges Mal renoviert worden. Manche Bewohner leben nach wie vor ohne Warmwasser oder moderne Sanitäranlagen. Wer hier zu Hause ist, gehört zu den sozial schwächsten Schichten Warschaus und damit häufig auch zu denen, die Pragas Statistik für Kleinkriminalität regelmäßig nach oben treiben. Entsprechend verrufen ist der Bezirk unter den Warschauern. Ohne triftigen Grund kommt hier niemand her.

Das könnte sich allerdings bald ändern. Schenkt man den Berichten der Medien Glauben, entwickelt sich ausgerechnet Praga in kultureller Hinsicht gerade zum „up-and-coming district" der Stadt. Es fallen Begriffe wie „Revival of the East Bank", „East Bank Art" (warsawvoice.pl, 2004) oder „Montmartre Warschaus" (*art*, 2004). Was ist dran an diesen Prophezeiungen? Was passiert in dem Bezirk gerade wirklich, mit welcher Tragweite? Und wer sind die Protagonisten?

WILLKOMMEN IN PRAGA

Wir begeben uns auf die Suche. Unsere Aufmerksamkeit gilt vorrangig Clubs oder Bars, denn sind in Praga Künstler aktiv, dann muss es auch ein Nachtleben geben. Eine erste Ortserkundung verläuft zunächst erfolglos, ist aber nicht uninteressant. Praga ist historisch gesehen das älteste zusammenhängend erhaltene Stadtviertel Warschaus. Die Häuserzeilen, die sich hier aneinander reihen, sind die einzigen, die den Zweiten Weltkrieg überstanden haben; deutlich sichtbare Einschusslöcher an vielen Fassaden erinnern an diese Zeit. Im Vergleich zu den breit gestreuten stalinistischen und postsozialistischen Neubauten, die heute das Bild Warschaus prägen, besitzt deshalb allein Praga noch eine Art authentischer Stadtstruktur mit Kiezcharakter. Die nachbarschaftlichen Kontakte sind eng. Man kennt sich, redet und trinkt miteinander und warnt den anderen gegebenenfalls vor der Polizeistreife in Zivil. Doch sozialer Romantizismus wäre angesichts des Stadtbezirks unangebracht. Denn gleichzeitig sind die Hinterhöfe dunkel, die

GENTRIFICATION IN PRAGA – WARSAW DISCOVERS ITS OTHER SIDE

ANNE DESCHKA

STRIKING OUT FOR NEW SHORES

When summer comes to Warsaw you can take a short sailing trip on the Vistula with the WARS: forty minutes upriver, then back to the landing stage. In order to follow the shifting views of the city you do not have to turn your head once. Although the river flows right through the middle of the city, Warsaw seems to lie exclusively on the west bank of the river. Promenades, traffic arteries, residential areas, the skyline – you see all this looking just in one direction.

The opposite side, on the other hand, resembles a nature reserve. A large number of densely overgrown sand banks and small clumps of trees line the bank here. Occasionally you see a few fishermen or a police launch, but nothing else – neither streets nor pedestrians. If it were not for the roofs of three blocks of flats to be seen in the background and the steady stream of cars, trains and tramcars crossing the bridges in both directions, you could be forgiven for thinking that the area east of the Vistula is uninhabited. But this is a misleading impression. Behind the inaccessible bank lies Praga, the other part of the city, in which some 100,000 inhabitants live on an area of some eleven square kilometres.

The way the two sides of the river fail to match reflects a dilemma of the Polish capital which was ignored by the town planners for decades. While the area west of the Vistula, with its tourist attractions, its night life and its high-rise office buildings, developed into the best part of Warsaw, Praga was neglected in every respect. To this day many of the dwellings in this former working-class district, most of them built at the beginning of the 20th century, have not been renovated once. There are still residents who live here without hot water or modern sanitation facilities. Those who are at home here belong to Warsaw's poorest and most deprived and are often among those who keep Praga's statistics for petty crime high. Hence the district's poor reputation among Varsovians. No one comes here unless they have a good reason to do so.

This could soon change, however. If the reports of local and international media are to be believed, Praga is in the process of becoming the city's "up-and-coming district" in cultural terms. There is talk of a "revival of the East Bank", "East Bank art" (warsawvoice.pl, 2004) and even "Warsaw's Montmartre" (*art*, 2004). Is there anything to these prophecies? What is really going on in the district and how significant is it? And who are the protagonists?

WELCOME TO PRAGA

We set off in search of answers. We are mainly on the lookout for clubs or bars, for if there are artists in Praga, there has to be a night life as well. Our first reconnaissance trip meets with no success, though it is not without interest. In historical terms Praga is the oldest quarter of Warsaw to survive as a cohesive whole. The rows of houses here are the only ones to have survived the Second World War; the bullet-scarred aspect of many facades is a reminder of those times. In comparison with the widespread Stalinist and modern, post-socialist buildings which make up the face of today's Warsaw, Praga alone still has a kind of authentic close-knit character. Relations between neighbours are intimate. People know one another, talk and drink with one another and, if the situation warrants it, warn one another if there are any plainclothes police about. Yet it would be wrong to romanticise the place. The courtyards are dark, the stairwells shabby, and the unemployment rate is high. The young people who hang about in the entranceways and adorn the walls with aggressive

Treppenhäuser schäbig und die Arbeitslosenquote ist hoch. Die Jugendlichen, die hier in den Toreinfahrten herumlungern und die Wände mit aggressiven Sprüchen verzieren, zählen zur Verlierergeneration Warschaus. Daran können auch die Streetworker wenig ändern, die sich hier regelmäßig die Nerven aufreiben. Gehörten ihre Großeltern noch zum arbeitenden Proletariat der Fabriken Pragas, repräsentieren die Eltern dieser Jugendlichen die postindustrielle Arbeiterklasse ohne Arbeit, die ihren Kindern wenig zu bieten hat. Entsprechend erwecken die Halbwüchsigen absolut nicht den Eindruck, Bewohner eines angesagten Stadtviertels zu sein. Und sie wissen auch nichts von den künstlerischen Szenen und Lokalitäten, auf die man in Praga angeblich zunehmend stößt. Auf unsere Fragen reagieren sie belustigt – und empfehlen uns fairerweise, unsere Kameras hier nicht so offen herumzutragen.

Bei unserer Spurensuche hilft uns letztlich der pure Zufall weiter. Und das Bedürfnis nach einer Tasse Kaffee. In der Ulica Zabkowska, einer recht belebten Straße, stoßen wir auf das Lysy Pingwin. Ein Aufsteller wirbt mit hausgemachtem Chili con Carne und Espresso, durch die Fensterfront schimmern ein paar bunte Sitzmöbel. Als wir das Café betreten, docken wir plötzlich an: an das neue Kulturnetzwerk Pragas.

DIE ERSTE SPUR

„Lysy Pingwin" heißt so viel wie glatzköpfiger Pinguin. Der Eigentümer ist Schwede. Er hielt Praga für einen interessanten Ort, an dem er irgendetwas machen wollte. Also mietete er die Räume einer ehemaligen Wäscherei, baute sie mit Hilfe von Freunden komplett um und eröffnete dort 2003 die Cafébar Lysy Pingwin. Das erfahren wir nicht von ihm selbst, sondern von Jacek, Servicekraft und Barmanager in einem. Seiner Beschreibung zufolge war das alles gar nicht schwer, nur bürokratisch etwas langwierig. Jaceks Credo ist der Spaßfaktor, der sich dabei für alle einstellte und auch weiterhin einstellen soll. Dafür gibt es nicht nur Tapas und nettes Design, sondern auch DJ-Parties am Wochenende. Der Plan scheint aufzugehen. Die Gäste kommen inzwischen aus allen Stadtteilen, ab und zu schnappt man gar englisches Smalltalk auf. Lysy Pingwin wurde von einem Stadtmagazin zu einer der spannendsten neuen Bars des Jahres 2004 gewählt.

Gar nicht oder nur zögerlich aber kommen die alteingesessenen Anwohner Pragas. Und das obwohl die Tür meistens offen steht und Jacek das gegenseitige Verhältnis als „entspannt" und „respektvoll" bezeichnet. Wundern muss man sich darüber nicht. Mit seinem Gastronomie- und Freizeitangebot, seinen Preisen und seinem Interieur wirkt das Lysy Pingwin in dieser Ecke wie ein Alien. Die Erklärung des Managers, durch die Eröffnung einer solchen Lokalität auch mit den Stereotypen über den Stadtteil brechen zu wollen, ist ehrlich gemeint. Aber es wird schnell klar, dass die Bar den unterschiedlichen Milieus, die hier aufeinander treffen, eher Kontur verleiht als sie aufzulösen. Jacek sieht das nicht so eng und schaut optimistisch in die Zukunft. Als Nächstes sollen die Räume fürs Boule-Spiel ausgebaut und die Küche professionalisiert werden. Außerdem gibt es um die Ecke diesen leeren Raum, aus dem man einen Plattenladen mit Chill-out-Bereich machen will. Praga in fünf Jahren? Darunter stellt er sich viele neue Leute an vielen neuen Orten vor, die viel neue Kultur mitbringen. Da gibt es für ihn kaum Zweifel, bedenke man, was in den letzten zwei Jahren schon entstanden sei: hier eine Kneipe, dort eine Galerie, da ein Theater. Seine Hand wandert über den Stadtplan Warschaus, den wir schnell noch vor ihm ausbreiten. Wo war der noch mal, dieser Club ein paar Tramstopps weiter? Kann er das einzeichnen?

PRAGA DE LUXE

Jaceks Markierung leitet uns vorbei an einer alten Wodkafabrik, die, reduziert auf 20 Prozent ihrer einstigen Produktionsfläche, wirklich noch Wodka destilliert – man kann ihn in einem kleinen Kiosk nebenan kaufen. Wir durchqueren ein paar heruntergekommene Straßenzüge, in deren Hinterhöfen bunte, mit Blumen und Kerzen geschmückte Marienstatuen zu sehen sind. Vor einer Häuserecke steht ein großes Kruzifix, unter dem sich ein paar Trinker auf ein Bier versammelt haben. Ein Laden macht mit seiner schrulligen Außendekoration auf sich aufmerksam. Seit mehr als 20 Jahren verkauft hier Erika Wisniewska Keramik & Kunstgewerbliches, vieles davon selbstgemacht. Die alte Dame hat fast vergessen, dass sie ursprünglich aus Deutschland kommt und direkt nach dem Krieg ihrem polnischen Ehemann nach Warschau gefolgt ist. Mit der Markierung auf unserer Karte kann sie wenig anfangen. Ja, ja, sie hat mal von dem Club gehört. Ihre Tochter war da wohl mal bei einer Tanzveranstaltung. Aber ansonsten – Veränderungen? Hier? Sie schüttelt verneinend den Kopf.

graffiti belong to Warsaw's loser generation. There is little the street workers can do to change this at whatever sacrifice to their nerves. If the grandparents still belonged to the working proletariat of Praga's factories, the parents of these young people represent the post-industrial working class – a class with no work and hence little to offer their children. So there is absolutely nothing about the teenagers to suggest they are inhabitants of an up-and-coming neighbourhood. Nor do they know anything of the artistic scenes and localities which are said to be springing up all over Praga. Their reaction to our questions is one of amusement – accompanied by a friendly warning not to sport our cameras so openly around here.

The next stage in our hunt for clues is the outcome of pure chance – and the need for a cup of coffee. In bustling Zabkowska Street we come across the Lysy Pingwin. A sign offers home-made chilli con carne and espresso, and through the window we see a few brightly coloured chairs. As we enter the café, we suddenly realize we have made the connection: this is part of Praga's new culture network!

THE FIRST CLUE

"Lysy Pingwin" means bald penguin. The proprietor is a Swede. He felt Praga to be an interesting place where he thought he could do something. He therefore rented the premises of a former laundry, converted them completely with the aid of friends, and opened the Lysy Pingwin Café in 2003. We do not learn of all this from him but from Jacek, who is bar manager and waiter rolled into one. According to him the whole thing was not all that hard; it was just the red tape that was a bit wearisome. Jacek believes in everybody having fun, which is what they did have and what they are to continue to have. You can not only enjoy tapas amid pleasant surroundings, but also attend DJ parties at the weekend. The plan seems to be working. The guests now come from all parts of the city, and occasionally you even hear snatches of English. One Warsaw magazine voted the Lysy Pingwin one of the capital's most exciting new bars of 2004.

Those who do not come – or only very sporadically – are the old-established denizens of Praga. This is in spite of the fact that the place is usually open and Jacek describes their mutual relations as "relaxed" and "based on respect". There is nothing really surprising about this. With its bill of fare and the range of activities on offer, its prices and its well designed interior, the Lysy Pingwin certainly creates an incongruous impression in this neck of the woods. The manager's explanation that the opening of such an establishment is a way of breaking with the stereotypes associated with Praga is sincerely meant. But it soon becomes clear that the bar tends rather to harden the divide between the two different milieus that come together here than to dissipate it. Jacek does not take such a narrow view and looks to the future with optimism. The next items on the agenda are the addition of an area where people can play boule and a more professional cuisine. Apart from that there is this empty property round the corner which they mean to turn into a record shop with a chill-out area. Will this be the face of Praga in five years' time? He reckons there will be a lot of new places with a lot of new people who will bring a lot in the way of new culture with them. He has no doubts at all on that score considering all the places that have sprung up in the last two years: here there's a pub, here there's a gallery, here there's a theatre. His hand moves across the street map which we hastily spread out before him. Where was it again, this club a few tram stops away? Could he mark it for us on the map?

PRAGA DE LUXE

Jacek's directions lead us past an old vodka distillery which, reduced to 20 per cent of its former production area, still really does make vodka which you can buy in a little kiosk next door. We cross a few dilapidated streets, in whose courtyards brightly painted madonnas adorned with flowers

An einer Kirche, wenige Meter entfernt, wirbt ein überdimensionales Porträt der Mutter Gottes für Radio Maria, einen katholischen Sender, der einer treuen Hörergemeinde täglich die Frohe Botschaft verkündet. Neben großformatigen Sparangeboten des neuen Carrefour-Einkaufszentrums ist die Heilige eine der wenigen markanten Werbeträger in dieser Gegend. Im Gegensatz zur anderen Stadtseite Warschaus, die einer einzigen Werbefläche gleicht, scheint man in Praga kaum Käuferpotentiale zu vermuten.

Noch ein paar Blocks geradeaus und wir stehen vor einem neuverputzten Gebäudekomplex. Hier müsste sie sein, diese neue Tanz-Location. Doch nichts weist von außen auf die Existenz eines Clubs hin. Wir versuchen uns durchzufragen. Unsere Hoffnung, dass Club oder Disko im Polnischen ähnlich klingt, geht leider nicht auf. Am Ende versuchen wir dem Pförtner mit Tanzbewegungen unser Anliegen klarzumachen, aber der schickt uns nur freundlich vom Hof.

Dabei sind wir völlig richtig, wie wir später erfahren. Hinter den Mauern dieser stillgelegten Fabrik befindet sich seit kurzem die Fabryka Trzciny, ein multifunktionales Kulturzentrum mit exklusivem Charakter. Wo einst Fleischwaren produziert wurden, kann man heute ins Theater gehen, Konzerte besuchen, Clubabende verbringen oder Release-Partys feiern. Die repräsentativen Räume, deren modernes Design geschickt mit der Industrievergangenheit spielt, können zudem für geschlossene Veranstaltungen jeder Art gemietet werden. Polnische Diplomatentreffen und Konferenzen der Konrad-Adenauer-Stiftung haben hier ebenso bereits stattgefunden wie Werbeevents des polnischen MTV-Senders.

Die Medien sind regelmäßig präsent und berichten über fast alles, was in der Fabryka Trzciny passiert. Angetrieben wird die hauseigene PR-Maschine durch den jungen Verkaufs- und PR-Manager Artur Ucher, mit dem wir uns wenige Tage später verabreden. Er führt den Erfolg des Hauses eher auf das Engagement des prominenten Eigentümers, Woiciech Trzcinski, zurück – der Komponist und TV-Produzent, nach dem die Kulturfabrik benannt ist.

Ucher versteht unsere ersten Orientierungsschwierigkeiten: Ja, wer nicht weiß, wo es ist, findet es nicht. Auf zufällige Laufkundschaft braucht er hier in Praga nicht zu setzen. Die Anwohner der Ulica Otwocka sind ihm zwar nicht unbekannt, wagen sich aber kaum herein. Und sie sind auch nicht die Zielgruppe. Werbeplakate für hauseigene Veranstaltungen werden in der Innenstadt platziert, nicht in Praga. Die Gäste der Fabryka Trzciny kommen aus anderen Stadtteilen und haben sich für das entsprechende Event vorher online registrieren lassen. Oder sie stehen ohnehin auf jeder VIP-Liste Warschaus. Als Manager von Trzcinskis privatem Kunsttempel ist Ucher daran gelegen, dem Besucher ein, wie er sagt, gehobenes kulturelles Niveau zu bieten. Geplant sind deshalb Clubkarten, die gewährleisten sollen, dass sich die Gäste miteinander wohl fühlen. Die Fabryka Trzciny setzt auf Exklusivität – so sehr, dass Ucher auch mit den anderen neuen Kulturaktivisten Pragas kaum in Berührung kommt. Er kennt weder sie noch die Lokalitäten, in denen sie sich treffen. Wie alle nächtlichen Besucher der Fabrik kommt und geht Ucher mit dem eigenen Auto oder per Taxi. Wenn er dann aus dem Fenster schaut, empfindet er den Stadtteil eigentlich als rückständig und trist. Es fehlt an Investoren, alles geschieht hier langsam, selbst die Bewohner bewegen sich mit einer für ihn ungewohnten Trägheit durch die Straßen. Zwar versteht Ucher, warum Künstler und Leute aus dem kreativen Business hierher ziehen: Praga ist neu und ungewöhnlich, man kann hier vieles ausprobieren. An eine steigende Popularität des Viertels glaubt er dennoch nicht. Und er führt an, was sich auch über die Fabryka Trzciny sagen ließe: Es sei ein schwer zugängliches Gebiet, das sich vielen verschließe. Seine Zukunft sieht der junge Manager deshalb nicht hier, in Praga, ebenso wenig in Warschau und schon gar nicht in Polen. Spanien wäre nach seiner Vorstellung, auch wenn er noch nie dort war. Er hegt ernsthafte Umzugspläne.

CLUBBING UNPLUGGED

Würde Artur Ucher morgen seine Koffer packen, niemand in Praga würde es bemerken. Nähme dagegen Arkadiusz Krawczyk seinen Hut und würde aus Praga verschwinden, wäre das schon eine andere Sache. Arkadiusz Krawczyk ist einer derjenigen, die Ucher nicht kennt, obwohl sie für Pragas momentane Entwicklung wichtige Antriebskräfte sind. Wir kennen ihn, wenn auch bislang nur vom Hörensagen, denn zu ihm gehört ein weiteres von Jaceks Kreuzchen auf unserem Stadtplan.

Krawczyk ist der Besitzer einer Bar in Pragas „Bermudadreieck". So wird ein Straßenkomplex genannt, der berüchtigt dafür ist, dass dort Dinge auf unerklärliche Weise verschwinden können.

and candles are to be seen. At one corner stands a large crucifix, under which a few drinkers have gathered for a beer. A shop attracts our attention with its quaint external decorations. For more than 20 years Erika Wisniewska has been selling ceramics and handicraft products here, many of them made on the premises. The old lady has almost forgotten that she originally came from Germany and followed her Polish husband to Warsaw just after the war. She cannot make much of the marks on our map. Yes, she has heard of such a club. She believes her daughter once went to a dance there. But otherwise – changes? Here? She shakes her head in denial.

At a church a few yards away an enormous image of the Madonna advertises Radio Maria, a Catholic station which broadcasts the glad tidings daily to its loyal following of listeners. Apart from the billboards proclaiming the special offers of the new Carrefour shopping mall the saint is one of the few conspicuous instances of advertising in this neighbourhood. Unlike the other side of Warsaw, which resembles one large billboard, no one seems to imagine there might be potential buyers in Praga.

After walking a few blocks further we come to a newly done up building complex. Surely this must be the new disco. But there are no external signs of a club within. We try asking people. Our hope that the Polish words for club or disco sound similar proves illusory. We end up imitating dance movements in an attempt to make the doorman understand what we are looking for, but he only sends us politely but firmly on our way.

And yet we are at the right place, as we later learn. It is only recently that the walls of this closed-down factory have housed the Fabryka Trzciny, a multi-functional cultural centre with exclusive character. In what used to be a meat-packing plant you can now go to the theatre, attend concerts, spend club evenings, or hold release parties. The imposing rooms, whose modern design cleverly plays on the industrial past, can also be rented for special functions of all kinds. Meetings of Polish diplomats and conferences of the Konrad Adenauer Foundation have taken place here, as have promotion events of Poland's MTV station.

The media are routinely present and report on almost everything that happens in the Fabryka Trzciny. The in-house PR machine is run by a young sales and PR manager, Artur Ucher, with whom we arrange an appointment for a few days later. He attributes the success of the establishment to the commitment of its prominent owner, Wojciech Trzcinski – a composer and TV producer after whom the culture factory is named.

Ucher understands our initial difficulties in finding the place. He agrees that if you don't know where it is you won't stumble across it. He doesn't expect any casual trade here in Praga anyway. The residents of Otwocka Street are not unknown to him, but they would never dare come here. Nor indeed are they the target group. Posters advertising forthcoming events are put up in the downtown area, not in Praga. The patrons of the Fabryka Trzciny come from other parts of town and have registered online for the relevant event in advance. Or they feature on every Warsaw VIP list. As manager of Trzcinski's private temple of art, Ucher is anxious to offer the visitor what he calls a high cultural standard. That is why he plans to introduce club cards to ensure that patrons find themselves in the right kind of company. The Fabryka Trzciny goes in for exclusiveness – to such an extent that Ucher hardly comes into contact with Praga's other new cultural activists. He knows neither them nor the places where they hang out. Like all night visitors to the factory Ucher comes and goes in his own car or by taxi. When he looks out of the window he finds the view backward and dismal. There is a lack of investors, everything here happens so slowly, even the residents walk along the streets with what he considers unnatural indolence. Ucher does understand why artists and people in the creative professions are moving here: Praga is a new and unusual environment in which one can try out a lot of things. But he has no faith in the district's rising popularity. And he points out what cannot be denied about the Fabryka Trzciny: it is in an out-of-the way location which for many might

Sagt man. Die Bar heißt U Krawca – Zum Schneider –, weil hier früher eine Schneiderwerkstatt war. Und so wird auch Krawczyk von allen genannt, die hier ein- und ausgehen: einfach Krawiec. Eine alte Schneiderpuppe steht als Reminiszenz noch im Fenster und erinnert uns daran, dass wir hier schon einmal vorbeigezogen sind, nichts ahnend. Denn auch hier gibt es kaum einen Hinweis darauf, was sich hinter der alten Ladentür verbirgt. Nur ein handgeschriebenes Schild mit Öffnungszeiten hängt da. Völlig überflüssig eigentlich. Alle Gäste wissen, dass nicht vor 19.00 Uhr geöffnet ist und ohnehin so lange ausgeschenkt wird, bis der Letzte gegangen ist. Und neue Gäste kommen meist als Freunde von alten, rein zufällig taucht hier niemand auf. Extra vorbei kommt ebenso niemand. Denn das U Krawca ist recht unspektakulär, steht in keinem Club-Magazin und bietet weder Tapas noch Chill-out-Sessions. Wer hierher kommt, hat die Wahl zwischen Bier, zwei Sorten Hauswein und Wodka. Bestenfalls gibt es dazu noch ein paar Erdnüsse. Ausgeschenkt wird von niemand anderem als Krawiec selbst oder seiner Frau Gabriela, die mit ihm zusammen den Laden betreibt.

Trotzdem ist die Bar stets gut besucht, selbst an Wochentagen. Das liegt nicht nur an den moderaten Preisen, sondern vor allem an der direkten Nachbarschaft zu einem der neuen Künstlerareale Pragas. Viele der Gäste, die sich hier einstellen, haben ihre Studios und Ateliers in dem alten Lagerhaus gleich nebenan. Und bestücken auch die Wände im U Krawca gelegentlich mit ihren Arbeiten. Die Bar ist schlicht das, was man in Berlin vor

zehn Jahren unter einer Künstlerkneipe verstanden hätte und was es in dieser einfachen Form inzwischen auch in Warschau-Downtown kaum mehr gibt. Die Porträtphotos, die wir bei unserem

Besuch vorfinden, zeigen Stammgäste der Bar. Alles Freunde, meint Krawiec dazu. Alles Menschen, die einfach nur mit sich selbst zu tun haben wollen. Ein Charakterzug, den Krawiec selbst meisterhaft zu verkörpern versteht. Einfach so aufkreuzen und Fragen stellen, das geht hier nicht. Es bedarf eines Dritten, der Krawiec kennt und uns nach zwei Runden Bier ganz beiläufig vorstellt. Und selbst dann ist es nicht leicht, von ihm Antworten zu bekommen. Krawiec gibt sich zugeknöpft und leicht nihilistisch. Ein spezielles Interesse habe er für Praga nicht. Die Bar hat er vor einem Jahr eröffnet, weil er mit irgendwas Geld verdienen musste und seine Frau hier aufgewachsen ist. Aber ihm sind die Standortvorteile natürlich bewusst: billige Mieten, weniger Korruption als in Downtown, das ästhetische Potential der Architektur, die authentische Stadtteilatmosphäre. Sicher schätzt er das. Nur mit den Menschen sei es nicht so einfach.

Denn neben einer langjährigen Arbeitertradition ist Praga auch durch eine soziale Tradition geprägt, die das nachbarschaftliche Miteinander bestimmten Codes und Hierarchien unterstellte. Und die hat für die Alten immer noch Gültigkeit. Schon für die jüngere Generation Pragas ist dieses Verhalten nur noch schwer zu begreifen, auch wenn sie es respektiert. Für neu Zugezogene ist es dagegen fast unmöglich, sich in das soziale Beziehungsnetz einzufügen. So herrscht eine Art Kluft zwischen den Repräsentanten des alten und des heutigen Praga, die für Konfliktpotential sorgt.

Krawiec steht irgendwo dazwischen. Durch seine Frau hat er einen besseren Zugang zu den alten Einwohnern als andere Neuankömmlinge. Er redet mit ihnen, sie akzeptieren ihn, ein paar sind zu Freunden geworden. Gleichzeitig sammelt er in seiner Bar die neue Einwohnerschaft aus freien Künstlern und Kulturproduzenten und bietet ih-

as well not exist. For this reason the young manager sees his future not here in Praga, nor in Warsaw either, nor even in Poland. He believes Spain would suit him, although he has never been there. He has serious plans about moving.

CLUBBING UNPLUGGED

If Artur Ucher were to pack his bags and go tomorrow, no one in Praga would notice. But if Arkadiusz Krawczyk were to suddenly drop everything and clear out that would be quite another matter. He is one of those whom Ucher does not know, although they provide much of the dynamic for Praga's current development. We know him, albeit only from hearsay, for his place is one of those Jacek marked with a cross on our street map.
Krawczyk is the proprietor of a bar in Praga's "Bermuda Triangle". This term refers to a maze of streets which is notorious for the fact that things have an inexplicable way of disappearing there. That's what people say, anyway. The bar is called U Krawca, or Tailor's, because the place used to be a tailor's workshop. And that is what everyone who comes and goes here calls Krawczyk – Krawiec (tailor). An old tailor's dummy still stands in the window as a reminder, and we recall passing it unwittingly before. For here too there is no indication of what the old shop door conceals. There is only a piece of paper on display with opening times written by hand. Quite unnecessarily. All the patrons know that it doesn't open before seven o'clock in the evening and continues to serve drinks until the last of them has gone. And the new patrons tend to be friends of existing ones – no one just happens to drop in. Nor does anyone make a special point of coming. U Krawca is eminently unspectacular, is not listed in any club magazine, and offers neither tapas nor chill-out sessions. Those who come here can choose between beer, two kinds of house wine, and vodka. The most you will get to go with it is a few peanuts. Serving at the bar is none other than Krawiec himself or his wife Gabriela, who runs the place with him.
Nevertheless the bar is always well frequented, even on weekdays. This is not just because of the moderate prices, but mainly because it is in the direct vicinity of one of Praga's new artists' colonies. Many of those who come here have their studios and ateliers in the old warehouse next door and have adorned the walls of U Krawca with some of their works. The bar is just what, ten years ago in Berlin, you would have called a typical artists' pub of a kind that, in this basic form, hardly exists any longer in Warsaw's downtown area. The photo portraits we find here during our visit feature the regulars. All of them friends, Krawiec comments. They are all people who just want to be among themselves – an attitude which Krawiec himself exemplifies to a degree. Simply turning up and asking questions is not acceptable here. We need to go through a third party who knows Krawiec, to whom we are casually introduced after two rounds of beer. And even then it is not easy to get any answers out of him. His manner is guarded and somewhat nihilistic. He says he has no special interest in Praga. He opened the bar a year ago as he had to earn money somehow, and his wife had grown up here. But of course he is aware of the district's advantages: cheap rents, less corruption than in the downtown area, the aesthetic potential of the architecture, the authentic neighbourhood atmosphere. Of course he appreciates these things. But getting along with the people is not so simple.
Apart from its long working-class tradition Praga is characterised by a social code which has always subordinated good-neighbourly relations to certain rituals and hierarchies. And for the elderly these still apply. Even the younger generation in Praga finds this behaviour hard to understand, even if they respect it. For newcomers, however, it is almost impossible to be adopted into the network of social relations. So there is a kind of gap between the representatives of the old and the new Praga, which is a potential source of conflict.
Krawiec finds himself somewhere in the middle. Through his wife he found it easier to make contact with the old inhabitants than with other newcomers. He talks to them, they accept him, and a few

nen Raum zur Milieupflege. Trotzdem ist es auch im U Krawca nicht so, dass sich die neue Boheme und Pragas Proletariat freundschaftlich zuprosten. Die Kneipe steht zwar jedem offen. Aber Krawiec weiß, dass sein Jamaika-Jazz nichts für die Ohren der alten Einwohner ist und sich das Bier auf der Straße immer noch billiger trinkt. Das zu ändern versuchen, weshalb? Er mag das wilde Leben, sagt er. An Sozialisierungsmaßnahmen liegt ihm nichts, und auch an Prognosen über die Zukunft Pragas ist er wenig interessiert. Was für ihn zählt, ist sein Alltag in dieser Bar, wo ihm Zigaretten, Alkohol und Stress die Gesundheit rauben. Wer weiß schon, wie es weitergeht? Dass Praga so nicht bleiben wird, ist ihm dennoch klar, die Veränderungen sind absehbar. Gegen den kulturellen Zuwachs hat Krawiec nichts einzuwenden, im Gegenteil. Aber dass Praga zu sehr in Mode kommt, das will er nicht. Auch wenn er es letztlich nicht ändern könnte, denn so sei es doch immer: In zehn Jahren werden hier die Yuppies sein, meint er, und zündet sich mit einem Schulterzucken die nächste Zigarette an.

Zugegeben, so viel desillusionierte Gelassenheit lässt uns nicht unbeeindruckt. Doch so gleichgültig wie Krawiec erscheint, sei er in Wirklichkeit nicht, bemerkt unser Begleiter nach Verlassen der Bar. Sonst hätte er nicht die Gründung von „Inzynierska" mit initiiert, einer Art Kulturinitiative für die Anwohner der gleichnamigen Straße.

KÜNSTLER ZUM ANFASSEN

„Inzynierska" ist das, wonach wir gesucht haben: das Herz des neuen Kulturnetzwerks von Praga, das langsam mehr und mehr Kunst in den Stadtteil pumpt. Das dazu eingerichtete Internetportal (www.inzynierska.pl) präsentiert alle ansässigen Künstler, Studios, Werkstätten und Galerien und verlinkt gegebenenfalls zu deren eigener Website. Das Design ist professionell, die Informationen sind auf dem letzten Stand, weitere Kontaktadressen ausreichend vorhanden, und das Forum wird rege frequentiert. Es gibt ein eigenes Logo, das samt Webadresse inzwischen auf allen Postkarten erscheint, die als Gratis-Werbeträger von den einzelnen Akteuren herausgegeben werden. Viele der Karten finden sich inzwischen auch in Verteilern auf der anderen Seite der Stadt, wo sie für zunehmende Aufmerksamkeit sorgen.

Zuletzt haben sich einige der „Inzynierska"-Mitstreiter an der „Warszawska Noc Europy", der „Europäischen Nacht Warschaus", beteiligt. Einzelne Museen und Galerien waren dafür bis spätabends geöffnet und durch einen Shuttlebus miteinander verbunden. Das Event wurde vom offiziellen Werbebüro der Stadt Warschau organisiert und von den wichtigsten Medienvertretern der Stadt betreut. Auf dem entsprechenden Flyer, der im gesamten Stadtgebiet auslag, erschien so die Adresse Inzynierska 3/4 gleichberechtigt neben der etablierter Kultureinrichtungen wie dem Kulturpalast oder dem Zentrum für Zeitgenössische Kunst. Ein geschickter Werbefeldzug, der die Beteiligten so gut wie nichts kostete. Das Inzynierska-Projekt mit der größten Öffentlichkeitswirkung ist diese Aktion dennoch nicht geworden. Diesen Platz hält nach wie vor das hauseigene Festival „S siedzi dla S siadów" – „Nachbarn für Nachbarn". Seit 2003 findet es regelmäßig im Frühjahr in den Straßen Pragas statt und verhilft der Initiative zu mehrtägiger Präsenz in den lokalen Medien. Auch wenn jedes Mal bis zuletzt unklar ist, ob es überhaupt finanziert werden kann. Geboten werden unter anderem Theaterveranstaltungen, Performances und Konzerte auch internationaler Künstler, meist in öffentlich zugänglichen Räumen oder unter freiem Himmel. Denn neben dem Wunsch, auch andere Warschauer einmal in die Straßen Pragas zu locken, ist das wichtigste Ziel des Festivals der Kontakt zu den Anwohnern, deren Weg ansonsten kaum zu den Künstlern führt. Wenn sich die Milieugrenzen auch nicht aufheben lassen, so will die Initiative zumindest dafür sorgen, dass die Einwohner wissen, wer ihre neuen Nachbarn überhaupt sind. In diesem Jahr geht man noch einen Schritt weiter und plant jenseits von Kunstprojekten ein offenes Symposium zur „Revitalisierung Pragas". Denn die geht alle gleichermaßen an, ob Alteingesessene oder Zuzügler.

DER SCHÖNE SCHEIN

Pragas „Revitalisierung" ist keine Begriffsschöpfung der Kulturaktivisten, sondern neuerdings ein erklärtes Ziel in Warschaus offiziellem Masterplan. Dafür sollen Gebäude saniert, die Infrastruktur verbessert und Investoren angeworben werden. Des Weiteren will man historische Potentiale Pragas aufbereiten und dem Tourismus zugänglich machen. Das ist die Theorie. Und die Praxis?

Wenn Jacek vom Lysy Pingwin morgens seinen Aufsteller nach draußen schiebt, dann fällt sein Blick tatsächlich auf neu gebaute oder renovierte Häuser. Auch das Gebäude, in dem sich seine Bar befindet, hat einen frischen Anstrich bekommen.

have become friends. At the same time it is the new inhabitants, the freelance artists and producers of culture, that his bar attracts, offering them a place to cultivate their milieu. Yet it is not the case that in U Krawca the new Bohemians and Praga's proletariat amiably raise their glasses to each other. The bar may be open to everybody, but Krawiec knows that his Jamaica jazz is not suited to the ears of the old inhabitants and that it is still cheaper to drink one's beer in the street. Why should he want to change that? He likes the casual way of life, he says. He thinks little of efforts to raise social standards, nor is he much interested in forecasts about the future of Praga. What counts for him is his daily life in this bar, where cigarettes, alcohol and stress are ruining his health. Who knows how things are going to develop? It's quite clear that Praga is not going to stay the way it is at present – the changes are foreseeable. Krawiec has nothing against cultural accretion, on the contrary. But he doesn't want to see Praga become too trendy. Not that he could do anything to change it; that was the way things always went. In ten years we'll have the yuppies here, he says with a shrug and lights his next cigarette.
Admittedly, all this calm disillusionment cannot fail to have an effect on us. But Krawiec is not so indifferent as he appears, remarks our companion after we have left the bar. Otherwise he would not be one of the founders of "Inzynierska", a kind of cultural initiative for the residents of the street of the same name.

ARTISTS IN THE FLESH

"Inzynierska" is what we have been looking for: the heart of Praga's new cultural network, which is steadily pumping more and more art into the neighbourhood. A specially set-up Internet portal (www.inzynierska.pl) presents all resident artists, studios, workshops and galleries, with links to their own websites if such exist. The design is professional, the information is up to date, there are plenty of additional contact addresses, and the forum is eagerly frequented. It has its own logo which now appears together with the Internet address on all postcards which are distributed free for publicity purposes by the individual participants. Many of the cards are now to be found in distribution lists on the other side of town, where they are attracting increasing attention.
Recently some of the "Inzynierska" group took part in the "Warszawska Noc Europy", or "Warsaw's Europe Night". Individual museums and galleries stayed open till late at night and were linked by a shuttle bus service. The event was organised by the PR department of the city of Warsaw and sponsored by the capital's main media representatives. The flyer distributed throughout the entire urban area featured the address Inzynierska 3/4 on equal terms with such established cultural institutions as the Palace of Culture or the Centre for Contemporary Art. It was a clever advertising campaign that cost the beneficiaries next to nothing. Yet it was not the Inzynierska project that gained the greatest publicity. That honour was still reserved for the home-grown festival "S siedzi dla S siadów", "Neighbours for Neighbours", a spring event held regularly in the streets of Praga since 2003 and helping the initiative to get several days' coverage in the local media. No one ever knows till the last moment whether the festival can be financed at all. The programme includes theatrical events, performances and concerts – some featuring international artists – generally held in premises open to the public or in the open air. Apart from a desire to lure the other Varsovians across the river onto the streets of Praga, the main aim of the festival is to reach out to the residents who have no other way of meeting artists. Even if it is not possible to break down the boundaries between milieus, the initiative should at least enable the inhabitants to find out who their new neighbours actually are. This year the organisers are taking it a step further and planning, in addition to the art projects, an open symposium on the "Revitalisation of Praga". For this concerns everyone equally, whether long-standing residents or newcomers.

KEEPING UP APPEARANCES

Praga's "revitalisation" is not just a new term invented by cultural activists, but a declared aim of Warsaw's official master plan. This involves renovating buildings, improving the infrastructure, and wooing investors. It is also intended to rediscover Praga's historical potential and make it accessible to tourism. That is the theory. How does it work in practice?
When Jacek sets up his Lysy Pingwin sign on the pavement every morning, his eyes fall on newly built or renovated houses. The building in which his bar is located has also received a fresh coat of paint. The new colours around him vary minimally between light beige and ochre, but all are basically shades of yellow. In this the house resembles

Die neuen Farbtöne um ihn herum variieren minimal zwischen Hellbeige und Ocker, gehören aber alle noch zur Familie des Gelb. Darin gleicht das Haus all den anderen renovierten Bauten in verschiedenen Teilen des Stadtviertels. Der Grund ist profan, doch aufschlussreich: Gelb ist die Farbe der Revitalisierung, denn gelbe Farbe ist billiger. Hier sparen nicht private Eigentümer, sondern die Stadt Warschau selbst. Die Mehrheit der Grundstücke Pragas liegt in ihrem Besitz.

Historisch authentisch sind diese Farben nicht. Doch da die Gebäude unter keinem rechtskräftigen Denkmalschutz stehen, muss man sich auch an keinerlei Auflagen halten. Potentiellen Käufern lässt man entsprechend freie Hand. Sie können zu Niedrigstpreisen Gebäude kaufen und bauen, was immer sie wollen. Vor kurzem wurden so große Teile von Pragas Binnenhafen Port Praski an einen privaten TV-Sender veräußert. Der neue Besitzer unternimmt zurzeit gar nichts, weil er weiß, dass sich der Wert des Geländes auch ohne sein Zutun täglich potenziert. Da, wo wirklich investiert wird, geschieht dies mit wenig Besonnenheit. Das Gebiet in der Nähe des Lysy Pingwin läuft inzwischen Gefahr, zu einer Art Mini-Ghetto aus modischen Appartements zu werden. Auch die Architektur des riesigen neuen Carrefour-Einkaufszentrums eine Straße weiter steht in keiner Beziehung zur ursprünglichen Baustruktur der Gegend. Vor kurzem musste nun auch das älteste Kino Pragas privaten Spekulantenträumen weichen. Man munkelt von einem Multiplex-Kino, das hier gebaut werden soll.

Pragas „Revitalisierung" ist momentan nicht mehr als eine verdeckte Kapitalschlacht, die eher zu Lasten des Stadtteils geht. Die Einwohner gewinnen dadurch nichts. Hinter den frisch getünchten Fassaden sieht es nicht anders aus als früher, denn wirklich saniert wurden die alten Häuser nicht. Auch leben die meisten der Mieter ohnehin in kommunalen Gebäuden, deren Renovierung für die Stadt enorm kostenintensiv wäre – nicht weil die Hälfte von ihnen hier längst keine Miete mehr zahlt, sondern weil man sie dazu alle kurz- oder langfristig in andere Wohnungen auslagern müsste. Doch solche Extraräume gibt es in Praga nicht, sie müssten von der Stadt erst gebaut werden, und zu diesem finanziellen Mehraufwand ist die Verwaltung nicht bereit. So wird sich in absehbarer Zeit an der Wohnsituation und damit auch den sozialen Verhältnissen der langjährigen Anwohnerschaft wenig ändern.

Die Betroffenen werden über all das kaum informiert, sie sind in die offiziellen Revitalisierungsprogramme nicht eingeweiht. Weitaus mehr darin verwickelt sind dagegen die Neuankömmlinge Pragas. Um leer stehende Flächen beanspruchen zu können, müssen sie sich zwangsläufig mit lokalen Besitzansprüchen, Instandsetzungsmaßnahmen und Nutzungsplänen auseinander setzen – auch die Betreiber von Lysy Pingwin, Fabryka Trzciny und U Krawca haben dies hinter sich.

Ihrem Verlangen nach Mitspracherecht können sich die Stadtplaner auf die Dauer nicht verschließen. Denn der Imagegewinn, den Praga durch den Zuzug von Künstlern und Kulturunternehmern erfährt, ist beiden Seiten bewusst. Gegenüber potentiellen Investoren wird ihre wachsende Präsenz von den Stadtverantwortlichen längst als profitabler Standortfaktor vermarktet, ohne ihnen im Gegenzug irgendeine Art von Förderung zu gewähren. Ein ungleiches Spiel.

PERSPEKTIVEN

Es ist also nicht verwunderlich, dass die Initiative „Inzynierska" das Thema Revitalisierung in ihr aktuelles Festivalprogramm aufgenommen hat, um auf damit verbundene Probleme und Chancen für Praga aufmerksam zu machen – sowohl gegenüber den Anwohnern als auch gegenüber der Warschauer Öffentlichkeit und Presse. Ob und wie sie die Interessen aller Beteiligten weiter vertreten können, hängt davon ab, wie schnell „Inzynierska" an Lobby gewinnt und wie weit sie ihr Netzwerk ausbauen kann. Denn weder ist die Zahl der Kulturpioniere Pragas bislang übermäßig hoch, noch haben zwangsläufig alle miteinander zu tun – wie das Beispiel der Fabryka Trzciny zeigt. Deren Besitzer pflegt völlig andere Kontakte und verfügt über eine ungleich größere Kapitalkraft, weshalb er sich hinsichtlich Programmplanung und Profilierung viel mehr an globalen Trends als an lokalen Maßgaben orientiert. Die Betreiber des Lysy Pingwin tun dies mit Tapas und Milchschaum in kleinerer Dimension zwar auch, agieren aber innerhalb eines festen nachbarschaftlichen Gefüges. Darin ähnelt ihre Bar wiederum dem Kiezcharakter von Krawiecs Kneipe, der allem Warschauer Globalisierungsgeist mit einem Schulterzucken begegnet.

Fabryka Trzciny, Lysy Pingwin, U Krawca: Allein anhand dieser drei neuen Lokalitäten zeigt sich, wie unterschiedlich die Kräfte und Interessen sind, die auf Pragas wachsendes Kulturleben einwirken. Eine gemeinsame Richtung lässt sich vorerst nicht aus-

all the other renovated structures in various parts of the district. The reason is banal, but suggestive: yellow is the colour of revitalisation because yellow paint is cheaper. The saving is made not by private owners but the city of Warsaw itself, to which most of the properties in Praga belong.

These colours have no historical authenticity. But since the buildings are not protected by law and have no heritage status, developers are subject to no restrictions. Potential buyers are given a free hand. They can buy up buildings at rock-bottom prices and build whatever they want on the sites. Not long ago large parts of Praga's river port, Port Praski, were sold to a private TV station. The new owner is doing nothing at all for the time being, because he knows that the value of the land is rising daily without any effort on his part. In cases where investment is really taking place, it is done in a haphazard fashion. The area around the Lysy Pingwin is now in danger of becoming a kind of mini-ghetto made up of fashionable apartments. Nor does the architecture of the huge new Carrefour shopping mall, just a block away, bear any relation to the original architectural concept for the area. Only recently Praga's oldest cinema had to make way for private speculators and their whims. It is said there are plans to build a multiplex cinema in its place.

At present Praga's "revitalisation" is nothing more than a covert battle for capital which is actually being waged at the district's expense. The inhabitants gain nothing from it. Behind the freshly painted facades all is as it was – the old houses have not really been renovated at all. In any case most tenants live in council flats whose renovation would cost the city a fortune – not because half of them have long ceased to pay rent, but because they would all have to be temporarily re-housed for a shorter or longer period of time. But since there is no spare accommodation in Praga the city would have to build it first, and the council is not prepared to incur such an expense. Thus little will change in the living and social conditions of the long-standing residents in the foreseeable future.

Those affected are barely informed about all this, as they are not privy to the official revitalisation programmes. On the other hand the newcomers to Praga are much more involved. In order to make use of empty properties they are forced to find out about local ownership claims, renovation measures and planning permission – the operators of the Lysy Pingwin, Fabryka Trzciny and U Krawca have got all this behind them.

In the long term the town planners cannot deny them a say in their own affairs. For the boost to Praga's image caused by the influx of artists and cultural entrepreneurs is well known to both sides. The city fathers have long been pointing out to potential investors that their growing presence is a factor in making the district a profitable location without granting them any kind of financial support in return. The deck is stacked.

PERSPECTIVES

It is not surprising that the "Inzynierska" initiative has included the revitalisation issue in its current festival programme. The idea is to draw the attention of local residents, on the one hand, and the general Warsaw public and press, on the other, to

the problems and opportunities the initiative represents for Praga. Whether and how it can continue to represent the interests of all concerned depends on how fast "Inzynierska" can acquire a lobby and how much it can expand its network. The number of Praga's cultural pioneers is still not all that large, nor do all of them necessarily have anything to do with one another – as shown by the example of the Fabryka Trzciny whose owner has quite different contacts and far more capital, which is why he is more geared to global trends than local requirements when it comes to programme planning and choice of profile. Although the operators of the Lysy

machen. Noch ist jeder dabei, sich selbst zu positionieren – auch gegenüber der proletarischen Mehrheit Pragas, die das Gesicht des Stadtteils nach wie vor bestimmt. Am Ende unserer Spurensuche haben wir fast alles durchstreift, was zu Pragas „Up-and-coming"-Erscheinung gehört: das Off-Theater, mit dessen Zuzug hier 2000 alles begann, die Hand voll Galerien, Ateliers und Läden, in denen sich die neuen Mitbewohner Pragas eingerichtet haben. Unser Stadtplan hat viele Kreuzchen bekommen.

Das Einzige, was sich unserer Recherche bis zuletzt verschließt, ist ein kleiner Ladenraum gleich neben Krawiecs Bar. Hier sollte der erste Club Pragas entstehen, erzählt man uns. Doch bislang ist nichts passiert. Es gab mal einen Interessenten, aber nach einer ersten Aufräumaktion ist ihm scheinbar die Luft ausgegangen. Oder das Geld. Zumindest hat er den Raum noch vorsorglich mit Brettern zugenagelt, so dass niemand ihn betreten oder von außen einsehen kann. Durch die Ritzen gähnt ein einziges schwarzes Loch. Passanten gehen gleichmütig vorbei.

Wie es wohl ausgesehen hätte in diesem Club? Wie in der Fabryka Trzciny oder wie bei Krawiec? Oder ganz anders? Und wer hier wohl aus und ein gegangen wäre? Darüber lässt sich nur spekulieren. Fest steht angesichts der vernagelten Ladenfront nur eins: Noch ist hier alles möglich. Wir setzen ein letztes Kreuzchen in unsere Karte: „potentieller Club". Man kann ja nie wissen.

Pingwin do something similar on a smaller scale with tapas and milk shakes, they are acting within a fixed neighbourhood context. This in turn gives their bar the air of being a "local", like that of Krawiec, who dismisses all talk of globalisation in a Warsaw context with a shrug of his shoulders.
Fabryka Trzciny, Lysy Pingwin, U Krawca: These three new localities alone show the variety of forces and interests that influence Praga's growing cultural life. A common direction is not discernible as yet. Everyone is still busy positioning themselves vis-à-vis Praga's proletarian majority, which still gives the district its character. By the end of our investigation we have touched on almost everything relating to Praga's "up-and-coming" aspect, including the Off Theatre – whose arrival here in the year 2000 marked the beginning of the process – and the handful of galleries, ateliers and shops in which Praga's new residents have established themselves. Our street map has acquired many crosses.

The one thing that has evaded our researches right up to the end is a small commercial property right next to Krawiec's bar. This, we are told, is where Praga's first club is going to be. But so far nothing has happened. There was one prospective buyer, but after an initial clean-up operation his enthusiasm seems to have run out. Or his cash. At least he took the precaution of boarding up the place so that no one can get in or view it from outside. All you can see through the cracks is a yawning blackness. People pass by indifferently.
What would this club have looked like? Like the Fabryka Trzciny or U Krawca? Or would it have been quite different from both of them? Who would have made up its clientele? All this can only be a matter of speculation. Faced with the boarded-up shop front the only conclusion you can draw is that this is a place where anything can happen. We put a final cross on our map: "Potential club". You never know.

DIE RUSSEN KOMMEN! ÜBER DIE GLOBALISIERUNG DES „PRINZIPS ABRAMOWITSCH"

SILKE STEETS

Moskau, 24. März 2004. Heute findet das Hinspiel im Viertelfinale der Champions League zwischen Arsenal und Chelsea London statt. Lokomotive Moskau, der russische Teilnehmer, war im Achtelfinale gegen den späteren Finalisten AS Monaco ausgeschieden. Aber das interessiert heute viele schon kaum mehr. Die kleine Bar in Moskaus Peripherie ist bis auf den letzten Platz gefüllt. An den Wänden hängen neben Wimpeln lokaler Fußballclubs ein Poster von Michael Jordan, ein Trikot von Manchester United und – direkt über der Theke – eine große Fahne von Chelsea London. Auf fünf Bildschirmen kann man das Match hier verfolgen. Dazu gibt es amerikanische Chicken Wings mit Heinz-Ketchup, australisches Bier und ein Gewinnspiel. Wer den Ausgang des Fußballmatchs richtig tippt, erhält einen Sixpack Foster's. Irgendwann fällt das 1:0 für Chelsea. Jubel bricht aus. Im suburbanen Moskau freut man sich für den noblen Club aus London. Das Spiel endet 1:1, und Chelsea hat sich in einem beeindruckenden Match gegen den Lokalrivalen Arsenal alle Chancen auf den Halbfinaleinzug bewahrt. Gefeiert wird dies nicht nur an der Stamford Bridge. Vor der Moskauer Sportbar singen ein paar Jugendliche: „Russland, wir lieben dich!"

Aber warum freut man sich in Moskaus Peripherie, wenn im Londoner Stadtderby ein Tor für Chelsea fällt? Es muss mit dem russischen Öltycoon Roman Abramowitsch zusammenhängen. In einem spektakulären Akt hatte Abramowitsch im Sommer 2003 den finanziell angeschlagenen FC Chelsea London aufgekauft. Der Preis: 210 Millionen EUR. Seither hat der mehrfache Milliardär einige Hundert Millionen EUR in Trainer und Spieler investiert. Trotzdem verwundert die Freude und der Ausdruck von nationalem Stolz unter jugendlichen Russen, wenn Chelsea siegt. Denn Abramowitsch gehört zu jenen gewieften Geschäftemachern, die sich während der Privatisierung der sowjetischen Staatsbetriebe mit durchaus zweifelhaften Methoden ein milliardenschweres Vermögen gesichert und anschließend Teile davon ins Ausland transferiert haben – unter anderem durch den Kauf eben jenes englischen Fußballclubs. Wäre es nicht patriotischer gewesen, wenn er mit seinem Kapital dem heimischen Fußball auf die Sprünge geholfen hätte?

Die folgenden Überlegungen beschäftigen sich mit der Bedeutung des Nationalen in der russischen Populärkultur. Nach dem Zusammenbruch des Sozialismus deutet vieles auf eine Wiederbelebung nationaler und ethno-kultureller Identitäten in Osteuropa und der ehemaligen Sowjetunion hin. Katherine Verdery hat deutlich gemacht, dass der postsozialistische Umbruch nicht nur Wirtschaft und Bürokratie betrifft, sondern das gesamte Leben der Menschen erfasst und so neue Bedeutungswelten und kulturelle Identitäten entstehen.[1] Das Nationale scheint dabei eine Schlüsselstellung einzunehmen. Vorsozialistische Narrative von nationaler Größe und Identität erleben eine Renaissance, Konflikte zwischen ethnischen Gruppierungen treten offen zutage. Die bekannteste Erklärung für diesen postsozialistischen Nationalismus lautet: Jahrzehntelang habe die Kommunistische Partei alte Rivalitäten unterdrückt und nivelliert, um einen geeinten, über die Idee des Nationalen hinausgehenden sozialistischen Staat zu formen; mit dem Ende des Sozialismus würden diese stets latent vorhandenen Differenzen wieder sichtbar.[2] Die Realität ist jedoch weitaus komplexer. Verdery etwa betont, dass nach dem Kollaps des Sozialismus in Osteuropa die Nation bzw. die neu gebildeten Staaten für die Bewohner die verlässlichste Größe im Chaos der Transformation gewesen seien, was eine territorial orientierte Identität erkläre.[3] Hinzu kommen vor allem in jüngster Zeit wach-

THE RUSSIANS ARE COMING! ON THE GLOBALISATION OF THE "ABRAMOVICH PRINCIPLE"

SILKE STEETS

Moscow, 24 March 2004. Today is the first leg of the quarter-final Champions League tie between the two London teams, Arsenal and Chelsea. Russia's Locomotive Moscow got to the last 16 but was eliminated by the eventual finalist, AS Monaco. But that hardly interests anyone any more. The little bar on the outskirts of Moscow is filled to capacity. Hanging on the walls, next to pennants of local football clubs, there is a poster of Michael Jordan, a Manchester United football shirt and – directly above the bar – a large Chelsea banner. There are five TV screens on which people can follow the match. Also on offer are American Chicken Wings with Heinz ketchup, Australian beer and a chance to win a six-pack of Foster's for correctly predicting the winner of the match. There are huge cheers as Chelsea take a 1:0 lead. People in suburban Moscow are rooting for the prestigious London club. The game ends 1:1; leaving Chelsea with every chance of making it to the semi-final thanks to an impressive performance against their local rivals. And the celebrations are not confined to Stamford Bridge. In front of a Moscow sports bar a few youths are singing: "Russia, we love you!"

But why this jubilation on the outskirts of Moscow when Chelsea score a goal in a London derby? It must have something to do with the Russian oil tycoon, Roman Abramovich. In summer 2003, Abramovich pulled off a spectacular coup, buying up Chelsea FC, who were in dire financial straits, for 210 million EUR. Since then the multi-billionaire has invested several hundred million euros in coaches and players. Yet the expressions of joy and national pride among young Russians when Chelsea win is still remarkable. Abramovich is, after all, one of those shrewd businessmen who amassed multi-billion fortunes during the privatisation of the Soviet state enterprises using highly dubious methods and subsequently transferred a large part of it abroad. He did this partly by buying the English football club in question. Would it not have been more patriotic to use his capital to give Russian football a boost?

The following remarks are concerned with the significance of national sentiments in Russian popular culture. After the collapse of socialism there have been many indications of a revival of national and ethno-cultural identities in Eastern Europe and the former Soviet Union. As Katherine Verdery has demonstrated, the post-socialist upheaval has not only affected the economy and bureaucracy, but people's whole lives, thus giving rise to new worlds of meaning and cultural identities.[1] The national element seems to occupy a key position in all this. Pre-socialist narratives of national greatness and identity are undergoing a renaissance, while conflicts between ethnic groupings are coming out into the open. The most frequently heard explanation for this post-socialist nationalism runs as follows: for decades the Communist Party suppressed and stamped out old rivalries in order to form a united socialist state that would supersede the national idea. When socialism came to an end these differences, which had always been latent, resurfaced.[2] The reality is far more complex, however. Verdery points out, for example, that after the collapse of socialism in Eastern Europe the population saw the nation or the newly formed state as the most reliable point of reference in the chaos of transformation, which explains the territorial sense of identity.[3] To this must be added the recent growth in the new states' global ties, which not only influence the economy and politics, but also culture and identity. How this has influenced the field of culture has been little studied so far. In western discourses on cultural globalisation Russia has always played a peripheral role.[4] Cultural currents have been mainly analysed as a move-

sende globale Verflechtungen der neuen Staaten, die nicht nur Wirtschaft und Politik, sondern auch Kultur und Identität beeinflussen. Wie dieser Einfluss im Feld der Kultur aussieht, wurde bisher wenig untersucht. In westlichen Diskursen über kulturelle Globalisierung nimmt Russland stets eine periphere Rolle ein.[4] Kulturelle Strömungen werden vorwiegend in ihrer Bewegung von West nach Ost analysiert. Ich möchte diese Perspektive hier umkehren: Was passiert, wenn man vom Osten in den Westen blickt? Welche Rolle spielt die Nation, wenn sich Russlands Populärkultur zur Welt ins Verhältnis setzt? Fußball als Teil einer globalisierten Popkultur scheint dafür hervorragendes Anschauungsmaterial zu liefern. Denn seit Abramowitsch Eigentümer des FC Chelsea ist, rückt der russische Fußball näher an das globale Zentrum. Nur: wie genau veränderte Abramowitschs Konsumrausch Russlands Verhältnis zur Welt?

ROMAN ABRAMOWITSCH & CO. ODER: DER IMAGINÄRE KONSUM IM NEUEN RUSSLAND

Treffen sich zwei Neue Russen, fragt der eine: „He, Vasia, wo hast du diese schöne Krawatte gekauft?" – „Bei Valentino. Hat mich 1 000 Dollar gekostet." – „Oh", sagt der andere abfällig, „ich kenne einen Laden, wo du genau die gleiche Krawatte bekommst, aber für 2 000 Dollar!"[5]

Roman Abramowitsch, ein Waisenkind aus der westsibirischen Provinz und Schulabbrecher, stieg in den 1990er Jahren während der Jelzin-Ära zum mächtigen Metall- und Ölmagnaten auf. Nach ersten unternehmerischen Gehversuchen mit Plastikspielzeug und Autoteilen hatte er 1992 das Ölgeschäft entdeckt. Sein Startkapital sollen 5000 Tonnen Heizöl gewesen sein, die er sich mit Hilfe gefälschter Dokumente angeeignet hatte.[6] Entscheidend für den Aufstieg Abramowitschs war seine Begegnung mit Boris Beresowski, dem zu Beginn der 1990er Jahre mächtigsten Tycoon Russlands. Beresowski führte Abramowitsch in die innersten Zirkel der Macht um den damaligen Staatspräsidenten Boris Jelzin ein und übertrug ihm wichtige Managementaufgaben. Der smarte Abramowitsch nutzte seine exponierte Stellung für zahlreiche Insidergeschäfte im Öl- und Metallsektor und für den Aufbau der Ölgesellschaft Sibneft, die er 1998 übernahm, nachdem sein Förderer Beresowski über Nacht ins Ausland hatte fliehen müssen. Wladimir Putin, mittlerweile im Amt des russischen Staatspräsidenten, hatte die Staatsanwälte auf Beresowski angesetzt. Zahlreiche Klagen, unter anderem wegen Betruges, Steuerhinterziehung und Geldwäsche, liefen gegen ihn. Das Beispiel seines Mentors vor Augen, suchte Abramowitsch Schutz vor etwaiger Verfolgung, indem er eine politische Karriere einschlug. Mit Erfolg, 1999 konnte er sich einen Sitz in der Duma sichern und damit die parlamentarische Immunität erlangen. Er hatte zuvor einen zweistelligen Millionenbetrag an Dollar investiert, um die 79 000 Einwohner der kleinen ostsibirischen Provinz Tschkotka davon zu überzeugen, ihn zum Gouverneur zu wählen. Ende der 1990er Jahre transferierte Abramowitsch große Teile seines Kapitals ins Ausland. In der Millhouse-Capital-Holding mit Sitz in London bündelte er seine Beteiligungen. Diese Gesellschaft hält heute unter anderem 88 Prozent der Anteile des Sibneft-Ölkonzerns, 26 Prozent der Fluggesellschaft Aeroflot sowie 50 Prozent des russischen Aluminium-Monopols Rusal, des weltweit zweitgrößten Aluminiumproduzenten.[7] Roman Abramowitsch belegte 2005 mit einem geschätzten Vermögen von 13,3 Milliarden Dollar Platz 21 in der *Forbes*-Liste der Dollar-Milliardäre.

Für Geschäftemacher wie Abramowitsch, die die wirtschaftliche und politische Umbruchphase der 1990er Jahre derart vorteilhaft für sich zu nutzen wussten, gibt es in Russland einen Namen: Wer in den letzten 15 Jahren reich geworden ist, gehört zu den „Neuen Russen". Der Begriff markiert in erster Linie einen ökonomischen Status, wird aber auch an der Ausprägung gewisser Einstellungen und Werte festgemacht, wie die Anthropologin Caroline Humphrey erklärt: „The term ‚New Russians' has acquired a definite and transferable meaning. It refers to an image of people with a new and alien mentality, people who are rapacious, materialist, and shockingly economically successful. In short, New Russians are ‚new' because they do not give precedence to various hoary Soviet values, which are still mostly seen in a rosy hue by everyone else: the value of honest labor, of supporting the *kollektive*, of respect for the working masses, of high-minded personal frugality, and above all the value of production of goods for the benefit of society as a whole. In this mode of talking, New Russians are presumed to be ‚corrupt'."[8] „Neue Russen" verkörpern also das Gegenteil der Werte, die für viele Menschen in Russland noch immer Gültigkeit besitzen. Und doch gibt es eine soziologisch interessante Verbindung zwischen Masse und Elite. Denn die Figur des Neuen Russen ist weniger Ausdruck einer Selbstcharakterisierung der ökonomisch Er-

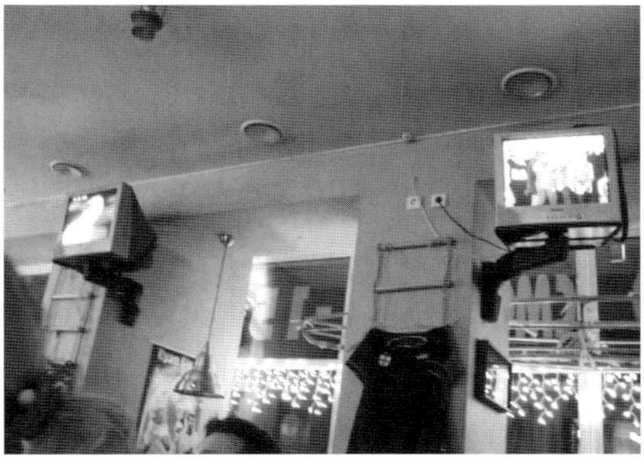

ment from west to east. I would like to reverse this perspective: What happens when one looks at the West through the eyes of the East? What role is played by the nation when Russia's popular culture is seen in relation to the world? As a part of a globalised pop culture, football would seem to provide excellent illustrative material. Since Abramovich has been the owner of Chelsea FC, Russian football has been moving closer to the global centre. But how exactly has Abramovich's spending spree altered Russia's relations with the world?

ROMAN ABRAMOVICH & CO. OR: IMAGINARY CONSUMPTION IN THE NEW RUSSIA

Two New Russians meet, and one asks: "Hey, Vasia, where did you get your nice tie?" – "At the Valentino store. Cost me 1 000 dollars." – "Phew" the other one says with contempt, "I know a place where you could get exactly the same tie for $ 2 000 dollars!"[5]

Roman Abramovich, an orphan and school drop-out from a West Siberian province, rose to become a powerful steel and oil magnate in the 1990s, during the Yeltsin era. After a few initial ventures with plastic toys and car parts he discovered the oil business in 1992. His starting capital appears to have been 5,000 tonnes of fuel oil, which he obtained with the aid of forged documents.[6] A key role in the rise of Abramovich was his meeting with Boris Berezovski, who in the early 1990s was Russia's most powerful tycoon. Berezovski introduced Abramovich to the innermost circles of power around the then President, Boris Yeltsin, and entrusted him with important management tasks. The astute Abramovich used his prominent position to clinch numerous insider deals in the oil and steel sectors and to build up the oil company Sibneft, of which he assumed control in 1998 after his patron Berezovski had had to flee the country overnight. Russia's new president, Vladimir Putin, had unleashed the public prosecutors on Berezovski, who had been facing numerous charges for fraud, tax evasion, money laundering and other offences. With the example of his mentor before him, Abramovich sought protection against possible prosecution by embarking on a political career. In this he was successful, securing a seat in the Duma in 1999 and thus gaining parliamentary immunity. He had previously invested an eight-digit sum in US dollars to convince the 79,000 inhabitants of the little East Siberian province of Chukotka to elect him as governor. In the late 1990s, Abramovich transferred a large amount of his capital abroad to the London-based Millhouse Capital Holding company. At present this company's holdings include 88 per cent of the stock in the Sibneft oil conglomerate, 26 per cent of the Aeroflot airline and 50 per cent of the Russian aluminium monopoly Rusal, the world's second largest aluminium producer.[7] In 2005, Roman Abramovich ranked 21st in the Forbes list of dollar billionaires with an estimated fortune of 13.3 billion dollars.

In Russia there is a name for wheeler-dealers like Abramovich who managed to exploit the economic and political transition phase of the 1990s to such great advantage for themselves: Those who have got rich in the past 15 years are called the "New Russians". The term mainly connotes economic status, but it is also associated with certain attitudes and values, as the anthropologist Caroline Humphrey explains: "The term 'New Russians' has acquired a definite and transferable meaning. It refers to an image of people with a new and alien mentality, people who are rapacious, materi-

folgreichen als vielmehr eine metaphernreiche Zuschreibung durch die gesellschaftliche Mitte. Der Begriff des Neuen Russen verdichtet all das, was sich – medial vermittelt – Arbeiter, Lehrer und Büroangestellte unter einem Neureichen vorstellen. Und das ist, idealtypisch gesprochen: ein Mann im Businessanzug mit Krawatte, Goldkette, mehreren Goldringen und einer Rolex-Armbanduhr, der einen Landrover-Jeep fährt, ständig mit seinem Handy telefoniert und sein Geld in Begleitung diverser weiblicher Models gedankenlos verprasst. Der Neue Russe ist – im Gegensatz zum sozialistischen Ideal des Neuen Menschen aus der Sowjetzeit – eine explizit männliche Figur, wenngleich mit durchaus schillerndem weiblichen Pendant: „Advertising directed to New Russians supposes a penumbra of ‚feminine' wives, mistresses, and high-class prostitutes, who emphatically do engage in work or business and whose time is pictured as being spent in consumption, homemaking, manicures, self-improvement, and so forth."[9] Abgesehen von diesem Frauenbild, das nur mehr wenig mit den noch zu Sowjetzeiten verbreiteten Vorstellungen von Emanzipation und Gleichberechtigung zu tun hat, tritt ein zweiter Aspekt in den Vordergrund: Gesellschaftlich sichtbar werden die Neuen Russen nicht durch das, was sie produzieren – das sind undurchsichtige, vermutlich illegale Geschäfte –, sondern durch das, was, und die Art und Weise, wie sie konsumieren. Die zentrale Bedeutung des Konsums im neuen Russland hebt auch der Anthropologe Serguei Alex Oushakine hervor. Er untersuchte Ende der 1990er Jahre die Assoziationen von sibirischen Teenagern zu Begriffen wie „Soviet Motherland" und „New Russia" anhand von 178 Aufsätzen. Oushakine zeigt, dass die Jugendlichen beide Begriffe nicht in ihrer politischen oder gesellschaftlichen Dimension auffassten, sondern mit ihnen hauptsächlich persönliche und imaginierte Konsummuster verbanden.[10] Zugespitzt formuliert: die Jugendlichen unterschieden zwischen der sowjetischen Vergangenheit und der russischen Gegenwart durch die Gegenüberstellung von „leeren sowjetischen Einkaufstaschen" und „üppig gefüllten postsowjetischen Läden".[11] Die Frage des Nationalen wird hier auf eine persönliche Alltagsebene gebracht und mit der Frage des Konsums verknüpft. Ins Zentrum der Aufmerksamkeit rückt so der neue russische Konsumstil, der nicht nur in den Aufsätzen der Jugendlichen, sondern auch in der medial vermittelten gesellschaftlichen Diskussion, am Stil der Neureichen festgemacht wird. Oushakine zeigt, ähnlich wie Humphrey, dass dieser Stil seine idealtypische Entsprechung in der Figur des neuen russischen Mannes findet: „Unlike in Soviet times, when shopping, or rather waiting in queues, was usually seen as the duty and prerogative of women, post-Soviet consumption is largly associated with the figure of the ‚new Russian man' (...)"[12] Die Haupterkenntnis Oushakines aber ist eine andere: Da die Jugendlichen keine direkten persönlichen Erfahrungen mit Neuen Russen hatten, zeichneten sie *imaginäre* Porträts dieses neuen Konsumstils und reproduzierten dabei ihre eigenen, erlernten Kulturmuster: „(...) I think, student's imaginary portraits of new Russians are interesting not because of their (non)correspondence with the ‚really' existing new Russians. Rather, they are interesting because it is these fantasies and envisioned ideals that define, frame and finally constrain the social and cultural expectations of the young generation. To put it differently, students' descriptions of the new Russian style to a large extent can be

alist, and shockingly economically successful. In short, New Russians are 'new' because they do not give precedence to various hoary Soviet values, which are still mostly seen in a rosy hue by everyone else: the value of honest labour, of supporting the *kollektive*, of respect for the working masses, of high-minded personal frugality, and above all the value of production of goods for the benefit of society as a whole. In this mode of talking, New Russians are presumed to be 'corrupt'."[8] "New Russians" thus embody the opposite of the values that still retain their validity for many people in Russia. And yet there is a sociologically interesting connection between mass and elite. The figure of the New Russian is not so much the expression of how the economically successful see themselves as a metaphorical attribution by the middle strata of society. The concept of the New Russian sums up everything which – through the prism of the media – workers, teachers and office workers imagine the nouveaux riches to be. The type may be ideally described as follows: a man in a business suit with a tie, a gold chain, several gold rings and a Rolex wristwatch, who drives a Land Rover Jeep, is always talking into a mobile phone and spends money lavishly in the company of various female models. The New Russian is – in contrast to the socialist ideal of the New Man from the Soviet period – an explicitly male figure, albeit with a somewhat enigmatic female counterpart: "Advertising directed to New Russians supposes a penumbra of 'feminine' wives, mistresses, and high-class prostitutes, who emphatically do engage in work or business and whose time is pictured as being spent in consumption, homemaking, manicures, self-improvement, and so forth."[9] Apart from this female role model, which has little to do with the still widespread Soviet-era notions of emancipation and equal rights, a second aspect stands out: the New Russians owe their high social profile not to what they produce – impenetrable and presumably illegal business deals – but to what they consume and how they consume it. The central importance of consumption in the new Russia is also highlighted by the anthropologist, Serguei Alex Oushakine, who in the late 1990s studied the associations of Siberian teenagers with concepts like "Soviet Motherland" and "New Russia" on the basis of 178 essays. Oushakine shows that the young people did not see these concepts in their political or social dimensions, but associated them with personal and imagined patterns of consumption.[10] To put it simply, the young people distinguished between the Soviet past and the Russian present in terms of "empty Soviet grocery-bags vs the full post-Soviet stores".[11] The question of national sentiment was reduced to a personal everyday level and linked to the question of consumption. The focus is thus on the new Russian style of consumption, which is firmly associated with the style of the nouveaux riches, not only in the young people's essays, but also in media discussions. Like Humphrey, Oushakine shows that this style finds its classic equivalent in the figure of the new Russian man: "Unlike in Soviet times, when shopping, or rather waiting in queues, was usually seen as the duty and prerogative of women, post-Soviet consumption is largely associated with the figure of the 'new Russian man' ..."[12] Oushakine's main finding, however, is another one. Since the young people had no direct personal experience of New Russians, they drew *imaginary* portraits of this new consumption style, reproducing their own, learned cultural pat-

seen as an example of what Marshall Shalins calls a ‚historical metaphor of a mystical reality' (...) These descriptions articulate an unfamiliar, ‚mythical' situation (e.g. patterns of wealthy consumption) by translating them into the already familiar vocabulary of metaphors and conceptions."[13]

Die Jugendlichen beschrieben also den imaginierten Luxusgeschmack der Neureichen im Vokabular eines für sie selbstverständlichen Notwendigkeitsgeschmacks. Obwohl sie immer wieder eine unbegrenzte Auswahl an Konsumgütern beschworen, füllten sie die neureichen Einkaufstüten mit derselben alten Wurst[14], wenngleich in besserer Verpackung. Wie unterschieden die Jugendlichen dann aber die Neureichen von den gewöhnlichen Russen? Wenn es keine außergewöhnlichen Konsumgüter sind, die die Differenz markieren, was ist es dann? Die Antwort ist einfach und doch erhellend: Es ist die *Quantität* der konsumierten Produkte. Exemplarisch dafür mag die Charakterisierung eines Neuen Russen durch einen 18-jährigen Jugendlichen stehen: „New Russian man – a 75-gram gold neck-chain, a 75-gram gold cross. A very expansive car, an expensive suit. Undoubtedly – a lot of intellect, common sense, and important connections."[15] Oushakine führt das, was er die „Quantität des Stils" nennt, auf zwei Ursachen zurück. Mit Bourdieu lassen sich die Schwierigkeiten der Jugendlichen, kulturelle Symbole zu finden, die die exzeptionelle ökonomische Stellung der neuen Reichen homolog im Feld der Kultur abbilden könnten, aus ihrer Mittelschichtsbiographie erklären.[16] Ihnen fehlt schlicht und einfach ein entsprechendes Vokabular. Eine zweite, diesem ersten Faktor vorgelagerte Ursache für die Dominanz des Quantitativen in der Beschreibung des Konsumstils der Neuen Russen findet Oushakine im generellen Fehlen einer vielfältigen postsowjetischen Symbolproduktion, die den neuen russischen Konsumstil auch mit distinktiven Merkmalen ausstatten könnte; er nennt dies „Culture of Symbolic Shortage"[17]. So kommt es, dass Neue Russen ihr Geld tatsächlich nicht in Gemälde, Literatur, Theater oder Stiftungen investieren, sondern in Goldketten (schon zu Sowjetzeiten war Gold ultimativer Ausdruck von Wohlstand), teure Autos und repräsentative Wohnungen – oder eben in Fußballclubs.

RUSSIAN FOOTBALL – WHO OWNS THE GAME?

Zu Beginn der russischen Fußballsaison im März 2004 veröffentlichte die Tageszeitung *Kommersant* eine Übersicht, die die Hauptsponsoren der russischen Erstligateams und den Umfang ihres jeweiligen jährlichen Engagements auflistete. Die russische Eisenbahngesellschaft JSC, Hauptsponsor von Lokomotive Moskau, führte die Rangliste mit einer Fördersumme von 25 Millionen US-Dollar an, gefolgt vom Ölkonzern Sibneft, der ZSKA Moskau 18 Millionen Dollar überwies, und dem Metallgiganten Norilsk Nickel, der Torpedo Metallurg, den heutigen FC Moskau, mit 10 Millionen Dollar unterstützte. Der Rest der 16 Erstligateams operierte mit Sponsorensummen im einstelligen Millionenbereich. Diese Liste war schnell veraltet. Noch im selben Monat gab Sibneft bekannt, 54 Millionen Dollar in den amtierenden russischen Meister ZSKA Moskau investieren zu wollen. Um herauszufinden, wer hinter dieser nennenswerten Sponsorensumme stand, bedurfte es wenig Phantasie, denn Sibneft gehört zu 88 Prozent Roman Abramowitsch. Doch welches Motiv verfolgte Abramowitsch mit diesem großzügigen Engagement? Versuchte er damit jene patriotisch gesinnten rus-

terns in the process: "... I think students' imaginary portraits of new Russians are interesting not because of their (non)correspondence with the 'really' existing new Russians. Rather, they are interesting because it is these fantasies and envisioned ideals that define, frame and finally constrain the social and cultural expectations of the young generation. To put it differently, students' descriptions of the new Russian style to a large extent can be seen as an example of what Marshall Shalins calls a 'historical metaphor of a mystical reality' ... These descriptions articulate an unfamiliar, 'mythical' situation (e.g. patterns of wealthy consumption) by translating them into the already familiar vocabulary of metaphors and conceptions."[13]
The young people thus described the imagined luxurious tastes of the nouveaux riches in terms of the taste of those who had never been able to satisfy anything more than basic needs, a situation which to them seemed self-evident. Although they repeatedly referred to the unlimited selection of consumer goods, they filled the shopping bags of the nouveaux riches with the same old sausage[14], albeit in better packaging. How then did the young people distinguish the nouveaux riches from ordinary Russians? If it is not out-of-the-way consumer goods that constitute the difference, what is it? The answer is simple and yet illuminating: it is the *quantity* of products consumed. An example of this is provided by this characterisation of a New Russian by an 18-year-old: "New Russian man – a 75-gram gold neck-chain, a 75-gram gold cross. A very expensive car, an expensive suit. Undoubtedly – a lot of intellect, common sense, and important connections."[15] Oushakine attributes what he calls the "quantity of style" to two causes. Like Bourdieu, he explains the difficulties experienced by young people in finding symbols to reproduce the exceptional economic situation of the nouveaux riches and match them in the cultural field in terms of their origins in the intermediate strata of society.[16] They simply lack the necessary vocabulary. The second, more basic cause of the dominance of the quantitative factor in the description of the New Russians' style of consumption is seen by Oushakine in the general absence of any productive source of post-Soviet symbolism that could provide that consumption with distinctive features. He calls this phenomenon the "culture of symbolic shortage".[17] This is why the New Russians do not in fact invest their money in paintings, literature, theatres or foundations, but in gold chains (even in Soviet times gold was the ultimate expression of affluence), expensive cars, fancy apartments – or football clubs.

RUSSIAN FOOTBALL – WHO OWNS THE GAME?

At the beginning of the Russian football season in March 2004 the business daily *Kommersant* published a list of the main sponsors of the Russian First Division teams, giving the extent of their annual contributions. The Russian railway company RZhD, the main sponsor of Locomotive Moscow, ranked first with a contribution of 25 million US dollars, followed by the oil giant Sibneft, which contributed 18 million dollars to TsSKA Moscow, and the mining conglomerate Norilsk Nickel, which supported Torpedo Metallurg (now Moscow FC) to the tune of 10 million dollars. The rest of the 16 First Division teams received sponsor contributions in the seven-digit range. This list was soon out of date. That same month Sibneft announced its intention of investing 54 million dollars in the reigning Russian champions, TsSKA Moscow. It did not

sischen Fans zu beruhigen, die sich darüber beklagt hatten, dass er vor Jahresfrist ein Vielfaches dieser Summe für den Kauf des FC Chelsea ausgegeben hatte, statt den einheimischen Fußball finanziell zu fördern? In den Augen des britischen Sportjournalisten Dan Brennan ist Abramowitschs Engagement im russischen Fußball Teil einer groß angelegten Strategie zur kontinuierlichen Umgestaltung der europäischen Fußballlandschaft. Brennan beschreibt, wie Abramowitsch seit seiner Übernahme des FC Chelsea Verbindungen zu anderen europäischen Spitzenclubs aufbaute. Im Zentrum dieser Verbindungen stehen der PSV Eindhoven (Niederlande), der FC Porto (Portugal) und ZSKA Moskau (Russland). „The strategy can enable the Blues [der FC Chelsea tritt traditionell in blauer Spielkleidung an; Anm. Steets] to establish a European conveyer belt for the Continent's best young talents, open up access to markets in Eastern Europe and South America, and also create a holding bay for surplus playing staff or Chelsea players in waiting."[18] Erste Früchte trug diese Strategie, so Brennan, mit dem Transfer des niederländischen Stürmerstars Arien Robben vom PSV Eindhoven zum FC Chelsea London zu Beginn der Saison 2004/05. Kostenpunkt: 21,5 Millionen EUR. Im Gegenzug soll Chelsea dem PSV bei der Verpflichtung des jungen brasilianischen Verteidigers Alex (er wechselte für fünf Millionen EUR vom brasilianischen Club FC Santos nach Eindhoven) behilflich gewesen sein. Als Chelsea kurz darauf mit dem Gedanken spielte, den ebenfalls hoch gehandelten peruanischen Stürmer Jefferson Farfan zu verpflichten, und dieser wenig später beim PSV Eindhoven unterschrieb, stand für Brennan fest: „(...) it all suggests that PSV – one of Europe's most prestigious clubs – is now a Chelsea's feeder club."[19] Ähnliches scheint für den Champions-League-Sieger von 2004, den FC Porto, zu gelten. Mit der Verpflichtung des portugiesischen Erfolgstrainers Jose Mourinho sicherte sich Chelsea auch die Option auf alle Nachwuchstalente, die Portos Fördersystem entspringen. Die portugiesischen Nationalspieler Paulo Ferreira (16 Millionen EUR) und Ricardo Carvalho (24,5 Millionen EUR), die mit Mourinho zum FC Chelsea wechselten, sind vermutlich nur die Vorhut dieses Talentflusses.

Die interessantesten Verbindungen aber, die der FC Chelsea etablierte, sieht Brennan in jenen zum ZSKA Moskau, dem russischen Meister von 2003 und dem für viele überraschenden UEFA-Cup-Sieger von 2005. Wenngleich es keine offiziellen Vereinbarungen zwischen den beiden Clubs gibt, ist die Männerfreundschaft zwischen Roman Abramowitsch und dessen altem Geschäftspartner Jewgenij Giner, dem Clubpräsidenten von ZSKA Moskau, kein Geheimnis. Das Sponsorenpaket in Höhe von 54 Millionen US-Dollar, das Abramowitsch im März 2004 schnürte, machte ihn zwar nicht zum Eigentümer des Clubs (was nach den Richtlinien des Europäischen Fußballverbands, UEFA, auch nicht erlaubt wäre), dennoch sicherte es ihm zweifelsohne einen gewissen Einfluss. Dieser Einfluss deutete sich bereits im Sommer 2003 an, kurz nachdem

require much imagination to guess who was behind this considerable sum, since Roman Abramovich has an 88 percent stake in Sibneft. But what was Abramovich's motive in making this generous contribution? Was he trying to appease the patriotically minded Russian fans who complained that a year before he had spent several times this sum to buy Chelsea FC instead of giving his financial support to Russian football? The British sports journalist, Dan Brennan, views Abramovich's commitment to Russian football as part of a grand strategy to change the face of European football. Brennan describes how, since his acquisition of Chelsea, Abramovich has established links with other top European clubs. The most important of these links are with PSV Eindhoven (Netherlands), Porto (Portugal) and TsSKA Moscow (Russia). "The strategy can enable the Blues [the traditional Chelsea colour (S.S.)] to establish a European conveyer belt for the Continent's best young talents, open up access to markets in Eastern Europe and South America, and also create a holding bay for surplus playing staff or Chelsea players in waiting."[18] According to Brennan, this strategy bore its first fruits with the transfer of the Dutch star striker Arien Robben from PSV Eindhoven to Chelsea at the beginning of the 2004/05 season at a cost of 21.5 million EUR. In return Chelsea are supposed to have helped PSV acquire the young Brazilian defender Alex (who was transferred for 5 million EUR from Santos FC in Brazil to Eindhoven). When shortly afterwards Chelsea were thinking of taking on the equally sought after Peruvian striker, Jefferson Farfan, and the latter signed for PSV Eindhoven not long afterwards, Brennan was convinced that: "... it all suggests that PSV – one of Europe's most prestigious clubs – is now a Chelsea feeder club."[19] The same seems to apply to Porto, the 2004 Champions League winners. By engaging the successful Portuguese coach, Jose Mourinho, Chelsea also secured an option on all the new football talents turned out by Porto's coaching and talent-seeking system. The Portuguese internationals, Paulo Ferreira (16 million EUR) and Ricardo Carvalho (24.5 million EUR), who switched to Chelsea with Mourinho, are probably only the vanguard of this flow of talent.

In Brennan's view, however, the most interesting links that Chelsea established were those with TsSKA Moscow, the Russian champions of 2003 who – to the surprise of many – won the UEFA Cup in 2005. Even if there are no official agreements between the two clubs, the friendship between Roman Abramovich and his old business partner, Yevgeni Giner, the club president of TsSKA Moscow, is no secret. The sponsorship package worth 54 million US dollars that Abramovich put together in March 2004 may not have made him the owner of the club (which the guidelines of the European Football Association, UEFA, would not have permitted anyway), but it definitely assured him of a certain influence. This influence made itself felt as early as summer 2003, shortly after Abramovich acquired FC Chelsea, when the Croatian star

Abramowitsch den FC Chelsea übernommen hatte. Damals unterschrieb der kroatische Stürmerstar Ivica Olic – durch die bis dahin für Russland als Rekord geltende Ablösesumme von 7,5 Millionen US-Dollar aus dem laufenden Vertrag mit Dynamo Zagreb freigekauft – beim ZSKA Moskau. In Moskau angekommen, erklärte Olic, er sehe den ZSKA als Sprungbrett zum FC Chelsea. Ein späterer Wechsel nach London sei ihm in den Vertragsverhandlungen sogar versprochen worden. Dan Brennan weiß von einem ähnlichen Angebot, das der brasilianische Stürmer Luis Fabiano erhalten habe. Auch ihm soll über den Umweg ZSKA Moskau eine Perspektive beim FC Chelsea London offeriert worden sein.[20] Wenngleich Jewgenij Giner den Einfluss seines Freundes Roman Abramowitsch öffentlich dementiert, ist für das russische Sportmagazin *Pro Sport* klar, dass der Chelsea-Eigner „the most influential figure in Russian football"[21] darstellt. Der Herausgeber des Magazins, Igor Poroschin, bringt es auf den Punkt: „There are only two clubs in Europe that can spend big now – TsSKA and Chelsea."[22]

Das war 2004. Mitte 2005 hatten die rasanten Veränderungen im russischen Fußball weitere Moskauer Erstligateams erfasst. Dem Rekordmeister Spartak Moskau beispielsweise gelangen mit den Millionen des Hauptsponsors Lukoil, dem größten Ölproduzenten des Landes, im Herbst 2004 gleich zwei Superdeals. Zuerst unterzeichnete der Mittelfeldstar und russische Nationalspieler Dmitri Alenitchev, der kurz zuvor mit dem FC Porto den Champions-League-Titel gewonnen hatte, bei Spartak, und schließlich konnte das argentinische Talent Fernando Cavenaghi für 8,6 Millionen EUR verpflichtet werden. Keinesfalls schlechter erging es dem erbittertsten Rivalen Spartaks aus vergangenen Tagen, dem Ex-KGB-Club Dynamo Moskau, der seinen eigenen „Abramovich-style sugar daddy"[23] gefunden hat. Sein Name: Alexei Fedorytschev. Der Düngemitteltycoon, dessen Konzern Fedcominvest bereits den AS Monaco sponsert, versprach Dynamo Moskau rund 220 Millionen EUR als Initialzündung. Der Verein verstärkte sich vor Beginn der Saison 2005 mit dem griechischen Europameister Georgios Seitaridis und mit nicht weniger als sechs Spielern der ersten portugiesischen Liga. Im Sommer 2005 bot Dynamo einer Meldung der Sportnachrichtenagentur sid zufolge 40 Millionen EUR Ablöse für den beim FC Bayern München unter Vertrag stehenden deutschen Mittelfeldstar Michael Ballack, der außerdem von Manchester United und Real Madrid umworben wurde. Auch der Bau einer neuen Fußballarena ist in Planung.[24] Das „Prinzip Abramowitsch" greift zunehmend in Russland: Während namhafte westliche Clubs durch die Krise der TV-Vermarktung (oder durch Missmanagement) teils mit erheblich kleineren Budgets operieren müssen, stärken in Russland finanzkräftige Oligarchen und Konzerne den Clubs den Rücken. Mit traumhaften Budgets machen sie eine Vielzahl erstklassiger Transfers möglich, was zweifellos zur Entwicklung und internationalen Anschlussfähigkeit des russischen Fußballs beiträgt. Worin aber liegt das Besondere dessen, was hier als „Prinzip Abramowitsch" bezeichnet werden soll? Es ist nicht die Tatsache, dass es so etwas wie Sponsoring (auch mit großen Summen) im Fußball gibt, sondern die Art und Weise, wie die Clubs ihr Geld für Spieler ausgeben, also die spezifische Ausprägung des Konsumverhaltens russischer (oder durch Russen geführter) Fußballclubs:

striker Ivica Olic – released from his contract with Dynamo Zagreb for the sum of 7.5 million US dollars, considered to be a record figure for Russia at the time – signed up with TsSKA Moscow. When he arrived in Moscow, Olic declared that he saw TsSKA as a stepping stone to FC Chelsea. He had even been promised a later transfer to London in the contract negotiations. Dan Brennan has heard of a similar offer made to the Brazilian striker, Luis Fabiano. He too seems to have been offered the prospect of going to Chelsea via TsSKA Moscow.[20] Although Yevgeni Giner publicly denies the influence of his friend, Roman Abramovich, the Russian sports magazine *Pro Sport* has no doubt that the Chelsea owner is "the most influential figure in Russian football".[21] The magazine's editor-in-chief, Igor Poroshin, put it succinctly: "There are only two clubs in Europe that can spend big now – TsSKA and Chelsea."[22]

That was in 2004. By mid-2005 the rapid changes in Russian football had overtaken other Moscow First Division teams. In autumn 2004, for example, supplied with millions from its main sponsor Lukoil, the country's largest oil producer, the record champions, Spartak Moscow, were able to clinch not one but two super deals. First the midfield star and Russian international, Dmitri Alenichev, who shortly before had won the Champions League title with FC Porto, signed up with Spartak, after which the talented Argentinean, Fernando Cavenaghi, was bought for 8.6 million EUR. No less fortunate was Spartak's bitterest rival of former times, the ex-KGB club Dynamo Moscow, which found its own "Abramovich-style sugar daddy".[23] His name is Alexei Fedorychev, the fertilizer tycoon, whose company Fedcominvest already sponsors AS Monaco. He has promised Dynamo Moscow around 220 million EUR for starters. Before the beginning of the 2005 season the club received reinforcements in the shape of Georgios Seitaridis of the European champions, Greece, and no fewer than six players from the Portuguese First Division. In summer 2005, the sports news agency SID reported that Dynamo had offered 40 million EUR to release the German midfield star Michael Ballack from his contract with FC Bayern Munich. Ballack had also been wooed by Manchester United and Real Madrid. The construction of a new football stadium is being planned.[24] The "Abramovich principle" is proving increasingly effective in Russia. While some big-name western clubs are being forced by the crisis in TV marketing (or by mismanagement) to operate with much smaller budgets, in Russia oligarchs and big companies with plenty of money to spend are giving the clubs a shot in the arm. Fabulous budgets open the way to a large number of first class transfers, which is undoubtedly contributing to Russian football's development and ability to climb the international ladder ties. But what is the defining feature of what we are calling here the "Abramovich principle"? It is not just the fact that there is such a thing as sponsoring (even with large sums) in football, but the way in which the clubs spend their money on players, i.e. the specific variety of consumer behaviour shown by Russian (or Russian-run) football clubs. Since the largesse bestowed by sponsors on Russian football in the last two years has shot up exponentially, it is less and less a matter of the actual sums paid for individual players. Or, if it is the sums that play the main role, it is not in a restrictive sense, but in the sense of compet-

Da die Sponsorensummen im russischen Fußball in den letzten beiden Jahren exponentiell in die Höhe geschossen sind, kommt es auf die Kosten für einen Spieler immer weniger an. Beziehungsweise: die Kosten könnten es sein, die in erster Linie zählen, aber nicht im Sinne der Restriktion, sondern im Sinne des Wettbewerbs um die beste Mannschaft. Was aus russischer Sicht gleichbedeutend zu sein scheint mit der teuersten Mannschaft. Abramowitsch macht es auf globaler Ebene vor. Der FC Chelsea ist mit einem Gesamttransferwert von über 390 Millionen EUR[25] die teuerste Mannschaft der Welt. Um den Titel auf russischer Ebene wird noch gestritten. Man kann das „Prinzip Abramowitsch" auch mit dem eingangs zitierten Witz umschreiben: Wenn ich die Wahl habe zwischen einer Krawatte, die 1 000 Dollar kostet, und einer – genauso gut, genauso schön –, die 2 000 Dollar kostet, warum soll ich mich dann mit der billigeren zufrieden geben?

Dass derartig rasante Entwicklungen im Fußball auch Auswirkungen auf Anhängerschaft und Fanstrukturen haben, liegt auf der Hand. Denn ein wahrer Fußballfan macht nicht nur die eigene Lebenssituation vom Tabellenstand des Lieblingsclubs abhängig[26], er identifiziert sich mit seinem Club auch, weil er für etwas steht, an das er glaubt: etwa für eine bestimmte Spielweise, für eine lokale Identität, für Geschichte, für Widerstand oder für eine bestimmte Art, einen Club zu führen. Deutlich wird dies beispielsweise an der bis heute andauernden Rivalität zwischen Dynamo und Spartak Moskau, denn Fußball zählte schon in der Sowjetunion zu den populärsten Sportarten.[27] Dynamo – 1923 durch den Geheimdienst KGB gegründet – war der erste sowjetische Sportclub und als solcher für die exzellente Ausbildung der Kader verantwortlich, weshalb er staatlicherseits stets besser und reichlicher bedacht wurde als irgendein anderer Verein. Spartak hingegen war immer unabhängig von staatlichen Strukturen und wurde einzig durch zivile Organisationen unterstützt – ein Grund, weshalb Spartak, besonders unter Arbeitern, immer der beliebteste Club des sowjetischen Fußballs war. Als „a small way of saying ‚No'" bezeichnet der Historiker Robert Edelman die Spartak-Anhängerschaft und bezieht sich auf den armenischen Anthropologen Levon Abramian: „In a Communist country (...) the football club you supported was a community to which you yourself chose to belong. The regime did not send you to support a club (...) It might be your only chance to choose a community, and, also, in that community you could express yourself as you wished (...)"[28] Diese Freiheit des Ausdrucks von Fansein führte auch außerhalb des Spielfeldes zu Auseinandersetzungen zwischen Dynamo und Spartak. Während eines Spiels der Rivalen ertönten „Kill the Cops"-Sprechchöre aus den Spartak-Reihen. Blutige Ausschreitungen waren keine Seltenheit. „Hatred of the structures of force was central to the fans' preference for Spartak."[29] Spartak stand für Opposition, für Protest.[30] Heute gibt es die Sowjetunion nicht mehr, und seit einigen Jahren scheint auch das Spartakfan-Sein seinen Reiz verloren zu haben. Zweifelhaften Entscheidungen der Vereinsführung folgte um das Jahr 2000 ein sportliches Chaos. Der einstige Serienmeister[31] bewegte sich in den letzten fünf Jahren vorwiegend im Niemandsland der Tabelle. Und in der Champions League spielen andere: Lokomotive Moskau zum Beispiel, ein Club, der in der sowjetischen Vergangenheit wenig in Er-

ing to put together the best team. Which in the Russian view seems to mean the most expensive team. Abramovich is demonstrating how this can be done at the global level. With a total transfer value of over 390 million EUR[25] Chelsea is the most expensive team in the world. In the Russian context it has yet to be established who deserves this honour. One can paraphrase the "Abramovich principle" in terms of the joke quoted earlier. If I have a choice between a tie that costs 1,000 dollars and one that looks just as good and costs 2,000 dollars, why should I content myself with the cheaper one?

The fact that such radical developments in football also affect supporters and the kind of people that become fans is obvious. A true football fan not only makes his own *joie de vivre* dependent on his favourite club's place in the league table[26], he also identifies with his club because it stands for something he believes in: for a certain way of playing, for a local identity, for history, for resistance, or for a certain way of running a club. This is clearly shown, for example, by the rivalry between Dynamo Moscow and Spartak Moscow that persists to this day, for football was one of the most popular sports in the Soviet Union.[27] Dynamo – founded in 1923 by the GPU (later KGB) – was the first Soviet sports club and as such responsible for the excellent training of the players, which is why it was always better and more lavishly endowed by the state than any other club. Spartak, on the other hand, had always been independent of state agencies, being supported only by civil organisations. This is one reason why Spartak was always the most popular club in Soviet football, especially among workers. "A small way of saying 'No'" is how the historian Robert Edelman refers to Spartak's followers, and he quotes the Armenian anthropologist Levon Abramian: "In a Communist country ... the football club you supported was a community to which you yourself chose to belong. The regime did not send you to support a club ... It might be your only chance to choose a community, and, also, in that community you could express yourself as you wished ..."[28]
This freedom of expression for fans led to conflicts between Dynamo and Spartak even off the playing field. At one match between the two rivals chants of "kill the cops" could be heard from the ranks of Spartak supporters. Bloody clashes were no rarity. "Hatred of the structures of force was central to the fans' preference for Spartak."[29]
Spartak stood for opposition, for protest.[30] Today the Soviet Union no longer exists, and for some years now being a Spartak fan seems to have lost its charm. Dubious decisions by the club management were followed about the year 2000 by a crisis in their sporting performance. Over the past five years the former champions[31] have been just about nowhere in the league table. And now others are playing in the Champions League. Locomotive Moscow, for example, a club, which made little impression in the Soviet past, has moved with the times. Since 2002 the club has had the most modern stadium in Russia[32], a purely football stadium without an athletics track, but with a giant video screen, state-of-the-art security equipment, and a VIP area. It is the key to success and winning new supporters. Football can also be experienced here by families at first hand in an exciting atmosphere without the fear of being threatened by fan violence. What the Locomotive stadium does not

scheinung getreten ist, die Zeichen der Zeit aber erkannt hat. Seit 2002 besitzt der Verein die modernste Arena Russlands[32], ein reines Fußballstadion ohne Leichtathletikbahn, aber mit Videowand, neuester Sicherheitstechnik und VIP-Bereich. Sie ist der Schlüssel zum Erfolg und zur Eroberung neuer Fanschichten. Fußball kann hier auch von Familien in großer atmosphärischer Dichte hautnah erlebt werden. Und ohne die Angst, von gewaltbereiten Fans bedroht zu werden. Was es im Lokomotive-Stadion nicht mehr gibt, sind die Stehplätze in der Fankurve, die einst Ort der Arbeiter waren. Sie sind dem Sicherheitsargument zum Opfer gefallen. In Russland folgt man dem internationalen Vorbild, oder, wie echte Fans es ausdrücken: „United we stand" war einmal, heute gilt: „Divided we sit".[33]

KULTURELLE GLOBALISIERUNG, DIE NATION UND DAS „PRINZIP ABRAMOWITSCH"

Trotz globaler Stadienarchitektur in Moskau steht man in Russland dem Phänomen der Globalisierung aus verschiedenen Gründen skeptisch gegenüber. Globalisierung wird als ein „vom Westen initiiertes und gelenktes politisches und ideologisches Projekt"[34] betrachtet. In der Idee der *global community* sieht man den Versuch der Verwestlichung bzw. Amerikanisierung „peripherer" nationaler Kulturen. Die ökonomische und politische Globalisierung wird als Mittel verstanden, Russland den Interessen des Westens, allen voran den Interessen der USA, zu unterwerfen.

Man kann diese Haltung als politische Pose einer im Verfall begriffenen Großmacht deuten oder es riskieren, einen Blick aus dem Osten auf den Westen zu werfen. Ich möchte Letzteres in Anlehnung an die Untersuchungen der Soziologin Hilary Pilkington wagen, um eine Antwort auf die Ausgangsfrage dieses Textes zu finden: Warum singen russische Jugendliche nach einem wichtigen Sieg von Chelsea London „Russland, wir lieben dich"?

Pilkington befragte 1997/98 insgesamt 270 russische Jugendliche im Alter von 15 bis 25 Jahren zu deren Umgang mit westlicher Musik und Kultur und kam zu dem Schluss, dass die bekannten Positionen westlicher Autoren im Diskurs über kulturelle Globalisierung unterkomplex sind. Insbesondere die Tatsache, dass die Debatte im Westen kulturelle Strömungen einzig in ihrer Bewegung vom „Zentrum" zur „Peripherie" erfasst und diese Peripherie als dasjenige versteht, was die Kultur der Metropole empfängt und nach ihren eigenen Besonderheiten rezipiert, erscheint Pilkington – trotz der Vielfalt der theoretischen Ansätze, die diesen Rezeptionsprozess zu erklären versuchen[35] – als zu einseitig. Neben der „Unangemessenheit des ‚Zentrum-Peripherie-Modells' kulturellen Austauschs" kritisiert sie den „Mangel in Bezug auf den Begriff des ‚Nationalen'" in westlichen Globalisierungsdebatten.[36] Im Umgang russischer Jugendlicher mit westlicher Musik und Kultur findet Pilkington vier dominante Narrative, die zeigen, wie die „periphere Position" Russlands im kulturellen Globalisierungsdiskurs in den Vorstellungen der Jugendlichen existiert bzw. mit ihnen konfligiert. Das erste Narrativ „Einbahnstraße auf dem Superhighway der globalen Information" drückt das Empfinden vieler Jugendlicher aus, dass die Zugehörigkeit zu einer globalen Jugendkultur nur um den Preis der Konsumtion westlicher Produkte zu haben ist. Zurück fließt nach ihrer Ansicht nichts: „Den einzigen gegenwärtigen Export von Russland in den Westen sahen die Jugendlichen in natürlichen Rohstoffen (in erster Linie Erdöl). Nur zwei kulturelle Exportartikel wurden überhaupt erwähnt: die Mafia und die Trinkgewohnheiten."[37] Das zweite Narrativ „Der Westen ist am besten" bezieht sich auf die Vorstellung, dass der Westen ein Modell der Modernität darstellt, dem es nachzueifern und den es einzuholen gilt. Gleichzeitig drückt es die Empfindung aus, Russland sei in ökonomischer, politischer und kultureller Hinsicht rückständig. Ganz anders das dritte Narrativ „Kulturimperialismus", das den Gedanken des Einholens als westliche Sichtweise entlarvt und ihn umkehrt: Wäre die russische Kultur im Westen stärker bekannt, würde sie langfristig auch als wertvoll anerkannt werden. Dazu komme es aber aufgrund der bereits erwähnten „kulturellen Einbahnstraße" nicht, was als „Kolonialisierung" und „kulturelle Nötigung"[38] durch den Westen beschrieben wird. Das vierte Narrativ „Verzerrte Spiegelungen" ist eng mit dem dritten verknüpft. Es betrachtet den Westen nicht als kulturell überlegen, sondern als unterlegen, und hält ihn deshalb nicht für nachahmenswert. Westliche Musik sei kommerzialisiert und daher minderwertig, betont wird der intellektuelle Anspruch russischer bzw. sowjetischer Kultur. In ihrer Analyse betont Pilkington, dass die von ihr aufgefundenen Narrative nicht mit westlichen Theorien kultureller Globalisierung zu erklären seien: „Die Hybridisierungstheorien räumen dem Konsumenten von Kultur zwar einen Vorrang ein,

have is the standing room in the fan section, where the workers used to gather. It has been sacrificed to security considerations. Russia is following the international model, or, as the real fans put it: The slogan used to be "United we stand" – now it's "Divided we sit".[33]

CULTURAL GLOBALISATION, THE NATION AND THE "ABRAMOVICH PRINCIPLE"

Global standards of stadium construction may prevail in Moscow, but most people in Russia are sceptical of the phenomenon of globalisation for various reasons. Globalisation is regarded as a "political and ideological project initiated and controlled by the West".[34] The idea of the "global community" is seen as an attempt at the Westernisation or Americanisation of "peripheral" national cultures. Economic and political globalisation is regarded as a means of subjecting Russia to the interests of the West in general and the U.S. in particular.

One can either interpret this attitude as the political pose of a great power in decline or try to look at the West through the eyes of the East. I would like to venture to do the latter on the basis of studies carried out by the sociologist Hilary Pilkington in order to find an answer to the question posed at the beginning of this article: Why should young Russians sing "Russia, we love you" after an important victory by Chelsea in London?

In 1997/98 Pilkington asked a total of 270 young Russians aged between 15 and 25 years about their attitudes to Western music and culture and came to the conclusion that the familiar positions of Western authors in the discourse on cultural globalisation were insufficiently sophisticated. The fact that the debate in the West registers cultural currents only in their movement from the "centre" to the "periphery" (the periphery being seen as that which receives the culture of the metropolis in accordance with its own peculiarities) seems to Pilkington – despite the multitude of theories attempting to explain the reception process[35] – to be too one-sided. In addition to the "inappropriateness of the 'centre-periphery model' of cultural exchange" she criticizes the "deficit in relation to the 'national' concept" in Western globalisation debates.[36] In the attitudes of young Russians to western music and culture Pilkington finds four dominant narratives which illustrate how Russia's "peripheral position" in the cultural globalisation discourse exists in the notions of young people or how it conflicts with them. The first narrative "The superhighway of global information – a one-way street" expresses the feeling of many young people that integration in the global youth culture can only be had at the price of consuming Western products. In their view there is no return flow: "All Russia currently exports to the West, in the young people's view, was natural resources (mainly oil). Only two cultural exports were mentioned at all: the mafia and drinking habits."[37] The second narrative "The West is best" refers to the notion that the West is a model of modernity to be emulated and caught up with. At the same time it expresses the feeling that Russia is backward in economic, political and cultural respects. A quite different

erfassen aber die Rezeption westlicher kultureller Formen bei russischen Jugendlichen nur unzureichend, die ihrerseits ziemlich klar zwischen ‚globalen' und ‚lokalen' Kulturen und kulturellen Produkten unterscheiden können. Westliche kulturelle Formen werden aus irgendeinem Grund an und für sich bereits als wahrhaft ‚global' betrachtet, während die russische Kultur spezifisch russisch bleibt: (...) [ein Jugendlicher wird zitiert, Anm. Steets] ‚Unsere Kultur ist grundsätzlich russisch (...), aber (...) es gibt einen Grund, warum die Beatles sich gleich über die ganze Welt verbreitet haben. Es ist etwas allgemein Menschliches und nicht etwas rein Englisches.'"[39] Mit anderen Worten: in Russland trennen die Jugendlichen sehr klar zwischen den globalen kulturellen Strömungen, die sie kennen und – wie die weitere Analyse von Pilkington zeigt – mit denen sie durchaus pragmatisch umzugehen wissen, und der russischen Kultur, die in ihrem Leben einen ganz eigenen, von westlichen Theorien kultureller Globalisierung unterschätzten Stellenwert einnimmt. In den Worten der Jugendlichen: „Bei russischer Musik ‚singt die Seele (...) und westliche Tanzmusik ist ‚Musik für die Füße'."[40] Das Nationale, auf dessen Bedeutung Pilkington in ihrer Studie so nachdrücklich hinweist, spielt auch im globalen Fußballgeschäft für die Identifikation der Fans eine entscheidende Rolle. Russland stellt in diesem Spiel derzeit einen zentralen Akteur, gewissermaßen den Spieler mit der Nummer zehn auf dem Trikot. Mit der medialen Wahrnehmung Abramowitschs rückt Russland ein Stück weit aus der – auch in den Narrativen der Jugendlichen ausgedrückten – „Peripherie" der Globalisierung ins „Zentrum", woraus ein weiteres Narrativ kultureller Globalisierung russischer Prägung entstehen könnte: Mit Abramowitsch exportiert Russland plötzlich mehr als Wodka, Öl und Mafia, mit Abramowitsch dringt Russland ein in das Herz europäischer Populärkultur und hinterlässt dort Spuren, russische Spuren. Vielleicht singen russische Jugendliche deshalb nach einem grandiosen Spiel von Chelsea London: „Russland, wir lieben dich!"

Bei unseren Feldforschungen in Moskaus Stadien und Sportbars haben uns viele Menschen unterstützt. Ihnen und besonders jenen, die uns für Interviews zur Verfügung standen, möchte ich ausdrücklich danken. Ein besonderes Dankeschön geht an Robert Edelman, ohne dessen Hilfe, Vermittlung und Anregungen uns vieles verschlossen geblieben wäre. Bis bald Bob!

ANMERKUNGEN

1 Verdery, Katherine: *The political life of dead bodies: reburial and post-socialist change.* New York 1999

2 Vgl. zur Einführung in die Diskussion um postsozialistische Identitäten und Nationalismus: Young, Craig/ Light, Duncan: „Place, national identity and post-socialist transformations: an introduction". In: *Political Geography.* Nr. 20/2001, S. 941–955

3 Verdery, Kathrine: *What was socialism and what comes next?* Princeton, NJ 1994

4 Pilkington, Hilary: „Popular Culture im Ost-West-Vergleich – Blick nach Westen? Kulturelle Globalisierung und russische Jugendkulturen". In: *Berliner Debatte Initial.* Nr. 5/6/2000, S. 153–162

5 Populärer russischer Witz, abgedruckt in: Oushakine, Serguei Alex: „The Quantity of Style. Imaginary Consumption in the New Russia". In: *Theory, Culture & Society.* Nr. 5/2000, Jg. 17, S. 114

6 Bornefeld, Andreas (01.08.2004): Wie entstanden Russlands große Vermögen? http://www.netstudien.de/Russland/abramowitsch.htm, 15.06.2005

7 Ebd.

8 Humphrey, Caroline: *The Unmaking of Soviet Life. Everyday Economies after Socialism.* Ithaca u. a. 2002, S. 177

9 Ebd., S. 178

10 Vgl. Oushakine, Serguei Alex: „The Quantity of Style", a. a. O.

11 Ebd., S. 101

12 Ebd., S. 102

13 Ebd., S. 99

14 Vgl. ebd. – Wurst ist ein symbolisch wichtiges Nahrungsmittel für die russische Gesellschaft, wie die kurze Abhandlung über den Konsum von Wurst im sozialistischen Moskau zu Beginn von Oushakines Text zeigt.

15 Ebd., S. 107

16 Vgl. Bourdieu, Pierre: *Die feinen Unterschiede. Kritik der gesellschaftlichen Urteilskraft.* Frankfurt/Main 1982

17 Oushakine, Serguei Alex: „The Quantity of Style", a. a. O., S. 110

18 Brennan, Dan (09.08.2004): All roads lead to Roman. http://soccernet.espn.go.com/, 15.06.2005

19 Ebd.

20 Ebd.

21 Ebd.

22 Zit. nach ebd.

23 Brennan, Dan (01.06.2005): The Russians are coming. http://soccernet.espn.go.com/, 15.06.2005

24 Ebd.

25 Alles rund um den Fußball – Transfermarkt. http://www.transfermarkt.de, 22.08.2005

26 Wie viel Liebe, Schmerz und Zerrissenheit mit einem Fußballclub (hier: Arsenal London) verbunden sein können, hat niemand besser beschrieben als Nick Hornby in seinem autobiographischen Roman *Fever Pitch* (1992).

view is expressed in the third narrative, "Cultural imperialism", which unmasks the notion of catching up as a Western view and reverses it. If Russian culture were better known in the West, its value would also be appreciated over time. This does not happen, however, because of the previously mentioned "cultural one-way street", which is described as "colonisation" and "cultural coercion"[38] by the West. The fourth narrative "Distorted reflections" is closely bound up with the third. It regards the West not as culturally superior, but inferior, and therefore does not consider it worth imitating. Western music is seen as commercialized and hence of inferior quality, while the intellectual claims of Russian/Soviet culture are stressed. In her analysis Pilkington points out that the narratives she discovered cannot be explained in terms of Western theories of cultural globalisation: "Although the hybridisation theories grant precedence to the consumer of culture, they are of limited help in understanding the reception of Western cultural forms by young Russians who are quite capable of distinguishing between 'global' and 'local' cultures and cultural products. For some reason Western cultural forms are basically regarded as truly 'global', whereas Russian culture remains specifically Russian. 'Our culture is basically Russian ...,' [a young person is quoted as saying, S.S.] 'but ... there is a reason why the Beatles spread over the whole world. They have something about them that is universally human and not just purely English.'"[39] In other words young people in Russia make a very clear distinction between the global cultural currents they know and – as Pilkington's analysis goes on to show – to which they have a perfectly pragmatic attitude, and Russian culture, which occupies a very special place in their lives and is underestimated by Western theories of cultural globalisation. In the words of the young people: "In Russian music 'the soul sings ... while Western dance music is 'music for the feet'."[40] The national element, on which Pilkington places such great emphasis in her study, also plays a crucial identification role for fans in the global football business. In this game Russia is currently playing a key role, that of the player with the number ten on his shirt, so to speak. Thanks to the media's perception of Abramovich, Russia is moving out of the global "periphery" – expressed in the young people's narratives – towards the "centre", which might give rise to another narrative: one of Russian-induced cultural globalisation. As a result of Abramovich's activities Russia is suddenly exporting more than vodka, oil and mafia gangs; thanks to Abramovich Russia is penetrating to the heart of European popular culture and leaving traces there, Russian traces. Perhaps that is why young Russians sing "Russia, we love you!" after a famous victory for Chelsea.

Many people have supported our field research about the sports arenas and sports bars in Moscow. We would like to thank all of them and especially the ones which have given us interviews. Special thanks go to Robert Edelman, without his help, mediation and stimulation many things would have been inaccessible. So long Bob!

NOTES

1 Verdery, Katherine: *The Political Life of Dead Bodies: Reburial and Post-socialist Change*. New York 1999

2 For an introduction to the discussion on post-socialist identities and nationalism see: Young, Craig/Light, Duncan: "Place, National Identity and Post-socialist Transformations: an Introduction". In: *Political Geography*, No. 20/2001, pp. 941–955

3 Verdery, Katherine: *What was socialism and what comes next?* Princeton, NJ 1994

4 Pilkington, Hilary: "Popular Culture im Ost-West-Vergleich – Blick nach Westen? Kulturelle Globalisierung und russische Jugendkulturen". In: *Berliner Debatte Initial*, No. 5/6/2000, pp. 153–162

5 Popular Russian joke quoted in: Oushakine, Serguei Alex: "The Quantity of Style: Imaginary Consumption in the New Russia". In: *Theory, Culture & Society*, No. 5/2000, Vol. 17, p. 114

6 Bornefeld, Andreas (01.08.2004): Wie entstanden Russlands große Vermögen? http://www.netstudien.de/Russland/ abramowitsch.htm, 15.06.2005

7 Ibid.

8 Humphrey, Caroline: *The Unmaking of Soviet Life. Everyday Economies after Socialism*, Ithaca/London 2002, p. 177

9 Ibid., p. 178

10 Cf. Oushakine, Serguei Alex: "The Quantity of Style", loc. cit.

11 Ibid., p. 101

12 Ibid., p. 102

13 Ibid., p. 99

14 Cf. ibid. Sausage is a food with symbolic importance for Russian society, as the brief discourse on the consumption of sausage in socialist Moscow at the beginning of Oushakine's text shows.

27 Vgl. Edelman, Robert: *Serious Fun. A History of Spectator Sports in the USSR.* New York/Oxford 1993

28 Abramian, zit. in: Edelman, Robert: „A Small Way of Saying ‚No': Moscow Working Men, Spartak Soccer, and the Communist Party, 1900–1945". In: *The American Historical Review.* Nr. 5/2002, Jg. 107, S. 1444

29 Ebd., S. 1455

30 Nicht nur in der Sowjetunion, auch in der DDR gab es Fußballmannschaften, die für Protest am System standen, wie beispielsweise BSG Chemie Leipzig. Vgl. Steets, Silke: „BSG Chemie Leipzig". In: Krehl, Reinhard/Steets, Silke/Wenzel, Jan (Hg.): *Leipzig Protestatlas. Text Bild Karte.* Leipzig 2005, S. 96–99

31 Spartak Moskau war zwölfmal sowjetischer Meister, neunmal Pokalsieger, in den 1990er Jahren gewann Spartak sieben der neun ausgetragenen russischen Meisterschaften.

32 Einige Daten: Fassungsvermögen: 30 000 Zuschauer; Planung: Bokov, Bush and partners (Moskau); Baukosten: über 100 Mio. US-Dollar. Vgl. „The Locomotive stadium". In: *Project Russia.* Nr. 27/2003, S. 24–29

33 Adam Brown beschreibt die Folgen der Stadienumgestaltung für die Fans exemplarisch für England in: Brown, Adam: „United we stand: some problems with fan democracy". In: ders. (Hg.): *Fanatics! Power, identity and fandom in football.* London/New York 1998, S. 50–68. Vgl. auch King, Anthony: *The End of the Terraces. The Transformation of English Football in the 1990s.* London/New York 1998

34 Pilkington, Hilary: „Popular Culture im Ost-West-Vergleich", a. a. O., S. 153

35 Theorien der Hybridisierung formulierten u. a. Stuart Hall und Homi K. Bhabha, das Konzept der Kreolisierung entwickelte Ulf Hannerz.

36 Pilkington, Hilary: „Popular Culture im Ost-West-Vergleich", a. a. O., S. 153

37 Ebd., S. 155

38 Ebd., S. 156

39 Ebd., S. 157

40 Ebd., S. 159

15 Ibid., p. 107

16 Cf. Bourdieu, Pierre: *Die feinen Unterschiede. Kritik der gesellschaftlichen Urteilskraft.* Frankfurt/Main 1982

17 Oushakine, Serguei Alex: "The Quantity of Style", loc. cit., p. 110

18 Brennan, Dan (09.08.2004): All roads lead to Roman. http://soccernet.espn.go.com/, 15.06.2005

19 Ibid.

20 Ibid.

21 Ibid.

22 Quoted in ibid.

23 Brennan, Dan (01.06.2005): The Russians are coming. http://soccernet.espn.go.com/, 15.06.2005

24 Ibid.

25 Alles rund um den Fussball – Transfermarkt. http://www.transfermarkt.de, 22.08.2005

26 How much love, pain and inner conflict can be bound up with a football club (in this case Arsenal) has never been better described than in Nick Hornby's autobiographical novel *Fever Pitch* (1992).

27 Cf. Edelman, Robert: *Serious Fun. A History of Spectator Sports in the USSR.* New York/Oxford 1993

28 Abramian, quoted in: Edelman, Robert: "A Small Way of Saying 'No': Moscow Working Men, Spartak Soccer, and the Communist Party, 1900–1945". In: *The American Historical Review.* No. 5/2002, Vol. 107, p. 1444

29 Ibid., p. 1455

30 Not only in the Soviet Union; in the GDR there were also football teams that stood for protest against the system, such as BSG Chemie Leipzig. Cf. Steets, Silke: "BSG Chemie Leipzig". In: Krehl, Reinhard/Steets, Silke/Wenzel, Jan (eds.): *Leipzig Protestatlas. Text Bild Karte.* Leipzig 2005, pp. 96–99

31 Spartak Moscow were Soviet champions twelve times and won the cup nine times. In the 1990s, Spartak were Russian champions seven out of nine times.

32 Some data: Capacity: 30,000 spectators; planning: Bokov, Bush and partners (Moscow); construction costs: over 100 million US dollars. Cf. "The Locomotive stadium". In: *Project Russia*, No. 27/2003, pp. 24–29

33 Taking England as an example, Adam Brown describes how stadium design affects fans in: Brown, Adam: "United we stand: Some Problems with Fan Democracy". In: Brown, Adam (ed.): *Fanatics! Power Identity and Fandom in Football*, London/New York 1998, pp. 50–68. Cf. King, Anthony: *The End of the Terraces. The Transformation of English Football in the 1990s.* London/New York 1998

34 Pilkington, Hilary: "Popular Culture im Ost-West-Vergleich", loc. cit., p. 153

35 Theories of hybridization have been formulated by Stuart Hall and Homi K. Bhabha amongst others; the concept of Creolization was developed by Ulf Hannerz.

36 Pilkington, Hilary: "Popular Culture im Ost-West-Vergleich", loc. cit., p. 153

37 Ibid., p. 155

38 Ibid., p. 156

39 Ibid., p. 157

40 Ibid., p. 159

DIE RÜCKKEHR DES MARKTES

THE RETURN OF THE MARKET

► SMOLENSK

ЕНСКАЯ
ЕЖДА
БРЮЧНЫЕ
КОСТЮМЫ
ПЛАТЬЯ
КОСТЮМЫ
ОТКРЫТО
РАЗМЕРЫ
42 72
БРЕСТСКИЙ ТРИКОТАЖ
ОДЕЖДА ДЛЯ ЖЕНЩИН
РАЗМЕРЫ 44-66
ПАВИЛЬОН № 19л
ЮБКИ

ПЕЧЕНЬЕ
КОНФЕТЫ
ШОКОЛАД
БОКС Л-10

ОТКРЫТО
Брюки женские

ПУНКТ
АПТЕЧНЫЙ ПУНКТ

КУРТКИ
ДЖИНСЫ
ДЖИНСЫ
Wrangler
Levi's
DIESEL
BOSS
Gee Jay
Gee Jay
ОТКРЫТО
ТОЛСТОВКИ
СВИТЕРА
ТРИКО
КУРТКИ
СПОРТ
КОСТЮМЫ
ОТКРЫТО
ЗАО СМОЛЕНСКАЯ ЧУЛОЧНАЯ ФАБРИКА
НОСКИ
ЧУЛКИ
КОЛГОТКИ
ДЛЯ ВСЕЙ СЕМЬИ
ГРУШКИ
ИГРУШКИ

МАСЛО
МОЛОЧНЫЕ ПРОДУКТЫ
БЕЛЬЕ
АНЖЕЛИКА
10-19
БЕЛЬЁ
ОТКРЫТО
БЕЛЬЕ
ОБУВЬ
ОТКРЫТО
ОТКРЫТО
ЖЕНСКАЯ
ОТКРЫТО
У нас всегда свежие фрукты и овощи

СЫРЫ
МАСЛО
МОЛОЧНЫЕ ПРОДУКТЫ
ОТКРЫТО

рукты
вощи

ОТКРЫТО

ОТКРЫТО
ДЕШЕВЫЕ
БАНАНЫ
!!!
ЗЕЛЕНЬ

REINVENTING CAPITALISM – DIE RÜCKKEHR DES MARKTES

REINVENTING CAPITALISM – THE RETURN OF THE MARKET

INFORMELLE NETZWERKE IN POST-KOMMUNISTISCHEN ÖKONOMIEN: EINE „TOPOGRAPHISCHE KARTE“

INFORMAL NETWORKS IN POST-COMMUNIST ECONOMIES: A “TOPOGRAPHICAL MAP“

INFORMELLE ÖKONOMIE? LASSEN SIE UNS LIEBER ÜBER EXTRAPOLARE WIRTSCHAFT SPRECHEN.

INFORMAL ECONOMY? LET US RATHER TALK ABOUT EXPOLARY ECONOMY.

REINVENTING CAPITALISM – DIE RÜCKKEHR DES MARKTES

REGINA BITTNER

Die Ein- und Ausgänge der Metrostation Ismailowski-Markt in Moskau quellen wie jeden Sonntag über von Menschen. Die meisten tragen riesige blau- oder rotkarierte Taschen, in Europa als „Balkanbags" bekannt, andere haben Plastiktüten mit den Logos internationaler Marken, nur wenige kommen mit Handtaschen wie zum Einkaufsbummel.

Der Ismailowski-Markt auf dem ehemaligen Olympiagelände ist eine riesige Anordnung aus Lagerhallen, provisorischen Ständen, offenen Märkten und einem halb fertig gestellten Themenpark. Die angegliederten Parkplätze sind für Busse und Lkws ausgelegt. Hier werden riesige Kartons und Taschen – wieder „Balkanbags" – verschnürt oder mit braunem Klebeband zugeklebt auf den Ladeflächen der Busse gestapelt. Es sind zum Teil noch Ikarus-Busse mit den Aufschriften „Saratow", „Krasnodar", „Smolensk". Die Businsassen haben einen schweren Tag hinter sich: Weite Reisen, zumeist über Nacht, unternehmen die Händler manchmal zweimal wöchentlich nach Moskau. Mit langen Einkaufszetteln stehen sie dann an den Geschäften, Kiosken und Ständen und kaufen große Mengen von derselben Warensorte, um sie später auf den heimischen Märkten weiterzuverkaufen.

Moskau ist seit Jahren ein *hub*, ein zentraler Umschlagplatz für den transnationalen Kofferhandel. Hier kreuzen sich die Wege von Händlern und Produkten aus China, Pakistan, der Türkei, Usbekistan, Tadschikistan und der Kaukasusregion. Die Waren, die angeboten werden, stammen aus Textil- und Ledermanufakturen in der Türkei und aus den Massenproduktionsstätten Chinas. Aber auch raubkopierte CDs, künstliche Blumen und Heimelektronik, Teppiche und Kosmetik findet man auf dem Ismailowski-Markt.

Die Wege zwischen den Ständen sind eng, kein Auto passt hindurch. Männer mit grauen Gesichtern ziehen riesige Karren hinter sich her, beladen mit notdürftig gestapelten Warenbergen. „Doroga!", rufen sie, um sich einen Weg durch die labyrinthischen Gänge zu bahnen, in die kaum Tageslicht dringt. Dazwischen schieben so genannte Peripathetik-Verkäufer ihre Wagen. Sie versorgen die Geschäftsleute auf dem Markt, die ihre Stände kaum verlassen können, mit Tee, Süßigkeiten und Sandwichs. Viele der Händler, die hier ihre Waren anbieten, nutzen das obere Geschoss ihrer Kioske zum Schlafen. Moskau ist teuer, und die Einkünfte auf dem Markt sind zu gering, um sich davon noch eine Unterkunft in der Metropole leisten zu können. Andere greifen auf vorhandene Migrantennetzwerke zurück: Wohnungen werden untereinander weitergegeben und saisonal genutzt.

REINVENTING CAPITALISM – THE RETURN OF THE MARKET

REGINA BITTNER

As is always the case on Sundays, the entrances and exits of the Ismailovski Market Metro station in Moscow are bubbling over with people. Most are carrying huge bags in red or blue check, known in Europe as "Balkan bags"; others have plastic bags bearing the logos of international brands and only a few come with handbags as if undertaking a shopping excursion.

The Ismailovski Market on the former Olympic site is a huge complex of warehouses, temporary stalls, open markets and a half-finished theme park. The adjoining car parks are designed for buses and lorries. Here huge boxes and bags – Balkan bags again – are tied up or sealed down with brown sticky tape and stacked onto the loading surfaces of the buses. Some of the buses are old Ikarus models that have Saratov, Krasnodar and Smolensk on their destination blinds. The bus passengers have a hard day behind them. The traders undertake long journeys to Moscow, usually through the night, sometimes twice a week. They then queue at the shops, kiosks and stalls, long shopping lists in their hands, and buy up large quantities of the same goods in order to sell them later on their home markets.

Moscow has been a hub for years, a central emporium for transnational shuttle traders. It is a meeting place for dealers and products from China, Pakistan, Turkey, Uzbekistan, Tajikistan and the Caucasus. The goods on offer come from textile and leather factories in Turkey and from the mass production sites of China. But also pirate CDs, artificial flowers and home electronics along with carpets and cosmetics are to be had at the Ismailovski market.

The spaces between the stalls are tight and a car cannot pass through them. Men with grey faces drag huge carts behind them, loaded with piles of goods stacked clumsily. They shout "doroga!" to free a path through the labyrinthine aisles, into which daylight is barely able to penetrate. In between them peripatetic traders push their carts. They provide the traders on the market, who can hardly leave their stalls, with tea, sweets and sandwiches. Many of the traders who offer their goods for sale here use the upper floors of their kiosks to sleep in. Moscow is expensive and the takings at the market are too low for them to be able to afford accommodation in the metropolis. Others use existing migrant networks, where flats are passed on between traders and used seasonally.

The Ismailovski market has consolidated its existence in spite of the efforts of the city authorities to drive the kiosks and stalls out of the city, because they disturb the new image of a global city. Here, in this huge emporium of goods, capital and people,

Der Ismailowski-Markt behauptet seine Existenz trotz der Bemühungen der Stadtregierung, die Kioske und Stände aus dem Stadtbild zu verdrängen, weil sie das neue Image einer *global city* stören. Hier, auf diesem riesigen Umschlagplatz von Waren, Kapital und Menschen, verdichten sich die riskanten Freiheiten der russischen Transformationsgesellschaft: Er steht für einen anderen Kapitalismus im östlichen Europa, einen Kapitalismus, der so gar nicht dem Bild des gezähmten und regulierten westlichen Markts entspricht und dessen Eigenschaften es erst noch zu definieren gilt.

Szenenwechsel. Der Kioskmarkt Kiseljowka in Smolensk befindet sich an der Endhaltestelle der Straßenbahn Nr. 7, mitten im Mikrorayon Papovka/Kiseljowka. Bis Ende der 1980er Jahre waren hier in sechs Reihen die der Plattenbausiedlung zugeordneten Garagen für die Moskvichs, Ladas und Saporochets untergebracht, die zugleich als Werkstätten dienten. Seit Mitte der 1990er Jahre beherbergen die Garagen Kioske. Sie gleichen nicht nur den Mangel an Einzelhandel und Konsumgütern in der Großwohnsiedlung aus, sondern bieten den arbeitslos gewordenen Einwohnern des Mikrorayons auch eine Chance, ihre magere Haushaltskasse aufzubessern. Neben Rentnern, die heute ihre selbst gezüchteten Kartoffeln und Möhren auf Holzkisten anbieten, um sich etwas zur Rente dazuzuverdienen, trifft man auf dem Kiseljowka-Markt auch ehemalige Buchhalter, Sekretäre oder Lehrer in zu Drogerien und Boutiquen umgebauten Garagen. Entweder sie sind selbst die Besitzer dieser Kioske oder sie arbeiten für den Inhaber einer Kioskkette, eine jener Personen, die in den Hochzeiten des Kioskhandels reich geworden sind. Dennoch übersteigt für viele das Einkommen hier das, was sie im Schuldienst oder im staatlichen Unternehmen verdienen würden. Wie gehen die Menschen im postsozialistischen Russland mit solchen biographischen Brüchen um? Was bedeutet der Wandel von der Arbeitergesellschaft zum Selbstunternehmertum für die individuellen Lebenswege?

Auch in Smolensk geht die Stadtregierung mittlerweile restriktiv gegen die Kioske vor. Während Anfang der 1990er Jahre der Mangel an Konsumgütern und die Sehnsucht nach westlichen Waren, und seien es nur die Imitationen aus China und der Türkei, die provisorischen Märkte expandieren ließen, unterliegen diese heute mehr und mehr staatlicher Regulation. Die Kioske waren Wegbereiter einer Kapitalisierung der Gesellschaft. Mit dem Wandel in den Konsummustern und der Konsolidierung gespaltener Einkommensverhältnisse möchte man sich nun auch der Provisorien eines „wilden Kapitalismus" entledigen. In Smolensk entstehen Minimärkte aus Fertigteilen, die zwar die kleinteilige Struktur der Kioske fortsetzen, aber dem Willen zur Regulation dieser ökonomischen Praktiken Folge leisten.

Erneuter Szenenwechsel. Der Istanbuler Stadtteil Laleli ist seit Anfang der 1990er Jahre ein Zentrum des transnationalen Textilhandels zwischen Ländern des ehemaligen Ostblocks und der Türkei. Die in der Türkei preiswert produzierten Textilien lockten, als die Grenzen geöffnet wurden, scharenweise Händlerinnen aus Russland nach Istanbul. Die kauften, so viel sie selbst in ihren Koffern tragen konnten, um die Waren dann in Moskau weiterzuverkaufen. Damit bedienten sie nicht nur die Nachfrage nach Konsumgütern in Russland, sondern verhalfen auch der türkischen Wirtschaft zu einem gigantischen Aufschwung. Anfangs noch als „Natascha trade" konnotiert und mit Prostitution verbunden, hat sich dieser Handel inzwischen professionalisiert. Hotels bieten den russischen Geschäftsfrauen organisierte Shop-Touren an, die je-

the risky freedoms of Russian transformation society are made manifest. The market stands for a different kind of capitalism in Eastern Europe, a capitalism that does not conform to the picture of the tamed and regulated Western market and whose characteristics first need to be defined.

A change of scene. The kiosk market of Kiselyovka in Smolensk is at the terminus of the No. 7 tramline, in the middle of the microrayon of Papovka/Kiselyovka. Up to the end of the 1980s there were six rows of garages attached to the prefabricated apartment blocks here for Moskvich, Lada and Zaporozhets cars; they also served as workshops. Since the mid-1990s the garages have housed kiosks. They not only compensate for the lack of retail facilities and consumer goods in the estate but also offer the unemployed inhabitants of the microrayon a chance to bolster their meagre household incomes. Alongside pensioners who nowadays offer their home-grown potatoes and carrots on wooden crates to supplement their pensions, the Kiselyovka market provides an outlet for former bookkeepers, secretaries and teachers in garages that have been converted into drugstores and boutiques. Either they are the owners of these kiosks themselves or they work for the owner of a chain of kiosks, one of those people who became rich in the boom days of the kiosk trade. Their takings here exceed what they would have earned as teachers or in state companies. How do people in post-socialist Russia handle such biographical caesuras? What does the transformation from a workers' society to entrepreneurship mean for the individual?

In Smolensk, too, the city authorities are now clamping down on the kiosks. While at the beginning of the 1990s the shortage of consumer goods and the desire for Western products, even if only for imitations from China and Turkey, allowed the temporary markets to expand, they are now subject increasingly to state regulation. The kiosks were pioneers of the capitalization of society. With the transformation in consumption patterns and the consolidation of income inequality the authorities now also want to do away with these outgrowths of "unbridled capitalism". In Smolensk, prefabricated mini markets are being built, which continue the small-scale structure of the kiosks but conform to the desire for regulation of these economic practices.

Another change of scene. The Istanbul district of Laleli has been a centre for the transnational textile trade between the countries of the former Eastern bloc and Turkey since the beginning of the 1990s. When the borders were opened, the cheaply produced textiles attracted female traders from Russia to Istanbul in droves. They bought as much as they could carry in their cases in order to sell the goods when they got back to Moscow. As a result they not only catered for the demand for consumer goods in Russia but also helped to trigger a massive upswing in the Turkish economy. Initially dubbed the "Natasha trade" and connected with prostitution, this trade has assumed professional dimensions in the meantime. Hotels offer the Russian businesswomen shop tours lasting from Sunday to Thursday – so that the goods can be sold on the Moscow market on Saturday, if the traders are not purchasing for regular shops, that is. Most of the businesspeople in Laleli can speak good Russian by now, the product range has been geared to the tastes and preferences of the Russian businesswomen, the advertising is bilingual and the dollar is the currency for transactions. The traders themselves mostly come from the rural regions of Turkey, often with a Kurdish background, or from Bulgaria, Bosnia and Macedonia: they are therefore themselves mi-

weils von Sonntag bis Donnerstag dauern – damit die Waren am Samstag auf dem Moskauer Markt verkauft werden können, wenn die Händlerinnen nicht reguläre Geschäfte bedienen. Die meisten der Händler in Laleli sprechen inzwischen gut russisch, das Sortiment haben sie auf den Geschmack und die Vorlieben der russischen Geschäftsfrauen abgestimmt, die Werbung ist zweisprachig und gehandelt wird in Dollar. Die Händler selbst kommen zumeist aus den ländlichen Regionen der Türkei, oft mit kurdischem Hintergrund, oder aus Bulgarien, Bosnien und Mazedonien; sie sind also selbst Migranten, die sich eine Existenz in der türkischen Metropole aufbauen wollen. Wie kommt ein solcher transnationaler Markt zustande und wofür steht er? Welche Institutionen regulieren diesen über Ländergrenzen hinweg sich etablierenden Warenaustausch?
Die drei Szenen zeigen unterschiedliche Schauplätze eines emergierenden Modells privatwirtschaftlicher transnationaler Beziehungen im östlichen Europa. Eine neue Geographie ist entstanden, die aus dem Fluss von Menschen-, Waren- und Kapitalströmen besteht. Eine Geographie, die bisherige Konzeptionen von Gesellschaft, gebunden an die räumlichen und zeitlichen Dispositive des Nationalstaates, in Frage stellt. Was sind die Konturen dieses neuen Kapitalismus, der so tiefgreifend den Alltag, die sozialen Beziehungen und Wertorientierungen verändert hat? Welche Institutionen des Zusammenlebens und des alltäglichen Verkehrs haben sich in Gesellschaften etabliert, in denen staatliche Regulationen geschwächt, Akteurskonstellationen im Fluss, Unsicherheiten und Unwägbarkeiten an der Tagesordnung sind? Was bedeuten Flexibilisierung und Mobilität für die Menschen im östlichen Europa?

NEUE MÄRKTE

Kofferhändler, Kioske und temporäre Märkte prägen die Stadtzentren, Grenzräume und wichtigsten Verkehrsknotenpunkte seit dem Fall des Eisernen Vorhangs. Kioske galten Anfang der 1990er Jahre als typische Erscheinung eines „Kapitalismus ohne Kapital". Die rechtlichen und strukturellen Unsicherheiten hatten insbesondere in Russland zu einer Zurückhaltung ausländischer Investoren geführt; Kapital musste also im Land selbst erbracht werden. Die Kioskmärkte stellten eine Möglichkeit des „Kapitalismus von unten" dar, bei dem jeder sein eigener Unternehmer werden konnte. Denn Kioske haben eine ganze Bandbreite von grenzüberschreitenden ökonomischen Aktivitäten zum Hintergrund: Der Verkäufer ist nur der Vorposten eines weit gespannten Netzwerkes, bestehend aus Pendlern, die die Waren einkaufen, Busunternehmen, Billigfluglinien, Frachtunternehmen und anderen kleinen Dienstleistern, Sicherheitspersonal, Schutzgeldeintreibern, Warenproduzenten, billigen Hotels, Pensionen und Wohnungsanbietern. Oft finden diese Aktivitäten aber auch in Personal- bzw. Familienunion statt.
Kioske existierten schon vor der Perestroika als mobile Handelseinrichtungen in den sowjetischen Städten. Meist an den Verkehrsknotenpunkten und U-Bahn-Stationen postiert, wurden hier vor allem Zigaretten und Wodka von „Babuschkas" verkauft – für viele Rentnerinnen überschüssige Güter, die sie aber im staatlichen Verteilungssystem zugeteilt bekamen und aus deren Tauschwert sie nun Nutzen ziehen wollten. Kioske waren Ausdruck der Existenz marktwirtschaftlicher Elemente unter planwirtschaftlichen Bedingungen. Viele der Händlerinnen entwickelten aus dieser Praxis ein

grants aiming to build up a livelihood for themselves in the Turkish metropolis. How does such a transnational market arise and what does it stand for? What institutions regulate this exchange of goods beyond national borders?
The three locations show differing settings for an emerging model of transnational, private-sector business relationships in eastern Europe. A new geography has arisen, consisting of the flow of people, goods and capital. A geography which calls existing concepts of society, bound to the spatial and geographical resources of the nation-state, into question. What are the contours of this new capitalism, which has changed everyday life, social relations and values in such a far-reaching way? What institutions of daily and social life have established themselves in societies in which state regulations have been weakened, the situations of important players are in flux and uncertainty is the order of the day? What do more flexibility and mobility mean for the people in eastern Europe?

NEW MARKETS

Shuttle traders, kiosks and temporary markets have been a characteristic feature of city centres, border areas and the most important transport intersections since the fall of the Iron Curtain. At the beginning of the 1990s, kiosks were regarded as a typical phenomenon of "capitalism without capital". Particularly in Russia the legal and structural uncertainties led to a reluctance on the part of foreign investors to invest; capital therefore had to be raised within the country itself. The kiosk markets represented an opportunity for "bottom-up capitalism", in which everyone could become his own entrepreneur. Kiosks involve a whole range of cross-border economic activities; the salesperson is only the outpost of a far-flung network, consisting of shuttle traders, who buy the goods, bus companies, low-cost airlines, shipping companies and other small service providers, security personnel, protection money collectors, manufacturers of goods, cheap hotels, guest houses and apartment providers. However, these activities are often carried out by one individual alone or within a family.
Even before *perestroika,* kiosks existed in the form of mobile commercial establishments in Soviet cities. Usually situated at transport intersections and underground railway stations, they offered mainly vodka and cigarettes sold by "babushkas" – for many women pensioners these were surplus goods which they were allocated in the state distribution system and from whose exchange value they now wished to benefit. Kiosks were elements of a market economy under the conditions of a planned economy. Many of the traders developed local market knowledge from this practice which they were able to utilise in post-socialist times. Studies on St. Petersburg, for example, show that right up to the late 1990s kiosks provided supplies to the population in the residential areas and dormitory towns outside the city centres.[1] The Kiselyovska market in Smolensk also fulfils this function. Located at the end of the tram lines and bus routes, these markets gave people the opportunity to purchase essential goods on their way home from the city. To date, there are relatively few large supermarkets in the provincial towns, which is certainly also due to the relatively low level of car ownership compared to western European cities.
Kiosks are flexible in a number of ways: they can adapt to the wishes of their customers quickly and they can be easily moved from one place to another. In addition,

Standortwissen, das ihnen in postsozialistischen Zeiten zugute kam. Studien zu St. Petersburg etwa beschreiben, dass bis in die späten 1990er Jahre Kioske die Versorgung der Bevölkerung in den Wohngebieten und Schlafstädten außerhalb der städtischen Zentren sicherten.[1] Auch der Kiseljowka-Markt in Smolensk hat im Grunde diese Funktion. An den Endstationen der Straßenbahn- und Buslinien gelegen, boten die Märkte den Menschen die Möglichkeit, auf dem Weg aus der Stadt nach Hause noch das Notwendige einzukaufen. Bis jetzt gibt es in den Provinzstädten nur wenige große Supermärkte, was sicherlich auch auf die – im Vergleich zu westeuropäischen Städten – relativ niedrige Motorisierungsrate zurückzuführen ist.

Kioske sind in mehrerer Hinsicht flexibel: Sie können sich den Wünschen der Kunden schnell anpassen, und sie können problemlos von einem Ort zum anderen verlagert werden. Ihre Besitzer haben zudem weniger Miet- und Unterhaltungskosten, trotz der Schutzgeldzahlungen, so dass sie ihre Ware preisgünstiger anbieten können als im Supermarkt. Je einträglicher Kioske in der ersten Periode der Transformation waren, umso schneller verschwanden sie von der Oberfläche der Stadt. Das Kapital, das hier akkumuliert wurde, konnte nun in feste Einzelhandelseinrichtungen investiert werden. Auch gehen die Stadtregierungen mittlerweile radikal gegen die temporären Märkte vor, da mit ihnen meist Kriminalität und Gewalt assoziiert werden. Waren die Kioske daher, wie Isolde Brade es behauptet, lediglich Mittler der neuen Marktwirtschaft?[2]

Kioske stellten eine Antwort des kleinen Mannes auf die radikalen gesellschaftlichen Umbrüche in Osteuropa nach 1990 dar. Unter dem Paradigma der „Transition" galten drei Prinzipien als richtungsweisend für den Umbau der ehemaligen sozialistischen Plan- und Mangelwirtschaften: Liberalisierung, Privatisierung und Demokratisierung.

Die radikale Privatisierung der ehemals volkseigenen Betriebe hatte nicht nur eine massenhafte Arbeitslosigkeit zur Folge, sie zerstörte auch die betrieblichen und staatlichen Fürsorgesysteme. Die Staatsbetriebe hatten für Wohnung, Urlaubsmöglichkeiten, Kinderbetreuung, den Bau von Infrastruktureinrichtungen und die Gesundheitsbetreuung ihrer Angestellten gesorgt. Erklärtes Ziel der so genannten Strukturanpassungsmaßnahmen von Weltbank und IWF war die Zerschlagung dieser Fürsorgesysteme; sie hätten vor allem die Mobilität der Arbeitskräfte gehemmt, hieß es. Während in den westeuropäischen Ländern langfristig Versicherungssysteme für den Fall von Arbeitslosigkeit, Krankheit etc. aufgebaut worden sind, stehen die Länder des Ostens nun vor den Trümmern der alten Sozialsysteme und vor der schwierigen Aufgabe, neue tragfähige Sozialsysteme zu entwickeln. Die Mehrheit der Menschen ist auf familiäre Netzwerke zurückgeworfen, die schon in der Ära des Staatssozialismus stark ausgeprägt waren.

Die Mobilisierung der Arbeitskräfte durch die radikale Privatisierung und die nachfolgende selektive Anpassung bestimmter arbeits- bzw. rohstoffintensiver Branchen und Standorte zog Entlassungen in außerordentlichen Größenordnungen nach sich. Den meisten der Menschen, die für Landwirtschaft und Industrie „unbrauchbar" geworden waren, standen nun drei Möglichkeiten offen: informelle Arbeit, die teilweise Rückkehr zu Formen der Subsistenzwirtschaft und das Einschlagen einer kriminellen Laufbahn.[3] Während die mittelosteuropäischen Länder die diesem Prozess geschul-

their owners pay lower rents and overheads, in spite of the protection money, so that they can offer their goods more cheaply than in supermarkets. The more profitable kiosks became in the first period of the transformation, the quicker they disappeared from the city. The capital that had been accumulated here could now be invested in fixed retail establishments. The city authorities are also now clamping down heavily on the temporary markets, as they are widely associated with crime and violence. Were the kiosks therefore, as Isolde Brade claims, just facilitators of the new market economy?[2]

Kiosks were a response of the man in the street to the radical social upheavals in eastern Europe after 1990. Under the paradigm of "transition", the former socialist planned economies, which had been plagued by shortages, were reconstructed on the basis of three key principles: liberalisation, privatisation and democratisation.

The radical privatisation of the former public companies not only led to mass unemployment, it also destroyed the corporate and state welfare systems. The state companies had provided accommodation, holidays, childcare, the construction of infrastructure and the healthcare of their staff. The declared aim of the so-called "structural adjustment measures" of the World Bank and IMF was the destruction of these welfare systems, since it was argued that they impaired labour mobility. While in the western European countries insurance systems have been built up over many decades to cover unemployment, illness etc., the countries of the east are now faced with the wreckage of the old social systems and the difficult task of developing new and sustainable ones. The majority of people have to fall back on family networks, which were already highly developed in the era of state socialism.

The mobilisation of labour through radical privatisation and the subsequent selective adjustment of certain labour and raw-material-intensive sectors and locations led to layoffs on an extraordinary scale. Most of the people who had become "unemployable" for agriculture and industry were now faced with three options: working in the "informal" economy, a partial return to forms of subsistence economy and criminal activities.[3] While the central and eastern European countries underwent a "transformation recession" caused by this process in the mid-1990s, the downturn in Russia lasted until the turn of the new century.

Here the state supported the jobs in the large industrial enterprises and state bureaucracies for a long time for political reasons but this was only possible at the cost of drastic reductions in wages. The privatisation of the economy – the supreme principle of transformation – primarily affected commerce, the craft professions and private services, while industry, as a protected area of large public-private enterprises, was excluded from this process. So the main issue here was not so much high unemployment as the decline in living standards. The income of many people was socially secure, but it fell drastically, as a result of which they were compelled to earn a living through a combination of informal jobs, the subsistence economy and formal employment.[4] The rapid opening-up of the world market enabled goods and labour to flow in and out, initially in an unregulated fashion. The considerable price and exchange rate differences gave rise to extensive cross-border trade and smuggling activities. Istanbul's district of Laleli reached its economic peak in these years and Moscow sank in a sea of kiosk markets. People from wide-ranging professions, who

dete „Transformationsrezession“ schon Mitte der 1990er Jahre durchliefen, verzögerte sich der Niedergang in Russland bis zur Jahrtausendwende.
Der Staat hatte hier die Arbeitsplätze in den industriellen Großbetrieben und staatlichen Verwaltungen aus politischen Gründen lange gestützt, was aber nur um den Preis drastischer Lohnsenkungen durchführbar war. Die Privatisierung der Wirtschaft, oberstes Prinzip der Transformation, betraf in Russland vor allem den Handel, das Handwerk und private Dienstleistungen; die Industrie war als geschützter Bereich staatlich-privater Großbetriebe davon ausgenommen. Daher stand hier nicht so sehr die hohe Arbeitslosigkeit als vielmehr der Niedergang des Lebensniveaus im Vordergrund. Das Einkommen vieler Menschen war zwar sozial sicher, aber drastisch gesunken, weshalb sie sich gezwungen sahen, ihren Lebensunterhalt durch eine Kombination von informellen Jobs, Subsistenzwirtschaft und formeller Beschäftigung zu sichern.[4] Die rasche Öffnung zum Weltmarkt erlaubte es, dass Waren und Arbeitskräfte zunächst ungeregelt zu- und abströmten. Die erheblichen Preis- und Wechselkursdifferenzen ließen einen umfangreichen grenzüberschreitenden Handel bzw. Schmuggel entstehen. In diesen Jahren erlebte Istanbuls Stadtteil Laleli seinen wirtschaftlichen Höhepunkt, und Moskau versank in einem Meer von Kioskmärkten. Menschen mit unterschiedlichsten Berufen, die zunächst meist nur ihr Einkommen mit einem Zuverdienst aufbessern wollten, pendelten zwischen Istanbul-Laleli und Moskau hin und her, um Unmengen von Textilien und Stoffen in Russland weiterzuverkaufen und damit die Nachfrage nach Konsumgütern zu decken. Dutzende von so genannten Pendelunternehmern, alleine oder mit zwei bis vier Partnern, importierten, was sie zu schleppen in der Lage waren. Dabei benutzten sie gewöhnliche Gepäckstücke (meist riesige Stofftaschen), die sie in einem Zugabteil, im Schiff oder Flugzeug verstauen konnten. Die Geographie des Kioskhandels besteht aus einem weit gespannten Netzwerk von Austauschbeziehungen – ein Geflecht aus dem Kapital russischer Emigranten, kapitalistischen Märkten zwischen Ostsee und Schwarzem Meer und dem Verkauf in den russischen Städten.[5]
Angesichts dieser Entwicklung vertritt die türkische Soziologin Deniz Yükseker die These, dass die Restrukturierung der Weltökonomie in den letzten Jahren zu einer Wiederbelebung des Marktmodells geführt habe, das Fernand Braudel in seiner Analyse des ökonomischen Lebens herausgearbeitet hat: Der Markt als Zone des kleinen Profits und eines stark ausgeprägten Wettbewerbs mit hohen persönlichen Risiken und Unsicherheiten steht dem Kapitalismus als Zone des besonderen Profits, der großen Kapitalkonzentration und Monopolisierung gegenüber. Transnationale Konzerne agieren heute ebenso über nationalstaatliche Grenzen hinweg wie der sich mehr und mehr entfaltende Pendlerhandel (*shuttle trade*). Zwei Prozesse sind es, die Deniz Yükseker für die Renaissance des Braudel'schen Marktmodells verantwortlich macht: zum einen die mit Migration, Flucht und Tourismus verbundene Ausbreitung von transnationalen sozialen Räumen, wo über Grenzen hinweg Menschen, Images, Waren und kulturelle Symbole einander kreuzen. Zum anderen erodiere, parallel zur Globalisierung der Ökonomie, die Regulationsfähigkeit nationaler Ökonomien. Der Nationalstaat wird immer unfähiger, Finanzströme auf seinem Territorium zu kontrollieren und gibt bewusst die Kontrolle in bestimmten ökonomischen Bereichen auf. Der Transnationalisierung von Finanzwirtschaft, Ökonomie und Arbeitsmarkt begegnen

initially only wanted to supplement their income with some additional earnings, commuted between Istanbul-Laleli and Moscow so that they could sell large quantities of textiles and fabrics in Russia and thus meet the demand for consumer goods. Dozens of so-called shuttle entrepreneurs, alone or with two to four partners, imported what they were able to carry with them. They used ordinary luggage, mostly huge carrier bags, which they were able to stash in a train compartment, a ship or an aeroplane. The geography of kiosk trade consists of a wide-spun network of exchange relationships – a nexus of the capital of Russian emigrants, capitalist markets between the Baltic and the Black Sea and the sale of goods in the Russian cities.[5]

In the light of this development the Turkish sociologist, Deniz Yükseker, argues that the restructuring of the world economy in the past few years has led to a revival of the market model posited by Fernand Braudel in his analysis of economic life: the market as a zone of small profits and highly developed competition with high personal risks and uncertainties is contrasted with capitalism as a zone of extraordinary profits, heavy concentration of capital and monopolisation. Today transnational companies act across national borders in the same way as the increasing shuttle trade. Deniz Yükseker makes two processes responsible for the renaissance of Braudel's market model: on the one hand, the spread of transnational social space associated with migration, refugees and tourism, where people, images, goods and cultural symbols meet across borders; on the other, the ability to regulate national economies has eroded in parallel with the globalisation of the economy. The nation-state is increasingly losing its capacity to control financial flows within its own territory and is consciously giving up control in certain economic fields. The transformation societies have responded to the trans-nationalization of the financial markets, the economy and the labour market in their own way: here the dismantling of the nation-state – in this case of state socialism – was an inevitable consequence of integration into the global economy.

The countries of the former Soviet Union and south-east Europe are a case study for the return of the market: it spreads out in areas in which states have lost their influence or into which multinational capital has not yet been able to penetrate.[6]

The flourishing of the new markets in Russia is due, above all, to the long transition between the disappearance of the old and the establishment of new economic regulations and tax systems. An economic development that equated the market with capitalism took stronger hold here than in the central European countries. Many studies on the transformation process have found that capitalism cannot, in fact, be reduced to its constituent element of the market alone, which has been the general tendency in central and eastern Europe. Rather, capitalism develops on the basis of numerous political-economic structures and practices as well as social institutions within the nation-state and dependencies at the local, regional and global levels. Against this backdrop scholars have debated the differences between managerial capitalism in the eastern European states and the Russian model. In their book *Making Capitalism without Capitalists* Gil Eyal, Ivan Szelenyi and Eleanor Townsley attempt to define the characteristics of the new capitalism in eastern Europe. Central to this is the question of what agents of capitalism can be detected if there is no property-owning class in the usual sense of the word. The authors argue that while in Poland or Hungary the former managers from industry form the new elite together with parts

die Transformationsgesellschaften auf besondere Weise: Die Demontage des Nationalstaates – in diesem Falle des Staatssozialismus – war hier nachgerade Bedingung der Integration in die globale Ökonomie.

Die Länder der ehemaligen Sowjetunion und Südosteuropas sind ein Fallbeispiel für die Rückkehr des Marktes: Er breitet sich in Sphären aus, in denen Staaten ihren Einfluss verloren haben oder in die das multinationale Kapital noch nicht hineindrängen konnte.[6]

Die Blüte der neuen Märkte ist in Russland vor allem der lang andauernden Phase zwischen dem Außerkrafttreten alter und dem Erlass neuer Wirtschaftsregulationen und Abgabesysteme zu verdanken. Hier griff stärker als in den mittelosteuropäischen Ländern eine wirtschaftliche Entwicklung, die Markt mit Kapitalismus gleichsetzte. Viele Studien zum Transformationsprozess stellen inzwischen heraus, dass Kapitalismus eben nicht nur auf seinen konstitutiven Teil, den Markt, reduziert werden kann, was sich als generelle Tendenz in Ost-und Mitteleuropa ausmachen lässt. Vielmehr entwickelt sich Kapitalismus auf der Grundlage zahlreicher politisch-ökonomischer Strukturen und Praktiken sowie sozialer Institutionen innerhalb des Nationalstaates und in Abhängigkeit von lokalen, regionalen und globalen Ebenen. Vor diesem Hintergrund diskutieren Forscher die Unterschiede zwischen einem Managerkapitalismus in mittelosteuropäischen Ländern und dem russischen Modell. Gil Eyal, Ivan Szelenyi und Eleanor Townsley versuchen in ihrem Buch *Making Capitalism without Capitalists,* die Eigenschaften des neuen Kapitalismus in Osteuropa zu definieren. Zentral ist dabei die Frage, welche Agenten des Kapitalismus sich ausmachen lassen, wenn es keine besitzende Klasse im eigentlichen Sinne gibt? Die Autoren arbeiten heraus, dass, während in Polen oder Ungarn die ehemaligen Manager der Industrie gemeinsam mit Teilen der Intelligenzija die neue Elite bilden und einen „Managerkapitalismus" in Gang gesetzt haben, Russlands Nomenklatura ihr politisches Kapital erfolgreich in privaten Reichtum oder, nach wie vor, in politische Macht umwandeln konnte. Anhand dieser Beobachtung entwickeln sie die These: „(...) if we see Central Europe as a system of capitalism without capitalists, the eastern European post-communist regimes might be characterized as systems of capitalists without capitalism."[7]

INFORMALISIERUNG

Auch wenn der Präsident der Europäischen Kommission am 29. Mai 2002 offiziell Russlands Status als Marktökonomie anerkannt hat, sind die Kosten der radikalen gesellschaftlichen Umbrüche im Land weiterhin unübersehbar. Die allgemeinen Lebensbedingungen haben sich drastisch verschlechtert. Ohne hier ausführlich auf die spezifischen Konstellationen russischer Privatisierung nach 1990 eingehen zu können[8] – der lang andauernde institutionelle Umbau der Gesellschaft und der Autoritätsverlust des Staates haben der Schattenwirtschaft, die viele Gesichter hat, neuen Raum gegeben.

Kioskkapitalisten sind nur ein Beispiel für die „Informalisierung" der Wirtschaft in Transformationsländern wie Russland. Hier findet sich vielerorts vor allem das Modell der Aufbesserung durch ein zweites Einkommen, während der Grundbedarf noch durch formelle Beschäftigung oder die Pension gedeckt wird. Das reicht vom Nachhilfeunterricht für die Tochter des Nachbarn über Reparaturen bis hin zum Handel mit

of the intelligentsia and have initiated a "managerial capitalism", Russia's nomenklatura was able to successfully convert its political capital into private wealth or, as before, into political power. Based on this observation they advance the proposition that "... if we see Central Europe as a system of capitalism without capitalists, the eastern European post-communist regimes might be characterized as systems of capitalists without capitalism."[7]

INFORMALISATION

Even if the president of the European Commission officially recognised Russia's status as a market economy on 29 May 2002, the costs of the radical social upheavals in the country continue to be clearly visible. General living standards have fallen drastically. Without being able to go into detail concerning the specific situation of Russian privatisation after 1990[8], the prolonged institutional reconstruction of society and the state's loss of authority have provided new scope for the black economy, which has many different guises.

Kiosk capitalists are only one example of the "Informalisation" of the economy in transformation countries like Russia. Prevalent here in many places is the supplementing of earnings by means of a second income, while basic needs continue to be met by formal employment or a pension. This ranges from extra tuition for the neighbour's daughter to repairs and trading in a very wide range of goods. The small-scale company or self-employment with a low level of technical equipment and capital provision is an answer to the disappearance of formal work – particularly for those who were most dependent on state socialism. In the wake of the long-term privatisation after 1990 there were huge movements from formal to informal work which, at least for international players like the World Bank, were regarded as a typical characteristic of labour market adjustment. According to the rhetoric of such players, the transformation was primarily about overcoming the rigidities of the old system. And it was precisely the informal sector that was seen as a welcome tool to give free rein to deregulation.[9]

Kiosk trade can be described as a market-based informal activity: there are low barriers to entry, and capital needs and profits are modest in return for a high work input. The social status of the activity is correspondingly low and self-exploitation or exploitation of workers are the order of the day.[10] It was possible to draw on the tradition of the "unofficial economy" in the former Soviet Union. Traditional attitudes and practices of "disobedience" vis-à-vis authority were widespread and deep-seated in social networks. Against the backdrop of a shortage economy, networks for the provision of resources, services and goods had arisen in the entire Eastern bloc. This parallel economy not only impinged on the daily life of the man in the street; the state economy, too, was permeated by these informal activities to a high degree. Informal relationships existed within wide-ranging family networks, but also and especially between friends, neighbours and colleagues. Informal channels were virtually essential in order to lead a normal life in the everyday socialist world. In this way people's social capital could be transformed in their daily interactions into a different type of capital. Alena Ledeneva has analysed the cultural peculiarities of *blat* – the Russian word for these specific exchange relationships – distinguishing them from relationships

verschiedensten Waren. Das kleine Unternehmen bzw. die kleine Selbständigkeit mit einem geringen Grad an technologischer Ausstattung und Kapitaleinsatz ist eine Antwort auf das Schwinden formeller Arbeit – insbesondere für diejenigen, die am meisten vom Staatssozialismus abhängig waren. Im Schatten der langfristigen Privatisierung in Russland nach 1990 fanden massive Verschiebungen von der formellen zur informellen Beschäftigung statt, die, zumindest für internationale Akteure wie die Weltbank, als typisches Merkmal der Arbeitsmarktanpassung galten. Nach der Rhetorik solcher Akteure ging es in erster Linie darum, die Erstarrung des alten Systems zu überwinden. Und gerade der informelle Sektor galt als willkommenes Ventil, um der Deregulierung freien Lauf zu lassen.[9]

Kioskhandel lässt sich als marktbezogene informelle Aktivität beschreiben: Der Marktzutritt ist leicht, der Kapitaleinsatz gering, die Gewinne sind, bei hohem Arbeitseinsatz, bescheiden. Die gesellschaftliche Anerkennung ist entsprechend gering, Selbstausbeutung oder Ausbeutung von Arbeitskräften sind an der Tagesordnung.[10] Dabei konnte an die Traditionen der zweiten Ökonomie in der ehemaligen Sowjetunion angeknüpft werden. Überkommene Haltungen und Praktiken des „Ungehorsams" gegenüber Autoritäten waren weit verbreitet und in sozialen Netzwerken gut verankert. Vor dem Hintergrund einer Mangelökonomie hatten sich im gesamten ehemaligen Ostblock Netzwerke der Versorgung mit Ressourcen, Dienstleistungen und Waren gebildet. Diese zweite Ökonomie betraf nicht nur das alltägliche Leben des „kleinen Mannes", auch die staatliche Ökonomie war hochgradig von informellen Aktivitäten durchsetzt. Informelle Beziehungen existierten innerhalb weitgreifender Familiennetzwerke, aber auch und vor allem zwischen Freunden, Nachbarn, Kollegen. Um ein normales Leben im sozialistischen Alltag zu führen, waren informelle Kanäle nahezu unerlässlich. Das soziale Kapital einer Person konnte insofern bei ihren alltäglichen Interaktionen in eine andere Kapitalsorte transformiert werden. Alena Ledeneva hat die kulturelle Besonderheit des *blat* – so das russische Wort für diese spezifischen Austauschbeziehungen – in Abgrenzung von Beziehungen analysiert, wie sie dem Schenken oder dem Warenaustausch zugrunde liegen. *blat* findet in einer Gemeinschaft statt, zwischen Menschen, die regelmäßig interagieren. *blat* ist insofern repetitiv, und die Partner sind einander bekannt. Die Reziprozität in *blat*-Beziehungen basiert auf einem beiderseitigen Verständnis von Fairness und Vertrauen, demzufolge jede Seite Verantwortung trägt für die Befriedigung der jeweils anderen. Weil es keine formellen Sanktionen und Regeln gibt, muss die wechselseitige Balance in *blat*-Beziehungen immer wieder neu hergestellt werden.[11]

Inwiefern haben sich nun diese Austauschbeziehungen nach 1990 verändert? Der Wandel des Sprichworts „Du hast nicht 100 Rubel, aber 100 Freunde" zu „Du hast nicht 100 Freunde, aber 100 Dollar" beschreibt zweifellos gut die radikale Monetarisierung sozialer Beziehungen. Er zeigt an, dass Geld nun zum realen Medium des Austauschs geworden ist – anstelle persönlicher Beziehungen und Netzwerke. Viele Studien machen jedoch darauf aufmerksam, dass sich zwar die Bedingungen der „economy of favours" verändert haben und damit auch der Charakter dieser informellen Netzwerke, dass sie aber nicht vollständig verschwunden ist.[12] Gerade in den schwierigen Zeiten der Transformation war und ist *blat* für diejenigen eine wichtige Ressource, die nicht über große Geldsummen verfügen. Sie sind abhängig vom sozialen Kapital – um ei-

based on making gifts or goods exchange. *Blat* takes place within a community, between people who interact regularly. In this sense *blat* is repetitive and the partners know each other. The reciprocity in *blat* relationships rests on a mutual concept of fairness and trust, based on which each side takes responsibility for the satisfaction of the other. Because there are no formal sanctions and rules, the mutual balance in *blat* relationships constantly needs to be recreated.[11]

To what extent have these exchange relationships changed since 1990? The change in the saying "You don't have 100 roubles, but 100 friends" to "You don't have 100 friends but 100 dollars" is undoubtedly a succinct description of the radical monetarisation of social relationships. It indicates that money has now become the real medium of exchange, in place of personal relationships and networks. However, many studies point out that, although the terms of the "economy of favours" have changed and with them the character of these informal networks, they have not disappeared entirely.[12] In the difficult times of transformation, *blat* was and still is an important resource for those who do not have access to large amounts of money. They are dependent on social capital to find a second job, obtain a loan or become a post-socialist entrepreneur. Whereas *blat* previously compensated for the shortage of goods, it now compensates for the shortage of money; for the majority it was probably what made survival possible during the turbulence of the transformation.

In addition, and this is what makes its continued existence understandable, these normative social relationships filled the gaps left behind by the collapse of state regulations and institutions in Russia. If economic relationships are not supported by state guarantees of property law and the sanctioning powers of social institutions, they can only function on the basis of mutual trust. In post-socialist Russia, however, mistrust and competition have led the small-scale entrepreneurs to withdraw to the closer circle of family, friends and relations – which among other effects has meant they are now locked into this circle and are subject to its social and moral norms.[13] By contrast an "economisation of relationships" (Alena Ledeneva) can be observed in the field of large-scale business.

SOCIAL MOBILITY

"I had to give up my job because my salary wasn't being paid any more. Everyone knows that happens very often nowadays and in many companies. I've been running my own business here on the market for six years now. And it is difficult to make a little profit with it, because we have to pay high taxes. The income here is only enough to survive. But as I am my own boss, I do have some advantages. I can take time off when I want to or just not work on a particular day. Most of the goods come from Moscow, while Ismailovski and Chernigovskaya are the cheapest places to buy goods. I go there by bus. How often I go depends on business, sometimes once or even twice a week or sometimes only once a month. I can't afford to go to Poland or Turkey, which is what most people did when they began their shuttle trade business in the mid-1990s, at a time when the conditions for it were good. Nowadays fewer and fewer people can afford to travel to Turkey. Those who began doing so in the early 1990s now have expensive kiosks and some have even opened shops. They are able to sell expensive goods, while I sell cheap ones.

nen zweiten Job zu finden, ein Darlehen zu bekommen oder ein postsozialistischer Selbstunternehmer zu werden. Hat *blat* vorher den Mangel an Waren ausgeglichen, so kompensiert er nun den Mangel an Geld und hat wahrscheinlich für die Mehrheit ein Überleben in den Turbulenzen der Transformation erst möglich gemacht.
Außerdem, und das macht ihr Fortbestehen erst nachvollziehbar, füllten diese normativ geprägten Sozialbeziehungen die Lücken, die mit dem Zusammenbruch von staatlichen Regulationen und Institutionen in Russland entstanden waren. Wenn Wirtschaftsbeziehungen nicht gestützt werden von staatlichen Garantien des Eigentumsrechts und der Sanktionsmacht offizieller Institutionen, dann können sie nur auf der Basis gegenseitigen Vertrauens funktionieren. Im postsozialistischen Russland haben jedoch Misstrauen und Konkurrenz die kleinen Unternehmer dazu veranlasst, sich in den engeren Kreis von Familie, Freundschaft und Verwandtschaft zurückzuziehen – was unter anderem zur Folge hat, dass sie nun in diesen Kreis eingeschlossen und seinen sozialmoralischen Normen unterworfen sind.[13] Demgegenüber ist im großen Geschäft eine „Ökonomisierung der Beziehungen" (Alena Ledeneva) zu beobachten.

SOZIALE MOBILITÄT

„Ich musste meine Stelle aufgeben, weil mir kein Gehalt mehr gezahlt wurde. Jeder weiß, dass das heute sehr oft und in vielen Unternehmen geschieht. Seit sechs Jahren betreibe ich hier auf dem Markt mein eigenes Geschäft. Und es ist schwer, ein wenig Profit damit zu machen, weil wir eine Menge Steuern zahlen müssen. Das Einkommen hier reicht nur zum Überleben. Aber da ich Selbstunternehmerin bin, habe ich doch ein paar Vorteile: Ich kann freimachen, wann ich möchte, oder eben an bestimmten Tagen nicht arbeiten. Die meisten Waren kommen aus Moskau, Ismailowski und Chernizovskaja sind die billigsten Märkte, um Waren einzukaufen. Ich fahre mit dem Bus dorthin. Wie oft ich fahre, hängt vom Handel ab, manchmal einmal, manchmal zweimal die Woche oder auch nur einmal im Monat. Ich kann es mir nicht leisten, in die Türkei oder nach Polen zu reisen, was die meisten Leute taten, als sie mit ihrem Pendlerhandel (*shuttle-trade business*) Mitte der 1990er Jahre anfingen, zu einem Zeitpunkt, als die Bedingungen dafür günstig waren. Inzwischen können es sich immer weniger Leute leisten, in die Türkei zu fahren. Die, die Anfang der 1990er damit begannen, haben heute teure Kioske, einige haben sogar Geschäfte eröffnet. Sie können teure Waren verkaufen, ich verkaufe billige.
Mein Eindruck ist, dass die Leute in jüngster Zeit weniger kaufen. Das hat weniger mit dem Wettbewerb zwischen den Verkäufern zu tun als vielmehr mit dem schwindenden Reichtum. Heute haben die Leute nur noch Geld, um ihre Wohnung zu bezahlen und Brot zu kaufen. Das Geschäft läuft nicht mehr so wie vorher, als mancher noch dachte: Ich möchte dieses Hemd haben, also kaufe ich es.
Während der Sowjetzeit habe ich in einer Fabrik gearbeitet. Ich wusste, dass ich immer mein monatliches Einkommen habe. Und wenn ich mir etwas Größeres leisten wollte, dann habe ich gespart, weil ich wusste, alles ist stabil, auch die Preise. Heute habe ich diese Möglichkeit nicht, weil ich nicht sicher bin, was morgen ist. Das Einkommen kann steigen oder fallen. Deshalb, ja, ich denke, es war besser vorher. Ich würde sogar wieder in einer Schlange anstehen, um Wurst oder Fleisch zu kaufen, weil ich zumindest wüsste, dass ich jeden Zwanzigsten des Monats ein stabiles

My impression is that people have been buying less recently. That has less to do with the competition between the sellers than with declining wealth. Today people only have money to pay their rent and buy bread. Business isn't like it used to be, when people thought to themselves: I like this shirt, so I'll buy it.
During the Soviet era I worked in a factory. I knew I would always get my monthly wages. And if I wanted to buy something big, I saved up, because I knew that everything was stable, including prices. I can't do that now because I'm not sure what tomorrow will bring. My income can rise or fall. So I tend to think things were better in the past. I would even stand in a queue again to buy meat or sausages if I knew that I would be getting a steady wage paid on the 20th of every month. I would never choose to sit here on the market, risk my health and waste my whole energy on bringing all the packages of goods here. I don't like this kind of life, but I don't have any choice."[14]

This woman trader is in her mid-forties, she sells clothes in a temporary stall on the Kalhozny market in Smolensk. Here, too, de-industrializsation and privatisation have increasingly led to the disappearance of formal work in the sense of socially secure and regulated employment. The woman trader is one of those entrepreneurs who have ventured into their own business in spite of the social risks involved. Social mobility is occurring here in both senses of the word: in terms of movement within the social space of a milieu, group or class and in terms of mobility in the sense of travel and commuting across national frontiers. Even if she does not travel to Poland or Turkey herself, the woman in Smolensk is part of a transnational shuttle trade network, whose social relationships are no longer organised within the context of the nation-state.

Even the Russian saleswoman in the leather store in Istanbul's Laleli district is part of this network. For her, social mobility means commuting back and forth between Moscow and Istanbul. She is married with two children. In spite of her family commitments she left her job as a trained nurse and set out to make money, as wages in Russia are too low. She shares an apartment near Laleli with three other Russian women. How did she come to do this? Friends who were there before her told her three years ago how it worked and she decided to follow them. She should have got involved in the trade at the beginning of the 1990s, when there were too few supplies in Russia. Now the markets are overflowing. Is this a school for capitalism? No, rather one for life. She has learned to adapt to the alien culture here and to build a life spanning two different worlds. Of course, this permanent travel creates problems for families and many have broken up as a result.[15] In Russia it is mainly the women who have set out on their travels, while the men remain at home with the children.

According to John Urry "social mobilities", as manifested in networks of people, information flows and flows of capital and goods, provide information on "sociology beyond society".[16] But the weakness of national regulations along with simultaneous integration into a global exchange system also gives rise to a risky environment in Russia. The radical mobilisation and flexibilisation of social relationships takes place in an environment which is still shaped by the experience of a closed society.

Travel restrictions at a national level were tightened further in the former Soviet Union by the restrictions of the *propiska* system between the various administrative districts (*oblasts*) and these restrictions extended to the almost non-existent social mo-

Einkommen habe. Ich würde es nie vorziehen, hier auf dem Markt zu sitzen, meine Gesundheit zu gefährden und meine ganze Energie darauf zu verschwenden, all die Pakete von Waren hierher zu bringen. Ich mag diese Art Leben nicht, aber ich habe keine Alternative."[14]

Die Händlerin ist Mitte 40, sie verkauft Kleidungsstücke in einem eher provisorischen Verkaufsstand auf dem Kalhozny-Markt in Smolensk. Deindustrialisierung und Privatisierung haben auch hier dafür gesorgt, dass formelle Arbeit im Sinne sozial abgesicherter und regulierter Arbeitsverhältnisse mehr und mehr verschwindet. Die Händlerin gehört zu jenen Selbstunternehmerinnen, die den Absprung ins eigene Unternehmen gewagt haben, trotz der sozialen Risiken, die damit verbunden sind. Soziale Mobilität findet hier im doppelten Sinne des Wortes statt: als Bewegung innerhalb des sozialen Raumes eines Milieus, einer Gruppe oder Klasse und als Mobilität im geographischen Sinne des Pendelns, des Unterwegsseins über nationalstaatliche Grenzen hinweg. Auch wenn sie selbst nicht nach Polen oder in die Türkei reist, ist die Händlerin in Smolensk doch Teil eines transnationalen Netzwerks des Pendlerhandels (*shuttle trade*), dessen soziale Beziehungen nicht mehr im Rahmen des Nationalstaates organisiert sind.

Auch die russische Verkäuferin im Ledergeschäft in Istanbul-Laleli gehört zu diesem Netzwerk. Soziale Mobilität bedeutet für sie, zwischen Moskau und Istanbul hin- und herzupendeln. Trotz Familie, sie ist verheiratet und hat zwei Kinder, hat sich die ausgebildete Krankenschwester auf den Weg gemacht, um Geld zu verdienen – die Löhne in Russland sind zu niedrig. Sie teilt sich mit drei anderen Russinnen ein Apartment ganz in der Nähe von Laleli. Wie sie dazu gekommen ist? Freunde, die zuerst da waren, haben ihr vor drei Jahren erzählt, wie das geht, und sie ist dem gefolgt. Sie hätte mit dem Handel schon Anfang der 1990er Jahre beginnen sollen, als es in Russland noch zu wenig Angebote gab. Jetzt sind die Märkte überfüllt. Ob es eine Schule des Kapitalismus ist? Nein, wohl eher eine fürs Leben. Sie hat hier gelernt, sich auf die andere Kultur einzustellen, ihr Leben zwischen zwei Welten einzurichten. Sicher bringt dieses dauernde Unterwegssein Probleme für die Familie mit sich, viele sind daran zerbrochen.[15] Es sind in Russland vor allem die Frauen, die sich auf den Weg gemacht haben, während die Männer zu Hause bei den Kindern bleiben.

„Social mobilities", wie sie sich in Netzwerken von Menschen, Flüssen von Informationen und Strömen von Waren und Kapital manifestieren, geben nach John Urry Hinweise auf eine „Sociology beyond society".[16] Aber die Schwäche nationalstaatlicher Regulation bei gleichzeitiger Integration in ein globales Austauschsystem bringt auch in Russland ein riskantes Umfeld hervor. Denn die radikale Mobilisierung und Flexibilisierung der sozialen Beziehungen vollzieht sich in einer Umgebung, die noch von den Erfahrungsbeständen einer geschlossenen Gesellschaft geprägt ist.

Reisebeschränkungen auf nationaler Ebene wurden in den Ländern der ehemaligen Sowjetunion noch verstärkt durch die Restriktionen des Propiska-Systems zwischen den einzelnen Oblasten, und diese Beschränkungen setzten sich fort in der nahezu nicht vorhandenen sozialen Mobilität: Arbeitsverträge galten sozusagen von der Wiege bis zur Bahre – was einerseits zu langfristigen sozialen Beziehungen mit Nachbarn, Kollegen und Freunden führte, andererseits aber auch zu sozialer Isolation und wenig Kontakt mit Fremden.[17]

bility. Work contracts were valid from the cradle to the grave so to speak – which led to long-term social relationships with neighbours, colleagues and friends but also to social isolation and little contact with outsiders.[17]

This system produced certain norms and values, which have survived until the present day. For one thing there are the norms of work, according to which only production is accorded a social value, because it is useful to the community, whereas traders merely work "for their own pockets". Taking this into account, it is not surprising that many people still have to overcome their own inbuilt resistance to standing at a corner and selling goods. Particularly for older women it is shameful to be seen by neighbours or family members on the Kiselyovska market. Moreover, the particular structure of the formerly closed society gives rise to particular "regimes of citizenship" in Russia. This involves communities, which extend from the brigade, understood as a collective, through the company, the district and the region up to Russia itself – and which in view of the permanent uncertainty within the country act as a last support in risky times. A clear distinction is made between "us" and "them". Traders are also regarded as threatening because their existence is based on the exchange of products across borders and they therefore call these last certainties into question.[18]

Is it then possible to talk of social mobility in terms of climbing the social ladder? Most of the kiosk operators we interviewed were previously in formal employment. Nurses, teachers, engineers, building workers – a wide range of professions is represented on the market. Either they were made redundant by the state company in which they had worked or the wages stopped being paid or were so low that setting up in a small business was the last remaining option for them. "The money that I earn here is only enough to survive. Before this market I worked in other markets and before that I worked in a factory. The markets may be insecure, but so are the factories. And at the market I am at least certain that I will earn some money by the end of the day."

What are the attitudes to moving into entrepreneurship in post-Soviet Russia? What does this social change mean for society?

The views of the kiosk traders in Smolensk present a mixed picture: "I can't say I've become unbelievably rich", explains a trader, "but I can at least claim that this is my business. I think I was moving in this direction throughout my life. I like talking to people and they like chatting to me. I like this market here. Of course there is a lot that is unsatisfactory here but I like my customers and they like me. I worked in an engineering company for 22 years and naturally I couldn't stay there. I was forced to come here. But even if the old company offered me a lot of money, I wouldn't go back. This is my vocation, my business."[19]

Others on the market are employees of operators of several kiosks. A young teacher, who because of her low salary as a state employee now prefers to work on the market as a saleswoman, lists the advantages for us: she no longer has to struggle with children who only help others with their homework in return for payment and she has a secure income as an employee, unlike the small-scale entrepreneurs in the garage kiosks. A young couple runs two kiosks in Smolensk selling trainers, mostly from China. Both studied economics. In today's Russia, they believe, qualifications no longer represent any capital.

Aus dieser Konstellation resultierten bestimmte Normen und Wertvorstellungen, die sich bis heute erhalten haben. Da sind zum einen die arbeitsgesellschaftlichen Normen, nach denen nur die Produktion gesellschaftliche Wertschätzung erfährt, weil sie der Gemeinschaft nützt, während Händler nur „in die eigene Tasche" wirtschaften. Vor diesem Hintergrund muss es nicht verwundern, dass es immer noch viele Menschen Überwindung kostet, sich an die Ecke zu stellen und Sachen zu verkaufen. Von ihren Nachbarn oder Familienangehörigen auf dem Kiseljowka-Markt gesehen zu werden, ist vor allem für ältere Frauen beschämend. Zum anderen resultieren aus der besonderen Konstellation der vormals geschlossenen Gesellschaft bestimmte „regimes of citizenship" in Russland. Dabei handelt es sich um Konstruktionen von Gemeinschaft, die von der Brigade, verstanden als Kollektiv, über das Unternehmen, den Distrikt und die Region bis hin zu Russland selbst reichen – und die, angesichts der permanenten Unsicherheit, im „Territorium" quasi einen letzten Halt in riskanten Zeiten versprechen. Zwischen einem „Wir" und den „Anderen" wird säuberlich unterschieden. Händler gelten auch deshalb als bedrohlich, weil ihre Existenz auf dem Austausch von Produkten über Grenzen hinweg beruht und sie diese quasi letzten Gewissheiten in Frage stellen.[18]

Lässt sich vor diesem Hintergrund von sozialer Mobilität im Sinne sozialen Aufstiegs reden? Die meisten der von uns interviewten Kioskbetreiber gingen bisher einer formell abgesicherten Beschäftigung nach. Krankenschwestern, Lehrer, Ingenieure, Bauarbeiter – ein breites Spektrum an Qualifikationen ist auf dem Markt versammelt. Entweder wurden sie von dem staatlichen Unternehmen, in dem sie beschäftigt waren, entlassen, oder die Löhne wurden nicht mehr bezahlt bzw. waren so gering, dass der Sprung ins kleine Unternehmen den letzten Ausweg darstellte. „Das Geld, das ich hier verdiene, reicht nur zum Überleben. Vor diesem Markt habe ich schon auf anderen Märkten gearbeitet, und zuvor war ich in einer Fabrik beschäftigt. Obwohl die Märkte unsicher sind, die Fabriken sind es nicht weniger. Und auf dem Markt bin ich mir zumindest sicher, dass am Ende des Tages etwas Geld herauskommt."

Wie wird der berufliche Wechsel zum Selbstunternehmertum im postsowjetischen Russland bewertet? Was bedeutet dieser soziale Wandel für die Gesellschaft?

Die Selbsteinschätzungen der Kioskhändler in Smolensk bieten ein eher kontroverses Bild: „Ich kann nicht sagen, dass ich unglaublich reich geworden bin", erzählt uns eine Händlerin, „aber ich behaupte schon, dass das mein Business ist. Das ganze Leben, denke ich, habe ich mich eigentlich in diese Richtung bewegt. Ich mag es, mit den Leuten zu reden, und sie mögen es, sich mit mir zu unterhalten. Ich mag diesen Markt hier. Sicher ist hier vieles mangelhaft, aber ich mag meine Kunden, und sie mögen mich. Ich habe 22 Jahre in einem Ingenieurbetrieb gearbeitet, und natürlich konnte ich dort nicht bleiben. Ich war gezwungen, hierher zu gehen. Aber selbst wenn das alte Unternehmen mir eine Menge Geld anbieten würde, ich käme nicht zurück. Das ist meine Berufung, mein Business."[19]

Andere auf dem Markt sind Angestellte von Betreibern mehrerer Kioske. Eine junge Lehrerin, die wegen ihres geringen Einkommens als Staatsangestellte nun lieber als Verkäuferin auf dem Markt arbeitet, zählt uns die Vorteile auf: Sie muss sich nicht mehr herumplagen mit Kindern, die nur noch gegen Geld anderen bei den Hausaufgaben helfen, und sie hat ein sicheres Einkommen als Angestellte, anders als die Kleinunter-

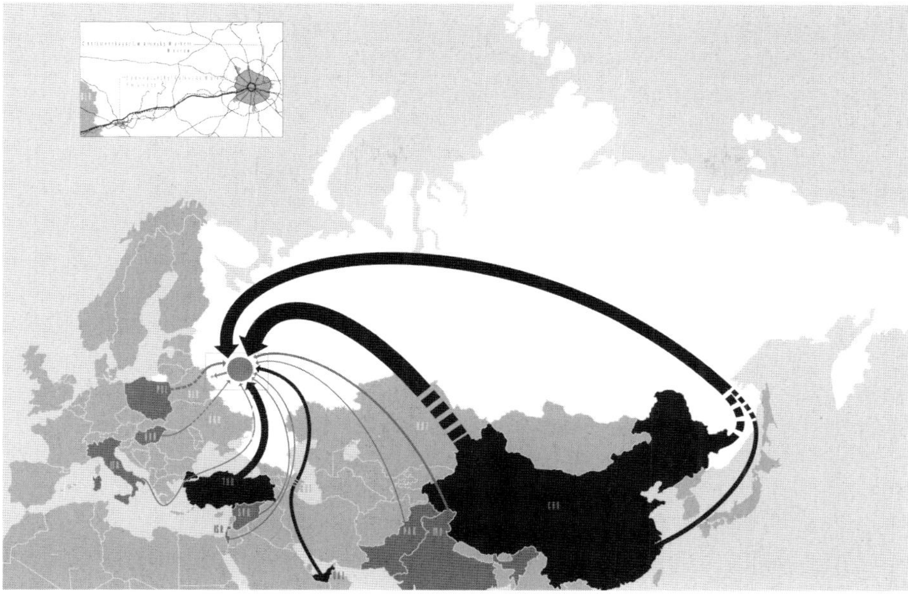

▲ KOFFERHANDEL / MOSKAU WARENUMSCHLAG
SHUTTLE TRADE / MOSCOW WHOLESALE
Karte / Map: Ana Maria Pradilla, Posade, Kate Nelson

▼ LOKALE MÄRKTE SMOLENSK
LOCAL MARKET SMOLENSK
Karte / Map: Ana Maria Pradilla, Posade, Kate Nelson

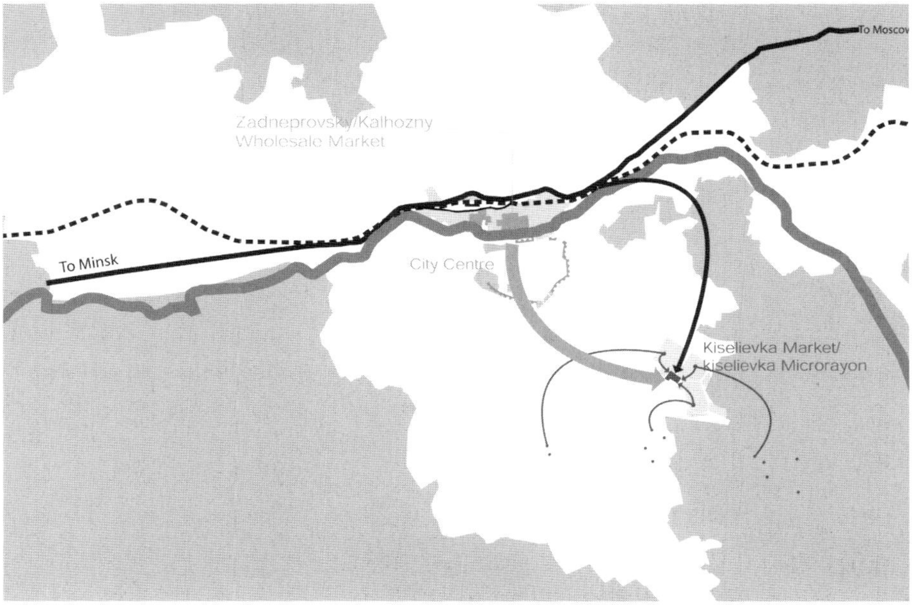

nehmer draußen in den Garagenkiosken. Ein jüngeres Pärchen betreibt zwei Kioske in Smolensk – sie verkaufen Turnschuhe, zumeist aus China. Beide haben Ökonomie studiert. Im heutigen Russland, meinen sie, sei eine Ausbildung kein Kapital mehr. Welche Kapitalsorten sind es dann, die gesellschaftlichen Aufstieg und Ansehen garantieren? Insbesondere von älteren Leuten hört man die Klage, heute drehe sich alles nur noch ums Geld. Ökonomisches Kapital besaß in kommunistischen Gesellschaften wenig Bedeutung, dagegen rangierten politisches und kulturelles Kapital an erster Stelle. Bereits in den 1970er Jahren, im Zuge poststalinistischer Reformen, beobachten Eyal, Szelenyi und Townsley allerdings eine Verschiebung innerhalb dieser Hierarchie: Während politisches Kapital nach wie vor für Aufstiegschancen entscheidend blieb, gewannen kulturelles und ökonomisches Kapital an Bedeutung – was auch zu wachsenden sozialen Ungleichheiten führte.[20] Der soziale Wandel, der nach 1990 einsetzte, hatte diese Veränderungen zur Voraussetzung: Aber während für die zentraleuropäischen Länder die Behauptung gelten mag, es hätten gerade nicht die Akteure der Schattenökonomie oder die ehemaligen Kader dank ihrer politischen Vormachtstellung den Platz der gesellschaftlichen Elite übernommen, sondern die Allianz aus kulturellen und ökonomischen Kapitalinhabern, sprich aus Intelligenzija und sozialistischem Management, trifft für Russland vielleicht ein anders Modell zu. Hier konnten ehemalige Kader ihre staatssozialistischen Privilegien erfolgreich in ökonomisches Kapital umwandeln, wenngleich auch die Manager der 1970er Jahre eine wichtige Rolle spielten. Denn die gut ausgebildeten Manager mittleren Alters waren es, die zur Neuinwertsetzung des ökonomischen Kapitals in Russland einen entscheidenden Beitrag leisteten.[21]

Viele Mitglieder der ehemaligen Nomenklatura sind Manager privater Unternehmen geworden, und in einigen Fällen wurden sie zudem sehr reich. Dennoch werden sie von den „Neuen Russen" unterschieden, auch wenn letztere aus der Produktion kommen, in ehemaligen sowjetischen Betrieben ihre Erfahrungen im Verhandeln, Geschäftemachen und Kontakteknüpfen gesammelt haben. Zumeist agieren sie heute als Unternehmer – im Import und Export, als Finanzberater oder als Banker. Nur wenige verdienen ihr Geld im produzierenden Sektor. Bei ihren ökonomischen Aktivitäten kooperieren und konkurrieren sie mit den Direktoren der Unternehmen, hochgekommenen Kleinhändlern, Regierungsbeamten etc.

Diese neuen Eliten vertraten im Verein mit internationalen Akteuren eine Ideologie der Monetarisierung, die vielleicht darüber Aufschluss gibt, warum sich der Mythos des Aufstiegs „vom Tellerwäscher/Kioskhändler zum Millionär" in Russland so hartnäckig hält. Der Monetarismus faszinierte insbesondere die technokratische Elite Osteuropas, waren sie es doch, die in ihrer Karriere und Entwicklung durch den Staatssozialismus massiv blockiert wurden und nun einen radikalen Umbau der Gesellschaft mit so wenig Staat wie möglich anstrebten. Monetarismus zielt darauf ab, die ökonomische Rolle des Staates massiv zu reduzieren. Wenn soziale Aktivitäten monetarisiert sind, müssen sie nicht länger vom Staat finanziert werden. Vor diesem Hintergrund gewinnen selbstunternehmerische Aktivitäten der Individuen eine zentrale Bedeutung. Eyal, Szelenyi und Townsley heben hervor, dass diese Strategie sich scheinbar als die passfähigste erwiesen hat, um die Turbulenzen der Transformation zu managen: „Marketize, monetarize and restore money to its status as universal currency,

What, then, are the types of capital that guarantee social advancement and prestige? Older people, in particular, complain that today everything revolves around money. Economic capital carried little clout in communist societies; by contrast, political and cultural capital was most important. However, Eyal, Szelenyi and Townsley observed a shift in this hierarchy as early as the 1970s in the wake of the post-Stalinist reforms: while political capital remained decisive for the opportunities of advancement, cultural and economic capital gained in importance – which also led to growing social inequalities.[20] The social transformation that began after 1990 was founded on these changes, but while for the central European countries the statement may hold true that it was *not* the players of the black economy or the former political class who became the new social elite thanks to their political power, but instead an alliance of the owners of cultural and economic capital, namely the intellegentsia and socialist management, a different model may well apply in Russia. Here the former political class was able to transform its state socialist privileges into economic capital, even if the managers of the 1970s also played an important role. It was the well-educated, middle-aged managers who made a decisive contribution to the revaluation of economic capital in Russia.[21]

Many members of the former nomenklatura became managers of private companies and in several cases they also became very rich. Nonetheless they are distinguished from the "New Russians", even if the latter come from the productive sector and gained their experience in negotiating, arranging deals and making contacts in former Soviet companies. They mostly work as businesspeople today – in the import and export sector, as financial advisers or as bankers. Only a few earn their money in the productive sector. In their economic activities they co-operate and compete with directors of companies, go-ahead shopkeepers and small merchants, government officials, etc.

In combination with international players these new elites put forward an ideology of monetarisation, which perhaps sheds light on why the legend of the rise from "a dishwasher/kiosk owner to a millionaire" has such persistent currency in Russia. Monetarism exerted a special fascination for the technocratic elite of eastern Europe, since they had been blocked in their careers and development by state socialism and now strove for a radical reconstruction of society with as small a state as possible. Monetarism is aimed at massively reducing the economic role of the state. If social activities are monetarised, they no longer need to be financed by the state. Hence the entrepreneurship activities of the individual take on crucial importance. Eyal, Szelenyi and Townsley highlight the fact that this strategy apparently proved the most effective in managing the turbulences of the transformation: "Marketize, monetarize and restore money to its status as universal currency, and then you will be able to know what is going on in society."[22]

In this context the "New Russians" should have become the shining lights of post-Soviet Russian society. Caroline Humphrey has pointed out the problems with the term "New Russians" and argues that it is more a description of a new mentality and a desirable status than of a definable social group. Certainly there are connotations associated with this term: it relates to a picture of people with a new and at the same time foreign mentality, people who are materialistic, greedy and alarming-

and then you will be able to know what is going on in society."[22]
In diesem Kontext müssten doch die „Neuen Russen" zur Lichtgestalt der postsowjetischen russischen Gesellschaft werden. Caroline Humphrey hat auf die Problematik des Begriffes der „Neuen Russen" hingewiesen und betont, dass es sich eher um die Beschreibung einer neuen Mentalität und eines erstrebenswerten Status als um eine abgrenzbare soziale Gruppe handelt. Sicher sind mit dieser Zuschreibung Bedeutungen verbunden: Der Begriff bezieht sich auf das Bild von Menschen mit einer neuen und zugleich fremden Mentalität, Menschen, die materialistisch, habgierig und ökonomisch erschreckend erfolgreich sind. „In short: new Russians are new because they do not give precedence to various hoary Soviet values (...) the value of honest labour, of supporting the *kollektive*, of respect for the working masses (...) These new people are understood not to be intrinsically other but indeed to have derived and spun away from us, the unmarked mainstream. Furthermore it is felt that they may indeed represent Russia's future."[23] Die Autorin hebt zugleich hervor, dass es sich bei diesem Begriff um ein kulturelles Konstrukt handelt, das zur identifikatorischen Abgrenzung benutzt wird. Sie sieht deshalb Parallelen zum „homo sovjeticus", gleichfalls eine rhetorische Figur, die, ähnlich den Neuen Russen, zahllose ironische Kommentare seitens der Intelligenzija inspirierte. Dennoch scheint die Figur der „Neuen Russen" eine Projektionsfläche für Sehnsüchte und Wünsche zu sein, die die postsowjetische Gesellschaft genährt hat. So tauchen in den Zukunftsvorstellungen russischer Jugendlicher genau die Insignien von Reichtum, Rücksichtslosigkeit und gnadenlosem Erfolg auf, die den Neuen Russen zugeschrieben werden: Villen im viktorianischen Stil am Rand der Stadt, verdunkelte Mercedes, schwere Barock- oder Empiremöbel.
Ist es dieses Lebensmodell, das einzig sozialen Aufstieg in der Transformationsgesellschaft garantiert? Die moralischen Skrupel der älteren Generation, die noch den „homo sovjeticus" lebten, spiegeln das Dilemma des sozialen Wandels in der postkommunistischen Gesellschaft wider, wo Privatisierung von Anfang an mehr war als die Rückführung von Eigentum an seine ehemaligen Besitzer und die Auflösung volkseigener Betriebe. Privatisierung ist eine Ideologie, die den Transformationsprozess der Gesellschaften in ganz Osteuropa bestimmte. Privatisierung nach dem Fall des Eisernen Vorhangs findet vor dem Hintergrund der Hinterlassenschaft eines, wie es Boris Groys nennt, „riesigen Imperiums kollektiver Gefühle statt, die zwecks der Herstellung einer individuellen kapitalistischen Seele zur privaten Aneignung freigegeben werden".[24]

SCHLUSS

Steht der Kioskhandel also für ein besonderes Modell postsozialistischen Kapitalismus? Ist er eine Metapher für die Ideologien der Transition – Übungsplatz für Deregulierung, Privatisierung und Flexibilisierung? Der Markt als Zone des kleinen Profits, hoher persönlicher Risiken und Unsicherheiten stellt den Lebensbereich eines Großteils der Menschen dar, die, aus staatlich garantierter Beschäftigung und Fürsorge entlassen, sich nun ein Auskommen als individualisierte Selbstunternehmer suchen müssen. Für die wenigsten ist das eine Erfolgsstory. Die Rückkehr des Marktes dort, wo Staaten ihre Regulationsfähigkeit verloren haben, hat eine Materialität gewonnen,

ly economically successful. "In short: new Russians are new because they do not give precedence to various hoary Soviet values ... the value of honest labour, of supporting the kollektive, of respect for the working masses ... These new people are understood not to be intrinsically other but indeed to have derived and spun away from us, the unmarked mainstream. Furthermore it is felt that they may indeed represent Russia's future."[23] The author also points out that this term is a cultural construct which is used for the purposes of identification and demarcation. She therefore draws a parallel with *homo sovieticus*, also a rhetorical figure which, rather like the New Russians, inspired countless ironic commentaries on the part of the intelligentsia. Nonetheless the figure of the New Russians seems to have become a target for projections fed by post-Soviet society. Hence young Russians' visions of the future contain precisely the insignia of wealth, ruthlessness and success associated with the New Russians: villas in Victorian style on the outskirts of the city, Mercedes with tinted glass, heavy Baroque or Empire furniture.

Is it only this lifestyle that can guarantee social advancement in the transformation society? The moral scruples of the older generation, who still live the life of *homo sovieticus*, reflect the dilemma of social transformation in post-communist society, where from the beginning privatisation was more than the return of property to its former owners and the dissolution of publicly-owned companies. Privatisation is an ideology which dominated the transformation process in the whole of eastern Europe. Privatisation after the fall of the Iron Curtain took place against the backdrop of the abandonment of what Boris Groys calls "a huge Empire of collective feelings, which are set free for private acquisition for the purposes of the creation of an individual capitalist soul."[24]

CONCLUSION

Does the kiosk trade therefore stand for a particular model of post-Soviet capitalism? Is it a metaphor for the ideologies of transition – the arena for deregulation, privatisation and flexibility? The market as a zone of limited profits, high personal risks and uncertainties defines the lives of a large part of the population who, deprived of state-guaranteed employment and welfare, now have to survive as individualised entrepreneurs. That is a success story for only a small number. The return of the market in areas where states have lost their capacity to regulate has resulted in a materiality which in the age of global mobility keeps thousands of people on the move: loaded with huge items of luggage they commute from one market to the next to generate an income from the narrow margin between purchasing, accommodation and transport costs. Below the level of transnational financial and capital flows, a new geography of working migrants, commuters and traders has grown up, whose social spaces are composed of closed networks of friendship and family which extend beyond national borders. In spite of the restrictive normative framework they offer their members, they represent the only hold in times of globalized uncertainty. In view of the predominance of the market ideology, it appears doubtful whether this will lead to a realisation of common problems and new forms of transnational solidarity.

die im Zeitalter globaler Mobilität Tausende von Menschen unterwegs sein lässt: Bepackt mit riesigem Gepäckstücken, reisen sie von einem Markt zum nächsten, um aus der geringen Spanne zwischen Einkauf, Unterbringungs- und Transportkosten und Verkauf ein Einkommen zu erwirtschaften. Unterhalb transnationaler Finanzströme und Kapitalflüsse hat sich eine neue Geographie der Arbeitsmigranten, Pendler und Händler entwickelt, deren soziale Räume aus geschlossenen Freundschafts- und Familiennetzwerken bestehen, die sich über Ländergrenzen hinweg aufspannen. Trotz des engen normativen Gerüstes, das sie ihren Mitgliedern bieten, stellen sie den einzigen Halt in Zeiten globalisierter Unsicherheiten dar. Ob sich daraus eine Wahrnehmung gemeinsamer Problemlagen und neue Formen transnationaler Solidarität entwickeln werden, scheint bei der Vorherrschaft der Marktideologie eher zweifelhaft.

ANMERKUNGEN

1 Papadopoulos, Alexander G./Axenov, Konstantin: „St. Petersburg: Kioske als Mittler der neuen Marktwirtschaft". In: Schneider-Sliwa, Rita (Hg.): *Städte im Umbruch*. Berlin 2003, S. 159

2 Vgl. Brade, Isolde/Axenov, Konstantin/Papadopoulos, Alexander G.: „Restructuring the Kiosk Trade in St. Petersburg: a new retail trade model for the post-Soviet period". In: *Geo Journal*. Nr. 4/1997, Jg. 42, S. 419–432

3 Hofbauer, Hannes: „Osteuropa: Die sozialen Folgen der Transformation". In: Komlosy, Andrea, u. a. (Hg.): *Ungeregelt und unterbezahlt. Der informelle Sektor in der Weltwirtschaft*. Frankfurt/Main 1997, S. 186

4 Neef, Rainer: „Zum Begriff und zu den sozialen Funktionen der Schattenwirtschaft in Osteuropa". In: *Soziale Welt*. Nr. 54, 2003, S. 263

5 Axenov/Papadoupoulos: „St. Petersburg: Kioske als Mittler der neuen Marktwirtschaft". a. a. O., S. 170

6 Yükseker, Deniz: ‚Embedding' Trust in a Transnational Trade Network: Capitalism, the market and Socialism. http://www.colbud.hu/honesty-trust/yukseker/pub01.doc

7 Eyal, Gil/Szelenyi, Ivan/Townsley, Eleanor: *Making Capitalism without Capitalists. The new ruling Elites in Eastern Europe*. London 2000, S. 166

8 Vgl. Ledeneva, Alena: *Russia's Economy of Favours*. Cambridge 1998, S. 193

9 Hofbauer, Hannes: „Osteuropa. Die sozialen Folgen der Transformation", a. a. O., S. 193

10 Altvater, Elmar/Mahnkopf, Birgit: *Globalisierung der Unsicherheit*. Münster 2002, S. 93

11 Ledeneva, Alena, a. a. O., S. 158 ff.

12 Arnstberg, Karl Olov/ Boren, Thomas: "Everyday Economy in Russia, Poland and Latvia. Introduction " In: Arnstberg, Karl Olov/ Boren, Thomas (Hg.) *Everyday Economy in Russia, Poland and Latvia*. Oslo 2003, S. 13 ff.

13 Siehe auch den Beitrag von Alena Ledeneva in diesem Band.

14 Interview mit einer Kioskhändlerin in Smolensk, geführt von Joanne Richardson und Oleg Kireev, März 2004

15 Interview mit einer russischen Geschäftsfrau in Istanbul, geführt von Ekaterina Vikulina, Januar 2005

16 Urry, John: *Sociology beyond Society. Mobilities for the twenty-first Century*. London 2000, S. 17

17 Busse, Sarah: „Strategies of Daily Life. Social Capital and the Informal Economy in Russia". In: *Sociological Imagination*. Nr. 2/3/2001, Jg. 38

18 Humphrey, Caroline: „Traders, Disorder and Citizenship Regimes in Provincial Russia". In: Buroway, Michael/Verdery, Katherine (Hg.): *Uncertain Transition. Ethnographies of Change in the Postsocialist World*. Oxford 1999, S. 22 ff.

19 Interview mit einer Kioskbetreiberin in Smolensk, geführt von Joanne Richardson und Oleg Kireev, März 2004

20 Eyal/Szelenyi/Townsley: *Making Capitalism without Capitalists*, a. a. O., S. 30

21 Ebd., S. 35

22 Ebd., S. 90

23 Humphrey, Caroline: „The Villas of the New Russians: A sketch of consumption and cultural identity in post-soviet landscapes". In: dies.: *The Unmaking of Soviet Life. Everyday Economies after Socialism*. London 2002, S. 177

24 Groys, Boris: „Privatisierungen oder künstliche Paradiese des Postkommunismus". In: ders.: *Privatisierungen. Zeitgenössische Kunst aus Osteuropa*. Frankfurt/Main 2004, S. 9

NOTES

1 Papadopoulos, Alexander G./Axenov, Konstantin: "St. Petersburg: Kioske als Mittler der neuen Marktwirtschaft". In: Schneider-Sliwa, Rita (ed.): *Städte im Umbruch*, Berlin 2003, p. 159

2 Cf. Brade, Isolde/Axenov, Konstantin/Papadopoulos, Alexander G.: "Restructuring the Kiosk Trade in St. Petersburg: a new retail trade model for the post-Soviet period". In: *Geo Journal*, vol. 42, No. 4/1997, pp. 419–432

3 Hofbauer, Hannes: "Osteuropa: Die sozialen Folgen der Transformation". In: Komlosy, Andrea, et al. (eds.): *Ungeregelt und unterbezahlt. Der informelle Sektor in der Weltwirtschaft*, Frankfurt/Main 1997, p. 186

4 Neef, Rainer: "Zum Begriff und zu den sozialen Funktionen der Schattenwirtschaft in Osteuropa". In: *Soziale Welt* 54 (2003), p. 263

5 Axenov/Papadoupoulos: "St. Petersburg: Kioske als Mittler der neuen Marktwirtschaft", loc cit., p. 170

6 Yükseker, Deniz: *'Embedding' Trust in a Transnational Trade Network: Capitalism, the Market and Socialism*, http://www.colbud.hu/honesty-trust/yukseker/pub01.doc

7 Eyal, Gil/Szelenyi, Ivan/Townsley, Eleanor: *Making Capitalism without Capitalists. The new ruling Elites in Eastern Europe*. London 2000, p. 166

8 Cf. Ledeneva, Alena: *Russia's Economy of Favours*. Cambridge 1998, p. 193

9 Hofbauer, Hannes: *Osteuropa. Die sozialen Folgen der Transformation*, loc cit., p. 193

10 Altvater, Elmar/Mahnkopf, Birgit: *Globalisierung der Unsicherheit*. Münster 2002, p. 93

11 Ledeneva, Alena, loc cit., pp. 158.

12 Arnstberg, Karl Olov/ Boren, Thomas: "Everyday Economy in Russia, Poland and Latvia. Introduction". In: Arnstberg, Karl Olov/ Boren, Thomas (eds.): *Everyday Economy in Russia, Poland and Latvia*. Oslo 2003, p. 13 ff.

13 See also the article by Alena Ledeneva in this volume

14 Interview with a kiosk owner in Smolensk conducted by Joanne Richardson and Oleg Kireev, March 2004

15 Interview with a Russian businesswoman in Istanbul, held by Ekaterina Vikulina, January, 2005

16 Urry, John: *Sociology beyond Society. Mobilities for the Twenty-first Century*. London 2000, p. 17

17 Busse, Sarah: "Strategies of Daily Life. Social Capital and the Informal Economy in Russia". In: *Sociological Imagination*, vol. 38, No. 2/3/2001

18 Humphrey, Caroline: "Traders, Disorder and Citizenship Regimes in Provincial Russia". In: Buroway, Michael/Verdery, Katherine (eds.): *Uncertain Transition. Ethnographies of Change in the Postsocialist World*. Oxford 1999, p. 22 ff.

19 Interview with a kiosk owner in Smolensk conducted by Joanne Richardson and Oleg Kireev, March 2004

20 Eyal/Szelenyi/Townsley: *Making Capitalism without Capitalists*, loc cit., p. 30

21 Ibid., p. 35

22 Ibid., p. 90

23 Humphrey, Caroline: "The Villas of the New Russians: A sketch of consumption and cultural identity in post-Soviet landscapes". In: Ibid.: *The Unmaking of Soviet Life. Everyday Economies after Socialism*. London 2002, p. 177

24 Groys, Boris: "Privatisierungen oder künstliche Paradiese des Postkommunismus". In: Ibid.: *Privatisierungen. Zeitgenössische Kunst aus Osteuropa*. Frankfurt/Main 2004, p. 9

INFORMELLE NETZWERKE IN POST-KOMMUNISTISCHEN ÖKONOMIEN: EINE „TOPOGRAPHISCHE KARTE"

ALENA LEDENEVA

Der Transformationsprozess in den postkommunistischen Staaten Mittel- und Osteuropas wird oft von Problemen eines aus sowjetischen Zeiten hinterlassenen Erbes der Schattenwirtschaft und eines Staates begleitet, der in seinem politischen Entscheidungsprozess von Partikularinteressen beherrscht wird und dessen Spielregeln in unzulässiger Weise von diesen Interessen diktiert werden. Der Staat kann von Oligarchen und räuberischen Eliten instrumentalisiert werden, in seinen formellen Institutionen können informelle Netzwerke wichtige Funktionen besetzen. Welche Bedeutung diesen informellen oder sozialen Netzwerken zukommt, ist nur sehr schwer zu erfassen.

Um bestimmen zu können, ob der Einfluss sozialer Netzwerke in postkommunistischen Ökonomien abnimmt, ob sie die Fremdbestimmung des Staates verstärken und ob die postkommunistischen Reformen den Charakter der sozialen Netzwerke verändern, muss man die sozialen Netzwerke auf einer „topographischen Karte", in der die verschiedenen Ansätze zur Untersuchung von Netzwerken eingetragen sind, verorten, ihren ambivalenten Charakter analysieren, die Schlüsselmerkmale der mit dem informellen Bereich der russischen Gesellschaft verbundenen Netzwerke definieren und die Aussichten für solch eine instrumentalisierte Nutzung sozialer Netzwerke unter postkommunistischen Bedingungen abschätzen.

Die meisten Untersuchungen zu postkommunistischen Netzwerken in den 1990er Jahren waren recht losgelöst vom allgemeinen Umfeld. Der Versuch von westlichen Spezialisten sowie den internationalen Finanzinstitutionen, die im Westen erprobten Ansätze einfach zu übertragen, führte in der Region zu keinen positiven Ergebnissen.[1] Es mussten also Alternativen gefunden werden. In gewisser Hinsicht schien die Fokussierung auf informelle Strukturen eine Antwort auf die Schwierigkeiten der Theorien des Übergangs zu geben. Bei der Beschäftigung mit der Frage, warum das westliche Modell nicht direkt auf die Transformationsökonomien übertragbar ist, wurde deutlich, dass die westlichen Beschreibungen außer Betracht ließen, wie stark die staatlich gelenkten Ökonomien auf die komplexen sozialen Netzwerke setzten, um wirtschaftliche Schwächen zu kompensieren. Meine eigenen Untersuchungen zur *blat*-Kultur (Nutzen persönlicher Netzwerke zur Beschaffung von Gütern und Dienstleistungen und von in der Sowjetunion produzierten Waren auf kurzem Wege) haben hier Erklärungsmöglichkeiten aufgezeigt.[2] Ich konnte nachweisen, dass sich der Transformationserfolg umgekehrt proportional zum Grad der Integration in die sowjetische Wirtschaft verhält. Die Staaten und früheren Sowjetrepubliken, die dem Sowjetre-

INFORMAL NETWORKS IN POST-COMMUNIST ECONOMIES: A "TOPOGRAPHICAL MAP"

ALENA LEDENEVA

The post-communist transition in Central and Eastern Europe is often associated with the Soviet legacy, informal economy and a "captured" state – a state in which particular group interests dominate the policy-making process, when these interests in an illicit way shape the rules of the game. The state can be captured by oligarchs and predatory elites, formal institutions can be penetrated by informal networks. Assessing the role of informal, or social, networks is perhaps most difficult.

In order to answer the questions of whether the impact of social networks in post-Communist economies is diminishing, whether they are conducive to state capture, and whether the post-Communist reforms change the nature of social networks, it is essential to "locate" social networks on the "topographical map" of approaches to the study of networks, analyse the ambiguous nature of networks, define the key features of networks that are associated with the informal workings of Russian society and assess the prospects of the instrumental use of social networks in post-Communist contexts.

Most of post-Communist network studies in the 1990s have been relatively unrelated to the general field. Once the initial "one size fits all" prescriptions of Western specialists and international financial institutions failed to deliver equally positive results throughout the region[1], some alternatives had to be found. In a way, focus on informality appeared to be a response to the difficulties of the theories of transition. In the search to find reasons why the Western model had not proved directly applicable to all the transition economies, it became apparent that Western prescriptions had not taken into account the fact that the command economy had relied heavily on complex social networks to compensate for its economic defects. My own research into *blat*, the use of personal networks for obtaining goods and services in short supply and for getting things done in Soviet Russia, has been given some explanatory power.[2] In fact, it could be argued that success of transformation is in a reverse proportion to the degree of integration with the Soviet economy. Countries and former Soviet republics that have been exposed to the Soviet regime for longer periods and in a more integrated way have been struggling through the 1990s and subject to state capture much more than those in which land was never collectivised (Poland) or where the private sector sustained itself throughout the Soviet rule (Hungary and Czechoslovakia), arguably due to a more substantial role that those informal networks and practices assumed in order to compensate for the deficiency of the planning systems. These networks had not only survived the transition, but in some cases – most nota-

gime für längere Zeit ausgesetzt und stärker in das System integriert waren, hatten in den 1990er Jahren große Anpassungsprobleme und waren wesentlich stärker dem Einfluss von Partikularinteressen ausgesetzt als diejenigen, deren Grund und Boden niemals kollektiviert wurde (Polen) oder in denen auch unter sowjetischer Herrschaft ein privater Sektor erhalten blieb (Ungarn und Tschechoslowakei). Die Erklärung dafür ist, dass die informellen Netzwerke und Praktiken eine sehr viel wichtigere Rolle bei der Kompensation der Defizite der planwirtschaftlichen Systeme spielten. Diese Netzwerke haben nicht nur den Transformationsprozess überlebt, sondern bildeten in einigen Fällen – am deutlichsten beim Privatisierungsprozess in Russland – auch die Kanäle, über die man seinen Einfluss auf den Staat geltend machte, Marktmechanismen außer Kraft setzte und die Schattenwirtschaft versorgte und damit sowohl die ökonomischen als auch die politischen Reformen behinderte.

Indem die Forschung bei der Untersuchung des postkommunistischen Übergangs ihre ganze Aufmerksamkeit auf die sozialen Netzwerke richtete, folgte sie in ihrer Betrachtungsweise westlichen Studien, die in anderen Zusammenhängen angestellt worden waren.[3] Dies schuf eine gewisse Kluft zwischen denen, die mit den Methoden zur Untersuchung von Netzwerken vertraut waren, und denen, die das Verständnis für die Funktionsweise von Netzwerken in der postkommunistischen Welt und für ihre Auswirkungen auf die entstehenden Märkte erst entwickeln mussten. Während die Forscher, die sich mit westlichen Ländern beschäftigen, bei der Untersuchung von Netzwerken bereits strenge methodologische Standards entwickelt haben und sogar über speziell für diese Zweck entwickelte Computerprogramme verfügen, sind Studien über Netzwerke in den entstehenden Marktwirtschaften sehr viel weniger strukturiert und basieren überwiegend auf qualitativen Methoden. Darüber hinaus decken die Untersuchungen in den postkommunistischen Gesellschaften ein breiteres Themenspektrum ab, da sie eine spontane Reaktion darauf sind, dass sich Netzwerke zu fast allen Aspekten des Transformationsprozesses bilden – angefangen von technischen und betrieblichen Netzwerken bis hin zu solchen, die Korruption in großem Maßstab ermöglichen oder das Überleben sichern. Ich werde in diesem Artikel verschiedene soziale Netzwerke betrachten, in denen Menschen miteinander agieren und die es in jeder Gesellschaft gibt. Ich werde dabei zeigen, dass soziale Netzwerke zwar überall ungefähr die gleiche Palette von Funktionen aufweisen, dass aber die Vergleichbarkeit von Netzwerken in den Transformationsgesellschaften aufgrund ihrer sehr spezifischen Funktionen, ihres Charakters und ihrer Einbettung in das sowjetische System stark eingeschränkt sein kann.

Die Versuche, diese Kluft zu überbrücken und eine Vergleichsbasis zu schaffen, zum Beispiel durch die Einbeziehung bestimmter Kategorien wie „soziales Kapital" in die Untersuchungen zu den entstehenden Märkten und Demokratien, haben gemischte Ergebnisse erbracht, die im Einzelnen später analysiert werden sollen. Endre Sik und Barry Wellman[4] argumentieren zum Beispiel auf der Grundlage ihrer eigenen Daten, dass Menschen in den kommunistischen Ländern Mittel- und Osteuropas auf das „Netzwerkkapital", also die Nutzung von Netzwerken, stärker vertrauten als Menschen in entwickelten kapitalistischen Ländern, was sich in der postkommunistischen Ära noch verstärkte. Die Ausbreitung und die Rolle des Netzwerkkapitals ist in verschiedenen Gesellschaften unterschiedlich; sie hängt von der jeweiligen Kultur der Gesell-

bly the privatisation process in Russia – had provided channels to capture the state, to substitute for the market mechanisms and to provide for the informal economy, thereby hindering both economic and political reforms.

In turning their attention to social networks, students of post-Communist transition stepped on the ground that has already been developed in Western studies but in different contexts.[3] This created a certain gap between those in possession of the method of studying networks and those in need of understanding the ways in which networks work in the post-Communist world and their implications for the emerging markets. Whilst scholars dealing with Western countries have developed the study of networks to the point where it is subject to fairly rigorous methodological standards – including the use of dedicated computer software – studies of networks in emerging market economies are far less structured and are predominantly based on qualitative methods. Furthermore, because studies of networks in post-communist societies evolved spontaneously as a response to the importance of networks to almost every aspect of transition, they cover a broader spectrum of topics – from technological networks and firm networks to networks that serve large-scale corruption and those used for survival. In this paper, I will consider social networks that are based on human interaction and penetrate every society. I will argue, however, that although the range of functions of social networks overall is fairly universal, the specific configuration of functions that networks perform in transition economies, the nature of social networks and their embeddedness in the Soviet system can undermine the potential comparability of social networks.

The attempts to bridge the gap and to build a base for comparisons, say by introducing categories such as social capital to the research into emerging markets and democracies, have produced mixed results for reasons that will be analysed in detail below. For example, on the basis of their data, Endre Sik and Barry Wellman[4] argue that people in the communist countries of Central and Eastern Europe used to rely on network capital – the use of networks – more than people in developed capitalist countries, and that they do so even more in the post-communist era. The scope and role of network capital varies among societies; it is a simultaneous function of a society's culture, its past and present social organisation, and the changing socio-economic situation.[5] The *volume* of an economic actor's[6] network capital is equal to the size and number of the networks that it can mobilise in case of need. The *value* of an actor's network capital is a function of the number and availability of network members, and the resources and amount of network capital that these members themselves possess. Sik and Wellman emphasise two ways in which network capital can operate in relation to the market and the state: as a substitute or as an addition. When network capital is a substitute, it is used as an institution independent from the dominant institutions – as when people exchange among themselves the goods and services needed for survival. In every society from ancient to modern times, various forms of network capital have persisted through altruism, barter and reciprocity.[7] Sik and Wellman describe several ways in which network capital was used as a substitute in communist countries: the reciprocal exchange of labor among workers to deal with routine problems, emergencies and the special case of house-building, and managers' reciprocal transactions in aid of their organisations. According to them, under com-

schaft, ihrer früheren und gegenwärtigen sozialen Organisation und der sich verändernden sozioökonomischen Situation ab.[5] Der *Umfang* des Netzwerkkapitals eines Akteurs der Wirtschaft[6] entspricht der Größe und der Zahl der Netzwerke, die er im Bedarfsfall aktivieren kann. Der *Wert* des Netzwerkkapitals des Akteurs wird von der Zahl und der Verfügbarkeit der Netzwerkmitglieder sowie von den Ressourcen und dem Netzwerkkapital, über das diese Mitglieder eigenständig verfügen, bestimmt. Sik und Wellman heben hervor, dass es zwei für das Netzwerkkapital mögliche Aktionsformen in Beziehung zum Markt und zum Staat geben kann: als Ersatz oder als Ergänzung. Wenn Netzwerkkapital ein Ersatz ist, wird es als eine von den herrschenden Institutionen unabhängige Einrichtung genutzt – zum Beispiel beim Austausch von zum Überleben benötigten Gütern und Dienstleistungen zwischen den Menschen. In jeder Gesellschaft haben sich im Laufe der Zeit bis in die Gegenwart verschiedene Formen von Netzwerkkapital auf der Grundlage von Altruismus, Tauschgeschäften und Reziprozität erhalten.[7] Sik und Wellman beschreiben unterschiedliche Arten, wie das Netzwerkkapital in den kommunistischen Ländern als Substitut benutzt wurde: der gegenseitige Austausch von Arbeitsleistungen unter den Mitarbeitern, um alltägliche Probleme, Notfälle und spezielle Situationen, wie zum Beispiel einen Hausbau, zu meistern, sowie die gegenseitigen Transaktionen von Managern als Unterstützung für ihre Organisationen. Die Autoren kommen zu dem Schluss, dass Netzwerkkapital unter kommunistischen und postkommunistischen Bedingungen im Allgemeinen eher eine Ergänzung war und ist, die im Rahmen von Staat und Markt funktioniert.[8]

Die Metapher vom „Kapital" hilft, den Einfluss von Netzwerken auf der Makroebene zu bestimmen, kann jedoch auf anderen Analyseebenen zu Fehlinterpretationen führen. Ob nun als Ergänzung oder als Substitut, Netzwerke spielen eine generell zweideutige Rolle, das heißt, sie können sowohl mit positiven als auch mit negativen Folgen für das soziale Kapital verbunden sein. Um diesen Punkt deutlicher herauszuarbeiten, wollen wir eine „topographische Karte" der bestehenden Sichtweisen auf Netzwerke erstellen. Im Ergebnis der Analyse zahlreicher Netzwerkuntersuchungen habe ich die bestehenden Ansätze geordnet, indem ich die Annahmen, die von den verschiedenen Autoren in ihrer Beurteilung der Netzwerke zugrunde gelegt wurden, offen lege:

1. *Persönliche* Netzwerke: Diese Betrachtungsweise trifft zu, wenn das Netzwerk als ein System von Knotenpunkten und Verbindungen organisiert ist, die um einen besonderen Kern gruppiert sind (oder um mehrere Kerne, wie das Beispiel der 1996 durchgeführten Studie zum persönlichen Netzwerk von St. Petersburger Lehrern zeigt[9]). ODER *Unpersönliche* Netzwerke: Diese Betrachtungsweise sieht die Netzwerke als ein dezentrales Organisationsprinzip (eine Firmen- oder Restaurantkette usw.).

2. Netzwerke werden von *innen* mit dem Interesse an ihnen selbst (in diesem Fall werden Einzeldaten über Netzwerke gesammelt) ODER von *außen* betrachtet, wenn ihre Auswirkungen in einem größeren Kontext in den Mittelpunkt der Studie gestellt werden. In diesem Fall werden sie als Instrumente oder Faktoren auf der Makroebene gesehen.

Die Überschneidung der Entscheidungen bezüglich der Fokussierung der Netzwerkanalogien ergibt vier grundlegende Betrachtungsweisen von Netzwerken, die wie folgt schematisch dargestellt werden können:

munism and post-communism, network capital was and is more commonly an addition, operating within the framework of the state and the market.[8]

The metaphor of "capital" is useful for assessing the impact of networks at the macro level but can be misleading at other levels of analysis. Apart from being an "addition" or "substitute," networks play a generically ambiguous role, i.e. can be associated with both positive and negative implications of social capital. To make this point clearer let us create a "topographical map" of existing perspectives on networks. Having analysed many studies of networks I have found a way of accommodating the existing perspectives by dissecting the basic assumptions that are implicitly or explicitly made about networks by the authors:

1. Networks are viewed as *personal* – that is, organised as a system of nodes and ties centered around a particular node (or around several nodes, as in the 1996 study of St. Petersburg teachers' personal networks for example[9]) – OR *impersonal* – that is, viewed as a de-centered organisational principle (a chain of restaurants, firms etc).

2. Networks are viewed *internally*, as interesting in themselves – in which case micro data on networks are collected – OR *externally*, when the implications of networks for the wider context become the focus of study – in which case networks are seen as an instrument or a factor at the macro level.

The intersection of choices made about the focus of the analysis of networks provides us with four principal perspectives on networks, illustrated in the following scheme:

Type of network / Focus on	Personal (Centered or multi-centered)	Impersonal (Decentered)
Internal constitution (Micro)	Sociability	Enabling structure
External influence (Macro)	Access to resources	Social capital

Because social networks can be viewed from all four perspectives and because the boundaries between these perspectives are construed by the analytical focus of a given researcher, it is crucial to see both the strengths and limitations of every perspective on the "map" and the linkages between different perspectives. Let us illustrate these linkages and an ambiguous and context-bound nature of networks in the context of the (post)communist order.

FROM "SOCIABILITY" TO "ACCESS TO RESOURCES"

In conventional sociological discourse the term "network" is used to designate social ties between people and to cover "sociability" (intersection of micro and personal perspective) – i.e. relationships with friends, leisure associates, and colleagues – and networking can be defined as connecting nodes and building up networks. Under certain conditions, however, as it used to be the case in the Soviet economy of short-

Netzwerktyp / Fokussierung auf	Persönlich (ein oder mehrere Zentren)	unpersönlich (dezentralisiert)
Interne Beschaffenheit (Mikroebene)	Soziabilität	Befähigungsstrukturen
Externe Einflüsse (Makroebene)	Ressourcenzugang	Soziales Kapital

Da soziale Netzwerke von allen vier Perspektiven her betrachtet werden können und die Grenzen zwischen diesen Perspektiven durch den analytischen Fokus des jeweiligen Forschers bestimmt werden, kommt es darauf an, sowohl die Stärken als auch die Grenzen jeder Perspektive auf der „Karte" zu berücksichtigen und die Verbindungen zwischen den verschiedenen Perspektiven in Betracht zu ziehen. Im Folgenden werden diese Verbindungen und der zweideutige und kontextgebundene Charakter von Netzwerken im Kontext (post)kommunistischer Verhältnisse verdeutlicht.

VON DER „SOZIABILITÄT" ZUM „ZUGANG ZU RESSOURCEN"

Normalerweise bezeichnet im soziologischen Diskurs der Begriff „Netzwerk" soziale Bindungen zwischen Menschen, wobei der Begriff der „Soziabilität" mit enthalten ist (zum Beispiel Schnittpunkt von „Mikroperspektive" und „persönlicher Perspektive"). Dazu zählen zum Beispiel das Verhältnis zu Freunden, Freizeitpartnern und Kollegen – während „Vernetzung" als Herstellen von Verbindungen und Aufbau von Netzwerken definiert werden kann. Unter bestimmten, in der sowjetischen Mangelwirtschaft herrschenden Bedingungen jedoch sind Freundschaft und Ausnutzen von Freundschaften nicht mehr klar voneinander getrennt. Von Freunden (und Bekannten) wurde erwartet, dass sie einem Zugang zu Gütern und Dienstleistungen, bei denen das Angebot nur unzureichend war, verschafften und sich untereinander noch auf andere Weise halfen. Das Aufbauen von persönlichen Kontakten und Geschäftskontakten (*networking*) erfolgte im Sinne des pragmatischen Gebrauchs von Netzwerken, und der Begriff „Netzwerk" wurde somit mehr als lediglich die Grundlage von Soziabilität. Persönliche Netzwerke bieten zusätzlich zur Soziabilität einen inoffiziellen, ungenehmigten Zugang zu institutionellen Ressourcen und schaffen damit bestimmte Formen des Ausgleichs oder der Vermittlung zwischen Staat und Gesellschaft, zwischen Öffentlichem und Privatem. Im sowjetischen Sprachgebrauch gibt es kein Wort für „Netzwerk" oder „sich vernetzen" (in akademischen Kreisen Russlands wird jetzt der technische Begriff *seti* [Netze] gebraucht), doch die am meisten verwendeten Ausdrücke, wie zum Beispiel *blat*, „die eigenen Leute" (*svoi liudi*), „Einer von uns" (*svoi*), und „Kreise gegenseitiger Abhängigkeit" (*krugovaia poruka*), weisen auf den exklusiven, in sich geschlossenen Charakter von Netzwerken und ihre berechnende Nutzung hin. Das bringt einen schnell dazu, zusätzlich zur Analyse ihrer funktionalen bzw. disfunktionalen Auswirkungen auf die Wirtschaft die Mikrodimensionen von Netzwerken zu betrachten: die Art der Bindungen, aus denen diese Netzwerke bestehen, ihre Offenheit/Geschlossenheit, die Normen und Ideen, die von diesen Netzwerken vermittelt werden. Es scheint tat-

age, friendship and the use of friendship become blurred. Friends (and acquaintances) were expected to provide each other with access to goods and services in short supply and help out in other ways, too. Networking acquires a connotation of the pragmatic use of networks, and the term "network," therefore, ceases to be just a basis for sociability. Along with sociability, personal networks also provide unauthorised access to institutional resources, and thereby form certain patterns of mediation between state and society, the public and the private. There is no Soviet word to denote "network" or "networking" (now a technical term *seti* is being used in academic circles in Russia), but the most related idioms – such as *blat*, "people of the circle" (*svoi liudi*), "one of us" (*svoi*), and "circles of mutual dependency" (*krugovaia poruka*) – carry connotations pointing to the exclusive (closed) nature of networks and their calculated use. This prompts one to look into the micro dimensions of networks – the nature of ties constituting networks, their openness/closeness, norms and ideas channeled by those networks – in addition to the analysis of their functional or dysfunctional implications for the economy. In fact, it appears to be the case that the role social networks play in a wider economy has a close correlation with the nature of ties, norms and ideas within a network.[10] The more dependent the formal economy is on personalised networks, the more instrumental the ties within social networks[11] are and the less developed the impersonal systems of trust are. In such economies the fact of belonging almost automatically provides a member of a social network with access to a whole variety of institutional resources available "for people of the circle only," while a wider social fabric is rather unwelcoming and even hostile. Needless to say, the legacy of such personal networks impedes the emergence of impersonal systems of trust and the development of a fully-fledged market economy in the post-Soviet period. This is not helped by the fact that the market economy does not work as it should for a variety of structural and macro-economic reasons, which makes the preservation of personal networks a perfectly rational economic response to a high-risk environment.

Once the sociability aspect of networks goes into the background the instrumental use of networks comes to the fore. Wellman argues in the introduction to *Networks in the Global Village* that the use of social networks is one of the five basic means by which people and institutions acquire necessary resources – along with market exchanges, state distributions, and to a lesser extent, self-provisioning and coercive appropriations.[12] "Just as people use their financial capital to purchase things on markets and their human capital to gain better access to markets and state distributions, they also use "network capital," their connections with people and organisations. Such network capital can assume many forms, such as altruistic, long lasting and multi-purpose relations; short-term instrumental relations; asymmetric patron-client relations; corrupt, exploitative unequal exchanges."[13] Despite the "anti-social" nature of many of these forms, Sik and Wellman's argument is that networks are an important form of social capital.

FROM "ACCESS TO RESOURCES" TO "SOCIAL CAPITAL"

The analogy between networks and financial capital is taken further by those using the concept of social capital (macro, impersonal perspective) in order to measure the

sächlich so, dass die Rolle, die soziale Netzwerke in der Wirtschaft spielen, stark vom Charakter der Bindungen, Normen und Ideen innerhalb eines Netzwerkes abhängen.[10] Je mehr die formale Wirtschaft von persönlichen Netzwerken abhängt, umso stärker instrumentalisiert sind die Bindungen innerhalb sozialer Netzwerke[11] und umso weniger entwickelt sind die unpersönlichen Vertrauenssysteme. In solchen Ökonomien eröffnet die Zugehörigkeit zu einem sozialen Netzwerk seinen Mitgliedern fast automatisch den Zugang zu einer ganzen Reihe von institutionellen Ressourcen, die „ausschließlich für Mitglieder dieses Kreises" zugänglich sind, während die nicht dem Netzwerk angehörenden Menschen eher unwillkommen sind und sogar als feindlich abgelehnt werden. Es muss wohl kaum erwähnt werden, dass das Vermächtnis solcher persönlichen Netzwerke das Entstehen unpersönlicher Vertrauenssysteme und die Entwicklung einer voll funktionierenden Marktwirtschaft in der postsowjetischen Zeit vereitelt hat. Die Tatsache, dass die Marktwirtschaft aufgrund einer ganzen Reihe von strukturellen und makroökonomischen Gründen nicht so funktioniert, wie sie es sollte – was wiederum die Bewahrung der persönlichen Netzwerke zu einer vollkommen rationalen wirtschaftlichen Antwort auf eine Welt mit hohen Risiken werden ließ –, erweist sich auch nicht als hilfreich.

Ist der Aspekt der Soziabilität erst einmal in den Hintergrund getreten, tritt der instrumentelle Gebrauch von Netzwerken in den Vordergrund. Wellman argumentiert in seiner Einleitung zu *Networks in the Global Village*, dass die Inanspruchnahme sozialer Netzwerke eine von fünf grundsätzlichen Möglichkeiten ist, über die sich Menschen und Institutionen Zugang zu den notwendigen Ressourcen verschaffen – neben Markttransaktionen, staatlichem Vertrieb und in einem geringerem Maße Selbstversorgung und gewaltsamer Aneignung.[12] „So wie Menschen ihr finanzielles Kapital zum Erwerb von Waren und ihr Humankapital für den besseren Zugang zu den Märkten und zum staatlichen Vertrieb nutzen, setzen sie ihr Netzwerkkapital, ihre Verbindungen mit Menschen und Organisationen ein. Solches Netzwerkkapital kann viele Formen annehmen: altruistische, lang andauernde und vielen Zwecken dienende Beziehungen; kurzzeitige formale Beziehungen; asymmetrische Patron-Klient-Beziehungen; und korrupte, ausbeuterische Tauschgeschäfte."[13] Trotz des „antisozialen" Charakters vieler dieser Formen argumentieren Sik und Wellman, dass Netzwerke eine wichtige Form des sozialen Kapitals darstellen.

VOM „ZUGANG ZU RESSOURCEN" ZUM „SOZIALEN KAPITAL"

Die Analogie zwischen Netzwerken und Finanzkapital wird ausführlicher von denen weiterverfolgt, die den Begriff des sozialen Kapitals verwenden (Makroebene, unpersönliche Perspektive), um den Einfluss von Netzwerken auf die ökonomische Leistung und die politische Teilhabe zu messen. Die bekanntesten Definitionen des sozialen Kapitals werden mit folgenden Autoren in Verbindung gebracht:

effect of networks on economic performance or political participation. The best known definitions of social capital are associated with the following authors:

Bourdieu (1986)	Coleman (1988)	Putnam (1993)
Social capital is "the aggregate of the actual or potential resources which are linked to possession of a durable network of more or less institutionalized relationships of mutual acquaintance and recognition – or in other words, to membership in a group – which provides each of its members with the backing of the collectivity-owned capital, a "credential" which entitles them to credit, in the various senses of the word."[14]	According to Coleman, "social capital is productive, making possible the achievement of certain ends that in its absence would not be possible."[15] Informal social relations can be critical in creating the potential for and conditioning the nature of social and economic activity. Coleman proposes to think of these relations as "social" capital. Social relations may have important effects on trust that may be critical to efficient exchange, important to the flow of information, and basic to the development of norms and effective social sanctioning.	Putnam sees social capital as those "features of social organisation, such as trust, norms, and networks, that can improve the efficiency of society by facilitating coordinate actions."[16] Putnam defined social capital as " ... features of social life—networks, norms, and trust—that enable participants to act together more effectively to pursue shared objectives."[17]

For Bourdieu, social capital is one of three forms of capital (economic, cultural and social) which taken together "explain the structure and dynamics of differentiated societies."[18] Fundamental structures that produce and reproduce access to social capital are *networks* of connections, which themselves are "the product of an endless effort at institution." If the ways of producing and reproducing of social capital in Bourdieu's account may appear vague, his understanding of how to measure social capital is clearer than that found in Coleman and Putnam. For Bourdieu, "the volume of the social capital possessed by a given agent ... depends on the size of the network of connections he can effectively mobilise and on the volume of the capital (economic, cultural or social) possessed in his own right by each of those to whom he is connected."[19]

Bourdieu and Coleman's conceptions of social capital emphasise the analogy with financial capital, seeing it as instrumental in the flow of goods and services to individuals and groups. Putnam, in contrast, has popularised a notion of social capital tied up with the production of collective goods such as "civic engagement" or a spirit of cooperation at a community or national level. For Putnam, associations, particularly those featuring face-to-face, horizontal relations among individuals, generate trust, norms of reciprocity, and a capacity for civic engagement which are essential to the functioning of a modern democracy.[20]

Bourdieu (1986)	Coleman (1988)	Putnam (1993)
Soziales Kapital ist „die Gesamtheit der vorhandenen oder potentiellen Ressourcen, die an den Besitz eines dauerhaften Netzes von mehr oder weniger institutionalisierten, von gegenseitigem Vertrauen und Anerkennung geprägten Beziehungen – oder, mit anderen Worten, an die Mitgliedschaft in einer Gruppe – gebunden sind, welches jedem seiner Mitglieder die Unterstützung durch gemeinschaftliches Kapital zukommen lässt und eine Referenz darstellt, die sie im weitesten Sinne kreditwürdig erscheinen lässt."[14]	Nach Coleman ist „soziales Kapital produktiv und ermöglicht Lösungen, die ohne es nicht möglich wären".[15] Informelle Sozialbeziehungen können entscheidend für das Potential zur Schaffung und Gestaltung sozialer und wirtschaftlicher Aktivitäten sein. Coleman schlägt vor, diese Beziehungen als „soziales" Kapital zu betrachten. Soziale Beziehungen können das Vertrauen stark beeinflussen, was entscheidend für einen effektiven Austausch, wichtig für den Informationsfluss und grundlegend für die Entwicklung von Normen und effektiver sozialer Kontrolle sein kann.	Putnam sieht soziales Kapital als „Merkmal sozialer Organisation wie Vertrauen, Normen und Vernetzung, die die Effektivität einer Gesellschaft erhöhen kann, indem sie abgestimmtes Handeln erleichtert".[16] Putnam definiert soziales Kapital als „(...) Merkmale des sozialen Lebens – Netzwerke, Normen, Vertrauen –, die die Mitglieder zu einem wirkungsvolleren Handeln und damit zum Erreichen gemeinsamer Ziele befähigen".[17]

Für Bourdieu ist das soziale Kapital eine der drei Kapitalformen (ökonomisches, kulturelles und soziales Kapital), die zusammen „die Struktur und Dynamik differenzierter Gesellschaften erklären".[18] Grundlegende Strukturen, die den Zugang zu sozialem Kapital herstellen und erhalten, sind Netzwerke von Verbindungen, die ihrerseits „das Produkt eines fortgesetzten Versuchs einer Institutionalisierung" sind. Wenn auch die Art und Weise der Produktion und Reproduktion sozialen Kapitals in der Darstellung Bourdieus vage erscheinen mag, so ist doch seine Vorstellung, wie soziales Kapital zu messen ist, klarer als die Colemans und Putnams. Für Bourdieu hängt „der Umfang des sozialen Kapitals, über das ein bestimmter Akteur verfügt (...) von der Größe des Netzes von Verbindungen, das er tatsächlich zu mobilisieren vermag, und von der Menge an Kapital (ökonomisches, kulturelles und soziales) ab, über das die mit ihm verbundenen Personen eigenständig verfügen können".[19]

Bourdieus und Colemans Konzeptionen des sozialen Kapitals betonen die Analogie zum Finanzkapital und sehen es als wesentlich an, um Güter und Dienstleistungen für Einzelpersonen und Gruppen anbieten zu können. Putnam hingegen betrachtet das soziale Kapital als etwas, das eng verknüpft ist mit der Produktion von kollektiven Gütern, wie zum Beispiel das „Bürgerengagement" oder der Gemeinschaftsgeist in Gruppen oder Nationen. Für Putnam schaffen Organisationen und dabei vor allem diejenigen, die die Menschen direkt miteinander in Kontakt bringen, horizontale Beziehungen zwischen ihnen, stellen Vertrauen her, führen auf Gegenseitigkeit beruhen-

Coleman's definition of social capital is somewhat problematic because social capital is defined in terms of its outcome and implies that social capital normally leads to "productive" outcomes.[21] However, Coleman himself does leave room for unproductive social capital. Regarding the productivity of social capital he notes that a given form of social capital that is valuable in facilitating certain actions may be useless or even harmful for others.[22]

Another important difference in Coleman's and Putnam's approach towards social capital is that Coleman uses the concept of social capital as a part of the theory of human action and applies it primarily at a micro level, while Putnam deploys social capital as a concept to study institutional and economic performance at regional level. Thus, the use of the concept of social capital ranges from the membership in networks and/or collectives (as in the case of Bourdieu) to the macro- and regional economic approach concentrating on the relationship between economic growth, democracy and social capital (as in Putnam's case). In the former case, relations themselves are treated as resources. In the latter case, the network location affects an individual's access to assets that are not in themselves characteristics of networks.[23] The multiple use of the concept and its context-bound nature makes the existing empirical studies of social capital incompatible in a comparative (capitalism vs. communism) or dynamical (communism vs. post-communism) perspective. To complete the description of our range of perspectives, let us move on to consider networks as "enabling structures".

FROM "SOCIAL CAPITAL" TO "ENABLING STRUCTURE"

Shifting our focus onto the membership in networks, we arrive at the fourth (micro, impersonal) perspective, which refers to a large number of people, groups, institutions, etc. that have a connection with each other and work together as a system.[24] It is used in relation to anything from a public telephone or television network to the supportive network of the extended family and global production networks.[25] Technically speaking, it is a system of nodes and ties representing a "web" principle of organisation. Thus, Manuel Castells promotes the idea of a network society[26] based on the new technologies and communicational networks characteristic of the information age, while Dirk Messner in *The Network Society*[27] focuses on social networks and excludes electronic networks, media networks, intra-firm networks or even production networks.[28] As emphasised by many authors, the perpetuating role of networks as 'enabling structures' has been particularly essential in the context of post-communist transformation. The enabling structure of networks has not only served the purposes of interpersonal or inter-enterprise survival/ success but also buffered the uncertainty of the post-communist transformation. As David Stark and Balazs Vedrez put it, network ties are a "resource both for navigating the uncertainties of post-socialism and for managing the new uncertainties of internationalisation of the economy." In their original sequence analysis of network formation, they provide substantial evidence that foreign investment and network evolution in Hungary are intertwined processes.[29] In their capacity as 'enabling structures', networks represent a third dimension to the existing dichotomy of the vertical (hierarchies) and the horizontal (markets) ones. Networks are neither vertical nor horizontal, their enabling quality resides

de Normen ein und entwickeln Fähigkeiten zu zivilgesellschaftlichem Engagement, was für das Funktionieren moderner Demokratien unerlässlich ist.[20]
Colemans Definition des sozialen Kapitals ist allerdings problematisch, weil es ergebnisbezogen definiert wird und damit impliziert, dass soziales Kapital normalerweise zu „produktiven" Ergebnissen führt.[21] Coleman selbst lässt jedoch Raum für unproduktives soziales Kapital. Zur Produktivität sozialen Kapitals schreibt er, dass eine bestimmte Form des sozialen Kapitals, dessen Wert daran gemessen wird, ob es bestimmte Handlungen erleichtert, nutzlos oder sogar schädlich für andere Handlungen sein kann.[22]
Ein weiterer wichtiger Unterschied zwischen Colemans und Putnams Ansätzen besteht darin, dass Coleman den Begriff des sozialen Kapitals als Teil der Theorie vom menschlichen Handeln verwendet und ihn vorrangig auf die Mikroebene anwendet, während Putnam soziales Kapital als Begriff zur Untersuchung institutioneller und wirtschaftlicher Leistung auf regionaler Ebene begreift. Folglich reicht die Anwendung des Begriffs des sozialen Kapitals von der Zugehörigkeit zu Netzwerken und/oder Kollektiven (wie im Falle Bourdieus) bis zum makro- und regional-ökonomischen Ansatz, der den Fokus auf die Zusammenhänge zwischen Wirtschaftswachstum, Demokratie und sozialem Kapital (wie im Falle Putnams) legt. Im ersten Fall werden die Beziehungen selbst als Ressource behandelt. Im letzteren beeinflusst der Ort eines Netzwerks den Zugang des Einzelnen zu Ressourcen, die an sich keine Merkmale von Netzwerken sind.[23] Der unterschiedliche Gebrauch des Begriffs des sozialen Kapitals und seine Kontextabhängigkeit führen dazu, dass die bestehenden empirischen Studien über soziales Kapital mit einer vergleichenden (Kapitalismus vs. Kommunismus) oder dynamischen (Kommunismus vs. Postkommunismus) Perspektive nicht vereinbar sind. Um die Beschreibung der Unterschiede in den Betrachtungsweisen zu vervollständigen, werden im Folgenden Netzwerke als „Befähigungsstrukturen" betrachtet.

VON „SOZIALEM KAPITAL" ZU „BEFÄHIGUNGSSTRUKTUREN"

Mit der Betrachtung der Mitgliedschaft in Netzwerken kommen wir zur vierten Perspektive (Mikroebene, unpersönlich). Sie bezieht sich auf eine große Zahl von Personen, Gruppen, Institutionen usw., die miteinander in Verbindung stehen und als System zusammenarbeiten.[24] Diese Perspektive kann alles Mögliche erfassen, angefangen von öffentlichen Telefon- und Fernsehkabelnetzen bis zu globalen Produktionsnetzen oder zum unterstützenden Netzwerk der Familie im weiteren Sinne.[25] Rein technisch handelt es sich um ein System aus Verbindungen und Knotenpunkten, die ein „vernetztes" Organisationsprinzip darstellen. Manuel Castells vertritt zum Beispiel die Idee einer Netzwerkgesellschaft[26], die auf den für das Informationszeitalter so typischen neuen Technologien und Kommunikationsnetzen beruht. Dirk Messner hingegen betrachtet in *The Network Society*[27] soziale Netzwerke und schließt elektronische Netze, Mediennetze, firmeninterne Netze und sogar Produktionsnetze aus.[28] Viele Autoren heben hervor, dass die fortdauernde Funktion von Netzwerken als „Befähigungsstrukturen" besonders im Kontext der postkommunistischen Transformation bedeutsam war. Diese Struktur von Netzwerken hat in den Beziehungen zwischen Einzelpersonen oder zwischen Betrieben nicht nur dem Ziel

in their ambiguity and their 'navigational' (between vertical and horizontal) capacity. Their logic is both to compensate for the defects of vertical and horizontal structures and to turn these defects into advantage of network members.

To re-iterate the points in *table 1*:

▸ Because networks stretch across all dimensions indicated in the table – networks serve both access and sociability, provide both a structure and its outcome (capital) – with insufficiently identifiable boundaries between these functions, they are inherently ambiguous in their impact on both micro and macro structures;

▸ Networks constitute a social form that cuts across conventional micro-macro divisions and personal-impersonal dimensions.

▸ The generic functions of networks coincide with all four perspectives on networks: "sociability", "access", "enabling structure", and "social capital", each of which can have both positive and negative implications.

Let us formulate the positive implications of the functioning of networks:

1. *Safety net (sociability).* Social networks are conducive to human co-operation and mutual help, providing sociability, emotional support, and assistance for routine domestic needs and health care.

2. *Survival kit at the micro-level (access).* Social networks constitute a basis for survival strategies. Co-operation is a way to cope while facing hardships. It is less costly, more effective, and more easily accessible than any other alternative – such as market purchases or acquiring state redistributions.[30]

3. *Beating the system (enabling structure).* Networks can be used as a means to avoid competition or to increase one's chances in it. Investing into and maintaining networks of partners represent a routine business strategy. For example, there are personal networks between buyers and sellers in local markets[31], and business executives often make personal deals to avoid the rigidities of contracts.[32]

4. *Compensatory effect (social capital).* Social networks compensate for the defects in formal systems – say in a high-risk environment or where impersonal systems of trust are not working as they should. By providing what formal systems cannot, networks not only enable their members to operate, but also contribute to their own reproduction.

In practice, social networks are operational both in the "access" mode (thus channeling the network/social capital to the macro-level in order to maintain existing formal institutions) and in the "sociability" mode (by servicing the social relationships at the micro-level that constitute networks); social networks are both a structure and its outcome. The ambiguous nature of networks, however, results in the fact that the "positive" implications of networks associated with access – flexibility, psychological support, reduced risks and transaction costs – may at the same time have "negative" implications for the economy, for the networks themselves and for the individual members.[33] Woolcock finds that: "high levels of social capital can be [...] "negative" in that it also places high particularistic demands on group members, thereby restricting individual expression and advancement, permits free riding on community resources; and negates, in those groups with a long history of marginalization through coercive non-market mechanisms the belief in the possibility of advancement through individual effort."[34] At the macro level, the predominance of networks does not nec-

des Überlebens/Erfolgs gedient, sondern federte ebenso die Unsicherheiten des postkommunistischen Übergangs ab. David Stark und Balazs Vedres formulierten sehr treffend, dass Netzwerkverbindungen eine „Stütze sowohl bei der Bewältigung der Unsicherheiten des Postsozialismus als auch bei den neuen Unsicherheiten der wirtschaftlichen Globalisierung" sind. In ihrer anfänglichen Untersuchungsserie zur Bildung von Netzwerken wiesen sie überzeugend nach, dass ein unmittelbarer Zusammenhang zwischen ausländischen Investitionen und der Entwicklung von Netzwerken in Ungarn besteht.[29] Mit ihrer Fähigkeit zur „Schaffung von Möglichkeiten" bilden Netzwerke eine dritte Dimension neben den beiden bestehenden Dimensionen, der vertikalen (Hierarchien) und der horizontalen (Märkte). Netzwerke sind weder horizontal noch vertikal, und die Fähigkeit zur Schaffung von Möglichkeiten liegt in ihrer Vielschichtigkeit und ihrer „Mobilität" (zwischen der Vertikalen und der Horizontalen). Ihre Logik besteht darin, die Schwächen der vertikalen und der horizontalen Strukturen zu kompensieren und die Schwächen in Vorteile für die Mitglieder des Netzwerkes zu verwandeln.

An dieser Stelle sollen die wesentlichen Punkte aus *Tabelle 1* noch einmal hervorgehoben werden:

- Da Netzwerke sich über alle in der Tabelle aufgeführten Bereiche erstrecken – Netzwerke dienen dem Zugang und der Pflege von Sozialkontakten, sie schaffen sowohl eine Struktur als auch dessen Ergebnis (Kapital) – und diese Bereiche nicht klar voneinander zu trennen sind, haben sie einen inhärent ambivalenten Einfluss auf die Mikro- und Makrostrukturen.
- Netzwerke stellen eine soziale Form dar, die sich zur konventionellen Unterteilung in „Mikro" und „Makro" sowie in „persönlich" und „unpersönlich" quer stellt.
- Die allgemeinen Funktionen von Netzwerken stimmen mit allen vier Perspektiven in Bezug auf Netzwerke überein: „Soziabilität", „Zugang", „Befähigungsstrukturen" und „soziales Kapital", wobei jede von ihnen negative oder positive Auswirkungen haben kann.

Worin bestehen die positiven Auswirkungen von Netzwerken?

1. *Sicherheitsnetz (Soziabilität).* Soziale Netzwerke fördern Kooperation und gegenseitige Hilfe zwischen den Menschen, sie bieten soziale Kommunikation, emotionale Unterstützung und Hilfe bei alltäglichen Problemen und Gesundheitsfragen.
2. *Überlebenssicherung auf der Mikroebene (Zugang).* Soziale Netzwerke bilden eine Grundlage für Überlebensstrategien. Zusammenzuarbeiten ist eine Möglichkeit, mit Entbehrungen zurechtzukommen. Netzwerke verursachen niedrigere Kosten, sind effektiver und leichter zugänglich als jede andere Alternative, zum Beispiel als der Einkauf zu Marktpreisen oder die Inanspruchnahme staatlicher Unterstützung.[30]
3. *Umgehung von Systemregeln (Befähigungsstrukturen).* Netzwerke können dazu genutzt werden, den Wettbewerb auszuschalten oder die eigenen Wettbewerbschancen zu erhöhen. Die Investition und Pflege von Netzwerken ist eine alltägliche Wirtschaftsstrategie. So bestehen zum Beispiel persönliche Netzwerke zwischen Käufern und Verkäufern auf lokaler Ebene[31], und Wirtschaftsvertreter schließen oft persönliche Abmachungen, um zum Beispiel das starre Korsett von Verträgen zu umgehen.[32]
4. *Kompensationseffekte (soziales Kapital).* Soziale Netzwerke kompensieren Lücken in den formellen Systemen. Das trifft insbesondere auf eine risikoreiche Umgebung

essarily improve or inhibit economic growth, as the contrast between Chinese and Russian recent developments illustrates. The impact of networks depends on their inner structure[35] and its projection onto the economy.

Similar ambivalence is characteristic of the role of informal networks in the Soviet system. Many scholars ranging from Merle Fainsod[36] to J. Arch Getty[37] viewed the significance of informal networks in the Soviet economy primarily as a hindrance to efficient governance. Others, building on the work of T. H. Rigby[38] and Graeme Gill[39], viewed personal networks as central to the workings of the system.[40] It seems essential to reveal both the functional and subversive roles of informal networks in the formal economy. On the one hand, personal networks became embedded in the institutional order to such an extent that agents stopped reflecting upon them, which in turn made them an integral part in the functioning of the economy. On the other hand, they also subverted the economy, especially its ideological and moral foundations. In other words, there is no linearity in the relationship between networks and functioning of the economy: any universal formula like "the more networks, the better" is unlikely to work. The reason for this is an ambiguous nature of networks, as there seems to be a reverse side to each of their "positive" implications. Let us now consider the "negative" implications of networks in more detail:

1. *High cost of implicit contract (the reverse side of sociability).* Even if one "inherits" a network, rather than builds one's own, the network does require maintenance and investment. Maintaining social ties (satisfying reciprocal demands and thus reproducing trust) generates cost. In other words, belonging to the network creates obligations towards the other members of the network, or implicit contract. Therefore, whatever advantages one receives from being embedded in a network (incurring less transaction costs) is counterbalanced by the obligations of the implicit contract.[41] These obligations, imposed by the relationships of trust and reciprocity, may force one to over-exploitation of one's resources (or access to resources) by other members of his network, which in turn can lead to a free-riding problem.

2. *Limits to individual action (the reverse side of access).* Membership in a closed social network (with consequent sanctions to enforce the implicit contract) can subject members to restrictive social regulations and limit their individual action. All kind of leveling pressures keep members in the same situation as their peers[42] and strong collective norms in communities may restrict the scope of individuals.[43] Non-compliance with the demands of membership can also result in a loss of reputation as a reliable member of the network.

3. *Lock-in effects (the reverse side of enabling structure).* It should be noted that the negative impact is strongly enhanced within the closed networks. It is the belonging to the closed networks, rather than networks in general, that reduces adaptive capacity and carries the dangers of lock-in effects. These lock-in effects may be strengthened by processes of cognitive dissonance in tight groups.[44] Individuals who make up a dense network tend to develop a commitment to one another and to their group. Information that disturbs the consensus of the group's perception of reality is likely to be rejected. Belonging to a network seems to yield positive results up to a certain threshold. Hence, the positive effects of being a member of a network are the same mechanisms that cause negative effects. The same processes of lock-in are found

oder auf Fälle zu, bei denen unpersönliche Vertrauenssysteme nicht so funktionieren, wie sie es sollten. Indem Netzwerke das leisten, was formelle Systeme nicht erbringen, eröffnen sie ihren Mitgliedern nicht nur Handlungsmöglichkeiten, sondern tragen auch zu ihrer eigenen Reproduktion bei.

In der Praxis funktionieren soziale Netzwerke sowohl im „Zugangsmodus" (und heben so Netzwerkkapital und soziales Kapital auf die Makroebene, um die bestehenden formellen Strukturen aufrechtzuerhalten) als auch im „Soziabilitätsmodus" (indem sie die sozialen Beziehungen der Mikroebene, aus denen Netzwerke bestehen, unterstützen). Soziale Netzwerke sind sowohl eine Struktur als auch das Ergebnis einer Struktur. Der ambivalente Charakter von Netzwerken ist in dem Umstand begründet, dass die mit dem Zugang zu Ressourcen verbundenen „positiven" Auswirkungen (Flexibilität, psychologische Unterstützung, verringerte Risiken und Kosten) zur gleichen Zeit „negative" Auswirkungen auf die Wirtschaft, das Netzwerk selbst und seine einzelnen Mitglieder haben kann.[33] Woolcock vertritt die Ansicht, dass „sich ein hohes Niveau an sozialem Kapital (...) ‚negativ' auswirken kann, indem die Gruppenmitglieder mit hohen, Partikularinteressen dienenden Anforderungen konfrontiert werden, wodurch die individuelle Entfaltung und Entwicklung eingeschränkt werden, während gleichzeitig der freie Zugriff auf die Gemeinschaftsressourcen ermöglicht wird. In Gruppen, die durch marktfremde Zwangsmechanismen marginalisiert wurden, wird so der Glaube an den Erfolg durch persönliche Anstrengung zunichte gemacht."[34] Auf der Makroebene verstärkt oder behindert das Vorherrschen von Netzwerkstrukturen nicht zwangsläufig die wirtschaftliche Entwicklung, wie die so unterschiedlichen gegenwärtigen Entwicklungen in China und Russland zeigen. Der Einfluss der Netzwerke hängt von ihrer inneren Struktur[35] und von ihrer Orientierung auf die Wirtschaft ab.

Die gleiche Ambivalenz charakterisiert auch die Rolle der informellen Netzwerke im sowjetischen System. Viele Forscher, von Merle Fainsod[36] bis zu J. Arch Getty[37], betrachteten die Netzwerke in der sowjetischen Wirtschaft vor allem als ein Hindernis für den Aufbau einer effizienten Verwaltung. Andere dagegen, die sich auf die Arbeit von T. H. Rigby[38] und Graeme Gill[39] stützen, sahen in persönlichen Netzwerken eine unabdingbare Voraussetzung für das Funktionieren des Systems.[40] Man muss daher beide Seiten, die funktionale als auch die subversive Rolle informeller Netzwerke, in formalen Systemen betrachten. Einerseits waren persönliche Netzwerke so fest in die institutionelle Ordnung eingebunden, dass die Akteure nicht mehr über sie nachdachten und die Netzwerke zu einem integralen Bestandteil der Wirtschaft wurden. Andererseits untergruben sie die Wirtschaft, vor allem ihre ideologische und moralische Grundlage. Das heißt mit anderen Worten, dass es keinen linearen Zusammenhang zwischen der Existenz von Netzwerken und dem Funktionieren der Wirtschaft gibt. Universallösungen wie „je mehr Netzwerke, desto besser" werden mit hoher Wahrscheinlichkeit nicht funktionieren. Das hängt mit dem ambivalenten Charakter von Netzwerken zusammen: Jede positive Auswirkung scheint auch immer eine Kehrseite zu haben. Im Folgenden seien die „negativen" Auswirkungen von Netzwerken genauer betrachtet:

1. *Hohe Kosten für implizite Verpflichtungen (Kehrseite der Soziabilität).* Selbst wenn man ein Netzwerk „erbt", statt es selbst zu schaffen, bedarf es der Pflege und des Ein-

at the level of sectors, localities and regions. Especially for de-industrialised regions, part of the problem is that they are locked-in to institutional structures that were relevant to an earlier phase of successful economic development but which now constitute a barrier to moving onto a new path of development.[45]

4. *The reverse side of social capital.* The adaptive ability seemingly intrinsic in network structures can be, however, reduced as a result of path-dependency effects.[46] Portes and Landolt suggest that the assumption that social capital is only positive is wrong and that there are also negative sides to social capital.[47] Portes and Sensenbrenner further argue that "it is important not to lose sight of the fact that the same social mechanisms that give rise to appropriable resources for individual use can also constrain action or even derail it from its original goals."[48] In other words, networks do not only organise and facilitate, they also divert and misappropriate the structures organising the economy's dominant functions and processes. For example, networks that have been used as a resource, say, in starting up businesses (studies of social capital emphasise this aspect of networks), can later become a serious obstacle for the further development of the business environment (skills of maintaining networks might not fit the context of competition, transparency, and market values). Finally, negative externalities from intense group membership result from the effects described by Olson.[49] When groups become too large and powerful, rent-seeking behavior and lobbying costs influence economic development negatively. However, Knack and Keefer[50] do not find empirical proof for this postulated negative relationship of Olson. It might be the case that both "too little" and "too much" social capital can impede economic performance, which suggests that social capital should be optimised and not maximised, and a careful analysis of the nature of social networks and their functions should be made.

In other words, because networks can work both for and against state and market institutions, the volume of network capital is not necessarily an "addition" to the economy, especially when networks are conducive to corruption.

Let us take the example of social networks that are associated with the informal workings of the economy. By serving the "economy of favors", social networks have a considerable bearing on the nature of both personal relations and institutions. Personal relationships become "colonised" and used for matters going far beyond sociability, while formal institutions get "informalized," which results in "privatising" the Soviet state, as Vladimir Shlapentokh put it[51] – or in the post-Soviet "state capture," using the terminology of the World Bank. There is literature on the sociology of organisations that looks into the impact of personal networks on organisations. What is less explored is the impact of the instrumentality of social networks on their nature and on the ideas and values channeled through them.

The exploitative use of social networks as well as the exploitative use of state or institutional resources is the basis of the economy of favors. Certain specific features by which such networks can be identified are as follows.

They are quite literally "in-formal", that is they operate on the basis of personal relationships but intertwine with the formal institutions (say, if a friend is also a colleague, a boss or a functionary in charge of distribution of a resource). In framing these networks, I follow the logic of Endre Sik and Pal Peter Toth's concept of the "hidden econ-

satzes. Die Pflege sozialer Beziehungen (Befriedigung gegenseitiger Ansprüche und damit Vertrauensbildung) verursacht Kosten. Das heißt mit anderen Worten, dass die Zugehörigkeit zu einem Netzwerk Verpflichtungen gegenüber anderen Mitgliedern mit sich bringt, eine Art impliziter Vertrag. Den Vorteilen, die die Zugehörigkeit zu einem Netzwerk bietet (einschließlich geringerer Transaktionskosten), stehen als Gegengewicht die Verpflichtungen dieses impliziten Vertrags gegenüber.[41] Diese auf Vertrauen und Gegenseitigkeit basierenden Verpflichtungen können zu einer übermäßigen Ausbeutung der eigenen Ressourcen (oder des Zugangs zu Ressourcen) durch andere Mitglieder des Netzwerks führen, was sich bis zum unkontrollierten und unbeschränkten Zugriff auf die Ressourcen entwickeln kann.

2. *Beschränkung des eigenen Handelns (Kehrseite des Zugangs).* Die Mitgliedschaft in einem geschlossenen sozialen Netzwerk (mit Sanktionsmöglichkeiten zur Durchsetzung des impliziten Vertrags) kann einzelne Mitglieder restriktiven sozialen Regeln unterwerfen und so ihr individuelles Handeln einschränken. Jede Art gleichmachenden Drucks führt dazu, dass sich alle in der gleichen Situation befinden,[42] wobei starke kollektive Normen in Gemeinschaften den Spielraum jedes Einzelnen einschränken können.[43] Die Nichterfüllung der Anforderungen als Mitglied eines Netzwerks kann auch dazu führen, dass das Ansehen als verlässliches Mitglied beschädigt wird.

3. *Eingeschlossensein (Kehrseite der Befähigungsstrukturen).* Es muss festgehalten werden, dass sich in geschlossenen Netzwerken negative Auswirkungen erheblich verstärken. Geschlossene Netzwerke neigen eher als andere Netzwerke dazu, die Anpassungsfähigkeit zu verringern und die Gefahr des Eingeschlossenseins zu vergrößern. Diese Wirkungen können durch eine selektive Wahrnehmung in Gruppen mit engen internen Verbindungen noch verstärkt werden.[44] Personen, die eng geknüpfte Netzwerke bilden, neigen dazu, Engagement für andere und die Gruppe zu entwickeln. Informationen, die den Konsens in der Wahrnehmung von Realität durch die Gruppe stören, werden ausgeblendet. Die Zugehörigkeit zu einem Netzwerk scheint bis zu einem gewissen Grad positive Auswirkungen zu haben. Den positiven wie auch den negativen Folgen scheinen also die gleichen Mechanismen zugrunde zu liegen. Auf der Ebene von Sektoren, von Ortschaften und Regionen zeigen sich die gleichen Auswirkungen des Eingeschlossenseins. Regionen mit rückläufiger industrieller Entwicklung leiden besonders unter dem Problem, dass sie in Verwaltungsstrukturen gefangen sind, die für die frühere Phase einer erfolgreichen wirtschaftlichen Entwicklung ausgelegt waren und die jetzt ein Hindernis auf dem Weg zu neuen Entwicklungen sind.[45]

4. *Die Kehrseite des sozialen Kapitals.* Die Netzwerkstrukturen eigentlich innewohnende Anpassungsfähigkeit kann sich im Ergebnis pfadabhängiger Effekte verringern.[46] Portes und Landolt gehen davon aus, dass die Annahme, soziales Kapital sei nur positiv, falsch sei und soziales Kapital auch negative Seiten habe.[47] Portes und Sensenbrenner stellen außerdem fest, dass „man nicht aus den Augen verlieren darf, wie derselbe soziale Mechanismus, der die Ressourcennutzung durch den Einzelnen förderte, diese auch einschränken, ja sogar von ihren ursprünglichen Zielen abbringen kann".[48] Anders ausgedrückt: Netzwerke bilden und begünstigen nicht nur die Strukturen, die zu den wirtschaftlich vorherrschenden Funktionen und Prozessen führen, sie stören und beschädigen diese auch. So können zum Beispiel Netzwerke, die bei

omy" and *Eurostat* classifications, which do not take account of housework, do-it-yourself activities, social work, the exchange of produce between households, crime or activities which count as productive but wh ch are not legal (e.g., the production of drugs and the trade in them). Under the category of "hidden" Endre Sik and Toth do list the unreported activities of registered enterprises and the activities of enterprises which, although not registered, conduct otherwise legal activities.[52] Following this logic, networks that serve the economy of favors are constituted by channels either penetrating or residing within formal structures. I thus exclude personal networks that serve domestic and do-it-yourself exchanges, and focus on favors that are given at the expense of institutional resources. These are so-called "favors of access" that serve to channel institutional resources into private pockets, thus constituting a parallel currency in an economy where money previously played only a limited role. Values and ideas channeled through these networks are associated with mutual help, beating the system, co-operation on a micro level to compensate for the unfairness or harshness of the macro order, or the notions of entitlement. In a Soviet context all these features are rooted in mutual parasitism between the state and the population: parasitism towards state resources on the part of the population and traditionally exploitative attitudes of the state towards its population. In the post-Soviet "piratisation"[53] of Russia, informal networks served the constituencies of grand corruption at the top involved in insider dealings for the benefit of cliques, clans or oligarchic groups.

The change of context during the post-communist reforms in Eastern Europe, Russia or post-Mao China and the subsequent change of role that informal networks play in an economy can be referred to the "dynamic puzzle"[54], i.e. the question of whether certain forms of social capital can be thought of as universally desirable regardless of historical context (i.e. does the evolution from industrial to post-industrial economic activity lead to a change in the form of social capital?) The literature on post-Communist transition seems also to indicate that the value of networks is not universal: in one political and economic framework they might play one role, but once that framework changes networks adapt and may function in different ways. One of the most conspicuous outcomes of the post-communist transformation in Russia is the spread of corruption that to some extent grew out of and was enhanced by the "monetarisation" or instrumental use of those network channels that already existed. In the economy where money did not play a role, informal exchanges were largely non-monetary, involved humanising relationship, and were more available for poor people. Once the informal exchanges within networks serving the economy of favors became monetarised the following tendencies can be noticed:

- Humanising relationship gave place to calculation of time and cost (*sociability*);
- Networks used for obtaining items of personal consumption became used for "making money" (*access*);
- Networks became less available for the poor and appropriated by the rich and powerful (as people say, the society in which one was connected at the bottom and lonely at the top has changed into the one in which one is lonely at the bottom and connected at the top. In Bourdieu's terms, *social capital* has become less accessible but its volume has increased dramatically);

der Gründung eines Unternehmens als Ressource genutzt wurden (Untersuchungen zum sozialen Kapital unterstreichen diesen Netzwerkaspekt), später ein ernsthaftes Hindernis für die weitere Entwicklung des geschäftlichen Umfeldes werden (die Fähigkeiten, die zur Erhaltung eines Netzwerks gebraucht werden, passen nicht unbedingt zu einem von Wettbewerb, Transparenz und Marktwert geprägten Kontext). Die von Olson beschriebenen Effekte führen darüber hinaus als Ergebnis von intensiver Gruppenmitgliedschaft zu negativen Außeneffekten.[49] Wenn Gruppen zu groß und stark werden, beeinflussen auf Korruption beruhende Versuche der Einkommensmaximierung („rent seeking behavior") und Kosten für Lobbyarbeit die wirtschaftliche Entwicklung negativ. Knack und Keefer[50] fanden jedoch keinen empirischen Beweis für diese von Olson postulierte negative Beziehung. Es ist durchaus möglich, dass sowohl „zu wenig" als auch „zu viel" soziales Kapital wirtschaftliche Leistung verhindert, was darauf hinweist, dass das soziale Kapital optimiert, nicht jedoch maximiert werden sollte und dass der Charakter von sozialen Netzwerken und ihren Funktionen einer sorgfältigen Analyse unterzogen werden muss.

Anders ausgedrückt: Da Netzwerke sowohl für als auch gegen staatliche und private Strukturen arbeiten können, ist der Umfang an Netzwerkkapital nicht einfach ein „Zusatz" zur Wirtschaft, besonders dann nicht, wenn Netzwerke zu Korruption führen.

Genannt sei an dieser Stelle das Beispiel sozialer Netzwerke, die mit informellen Formen wirtschaftlicher Aktivität verbunden sind. Da sie der Günstlingswirtschaft in die Hände spielen, üben soziale Netzwerke einen großen Einfluss auf die persönlichen Beziehungen wie auch auf die Institutionen aus. Persönliche Beziehungen werden dabei „besetzt" und für Zwecke genutzt, die weit über die soziable Komponente hinausgehen, während formale Institutionen mit informellen Strukturen durchdrungen werden, was zu einer „Privatisierung" des Sowjetstaates, wie es Vladimir Shlapentokh so treffend ausdrückte[51], bzw. zu einer postsowjetischen Instrumentalisierung des Staates durch privilegierte Gruppen („state capture") führte, um die Terminologie der Weltbank zu benutzen. Zur Soziologie von Organisationen gibt es Literatur, die den Einfluss persönlicher Netzwerke auf Organisationen untersucht. Weniger erforscht wurde dagegen der Einfluss, den die Instrumentalisierung sozialer Netzwerke auf ihren eigenen Charakter und die durch das Netzwerk verbreiteten und geförderten Ideen und Werte hat.

Die ausbeuterische Nutzung sozialer Netzwerke ist ebenso wie die ausbeuterische Nutzung staatlicher oder institutioneller Ressourcen die Basis von Günstlingswirtschaft. Einige besondere Merkmale, mit denen diese Netzwerke charakterisiert werden können, sollen im Folgenden benannt werden:

Sie sind im wörtlichen Sinne „in-formell", das heißt, sie funktionieren auf der Grundlage persönlicher Beziehungen, sind jedoch mit formalen Strukturen verflochten (zum Beispiel der Freund, der gleichzeitig auch ein Kollege, ein Vorgesetzter oder ein mit der Verteilung einer Ressource betrauter Angestellter ist). Zur Charakterisierung dieser Netzwerke folge ich hier der Logik des von Endre Sik und Pal Peter entwickelten Konzepts der „versteckten Wirtschaft" und der *Eurostat*-Klassifikation, die Hausarbeit, Eigenleistung, gesellschaftliche Arbeit, Warenaustausch zwischen Haushalten, Kriminalität und als produktiv geltende, jedoch illegale Aktivitäten (wie Herstellung von Drogen und Handel mit ihnen) nicht einbeziehen. In der Kategorie „versteckt" führen

- Networks became more "closed" turning into clubs and circles[55] (*enabling structures*).

The latter point is important. In fact, it can be argued that although there might not be any linear correlation between types of social capital and economic and political development, the implications of networks do depend on their inner structure – "open" or "closed" – on the ideas and values they channel, and on the practices they organise. Below I illustrate this point by outlining the generic features of networks that serve the economy of favors, relying on my own research[56], in contrast to the features of networks characteristic in the network society, as suggested by Manuel Castells.[57] These are the ideal types that can be used for assessing the role of networks in Soviet times, their transformation in the post-Soviet Russian and prospects for change.

Networks in the Economy of Favors	Networks in the Network Society
Existing structures grounded in the past	Emerging structures permeating all societies
Networks account for anti-modern nature of institutions	Networks are the institutions of the information age, enabling and innovative
Socio-political basis: statism	Socio-political basis: global capitalism
Networks are exploitative of the state, parasitic on state property	Networks transcend all states
Networks are personalised, based on a priori existing social contacts	Networks (both technological and social) are of an impersonal nature
Networks of "svoi liudi" bound by mutual obligations and closed to outsiders	Networks imply openness, dynamism and flexibility for individuals, firms and countries
Discipline imposed by ethics, etiquette and unwritten rules	Discipline imposed by global financial markets, military technology, control of knowledge
Unwritten rules are followed more than laws	The only rule is that there are no rules – laws are enforced with difficulty by global and national institutions
Ambivalent relationship between networks and the socio-economic order: networks are both functional and subversive	Networks generate a new order (assumes decline of the state)

Endre Sik and Pal Peter die nicht erfassten Aktivitäten offiziell ins Register eingetragener Unternehmen sowie die Aktivitäten von Unternehmen, die zwar nicht eingetragen sind, sich ansonsten jedoch mit legalen Geschäften befassen.[52] Dieser Logik zufolge bestehen die Netzwerke, die der Günstlingswirtschaft zuarbeiten, aus Kanälen, die innerhalb formaler Strukturen schon vorhanden sind oder in diese hineinreichen. Ich lasse hier persönliche Netzwerke außer Acht, da sie dem Austausch von Eigenleistungen und häuslichen Tätigkeiten dienen, und beschränke mich auf diejenigen, die auf Kosten institutioneller Ressourcen existieren. Diese auch als „Türöffner" bezeichneten Netze dienen dazu, institutionelle Ressourcen in private Taschen zu lenken. Sie stellen somit eine Art Parallelwährung in einer Wirtschaft dar, in der Geld früher nur eine begrenzte Rolle gespielt hat. Diese Netzwerke hatten Werte und Ideen, die etwas mit gegenseitiger Hilfe, systemkritischem Verhalten und der Zusammenarbeit auf der Mikroebene zu tun hatten, um die mangelnde Fairness und die größere Härte auf der Makroebene zu kompensieren; sie hingen außerdem mit der Vorstellung eines berechtigten Anspruches zusammen. Im Kontext der Sowjetunion entstanden all diese Eigenschaften aus einer gegenseitigen parasitären Bindung zwischen Staat und Bevölkerung: parasitäre Haltung der Bevölkerung, die die staatlichen Ressourcen für sich nutzt, und der Staat mit seinem traditionell ausbeuterischen Verhalten gegenüber seiner Bevölkerung. Während der postsowjetischen „Piratisierung"[53] Russlands waren informelle Netzwerke der Nährboden für Korruption im großen Stil und auf höchster Ebene, deren Insidergeschäfte der Bereicherung von Cliquen, Klans und Oligarchien dienten.

Die Änderung der Rahmenbedingungen infolge der postkommunistischen Reformen in Osteuropa und Russland oder auch in China nach dem Tode Mao Tse-Tungs und die damit einhergehende Veränderung der Rolle, die informelle Netzwerke in einem Wirtschaftsgefüge spielten, können mit einem „dynamischen Puzzle"[54] in Verbindung gebracht werden, das heißt mit der Frage, ob bestimmte Formen des sozialen Kapitals unabhängig vom historischen Kontext als allgemein wünschenswert angesehen werden können. (Führt zum Beispiel der Übergang von einer industriellen zu einer postindustriellen Wirtschaftstätigkeit zu einer Veränderung der Form des sozialen Kapitals?) Der Literatur über die Phase der postkommunistischen Transformation lässt sich entnehmen, dass der Wert von Netzwerken nicht allgemein gültig ist: In einem ganz bestimmten politischen und wirtschaftlichen Kontext scheinen sie eine bestimmte Rolle zu spielen, doch wenn sich die Bedingungen ändern, passen sie sich an und können auf ganz andere Weise funktionieren. Eines der hervorstechendsten Ergebnisse des postkommunistischen Übergangs in Russland ist die Verbreitung der Korruption, die überall aufblühte und durch die „Monetarisierung" oder Instrumentarisierung bereits existierender Netzwerke noch verstärkt wurde. In einer Wirtschaft, in der Geld keine Rolle spielte, fanden die informellen Tauschgeschäfte meist ohne Geld statt. Sie beruhten auf den persönlichen Beziehungen und waren damit armen Menschen leichter zugänglich. Mit der „Monetarisierung" der informellen Tauschgeschäfte innerhalb der Netzwerke, die die Günstlingswirtschaft förderten, lassen sich folgende Tendenzen beobachten:

- Persönliche Beziehungen zueinander machten der Berechnung von Zeit- und Kostenaufwand Platz (*Soziabilität*).

Fragmentation of the state, with state institutions being "colonised" by antagonistic networks	The new state will be a decentralised network state (devolution of power and resources to regions, local governments and NGOs, initiated by the state)
Indicators of economy of favors: diversion in workings of formal institutions (ineffectiveness of the rule of law, oversized informal economy, spread of corruption and customary practices)	Indicators of network society: number of communication devices (telephone lines, TV, PCs, Internet hosts etc.)

It follows from the evidence provided by Castells and Kizelyova[58] that some features of the network society model are already visible in Russia. My own views on the possibilities of a smooth transition in Russia to a network society are rather pessimistic. There is evidence that even emerging networks of a "network society" type still have the features of Soviet informal networks.[59] For a fully-fledged market and democracy to emerge, networks will have to cease being exploitative of friendships and of institutional resources – features that have been described as somewhat inherent to the Russian character.[60] So far this has not been the case. Social networks have become linkages between Soviet and post-Soviet society and have been held responsible not only for their "safety net", "survival kit", "enabling" and "compensatory" functions but also for their aggressive and instrumental use in barter and the shadow economy, arrears and tax games, corrupt exchanges and criminalised contexts. These have had important implications for the state, market and civil society during the "formative" period. To sum up:

- Networks have been conducive to state capture and corruption. The organised groups that breached the state monopoly of legitimate violence and took over the function of conflict-resolution and law and contract enforcement in the private sector of the economy used a ramified network of informal control and forced sanctions (gangs, private protection firms, etc).[61] They also offered, among other things, services of "solving problems" through informal channels in local and regional authorities, tax inspection offices and the state coercive institutions.
- Networks have undermined the free-market principles of profitability and open competition. The "favors of access" given to "people of the circle" are likely to account for the super-profits made on the Russian market, for the 1995 loans-for-shares auctions, GKO-pyramids and the notorious role of "authorised" banks in covering state budget deficits before the 1998, as well as for large-scale corruption.[62] The anti-bankruptcy alliances between industrial firms and local authorities, the spread of financial scheming, complex ownership schemes and so-called "authorised" business structures etc. all indicate the crucial role of informal networks in the Russian "market".[63]
- Networks of mutual help and informal exchange – developed under the Soviet regime outside the state and the market domain – did not contribute, as some would perhaps expect, towards the constitution of civil society because of the exploitative nature of informal associations and the parasitic use of state and non-state resources.[64]

- Die Netzwerke, die zur Beschaffung von Gütern des eigenen Bedarfs dienten, wurden nun zum „Geld verdienen" verwendet (*Zugang*).
- Die Netzwerke wurden für Arme weniger zugänglich, während die Reichen und Mächtigen sich diese Netzwerke aneigneten. (Die Gesellschaft veränderte sich von einer Struktur, in der man an der Basis zusammenhält und an der Spitze einsam ist, in eine Gesellschaft, in der man an der Spitze zusammenhält und an der Basis einsam ist. Bourdieu zufolge wurde der Zugang zu „sozialem Kapital" erschwert, während es gleichzeitig an Umfang drastisch zugenommen hat.)
- Netzwerke wurden „geschlossener" und verwandelten sich in Klubs oder Zirkel[55] (*Befähigungsstrukturen*).

Der letzte Punkt ist wichtig, denn auch ohne direkten Zusammenhang zwischen den verschiedenen Arten des sozialen Kapitals und der wirtschaftlichen und politischen Entwicklung hängen die Auswirkungen von Netzwerken offensichtlich von ihrer inneren Struktur („offen" oder „geschlossen"), den verbindenden Ideen und Werten und den Aktivitäten, die sie organisieren, ab. Im Folgenden werde ich diesen Punkt durch die Herausarbeitung der für Netzwerke der Günstlingswirtschaft charakteristischen Merkmale verdeutlichen, wobei ich mich auf meine eigenen Forschungsergebnisse stützen werde.[56] Demgegenüber stehen die Merkmale von Netzwerken einer vernetzten Gesellschaft, wie sie von Manuel Castells erarbeitet wurden.[57] Es sind Idealtypen, mit denen sich die Bedeutung von Netzwerken zu sowjetischer Zeit, ihre Umgestaltung im postsowjetischen Russland und ihre erwartete Veränderung abschätzen lassen.

Netzwerke in Günstlingswirtschaften	Netzwerke in vernetzten Gesellschaften
Bestehende Strukturen leiten sich aus der Vergangenheit ab	Die entstehenden Strukturen durchdringen alle Gesellschaften
Die Netzwerke sind für die veralteten Strukturen der Institutionen verantwortlich	Netzwerke sind die Institutionen des Informationszeitalters, ergebnisorientiert und innovativ
Soziopolitische Grundlage: Dirigismus	Soziopolitische Grundlage: globalisierter Kapitalismus
Netzwerke beuten den Staat aus und sind parasitär in Bezug auf das Staatseigentum	Netzwerke bestehen über Staatsgrenzen hinweg
Netzwerke sind personalisiert, sie gründen sich a priori auf bestehende soziale Kontakte	Netzwerke (sowohl technischer als auch sozialer Natur) sind unpersönlich

These tendencies illustrate the closed nature of networks in Russia in the 1990s as well as all four types of negative implications that networks can have. Moreover, Sik and Wellman argue that the need to use networks to compensate for the permeability, fluidity and uncertainty of post-communism have fostered even greater reliance on networks. The implications of closed networks in post-communist contexts need to be explored further and related to the findings of network studies elsewhere. To sum up the discussion of the closed networks serving the economy of favors, the following hypotheses can be formulated for further consideration:

- As follows from the table on page 321/323, "closed" networks are essentially different from the networks characteristic for the "network society";
- "Closed" networks have proved sustainable in a post-Communist context, and the World Bank survey on state capture indicates that only a limited constituency for "opening up" exists in Russia[65];
- There are vested interests in sustaining the influence of personalised and closed networks in Russia and consequently the resistance towards Russia's integration into the international community. In Russia's political climate, the closed nature of networks impedes internationalisation and substantial change. Rather, by reproducing themselves (and their links to the state system that originally empowered them) these networks adapt, reinvent and reinforce the forms of their integration into the political and economic system. It is these forms that are essential to grasp in order to understand, for example, how *guanxi* and *blat* networks which on the surface of things were similarly integrated into the state centralized systems in China and Russia, now generate *guanxi* capitalism and use the networks' capacity to back up the state-driven reform in one case, and undermine state capacity in the other.

NOTES

1 Stiglitz, Joseph, *Globalisation and its Discontents*. New York 2002

2 Ledeneva, Alena: *Russia's Economy of Favours*. Cambridge 1998

3 Studies of networks are a wide-ranging and multidisciplinary field. Its mainstream dimension, "social network analysis", is grounded in a specific technique used to analyse network data. It is focused on concepts of centrality, cohesion, cores, prestige, roles, personal and occupational ties in the allocation of resources etc. (see, for example, Wellman, B./Berkowitz, S. D.: *Social Structures: A Network Approach*. Cambridge 1988) Network analysis is concerned with how to locate people in various kinds of networks, how to estimate who and what they know, the resources to which they have access and the social constraints affecting their behavior. Network analysis uses graph theory and models such as p1 and its relatives. Software packages have been developed to analyse network data, such as UCINET and Krackplot. The field has been booming in the USA and the UK and has achieved a high degree of formalization (see for example Wasserman, S./Faust, D.: *Social Network Analysis: Methods and Applications*, CUP, 1994). Social network analysis is also widely used in business studies and management, see for example Barabasi, Albert-Laszlo: *Linked: The New Science of Networks*. Perseus, 2002.

4 Sik, Endre/Wellman, Barry: "Network capital in capitalist, communist and post-communist countries." In: Wellman, Barry (ed.): *Networks in the Global Village*. Boulder, CO 1999, pp. 225–255

5 Granovetter, Mark: "The strength of weak ties." In: *American Journal of Sociology*, vol. 78, 1973, pp. 1360–1380; Granovetter, Mark: "Economic action and social structure: the problem of embeddedness." In: *American Journal of Sociology*, vol. 91, 1985, pp. 481–510

6 An economic actor could be a person, household, organisation, state, etc.

7 Polanyi, K.: *The Great Transformation*. New York 1944

8 Sik/Wellman, as in footnote 4

Netzwerke, die nach dem Prinzip „svoi liudi" (die eigenen Leute) funktionieren, werden durch gegenseitige Verpflichtungen zusammengehalten und sind für Außenstehende unzugänglich	Netzwerke sind offen, dynamisch und flexibel gegenüber Personen, Unternehmen und Staaten
Disziplin gründet sich auf ethische Grundsätze, Etikette und ungeschriebene Regeln	Disziplin gründet sich auf den Druck der globalen Finanzmärkte, auf militärische Stärke und die Kontrolle von Wissen und Erkenntnis
Ungeschriebene Regeln stehen über den Gesetzen	Die einzige Regel ist, dass es keine Regeln gibt – Gesetze können nur unter Schwierigkeiten durch globale und nationale Institutionen durchgesetzt werden
Ambivalente Beziehung der Netzwerke zur sozio-ökonomischen Ordnung: Netzwerke sind sowohl funktional als auch subversiv	Netzwerke schaffen eine neue Ordnung (bei angenommener Reduzierung der Rolle des Staates)
Es kommt zu staatlicher Zersplitterung mit einer „Kolonialisierung" staatlicher Institutionen durch antagonistisch arbeitende Netzwerke	Der neue Staat wird ein dezentralisierter vernetzter Staat sein (vom Staat initiierte Übertragung von Macht und Ressourcen auf Regionen, Kommunalverwaltungen und Nichtregierungsorganisationen)
Indikatoren für Günstlingswirtschaft: ungenügendes Funktionieren der offiziellen Institutionen (Ineffektivität der Gesetze, starke Schattenwirtschaft, verbreitete Korruption und Gewohnheitsrechte)	Indikatoren für vernetzte Gesellschaft: Anzahl an Kommunikationsgeräten (Telefonanschlüsse, Fernsehen, PCs, Internetanschlüsse usw.)

Aus den Beweisführungen Castells' und Kizelyovas[58] ergibt sich, dass gewisse Merkmale des Modells der vernetzten Gesellschaft in Russland bereits sichtbar sind. Ich selbst schätze die Möglichkeit eines reibungslosen Übergangs zu einer vernetzten Gesellschaft in Russland eher pessimistisch ein. Es zeigt sich deutlich, dass selbst die entstehenden Netzwerke vom Typus der „vernetzten Gesellschaft" noch die Merkmale sowjetischer informeller Netzwerke aufweisen.[59] Für die Entstehung eines voll funktionsfähigen Marktes und einer Demokratie müssen Netzwerke aufhören, Freundschaften und institutionelle Ressourcen ausbeuterisch zu nutzen – doch gerade diese Merkmale wurden als integrale Bestandteile des russischen Charakters beschrieben.[60] Dies ist bisher jedoch noch nicht eingetreten. Die sozialen Netzwerke sind zu Bindegliedern zwischen der sowjetischen und der postsowjetischen Gesellschaft geworden, sie stellen nicht nur ein „Sicherungsnetz" dar, sind nicht nur eine Art „Überlebenshilfe", verleihen ihren Mitgliedern nicht nur „Fähigkeiten" und schaffen nicht nur Ausgleich, sondern sie stehen auch für die aggressive und instrumentalisierte Nutzung für Tauschgeschäfte und Schattenwirtschaft, für Schulden und Zollbetrug,

9 Lonkila, Markku: *Social Networks in Post-Soviet Russia.* Helsinki 1999 ; Risto, Alapuro: "Categories, networks and civil society: teachers' social ties in St Petersburg." In: *Civil Society in the European North: Concept and Context.* St Petersburg 1996, pp. 109–116

10 For example, Li Bennich-Bjorkman illustrated the variation in state capture in the Baltic states by showing that "old" networks (anti-communist, student movement) in Estonia have contributed toward the development of the party politics and transparency of the economy whereas "new" networks in Latvia have become a cause for exclusivity and corruption. See Bennich-Bjorkman, Li: "Explaining State Capture in Estonia and Latvia: Identity, International Role Models and Political Formation." In: *The Baltics: Culture, Society, Politics.* 2002

11 The instrumental use of networks is usually "misrecognised" by the members. The aspect of misrecognition is not considered in this paper. For details see Ledeneva, A.: *Russia's Economy of Favours.* Cambridge 1998

12 Wellman, B. (ed.): *Networks in the Global Village.* Boulder, CO 1999, pp. 4–12

13 Sik/Wellman, as in footnote 4

14 Bourdieu, Pierre: "The Forms of Capital." In: Richardson, John G. (ed.): *Handbook of Theory and Research for the Sociology of Education.* New York 1986, pp. 248–249

15 Coleman, J.S.: "Social capital in the creation of human capital." In: *American journal of sociology.* 1988, vol. 94, pp. 95–120, p. 98

16 Putnam, R.D./Leonardi, R./Nanetti, R.Y.: *Making Democracy Work: Civic Traditions in Modern Italy.* Princeton, New Jersey 1993, p. 167

17 Putnam, Robert D. "Tuning In, Tuning Out: The Strange Disappearance of Social Capital in America." In: *PS,* 1995, 28(4), pp. 664–683, p. 664–665

18 Bourdieu, Pierre/Wacquant, Loïc : *An Introduction to Reflexive Sociology.* Chicago 1992, p.119

19 Bourdieu, as in footnote 14, p. 249

20 See Putnam, as in footnote 16 and Putnam, Robert D.: "Bowling Alone: America's Declining Social Capital." In: *Journal of Democracy,* 6(1), pp. 65–78

21 Bebbington, A./Perreault, T.: "Social capital, development and access to resources in highland Ecuador." In: *Economic geography,* 1999, vol. 75.4, pp. 395–418; Portes, A./Sensenbrenner, J.: "Embeddedness and immigration: notes on the social determinants of economic action." In: *American journal of sociology,* 1993, vol. 98.6, pp. 1320–1350

22 Coleman, as in footnote 15, pp. 98, 105

23 Burt, R.: "The social structure of competition." In: Nohria, N./Eccles, R. (eds.): *Networks and organisations, structure, form and action.* Boston MA 1992; Burt, Ronald S.: "The Contingent Value of Social Capital." In: *Administrative Science Quarterly,* 1997, 42, pp. 339–365

24 *Collins Cobuild English Language Dictionary.* London & Glasgow 1987, p. 966. See also Wellman, B./Berkowitz, S. D.: *Social Structures: A Network Approach.* Cambridge 1988

25 Held, D./McGrew, A./Goldblatt, D./Perraton, J.: *Global Transformations: Politics, Economics and Culture.* (Ort?) 1999, pp. 259–282

26 Castells, M.: *The Rise of Network Society.* Oxford 1996, p. 165

27 Messner, D.: *The Network Society: Economic Development and International Competitiveness as problems of Social Governance.* London 1997

28 Perkmann, M.: "The two network societies." In: *Economy and Society.* Vol. 28, No. 4, 1999 (pp. 615–628), p. 620

29 Stark, D./Vedrez, B.: "The social times of networks spaces: sequence analysis of network formation and foreign investment", presented at the Workshop on Networks and Markets (Santa Fe Institute, May 2003). Quoted from the manuscript, p. 4

30 Polanyi, K.: "The Economy as Instituted Process." In: Polanyi, Karl/Arensberg, Conrad/Pearson, H. (eds.): *Trade and Market in the Early Empires.* Glencoe, IL1957, pp. 243–270; Wellman, Barry/Wortley, Scot: "Different Strokes from Different Folks: Community Ties and Social Support." In: *American Journal of Sociology,* 1990, 96, pp. 558–588

31 See Plattner, Stuart: "Economic Behaviour in Markets." In: Plattner, Stuart (ed.): *Economic Anthropology.* Stanford 1989, pp. 210–221; White, Harrison: *Identity and Control.* Princeton 1992

32 See Macaulay, Stewart: "Non-Contractual Relations in Business: A Preliminary Study." In: Granovetter, Mark/Swedberg, Richard (eds.): *The Sociology of Economic Life.* Boulder 1992; Burt, Ronald S.: *Structural Holes.* Chicago 1992

33 The "positive" and "negative" implications are referred to in inverted commas because their evaluation depends on whether the interests of networks are consistent with the interests of the economy and on the concrete perspective from which the assessment is made. For example, limits that the group or community puts on individuality cannot be seen as outright negative. Studies of stress lev-

für korrupte Tauschgeschäfte und kriminelle Zusammenhänge. Das hatte während der „prägenden" Zeit entscheidenden Einfluss auf den Staat, den Markt und die Zivilgesellschaft.

Zusammenfassend kann man sagen:

- Die Netzwerke haben zur Instrumentalisierung des Staates durch privilegierte Gruppen beigetragen und die Korruption gefördert. Organisierte Gruppen, die das staatliche Gewaltmonopol aufgebrochen und die Funktion als Konfliktlöser, Gesetzeshüter und Vertragswächter im privatwirtschaftlichen Sektor übernahmen, nutzten ein weit verzweigtes Netz informeller Kontrollen und gewaltsamer Sanktionen (Gangs, private Sicherheitsdienste usw.)[61] und boten unter anderem auch „Problemlösung" durch die Nutzung informeller Kontakte zu lokalen und regionalen Behörden, Steuerinspektoren und Strafanstalten an.
- Die Netzwerke haben die marktwirtschaftlichen Prinzipien von Gewinnorientierung und freiem Wettbewerb untergraben. Der „Vortritt", der den „Eingeweihten" gegeben wurde, ist verantwortlich für die auf dem russischen Markt erzielten Superprofite, für die 1995 in der zweiten Privatisierungswelle eingeführte Praxis der Verpfändung von Aktienpaketen gegen Kredite („loans for shares"-Programm), für die GKO-Pyramiden, für die berüchtigte Rolle „autorisierter" Banken bei der Übernahme der Staatsdefizite vor 1998 und für Korruption auf den höchsten Ebenen.[62] Die Anti-Bankrott-Allianzen zwischen Industrieunternehmen und örtlichen Behörden, die weit verbreiteten finanziellen Machenschaften, die komplizierten Eigentumsstrukturen und die so genannten „autorisierten" Unternehmensstrukturen usw. zeigen, welch entscheidende Bedeutung informelle Netzwerke auf dem russischen Markt haben.[63]
- Die Netzwerke, die der gegenseitigen Hilfe und dem informellen Austausch dienten und die sich in der Zeit des Sowjetregimes abseits von Staat und Markt entwickelt hatten, trugen nicht (wie vielleicht manche erwartet hatten) zum Aufbau einer Zivilgesellschaft bei. Diese informellen Zusammenschlüsse waren vielmehr ausbeuterischer Natur und beuteten in parasitärer Weise die staatlichen und nichtstaatlichen Ressourcen aus.[64]

Diese Tendenzen verdeutlichen den geschlossenen Charakter russischer Netzwerke in den 1990er, Jahren, in ihnen treten die vier Arten negativer Auswirkungen in Erscheinung, die Netzwerke haben können. Außerdem, so meinen Sik and Wellman, hat die Nachfrage nach Netzwerken, um die Unbeständigkeit, Unstetigkeit und Unsicherheit des Postkommunismus zu kompensieren, das Vertrauen in Netzwerke sogar noch gestärkt. Die Auswirkungen der geschlossenen Netzwerke in postkommunistischen Gesellschaften sollten näher beleuchtet und mit den Ergebnissen der Untersuchungen zu anderen Netzwerken verknüpft werden.

Um die Diskussion zu geschlossenen Netzwerken in Günstlingswirtschaften zusammenzufassen, können folgende Hypothesen für eine weitere Betrachtung formuliert werden:

- Wie aus der Tabelle 324/326 hervorgeht, unterscheiden sich „geschlossene" Netzwerke grundsätzlich von denen einer „vernetzten Gesellschaft".
- „Geschlossene" Netzwerke zeigen Beharrungsvermögen im postkommunistischen Kontext, und der Bericht der Weltbank zur Instrumentalisierung des Staates durch

els indicate that stress is much higher in so-called "atomised" societies than in networkbased societies where individuals might be subject to certain restrictions imposed by networks.

34 Woolcock, Michael: "Social Capital and Economic Development: Toward a Theoretical Synthesis and Policy Framework." In: *Theory and Society*. 1998, 27, pp. 151–208, p. 165

35 The genesis and the functions of networks are somewhat reflected in the nature of the structure (nodes, ties and the "maintenance cost" of the network) that should be explicated. For example, whether one inherits or invests into a self-made network will define the nature of the ties and nodes and the functions of this network. Whether business is the result of an existing network or a network is the outcome of business is not perhaps the most important question. It's much more crucial to see the dynamic process in which social relationships facilitate or impede the development of market institutions.

36 Fainsod, M.: *How Russia is Ruled*. Cambridge, MA 1963

37 Getty, J.A.: *Origins of the Great Purge: The Soviet Communist party Reconsidered, 1933–1938*. New York 1986

38 Rigby, T.H.: "Early provincial cliques and the rise of Stalin." In: *Soviet Studies*, 33, No. 1, January, 1981; "Was Stalin a disloyal patron?" In: *Soviet Studies*, 38, No. 3, July 1986

39 Gill, G.: *The Origins of the Stalinist Political System*. New York 1990

40 Easter, Gerald M.: *Reconstructing the State: Personal Networks and Elite Identity in Soviet Russia*. Cambridge 1999

41 In Bourdieu's terms, such implicit contract consists of "institutional rites" and gift giving that transform "contingent relations, such as those of neighborhood, the workplace, or even kinship, into relationships that are *at once necessary and elective*, implying durable obligations subjectively felt" (Bourdieu, as in footnote 14, pp. 249–50 – my italics).

42 See Ledeneva, A.: "Genealogy of *krugovaya poruka*: forced trust as a feature of Russian political culture." In: Markova, I. (ed.): *Trust and Democratic Transition in Post-Communist Europe*. Oxford 2004

43 Portes/Sensenbrenner, as in footnote 21

44 Meyerson, E.M.: "Human capital, social capital and compensation: the relative contribution of social contacts to managers' incomes." In: *Acta sociologica*, 1994, vol. 37, pp. 383–399

45 In a study on the banking sector Uzzi finds that firms are more likely to get loans and receive lower interest rates on loans if their network of bank ties has a mix of embedded ties and arm's-length ties, see Uzzi, B.: "Embeddedness in the making of financial capital: how social relations and networks benefit firms seeking financing." In: *American sociological review*. 1999, vol. 64.4, pp. 481–505

46 Stark, David/Bruszt, Laszlo: *Postsocialist Pathways: transforming Politics and property in East Central Europe*. pp. 7–8, 82–3; Stark, David/Bruszt, Laszlo: "One Way or Multiple Paths?; For a Comparative Sociology of European Capitalism." In: *American Journal of Sociology*, Vol. 106, No. 4, January 2001

47 Portes, Alejandro/Landolt, Patricia: "The downside of social capital." In: *The American prospect*. 1996, 26, pp. 18–21

48 Portes, A./Sensenbrenner, J.: "Embeddedness and immigration: notes on the social determinants of economic action." In: *American journal of sociology*. 1993, vol. 98.6, pp. 1320–1350, p. 1338

49 Olson, M.: *The Rise and Decline of Nations*. New Haven 1982

50 Knack, Stephen/Keefer, Philip: "Does social capital have an economic pay-off? A cross country investigation." In: *Quarterly journal of economics*. 1997, vol. 112.4, pp. 1251–1288

51 Shlapentokh, Vladimir: *Public and Private Life of the Soviet People*. New York 1989

52 Sik, Endre/Toth, Istvan Janos: "Some elements of the hidden economy in Hungary today." In: Kolosi, Tamas/Toth, Istvan Janos/Vukovich, Gyorgy (eds.): *Social Report 1998*. Budapest 1999, p. 100. See also Sik, E. (1994): "Network capital in capitalist, Communist and post-Communist societies." In: *International Contributions to Labor Studies*, No. 4, pp. 73–93

53 Goldman, Marshall I.: *The Piratisation of Russia: Russian Reform Goes Awry*. New York 2003

54 Fedderke et al. (1999) address three puzzles associated with the concept of social capital. First, they pose the question whether more social capital is always better for purposes of economic growth (non linearity issue), whether over time economic development may bring the need for different forms of social capital (dynamic puzzle) and whether any society at a given point in time is likely to be characterised by rival, competing forms of social capital, and that it matters which comes to predominate (local optima puzzle). See Fedderke, J./De Kadt, R./Luiz, J.: "Economic growth and social capital: a critical reflection." In: *Theory and Society*. 1999, vol. 28, pp. 709–745

55 Clubs and circles may in turn transform into ambitious cliques thus creating "parallel power systems." Wedel, Janine R.: *Collision and Collusion: The Strange Case of Western Aid to Eastern Europe 1989—1998*. New York 1998

56 My research was prompted by the question "what kind of networks existed under the Soviet regime and do they continue to exist", see Ledeneva, as in footnote2

privilegierte Gruppen (*state capture*) sieht nur geringe Tendenzen für eine Öffnung in Russland.[65]

▸ Es besteht in Russland ein ausgeprägtes Interesse, den Einfluss der persönlichen und geschlossenen Netzwerke zu erhalten, folglich ist der Widerstand gegen eine Integration Russlands in die internationale Gemeinschaft groß. Im politischen Klima Russlands verhindert die Abgeschlossenheit der Netzwerke eine Internationalisierung sowie einen grundlegenden Wandel, und es ist eher so, dass sich diese Netzwerke durch die eigene Reproduktion (und der Bindungen an das staatliche System, das diese ursprünglich hat stark werden lassen) anpassen und die Formen ihrer Integration in das politische und wirtschaftliche System neu gestalten und verstärken. Diese Formen müssen in Betracht gezogen werden, wenn man verstehen will, warum zum Beispiel *guanxi*- und *blat*-Netzwerke, die oberflächlich betrachtet in gleicher Weise in die zentralisierten Staatssysteme Chinas und Russlands integriert waren, jetzt in dem einen Staat einen *guanxi*-Kapitalismus hervorbringen und dabei Netzwerkkapazitäten nutzen, um die staatlichen Reformen zu stützen, während sie in dem anderen Staat die staatliche Autorität unterminieren.

ANMERKUNGEN

1 Stiglitz, Joseph: *Globalisation and its Discontents*. New York 2002

2 Ledeneva, Alena: *Russia's Economy of Favours*. Cambridge 1998

3 Studien über Netzwerke sind ein umfassendes und multidisziplinäres Forschungsfeld. Die Hauptrichtung „Analyse sozialer Netzwerke" beruht auf einer spezifischen Technik zur Analyse von Netzwerkdaten. Sie bezieht sich auf Konzepte von Zentralität, Kohäsion, Zentren, Prestige, Rollenverhalten, persönliche und berufliche Bindungen in der Ressourcenallokation usw. (siehe zum Beispiel Wellman B./Berkowitz, S. D.: *Social Structures: A Network Approach*. Cambridge 1988). Netzwerkanalysen beschäftigen sich mit den Fragen, wie Menschen in verschiedenen Netzwerken verortet werden können und wie abgeschätzt werden kann, wen sie kennen, was sie wissen, zu welchen Ressourcen sie Zugang haben und welche sozialen Zwänge ihr Verhalten beeinflussen. Netzwerkanalysen nutzen die Graphentheorie und Modelle wie p1 und verwandte Verfahren. Es wurden Software-Anwendungen zur Netzwerkanalyse wie UCINET und Krackplot entwickelt. Das Forschungsfeld entwickelte sich besonders in den USA und in Großbritannien und erreichte einen hohen Formalisierungsgrad (siehe zum Beispiel Wasserman, S./ Faust, D.: *Social Network Analysis: Methods and Applications*, CUP, 1994). Die Analyse sozialer Netzwerke ist in Wirtschaftsstudien und im Management ebenfalls weit verbreitet, siehe zum Beispiel Barabasi, Albert-Laszlo: *Linked: The New Science of Networks*. Perseus, 2002.

4 Sik, Endre/Wellman, Barry: „Network capital in capitalist, communist and post-communist countries". In: Wellman, Barry (Hg.): *Networks in the Global Village*. Boulder, CO, 1999, S. 225–255

5 Granovetter, Mark: „The strength of weak ties". In: *American Journal of Sociology*. Band 78, 1973, S. 1360–1380; ders.: „Economic action and social structure: the problem of embeddedness". In: ebd., Band 91, 1985, S. 481–510

6 Ein wirtschaftlicher Akteur kann eine Person, eine Familie, eine Organisation, ein Staat usw. sein.

7 Polanyi, K.: *The Great Transformation*. New York 1944

8 Sik/Wellman, wie Fußnote 4

9 Lonkila, Markku: *Social Networks in Post-Soviet Russia*. Helsinki 1999; Risto, Alapuro: „Categories, networks and civil society: teachers' social ties in St Petersburg". In: *Civil Society in the European North: Concept and Context*. St. Petersburg 1996, S. 109–116

10 Li Bennich-Bjorkman zeigt zum Beispiel Unterschiede in der Vereinnahmung des Staates in den Baltischen Ländern; sie weist nach, dass „alte" Netzwerke (Antikommunisten, Studentenbewegung) in Estland zu einer Entwicklung politischer Parteien und transparenter Wirtschaft beigetragen haben, während „neue" Netzwerke in Lettland Grund für Exklusivität und Korruption wurden. Siehe dazu Bennich-Bjorkman, Li: „Explaining State Capture in Estonia and Latvia: Identity, International Role Models and Political Formation". In: *The Baltics: Culture, Society, Politics*, 2002

57 Castells, M.: *The Rise of Network Society*. Oxford 1996

58 Castells, M./Kizelyova, E. (1998): "Russia and the network society: an analytical exploration", paper prepared for the Conference on "Russia at the End of the 20th Century", School of Humanities and Sciences, Stanford University, 5–7 November, available on the website www.stanford.edu.

59 See Li Bennich-Bjorkman's research of the networks of political elite in Latvia as in footnote 10

60 Kasianova, Kseniya: *O Russkom Natsional'nom Kharaktere*. Moskva 1994

61 See Volkov, Vadim: *Violent Entrepreneurship*. Ithaca, NY 2002

62 See Pleines, Heiko: "Large-Scale Corruption in the Russian Banking Sector" and other articles in Ledeneva, Alena/Kurkchiyan, Marina: *Economic Crime in Russia*. Kluwer Law International, 2000

63 Woolcock (1998) as in footnote 34 uses the term "amoral familism" to describe the presence of social integration within a group but no linkages outside this group. In his view, "amoral familism" undermines the efficiency of all forms of economic exchange by increasing transaction costs. On the other hand there is amoral individualism. In this case there is no familial or generalised trust at all and only narrow self-interested individuals exist. Individuals are not embedded in a cohesive social network. The term first used in Banfield, Edward: *The Moral Basis of a Backward Society*. Chicago 1958

64 See Ledeneva, A.: "Informal networks and civil society in post-Soviet society." In: *Pro et Contra*. Special issue on Civil Society, Fall 1997

65 See the types of firms in the survey by Hellman, Joel/Jones, Geraint/Kaufmann, Daniel/Shankerman, Mark: *Measuring Governance, Corruption, and State Capture*. World Bank Paper, April 2000

LITERATURE

Baker, Wayne E.: "Illicit Networks". In: *American Sociological Review*. Vol. 58, 1993, pp. 837–860

Baker, Wayne E.: *Achieving Success Through Social Capital*. Jossey-Bass, 2000

Biggart, N.W./M.F. Guillén: "Developing difference: social organisation and the rise of the auto industries of South Korea, Taiwan, Spain and Argentina". In: *American sociological review*, vol. 64, 1999, p. 722–747

Bovenberg, L.: "On the cutting edge between policy and academia: challenges for public economists". In: *De Economist*, vol. 148.3, 2000, pp. 295–329

Buchanan, Mark: *Nexus: The Groundbreaking Science of Networks*. New York 2002

Cohen, Don /Prusak, Laurence: *In Good Company: How Social Capital Makes Organizations Work*. Watertown, MA 2001

Coleman, J.S.: *Foundations of social theory*. Cambridge 1990

Coleman, J. S. : "The Rational Reconstruction of Society". In: *American Sociological Review* 58, 1993, pp.1–15

Coles, N.: "It's not What you Know-It's Who You Know that Counts." In: *British Journal of Criminology*. 41, 2001, pp. 580–594

Foley, Michael W./Edwards, Bob: "Beyond Tocqueville: Civil Society and Social Capital in Comparative Perspective." In: *American Behavioral Scientist* 42, 1998, 1: 5–20

Foley, Michael W./Edwards, Bob: "The Paradox of Civil Society." In: *Journal of Democracy* (Summer 1996), 7,3: 38–52

Foley, Michael W./Edwards, Bob: "Escape from Politics? Social Theory and the Social Capital Debate." In: *American Behavioral Scientist* 40,6, 1997, pp. 550–561

Fukuyama, Francis: "Social Capital and the Global Economy." In: *Foreign Affairs*. September/October 1995, pp. 89–103

Glasmeier, A.: "Technological discontinuities and flexible production: the case of Switzerland and the world watch industry." In: *Research policy*, vol. 20, 1991, pp. 469–485

Grabher, G.: "The weakness of strong ties: the lock-in of regional development in the Ruhr area." In: Grabher, G. (ed.): *The embedded firm, on the socioeconomics of industrial networks*. London 1993, pp. 255–277

Inglehart, R./Baker, W.: "Modernization, cultural change and the persistence of traditional values." In: *American sociological review*, vol. 65, 2000, pp. 19–51

McAndrew, D.: "The Structural Analysis of Criminal Networks." In: Canter, D./Alison, L. (eds.): *The Social Psychology of Crime*. Aldershot 1999, pp. 52–92.

North, D.C.: "Institutions." In: *Journal of economic perspectives*, 5.1, 1991, pp. 97–112.

Padgett, John/Bonacich, Philip/Skvoretz, John/Scott, J.: *Social Network Analysis*. Chicago 2000

Platteau, J.P.: "Behind the market stage, where real societies exist, Part II: The role of moral norms." In: *Journal of development studies*, vol. 30.3, 1994, pp. 753–817

11 Der instrumentelle Gebrauch von Netzwerken wird von seinen Mitgliedern normalerweise nicht anerkannt. Der Aspekt der Nichtanerkennung wird in diesem Artikel nicht behandelt. Für Einzelheiten hierzu siehe auch Ledeneva, wie Fußnote 2

12 Wellman, B. (Hg.): *Networks in the Global Village*. Boulder, CO, 1999, S. 4–12

13 Sik/Wellman, wie Fußnote 4

14 Bourdieu, Pierre: „The Forms of Capital". In: Richardson, John G. (Hg.): *Handbook of Theory and Research for the Sociology of Education*. New York 1986, S. 248 f.

15 Coleman, J. S.: „Social capital in the creation of human capital". In: *American Journal of Sociology*. Band 94, 1988, S. 95–120, hier S. 98

16 Putnam, Robert D./Leonardi, R./Nanetti, R. Y.: *Making Democracy Work: Civic Traditions in Modern Italy*. Princeton, New Jersey 1993, S. 167

17 Putnam, Robert D.: „Tuning In, Tuning Out: The Strange Disappearance of Social Capital in America." In: *PS*. Heft 28 (4), 1995, S. 664–683, hier S. 664 f.

18 Bourdieu, Pierre/Wacquant, Loïc: *An Introduction to Reflexive Sociology*. Chicago 1992, S. 119

19 Bourdieu 1986, siehe Fußnote 14, S. 249

20 Siehe Putnam 1993, wie in Fußnote 16 und Putnam, Robert D.: „Bowling Alone: America's Declining Social Capital". In: *Journal of Democracy*. Heft 6 (1), 1995, S. 65–78

21 Bebbington, A./Perreault, T.: „Social capital, development and access to resources in highland Ecuador". In: *Economic geography*. Band 75.4, 1999, S. 395–418; Portes, A./Sensenbrenner, J.: „Embeddedness and immigration: notes on the social determinants of economic action". In: *American Journal of Sociology*. Band 98.6, 1993, S. 1320–1350

22 Coleman 1988, wie in Fußnote 15, hier S. 98 und S. 105

23 Burt, R.: „The social structure of competition". In: Nohria, N./ Eccles, R. (Hg.): *Networks and organisations, structure, form and action*. Boston, MA 1992; Burt, Ronald S.: „The Contingent Value of Social Capital". In: *Administrative Science Quarterly*. 42, 1997, S. 339–365

24 *Collins Cobuild English Language Dictionary*. London/Glasgow 1987, S. 966. Siehe auch Wellman, B./ Berkowitz, S. D.: *Social Structures: A Network Approach*. Cambridge 1988

25 Held, D./McGrew, A./Goldblatt, D./Perraton, J.: *Global Transformations: Politics, Economics and Culture*. (Ort???) 1999, S. 259–282

26 Castells, Manuel: *The Rise of Network Society*. Oxford 1996, S. 165

27 Messner, Dirk: *The Network Society: Economic Development and International Competitiveness as problems of Social Governance*. London 1997

28 Perkmann, M.: „The two network societies". In: *Economy and Society*. Band 28, Nr. 4, 1999, S. 615–628, hier S. 620

29 Stark, David/Vedres, Balazs: *The social times of networks spaces: sequence analysis of network formation and foreign investment*. Vorgestellt auf dem Workshop über Netzwerke und Märkte (Santa Fe Institute, Mai 2003). Zitiert aus dem Manuskript, S. 4

30 Polanyi, Karl: „The Economy as Instituted Process". In: Polanyi, Karl/Arensberg, Conrad/Pearson H. (Hg.): *Trade and Market in the Early Empires*. Glencoe, IL, 1957, S. 243–270; Wellman, Barry/Wortley, Scot: „Different Strokes from Different Folks: Community Ties and Social Support". In: *American Journal of Sociology*. Heft 96, 1990, S. 558–588

31 Siehe Plattner, Stuart: „Economic Behaviour in Markets". In: ders. (Hg.): *Economic Anthropology*. Stanford 1989, S. 210–221; White, Harrison: *Identity and Control*. Princeton 1992

32 Siehe Macaulay, Stewart: „Non-Contractual Relations in Business: A Preliminary Study". In: Granovetter, Mark/Swedberg, Richard: *The Sociology of Economic Life*. Boulder 1992, S. 265–283; Burt, Ronald S.: *Structural Holes*. Chicago 1992

33 Die Begriffe „positiv" und „negativ" sind in Anführungszeichen gesetzt, da die Beurteilung von der Übereinstimmung der Netzwerk- und Wirtschaftsinteressen sowie von der konkreten Perspektive abhängt. So kann zum Beispiel eine Begrenzung der individuellen Entwicklung durch eine Gruppe oder Gemeinschaft nicht nur als negativ gesehen werden. Untersuchungen über Stress haben gezeigt, dass dieser in so genannten „zersplitterten" Gesellschaften wesentlich größer ist als in netzwerkbasierten Gesellschaften, in denen das Individuum durch Regeln des Netzwerkes eingeschränkt sein kann.

34 Woolcock, Michael: „Social Capital and Economic Development: Toward a Theoretical Synthesis and Policy Framework". In: *Theory and Society*. Heft 27, 1998, S. 151–208, hier S. 165

35 Die Bildung und die Funktionen von Netzwerken spiegeln sich auf gewisse Art in der Struktur wieder (Knotenpunkte, Verbindungen und „Unterhaltskosten" des Netzwerkes), was näher erläutert werden muss: Ob man ein Netzwerk erbt oder in ein selbst geschaffenes Netzwerk investiert, beeinflusst die Bindungen, die Knotenpunkte und die Funktionen dieses Netzwerkes. Ob die Geschäftsbeziehung das Ergebnis eines existierenden Netzwerkes oder das Netzwerk das Ergebnis einer Geschäftsbeziehung

Platteau, J.P.: "Behind the market stage, where real societies exist, Part I: the role of public and private order institutions:" In: *Journal of development studies*, vol. 30.3, 1994a, pp. 533–577
Portes, Alejandro: "Social Capital: Its Origins and Applications in Modern Sociology." In: *Annual Review of Sociology*, 24, 1998, pp.1–24
Putnam, Robert D.:*Making Democracy Work: Civic Traditions in Modern Italy*. Princeton, NJ 1993Putnam, Robert D.: "The Strange Disappearance of Civic America." In: *American Prospect*, 24 (Winter 1996), pp. 34–48
Shapiro, S.P.: "The social control of impersonal trust." In: *American journal of sociology*, vol. 93.3, 1987, pp. 623—658
Sparrow, M.: "The Application of Network Analysis to Criminal Intelligence: An assessment of the Prospects." In: *Social Networks*. 13, 1991, pp. 251–274
Skocpol, Theda: "Unraveling From Above." In: *The American Prospect*, 25, 1996, pp. 20–25
Tilly, Charles:*Durable Inequality*. Berkeley/Los Angeles 1998
Uzzi, B.: "The sources and consequences of embeddedness for the economic performance of organisations: the network effect." In: *American sociological review*, vol. 61.4, 1996, pp. 674–698
Uzzi, B.: "Social structure and competition in interfirm networks: the paradox of embeddedness." In: *Administrative science quarterly*, vol. 42, 1997, pp. 35–67
Wall, Ellen/Ferrazzi, Gabriele/Schryer, Frans: "Getting the goods on social capital," *Rural Sociology*, 63,2, 1998, pp. 300–322.

ist, ist vielleicht nicht die wichtigste Frage. Viel wichtiger ist es, den dynamischen Prozess zu beobachten, bei dem soziale Beziehungen die Entwicklung von Marktinstitutionen erleichtern oder verhindern.

36 Fainsod, Merle: *How Russia is Ruled*. Cambridge, MA 1963

37 Getty, J. Arch: *Origins of the Great Purge: The Soviet Communist party Reconsidered, 1933–1938*. New York 1986

38 Rigby, T. H.: „Early provincial cliques and the rise of Stalin". In: *Soviet Studies*. Jg. 33, Nr. 1, Januar 1981; ders.: „Was Stalin a disloyal patron?". In: *Soviet Studies*. Jg. 38, Nr. 3, Juli 1986

39 Gill, Graeme: *The Origins of the Stalinist Political System*. New York 1990

40 Easter, Gerald M.: *Reconstructing the State: Personal Networks and Elite Identity in Soviet Russia*. Cambridge 1999

41 Mit den Worten Bourdieus ausgedrückt, bestehen solche impliziten Verträge aus „institutionalisieren Riten" und Geschenken, „durch die zufällige Beziehungen in der Nachbarschaft, am Arbeitsplatz oder sogar in der Verwandtschaft sich in Beziehungen verwandeln, die *zugleich notwendig und ausgesucht* sind und subjektiv empfundene dauerhafte Verpflichtungen schaffen". Bourdieu 1986 wie in Fußnote 14, S. 249 f. (Hervorhebung durch die Autorin)

42 Siehe Ledeneva, Alena: „Genealogy of *krugovaya poruka*: forced trust as a feature of Russian political culture". In: Markova, I. (Hg.): *Trust and Democratic Transition in Post-Communist Europe*. Oxford 2004

43 Portes/Sensenbrenner, 1993, wie in Fußnote 21

44 Meyerson, E. M.: „Human capital, social capital and compensation: the relative contribution of social contacts to managers' incomes". In: *Acta sociologica*. Band 37, 1994, S. 383–399

45 Bei einer Untersuchung des Banksektors fand Uzzi, dass Firmen eher Kredite und diese zu niedrigeren Zinsen erhalten, wenn ihr Verbindungsnetz zu den Banken eine Mischung aus eingebetteten und außen-, aber nicht fernstehenden Beziehungen aufweist. Siehe Uzzi, B.: „Embeddedness in the making of financial capital: how social relations and networks benefit firms seeking financing". In: *American Sociological Review*. Band 64.4, 1999, S. 481–505

46 Stark, David/Bruszt, Laszlo (Hg.): *Postsocialist Pathways: transforming Politics and property in East Central Europe*. Cambridge 1998, S. 7 f., S. 82 f.; dies.: „One Way or Multiple Paths? For a Comparative Sociology of European Capitalism". In: *American Journal of Sociology*. Band 106, Nr. 4, Januar 2001

47 Portes, Alejandro/Landolt, Patricia: „The downside of social capital". In: *The American prospect*. Heft 26, 1996, S. 18–21

48 Portes/Sensenbrenner, 1993, wie in Fußnote 21, hier S. 1338

49 Olson, M.: *The Rise and Decline of Nations*. New Haven 1982

50 Knack, Stephen/Keefer, Philip: „Does social capital have an economic pay-off? A cross country investigation". In: *Quarterly journal of economics*. Band 112.4, 1997, S. 1251–1288

51 Shlapentokh, Vladimir: *Public and Private Life of the Soviet People*. New York 1989

52 Sik, Endre/Toth, Istvan Janos: „Some elements of the hidden economy in Hungary today". In: Kolosi, Tamas/Toth, Istvan Janos/Vukovich, Gyorgy (Hg.): *Social Report 1998*. Budapest 1999, S. 100. Siehe auch Sik, Endre: „Network capital in capitalist, Communist and post-Communist societies". In: *International Contributions to Labor Studies*. Heft 4, 1994, S. 73–93

53 Goldman, Marshall I.: *The Piratisation of Russia: Russian Reform Goes Awry*. New York 2003

54 Fedderke et al. (1999) benennen drei Puzzles, die mit dem Konzept des sozialen Kapitals verknüpft sind. Zuerst stellen sie die Frage, ob ein Mehr an sozialem Kapital stets besser für das wirtschaftliche Wachstum ist (Problem der Nicht-Linearität), ob wirtschaftliche Entwicklung mit der Zeit den Bedarf nach einer Differenzierung von Formen sozialen Kapitals weckt (dynamisches Puzzle) und ob jede Gesellschaft zu einem gegebenen Zeitpunkt über rivalisierende, wettbewerbsorientierte Formen sozialen Kapitals charakterisiert wird. Dabei ist dann entscheidend, welche die Vorherrschaft übernimmt (Puzzle des lokalen Optimums). Siehe hierzu Fedderke, J./De Kadt, R./Luiz, J.: „Economic growth and social capital: a critical reflection". In: *Theory and Society*. Band 28, 1999, S. 709–745

55 Klubs und Zirkel wiederum können sich in ambitionierte Cliquen verwandeln, die so „parallele Machtstrukturen" aufbauen. Wedel, Janine R.: *Collision and Collusion: The Strange Case of Western Aid to Eastern Europe 1989–1998*. New York 1998

56 Meine Untersuchung ging von der Frage aus: „Welche Arten von Netzwerken gab es unter den Bedingungen des sowjetischen Regimes und existieren diese weiterhin?" Siehe dazu Ledeneva, 1998 wie in Fußnote 2

57 Castells, Manuel: *The Rise of Network Society*. Oxford 1996

58 Castells, Manuel/Kizelyova, E.: „Russia and the network society: an analytical exploration". Beitrag zur Konferenz: „Russia at the End of the 20th Century". Stanford University, 5.–7. November 1998. http://www.stanford.edu

59 Vgl. die Untersuchung von Li Bennich-Bjorkman zu den Netzwerken der politischen Elite Lettlands, wie in Fußnote 10

60 Kasianova, Kseniya: *O Russkom Natsional'nom Kharaktere.* Moskau 1994

61 Siehe Volkov, Vadim: *Violent Entrepreneurship.* Ithaca, NY 2002

62 Siehe Pleines, Heiko: „Large-Scale Corruption in the Russian Banking Sector", sowie andere Artikel in: Ledeneva, Alena/Kurkchiyan, Marina: *Economic Crime in Russia.* 2000

63 Woolcock (1998, wie in Fußnote 34) benutzt den Begriff der „unmoralischen Familiarität", um die soziale Integration in eine Gruppe ohne Außenverbindungen zu beschreiben. Seiner Ansicht nach untergräbt unmoralische Familiarität die Effizienz aller Formen wirtschaftlichen Austausches durch steigende Transaktionskosten. Auf der anderen Seite steht der unmoralische Individualismus. In diesem Fall gibt es weder familiäres noch generalisiertes Vertrauen, sondern nur egozentrische Individuen, die nicht in zusammenhaltende soziale Netzwerke eingespannt sind. Banfield, Edward: *The Moral Basis of a Backward Society.* Chicago 1958, benutzte diesen Ausdruck zuerst.

64 Siehe Ledeneva, Alena: „Informal networks and civil society in post-Soviet society". In: *Pro et Contra.* Sonderausgabe zur Zivilgesellschaft, Herbst 1997

65 Siehe die Unternehmensarten in der Untersuchung von Hellman, Joel/Jones, Geraint/Kaufmann, Daniel/Shankerman, Mark: *Measuring Governance, Corruption, and State Capture.* World Bank Paper, April 2000

LITERATUR

Baker, Wayne E.: „Illicit Networks". In: *American Sociological Review.* Band 58, 1993, S. 837–860

Baker, Wayne E.: *Achieving Success Through Social Capital.* Jossey-Bass, 2000

Biggart, N. W./Guillén, M. F.: „Developing difference: social organisation and the rise of the auto industries of South Korea, Taiwan, Spain and Argentina". In: *American sociological review.* Band 64, 1999, S. 722–747

Bovenberg, L.: „On the cutting edge between policy and academia: challenges for public economists". In: *De Economist.* Band 148.3, 2000, S. 295–329

Buchanan, Mark: *Nexus: The Groundbreaking Science of Networks.* New York 2002

Coleman, J. S.: *Foundations of social theory,* Cambridge 1990

Coleman, James: „The Rational Reconstruction of Society". In: *American Sociological Review.* 58, 1993, S. 1–15

Coles, N.: „It's not What you Know-It's Who You Know that Counts". In: *British Journal of Criminology.* 41, 2001, S. 580–594

Don Cohen/Prusak, Laurence: *In Good Company: How Social Capital Makes Organizations Work.* Watertown, MA 2001

Foley, Michael W./Edwards, Bob: „Beyond Tocqueville: Civil Society and Social Capital in Comparative Perspective". In: *American Behavioral Scientist.* 42, 1981, S. 5–20

Foley, Michael W./Edwards, Bob: „The Paradox of Civil Society". In: *Journal of Democracy.* Sommer 1996, 7,3, S. 38–52

Foley, Michael W./Edwards, Bob: „Escape from Politics? Social Theory and the Social Capital Debate". In: *American Behavioral Scientist.* 40,6, 1997, S. 550–561

Fukuyama, Francis: „Social Capital and the Global Economy". In: *Foreign Affairs.* September/Oktober 1995, S. 89–103

Glasmeier, A.: „Technological discontinuities and flexible production: the case of Switzerland and the world watch industry". In: *Research policy.* 1991, Band 20, S. 469–485

Grabher, G.: „The weakness of strong ties: the lock-in of regional development in the Ruhr area". In: Grabher, G. (Hg.): *The embedded firm, on the socioeconomics of industrial networks.* London 1993, S. 255–277

Inglehart, R./Baker, W.: „Modernization, cultural change and the persistence of traditional values". In: *American sociological review.* Band 65, 2000, S. 19–51

John Padgett/Bonacich, Philip (UCLA)/Skvoretz, John/Scott, J.: *Social Network Analysis.* Chicago 2000

McAndrew, D.: „The Structural Analysis of Criminal Networks". In: D. Canter/Alison, L. (Hg.): *The Social Psychology of Crime.* Aldershot 1999, S. 52–92

North, D. C.: „Institutions". In: *Journal of economic perspectives.* 1991, 5.1, S. 97–112

Platteau, J. P.: „Behind the market stage, where real societies exist, Part II: The role of moral norms". In: *Journal of development studies.* 1994, Band 30.3, S. 753–817

Platteau, J. P.: „Behind the market stage, where real societies exist, Part I: the role of public and private order institutions". In: *Journal of development studies.* 1994a, Band 30.3, S. 533–577

Portes, Alejandro: „Social Capital: Its Origins and Applications in Modern Sociology". In: *Annual Review of Sociology.* 1998, 24, S. 1–24

Putnam, Robert D.: *Making Democracy Work: Civic Traditions in Modern Italy.* Princeton, New Jersey 1993

Putnam, Robert D.: „The Strange Disappearance of Civic America". In: *American Prospect.* 24 (Winter 1996), S. 34–48

Shapiro, S. P.: „The social control of impersonal trust". In: *American journal of sociology.* 1987, Band 93.3, S. 623–658

Skocpol, Theda: „Unraveling From Above". In: *The American Prospect.* 1996, 25, S. 20–25

Sparrow, M.: „The Application of Network Analysis to Criminal Intelligence: An assessment of the Prospects". In: *Social Networks.* 1991, 13, S. 251–74

Tilly, Charles: „Durable Inequality". Berkeley/Los Angeles 1998

Uzzi, B.: „The sources and consequences of embeddedness for the economic performance of organisations: the network effect". In: *American sociological review.* 1996, Band 61.4, S. 674–698

Uzzi, B.: „Social structure and competition in interfirm networks: the paradox of embeddedness". In: *Administrative science quarterly.* Band 42, 1997, S. 35–67

Wall, Ellen/Ferrazzi, Gabriele /Schryer, Frans: „Getting the goods on social capital". In: *Rural Sociology.* 63,2, 1998, S. 300–322

СУМКИ
СУМКИ
Овощи
фрукты

INFORMELLE ÖKONOMIE? LASSEN SIE UNS LIEBER ÜBER EXTRAPOLARE WIRTSCHAFT SPRECHEN.

TEODOR SHANIN IM GESPRÄCH MIT JOANNE RICHARDSON UND REGINA BITTNER

Teodor Shanin ist einer der bedeutendsten Theoretiker der „Kleinbauernstudien" (*peasantology*) und untersucht seit vielen Jahren die Lebensumstände der russischen Bauernschaft und die Dynamik der informellen Wirtschaft. Aus seiner Feder stammen *Die informelle Wirtschaft: Russland und die Welt* (in Russisch), *Defining Peasants* (1990), *The Theory of Peasant Economy* (1986), das zweibändige Werk *Russia as a Developing Society* (1986) und *Revolution as a Moment of Truth* (1987), *Late Marx and the Russian Road* (1984), *The Awkward Class* (1972) und *Peasants and Peasant Societies* (1971). Er wurde in Vilnius geboren, studierte Soziologie in Jerusalem und Birmingham, wirkte 25 Jahre lang als Professor für Soziologie an der Universität Manchester und ist jetzt Rektor der Moskauer Graduiertenuniversität für Sozial- und Wirtschaftswissenschaften (Moscow School of Social and Economic Sciences).

JR: Können Sie uns erklären, was man unter informeller Wirtschaft versteht?

TS: Es handelt sich um ein Wirtschaftssystem, das nicht wie etwa der Kapitalismus auf Gewinnmaximierung und Profitieren von der Arbeit anderer beruht, sondern auf der Sicherung des wirtschaftlichen Überlebens auf verschiedenen Wegen, unter anderem durch die Ausnutzung kultureller oder familiärer Beziehungen. Dazu gehören zum Beispiel Kreditvergabe innerhalb der Verwandtschaft, Beschäftigung von Familienmitgliedern usw. Darum ist die Familie die zentrale Einheit eines solchen Wirtschaftsystems. Tschajanow hat eine umfangreiche Analyse der Familienwirtschaft vorgelegt und herausgearbeitet, in welchen Bereichen sie sich vom kapitalistischen oder planwirtschaftlichen System unterscheidet. Ich denke, dass seine Theorie und seine Modelle immer noch gültig sind. Sie sind die beste verfügbare Methode zum Verständnis der informellen Wirtschaft. Mit der üblichen Unterscheidung zwischen staatlich gelenktem und kapitalistischem System lässt sich die Frage, was eine natürliche Wirtschaft ist, nicht zufriedenstellend beantworten. Eine Unterteilung in große und kleine Wirtschaftseinheiten trägt ebenfalls nicht viel zur Erklärung der informellen Wirtschaft bei.

JR: Sie sagten in einem früheren Interview, dass die informelle Wirtschaft weder kapitalistisch noch kommunistisch sei. Können Sie uns erklären, was Sie damit meinten?

TS: Ich meinte damit, dass sie im Wesentlichen eine Familienwirtschaft ist. Sie agiert innerhalb eines Netzes, das größer als das der Familie ist, da es Freundschaften und ähnliche Beziehungen mit einschließt. Es ist eine parallele Ökonomie, die weder kapitalistisch noch kommunistisch ist, da sie sich sowohl im kapitalistischen als auch im sowjetischen System herausbilden konnte. Und sie hat ja in der Tat in beiden Systemen bestanden und kann sich in anderen Systemen ebenfalls entwickeln. Hier finde ich Tschajanow sehr nützlich: Anstatt die Wirtschaftssysteme verschiedener Länder zu definieren (dieser ist ein kommunistischer, jener ein kapitalistischer oder ein feudaler Staat), spricht er von grundlegenden ökonomischen Modellen und geht davon aus, dass unterschiedliche Wirtschaftssysteme dieser Art nebeneinander existieren und in Wechselbeziehung zueinander treten können, was ja auch tatsächlich geschieht. Selbst in einem Land mit dem Kapitalismus als vorherrschender Wirtschaftsform heißt das nicht, dass alle Wirtschaftsformen in diesem Land kapitalistisch sind. Es gibt „Inseln", die anders sind und nach ihrer eigenen Logik funktionieren. Auch in sozialistischen Wirtschaftssystemen oder, besser gesagt, in

INFORMAL ECONOMY? LET US RATHER TALK ABOUT EXPOLARY ECONOMY.

TEODOR SHANIN IN CONVERSATION WITH JOANNE RICHARDSON AND REGINA BITTNER

Teodor Shanin is one of the most important theorists of what has become known as "peasantology" and a long-time researcher into the life of the Russian peasantry and the dynamics of the informal economy. He is the author of Informal Economies: *Russia and the World* (in Russian), *Defining Peasants* (1990), *The Theory of Peasant Economy* (1986), the two-volume work *Russia as a Developing Society* (1986) and *Revolution as a Moment of Truth* (1987), *Late Marx and the Russian Road* (1984), *The Awkward Class* (1972), and *Peasants and Peasant Societies* (1971). Born in Vilnius, he studied sociology in Jerusalem and Birmingham, served for a quarter of a century as Professor of Sociology at the University of Manchester and is currently the rector of a post-graduate university, the Moscow School of Social and Economic Sciences.

JR: Can you explain what the informal economy is?

TS: It's an economic system that is not based, as capitalism is, on the maximization of profit and the use of the labour of others, but rather on solving economic problems of survival through a variety of methods – partly cultural, partly family relations. It includes such things as credit on a kinship basis, employment on a family basis, etc. That is why the core unit of such an economy is the family. Chayanov created a systematic analysis of the family economy and ways in which the family economy is different from a capitalist economy or a state planned economy. I think his theory and models are still valid and constitute the best method we have for understanding the informal economy. The usual division between state-run and capitalist economy doesn't quite answer the question about what a natural economy is. Its division between large and small economic units is not a division that explains much about the informal economy either.

JR: You said in an earlier interview that the informal economy is neither capitalist nor communist. Can you explain what you meant?

TS: I meant that it is fundamentally a family economy, within a network that is broader than a family because it includes friendships and these types of relations. It is a parallel economy, neither capitalist nor communist because it can thrive in both capitalism and in the Soviet system – indeed it has worked in both systems and can work in other systems as well. This is where I find Chayanov so useful because instead of defining different countries' economies – this one is communist, this is a capitalist or a feudal country – he spoke of fundamental economic models and assumed that various economies of this kind may work together and indeed do work together and interlink. Even in a country where there is a dominant economy like capitalism, this doesn't mean that all the economics in that country is capitalist. There are "islands" of something else, which operate under their own logic. Also, in a socialist economy, or better to call it a state-run economy, "other" economies can act in parallel. I would say indeed that the informal economy is a necessary element ... for the other types of economy; in the past if the informal economy of the Soviet Union had stopped, the Soviet Union would have collapsed economically. Also later, if all of a sudden the informal economy had stopped in the early 1990s in Russia, half the population would have died of hunger. By the way, I once suggested that "expolary" might be a much better definition than "informal" economy. But it wasn't accepted by the academic community, which had already adopted the word "informal economy", and I was not ready to spend time

Planwirtschaften existieren parallel „andere" Ökonomien. Ich will damit sagen, dass die informelle Wirtschaft in der Tat ein notwendiges Element für die anderen Bereiche der Wirtschaft ist. Die Sowjetunion wäre wirtschaftlich kollabiert, wenn ihre informelle Wirtschaft aufgehört hätte zu funktionieren. Und hätte später, Anfang der 1990er Jahre, die informelle Wirtschaft in Russland plötzlich ausgesetzt, wäre die Hälfte der Bevölkerung verhungert. Übrigens hatte ich einmal vorgeschlagen, dass die Bezeichnung „extrapolare Wirtschaft" sehr viel treffender wäre als „informelle Wirtschaft". Doch das wurde von der Wissenschaft nicht akzeptiert. Sie hatte bereits den Terminus „informelle Wirtschaft" angenommen, und ich war nicht bereit, meine Zeit mit dem Kampf um Worte zu verbringen. Ich benutzte „extrapolares Wirtschaftssystem", da man damals über zwei Pole sprach: das kapitalistische Wirtschaftssystem als Idealmodell der westlichen Welt und das planwirtschaftliche System als Idealmodell des sowjetischen Blocks. Wenn man eine solche Gesellschaft in einem Modell darstellen wollte, verglich man sie gewöhnlich mit Ländern, die dem einen oder dem andern Pol näher kamen. Gab es eine Krise, griff die Regierung zu „Reformen", d. h. die Wirtschaft des Landes wurde entweder in Richtung einer stärkeren staatlichen Kontrolle oder in Richtung einer Privatisierung umorientiert. Ich sprach daraufhin von einem dritten Wirtschaftstyp, den man normalerweise vergisst, obwohl die Mehrheit der Weltbevölkerung im Augenblick in ihm lebt. Und diese dritte Variante ist weder der Pol des Kapitalismus noch der Pol des Staates, noch irgendwo zwischen beiden Polen angesiedelt, sondern sie liegt außerhalb dieser Pole und ist daher „extrapolar".

JR: Für mich besteht die informelle Wirtschaft aus sehr verschiedenen Elementen. Dazu gehört zum Beispiel die informelle Arbeit, bei der Menschen unterhalb des Mindesteinkommens, als Saisonkräfte oder ohne soziale Absicherung arbeiten. Diese Arbeit ist unsicher, und es gibt gegenwärtig in den westeuropäischen Ländern die Tendenz, Frauen aus Rumänien oder anderen Staaten als Saisonarbeiterinnen ins Land zu holen. Sie erhalten sehr geringe Löhne und haben keine Verträge, die Arbeitsbedingungen sind wie in einem Gefängnis. Sie ist ein fester Bestandteil des kapitalistischen Wirtschaftssystems, da sich die Unternehmen zur Senkung ihrer Produktionskosten auf Staaten stützen müssen, die noch nicht oder noch nicht völlig kapitalistisch und somit eine Quelle billiger, informeller Arbeitskräfte sind. Auf der anderen Seite gibt es den Schwarzmarkt oder den Waffen- und Drogenhandel, der nicht nur informell, sondern einfach illegal ist. Viel Arbeit und viel Handel werden oft nicht registriert und ohne jedes Dokument abgewickelt. Da ist z. B. die landwirtschaftliche Produktion nur für den Eigenbedarf. Oder der Transithandel, der die ineffiziente Verteilung von Gütern ausnutzt, indem er sie billig in einem Land kauft und teurer in einem anderen verkauft. Betrachten Sie all diese sehr verschiedenen Aktivitäten als Teile der informellen Wirtschaft?

TS: Ja. Also, nicht wirklich alle, aber fast alle. Man kann sogar sagen, dass die informelle Wirtschaft die der familiären Überlebensstrategien ist. Aus der Sicht des Kapitalisten oder des Staates kann sie nicht richtig erfasst werden, obwohl beide die informellen Wirtschaftssysteme nutzen.
Wenn man sie mit den Augen von Unternehmern oder Behörden, also von oben nach unten betrachtet, nimmt man nur die Massen von Menschen wahr, die von den großen Wirtschaftssystemen kapitalistischer oder staatlicher Natur ausgenutzt werden. Doch wenn man sie von unten nach oben betrachtet, stellt man fest, dass es spezifische Arten von Wirtschaftssystemen gibt, die von den verschiedenen Aspekten familiärer Überlebensstrategien bestimmt werden. Das ist die informelle Wirtschaft unserer Zeit.

JR: Glauben Sie, dass die *blat*-Ökonomie, d. h. die Günstlingswirtschaft der sowjetischen Zeit, Teil der informellen Wirtschaft war?

TS: Ohne Zweifel war die *blat*-Ökonomie ein Teil der informellen Wirtschaft, obwohl ich sagen muss, dass einige ihrer Bereiche nicht zwangsläufig zu ihr gehörten. Oft war sie ein Teil der staatlichen Wirtschaft und sorgte dafür, dass diese funktionierte. Wie ich schon sagte, hängt das von der Perspektive ab, aus der man einen wirtschaftlichen Prozess betrachtet: Schaut man auf ihn mit den Augen der Mehrheit der Bevölkerung, die mit dem eigenen Überleben beschäftigt ist, oder schaut man mit den Augen eines Ökonomen, eines Unternehmers oder eines Politikers, die alle von oben auf diesen Prozess blicken und von denen James Scott sagte, dass sie „mit den Augen des Staates" die Dinge betrachten. Daher ist es nicht verwunderlich, dass die informelle Wirtschaft am klarsten gesehen wird

fighting over it. I used expolary economy because in those days people were speaking about two poles – the capitalist economy, which was the ideal model of the Western world, and the state economy, which was the ideal model of the Soviet bloc – and usually when you wanted to model such a society you described it on a scale with countries closer to one pole or the other. When a crisis hit a country, its government policies "reformed", i.e. moved it either in the direction of state control or in the direction of privatisation. What I said then was that there was a third type of economy, which people usually forget but in which the majority of the population of the world actually live. And the third possibility is neither the pole of capitalism nor the pole of the state, nor the movement in between the poles, but somewhere outside all this, so "ex-polar".

JR: For me there are very different elements that make up the informal economy. For instance, there is informal labour, which is people working below the minimum wage, or seasonally, or those who have no social guarantees. This is a kind of precarious work, and now there is a trend for Western European countries to use women from Romania and other countries for seasonal work, and they are paid really low wages, they don't have contracts, they are kept in almost prison conditions – and this is very much part of the capitalist economy because for corporations to be able to produce cheap commodities they need to rely on countries that are not yet or not quite yet capitalist as a source of cheap informal labour power. On the other hand there is also the black market, or the sale of arms and drugs, which is not just informal but illegal. There is a lot of unregistered and undocumented labour and trade. There is subsistence farming. There is the shuttle trade, which is managing inefficient flows of commodities, buying cheap in one country and selling more expensive in another. Do you think of all of these very different types of activities as part of the informal economy?

TS: Yes. Well, not absolutely everything, but most of it. You can even say that the informal economy is the economy that you see not from the point of view of a capitalist or a state that is exploiting informal economies, but that it is the economy of family strategies of survival. If you see it only through the eyes of the capitalists or state officials, so to speak from the top down, then all you see are masses of people used by large economies of a capitalist or state nature. But if you see it from the bottom up, you notice that these are specific types of economy, and there are categories that encompass various aspects of family strategy of survival. This is the informal economy of our times.

JR: Do you think *blat*, or the economy of favours and acquaintances, as it functioned during Soviet times was part of the informal economy?

TS: No doubt *blat* was part of the informal economy, though I must say that some of the *blat* was not necessarily informal economy. It was often part of the state economy, making sure that the state economy worked. It is, as I said, a question of through which eyes you look at the economic process. Do you look at the economic process through the eyes of the majority of the population, which is involved in surviving, or through the eyes of the economist, or the eyes of the owner, or the eyes of the politicians who all look at it from the top down (James Scott called it "seeing like the state"). This is why it's not accidental that the informal economy is seen most clearly ... by ethnographers and people who go "into the field". If you ask an economist "from above" what an informal economy is, it often disappears before him, as if he really doesn't see it. I saw it a short time ago – during a debate in the Duma – when the expression "informal economy" very slowly reached them, whereupon some economists and politicians seized on the idea and said, "How wonderful, let's tax it", quite forgetting that it relates to the poorest people and the worst problems politicians have failed to resolve.

von Ethnographen und von den Menschen, „die an die Basis gehen". Wenn man einen Ökonomen „von oben" fragt, was informelle Wirtschaft ist, kann er sie oft nicht beschreiben, es ist, als ob er sie wirklich nicht sieht. Ich konnte dies vor kurzem während einer Debatte in der Duma beobachten, als der Ausdruck „informelle Wirtschaft" sehr langsam in der Diskussion auftauchte, woraufhin einige Ökonomen und Politiker die Idee aufgriffen und sagten: „Wie wunderbar, das können wir besteuern", und dabei völlig vergaßen, dass die informelle Wirtschaft die ärmsten Menschen betrifft und etwas mit den schlimmsten Problemen zu tun hat, die eben diese Politiker zu lösen nicht in der Lage waren.

JR: Sie wissen doch aber, dass nun selbst der IWF alle möglichen Studien darüber hat, wie die informelle Wirtschaft funktioniert. Die führenden Institutionen des globalen Kapitalismus haben ein starkes Interesse an der informellen Wirtschaft im Allgemeinen und am Transithandel im Besonderen. Da in manchen Ländern der Anteil der informellen Wirtschaft beinahe 50 Prozent des BIP ausmacht, müssen sie die informelle Wirtschaft in Betracht ziehen und beobachten, um herauszufinden, wie sich diese Prozesse steuern lassen und wie man von ihnen profitieren kann.

TS: Dazu kann ich zwei Dinge sagen. Erstens hoffe ich, dass sie mit ihren Untersuchungen scheitern werden. Je klarer sie scheitern, desto besser werden die Menschen leben, besonders diejenigen, für die die informelle Wirtschaft ein Schutzschild ist. Zweitens würde ich Ihnen gern erläutern, wie meine Forschungsgruppe informelle Wirtschaftssysteme untersucht hat. Wir führten die Untersuchungen vor zehn Jahren in verschiedenen russischen Dörfern durch. Meine Kollegen, die die Felduntersuchungen durchführen sollten, gingen in diese Dörfer und lebten dort fast ein ganzes Jahr lang, ohne irgendwelche Forschungen zu betreiben, sondern nur, damit die Leute sie sehen und die Überzeugung gewinnen konnten, dass sie weder Staatsbeamte noch Betrüger oder Ganoven sind, sondern ganz normale Menschen, die gern mit ihnen lebten und die man sympathisch finden konnte. Ihre „Legende" war, dass sie die Geschichte des Dorfes schreiben wollten. Sie begannen, mit den Leuten zu arbeiten, und entwickelten schließlich ein System, in dem die Bauern ihre Einkommensverhältnisse usw. aufschrieben. Und dann passierte etwas sehr Interessantes. Von Mal zu Mal schien der Anteil der informellen Wirtschaft in der Familie zu steigen, nicht weil er wirklich anwuchs, sondern weil die Menschen meinen Kollegen mehr und mehr vertrauten und weil sie bereit waren, offen zu sprechen und ihnen ein Bild ihrer wahren Lage zu geben. Wir haben Budgetstudien von einer recht großen Anzahl von Familien, und ich werde sie nicht veröffentlichen, weil ich ein Humanist bin, oder ein Sozialist, oder wie heißt das jetzt?

JR: Sie sagten in einem früheren Interview, dass die informelle Wirtschaft den Menschen die Möglichkeit gebe, Herr ihres eigenen Lebens zu werden.

TS: Ja, aber man sollte das auch nicht überbewerten. Wie jede Aussage kann sie lächerlich oder falsch werden, wenn man sie zu weit treibt. Es dürfte jedem klar sein, dass die in der informellen Wirtschaft tätigen Menschen in den meisten Fällen zum ärmsten und mittellosesten Teil der Bevölkerung eines Landes gehören. Unter diesen Umständen ist es dumm, davon zu sprechen, dass man frei oder befreit sei, denn unter den Bedingungen der kapitalistischen Wirtschaft ist die eigene Freiheit oftmals das Geld, das man in der Tasche hat. Das ist jedoch nicht die ganze Wahrheit. Es gibt dazu noch eine zweite Geschichte. Wenn jemand ärmer ist als andere Mitglieder der Gesellschaft, ist die Tatsache, dass er selbst wirtschaftlich tätig werden kann, ein beträchtlicher Vorteil gegenüber anderen, die keine Möglichkeit zur Familienwirtschaft haben. Ich habe einige Zeit in den *favelas* von Rio de Janeiro gelebt. Mir wurde dutzende Male gesagt, ich solle nicht in die *favelas* gehen, da sie gefährlich und dreckig seien und dort schreckliche Menschen leben. Mir wurde das von Soziologen gesagt, die in ein oder zwei Kilometern Entfernung von den *favelas* lebten. Ich schloss mich trotzdem einigen Anthropologen an, die über die *favelas* arbeiteten. Eines wurde deutlich: Die Menschen in den *favelas* lebten häufig besser als die Industriearbeiter. Diese Leute sind ohne jeden Zweifel besser in der Lage, ihre Probleme zu lösen, und ihre autonomen Familienstrategien ermöglichen es ihnen, ihr Leben in ihrem Sinne zu gestalten. Wenn ich von staatlicher Seite um Rat gefragt werde, was denn mit „solchen Leuten" zu machen sei, gebe ich oft zur Antwort: Tun Sie bloß nichts, denn Ihr Eingreifen hat oft negative Folgen.

RB: Ich möchte noch einmal auf die Frage zurückkommen, wie die informelle Wirtschaft Bedingun-

JR: But you know that now even the International Monetary Fund has all kinds of studies about how the informal economy works, and its very strange for them to study such an imprecise thing because they can either study it by making a few thousand surveys and then abstracting by multiplying the numbers into millions, or they can make hypotheses about its size by measuring the lacks and gaps in the official economy (since more money is being spent than is being made). So the leading institutions of global capitalism have a strong interest in the informal economy and the shuttle trade in particular. Because they feel that since in some countries the value is almost 50 per cent of their GDP, they have to take this into account and observe it in order to learn how to regulate it and profit from it.

TS: I can say two things. First, I hope they will fail in their research. Because the more they fail, the better human beings may live, especially that group of human beings for whom the informal economy is their shield. The second thing I would like to tell you is how my research team studied the informal economy. We did it 10 years ago in different villages in Russia. My colleagues who went into the field lived in those villages for nearly a year without doing any research but just letting people watch them, letting people get used to the idea that they are not officers of the state or people who will sell them down the river, but normal human beings who liked them and who could be liked. Their "legend" was that they came to write the history of the village. They started to work with people and eventually they set up a system in which the peasants themselves wrote their own budgets, etc. And then something very interesting happened. From budget to budget it seemed that the share of the informal economy in the family increased – not because it really went up, but because people began to trust my colleagues more and more and were ready to open up and give them real figures. We have budget studies of quite a large number of families. And I am not going to publish it for the reasons of being a humanist, or being a socialist, or how do I call it now?

JR: You said in an earlier interview that the informal economy was an opportunity for people to become masters of their own lives.

TS: Yes, but one should not overstate that. Like every statement, it can be made ridiculous and wrong if you push it too far. It goes without saying that the people involved in the informal economy are in most cases the poorest and most destitute part of the population of a country. In those conditions, to speak about being free and liberated is silly, because in the conditions of a capitalist economy your freedom is often the money in your pocket. However, this is not the whole story. There is a second story to it. In the condition in which you are poorer than other parts of the population the fact that you can run your own economy gives you considerable advantage over people who cannot run their own family economy. I spent some time in the *favelas* of Rio de Janeiro. I was told dozens of times that I shouldn't go to the *favelas* because it's dangerous, because it's dirty, because terrible people live there. I was told this by sociologists living at a distance of 1 or 2 kilometres from the *favelas*. All the same I went with some anthropologists who had studied the *favelas*. One thing was clear: the people in the *favelas* often lived better than the workers who worked in industry. There could be no doubt about the capacity of the people in the *favelas* to better solve their own problems, and it was their autonomous family strategy that made them able to run their lives the best they knew how. I must say that often when I was asked to advise bodies of a governmental nature as to what might be done for "these people", my answer was: Just get out, because your interference is so often negative.

RB: I would like to come back to the question of how the informal economy creates a situation in which people feel they are free to make their own

gen schaffen kann, unter denen sich Menschen frei fühlen und ihr eigenes Leben führen. Ich würde gern eine Frage stellen, die mehr auf das Selbstverständnis der Menschen zielt. Wir haben eine Feldforschung auf einem Markt in Smolensk durchgeführt, und eine der Frauen, mit denen wir gesprochen haben, sagte uns, dass sie sich schämte, hier in einer Ecke zu stehen und all dieses Zeug zu verkaufen, während sie früher eine Arbeiterin und Produzentin von Gütern gewesen sei. Sie war wirklich stolz auf diese Vergangenheit, stolz darauf, einer Arbeitergesellschaft angehört zu haben. Mir scheint, dass es viele Vorbehalte gegen diese neue Erfahrung gibt, nur zu handeln, an einer Ecke zu stehen und irgendetwas zu verkaufen. Daher hege ich einige Zweifel an der These, dass Menschen sich freier fühlen, weil sie ihr eigenes Leben gestalten.

TS: Wenn man vom Selbstverständnis der Menschen redet, muss man davon ausgehen, dass sie durch ihre Erziehung beeinflusst sind. Die von Ihnen befragte Frau ist im sowjetischen System aufgewachsen. Dort hatte man ihr gesagt, dass man auf seinen erarbeiteten Lohn stolz sein könne und dass es furchtbar sei, an einer Ecke zu stehen und Waren zu verkaufen. Eine Identität bildet sich auf verschiedenen Wegen heraus. Diese Frau hatte gelernt, auf diese Weise zu denken, während ihre Kinder vielleicht schon anders denken. Natürlich gibt es andere Menschen, die sich dem Sowjetregime widersetzt haben und für die es eine Befreiung war, ihren eigenen Entscheidungen zu folgen. Man sollte auch unterscheiden zwischen dem, was die Menschen über sich selbst denken, und dem, was sie in Wirklichkeit sind. Wenn ich an einer Ecke stehen und etwas verkaufen müsste, hätte ich damit auch Probleme, da man mir stets eingetrichtert hat, ich solle „etwas Richtiges" tun, und an einer Ecke zu stehen gehört nicht dazu. Warum sollte ich also annehmen, ich wäre irgendwie anders als diese Frau, die sie interviewten. Ich hatte vor einiger Zeit eine Auseinandersetzung mit einem Kollegen, der Manager für eines der größten Unternehmen Russlands schult. Er fragte mich, warum ich nichts anderes mache im Leben. Ich sagte ihm – bitte verzeihen sie mir meinen Konservatismus –, dass den Leuten zu erzählen, wie man im Aktiengeschäft spekuliert und sehr schnell sehr reich wird, nicht zu den Dingen gehört, mit denen ich die mir nahe stehenden Menschen gern beschäftigt sehen würde. Ich denke also, ihre Marktfrau und ich haben eines gemeinsam, denn auf einer anderen Ebene hat sie ihren Protest gegen das Maß an Selbstausbeutung, das uns das neue System abverlangt, formuliert. Es gibt jedoch einen grundsätzlichen Test. Wenn man sie fragte: „Würden Sie wieder in der Fabrik arbeiten wollen, wenn der Lohn gering wäre, Sie jedoch die gleiche Sicherheit wie zu Zeiten der Sowjetunion hätten?", bekommt man die Antwort.

JR: Wir haben sie tatsächlich gefragt und sie hat uns mit „Ja" geantwortet.

TS: Sie sagte „Ja" – interessant. Doch einfach nur die Antwort auf diese Frage ist nicht immer ausreichend. Ich hätte sie gern dabei gesehen, Gesten können anderes „sagen" als Worte. Aber ich gebe gerne zu, dass die Mehrheit der Sowjetbürger nicht unbedingt unglücklich war. Sie hatten eine feste Arbeit und am Ende eine feste Rente. Das war nicht unbedingt ein schlechtes Leben. Ich würde nicht sagen, dass der heutige Kapitalismus besser ist, als es der Sozialismus war. Für einige Leute ist er es, aber nicht für alle.

RB: Ich habe ein Frage zum Vergleich der informellen Wirtschaft in der Sowjetunion mit der in Lateinamerika. In der Sowjetunion und in anderen ehemals sozialistischen Ländern herrschte eine ganz besondere Situation, die von staatlicher Regulierung und von aus der Industriegesellschaft herkommenden Institutionen geprägt war und sich somit sehr von der in Lateinamerika unterschied. Meine Frage zielt auf die Wurzeln dieser Gesellschaft, da die Mentalität der Menschen von ihrem Vertrauen in die behördliche und staatliche Regulierung bestimmt wurde. In welcher Form beeinflusst diese frühere spezifische Situation ihre jetzigen wirtschaftlichen Praktiken? Gibt es in den ehemals sozialistischen Staaten vielleicht ein neues Verständnis von informeller Wirtschaft, das sich von dem in Lateinamerika unterscheidet?

TS: Ich denke, dass in der Zeit des Sowjetregimes die Menschen in ihrer natürlichen Fähigkeit des Erlernens informeller Wirtschaftspraktiken beschränkt wurden. Im Vergleich dazu sind die Menschen in Lateinamerika einfach durch die Wendungen des Lebens besser auf die informelle Wirtschaft vorbereitet. Wenn ein Nachbar auf diese Weise lebt, kann er zum Lehrer werden, auch die Eltern oder die Familie sind Lehrer und Helfer – in diesem Sinne war es für einen Bürger der Sowjetunion schwieriger, mit der informellen Wirtschaft vertraut zu werden.

living. If I may, I would like to ask a question that is more about people's self-understanding. We did field research in a market in Smolensk, and one of the women we talked to said she felt it was a shame for her to stand in a corner and sell all this stuff and that it went against her past background of being a worker and a producer of goods – and she was really proud of this sort of experience and of belonging to a workers' society. It seems to me that there are a lot of reservations about this new experience of being only a trader and standing on the corner selling some stuff, and that's why I have some doubts concerning this idea that people feel freer because they are making their own living.

TS: If you're talking about people's self-understanding, you first of all have to acknowledge that it was influenced by the ways in which they were educated. The lady you interviewed grew up in a Soviet system in which she was told that there is pride in wage-working, and that standing on a corner selling merchandise is terrible. The ways in which you develop your identity differ. She has been trained to think this way. Her children may think otherwise. Of course, there are other people who objected to the Soviet regime and for whom it was liberation to be able follow their own choices. One should also make a distinction between what people think about themselves and what they really are. If I had to stand on a corner and sell goods, I would also find it very difficult because I was trained to think that I have to do "something real" and this does not mean standing on a corner. So why should I expect to be any different from the woman you interviewed? I had an argument some time ago with a colleague who is training businessmen for one of the major industries of Russia and who asked why I am doing what I am doing. I said because to me – forgive me for my conservativism – the fact that you tell people how to speculate on the stock market and become very rich very quickly is not a thing I would like people who are close to me to do. So I think your woman in the market and I ... have something in common. On another level, I think that what she was saying is her protest against the level of self-exploitation that the new system demands. Still, there is a fundamental test to it all. Usually, if you ask, "Would you like to go back to the factory if the income is modest but there is stability like in the Soviet Union time?" you will get the answer.

JR: Actually, we did ask and she said "yes".

TS: She said yes – interesting. Even so, such an answer to the question is not always sufficient. I would like to see her act; actions may "say" something different than words. But I would easily accept the fact that a majority of Soviet people did not necessarily feel unhappy. They had a steady job and a steady pension at the end. It was not necessarily a bad life. I would not say that capitalism today is better than state socialism was. To some people it is, but not to all.

RB: I have a question related to a comparison of the informal economy in the Soviet Union and Latin America. The fact that in the Soviet Union and other former socialist countries there was a very specific situation of state regulation and institutions that emerged from industrial society is a very different case than in Latin America. My question is about the roots of this society, because people's mentality was shaped by their reliance on institutional and government regulation. How does this specific situation from the past shape their economic practices now? This is to say that maybe there is a new understanding of informality in former socialist countries that is different, for instance, from what happens in the informal economy in Latin America.

TS: I think that the period of the Soviet regime limited people's natural self-training for the informal economy. In Latin America, by comparison, people are more prepared for the informal economy by the facts of life. The fact that your neighbour is liv-

Das erklärt auch, warum die erste Welle des Zerfalls der sowjetischen Wirtschaft solch ein Schock war und solch dramatische Auswirkungen hatte. Doch selbst in den ersten, besonders schlechten Jahren, zwischen 1991 und 1995, gab es in Russland keine Hungersnot. Das heißt, dass sich die Leute schneller anpassten als erwartet. Als die Regierung fast vollständig aus dem öffentlichen Leben verschwand, fanden sie eigene Wege, sich über Wasser zu halten. Ich hatte 1991 einen merkwürdigen Besuch eines amerikanischen Professors. Er kam zu mir nach Moskau, da er gehört hatte, dass ich „ein Spezialist für die Landwirtschaft" sei. Er fragte mich, was man angesichts der Hungersnot in Russland tun solle. Ich antwortete ihm, dass es in Russland keine Hungersnot gebe. Er erwiderte: „Wie können Sie so etwas sagen? Unsere statistischen Erhebungen zeigen, dass die Nahrungsmittelproduktion gesunken ist." Ich sagte ihm, dass im Moment 22 unserer Mitarbeiter in russischen Dörfern Informationen sammeln und dass es dort keinerlei Anzeichen von Hunger gebe. Natürlich habe sich die Ernährungslage verschlechtert, aber Hunger könne man nicht so leicht verbergen, man sehe es in den Gesichtern der Menschen, man sehe es besonders bei den Kindern. Meine Antwort missfiel ihm deutlich, und er sagte: „Ich werde meine Frage anders formulieren: Was soll man Ihrer Meinung nach tun, wenn demnächst in Russland eine Hungersnot ausbricht?" Ich sagte ihm, dass es in Russland keine Hungersnot geben werde und dass ich durch Leute vor Ort über die reale Situation informiert sei. Zuerst verstand ich gar nicht, was hinter all diesen Fragen steckte, bis zwei Monate später Waggonladungen mit Nahrungsmitteln für das hungernde Russland eintrafen. Wenige Tage später wurden Lebensmittel und Zigaretten mit der Aufschrift „Hilfslieferung aus den Vereinigten Staaten" in Berlin verkauft – die Lieferungen waren direkt in die Hände der Mafia gelangt.

JR: Ist die Mafia auch ein Teil der informellen Wirtschaft?

TS: Sie ist eine Form der informellen Wirtschaft, obwohl ich sagen muss, dass ein großer Teil der russischen Mafia nicht mehr Teil der informellen Wirtschaft ist, sondern inzwischen zur offiziellen kapitalistischen Wirtschaft gehört. Sie handeln illegal, doch ist der Kapitalismus nicht unbedingt ein formalisiertes legales System. Max Webers Modell lässt sich hier nicht voll anwenden. In Russland gibt es eine ganze Reihe von illegalen Bereichen in der kapitalistischen Wirtschaft, und die Mafia ist ein Teil davon. Das kann in der informellen Wirtschaft beginnen, wächst sich dann aber oft zu einem illegalen kapitalistischen Wirtschaftsbereich aus, der parallel zur legalen kapitalistischen Wirtschaft existiert.

JR: Glauben Sie, dass 1998 eine kritische Zeit oder ein Wendepunkt war, nach dem die normalere Phase des Kapitalismus mit einer sich herausbildenden Kapitalistenklasse begann? Ich stelle diese Frage, weil mir Boris Kagarlitzki gestern sagte, dass nach diesem Wendepunkt 1998 die Entwicklung in Richtung auf einen im Inneren kohärenteren Kapitalismus verlief, trotz der Tatsache, dass Russland vor 1998 nicht wirklich kapitalistisch war, trotz der Günstlingswirtschaft und der Kämpfe zwischen Managern und Besitzern, trotz der weit verbreiteten Schattenwirtschaft und so weiter.

TS: Ich werde mit etwas anderem beginnen, wenn Sie erlauben, und dann auf ihre Frage zurückkommen. Ich denke, dass die Ereignisse von 1998 auf die informelle Wirtschaft nur geringe Auswirkungen hatten. Wie gering die Auswirkungen dieses Zusammenbruchs waren, ist wirklich erstaunlich. Kurz nach diesen katastrophalen Ereignissen fuhr ich nach Wolgograd (ehemals Stalingrad) und kam dort in eine saubere, geordnete und gut funktionierende Stadt. Man hatte das Gefühl, dass offensichtlich nichts Wesentliches passiert sei, was angesichts meiner Moskauer Erfahrungen einfach unglaublich war. Ich ging auf den Markt, und dort gab es überall Nahrungsmittel aus der Region zu relativ moderaten Preisen. Ich fragte: Welche Auswirkungen hatte der Zusammenbruch hier? Und man antwortete mir: Wieso sollen Änderungen im Wechselkurs zum Dollar uns hier betreffen?
Zweitens glaube ich, dass die Ereignisse von 1998 die Entwicklung des russischen Kapitalismus gefördert haben. Viele westliche Kapitalisten, die in Russland investiert hatten, verließen das Land nach diesem Zusammenbruch. Ich gehe bei mir in einem Geschäft einkaufen, das vorrangig für Ausländer bestimmt ist. Innerhalb weniger Monate stellte ich fest, dass dort mehr und mehr russische Produkte verkauft wurden und somit auch russische Kunden kamen. Die russischen Kapitalisten hatten diese Chance genutzt und die Lücke gefüllt, und das hat die russische kapitalistische Wirtschaft gestärkt. Als die Ausländer zurück kamen (oft hatten sie festgestellt, dass sie einen Fehler began-

ing this way means that your neighbour will teach you, your parents and family may teach you too or help you – so in this sense it has been more difficult for the Soviet citizenry to get into the informal economy. This explains why the first stage of disintegration of the Soviet economy was such a shock and led to such difficult results. But even in the first years, the particularly bad years, between 1991 and 1995, there was no famine in Russia, which means that people adjusted faster than expected. The moment when the government all but disappeared they found ways to sort themselves out. I had a funny visit from an American professor in 1991. He came to me in Moscow because he said that he had heard that I was "a specialist in agriculture". He asked me what one should do in view of famine in Russia. I answered that there was no famine in Russia. He responded, "How can you say that? Our statistics show that the production of food has dropped." I said at the moment we have 22 people in Russian villages collecting information. And there is no sign of hunger. Of course, their diet has worsened, but the one thing you cannot hide easily is hunger; you see it in the faces of the people on the street, you see it especially in the children. He was clearly displeased with me and said, "I will reformulate the question: What do you think one should do when famine begins shortly in Russia?" I said famine will not begin in Russia. I have people reporting to me about the situation as it is. At first I could not ... understand what was behind all these questions until two months later when we started to get trainloads of food for the starving Russians. A few days later the food and cigarettes with stamps "Help from United States" were being sold in Berlin – the trainloads went directly into mafia hands.

JR: And is the mafia also a part of the informal economy?

TS: It is a form of informal economy, though I must say that by now much of Russia's mafia is no longer simply an informal economy becoming part of the formal capitalist economy. It acts illegally, but capitalism – and Max Weber's model was not necessarily effective here – is not necessarily a formalised legal system. In Russia there are a lot of illegal elements of a capitalist economy, and the mafia is one part of it. It may start as an informal economy, but it often grows into a form of illegal capitalist economy parallel to the legal capitalist one.

RB: What do you think about this phrase by Szelenyi, capitalism without capitalists? Is the development of capitalism with a lack of the property classes a description of what is happening in Eastern European countries?

TS: Yes, but we can already look back at it. Maybe 10 years ago it was right. But at the moment capitalism in Russia is definitely not capitalism without capitalists. "Capitalism without capitalists" illustrated a transitional period.

JR: Do you think 1998 was a critical time or turning point for this more normal phase of capitalism with a capitalist class emerging? I am asking because Boris Kagarlitsky said to me yesterday that, although before 1998 Russia was not really capitalist because of its barter economy, struggles between managers and owners, high degrees of informality and so on – that after the turning point of 1998 it started moving towards a more internally coherent capitalism according to its definition.

TS: I will begin with something else, with your permission, and then come back to the question. I think that what happened in 1998 was of little significance to the informal economy. The extent to which the crash didn't influence anything at all was staggering. Shortly after this fundamental disaster I went to Volgograd (ex-Stalingrad), and I found a city which was clean, orderly and well run. What was obvious was the feeling that nothing much had happened, which was unbelievable in the context of my Moscow experience. I went to a market in Volgograd. The market was full of locally produced food. The prices were relatively inexpensive. And I asked: What was the effect of the collapse? And the answers were: Why should change in the price of dollars influence us here? Secondly, I think that what happened in 1998 helped the development of Russian capitalism. Many capitalists from the West who invested in Russia ran from Russia after the crash. I shop nearby in a shop that used to be mostly for foreigners. Within a few months I noticed that the products there became Russian and then the people there became Russian. Russian capitalists took the opportunity to step in, and this strengthened the Russian capitalist economy. When the foreigners started to come back (often realising they made a mistake and they should have shown some nerve), space was already taken up by Russian capitalists. Ever since, you can speak of an increasingly well-

gen hatten und einfach die Nerven hätten behalten sollen), war ihr Platz bereits von russischen Kapitalisten besetzt. Von da an kann man von einem zunehmend besser organisierten russischen Handelskapitalismus sprechen. Ich denke also auch, dass 1998 ein bedeutender Moment des Übergangs war. Außerdem sollte man stets vor Augen haben, dass sich für die Mehrheit der Bevölkerung nichts verändert hat. Man stelle sich einmal vor, was passierte, wenn der westliche Kapitalismus einzelne Länder aufgeben würde! Russland hat gezeigt, dass es für die Entwicklung des lokalen Kapitalismus nichts Besseres geben kann. Auch der informellen Wirtschaft würde wenig passieren.

RB: Denken Sie, dass es nach 1998 eine Bewegung in Richtung auf eine staatliche Regulierung der russischen Wirtschaft gab?

TS: Nicht nach 1998, aber in den letzten drei Jahren gab es eine zunehmende Zentralisierung der Wirtschaft, eine steigende Einflussnahme und den Ruf nach staatlicher Kontrolle. Die neue Führung sieht die Zukunft Russlands eindeutig als eine Art staatskapitalistische Wirtschaft.

JR: Ich möchte Sie etwas zum Transithandel (*shuttle trade*) fragen, der einen sehr großen Teil der russischen Wirtschaft ausmacht. Ich kann mich an einen Artikel erinnern, der davon sprach, dass die Transithändler die halbe russische Bevölkerung mit Essen und Kleidung versorgen. Haben Sie Untersuchungen auf diesem Gebiet durchgeführt und können Sie auf die sich verändernde Bedeutung des Transithandels in den letzten Jahren, in denen sich der Kapitalismus in Russland entwickelt hat, eingehen?

TS: Ich habe auf diesem Gebiet nicht gearbeitet, und ich habe auch nie Studien gesehen, die ausreichend systematisch sind und die Frage beantworten können, ob nun die Hälfte oder ein Viertel der Versorgung über den Transithandel erfolgen. Ohne Zweifel hat dieser Bereich einen großen Anteil. Ich denke, der Transithandel nimmt im Augenblick ab. Auf den Märkten sieht man nicht so sehr Handelswaren aus dem Ausland als vielmehr russische Waren mit ausländischen Etiketten. Es gibt sehr viele Güter, bei denen russische Produzenten ziemlich gut sind. Es gibt noch einige Dinge, die russische Produzenten nicht herstellen, wie etwa Lederwaren. In diesem Bereich haben sie dann auch mehr Transithandel.

JR: Ich habe eine Frau interviewt, die Transithandel betrieb, wobei dieser Begriff vielleicht nicht ganz passend ist, weil sie nur zwischen Smolensk und Moskau pendelte. Sie sagte mir, dass die meisten Waren auf dem Smolensker Markt aus Moskau kämen und dass es nur sehr wenige Leute gäbe, die ihre Waren in der Türkei holen würden. Der Transithandel mit der Türkei kam 1995 und 1996 in Gang. Die damaligen Händler stehen sich jetzt sehr gut und können es sich leisten, ihre Reisen mit dem Flugzeug zu machen. Die meisten Leute jedoch, die wie diese Frau relativ spät mit ihren Pendelreisen begannen, können sich so etwas nicht leisten. Sie fährt nur einige Male im Monat nach Moskau und bringt Waren zum Verkauf nach Smolensk. Diese Frau unterschied also zwischen den Leuten, die international agieren, regelmäßig in die Türkei oder nach China fahren und sich das leisten können, weil sie sich in diesem Bereich bereits vor längerer Zeit etabliert haben, und den Neueinsteigern, die sich Auslandsfahrten nicht leisten können und daher Güter zwischen den verschiedenen Städten Russlands transportieren.

TS: Manchmal hat man es auch mit einer Entwicklung des Kapitalismus im engeren Sinne des Wortes, also außerhalb der informellen Wirtschaft, zu tun. Der IWF geht in der Tat davon aus, dass sich nach einer bestimmten Zeit alle informellen Bereiche der Wirtschaft in kapitalistische Strukturen verwandeln und damit „das Problem gelöst" wäre. Diese Sichtweise unterschätzt die Überlebensfähigkeit der informellen Wirtschaft und die sozialen und wirtschaftlichen Gründe, die ihr zugrunde liegen. Sie beachtet auch nicht die Möglichkeit einer Reformierung der informellen Wirtschaft, d. h. der Herausbildung neuer Formen ohne Änderung der Grundsubstanz. Nehmen wir ein Beispiel aus Russland: Wir bemerken hier einen schnellen Anstieg der Zahl nichtrussischer Arbeitskräfte, die illegal in Russland leben und in ihrer sozialen Organisationsweise „informell" sind. Die „formale" kapitalistische Wirtschaft bedient sich dieser Situation, bezahlt sie äußerst schlecht und presst aus ihnen alles heraus. Nichtsdestotrotz liegt das Hauptfeld der informellen Wirtschaft weiterhin eher im Handel als in der Produktion. Die von Ihnen interviewte Frau hatte ohne Zweifel Recht mit ihrer Unterscheidung zwischen internationalem Transithandel und dem Transithandel innerhalb Russlands, der sich die Unterschiede im Preis- und Lohnniveau zwischen dem reicheren Moskau und den sehr viel ärmeren russischen „Provinzen" zu Nutze macht.

organised Russian merchant capitalism. So I agree that 1998 was an important moment of transition. But I think it is useful to remember that for the majority of the population nothing changed. I think if you want to test what would happen if Western capitalism were to abandon certain countries, Russia has shown that nothing better could have happened for the development of local capitalism. Also, little would happen to the informal economy.

RB: Do you think that after 1998 there was a shift towards a regulation of the economy of Russia from above?

TS: Not after 1998, but during the past three years there has been a growing centralization of the economy, a growing interference and call for control of government. Clearly the new leadership is seeing the future of Russia as a kind of state capitalist economy.

JR: I would like to ask a question about the shuttle trade, which is a very large portion of the Russian economy. I remember one article which said that the shuttlers are providing clothing and food for half of the Russian population. I am wondering if you've done any research on the shuttle trade and if you can comment on the changing significance of the shuttle trade during the last few years as capitalism in Russia became more established?

TS: I didn't work on it and I have never seen sufficient systematic research to answer the question "Is it half or is it a quarter?" There is no doubt that it's a large sum. I think the shuttle trade is actually decreasing. If you watch the markets, it is not so much the shuttle trade but foreign tags on quite a lot of Russian production. There are very many things that Russian producers produce fairly well. There are still a few things that the Russians don't produce, like leather goods. So you have in this field more shuttle trade.

JR: I interviewed a woman shuttler, actually maybe this is not a correct term because she's travelling only from Smolensk to Moscow, and she said that most of the things in the Smolensk market are coming from Moscow and that there are very few people who are going to Turkey because the period when the shuttle trade with Turkey was established was 1995 and 1996, and those people are already quite well off and can afford to continue making these trips by flying, but most people who began the shuttle trade relatively late like she did can't afford to make these kinds of trips and therefore she comes only to Moscow a few times a month and brings things to sell in Smolensk. She made a distinction between the international shuttle trade, between those people who are going to Turkey and China, who can afford to do it only because they had been established in the field for a long time, and the newcomers who can't afford to go abroad and are therefore shuttling goods between different cities in Russia.

TS: Sometimes you have a development of capitalism in the strict sense, that is in the narrow sense of that definition, out of the informal economy. Indeed, the IMF believed that, given time, all informal economy would develop into capitalist economies and the "problem" would be "solved". This view underestimated the survival abilities of the informal economy and the social as well as economic reasons for it. Also, it disregarded the ability of the informal economy to reform that is to establish new forms without changing its substance. To take a Russian example, we now have rapid growth in the non-Russian labour force, which is illegal and "informal" in its social organisation, but on the increase because it serves a particular way for the "formal" capitalist economy to squeeze such labour through underpayment. However, now as before the most significant field in which the informal economy proceeds to blossom is still trade rather than production. The woman you interviewed was doubtlessly right in making a distinction between international shuttle trade and shuttle trade inside Russia, which is based on price and wage differences between the richer Moscow and much poorer "provinces" of Russia.

DIE POST-SOZIALISTISCHE STADT

THE POST-SOCIALIST CITY

► MINSK

ПАЛАЦ РЭСПУБЛІКІ

ЯПОНСКА
104,6 FM
Marlbor
Lights
КУРЕНИЕ ОПАСНО ДЛЯ ЗДОРОВ

ВИТЯ, ТЫ СПАС НАС, ТАК
15.08.90
ЗАЧЕМ ТЫ УШЁЛ
ТЫ ЗНАЛ ЧТО БУ-ДЕТ ПЛОХО, НО НЕ ЗНАЛ ЧТО ТАК СКО-РО!
В.ЦОЙ
ЦОЙ

БИС

МЕБЕЛЬ

► **SMOLENSK**

РЫЛЕНКОВА
53

ИВАН

ПОПОВА
НЕ ВХОДИ

STADTPLANUNG NACH DEM ENDE DES KOMMUNISMUS
URBAN PLANNING AFTER COMMUNISM

MIKRORAYONS, SMOLENSK – VON DER KOLLEKTIVEN HOFFNUNG ZUM TRAUM VOM PRIVATEN GLÜCK
MICRORAYONS, SMOLENSK – FROM COLLECTIVE HOPE TO THE DREAM OF PRIVATE HAPPINESS

RÜCKZUG INS WOHNZIMMER
RETREAT INTO THE LIVING ROOM

ÖFFENTLICHER RAUM, MINSK – RÄUME DES JUBELS UND DIE ENTSTEHUNG NEUER ÖFFENTLICHKEITEN
PUBLIC SPACES IN MINSK – SETTINGS FOR JUBILATION AND THE EMERGENCE OF NEW KINDS OF PUBLIC

„EINE GUTE GESELLSCHAFT“
„A GOOD SOCIETY“

AKTIVITÄTEN DER POLITISCHEN OPPOSITION IN MINSK: EIN BERICHT
OPPOSITIONAL POLITICAL ACTIVITIES IN MINSK: A REPORT

DIGITALE TECHNOLOGIEN DER KONTROLLE – FALLSTUDIE ZUM VIRTUELLEN ÖFFENTLICHEN RAUM IN WEISSRUSSLAND
DIGITAL TECHNOLOGIES OF CONTROL – CASE STUDY ON THE BELARUSIAN VIRTUAL PUBLIC SPACE

STADTPLANUNG NACH DEM ENDE DES KOMMUNISMUS

BART GOLDHOORN

Man kann das Phänomen der russischen Stadt ohne Kenntnis der sowjetischen Stadt einfach nicht verstehen. Im Unterschied zu anderen ehemals kommunistisch regierten Städten in Osteuropa wurden die größten Bereiche von russischen Städten zu Zeiten der Sowjetunion erbaut, als Russland einen Prozess ungezügelter Urbanisierung durchlief. Außerdem muss man wissen, dass eine russische Stadt im 19. Jahrhundert vor allem aus Holzhäusern bestand. Da Holzgebäude nun einmal schneller verfallen oder gar abbrennen, haben selbst Städte mit einer jahrhundertealten Geschichte nicht viel an historischer Architektur aufzuweisen, mit Ausnahme einiger weniger Villen aus dem 18. und 19. Jahrhundert, einiger Kirchen und vielleicht eines rekonstruierten Kremls. Die große Ausnahme ist natürlich St. Petersburg, aber selbst das vorrevolutionäre Erbe Moskaus ist, verglichen mit der Gesamtgröße der Stadt, äußerst bescheiden.

DAS SOWJETISCHE ERBE

Auch wenn westliche Architekten von der russischen Architektur im Allgemeinen die Experimente des Konstruktivismus und den stalinistischen Klassizismus am ehesten kennen, besteht der größte Teil einer russischen Stadt aus industriell gefertigten Wohngebäuden. Dieser Gebäudetyp wurde von Chruschtschow in den 1960er Jahren eingeführt. Es war ein Versuch, die Bauproduktion zu steigern und die Bedürfnisse der wachsenden Stadtbevölkerung zu befriedigen. Seitdem waren nicht Architekten, sondern Bauingenieure die treibenden Kräfte der urbanen Entwicklung. Wenn man einen Querschnitt durch eine russische Stadt machen würde, könnte man die Entwicklungen der Bautechnik zurückverfolgen – je weiter vom Zentrum entfernt, desto höher die Gebäude. Sowjetische Städteplaner sahen keinen Grund, warum Wohngebäude unterschiedlich hoch sein sollten – das hätte ja im Widerspruch zu den von Chruschtschow postulierten Prinzipien der Rationalisierung im Wohnungsbau gestanden. Deshalb befinden sich die höchsten Gebäude in den Vororten, denn sie wurden als letzte gebaut. Ein Querschnitt durch eine russische Stadt ist sozusagen das Gegenteil einer amerikanischen Stadt mit Hochhäusern im Zentrum und endlosen zersiedelten Vororten. Das Zentrum einer russischen Stadt wird von relativ niedrigen Gebäuden beherrscht, während sich die höchsten Gebäude an der Stadtgrenze befinden, wo die Besiedlung abrupt endet. Viele Städte werden von ihrer Umgebung durch eine Ringstraße geradezu abgeschnitten, die oft die über 100 Kilometer lange Moskauer Ringstraße zum Vorbild hat.

URBAN PLANNING AFTER COMMUNISM

BART GOLDHOORN

One cannot understand the Russian city without knowledge of the Soviet city. In contrast with other former communist Eastern European cities the greater part of the Russian city was constructed in the Soviet period, when Russia underwent a process of unbridled urbanisation. Furthermore, one should understand that the 19th century Russian city consisted primarily of wooden buildings. Since wooden buildings tend to fall apart or burn down regularly, even cities boosting a history of many centuries have not much historical architecture to show for except a number of 18th and19th century mansions, a number of churches and sometimes a reconstructed Kremlin. The big exception is of course St. Petersburg, but even Moscow's pre-revolutionary part is extremely small compared to the overall size of the city.

THE SOVIET HERITAGE

Although Western architects tend to know Russian architecture best for its constructivist experiments and Stalinist classicism, the main part of the Russian city is made of pre-fabricated apartment buildings. This type of housing was introduced by Khrutchev in the 1960s in an attempt to rise the building production and fulfil the need of the growing urban population. From this time on, not architects but the construction industry became the leading force for urban development. When one would make a cross section through the Russian city one can trace back the developments in construction technology – the further from the centre, the higher the buildings. In Soviet city planning there was no reason why one should build housing blocks of various heights – this would actually contradict the principles of rationalisation of the housing industry introduced by Khrutchev. Thus we see the highest buildings at the outskirts of the cities, since these we built last. When one would make a cross section through the Russian city, one gets the inverse of that of the American city, with its high-rise downtown and endless suburban sprawl. The centre of the Russian city is relatively low-rise, whereas at its border, here its buildings are the highest, it ends abruptly. At this point many cities are closed off from the surrounding countryside by a ring road, modelled after the more then 100 km long Moscow Ring Road.
The copying of this model can have strange results. I remember arriving to Yekaterinburg by airplane. Somewhere between the airport and the city we crossed a huge fly-over. The taxi driver told me that this was the Yekaterinburg ring road, which had been under construction for decades. Later I saw the project in the office of the chief architect – a huge circle surrounding the city on a distance of several kilometres, its

Die Nachahmung dieses Modells hat eigenartige Ergebnisse hervorgebracht. Ich erinnere mich an einen Flug nach Jekaterinburg. Irgendwo zwischen Flughafen und Stadt passierten wir eine riesige Überführung. Der Taxifahrer erzählte mir, dass dies die Ringstraße von Jekaterinburg sei, an der seit Jahrzehnten gebaut würde. Später sah ich das Projekt im Büro des Chefarchitekten – ein gigantischer Ring, der die Stadt in einer Entfernung von mehreren Kilometern umschließt und dessen Größe eindeutig die Lage Jekaterinburgs zwischen Asien und Europa widerspiegeln sollte; die Behörden wollten den Verkehr zwischen diesen beiden Kontinenten nicht in ihrer Stadt haben.

Der radikale Kontrast zwischen Stadt und Land hat natürlich mit dem völligen Fehlen von Privathäusern in der Stadt zu tun. (Es gibt Ausnahmen, z. B. einige Holzhäuser aus vorrevolutionärer Zeit in den Stadtzentren und natürlich das Melnikow-Haus, das einzige zu Sowjetzeiten errichtete Privathaus.)

Anstelle von Privathäusern kennen russische Städte das Datschenwesen. An sich ist das eine sehr interessante Erfindung – man hat eine Wohnung in der Stadt, effizient organisiert und mit guter Infrastruktur, und außerdem einen Garten mit Häuschen auf dem Land. Verglichen mit den bescheidenen Ausmaßen europäischer Landschaften ist Russland ein Riesenterritorium mit einer begrenzten Anzahl hoch verdichteter Großstädte, umgeben von einer aus Datschen bestehenden Parallelstadt. Der Radius der Datschenstadt kann sich über wenige Dutzend Kilometer erstrecken, aber auch, wie im Fall von Moskau, bis zu 400 Kilometer umfassen. Man fährt an jedem Sommerwochenende entweder mit dem Auto oder mit der Vorortbahn, der so genannten Elektritschka, zum Garten. Mitunter wohnen Frauen und Kinder den ganzen Sommer über dort. Das ist auch der Hauptgrund, warum man ein Auto hat – angesichts der großen Entfernungen und des schlechten Straßenzustandes sind bei Reisen zwischen den Städten Eisenbahn und Flugzeug vorzuziehen. In der Stadt werden Autos in großen Garagenkomplexen geparkt, die sich in Übereinstimmung mit der russischen Stadtplanung außerhalb der Wohnviertel auf separaten Grundstücken mit an KZs erinnernden Wachtürmen für den Sicherheitsdienst befinden. Neben der Garage ist der Balkon das Bindeglied zwischen Datsche und Wohnung. Er wird nicht als Sitzplatz im Freien genutzt, sondern ist oftmals von Glas umschlossen und dient dazu, die Ernte aus dem eigenen Garten zu lagern.

VERÄNDERUNGEN

Wie also hat sich dieses Modell einer Stadt unter dem Einfluss des Übergangs von der Plan- zur Marktwirtschaft gewandelt? Zunächst einmal ist festzuhalten, dass das sowjetische Modell noch längst nicht ausgestorben ist. Besonders in den reichsten Städten das Landes, z. B. in Moskau und St. Petersburg, aber auch in Kasan, geht der industrielle Wohnungsbau mit seinen „Plattenbauten" ungehemmt weiter, wohingegen er in Osteuropa ein radikales Ende gefunden hat. Wenn man sich die Zahlen des jährlichen Bauvolumens ansieht, stellt man fest, dass immer noch dieselben Wohnungsbauunternehmen wie zu Sowjetzeiten den größten Teil der Wohnfläche produzieren, und das mit praktisch unveränderten Typenbauten, die in den 1980er Jahren entworfen wurden und so phantasievolle Namen wie P44 T trugen. Die Marktwirtschaft hat das Monopol dieser Industriegiganten nicht gebrochen, so dass die Mehr-

size clearly meant to reflect the position of Yekaterinburg between Asia and Europe – the authorities did not want the traffic between these continents going through their city.
The radical contrast between city and countryside of course also had everything to do with the complete absence of private houses in the city. (There are exceptions`, some remaining pre-revolutionary wooden houses around the city centres and of course the Melnikov house – the only private house constructed in the Soviet city).
Instead of this the Russian city has the system of the dacha. In itself this is a very interesting invention – to have an apartment in the city, efficiently organised with a good infrastructure, and a garden with a small house in the countryside. Compared to the small scale European landscape Russia is a vast territory by a limited number of big cities with high density, each of them surrounded by a parallel city of dachas. The radius of the dacha city can be from some tens up to 400 kilometres in the case of Moscow. One drives to one's garden by car or by train (the so-called elektrichka) every summer weekend, wife and children might even live there the whole summer. This is actually also the main reason one has a car – considering the long distances and the bad state of the roads one prefers to use train or airplane to travel between cities. In the city cars are kept in huge garage complexes that in accordance with Russian urban planning law are located outside the housing areas in separate compounds with concentration camp like watchtowers for the guards. Apart from the garage the intermediary between dacha and apartment is the balcony which is not used to sit outside but preferably closed off by glass in order to store the produce of the dacha.

CHANGES

So how has this model of the city changed under influence of the changes from a centrally planned to a market economy? First of all it must be said that the Soviet model is far from extinct. Especially in the richest cities such as Moscow and Petersburg, but also Kazan, the 'Plattenbau' districts, the construction of which has radically ceased in Eastern Europe, is still proceeding full speed: if one looks at the yearly construction figures, one sees that the majority of square meters is still being produced by the same housing factories that did this in Soviet times, using practically the same housing types as those that were designed in the 1980s with illustrious names as P44T or ... (?) The market economy has not broken the monopoly of these industrial giants, and there is not much to choose from by the majority of the population. Alternatives to these housing blocks are still very rare, and because of their rareness prohibitively expensive. As a result, the population thinks that it is actually very expensive to build other typologies then the standard flat, and there is no pressure on the construction industry to change its production.
When in the second half of the 1990s the architects of the housing design institute TSNIIP Zhilishi actually worked out very detailed plans for cheap low-rise housing with smart and economic floor plans, developers were quick to construct houses according to this scheme and sell them for exorbitant prices. Since the amount of people being able to afford these prices is very low, this type of housing has never been developed on a big scale. This would not be such a big problem if the pre-fab houses we were actually being improved, but this is rarely the case. To give an example

heit der Bevölkerung kaum eine Wahl hat. Alternativen zu diesen Wohnblöcken sind nach wie vor selten, und weil sie so selten sind, sind sie unverschämt teuer. Eine Folge davon ist auch, dass die Bevölkerung der Meinung ist, alles außer den Standardwohnungen sei sehr teuer, so dass die Bauunternehmen auch nicht unter Druck stehen, ihre Produktion zu ändern.
Als in der zweiten Hälfte der 1990er Jahre die Architekten des Zentralen Forschungsinstituts für Wohnraumprojektierung (ZNIIPSh) daran gingen, detaillierte Entwürfe für preiswerte niedriggeschossige Wohnbauten mit günstigen und wirtschaftlichen Grundrissen zu erarbeiten, waren Entwicklungsgesellschaften schnell dabei, Wohnungen nach diesen Entwürfen zu bauen und zu exorbitanten Preisen zu verkaufen. Da die Anzahl derjenigen, die sich solche Preise leisten können, sehr gering ist, wurden solche Wohnungen nie zu einer Massenerscheinung. Das wäre kein großes Problem, wenn die Plattenbauproduktion wenigstens verbessert würde, aber das ist selten der Fall. Nur ein Beispiel: Die Fenster in solchen Häusern sind meist so weit oben, dass man auf einem normalen Stuhl sitzend kaum hinausschauen kann. So unbequem das für die Bewohner ist, so bequem ist das für das Werk, weil sich die Fensteröffnung in der Mitte der Fassadenplatte befindet.
Das heißt jedoch nicht, dass sich in einer russischen Stadt nichts ändert – es heißt nur, dass sich Veränderungen jedenfalls nicht im Wohnungsbau abspielen und dass sie sich auf die Wohnsituation für die Mehrheit der Menschen, die sich nur eine Standardwohnung leisten können, nicht auswirken. Trotzdem gibt es tatsächlich zwei Bereiche, in denen immense Veränderungen zu beobachten sind: die Innenstädte und das Land.

LEBEN AUF DEM LANDE

Anfang der 1990er Jahre herrschte auf den Datschen der sowjetischen Städte fieberhafte Betriebsamkeit. Einerseits waren die Stadtbewohner aktiv, die sich in Zeiten gravierender Unterversorgung zunehmend auf Dinge verlegten, die sie selbst auf ihren kleinen Grundstücken anbauen konnten, und andererseits waren es die Neureichen, die angesichts einer galoppierenden Inflation ihr Geld lieber in Ziegelsteine investierten. Dieses Baumaterial war zu Sowjetzeiten immer knapp gewesen und stand praktisch nur für Parteibauten zur Verfügung; jetzt führte dessen Status dazu, dass sich einige entschlossen, der Stadt endlich den Rücken zu kehren und auf dem Land Minipaläste zu bauen. Mit Eigenheimen, errichtet im eklektischen Stile der Villen des 19. Jahrhunderts mit ihren Türmen und dicken Mauern, meinte man, eine Garantie für Stabilität und Glück zu haben. Allerdings hielt dieser Traum nicht lange an. Mangels durchdachter Planung haben es viele nicht geschafft, ihr Haus zu Ende zu bauen, bevor das Geld ausging, da sie nicht berücksichtigt hatten, dass man mehr als Ziegelsteine benötigt, um sich ein gemütliches Heim zu schaffen. Andere wurden mit dem Bau zwar fertig, mussten aber bald feststellen, dass ein Leben weit weg von der Stadt, in einer Gegend ohne Schulen und Geschäfte im Sommer ganz angenehm, aber in den übrigen Monaten des Jahres ziemlich anstrengend ist. Innerhalb weniger Jahre sah es in der Umgebung russischer Großstädte aus wie in einem Ziegelstein-Pompeji – überall standen Ruinen und halbfertige Häuser in der Landschaft. Suburbanisierung, die viele, darunter auch amerikanische Berater der russischen Regierung, als Patent-

– windows in these houses tend to be situated so high that even sitting on a normal chair one can hardly look outside. As much as it inconvenient for the user, this is convenient for the factory, since the opening is located in the middle of the panel used in the construction of the facade.
This all doesn't mean that nothing changes in the Russian city – it only means that the changes are not taking place in the area of housing and do not affect the housing conditions for the majority of people that can only afford to live in the standard buildings. Having said this, one can define two areas that are actually changing immensely: the inner city and the countryside.

THE COUNTRYSIDE

In the beginning of the 1990s, the dacha landscape of the Soviet cities was buzzing with feverish activity. On the one hand, there were the city dwellers that in these times of big deficits increasingly relied on the produce they could grow themselves on their small plots of land, on the other hand, there were the New Rich who as a result of the enormous inflation were converting their money in red bricks. This material had been very scarce in Soviet times and was only issued for Party buildings – now its status led to a preference for this material for those who decided that finally they could flee the city and build their little palaces in the countryside. Modelled after eclectic 19th century villas with towers and thick walls, they believed that building their own home would be the guarantee for stability and happiness. Alas this dream didn't last very long. Due to the lack of planning many just didn't manage to finish their cottage before their money evaporated (not realising that one needs more then red brick to build a comfortable house), others who actually managed to finish it found out that living in a big distance from the city in an area without schools and shops might be OK for the summer months, but is quite hard in the rest of the year. Within a few years the surroundings of big Russian cities looked like a redbrick Pompeii – ruins of unfinished houses were scattered along the landscape. Suburbanisation, seen by many, including American consultants to the Russian government, as the panacea for the problems of the Russian city, never really came off the ground. The Russian city was just not designed for this. In Moscow this is most obvious: The ring road works as a wall – even if now only a limited number of people travel in and out the city every day, this already leads to endless traffic jams at the limited number of flyovers.

THE CITY CENTRE

The biggest and most impressive changes are seen in the city centres. In order to understand the importance of the changes here, one must realize that Soviet city planning had left the city centres alone. With the increase of production as its main aim, it concentrated its efforts on the outskirts of the city, where it built factories and the housing for the people working in them. Many ministries, such as the ministry of light industry and the ministry of nuclear energy, had their own urban planning offices that were constructing new housing districts and even new cities.
This all changed with the emergence of the market economy. The city centre suddenly got a completely new meaning as a centre of communication, trade and shopping – to be short - as a market and a place of identification. It is probably no coincidence

lösung für die Probleme der russischen Städte gesehen hatten, konnte nicht funktionieren. Aufgrund ihrer Anlage eignen sich russische Städte dafür einfach nicht. Am deutlichsten sieht man das in Moskau. Die Ringautobahn wirkt als Barriere – selbst wenn die Zahl der Pendler relativ gering ist, führt dies schon heute zu endlosen Staus an den wenigen Anschlussstellen.

DAS STADTZENTRUM

Die größten und deutlichsten Veränderungen findet man in den Stadtzentren. Will man die Bedeutung der Veränderungen hier verstehen, muss man wissen, dass Stadtplaner zu Sowjetzeiten die Stadtzentren nicht angerührt haben. Da das wichtigste Ziel die Steigerung der Produktion war, konzentrierte man sich auf die Vororte, wo Fabriken und Wohnungen für die dort Beschäftigten errichtet wurden. Viele Ministerien, wie zum Beispiel das Ministerium für Leichtindustrie und das Ministerium für Kernenergie, hatten eigene Bauabteilungen, deren Aufgabe der Bau neuer Wohngebiete, ja ganzer neuer Städte war.
All das änderte sich mit der Herausbildung der Marktwirtschaft. Das Stadtzentrum erhielt plötzlich eine völlig neue Bedeutung als Zentrum der Kommunikation, des Handels und des Einkaufens oder, kurz gesagt, als Markt und Identifikationsort. Es ist wahrscheinlich kein Zufall, dass sich das anschaulichste Beispiel für diese Entwicklung in Nishni Nowgorod findet, einer Provinzstadt mit 1,5 Millionen Einwohnern 800 Kilometer östlich von Moskau. In enger Zusammenarbeit mit kleinen Bauunternehmen leiteten die Architekten der Stadt einen Prozess der „behutsamen Stadterneuerung" ein, um den Bedürfnissen der neuen Elite gerecht zu werden, die ihre Landhäuser aufgab und in die Stadt zurückkehrte. Im Unterschied zu Moskau und St. Petersburg, jedoch ganz ähnlich wie in anderen russischen Provinzstädten, bestand ein Großteil des Zentrums von Nishni Nowgorod aus Holzhäusern, die aufgrund der Vernachlässigung zu Sowjetzeiten extrem baufällig waren. Auch wenn es nicht möglich war, sie alle zu retten, hatten die Architekten doch versucht, die Struktur der Stadt weitestgehend intakt zu halten, indem sie neue Gebäude zwischen die alten Holzhäuser setzten. Auch wenn das nicht immer zu befriedigenden Ergebnissen führte, war es doch einer der wenigen Versuche, eine Vision urbanen Bauens in die Arbeit der kommunalen Planungsbehörden unter Leitung des Chefarchitekten Alexander Charitonow einfließen zu lassen.
Am bemerkenswertesten daran ist, dass das Stadtzentrum in den Augen der Bewohner zunehmend an Bedeutung gewann. Zu Sowjetzeiten hatte kaum jemand die Schönheit der Stadt wahrgenommen. Heute ist das Stadtzentrum, dass sehr malerisch auf einer Anhöhe am Zusammenfluss von Wolga und Oka liegt, Stolz und Identifikationspunkt der Bevölkerung. Kurz gesagt, Nishni Nowgorod war in der zweiten Hälfte der 1990er Jahre so etwas wie der Traum jedes Reformers oder westlichen Beraters: Pluriformität statt Totalitarismus, Kleinteiligkeit statt Gigantomanie, lokale Kultur statt Zentralismus. Allerdings war die Stadt eine Ausnahme, und rückblickend wird klar, dass ein Großteil des Erfolges der Nishni Nowgoroder Schule auf ihren Mentor Alexander Charitonow zurückgeht, der im Jahr 2000 auf tragische Weise bei einem Verkehrsunfall ums Leben kam.

that the most vivid example of this development took place in Nizhniy Novgorod, a provincial town of 1,5 million 800 kilometres east of Moscow. In close cooperation with small building firms – the local architects started a process of 'behutsame Stadterneurung", catering to the need of the new elite that actually came back to the city, leaving their cottages behind. Other than Moscow and Petersburg, and quite similar to many provincial Russian cities, a large part of the centre of the Nizhniy Novgorod consisted of wooden houses that were almost falling apart since they had not been taken care of in the Soviet era. Although it was not possible to rescue them all, architects tried to keep the structure of the city intact as much as possible by constructing new buildings amongst the older ones.[1] Although not always leading to satisfactory results, this was one of the few attempts to actually incorporate a vision of urban design in the work of the municipal planning department, headed by the leading local architect Aleksandr Kharitonov.
The most remarkable of this all is the meaning which the city centre got in the eyes of the cities' inhabitants. In Soviet times nobody would actually see the beauty of the city. Now the city centre, which is actually beautifully located on a high riverbank on the junction of the Volga and Oka rivers, has become the focus point of pride and identification of the population. In short – Nizhniy Novgorod in the second half of the 1990s was like a dream for every reformer or Western consultant: pluriformity instead of totalitarianism, small scale instead of gigantism, and local culture instead of centralism. However, with this the city was an exception, and in retrospect it is clear that a large part of the success of the Nizhniy Novgorod school can be attributed to its leader Aleksandr Kharitonov, who tragically died in a car accident in 2000.

GENPLAN

The main instrument for urban design in the Soviet Union was the so-called Genplan – a big plan of the city on which its future development was projected. Each city would have such a plan, designed by a central institute in Moscow or St. Petersburg, where there were specialists needed for its various components. The plan was sent to the city and put on the wall in the office of the chief architect (head of the urban planning department), and would serve as a blueprint for the future of the city. Theoretically, under communist rule this system worked: in the end, the whole planning process and its financing was in the hands of one organisation, so there was just the question of speed – how fast can you fulfil the plan.
Still, anyone who has visited Russia knows that practice differed somewhat from this ideal – disorder often seems to prevail over order, and it is difficult to understand what were the intentions of the urban designers. If this even was the case in Soviet times, it is not difficult to predict what happened after that, when the means for realising the Genplan were not any more in the hands of the municipality, but that for the realisation of the plan the city depends on the money of private developers. In fact it meant that the Genplan completely lost its meaning as a planning instrument, and as a result the chief architects were empty-handed – they had no planning instrument any more. What exists in large quantities are regulations and norms. This was already the case in the Soviet Union - being in the end nothing else than a total bureaucracy. In communist society these norms had a specific character. They were

GENERALBEBAUUNGSPLAN

Das wichtigste Instrument in der Städteplanung der Sowjetunion war der so genannte Generalbebauungsplan, ein Riesenplan, der künftige Entwicklungen widerspiegeln sollte. Jede Stadt verfügte über einen solchen Generalbebauungsplan, aufgestellt von einem Zentralinstitut in Moskau oder St. Petersburg, wo es die für die einzelnen Bereiche erforderlichen Experten gab. Der Plan wurde dann der betreffenden Stadt ausgehändigt, wo ihn der Chefarchitekt, also der Leiter der kommunalen Bauabteilung, an die Wand hängte, um ihn als Vorgabe für die Zukunft der Stadt zu benutzen. Unter kommunistischer Herrschaft hat dieses System auch, zumindest theoretisch, funktioniert: Letztendlich lag der gesamte Planungsprozess und seine Finanzierung in der Verantwortung einer einzigen Stelle, so dass die entscheidende Frage lediglich das Tempo war, mit dem der Plan umgesetzt werden konnte.

Wer jedoch jemals in Russland war, weiß, dass die Praxis von diesem Ideal etwas abwich. Unordnung siegte oft über Ordnung, und es war schwer, die Absichten der Stadtplaner zu erkennen. Wenn das schon zu Sowjetzeiten so war, kann man sich leicht ausmalen, was passierte, als die Stadtverwaltung nicht mehr über die Mittel zur Umsetzung des Generalbebauungsplans verfügte, sondern nun vom Geld privater Entwickler abhing. Es lief darauf hinaus, dass der Generalbebauungsplan seine Bedeutung als Planungsinstrument vollständig verlor und die Chefarchitekten nun mit leeren Händen dastanden.

Was es dagegen reichlich gab, waren Vorschriften und Normen. Das war schon in der Sowjetunion so, die am Ende nichts weiter war als Bürokratie pur. In der kommunistischen Gesellschaft hatten Normen einen besonderen Charakter. Sie wurden von führenden Experten des Landes an so genannten Unionsforschungsinstituten für Projektierung (WNIIP) in Moskau aufgestellt. Da ihre Arbeit auf wissenschaftlichen Methoden basierte und den Interessen der Arbeiterklasse dienen sollte, konnte das Ergebnis nur die reine Wahrheit sein. Diese Wahrheit stand im Gegensatz zur kapitalistischen Unwahrheit, wo die freien Kräfte des Marktes zu unwissenschaftlichen und antisozialistischen Ergebnissen führen mussten. Logischerweise war dann jeder, der gegen diese Wahrheit opponierte, ein Feind des Volkes. Normen setzten also keine Grenzen, sondern schrieben vor, wie etwas zu machen war.

Die Transformation in den 1990er Jahren bedeutete nicht, dass die sowjetischen Normen aufgegeben wurden. Im Gegenteil – nun kamen neue Normen und Vorschriften hinzu. Ein wichtiger Grund für die Herausbildung von Glasnost und Perestroika war der Protest der Bevölkerung gegen die Zerstörung historischer Stadtkerne und die Umweltverschmutzung durch die Industrie. Statt einer Deregulierung führte die Perestroika zur Gründung von noch mehr Komitees, Räten und Instituten, die den Planungsprozess regeln wollten. Der letzte Nagel am Sarg der Stadtplanung waren die Reformen zur Etablierung des freien Marktes, in deren Folge sich die Gehälter der Fachleute in den Verwaltungen aufgrund der Inflation in nichts auflösten. Da die Ideologie des freien Marktes allenthalben propagiert wurde und sich die Regierung weigerte, für Verluste aufzukommen, beschlossen diese Fachverwaltungen, ebenfalls auf der Grundlage des freien Marktes tätig zu werden. Da sie über ein Monopol verfügten, hatten sie dabei auch Erfolg. Anstatt ein Planungsinstrument zu nutzen, arbeiten die Planungsbehörden jetzt mit einem diffusen Konglomerat von Instanzen zusam-

worked out by so-called "all-union scientific research design institutes" (VNIIP: vsesoyuznie nauchni-issledovatelskie instituti proektirovanii) in Moscow, by the best specialists of the country. Since their work was based on scientific methods and aimed to serve the interests of the working class, the outcome could unavoidably only be the Truth (Pravda). This Truth was opposed to the capitalist Untruth, where the free forces of the market would lead to non-scientific and anti-socialist outcome. Logically anybody who would oppose this truth was an enemy of the people. As a result these norms didn't have the character of limitations, but of prescriptions: a norm means – this is the way to do it.

The changes of the 1990s didn't mean that Soviet norms were abandoned. On the contrary – they were superimposed with new norms and regulations. This was the result of the fact that an important reason for the occurrence of glasnost and perestroika was related to the population's protest against the demolition of historic cities and the industrial pollution of the environment. Instead of de-regulation perestroika led to more committees, councils and institutes regulation the planning process. The last nail to the coffin of urban planning was the introduction of free market reforms, when the salaries of the specialists working in these institutions evaporated under the influence of inflation. Since free market ideology was propagated everywhere and the government refused to compensate these losses, these institutions decided that they could also operate on the basis of the market, and since they had a monopoly, they were quite successful in this. Instead of using a planning instrument, the planning authorities now work with a diffuse agglomerate of instances that should be visited to get an approval. These organisations prefer not to make their demands known on paper, they'd rather speak with you in person. Since the regulations are not coordinated, it has in fact become virtually impossible to build anything without breaking one or another regulation, meaning that somewhere one should try to 'convince' a regulator by offering extra compensation.

As a result of this, urban planning has become virtually impossible. Urban planning means that at an early stage of planning, limitations are introduced that guarantee that buildings that are constructed together form a certain urban entity which corresponds with the vision of the urban designer. In the reality of today's planning process, nobody is interested in the implementation of these limitations – if they are used, then they are only meant to be part of negotiations in a later stage. All parties involved in the process, (except for the architect) are actually happy about this, because the uncertainty of the process allows them to find the constellation that is most profitable to all parties involved: the investor, the city and the multiple approving bodies. All understand this as a play in which one can become lucky and get rich. And is this not all that capitalism is about – a big casino?

One has to understand this phenomenon as a legacy of Soviet rule, where the identification of the individual with the state was completely absent. Everybody understood the state system as a big theatre in which you were forced to take part, but that was not part of your system of values. A well-known saying expresses this: 'The state pretends to pay us, we pretend to be working". This differs strongly from the Western European mentality: when you are confronted with regulations here, a civil servant will start to explain to you why this rule is important for the common good.

men, von denen Genehmigungen einzuholen sind. Diese Organisationen ziehen es vor, ihre Forderungen nicht zu veröffentlichen; sie sprechen lieber mit den Betroffenen direkt. Da es keine Koordinierung der Vorschriften gibt, ist es faktisch unmöglich geworden, irgendetwas zu bauen, ohne die eine oder andere Vorschrift zu verletzen. Das bedeutet im Gegenzug, dass man einen der Zuständigen „überzeugen" muss, indem man eine Zusatzvergütung anbietet.

Stadtplanung ist unter diesen Umständen praktisch unmöglich geworden. Stadtplanung bedeutet ja, in einer frühen Planungsphase Grenzen zu definieren, um zu sichern, dass die zu errichtenden Gebäude eine bestimmte urbane Einheit bilden, die in Übereinstimmung mit den Visionen der Stadtplaner steht. Die Realität sieht heute jedoch so aus, dass niemand an der Einhaltung solcher Grenzen interessiert ist – wenn sie überhaupt zur Sprache kommen, dann nur, um in einer späteren Phase als Verhandlungsmasse eingesetzt zu werden. Alle Beteiligten (mit Ausnahme des Architekten) sind auch ganz zufrieden mit diesem Zustand, denn die Unsicherheit des Gesamtprozesses ermöglicht es ihnen, eine Konstellation zu finden, die schließlich für alle Beteiligten am profitabelsten ist – für den Investor, die Stadt und die zahlreichen Genehmigungsbehörden. Alle sehen das als Spiel, in dem man Glück haben und reich werden kann. Und geht es im Kapitalismus nicht schließlich genau darum, dass alles als großes Kasino zu betrachten ist?

Man muss dieses Phänomen als Erbe der Sowjetherrschaft begreifen, wo die Identifikation des Einzelnen mit dem Staat völlig fehlte. Jeder sah das staatliche System als ein großes Theater, an dem man teilnehmen musste, ohne dass man es als Teil des eigenen Wertesystems betrachtete. Ein bekannte Redewendung dazu lautet: „Der Staat tut so, als bezahlte er uns; wir tun so, als ob wir arbeiteten." Das unterscheidet sich massiv von der westeuropäischen Mentalität: Wenn man hier mit Vorschriften konfrontiert wird, erklärt ein Beamter, warum diese Vorschrift im allgemeinen Interesse ist. In Russland erzählt er stattdessen, dass er die Regeln nicht gemacht hat, dass sie natürlich willkürlich sind und dass es, wenn man das wirklich will, einen Weg gibt, dieses Einzelproblem zu lösen. Wenn diese Missachtung des Rechts auch irgendwie sehr menschlich ist, so bedeutet es nichts Gutes für die Stadtplanung, die ja ein direkter Ausdruck des öffentlichen Interesses sein sollte.

Die Architektur, die aus diesem Übermaß dysfunktionaler Regeln entsteht, folgt dem Weg des geringsten Widerstandes. Architektur wird ebenfalls zur Verhandlungsmasse. Es ist sicher keine Überraschung, dass der Geschmack vieler hochrangiger Politiker (darunter auch der Moskauer Bürgermeister) von dieser Tatsache beeinflusst wird. Da die Bevölkerung im Allgemeinen des Modernismus im sowjetischen Stil überdrüssig ist, passen sich Politiker lieber dem Geschmack der Öffentlichkeit an. Beamte wiederum lassen sich nicht gern von ihren Vorgesetzten kritisieren, und wenn man eine Baugenehmigung braucht, vereinfacht es die Dinge, wenn das Gebäude irgendwie historisch aussieht. Das erklärt, warum viele Bauten im demokratischen Russland mit seinem freien Markt denen der Stalinzeit ähneln. Der sozialistische Realismus hat im kapitalistischem Realismus einen würdigen Nachfolger gefunden.

In Russia he will tell you that he didn't make up the rules, that of course they are arbitrary, and that if you really want to, there is always a way to solve your individual problem. Although this disrespect for the law is in a way very humane, it is very bad for urban planning, being a direct expression of public interest.
The architecture that results from this overwhelming amount of dysfunctional rules takes the line of least resistance. Architecture also becomes a part of the negotiations. It might be no surprise that the taste of many high-positioned politicians (including, for instance, the mayor of Moscow) is strongly influenced by the fact that since the population in general is fed up with Soviet-style modernism, politicians tend to follow public taste and civil servants don't like to be critisized by their bosses, in order to get a building approved, this is easier when it looks historical. This explains why much of the architecture in a free-market democratic Russia is similar to that of the Stalin era. Socialist realism has found its successor in Capitalist Realism.

MIKRORAYONS, SMOLENSK – VON DER KOLLEKTIVEN HOFFNUNG ZUM TRAUM VOM PRIVATEN GLÜCK

KAI VÖCKLER

Ein Großteil der 340 000 Einwohner von Smolensk lebt in Plattenbauten. Diese befinden sich in den Außenbezirken der Stadt und sind durch eine Straßenbahn und ein privat betriebenes Minivan-Bussystem mit dem Stadtzentrum verbunden. Es wird immer noch gebaut, neue zwölfgeschossige Wohnscheiben entstehen, denn es herrscht Wohnungsmangel – allerdings handelt es sich größtenteils um Eigentumswohnungen für Besserverdienende. Daneben erheben sich die Wohnblocks aus der sozialistischen Ära, die seit Ende der 1950er Jahre entstanden sind und deren baulicher Zustand besorgniserregend ist. In ihnen reiht sich Wohneinheit an Wohneinheit, hermetisch abgeschlossen voneinander, teilweise mit Stahltüren verriegelt. Die Flure sind mit Graffiti verschmiert, die Briefkästen demoliert, und die freien Flächen zwischen den Wohnbauten wirken verwahrlost – neben einem ausgebrannten Autowrack sieht man aber auch ein älteres Paar, das gerade Spielgeräte eines Kinderspielplatzes neu streicht, und Hausfrauen, die ihre Wäsche aufhängen. Was heute als Betontristesse erscheint, war einst Teil einer großen Erzählung, eines großen städtebaulichen Planes, nach dem es weder Armut noch Ausgrenzung geben sollte. Mehrere Wohnblocks formten Bezirke, so genannte Mikrorayons. Als selbständige Einheiten verknüpften diese das Wohnen mit öffentlichen Dienstleistungen des Alltags: In den Flachbauten zwischen den Wohnblocks befanden sich Kindergärten, medizinische Versorgung, Sportstätten, kulturelle Einrichtungen und Einkaufsstätten. Ihre Größe war auf das Einzugsgebiet einer Achtklassenschule ausgerichtet. So konnten die Bewohner alle Erledigungen des Alltags zu Fuß bewältigen.

Für den sozialistischen Menschen war Wohnen keine Privatangelegenheit. Die sozialräumliche Struktur sozialistischer Städte basierte auf einer funktionalen Differenzierung der sozialen Rollen des Individuums: Betrieb, Wohnung und Datsche formten eine lebensweltliche und räumliche Triade, in der die Wohnung der faktische und ideologische Ort des kleinsten Grundkollektivs, der sozialistischen Kleinfamilie, war. Als das politisch-gesellschaftliche System der Sowjetunion zusammenbrach, geriet diese Beziehung aus den Fugen, das Verständnis von Wohnen wandelte sich. Mit der Möglichkeit der Eigentumsbildung, der Privatisierung der eigenen Wohnung, wurde diese zum Ort privater Freiheit und zu einem Schlüsselelement für Wohlstand.

Der von Wladimir Makanin 1998 veröffentlichte Roman *Underground oder Ein Held unserer Zeit* beschreibt eindringlich die Verwerfungen der postsowjetischen Gesellschaft zu Beginn der 1990er Jahre. Nicht von ungefähr spielt ein Wohnheim in der Peripherie Moskaus die zentrale Rolle. Hier fristet der Protagonist des Romans sein Leben

MICRORAYONS, SMOLENSK – FROM COLLECTIVE HOPE TO THE DREAM OF PRIVATE HAPPINESS

KAI VÖCKLER

A large proportion of Smolensk's 340,000 inhabitants live in concrete blocks made of prefabricated elements. These are located in the city's outlying districts and are linked to the city centre by tram and a privately operated minivan bus service. Building continues, as there is still a housing shortage. New twelve-storey apartment houses are going up, although these are largely owner-occupied flats for the better-off. Next to them stand blocks of flats from the socialist era, some of them dating back as far as the late 1950s, whose state of repair gives rise to concern. Inside it is one dwelling unit next to another, each hermetically sealed off from its neighbours, some of them secured with steel doors. The entrance halls are defaced with graffiti, the letterboxes demolished, and the open areas between the blocks have an abandoned air – next to the burnt-out shell of a car one can also see an elderly couple engaged in repainting the apparatus of a children's playground and housewives hanging up their washing. What appears today to be a dismal concrete jungle was once part of a larger narrative, a grand town planning concept under which there was to be neither poverty nor social exclusion . Several blocks of flats formed a small district (Russian: rayon) known as a microrayon. These were autonomous units combining dwelling facilities with everyday public services. Between the blocks of flats there were low buildings containing kindergartens, first aid stations, sports facilities, cultural institutions and shops. Their size corresponded to the catchment area of an eight-grade school, so that the residents could do all their everyday errands on foot.

Under socialism home life was not a private matter. The structural layout of socialist towns was based on a functional differentiation of the social roles of the individual: workplace, flat and dacha (summer chalet, usually wooden and hand-built) formed the three pillars of a self-contained world in which the flat was the actual and ideological site of the smallest basic collective, the socialist nuclear family. When the political and social system of the Soviet Union collapsed this structure disappeared with it, and the whole concept of home life changed. As people became able to acquire property, including their own flat, the latter became a locus of privacy and freedom and a key element of affluence.

The novel *Underground or A Hero of our Time*, published by Vladimir Makanin in 1998, vividly describes the upheavals of post-Soviet society in the early 1990s. It is no accident that an apartment house on the outskirts of Moscow plays the central role. Here the novel's protagonist spends his time acting as a "watchman" for flats belonging to better-off tenants when they are away abroad. The fear is not only of burglars but

als „Wächter" von Wohnungen bessergestellter Mieter, die auf Auslandsreise sind. Nicht nur Einbrüche, auch die Nachbarn sind zu fürchten, denn Wohnraum ist knapp: „Wenn die Nachbarn von diesem Zimmerchen Wind bekämen – die zur Rechten oder zur Linken (je nachdem, wer als erster davon erführe) –, würden sie die Wand durchbrechen und den kleinen Raum eilends ihren beiden vorhandenen angliedern. Die Tür zu diesem Nebenzimmer würden sie ganz einfach vernageln. Vielleicht sogar zumauern. Käme man dann am nächsten Tag, so würde einen die wunderschöne, kahle Wand anschauen, frisch gestrichen. ‚Aber war hier nicht meine Tür?' würde man fragen. Da würden die nur die Achseln zucken: Keine Ahnung. ‚Aber die Tür kann doch nicht verschwunden sein?' Doch dieser Hund, dieser Arsch, der sie zugemauert und sich das Zimmerchen einverleibt hat, wird dich auch noch fragen (ein bisschen verwundert): ‚Suchen Sie auf dem richtigen Stockwerk? Haben Sie sich nicht geirrt?', und dich in den nächsten Stock schicken, wo du wie ein Narr herumtapsen wirst."[1]
Die Geschichte steht für die Orientierungslosigkeit und Unsicherheit des postsowjetischen Großstadtbewohners angesichts der neuen Verhältnisse. Insbesondere die Privatisierung der einstmals sicher geglaubten Wohnungen treibt ihn um. Makanin beschreibt die Auseinandersetzungen und Feindseligkeiten zwischen den Bewohnern, die mit den neuen Eigentumsverhältnissen um sich greifen: „Man grüßte nicht und schrie mich auf dem Gang unverschämt an; tief drinnen in ihrer beklommenen Seele (ich spürte es) mühte sich aber ein feines Stimmchen, ertönte der wehmütige plebejische Schrei: *Sie werden uns doch alle betrügen,* sowohl mit der Wohnung wie auch mit dem Eigentum. Es sind liebe, vertraute Menschen, aber sie werden uns anschmieren. Wann wären wir einmal nicht angeschmiert worden? Die bittere Gewissheit bedrückte sie bereits, und das Gefühl, unausweichlich (in der Zukunft) betrogen zu werden, löste beizeiten ihre Schutzinstinkte aus. Allein schon der Gedanke, dass du betrogen worden bist, es einem anderen jedoch gelungen ist, zu einem Spottpreis (und mit etwas Beeilung) Eigentum zu erwerben und damit einen nigelnagelneuen Lebenssinn! Allein schon dieser Gedanke kann einen Menschen aus dem Wohnheim krank machen. Falejew wurde rausgeschmissen: Er wohnte im zweiten Stock bei einer Verwandten, ohne Berechtigung, schon seit fünf Jahren. Falejew hatte geschworen, dass er nicht die Absicht habe, sich polizeilich zu melden, keinen Anspruch stelle (und an der Privatisierung nicht teilnehme), aber es wurde ihm barsch gesagt: Geh zurück nach Rschew. Und er ging. Die beiden Gnadenbrotempfänger aus dem sechsten Stock wurden rausgeschmissen. Der nicht gemeldete Elektriker Kolja im siebten Stock wurde kollektiv bei der Miliz angezeigt. Dann entdeckte man den alten Nisowski, der im ersten Stock hauste, und drängte ihn hinaus, der unglückliche, vergessliche Greis war als Dauergast geblieben, wohnte in einem Kämmerchen, aber nein, raus mit dir! (Wen er ursprünglich besucht hatte, wusste der Alte nicht mehr. Es war so viele Jahre her. Auch die, zu denen er gekommen war, hatten es vergessen.) Hatte man mit geschärftem Spürsinn mögliche Anwärter auf Q-Meter entdeckt, so wurden sie aus dem Wohnheim wie aus einer Tube gequetscht. (...) Besonders diejenigen, die ein gutes Stück älter waren, erinnerten sich nun an die auf alle gleichmäßig verteilte sowjetische Armut wie an das himmlische Manna."[2]

also of the neighbours, for housing is scarce: "If the neighbours were to get wind of this little room – those on the right or those on the left (depending on who found out first) – they would instantly break through the wall and annexe it to their two existing ones. They would quite simply board up the door to this adjoining room, perhaps even wall it up. Then, if you were to come next day you would be confronted with a beautiful, freshly painted bare wall. 'But didn't my door use to be here?' you would ask. They would just shrug their shoulders. No idea. 'But the door can't just have disappeared?' Then this swine, this bastard who has annexed the room and walled it off, will go on to ask you in a slightly surprised tone: 'Are you looking on the right floor? Are you sure you're not mistaken?', and send you to the next floor where you will wander around like a fool."[1]

The story represents the disorientation and insecurity of the post-Soviet city dweller in the face of the new realities. He is especially haunted by the privatisation of the flats once believed to be so secure. Makanin describes the conflicts and hostilities between the residents as they grapple with the new system of property: "They didn't greet me but shouted rudely at me in the corridor; deep down in their anxiety-ridden soul (I felt it) a tiny voice was struggling to be heard, to utter the plaintive plebeian cry: *They're going to cheat us all,* both with the flats and the property. They are nice people and we know them, but they'll take us for a ride. When was there ever a time when we weren't taken for a ride? The bitter certainty was already oppressing them, and the feeling that they were bound to be cheated at some future date soon mobilised their instinct for self-preservation. The very thought that you have been cheated while another has managed to acquire property for a song (more or less overnight) and is now full of the joys of life! The very thought is enough to make any occupant of the apartment house sick. Faleyev was thrown out. He had lived unregistered with a relative on the second floor for five years. Faleyev had sworn that he had no intention of registering with the police, was not going to make any claims (nor take part in the privatisation), but they told him bluntly to go back to Rzhev. And he went. The two on the sixth floor who'd been living on charity were thrown out. The unregistered electrician Kolya on the seventh floor was collectively reported to the Militia. Then they found old Nizovski, who squatted on the first floor, and forced him to leave. The unfortunate, forgetful old man had remained as a permanent guest, living in a cubby hole. But oh no, it was out you get! (The old man could no longer remember whom he had originally been visiting. Too many years had passed. Those who had invited him had also forgotten.) As soon as the presence of prospective buyers of living space was sensed in the offing, the existing occupants were squeezed out of the apartment house like toothpaste from a tube. (...) Those who were getting on in years now remembered the equitably shared poverty of Soviet times as though it were manna from heaven."[2]

HOME LIFE UNDER SOCIALISM

Under socialism having a home to live in was considered to be one of the most important social needs that not only had to be met but re-ordered and designed with a view to the development of a communist society and to foster the emergence of a "New Man". Thus centrally organised housing was a key element in Soviet propa-

WOHNEN IM SOZIALISMUS

Wohnen galt im Sozialismus als eines der wichtigsten gesellschaftlichen Bedürfnisse, das nicht nur zu erfüllen, sondern im Sinne der Entwicklung hin zu einer kommunistischen Gesellschaft, zur Erziehung eines „Neuen Menschen" zu gestalten und neu zu ordnen war. Daher war das zentralistisch organisierte Wohnungswesen ein Kernstück der sowjetischen Propaganda. Die öffentliche Versorgung mit Wohnraum erschien als geeignetes Mittel, die gewünschte Gleichheit der Lebensverhältnisse und eine egalitäre Lebensweise sicherzustellen. Die Revolutionierung der Lebensweise zielte auch auf das häusliche Leben, wie Erhard Stölting ausführt: Die Individuen sollten aus ihren traditionellen familiären Bindungen herausgelöst und in die kollektiv-gesellschaftliche Organisation eingegliedert werden.[3] Das Familienleben selbst sollte vergesellschaftet, überhaupt die Privatsphäre aufgelöst werden. Ernährung, Kindererziehung und gesellige Kommunikation hatten außerhalb der eigenen vier Wände stattzufinden. Und diese veränderte Lebensweise sollte durch die Architektur mitgeformt werden, der vergesellschaftete Alltag sein Gegenstück in Gemeinschaftshäusern finden. Entsprechend entwickelte die Architektenschaft nach der Oktoberrevolution utopische Entwürfe für Kommunehäuser, von denen nur vereinzelte Exemplare wie das Narkomfin-Gebäude (1928–1930) von Moisei Ginzburg und Ignati Milinis in Moskau realisiert wurden.[4] Inspiriert durch die sozialutopischen Entwürfe des 19. Jahrhunderts, etwa die „phalanstères" von Charles Fourier, entwickelte man radikal-kollektivistische Konzeptionen des Wohnungswesens. Ein oft dokumentiertes Beispiel ist das Projekt einer „Hauskommune" für 1680 Personen von M. Barschtsch und W. Wladimirow, das diese 1929 entworfen haben: Sie sollte aus einem Hauptblock für 1000 erwachsene Personen bestehen, dazu kamen zwei Gebäudeflügel für 320 Kinder im Alter von acht bis 16 Jahren sowie drei Querflügel für 360 Kinder im Vorschulalter. In den unteren Geschossen waren Dienstleistungseinrichtungen aller Art vorgesehen, im Hauptblock individuelle Schlafkabinen von sechs Quadratmetern Größe. Die Konzeption der Hauskommune beruhte auf einer völligen Ausschließung der Familie und des individuellen Haushalts.[5] Diese Absicht, die bürgerliche Familie aufzulösen, lag auch begründet in der Einbindung der Frau in den Produktionsprozess, wie sie von Marx, Engels und Lenin gefordert wurde; die gesellschaftliche statt der häuslichen Kindererziehung zielte auf die Gestaltung des „Neuen Menschen".

Allerdings war die Bautätigkeit in den 1920er Jahren geringfügig; vielmehr wurden die Wohnungssuchenden in die großräumigen Wohnungen des Adels und des Bürgertums eingewiesen. In der Gemeinschaftswohnung, der „Kommunalka", lebten unterschiedliche Wohnparteien zusammen, Paare, Einzelpersonen, Familien, und nutzten Küche und sanitäre Einrichtungen kollektiv – eine Wohnform, die bis heute fortbesteht. Zumeist bedeutete dies, dass einer Familie ein Zimmer zur Verfügung stand. In den beengten Verhältnissen blieb kaum etwas verborgen, was durchaus den Intentionen des Staates entsprach. Insbesondere im Stalinismus herrschte ein Klima wechselseitigen Misstrauens, das sich bis in die intimsten Bereiche erstreckte; die Bespitzelung untereinander verhinderte Privatheit. Die bourgeoisen Wohnungen sollten zu Zellen kommunistischer Kultur werden.[6] Stölting sieht hier den zentralen Widerspruch der sozialistischen Gesellschaft angelegt; er resultierte aus dem prinzipiellen Misstrauen gegenüber dem Privaten, das als Quelle unkontrollierter Widerständigkeit gegen den

ganda. The public provision of housing seemed to be a suitable means of ensuring the desired equality of living conditions and an egalitarian way of life. Revolutionising the way people lived extended to their home life, as Erhard Stölting points out. The individual was to be detached from his traditional family ties and integrated in a collectively organised society.[3] Family life itself was to be socialised; indeed the private sphere was to disappear altogether. Eating, raising children and socialising had to take place outside one's own four walls. And one of the things that helped shape this changed way of life was architecture in that it gave everyday socialised existence a counterpart in communal houses. After the October Revolution architects accordingly developed utopian blueprints for communal houses, of which only a few, such as the Narkomfin (Finance Ministry) Building (1928–1930) by Moisei Ginzburg and Ignati Milinis in Moscow, were realised.[4] Inspired by the social utopian designs of the 19th century, such as Charles Fourier's *phalanstères*, radical concepts of collectivist living were developed. A well documented example of this is the project for a "house commune" for 1,680 persons by Mikhail Barshch and Vyacheslav Vladimirov, which they designed in 1929. It was to consist of a main block for 1,000 adults, plus two wings for 320 children aged 8 to 16, and three transverse wings for 360 children of pre-school age. The lower floors were intended for service facilities of all kinds, while the main block contained individual sleeping cubicles of six square metres each. The concept of the house commune was based on a complete rejection of the family and the individual household.[5] This intention of dissolving the bourgeois family was also justified in terms of the integration of women into the production process, as Marx, Engels and Lenin had called for; having children raised by the community instead of in the parental home was a step towards the emergence of the "New Man".

However, there was little construction activity in the 1920s. Instead those in search of housing were assigned to the spacious apartments of the nobility and bourgeoisie. In the communal flat, or *kommunalka*, different occupants lived together – couples, single persons, families – and used the kitchen and sanitary facilities collectively, a way of living that persists to this day. This usually meant that a family had the use of one room. Under these cramped conditions it was hardly possible to conceal anything, which was quite in accord with the government's intentions. Under Stalinism in particular a climate of mutual distrust prevailed, which extended to the most intimate spheres, and with people spying on one another there could hardly be any privacy. The bourgeois apartments were to become cells of communist culture.[6] This is where Stölting sees the central contradiction of socialist society, namely the programmatic distrust of the private sphere, which was seen as a source of uncontrolled obstructiveness to the guiding hand of the state. The private sphere was to be overcome on the one hand by a propaganda-induced enthusiasm, in which the individual would become submerged in the mass, and on the other by a system of seamless surveillance based on the assumption that everyone had something to hide.[7] This was not to change until after Stalin's death. Although the housing shortage had caused construction to increase even during Stalin's lifetime, it was Nikita Khrushchev's speech at the All-Union Conference of Construction Workers and Architects in 1954 that ushered in a new era. From now on there was a promise of a state-guaranteed entitlement to a minimum dwelling which also permitted a certain measure of

steuernden Eingriff des Staates galt. Das Private sollte einerseits überwunden werden durch eine propagierte Begeisterung, in der das Individuum in der Masse aufgeht, und andererseits durch die lückenlose Überwachung, in der Annahme, dass jeder etwas zu verbergen habe.[7] Das sollte sich erst nach Stalins Tod ändern. Zwar wurde wegen des Wohnungsmangels noch zu Stalins Lebzeiten die Produktion von Wohnraum erhöht, aber erst Nikita Chruschtschow leitete mit seiner Rede auf der Allunionstagung der Bauarbeiter und Architekten 1954 die Wende ein: Fortan galt das Versprechen eines staatlich garantierten Anspruchs auf eine Minimalwohnung, der auch ein gewisses Maß an Privatheit zuließ. Chruschtschow und die späteren Sowjetführer versuchten, den Ansprüchen auf Wohnen und Konsum Rechnung zu tragen. Doch bis zuletzt konnte dieses Versprechen nicht eingelöst werden.[8] Wichtige infrastrukturelle Maßnahmen wurden immer wieder aufgeschoben, es herrschte Wohnungsmangel bis zum letzten Tag der Sowjetunion. Und Knappheit produziert Ungleichheit: Das Versprechen, dass alle das Gleiche bekommen würden, war nicht aufrechtzuerhalten – es musste entschieden werden, wer bevorzugt wird.[8]

Betrachtet man die sowjetische Stadtentwicklung, so lässt sich feststellen, dass der sowjetische Städtebau eigentlich erst Ende der 1920er Jahre beginnt, etwa zu der Zeit, als der erste Fünfjahresplan (1927–1932) veröffentlicht wird. Den Hintergrund bildeten die intensivierte Industrialisierung und die Zwangskollektivierung der Landwirtschaft, eine radikale Modernisierung, die einen rasanten Verstädterungsprozess zur Folge hatte. Der Historiker Thomas Bohn zeigt die Wohnideologien auf, die den unterschiedlichen Stadien des sozialen Wandlungsprozesses entsprechen. Die sowjetische Gesellschaft wird ihm zufolge Ende der 1920er Jahre mobilisiert, danach atomisiert und schließlich konsolidiert. Als Etappen dieses Prozesses sind die Nivellierung der Bevölkerung (Verstaatlichung der Industrie, Kollektivierung der Landwirtschaft, Liquidierung der Klassenfeinde), der Elitenaustausch (Proletarisierung der Landflüchtigen, Aufstieg von Fachkräften, Parteisäuberungen) und die Etablierung neuer Hierarchien (Nomenklatura, Arbeiterdynastien, Intelligenz als Klassenmacht) festzuhalten. Dem entspricht der städtebauliche Diskurs, der zunächst auf utopische Lebensentwürfe rekurriert, sich Mitte der 1940er Jahre auf die Erfüllung von Grundbedürfnissen konzentriert und seit den 1960er Jahren die individuelle Selbstentfaltung thematisiert. Dazu finden sich die jeweiligen Wohnformen: zunächst das Kommunehaus, dann die Gemeinschaftswohnung („Kommunalka") und schließlich der Mikrorayon mit der Minimalwohnung.[9]

DIE SOZIALISTISCHE STADT

In den sozialistischen Ländern hat die Stadtentwicklung die urbane Struktur sehr viel stärker verändert als in den westeuropäischen Ländern. Die ideologischen Ziele waren auch höher gesteckt, schließlich sollte eine neue Gesellschaftsform geschaffen werden. Ausgehend von den im *Kommunistischen Manifest* erhobenen Forderungen „Vereinigung des Betriebs von Ackerbau und Industrie, Hinwirken auf die allmähliche Beseitigung des Unterschieds von Stadt und Land", stellte sich für die Architekten in der Sowjetunion die Frage nach den Spezifika der sozialistischen Stadtentwicklung.[10] Eine Frage, um die Ende der 1920er Jahre eine scharfe Debatte zwischen „Urbanisten" und „Desurbanisten" entbrannte. Beiden gemeinsam war die Vorstellung einer „Dezentralisierung" und damit Verkleinerung, wenn nicht sogar Auflösung der beste-

privacy. Khrushchev and the later Soviet leaders tried to do justice to the claims for housing and consumption. But right to the end this promise (the promise of a minimum dwelling for all?) proved impossible to keep.[8] Important infrastructure projects were repeatedly postponed, and the housing shortage persisted up to the last day of the Soviet Union's existence. And scarcity generates inequality: The promise that everyone would receive the same was impossible to honour – it had to be decided who was going to get preferential treatment.[8]

When we look at the history of Soviet urban development, it may be said that it did not really get under way until the late 1920s, round about the start of the first Five-Year Plan (1927–1932). The background was provided by intensified industrialisation and the forced collectivisation of agriculture, a radical modernisation resulting in a rapid process of urbanisation. The historian Thomas Bohn identifies the housing ideologies corresponding to the various stages in the process of social transformation. In his view Soviet society was mobilised in the late 1920s, then atomised, and finally consolidated. The stages of this process were the levelling of the population (nationalisation of industry, collectivisation of agriculture, liquidation of class enemies); the replacement of the old elites with new ones (proletarianisation of those fleeing the land, the rise of a new class of experts, party purges); and the establishment of new hierarchies (nomenklatura, worker dynasties, the intelligentsia as a social force with class status). These stages correspond to the deliberations of the town planners, who initially resorted to utopian projects, then concentrated on meeting basic needs in the mid-1940s, and finally stressed the development of the individual from the 1960s on. Each stage had its appropriate form of housing: first the communal house, then the communal flat (*kommunalka*), and finally the microrayon with the minimum dwelling.[9]

THE SOCIALIST CITY

In the socialist countries urban development did much more to change the structure of cities than in Western Europe. The ideological aims were set much higher, as nothing less than a new form of society was to be created. Proceeding from the demands raised in the *Communist Manifesto* for the "combination of agriculture with manufacturing industry; gradual abolition of the distinction between town and country", architects in the Soviet Union were faced with the question of the specifics of socialist urban development.[10] This question triggered a lively debate between "urbanists" and "disurbanists" in the late 1920s. Common to both sides was the idea of "decentralization", i.e. reducing the size of if not actually dissolving the existing towns, and the aim of abolishing the differences between town and country. This must be seen against the background of a strong migration movement – between 1926 and 1939 the urban population of the Soviet Union doubled. Both tendencies assumed the socialist towns would have a completely new and autonomous character and that the family as an economic unit would disappear. Like many of their western colleagues they believed that social processes could be steered by means of architecture and town planning. The overcoming of class differences was conceived in these terms: the disappearance of the contradiction between centre and periphery, between bourgeois residential quarter and working-class slum, and ultimately the abolition of the

henden Städte und das Ziel, die Unterschiede von Stadt und Land aufzuheben. Dies ist vor dem Hintergrund eines starken Migrationsdrucks zu sehen – von 1926 bis 1939 verdoppelte sich die Stadtbevölkerung in der Sowjetunion. Beide Richtungen gingen vom völlig neuen und eigenständigen Charakter der sozialistischen Städte und vom Absterben der Familie als Wirtschaftseinheit aus. Wie viele ihrer westlichen Kollegen vertraten sie die Auffassung, dass sich soziale Prozesse durch Architektur und Städtebau steuern lassen. Die Überwindung der Klassengegensätze wurde in stadtplanerischen Kategorien gedacht: als Verschwinden des Gegensatzes von Zentrum und Peripherie, von bürgerlichem Villenviertel und Arbeiterslum und in letzter Konsequenz als Aufhebung des Gegensatzes von Stadt und Land. Die Urbanisten entwickelten ihre Konzeption der „Städtekommunen", die eine konzentrierte Organisation von Hauskommunen in Wohnkombinaten (als kleinsten Wohneinheiten der Siedlungsstruktur) vorsah. Die Desurbanisten dagegen lehnten jede Form von Zentren ab und entwarfen „Besiedlungslinien" entlang von Versorgungseinheiten, in einer dezentralisierten Siedlungsweise aus standardisierten und flexiblen Wohnungseinheiten. Kurz gesagt: Super-Gemeinschaftshäuser als gesellschaftlich-räumliche Keimzelle bei den Urbanisten und mobile, lineare Bandstädte aus entsprechend den Erfordernissen flexibel kombinierbaren Ein-Personen-Häusern bei den Desurbanisten.[11] Diese Konzeptionen blieben weitgehend folgenlos, sieht man von der im ersten Fünfjahresplans verankerten Idee ab, die sozialistische Stadt („Sozgorod") aus Wohnkombinaten gleichen Typs zu schaffen.[12]
Der 1935 ratifizierte „Allgemeine Plan zur Umgestaltung Moskaus", der die planerischen Vorstellungen über den Wiederaufbau der sowjetischen Städte nach dem Zweiten Weltkrieg bestimmte, suchte den Kompromiss zwischen utopischer Diskussion und dem zu diesem Zeitpunkt vorherrschenden akademischen Traditionalismus, der jetzt die Werte des Bürgertums zu bewahren und neu zu interpretieren suchte. Erstmalig wurde im Generalplan eine sowjetische Variante der „Nachbarschaft" propagiert: der schon erwähnte „Mikrorayon". Diese aus mehreren Wohnblocks zusammengesetzten Mikrobezirke waren als selbständige Einheiten konzipiert; sie sollten zwischen 30 und 50 Hektar umfassen und eine Einwohnerzahl von 5000 bis 15000 haben. Als gesetzlich festgelegte Grundlage der Wohngebietskonzeptionen wurde der Mikrorayon in der Chruschtschow-Ära ein wesentliches Kriterium bei der Planung und prägt bis heute nachhaltig das Bild der osteuropäischen Städte. Die Idee des Mikrobezirks – und ihre Umsetzung in die städtebauliche Praxis – kann als einer der wichtigsten Beiträge der Sowjetunion zur Organisation des städtischen Lebens bewertet werden.[13]

VERSTÄDTERUNG OHNE STADT

Dabei ist nicht zu übersehen, dass das im Sozialismus geschaffene Raumgefüge sich deutlich von dem der westeuropäischen Länder unterscheidet, wenngleich diese Tatsache hinsichtlich ihrer Auswirkung auf die derzeitige Stadtentwicklung unterschiedlich bewertet wird.[14] In der Sowjetunion wurden über tausend neue Städte gegründet, meist in der Nähe von Rohstoffquellen. Es fand eine weitgehend homogene Raumentwicklung statt, die mit einer im Vergleich zu Westeuropa deutlich geringeren räumlichen Konzentration einherging – Resultat der spezifisch sozialistischen Entwicklung, die auf ein massives Wachstum von Arbeitsplätzen im Industriesektor gründete. Durch die Industrialisierungskampagne und die Kollektivierung ab 1929 wurde

distinction between town and country. The town planners developed their concept of "city communes", which provided for a concentrated organisation of house communes in housing combines (as the smallest housing units of the settlement structure). The disurbanists on the other hand rejected every form of centre and drew up plans for "linear settlements" along provisioning units, in a decentralised mode of settlement composed of standardised and flexible housing units. In short, the urbanists saw the nucleus of social life in super communal houses, while the disurbanists saw it in mobile, linear or "ribbon" towns composed of one-person houses that could be flexibly combined as required.[11] For the most part these concepts did not lead to anything, apart from the idea – enshrined in the first Five-Year Plan – of creating the socialist city (*sotsgorod*) out of housing combines of the same type.[12]
The "General Plan for the Reconstruction of Moscow", which was adopted in 1935 and formed the theoretical basis for planning the reconstruction of Soviet cities after the Second World War, sought a compromise between utopian discussion and the academic traditionalism prevailing at the time, which was now trying to preserve the values of the bourgeoisie and reinterpret them. For the first time the General Plan propagated a Soviet variant of the "neighbourhood": the "microrayon" mentioned above. These microdistricts composed of several blocks of flats were conceived as autonomous units; they were to cover between 30 and 50 hectares and have a population of 5,000 to 15,000. As the legally fixed basis of the concept of the residential area, the microrayon became an important planning criterion of the Khrushchev era and has left its mark on East European cities to this day. The idea of the microdistrict, and its application in practice, may be seen as one of the most important contributions of the Soviet Union to the organisation of urban life.[13]

URBANISATION WITHOUT CITIES

Yet there can be no overlooking the fact that the regional structure created under socialism differed markedly from that of the West European countries, even if this fact is variously interpreted with regard to its effect on the current urban development.[14] In the Soviet Union over a thousand new towns were founded, mainly at sites where natural resources were located. A largely homogeneous process of regional development took place, accompanied by a much lower degree of concentration as a result of its specifically socialist nature, which was founded on the massive growth of jobs in the industrial sector. During the industrialisation and collectivisation campaigns begun in 1929 the peasant culture was systematically destroyed, with the familiar devastating results: famines claiming millions of lives, a sharp drop in agricultural productivity, and deportations and executions of those unwilling to comply. This released the labour required for industrialisation – a mobilised population that was quick to change jobs, was not acclimatised to city ways, and found correspondingly little support in the urban networks.[15] In Marxist thought, urban life had a special importance as a progressive force opposed to the "idiocy of rural life" (Marx/Engels) and was also expected to promote a collective identity.[16] The aim was therefore the complete urbanisation of the entire territory so that, in addition to the new industrial towns, agrarian towns ("agrotowns") were also developed for the collectivised agriculture. A large part of the urban population consisted of migrants from the country-

systematisch die bäuerliche Kultur zerstört, mit den bekannten verheerenden Folgen: Hungersnöte mit Millionen von Toten, Einbruch der landwirtschaftlichen Produktivität, Deportationen und Hinrichtungen von Nichtwillfährigen. Damit wurden die Arbeiter freigesetzt, die man für die Industrialisierung benötigte – eine mobilisierte Bevölkerung, die rasch die Arbeitsstellen wechselte, nicht städtisch sozialisiert war und entsprechend wenig Rückhalt in den städtischen Netzwerken fand.[15] Städtisches Leben hatte im Marxismus eine besondere Bedeutung als progressive, dem „Idiotismus des Landlebens" (Marx/Engels) entgegengesetzte Kraft, die zudem eine kollektive Identität befördern sollte.[16] Ziel war daher die vollständige Urbanisierung des gesamten Territoriums, und dazu entwickelte man neben neuen Industriestädten auch agrartechnologische Städte („Agrostädte") für die kollektivierte Landwirtschaft. Ein Großteil der städtischen Bevölkerung bestand aus Landmigranten, die häufig in den „Neuen Städten" im ländlichen Raum wohnten – eine Verstädterung der bäuerlichen Lebensweise und, umgekehrt, eine Ruralisierung der Städte.[17] Städte konnten daher in ihrer Struktur und ihrer Form von Urbanität stark voneinander abweichen. Die sozialistische Stadt, so Thomas Bohn, war ein Phänomen der nachholenden Modernisierung unter den Vorzeichen einer Industrialisierung, die auf der Verstaatlichung von Ressourcen und Einrichtungen gründete. Durch eine bäuerlich sozialisierte Bevölkerung geprägt und ohne starkes Bürgertum und Zivilgesellschaft, hat die sowjetische – wie auch die altrussische – Stadt nie der „okzidentalen Stadt" (Max Weber) mit ihrem sich selbst verwaltenden städtischen Bürgertum entsprochen.[18] So haben sich räumliche Muster, physische und soziale Strukturen herausgebildet, die auf die Entwicklung der postsozialistischen Stadt einen nachhaltigen Einfluss ausüben.

UNTERURBANISIERUNG

Städte galten im Sozialismus als Instrument zur Steigerung der industriellen Produktion. Dienstleistungen und infrastrukturelle Maßnahmen dagegen wurden als „nicht-produktiv" angesehen. Entsprechend investierte man in den „nicht-produktiven" Sektor – Wohnungsbau, Schulen, Kindergärten, Krankenhäuser, Kaufhallen – immer weniger, um die Investitionen in die Industrialisierung zu maximieren. Das hatte zur Folge, dass wichtige Investitionen ausblieben – die schlechte Verkehrsanbindung der randstädtischen Mikrorayons in Smolensk während der Sowjetzeit ist ein Beispiel dafür. Oftmals konnten die versprochenen öffentlichen Dienstleistungen nicht oder erst verspätet bereitgestellt werden. Ein weiteres wichtiges Merkmal sozialistischen Stadtlebens war es, dass nicht die Stadt, sondern die Betriebe die eigentlichen Orte der Vergesellschaftung bildeten – sie gewährleisteten für ihre Beschäftigten die Versorgung mit Wohnraum, Kindergärten sowie Einkaufsstätten und organisierten Urlaub und Freizeitaktivitäten. Daher fanden die Menschen, wiewohl sie oftmals im gleichen Gebäude lebten, ihren gemeinschaftsstiftenden Bezugspunkt am Arbeitsplatz und nicht am Wohnort. Die Betriebswohnsiedlung, der an einen Wirtschaftszweig gebundene Wohnungsbau (finanziert durch das jeweilig zuständige Industrieministerium), war nicht nur unter Industriebetrieben weit verbreitet, sondern auch bei ganz anderen Einrichtungen und Organisationen. Der Anteil dieser Wohnungen betrug in den Städten oft mehr als 50 Prozent. Daneben gab es die Gemeinschaftswohnungen sowie wenige genossenschaftliche Wohnungsfonds, die die Möglichkeit boten, durch ein-

side who often lived in the rural parts of the "New Towns", which may have been an urbanisation of the peasant way of life, but it was also a ruralisation of the towns.[17] Towns could therefore differ greatly in their structure and urban character. The socialist city, according to Thomas Bohn, was a phenomenon born of belated modernisation in the shape of an industrialisation based on the nationalisation of resources and institutions. Characterised by a basically peasant population and without a strong middle class or civil society, the Soviet city has never – any more than the old Russian city – corresponded to Max Weber's "occidental city" with its self-governing citizenry.[18] Thus spatial patterns have emerged together with physical and social structures that exercise a lasting influence on the development of the post-socialist city.

UNDER-URBANISATION

Under socialism, towns were seen as an instrument for raising industrial production. Services and infrastructure projects on the other hand were regarded as "non-productive". Accordingly less and less was invested in the "non-productive" sector – housing construction, schools, kindergartens, hospitals, supermarkets – so as to maximize the investments in industrialisation. The result was that important investments were not made – the poor transport links with the outlying microrayons of Smolensk during the Soviet period are an example of this. Often the promised public services could not be provided or only after a delay. Another important feature of socialist city life was that it was not the city but the enterprises that were the real loci of socialisation – they provided their employees with housing, kindergartens, shops and organised vacations and leisure activities. Thus people, although they often might live in the same building, identified with the community at the workplace, not that of their home neighbourhood. The housing estate attached to a particular branch of industry (financed by the relevant ministry), was a widespread phenomenon, and not just among industrial enterprises, but also among quite different institutions and organisations. The proportion of such flats in the towns was often more than 50 per cent. There were also the communal flats as well as a few cooperative housing funds which gave people an opportunity of getting a flat quicker by making their own capital contribution – a variant mainly opted for by university graduates and industrial managers.[19]

Thanks to the state ownership of land, the concentration of the construction industry, and state financing, a great number of very large residential districts were built and concentrated in certain areas. This urbanisation was based on centralized investment in infrastructure. But it failed to achieve a truly urban character. There was little diversity in the urban services and hardly any urban density. In view of the new ownership situation the marginalised members of the middle social strata moved to the new housing estates on the outskirts which were better provided for, whereas the new elite, the "nomenklatura" (party leaders, directors of the state economy and top administrators), lived in privileged enclaves, some of which were located in the downtown areas. What remained were the dropouts of socialist society – misfits and dissidents, former criminals – who withdrew to the crumbling inner cities. This led to a dissolution of social networks and neighbourhoods – in so far as there were any – which for most of the population were replaced by workplace-based communities. Most people now lived in the new housing estates with their colleagues from work,

gebrachtes Eigenkapital schneller an eine Wohnung zu kommen – eine Möglichkeit, die hauptsächlich Akademiker und kaufmännische Angestellte nutzten.[19]
Durch das staatliche Eigentum an Grund und Boden, die Konzentration der Bauindustrie und die Finanzierung durch die staatliche Hand konnte eine Vielzahl sehr großer Wohnbezirke errichtet werden, die zudem räumlich konzentriert waren. Diese Urbanisierung basierte auf der Zentralisierung der infrastrukturellen Investitionen. Allerdings entwickelte sich kaum „Urbanität"; es gab wenig Diversität in den städtischen Dienstleistungen, kaum städtische Dichte. Die marginalisierte Mittelschicht wich aufgrund der neuen Eigentumsverhältnisse auf die besser ausgestatteten, randstädtischen Neubausiedlungen aus, während die neue Elite, die „Nomenklatura" (Parteiführung, Direktoren der staatlichen Ökonomie und Leiter der öffentlichen Verwaltung), in privilegierten Enklaven wohnte, die sich teilweise auch in der Innenstadt befanden. Übrig blieben die aus der sozialistischen Gesellschaft Herausgefallenen – Unangepasste und Dissidenten, auch frühere Kriminelle – die sich in die verwahrlosten Innenstadtkerne zurückzogen. Damit lösten sich – insoweit sie überhaupt bestanden – soziale Netzwerke und Nachbarschaften auf; für den größten Teil der Bevölkerung wurden sie durch arbeitsplatzbasierte Gemeinschaften ersetzt. Zumeist wohnte man nun in den neuen Wohnsiedlungen mit den Arbeitskollegen zusammen, was eine hohe soziale Homogenität zur Folge hatte. Das alles führte zu einer spezifischen Form von Urbanität, die Ivan Szelenyi als „under-urbanisation" (Unterurbanisierung) bezeichnet.[20] Sie steht im Gegensatz zum westlichen Entwicklungsmodell, wo das schnelle Wachstum von Arbeitsplätzen mit dem Ausbau der Infrastruktur und der Dienstleistungen verbunden war, die Ökonomisierung des Raums eine größere Vielfalt an Konsumangeboten hervorbrachte und der städtische Raum zugleich durch soziale Distinktion und die damit verbundenen Segregationserscheinungen geprägt wurde.

KOLLEKTIVE HOFFNUNG

Die sozialistische Stadtplanung hat räumlich konzentrierte, große Wohnbezirke geschaffen, die weitgehend homogen waren in der Zusammensetzung ihrer Bewohner. Unbestreitbar war die soziale Segregation hier sehr viel geringer als in den westlichen Gesellschaften. Die sozialistische Wohnungspolitik basierte auf dem Grundsatz, dass Haushalte Wohnraum nicht über eine administrativ definierte Norm hinaus benutzen durften (davon war die politisch-militärische, industrielle und intellektuelle Elite ausgenommen).[21] Ihr lagen egalitäre Prinzipien zugrunde; die öffentliche Versorgung mit Wohnraum sollte, wie gesagt, die Gleichheit der Lebensverhältnisse gewährleisten. György Enyedi hat darauf hingewiesen, dass Egalitarismus im Zeichen von Knappheit Ungleichheit produziert: Wenn nicht alle gleichermaßen versorgt werden können, dann muss die staatliche Verwaltung entscheiden, wer bevorzugt wird.[22] Angesichts des bis heute in Russland bestehenden Wohnraummangels stellt der „Besitz" einer Wohnung ein Privileg dar – denn wer im Sozialismus eine Wohnung erhielt, war quasi unkündbar, was einem Eigentumsverhältnis nahe kam. Begünstigt wurden diejenigen, die sich dem Staat und der Obrigkeit gegenüber loyal verhielten. Da die Wohnungen in den Neubausiedlungen mit Warmwasser und Fernheizung über einen weit höheren Standard verfügten als die Altbauwohnungen, war die Zufriedenheit mit den neuen Verhältnissen groß. „Wohlstand als öffentlicher Zweck, Glück, so könnten wir sagen, für die Werktäti-

ПРИШЛО ВРЕМЯ ВОПЛОТИТЬ МЕЧТУ!
CAMEL
4 поездки для 4 друзей!
Условия внутри пачки
МИНЗДРАВ РОССИИ ПРЕДУПРЕЖДАЕТ: КУРЕНИЕ ВРЕДИТ ВАШЕМУ ЗДОРОВЬЮ

ДМБ 93

gen, die Mehrheit, den Durchschnitt, das war zur Rechtfertigung staatlicher Intervention geworden", schreibt György Konrád in seinem „Rückblick auf die Beglückung", „das Tor zum Glück war die Tür zum Flur einer Wohnung, wofür der Bürger nach Verdienst und Bedarf vom Wohnungsamt einen Schlüssel erhielt. Und ein junges Pärchen fühlte sich glücklich, wenn ihm ein solcher Schlüssel ausgehändigt, ein solches Leben in einer Plattenbausiedlung ermöglicht wurde."[23] Jeder Hausbewohner konnte sich leicht vorstellen, wie sein Nachbar lebte, denn zur Idee der Gleichheit passten die standardisierte Bauweise und die Typisierung der Gebäude wie auch die einheitliche Planung der Mikrorayons nach den Prinzipien der Nachbarschaftseinheit.

Überhaupt war es verpönt, sich zu exponieren. Die Auflösung der bürgerlichen Klasse als distinkter sozialer Kategorie und die massive Proletarisierung, in der die meisten Menschen Angestellte des Staates waren, hatte eine „Mittelschicht" entstehen lassen, die sich als eine Gesellschaft von Gleichen begriff. „Der Mensch der Neubausiedlung, der werktätige, kollektive, sozialistische Mensch ist jemand, dem für sein Kind ein Spielplatz und für sein Auto ein Parkplatz zur Verfügung steht, dessen Frau zu dem ihr trauten Friseur nicht weit gehen muss. (...) Wenn der neue Mensch, der Aktivist, außer seiner Wohnung im Sommer noch einen Urlaubsplatz im familiären Erholungsheim der Gewerkschaften bekam, am Gewässer oder im Gebirge gelegen, dann fehlte ihm nicht viel, um vollends glücklich zu sein", so György Konrád; aber es gab „noch ein anderes Problem. Es war dort erschreckend langweilig. Und Langeweile macht nicht glücklich. Zwischen den Häusern fegt der Wind hin und her; wenn der Bewohner auf die Straße geht, um einen Spaziergang zu machen, findet er nichts, was ihn fesseln würde. Der Passant auf dem Bürgersteig will etwas sehen; Schaufenster und Gaststätten erregen die Phantasie, die bloße Wand nicht. Aus der Abschaffung der *rue corridor* resultiert Heimatlosigkeit."[24] Konrád schlägt daher vor, dass in demokratischen Gesellschaften die Individuen zwischen verschiedenen Umgebungen wählen sollten, bis sie ihre Gegend zum Wohnen gefunden haben. Ein Glück für denjenigen, dem dies möglich ist – für die meisten Bewohner der russischen Mikrorayons ist es schon aus Geldgründen nicht machbar.

PRIVATISIERUNG

Nach dem Zusammenbruch der Sowjetunion wurden die durch die staatliche Förderung verdeckten Missstände sichtbar: Die Gebäude waren nicht instand gehalten worden; die Bausubstanz der in den 40 Jahren zuvor errichteten Wohnsiedlungen ist extrem baufällig. Es kommt immer wieder zu Unterbrechungen bei der Warmwasserversorgung, weil die alten Leitungen brechen. Obgleich alle Wohnungen mit Strom und Fernheizung versorgt sind, weisen viele von ihnen große Mängel auf. Die Fenster sind schlecht abgedichtet, die Heizkörper sind oftmals zu klein dimensioniert und verfügen über kein Thermostat, mit dem sie sich regulieren ließen. Die Mieten sind nicht kostendeckend. Es fehlt eine eindeutige Abgrenzung der Verantwortlichkeiten. Und es herrscht nach wie vor Wohnungsknappheit. Der russische Staat hat sich dieser Probleme zu entledigen versucht, indem er den staatlichen Wohnungsbestand den Kommunen übergab.[25] Diese übernahmen außerdem die angegliederte Dienstleistungsstruktur. Auch Unternehmen, insbesondere jene, die privatisiert werden sollten, und gesellschaftliche Organisationen wurden angehalten, ihren Wohnungsbestand zu

which resulted in a high degree of social homogeneity. All this led to a specific form of city life that Ivan Szelenyi calls "under-urbanisation".[20] It contrasts with the western development model, where the rapid growth of jobs was linked to the expansion of infrastructure and services, and the economic development of a region led to a greater variety of consumer goods, which at the same time led to greater social distinctions and segregation phenomena.

COLLECTIVE HOPE

Socialist town planning created large, densely populated residential districts that were largely homogeneous as regards the composition of their residents. There is no denying that there was much less social segregation here than in western societies. Socialist housing policy was based on the principle that households were not entitled to living space in excess of an administratively defined norm (this did not include the political, military, industrial and intellectual elites).[21] It was based on egalitarian principles, the public provision of housing being supposed, as was said above, to guarantee equality of living conditions. György Enyedi has pointed out that egalitarianism under conditions of scarcity produces inequality: If equal provision cannot be made for all, the state administration must decide who gets preference.[22] (see page 1) In view of the housing shortage (that still exists in Russia) the "ownership" of a flat constituted a privilege – for under socialism anyone who received a flat could practically never be given notice, which was something very close to ownership. Preference was given to those who showed loyalty to the state and the authorities. Since the flats in the new housing schemes had hot water and district heating of a much higher standard than in the old buildings, people were very contented with their new circumstances. "Prosperity as the aim of public policy, happiness, it might be said, for the working people, the majority, the average people, that became the justification for state intervention," writes György Konrád in his *Rückblick auf die Beglückung* (Compulsory Happiness in Retrospect), "the gate to happiness was the door to the entrance hall of a flat, for which the citizen received a key from the public housing agency according to his merits and requirements. And a young couple were happy to be given such a key that made it possible to live in a new estate made up of concrete blocks."[23] Every resident of the building could easily imagine how his neighbour lived, for the idea of equality was matched by the standardised construction of every building and the uniform planning of microrayons according to the principles of the neighbourhood unit.

There was a general taboo on anything that would make one stand out. The dissolution of the bourgeois class as a distinct social category and the mass proletarianisation whereby most people became employees of the state, had led to the emergence of a "middle stratum" which saw itself as a society of equals. "The man in the new housing estate, the working, collective, socialist man, is someone who has access to a playground for his child and a parking space for his car, whose wife does not have far to go to her regular hairdresser. (...) If in addition to his flat the new man, the activist, got a summer vacation place in the trade union's family recreation home at the seaside or in the mountains, it didn't take much more to make him perfectly happy," says György Konrád, but there was "another problem. Life was terribly boring. And

übergeben – was sie bereitwillig taten, um sich von der „Bürde" der kostenträchtigen Aufgabe und der sozialen Verantwortung zu befreien. In der Folge führte dies zu andauernden Konflikten zwischen der russischen Regierung und der lokalen Politik, beispielsweise um die Kontrolle ausländischer Eigentümer oder die Einhaltung von Mieterrechten.[26] Insbesondere die Intransparenz des derzeitigen Wohnungsmarktes ist der russischen Regierung ein Dorn im Auge – von den jährlich etwa 4 Milliarden Euro Subventionen kommen gerade 120 Millionen bei den Haushalten an, der Rest wird von den Wohnungsgesellschaften und den an der Wohnungswirtschaft beteiligten Firmen verbraucht.[27]

Mit dem Gesetz „Über die Privatisierung des Wohnungsfonds der RFSFR" wurde 1991 die Privatisierungskampagne gestartet. Mieter konnten, auf freiwilliger Basis, die von ihnen bewohnte Wohnung erwerben. Anfangs wurde ein kleines Entgelt verlangt, das später ganz entfiel. Es ergeben sich marginale Verwaltungsgebühren in Höhe von 1000 Rubel (ca. 33 EUR), und die Belastung durch die Vermögenssteuer fällt kaum ins Gewicht.[28] Die Betriebskosten liegen deutlich unterhalb der Miete. Durch eine rasche und nahezu kostenlose Privatisierung sollten die laufenden Kosten, aber auch die anfallenden Sanierungskosten auf die Privateigentümer abgewälzt werden. Dies ist nur bedingt gelungen. Da ein Großteil der russischen Bevölkerung lediglich über geringfügige Einkommen verfügt, müssen nach wie vor Heizung, Elektrizität und Wasserversorgung staatlich subventioniert werden (allerdings sollen die Subventionen bis 2010 abgebaut werden).[29] Auch wurde das Wohneigentum vom Gesetzgeber nicht mit der Verantwortung des Eigentümers für seinen Besitz verknüpft; die gemeinsame Verwaltung durch Eigentümergemeinschaften findet nahezu nicht statt. Faktisch wird das Hauseigentum durch die lokalen Behörden betreut und nicht durch von den Eigentümern beauftragte Hausverwaltungen.

Der Privatisierungsprozess ging zunächst rasch vonstatten. Dabei waren es hauptsächlich Objekte in gut erschlossenen Gegenden und in Ziegelbauweise, die besonders begehrt waren – auch in Smolensk vornehmlich die innerstädtischen Wohnungen. Die Mieter der Plattenbauten waren zurückhaltender, denn gegen den Erwerb sprach, dass nach wie vor ein hoher Mietschutz besteht und sie zu Recht befürchteten, beträchtliche Renovierungskosten mittragen zu müssen. Das betrifft insbesondere die fünfgeschossigen Bauten aus der ersten Bauphase von 1956 bis 1970, die etwa 15 Prozent des russischen Wohnflächenbestands ausmachen und nach deutschen Maßstäben abrissreif sind.[30] Der Chefarchitekt von Smolensk bestätigte auf Nachfrage, dass die Stadt in den alten Mikrorayons keinerlei Sanierungsmaßnahmen durchführen wird.

Die Massenprivatisierung von Wohnungen erfolgte in Smolensk vor allem in der zweiten Hälfte der 1990er Jahre. 2001 befanden sich 38 Prozent der Wohnfläche in privatem Besitz.[31] Dieser Wert liegt unterhalb des Anteils von Privateigentümern in Russland insgesamt, der 2003 schon 59 Prozent betrug.[32]

In den 1990er Jahren wurde der staatliche Wohnungsbau für Bevölkerungsschichten mit niedrigem oder durchschnittlichem Einkommen stark reduziert. Derzeitig gibt es, wie das Stadtplanungsamt darlegt, drei Varianten des Wohnbaus in Smolensk: erstens den mittlerweile auch stattfindenden privaten Einfamilienhausbau – knapp sieben Prozent der Gesamtwohnfläche, die zwischen 1995 und 2001 bebaut wurde –; zweitens den staatlich finanzierten Wohnungsbau, der durch private Investoren durch-

boredom does not make for happiness. The blocks are swept by gusts of wind. If a resident goes out into the street for a walk he will find nothing to attract his attention. The passer-by on the pavement wants to see something. Shop windows and restaurants stimulate the imagination, but a bare wall doesn't. The abolition of the *rue corridor* led to a sense of homelessness."[24] That is why Konrád proposes that in democratic societies individuals should be able to choose between various environments, they should be able to look until they find a location that suits them. This is fine for those who can afford it, but most residents of Russian microrayons can't.

PRIVATISATION

After the collapse of the Soviet Union the deficiencies concealed by state subsidisation became plain to see. As it was not kept in good repair, the building stock of the housing estates built in the past 40 years is extremely dilapidated. There are constant interruptions in the hot water supply because the old pipes keep bursting. Although all flats are provided with electricity and district heating, many of them have grave defects. The windows are poorly insulated, while the radiators are often too small and have no thermostat to regulate them. The rents do not cover the costs of upkeep. There is no clear division of responsibility. And the housing shortage persists. The Russian government has tried to get rid of these problems by handing over state-owned housing to the municipalities[25], which also took over the attached service structure. State enterprises, especially those earmarked for privatisation , and social organisations were also asked to hand over their housing stock – which they were quite prepared to do to free themselves of the "burden" of this costly social responsibility. The result has been constant conflicts between the Russian government and the local authorities over such things as the control of foreign owners or the observance of tenants' rights.[26] Furthermore the opaque nature of today's housing market is a thorn in the flesh of the Russian government – of an annual total of 4 billion euros paid out in subsidies just 120 million reaches the households, the rest being swallowed up by the housing associations and their contractors.[27]

The passing of the law "On the Privatisation of Housing Funds in the RFSFR" in 1991 marked the start of the privatisation campaign. Tenants were allowed to become owners of the flat they occupied. Initially a small sum was charged, but this was later abandoned. There are marginal administrative charges coming to 1,000 roubles (about 33 euros), and the wealth tax is insignificant.[28] The cost of upkeep is well below the rent. Privatisation was supposed to be carried out quickly and at almost no cost so that both the running costs and the costs of repairs could be passed on to the private owners. This has only been partly successful. As a large part of the Russian population have a low income, heating, electricity and water supply still have to be subsidized by the state (although the subsidies are to be abolished by 2010).[29] Nor did the legislation make home owners responsible for their property, and there is as good as no joint administration by the homeowners' associations. In fact, home ownership is supervised by the local authorities and not by estate agents employed by the owners.

The privatisation process got off to a good start. Most sought after were brick-built flats in well developed areas and these – in Smolensk as elsewhere – were mainly in the downtown area. The tenants of the concrete blocks were more cautious about

geführt wird. In der Regel wird hier das Grundstück – das sich nach wie vor in städtischem Besitz befindet – den Investoren kostenlos zur Verfügung gestellt; außerdem beteiligt sich die Stadt an den Baukosten und überlässt fünf Prozent der Wohnungen dem Investor. Dessen Profit errechnet sich aus dem Verkauf der Wohnungen und dem Überschuss aus der finanziellen Beteiligung der Kommune. Die restlichen Wohnungen werden dann zugeteilt, wobei die Auswahlkriterien undurchsichtig sind. Drittens gibt es die Zusammenarbeit mit privaten Investoren bei der Durchführung von Wohnbauprojekten. Die Stadt stellt auch hier das Grundstück kostenlos zur Verfügung, allerdings übernimmt der Investor alle Baukosten. Dafür erhält die Stadt zehn Prozent der Wohnungen, die sie verkauft, um mit den Erlösen den sozialen Wohnungsbau zu finanzieren – so zumindest die Absicht. Das Problem bei dieser Vorgehensweise ist offensichtlich: Die öffentliche Hand reguliert einerseits das Marktgeschehen, andererseits ist sie selbst in dieses involviert.[33] Entsprechend undurchsichtig ist das Verhältnis von privatem Investor und lokaler Verwaltung. Letztere steht vor der schwierigen Aufgabe, die Balance zwischen ökonomischen und sozialen Notwendigkeiten zu halten – bei permanenter Verschlechterung der allgemeinen Lebensverhältnisse. Der Wunsch, einerseits alles zu kontrollieren und andererseits direkt am ökonomischen Prozess zu partizipieren, dürfte typisch für die unentschiedene Rolle des Staates innerhalb des Transformationsprozesses sein.

TRANSITRAUM MIKRORAYON

Wird die Wohnung zur Ware, deren Wert vom Immobilienmarkt bestimmt wird, kann sie zu einer Quelle des Einkommens und des Wohlstands werden.[34] Die Privatisierung hat zu einer Umstrukturierung und Umverteilung des Wohnungsbestands geführt, ein Prozess, der mit der Segregation der Bevölkerung je nach Einkommen verbunden ist. Wie eine Untersuchung von Angela Harutyunyan und Samuel G. R. Johnston zeigt, ist dies auch in den Mikrorayons von Smolensk der Fall.[35] Besserverdienende sind in die attraktiveren innerstädtischen Wohnungen gezogen; dagegen versuchen Arbeitslose und Pensionäre, mit primitivsten Formen der Subsistenzwirtschaft ihr Auskommen zu sichern, wenn sie nicht sogar auf das Land ausweichen – auch dies Ausdruck einer katastrophalen Verschlechterung der Lebensverhältnisse in Russland, wo 29 Prozent der Bevölkerung, also etwa 42 Millionen Menschen, auf diese Weise zu überleben versuchen.[36] Die Städte verlieren an Attraktivität, so überstieg in Russland 1991 erstmalig der Wegzug städtischer Einwohner den Zuzug.[37] Und es suchen immer noch Millionen von Menschen eine Wohnung, die Zahl der Haushalte nimmt aus politischen Gründen zu – in die Smolensker Mikrorayons etwa drängen zunehmend russische Migranten aus den baltischen Staaten und Militärangehörige, die repatriiert werden. Die einst homogenen Hausgemeinschaften haben sich aufgelöst, stattdessen betrachten viele der neu Zugezogenen die in der Sowjetzeit errichteten Mikrorayons nur als Durchgangsstation. Für die, die dageblieben sind, ist die eigene Wohnung zum Rückzugsort geworden, wo man vom privaten Glück nur träumen kann und die Älteren den hoffnungsvollen Versprechungen der Sowjetzeit nachtrauern.

Bei der Wahl der Wohnung beginnt „Nachbarschaft" in einem neuen Sinne maßgeblich zu werden: Man sucht jetzt die Nähe sozial Gleichgestellter. Nicht mehr der Arbeitsplatz, sondern der Wohnort mit seiner lokalen Gemeinschaft bildet den Fokus eines

ownership, realising that a high degree of tenant protection remained in force and rightly fearing they would have to bear a share of the considerable renovation costs. This applied particularly to the five-storey blocks dating from the first construction phase from 1956 to 1970, which make up about 15 per cent of Russia's total living space and by German standards would be due for demolition.[30] When pressed, the city architect of Smolensk confirmed that the city would not carry out any renovation work in the old microrayons.

In Smolensk the mass privatisation of flats took place mainly in the second half of the 1990s. In 2001, 38 per cent of the living space was privately owned.[31] This figure is below the proportion of private owners in Russia as a whole, which in 2003 was already 59 per cent.[32]

In the 1990s, state housing construction for sections of the population with low or average incomes was sharply reduced. At present, according to the Town Planning Office, there are three types of housing construction going on in Smolensk. Firstly, the construction of private single-family houses which is currently taking place. These houses, built between 1995 and 2001, account for just under seven per cent of the total living space. Secondly, there is the state-financed housing construction which is carried out by private investors. In general the land – which continues to be owned by the city – is made available to investors free of charge. Furthermore the city also covers part of the construction costs and lets the investor have five per cent of the flats. The latter's profit comes from the sale of the flats and the surplus from the financial participation of the municipality. The remaining flats are then allocated on the basis of opaque selection criteria. Thirdly, there are the housing projects implemented in cooperation with private investors. The city makes the land available free of charge, while the investor assumes all construction costs. For this the city receives ten per cent of the flats it sells in order to finance social housing construction with the proceeds – such at least is the intention. The problem with this approach is obvious. The local authorities regulate the market transactions while being themselves involved in them.[33] The relations between private investors and the local administration are correspondingly murky. The latter are faced with the difficult task of maintaining a balance between economic and social necessities at a time when general living conditions are in a state of permanent deterioration. The desire to control everything, on the one hand, and to participate directly in the economic process, on the other, is probably typical of the ambiguous role of the state in the transformation process.

THE MICRORAYON AS A TEMPORARY STOP

Once the flat becomes a commodity whose value is determined by the property market, it can also be a source of income and of prosperity.[34] Privatisation has led to a restructuring and redistribution of the housing stock, a process connected with the segregation of the population according to income. As a study by Angela Harutyunian and Samuel G. R. Johnston shows, this is also the case in the microrayons of Smolensk.[35] The better-off have moved to the more attractive downtown flats, while the unemployed and *pensioners* struggle to get by with the most primitive forms of subsistence economy, and in some cases even seek refuge in the countryside – this too being an expression of the catastrophic deterioration of living conditions in Rus-

individuellen Lebens. Damit geht eine Depolitisierung der Arbeitsverhältnisse einher, aber von einer Verantwortung gegenüber dem Wohnort kann nicht die Rede sein. Zu groß sind die Probleme der meisten Menschen: Armut, Arbeitslosigkeit und fehlende Zukunftsperspektiven haben zu Apathie und Frustration geführt. Michael Harloe sieht hier die Tendenz einer „Palermoisierung" der Verhältnisse: ein mangelndes Vertrauen in die staatlichen Institutionen, kaum vorhandene zivilgesellschaftliche Prozesse, zumeist ineffiziente öffentliche Verwaltungen, die selbst als Unternehmer auftreten und öffentliche Gelder zur Profitmaximierung nutzen, Klientelismus, der die ehemaligen Mitglieder der Nomenklatura, die Direktoren der vormals staatlichen Betriebe und die erfolgreichen Unternehmer der zweiten oder Schattenökonomie begünstigt und vernetzt. Privatisierung, so Harloe, führt nicht zwangsläufig zu einer Marktwirtschaft; vielmehr lässt sich angesichts der russischen Verhältnisse von einer Entwicklung von der Planwirtschaft zur Klanwirtschaft sprechen. In hohem Maße hängt es von den lokalen Autoritäten ab, von ihrer Integrität und Professionalität, die negativen Aspekte des Transformationsprozesses abzuwenden.

Die Netzwerke, die aufgebaut, und die Fertigkeiten und Verhaltensweisen, die in der Schattenökonomie der Sowjetunion erlernt wurden, stellen eine Form des sozialen Kapitals dar, das jetzt genutzt wird, um sich eine Position in der neuen Ökonomie zu erkämpfen.[38] So wie früher die meisten Russen ihre reichen Beziehungsnetzwerke aktivierten, um die Probleme der Mangelwirtschaft zu bekämpfen, werden diese heute genutzt, um die Schwierigkeiten der Marktwirtschaft zu meistern. Dazu müssen, wenn es an finanziellem Kapital fehlt, alle Ressourcen ausgeschöpft werden: das soziale Kapital (Beziehungsnetzwerke), physisches Kapital (Apartments, Automobile, Datschen, Rechte am Land auf die Erträge aus Subsistenzwirtschaft) und menschliches Kapital (intellektuelle und handwerkliche Fähigkeiten).[39] Die sozio-räumliche Struktur der postsozialistischen Stadt wird einerseits durch ihren ökonomischen Wert bestimmt – begründet in der Einführung des Wohneigentums 1991 und des Eigentums an Grund und Boden 2001 –, mit den entsprechenden Umverteilungen und der damit verbundenen Aufspaltung der Gesellschaft. Andererseits ist die postsozialistische Stadt auch weiterhin durch einen sozialen Wert charakterisiert: durch die unsichtbaren Netzwerke, in die die Bevölkerung mehr oder weniger gut eingebettet ist.[40] Damit geht ein enormes Wachstum von städtischer Diversität und Marginalität und die Entstehung von Basarökonomien einher, die Ivan Szelenyi die Frage stellen lassen, ob hier nicht die Entwicklung hin zu einer „over-urbanisation" (Überurbanisierung) wie in der Dritten Welt prognostiziert werden kann.[41] Erhard Stölting erkennt in dem Rückzug auf das Land und der überlebensnotwendigen Subsistenzwirtschaft sogar eine Tendenz zur „Gegenurbanisierung", allerdings nicht als raumgreifende Form der Suburbanisierung in der Fortsetzung eines industriellen Dezentralisierungsprozesses wie in den westlichen Ländern, sondern vielmehr als eine Folge der wirtschaftlichen Ausnahmesituation – bezeichnenderweise eine Umkehr des von Stalin durchgepeitschten Industrialisierungs- und Urbanisierungsprozesses.[42] Es bleibt ungewiss, wohin sich die postsozialistischen Städte entwickeln. Unbestreitbar aber bestehen große Konfliktpotentiale, denn die zentrifugalen Kräfte der neuen Ökonomie bewirken, dass die im Versprechen auf ein besseres Leben zusammengehaltenen Gemeinschaften auseinander brechen. Es entstehen privilegierte Zentren und ausgegrenzte Räume, wobei die Dezentralisierungseffekte

sia, where 29 per cent of the population, or some 42 million people, try to survive in this way.[36] The cities are losing their attractiveness. In 1991, for the first time ever in Russia, the number of people who left the cities exceeded the number of those who moved to them.[37] And millions of people are still seeking flats as the number of households is increasing for political reasons – Russian migrants from the Baltic states and repatriated members of the armed forces are increasingly moving into the microrayons of Smolensk. The once homogeneous house communities have been broken up, and many of the newcomers regard the microrayons built in the Soviet period only as a temporary stop. For those of the original occupants who have remained, their own flat has become a place of refuge, where they can only dream of private happiness and, in the case of the older ones, mourn for the hopes and promises of the Soviet period.

For those choosing a flat "neighbourhood" – understood in a new way – is beginning to be the decisive factor. People now want to live next to their social equals. It is no longer the workplace but the place of residence, the local community, that is the focus of an individual's life. This is accompanied by a depoliticisation of the workplace, but there is no question of anyone feeling a sense of responsibility towards their place of residence. The problems facing most people are just too great: poverty, unemployment and the lack of future prospects have led to apathy and frustration. This is where Michael Harloe sees a tendency towards a "Palermoisation" of the situation: a lack of trust in state institutions; a civil society that is more or less non-existent; generally inefficient public administrations that assume the role of entrepreneur themselves and use public funds to maximize their own profit; and cronyism, which favours and links up the former members of the nomenklatura, the directors of the former state enterprises and the successful entrepreneurs of the second or shadow economy. According to Harloe, privatisation does not necessarily lead to a market economy – the situation in Russia is more like a transition from a planned economy to a clan economy. It is largely up to the local authorities, to their integrity and professionalism, to avert the negative aspects of the transformation process.

The networks created and the skills and modes of behaviour acquired in the shadow economy of the Soviet Union constitute a form of social capital that is now being used to jockey for a position in the new economy.[38] Just as most Russians used to activate their extensive networks of contacts in order to cope with the problems of economic scarcity in the past, these contacts are now being used to master the difficulties of the market economy. In the absence of financial capital, all resources must be directed to this end: social capital (networks of contacts); physical capital (apartments, cars, dachas, the right to own land, what can be wrested from the subsistence economy); and human capital (intellectual and artisan skills).[39] The socio-spatial structure of the post-socialist city is determined, on the one hand, by its economic value – based on the introduction of home ownership in 1991 and land ownership in 2001 – with all the redistribution and social fissures this entails. On the other hand, the post-socialist city continues to be characterised by its social value: through the invisible networks to which most of the population has some kind of connection.[40] This is accompanied by an enormous growth of urban diversity and marginality and the emergence of bazaar economies, which leads Ivan Szelenyi to ask whether one

auf einen weitgehend urbanisierten Raum und eine mobilisierte Bevölkerung treffen, für die die Bindung an den Ort kaum eine Bedeutung hatte – und die jetzt dort, im Mikrorayon, wie in der Falle sitzt.[43] Seine Bewohner müssen für sich bestimmen, ob sie weiterhin auf den zentralistisch organisierten Staat und seine Autoritäten vertrauen oder ob sie die neu gewonnene Freiheit selbst gestalten wollen.

ANMERKUNGEN

1 Makanin, Wladimir: *Underground oder Ein Held unserer Zeit.* München 2003, S. 253 f.

2 Ebd., S. 357 f.

3 Vgl. Stölting, Erhard: „Stadt und Gesellschaft in Russland". In: Berking, Helmuth/Faber, Richard (Hg.): *Städte im Globalisierungsdiskurs.* Würzburg 2002

4 Vgl. Leiprecht, Helga: „Ein neues Haus für eine neue Welt". In: *Du.* Nr. 12/2003, Jg. 742; vgl. auch Buchli, Victor: *An Archaeology of Socialism.* Oxford, New York 2000

5 Vgl. Goldzamt, Edmund: *Städtebau sozialistischer Länder.* Berlin/Ost 1973

6 Vgl. Leiprecht, a. a. O.

7 Vgl. Stölting, a. a. O.

8 Vgl. Enyedi, György: „Urbanisation under Socialism". In: Andrusz, Gregory/Harloe, Michael/Szelenyi, Ivan (Hg.): *Cities after Socialism. Urban and Regional Change and Conflict in Post-Socialist Societies.* Oxford/Cambridge 1996

9 Vgl. Bohn, Thomas: „‚Bau auf...'. Der Maurer Denis Bulachow". In: Satjukow, Silke/Gries, Rainer (Hg.): *Sozialistische Helden. Eine Kulturgeschichte von Propagandafiguren in Osteuropa und der DDR.* Berlin 2002

10 Marx, Karl/Engels, Friedrich: „Das Kommunistische Manifest". In: dies., *Ausgewählte Werke.* Bindlach o. J., S. 47; vgl. auch Miljutin, Nikolaj A.: *Sozgorod. Die Planung der neuen Stadt.* Basel u. a. 1992

11 Vgl. Chan-Magomedow, Selim O.: *Pioniere der sowjetischen Architektur.* Dresden 1983; Goldzamt, a. a. O.; Gradow, G. A.: *Stadt und Lebensweise.* Berlin/Ost 1969 (?); Kaltenbrunner, Robert: *Minhang, Shanghai: Die Satellitenstadt als intermediäre Planung. Chinas Architekten zwischen kompetitivem Anspruch und parteipolitischer Realität.* Berlin 1993; Kopp, Anatole: *Town and Revolution. Soviet Architecture and City Planning 1917–1935.* New York 1970; Pistorius, Elke: „Das Sozgorod-Ideal". In: *StadtBauwelt* 128. Bauwelt, Nr. 48/1995

12 Für die Stadtplanung waren nicht die als unrealistisch angesehenen Theorien der Urbanisten und Desurbanisten maßgeblich, sondern pragmatischere Konzeptionen wie Nikolaj A. Miljutins „Sozgorod"-Bandstadtkonzept (1930) mit seinem „fließenden Funktionsschema" parallel zueinander verlaufender funktionaler Zonen und Nikolaj A. Ladowskis parabelförmiges Stadtentwicklungsschema, welches ein an der Achse der Parabel entlangwachsendes, gesamtstädtisches Zentrum mit einschloss, das der Reihe nach von Wohn-, Grün- und Industriezonen umschlossen wird.

13 Kaltenbrunner, a. a. O., S. 58

14 Vgl. Andruzs/Harloe/Szelenyi (Hg.), a. a. O.

15 Vgl. Stölting, a. a. O.

16 Marx/Engels, a. a. O., S. 35

17 Vgl. Bittner, Regina/Vöckler, Kai: „Die postsozialistische Stadt". In: *UmBau.* Nr. 20/2003

18 Vgl. Bohn, Thomas: *„Von der Sowjetunion lernen, heißt siegen lernen." – Potemkinsche Dörfer und ostdeutsche Stadtplanung in der Nachkriegszeit.* Unveröffentlichtes Manuskript; vgl. dazu Weber, Max: *Wirtschaft und Gesellschaft. Die Stadt.* Tübingen 2000

19 Vgl. Brade, Isolde/Wendina, Olga: „Der Immobilienmarkt in Moskau. Grundtendenzen der 90er Jahre". In: *EUROPA REGIONAL.* Nr. 4/1996

20 Vgl. Szelenyi, Ivan: „Cities under socialism – and after". In: Andruzs/Harloe/Szelenyi (Hg.), a. a. O.

21 Vgl. Andrusz, Gregory: „Structural Change and Boundary Instability". In: Andruzs/Harloe/Szelenyi (Hg.), a. a. O.

22 Vgl. Enyedi, a. a. O.

23 Konrád, György: „Rückblick auf die Beglückung". In: Schneider, Romana/Stegers, Rudolf: *Glück, Stadt, Raum in Europa 1945 bis 2000.* Basel/Berlin/Boston 2002, S. 8

24 Ebd., S. 8 ff.

25 Vgl. Goedecke, Stefanie: „Neue Wege in der russischen Wohnungswirtschaft". In: *OSTEUROPA-WIRTSCHAFT.* Nr. 3/2001

26 Vgl. Marcuse, Peter: „Privatisation and its Discontents: Property Rights in Land and Housing in the Transition in Eastern Europe". In: Andruzs/Harloe/Szelenyi (Hg.), a. a. O.

27 Vgl. Goedecke, a. a. O.

cannot predict a tendency towards "over-urbanisation" here, as in the Third World.[41] Erhard Stölting even sees in the retreat to the countryside and the resort to the subsistence economy in order to survive a tendency to "counter-urbanisation", although not in the form of suburban sprawl as a continuation of the process of industrial decentralisation as in the western countries, but as a consequence of an economic state of emergency that marks a significant departure from the industrialisation and urbanisation process forced through by Stalin.[42] It remains uncertain how the post-socialist cities will continue to develop. There can be no doubt, however, that a great potential for conflict remains, as the centrifugal forces of the new economy are causing the communities held together by the promise of a better life to break up. While privileged centres and cordoned-off areas are springing up, the effects of decentralisation are hitting a largely urbanized area and a mobilised population, to whom neighbourhood ties never meant anything – and who now find themselves trapped in the microrayon.[43] Its residents must decide for themselves whether to continue to put their trust in the centrally organised state and its authorities or whether they want to take advantage of their newly won freedom.

NOTES

1 Makanin, Vladimir: *Underground oder Ein Held unserer Zeit*, Munich 2003, p. 253ff.

2 Ibid., p. 357f.

3 Cf. Stölting, Erhard: "Stadt und Gesellschaft in Russland" in Berking, Helmuth/Faber, Richard (eds.): *Städte im Globalisierungsdiskurs*, Würzburg 2002

4 Cf. Leiprecht, Helga: "Ein neues Haus für eine neue Welt" in *Du* No. 12/2003, Vol. 742; cf. also Buchli, Victor: *An Archaeology of Socialism*, Oxford, New York 2000

5 Cf. Goldzamt, Edmund: *Städtebau sozialistischer Länder*, Berlin (East) 1973

6 Cf. Leiprecht, loc cit.

7 Cf. Stölting, loc cit.

8 Cf. Enyedi, György: "Urbanisation under Socialism" in Andruzs, Gregory/Harloe, Michael/Szelenyi, Ivan (eds.): *Cities after Socialism. Urban and Regional Change and Conflict in Post-Socialist Societies*, Oxford/Cambridge 1996

9 Cf. Bohn, Thomas: "'Bau auf...'. Der Maurer Denis Bulachow" in Satjukow, Silke/Gries, Rainer (eds.): *Sozialistische Helden. Eine Kulturgeschichte von Propagandafiguren in Osteuropa und der DDR*. Berlin 2002

10 Marx, Karl/Engels, Friedrich: "Das Kommunistische Manifest" in *Ausgewählte Werke*. Bindlach n.d., p. 47; cf. also Miljutin, Nikolaj A.: *Sozgorod. Die Planung der neuen Stadt*, Basel/Berlin/Boston 1992

11 Cf. Chan-Magomedow, Selim O.: *Pioniere der sowjetischen Architektur*, Dresden 1983; Goldzamt, loc cit.; Gradow, G. A.: *Stadt und Lebensweise*, Berlin(East) 1969 (?);Kaltenbrunner, Robert: *Minhang, Shanghai: Die Satellitenstadt als intermediäre Planung. Chinas Architekten zwischen kompetitivem Anspruch und parteipolitischer Realität*, Berlin 1993; Kopp, Anatole: *Town and Revolution. Soviet Architecture and City Planning 1917–1935*, New York 1970; Pistorius, Elke: "Das Sozgorod-Ideal" in *StadtBauwelt* 128, Bauwelt, No. 48/1995

12 Town planning was not determined by the theories of the urbanists and disurbanists, which were regarded as unrealistic, but by more pragmatic notions, such as Nikolai A. Milyutin's *Sotsgorod* concept of the linear town (1930), with its "flowing functional scheme" of parallel functional zones, and Nikolai A. Ladovski's parabolic urban development scheme, which included a holistic city centre growing along the axis of the parabola and enclosed by successive residential, green and industrial zones.

13 Kaltenbrunner, loc cit., p. 58

14 Cf. Andruzs/Harloe/Szelenyi (eds.), loc cit.

15 Cf. Stölting, loc cit.

16 Marx/Engels, loc cit., p. 35

17 Cf. Bittner, Regina/Vöckler, Kai: "Die postsozialistische Stadt" in *UmBau*, No. 20/2003

18 Cf. Bohn, Thomas: *"Von der Sowjetunion lernen, heißt siegen lernen." – Potemkinsche Dörfer und ostdeutsche Stadtplanung in der Nachkriegszeit* (unpublished manuscript); cf. Weber, Max: *Wirtschaft und Gesellschaft. Die Stadt*, Tübingen 2000

28 Vgl. Lodahl, Maria: Wohnungsmarkt in Russland: Enttäuschende Bilanz. Wochenbericht des DIW Berlin 22/01. http://www.diw.de/deutsch/publikationen/wochenbericht

29 Vgl. Goedecke, a. a. O.

30 Ebd.

31 Vgl. Piterski, Dmitri: *Studie zum Thema Smolensk – Mikrorayons: Withdrawal to the Living Room.* Unveröffentl. Manuskript 2003

32 Vgl. Sivaev, Sergey: Housing Sector Reforms (1998–2000). http://www.urbaneconomics.ru/eng/publications

33 Ebd.

34 Vgl. Struyk, Raymond J.: „Housing Privatisation in the Former Soviet Bloc to 1995". In: Andruzs/Harloe/Szelenyi (Hg.), a. a. O.

35 Vgl. Harutyunian, Angela/Johnston, Samuel G. R.: *Privacy and Neighbourhood.* Dokumentation 2. Trimester Bauhaus-Kolleg V, 2004. Siehe auch den Beitrag von Angela Harutyunian in diesem Band

36 Vgl. Kapustin, Boris: „Russland als postmoderne Gesellschaft". In: *Berliner Debatte INITIAL 11.* Nr. 5/6/2000

37 Vgl. Stölting, a. a. O.

38 Vgl. Harloe, Michael: „Cities in Transition". In: Andruzs/Harloe/Szelenyi (Hg.), a. a. O.

39 Vgl. Busse, Sarah: „Strategies of Daily Life: Social Capital and the Informal Economy in Russia". In: *Sociological Imagination.* Nr. 3/2001

40 Vgl. Harloe, a. a. O.; siehe auch den Beitrag von Regina Bittner in diesem Band.

41 Vgl. Szelenyi, a. a. O.

42 Vgl. Stölting, a. a. O.

43 Vgl. Bittner/Vöckler, a. a. O.

19 Cf. Brade, Isolde/Wendina, Olga: "Der Immobilienmarkt in Moskau. Grundtendenzen der 90er Jahre" in *EUROPA REGIONAL* No. 4/1996
20 Cf. Szelenyi, Ivan: "Cities under socialism – and after" in Andruzs/Harloe/Szelenyi (eds.), loc cit.
21 Cf. Andruzs, Gregory: "Structural Change and Boundary Instability" in Andruzs/Harloe/Szelenyi (eds.), loc cit.
22 Cf. Enyedi, loc cit.
23 Konrád, György: "Rückblick auf die Beglückung" in Schneider, Romana/Stegers, Rudolf: *Glück, Stadt, Raum in Europa 1945 bis 2000,* Basel/Berlin/Boston 2002, p. 8
24 Ibid., p. 8ff.
25 Cf. Goedecke, Stefanie: "Neue Wege in der russischen Wohnungswirtschaft" in *OSTEUROPA-WIRTSCHAFT* No. 3/2001
26 Cf. Marcuse, Peter: "Privatisation and its Discontents: Property Rights in Land and Housing in the Transition in Eastern Europe" in Andruzs/Harloe/Szelenyi (eds.), loc cit.
27 Cf. Goedecke, loc cit.
28 Cf. Lodahl, Maria: Wohnungsmarkt in Russland: Enttäuschende Bilanz. Wochenbericht des DIW Berlin 22/01. http://www.diw.de/deutsch/publikationen/wochenbericht
29 Cf. Goedecke, loc cit.
30 Ibid.
31 Cf. Piterski, Dmitri: *Studie zum Thema Smolensk – Mikrorayons: Withdrawal to the Living Room* (unpublished manuscript) 2003
32 Cf. Sivaev, Sergey: Housing Sector Reforms (1998–2000). http://www.urbaneconomics.ru/eng/publications
33 Ibid.
34 Cf. Struyk, Raymond J.: "Housing Privatisation in the Former Soviet Bloc to 1995" in Andruzs/Harloe/Szelenyi (eds.), loc cit.
35 Cf. Harutyunian, Angela/Johnston, Samuel G. R.: *Privacy and Neighbourhood.* Documentation 2nd term Bauhaus Kolleg V, 2004. See also the essay by Angela Harutyunian in this volume.
36 Cf. Kapustin, Boris: "Russland als postmoderne Gesellschaft" in *Berliner Debatte INITIAL 11.* No. 5/6/2000
37 Cf. Stölting, loc cit.
38 Cf. Harloe, Michael: "Cities in Transition" in Andruzs/Harloe/Szelenyi (eds.), loc cit.
39 Cf. Busse, Sarah: "Strategies of Daily Life: Social Capital and the Informal Economy in Russia" in *Sociological Imagination* No. 3/2001
40 Cf. Harloe, loc cit.; see also the essay by Regina Bittner in this volume
41 Cf. Szelenyi, loc cit.
42 Cf. Stölting, loc cit.
43 Cf. Bittner/Vöckler, loc cit.

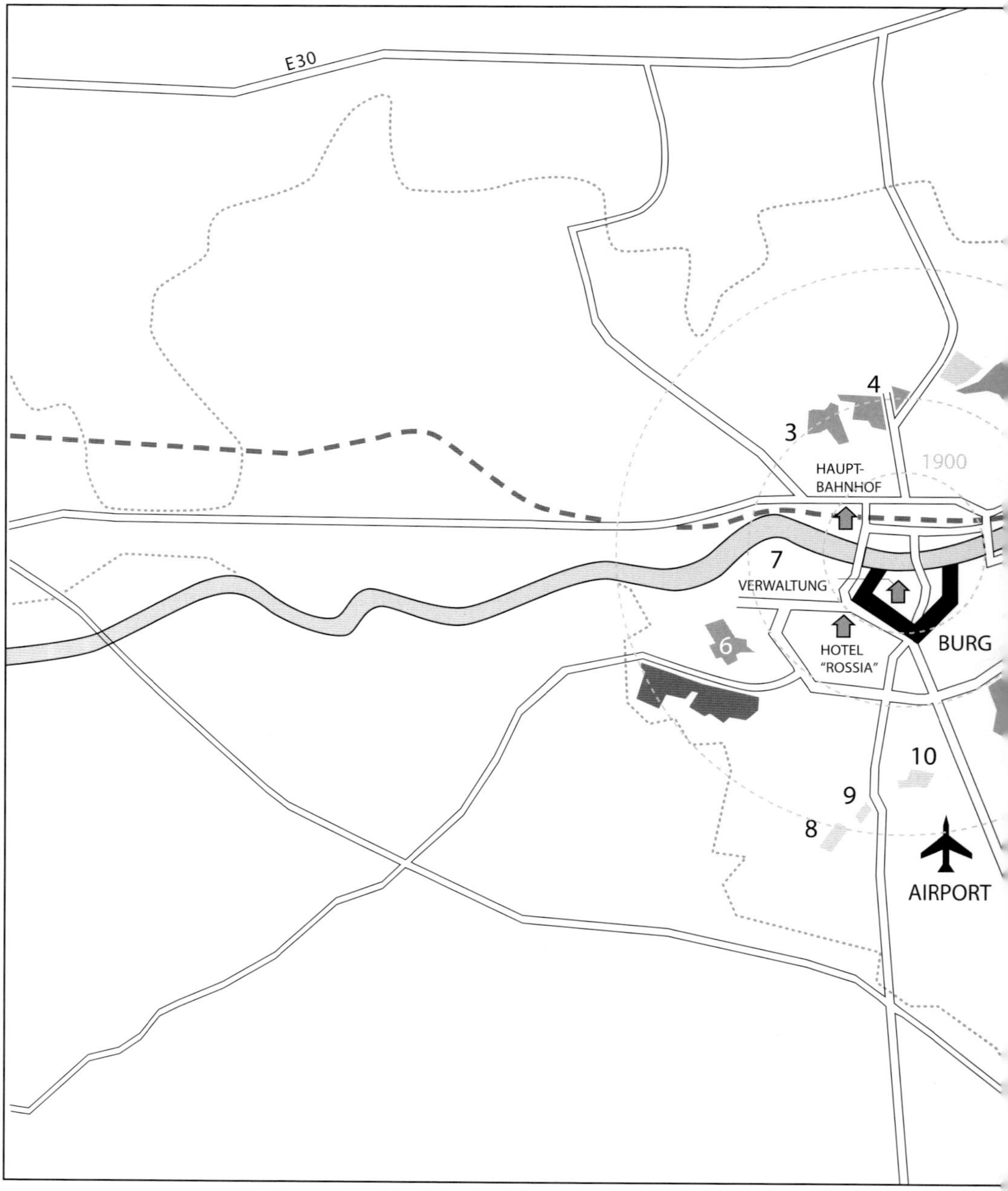

DIE ENTWICKLUNGSSTRUKTUR VON SMOLENSK IST PROTOTYPISCH FÜR RUSSISCHE STÄDTE.
THE DEVELOPMENT STRUCTURE OF SMOLENSK IS PROTO-TYPICAL FOR RUSSIAN CITIES.
Karte Map: Dmitrij Piterski, Kai Vöckler, Rainer Mühr

ZENTRALE GEBÄUDE

FLUGHAFEN

BAHN

STADTGRENZE

HAUPTSTRASSEN

FLUSS DNJEPR

MIKRORAYONS

1 - POPOWKA
2 - KISELJOWKA
3 - KOROLJOWKA
4 - SITNIKI
5 - SCHTSCHOTKINO
6 - KLOWSKAJASTRASSE

DATSCHEN UND EINFAMILIENHÄUSER

7 - MALOKRASNOFLOTSKAJA STRASSE
8 - SAGORJE-1
9 - SAGORJE-2
10 - "SCHKADOWKA"

INDUSTRIEGEBIETE

BURG (KREML)

RÜCKZUG INS WOHNZIMMER

ANGELA HARUTYUNYAN

EINLEITUNG

In Zeiten des Wandels befinden sich Gesellschaften oft in einer Art Niemandsland zwischen alten und neuen Paradigmen, und sowohl das gesellschaftliche Makrolevel (politisch und sozial) als auch das Mikrolevel (das Individuum) sind betroffen. Der Alltag einschließlich der Art und Weise, wie Mitmenschen miteinander umgehen und kommunizieren, aber auch ihre Einstellung zu alten Lebensweisen verändern sich oft drastisch. Jeder Umbruch zwingt den Einzelnen dazu, seinen Lebensstil und auch seine Überzeugungen zu überdenken. Im postsowjetischen Raum wird die Entwicklung vom Sozialismus zum Postsozialismus von den Erscheinungen Migration und Instabilität sowie dem Triumph des privaten über den öffentlichen Raum begleitet.

Um diese Entwicklung zu verstehen, ist es von Nutzen, auf Makro- und Mikroebene zu untersuchen, wie der staatliche Wohnungsbau in der Vergangenheit wahrgenommen wurde und wie man heute zu ihm steht. Diese Arbeit befasst sich sowohl mit Aspekten der Städteplanung und Privatisierung als auch mit den Gedanken Betroffener zu diesem Thema, insbesondere mit ihrer Reaktion auf den Rückzug ihrer Nachbarn aus der Gemeinschaft in die Privatsphäre. Sie versucht, diese Entwicklung zu erklären und zeichnet zu diesem Zweck die Veränderungen auf, die der russische staatliche Wohnungsbau in den letzten zehn Jahren durchgemacht hat.

Zu Sowjetzeiten forderte der Ideologieapparat des Staates, dass sowohl Öffentlichkeit als auch Privatsphäre Bestandteile des kollektiven Lebens sein sollten. Nach dem Zusammenbruch der Sowjetunion mussten beide Begriffe folglich neu definiert werden.

Um die Auswirkungen des Wandels, die durch politische und soziale Veränderungen herbeigeführte Instabilität, aber auch den gescheiterten Traum von einer besseren, kapitalistischen Zukunft verständlicher zu machen, untersucht diese Arbeit, wie sich das Wohnungswesen in Smolensk in jüngster Vergangenheit verändert hat. Dabei zieht sie Faktoren wie etwa die Privatisierung von Eigentum, eines der Hauptcharakteristika der postsowjetischen Umbruchphase, in Betracht. Und sie weist auf einen Trend hin, nämlich den Rückzug der Bewohner von Smolensk aus dem gemeinschaftlichen Leben in ihre eigenen vier Wände.

Die Arbeit untersucht eine Reihe von Fragen und in einigen Fällen liefert sie Antworten. So wird im Laufe der Untersuchung zum Beispiel deutlich, dass Auffassungen von Nachbarschaft und Gemeinschaft mehr oder weniger unverändert geblieben sind.

Kann man die Wohngegenden in Smolensk heute noch als Nachbarschaften bezeichnen? Sind die Mikrorayons und die *Chruschtschowkas* Transiträume, Übergangslager für eine neue Generation von Migranten geworden? Ist es ein Widerspruch, Teil einer Gemeinschaft sein zu wollen, aber Aspekte des Gemeinschaftslebens abzulehnen? Wie haben sich kollektive Vorstellungen geändert, wie denkt man in Smolensk heute über Wohnen, Arbeiten und Freizeitgestaltung? Inwieweit können die Mikrorayons noch das sozialistische Versprechen eines besseren Lebens einlösen, nach der Transformation, die sie und ihre Bewohner in den letzten Jahren durchlaufen haben?

Diese Arbeit versucht zu zeigen, wie der im postsowjetischen Raum stattfindende Transformationsprozess die Stadt Smolensk verändert hat. Hierfür wertet sie Interviews aus, die im Rahmen einer Forschungsreise mit einigen Einwohnern sowie mit Repräsentanten der örtlichen städteplanerischen Abteilung geführt wurden, und greift auf Sekundärmaterial zurück.

RETREAT INTO THE LIVING ROOM

ANGELA HARUTYUNYAN

INTRODUCTION

Periods of transition thrust societies into a state of inbetweeness and affect societies not only on a macro (political and social) level but also on a micro (personal) level. People's lives change, including their interaction and communication as well as their attitude towards their former way of life. Any process of transition forces people to reevaluate their lives as well as their basic believes. The transition from Socialism to Postsocialism that has been taking place in the post-Soviet space is accompanied by the phenomena migration, instability and the triumph of the private over the public sphere.

To understand this development it is useful to discuss the changing attitude towards public housing both on a macro and a micro level. Therefore, this project focuses on urban planning and privatisation as well as on people's thoughts about and reaction to their neighbours' retreat from the public into the private realm. It tries to understand this process by exploring the changes that have been affecting the public housing sector in Russia during the past decade.

During Soviet times, the state's ideological apparatus propagated that the public sphere and public space are part of collective life. After the collapse of the Soviet Union it became necessary to redefine both.

In order to better understand what effects the process of transition, the instability caused by political and social developments of the recent past as well as the failed dream of a brighter Capitalist future have had, this project examines the changes the housing sector underwent in Smolensk in the recent past. It takes developments such as privatisation, a key element of the post-Soviet process of transformation, into consideration. It will show that the retreat from the communal space into the private living room is a major trend in Smolensk today.

This project explores a number of questions and in some cases it answers them. During the investigation it becomes clear, for example, that concepts of neighbourhood and community remain fairly stable.

Is it still possible to call the residential areas in Smolensk neighbourhoods? Have microrayons and *khrushchevkas* become a transit space for a new generation of migrants? Does the desire to live in a community contradict the simultaneous rejection of some aspects of it? How have collective ideas about living, working and leisure changed in Smolensk? How do the changes that have been affecting microrayons and their residents clash with the Socialist narrative of a better life implied in the structure of microrayons?

This project attempts to make the impact that the process of transformation has been having on Smolensk visible. To do so, it draws largely on interviews with residents and officials of the city's urban planning department that were conducted during a field trip to Smolensk as well as secondary sources.

NEIGHBOURHOOD

According to sociological research from the early 20th century, the average resident of a city with one million inhabitants comes into contact with other people 300 times each day. As the amount of contacts increases they become increasingly superficial and more and more urban dwellers feel isolated and lonely. The rapid urbanisation that was part of Modernity caused many people to withdraw from the public sphere and lived in seclusion. The swift transformation that Russian society underwent after the October Revolution turned the feudalist, backward state into a highly industrialised power.

Industrialisation and the plan to move as many people as possible from rural areas to the new industrial centers were crucial aspects of Socialist

NACHBARSCHAFT

Soziologische Studien des frühen zwanzigsten Jahrhunderts weisen darauf hin, dass jeder Bewohner einer Stadt, die mehr als eine Million Einwohner zählt, im Schnitt mit 300 Menschen am Tag in Berührung kommt. Je größer die Anzahl der Kontakte ist, desto oberflächlicher werden sie, und der Städter fühlt sich folglich mehr und mehr isoliert und einsam. Die unaufhaltsame Industrialisierung, die in der Moderne stattfand, hatte zur Folge, dass das Individuum sich absonderte und vereinsamte. Die rasanten Veränderungen, die die russische Gesellschaft nach der Oktoberrevolution durchlief, verwandelten den rückständigen feudalistischen Staat in eine Industriemacht.

Die Industrialisierung und der Plan, so viele Landbewohner wie möglich in die neuen Industriezentren umzusiedeln, bildeten die Eckpfeiler der sowjetischen Ideologie. Sozialistische Reformer wollten starke Gemeinschaften schaffen und den Alltag, oder *byt,* völlig neu gestalten. Er sollte soweit wie möglich im öffentlichen Raum stattfinden, damit niemand sich isolieren oder absondern konnte. Ihr Kampf gegen die Häuslichkeit und die Privatsphäre hatte jedoch den entgegengesetzten Effekt: Man ärgerte sich mehr und mehr über den Mangel an Privatsphäre. Der sozialistische Traum von friedlich miteinander lebenden Menschen, die in einem Gemeinschaftshaus Küche, Wohnzimmer und Kinderzimmer teilen, blieb unerfüllt. Das Haus Narkomfin in Moskau, entworfen vom konstruktivistischen Architekten Moisei Ginzburg, ist eines der wenigen Gemeinschaftshäuser, die gebaut wurden.[1]

Mehr und mehr sowjetische Städteplaner begannen am Mikrorayon Gefallen zu finden, nachdem Nikita Kruschtschow den Stalinismus verurteilt und in seiner berühmten Rede an die Gewerkschaft der Architekten und Bauarbeiter Mitte der fünfziger Jahre eine neue Richtlinie bezüglich dem staatlichen Wohnungsbau vorgestellt hatte. Im Gegensatz zu Gemeinschaftshäusern bestanden Mikrorayons aus separaten Wohnungen, welche den Bewohnern wenigstens etwas Privatsphäre zugestanden. Gleichzeitig wurde der öffentliche oder gemeinschaftliche Raum von Mikrorayons bewusst so angelegt, dass man dort auf seine Nachbarn traf und sich animiert fühlte, miteinander Zeit zu verbringen oder an Gemeinschaftsaktivitäten teilzunehmen. Somit unterschieden sich Mikrorayons von den *kommunalkas* der Ära Stalin, denn obwohl Letztere das Leben der Menschen transparent machen sollten, fehlten ihnen die räumlichen Strukturen – zum Beispiel Gemeinschaftsräume oder Sitzgelegenheiten im Hof –, die nachbarschaftliche Beziehungen gefördert hätten. Davon abgesehen, war die gesamte Epoche nicht sonderlich kommunikationsfördernd, da ein einziges, beiläufiges Wort einem das Leben kosten konnte.

Zu den Wohnblocks der Chruschtschow-Ära gehörte für gewöhnlich ein großer Hof (einschließlich eines Spielplatzes und kleiner, offener Hütten bzw. *besetki*), der die Bewohner dazu anhalten sollte, miteinander Zeit zu verbringen. Gleichermaßen sollte das Putzen der Gemeinschaftsbereiche (*subotniki*), wie zum Beispiel des Hofes und des Treppenhauses an Samstagen, die Menschen zusammenbringen und so einen Austausch unter den Nachbarn fördern.

Die Häuserblocks bildeten nur ein Element eines Mikrorayons, der darüber hinaus über eine Infrastruktur verfügte, welche die alltäglichen Bedürfnisse seiner Bewohner deckte. Man lebte und arbeitete hier und verbrachte auch die Freizeit innerhalb des räumlich begrenzten Mikrorayons. Zu jedem Mikrorayon gehörte ein eigener Kindergarten, eine Schule, Einkaufsmöglichkeiten und Büros, Fabriken und Erholungsparks. Mikrorayons wurden üblicherweise für eine bestimmte soziale Gruppe gebaut, was erklärt, warum die Bewohner oft eine homogene Gruppe bildeten. Die Bewohner eines jeden Mikrorayons übten ähnliche Berufe aus, und deshalb waren einige – meistens die außerhalb der Stadtgrenze gelegenen – von mehr Fabriken umgeben als andere. In den für Intellektuelle und Akademiker gebauten Mikrorayons gab es mehr Schulen und Büros als in anderen. Da die Bewohner eines Mikrorayons diesen nicht verlassen mussten, um zur Arbeit zu gehen oder ihre Freizeit zu verbringen, und da es ihre Pflicht war, an gemeinschaftlichen Aktivitäten teilzunehmen, waren die Beziehungen zwischen Nachbarn und den Bewohnern eines ganzen Häuserblocks oft eng.

In den späten achtziger und frühen neunziger Jahren, als die Perestroika sich dem Ende neigte und die Phase der Unabhängigkeit begann, bekamen die Bewohner der Mikrorayons die Migration ihrer Nachbarn, aber auch andere Entwicklungen innerhalb der Nachbarschaft zu spüren. Insbesondere zu Beginn der neunziger Jahre verließen viele auf der Suche nach besseren Jobs und einem besseren Leben Smolensk und zogen nach Moskau oder in eine andere russische Großstadt. Andere zogen einfach aus den Mikrorayons weg, da sie jetzt mehr verdienten und in einem größeren und komfortableren Heim leben wollten. Im Ange-

ideology. Socialist reformers were keen on creating strong communities and reforming everyday life or *byt*. They wanted to integrate – at least on the surface – people's everyday life into the public sphere and leave no room for feelings like isolation or segregation. Yet, their war on domesticity and privacy had just the opposite effect: people increasingly resented the lack of personal space. The utopian idea of people living peacefully in communal houses that featured communal kitchens, living rooms and children's dorms was never realised. The Narkomfin House in Moscow, which was designed by the Constructivist architect Moisei Ginzburg, is one of the few communal houses that were actually built.[1]

The concept of microrayons gained popularity among Soviet urban planners when Nikita Chruschtschow denounced Stalinism and introduced a new public housing policy in his famous address to the Union of Architects and Builders in the mid 1950s. Unlike communal houses, microrayons consisted of single-family apartments that allowed residents to enjoy a certain level of privacy. At the same time, the public space of microrayons was especially designed to bring people together and to encourage them to spend their leisure time together or engage in communal activities. Microrayons differed from Stalinist *kommunalkas*, which were supposed to make the lives of residents transparent but which lacked the spatial structures, such as communal lounges or sitting areas in the yards that would have encouraged interaction between neighbours. Besides, at that time it was dangerous to communicate with anyone as a casually uttered word could cost people their lives.

The housing blocks of the Chruschtschow era typically featured a big yard (including a playground and small huts or *bisetki*) that encouraged residents to socialise with each other. Cleaning the common spaces (*subotniki*) such as the yard and the staircase on Saturdays was another way of bringing people together and promoting communication between neighbours.

Apartment blocks were not the only element of a microrayon as they featured an infrastructure that accommodated all of people's everyday needs. People lived and worked here and they also spent their leisure time within the limited realm of the microrayon. Each one had its own kindergarten, a school, shopping facilities, offices, factories and recreational parks. Because microrayons were designed to accommodate a specific social group, the residents typically formed a homogeneous group. The residents of each microrayon worked in the same field, which explains why some microrayons – mostly the ones located far from the city center – were surrounded by more factories than others. The microrayons that were built to accommodate the intelligentsia featured more schools and offices. Since residents did no have to leave the microrayon for either work or leisure, and because they were obliged to participate in communal activities, the ties between neighbours and, in fact, all residents were often strong.

During the late 1980s and early 1990s, during the final years of Perestroika and the early years of independence, people started to feel the impact of their neighbours' migration and their experience of the community began to change. Especially during the early nineties many people were looking for better lives or jobs and moved from Smolensk to Moscow or other large Russian cities. Others simply left the microrayons because they were making more money and wanted to live in a bigger, more comfortable home. The initial optimism that had been triggered by the promise of change was soon replaced by harsh reality. Due to the migration and the social repositioning that many people experienced, the original desire and need for privacy was subsequently replaced by feelings of confusion and isolation. Conflicts, denunciations and the invasion of privacy had been part of people's lives and since people no longer experienced these undesirable aspects of communal living they began to see its advantages. According to Liudmila Ivanovna, a teacher from Smolensk, it was never a problem in the past to borrow household equipment from neighbours, get groceries that you forgot to buy from them or even ask them for a small favour. Everybody – depending on their ability, their special skills or professional experience – was willing to help each other.

Liudmila Ivanovna, who experienced that members of a social class or people with the same occupation formed a community, confirmed the hypothesis that the residents of microrayons in Smolensk are becoming increasingly nostalgic. According to her, people felt more comfortable before Perestroika because everyone earned the "same amount of money, had the same expenses and shared the same joys and sorrows". But she also admits that meaningful interaction was rare.

Since the mid-nineties, it has become popular to move out of microrayon apartments and into new-

sicht der neuen, harten Realität schwand der anfängliche Optimismus der Bevölkerung bald. Viele bekamen Migration und soziale Repositionierung am eigenen Leib zu spüren, und das ursprüngliche Bedürfnis und Verlangen nach einer Privatsphäre wich Gefühlen der Verwirrung und Isolation. Konflikte und Denunzierungen waren nun nicht mehr an der Tagesordnung und die Privatsphäre des Einzelnen wurde nicht mehr verletzt. Dies hatte zur Folge, dass man sich bald nur noch an die Vorteile des kollektiven Zusammenlebens erinnerte. Liudmila Ivanovna, eine Lehrerin aus Smolensk, weist darauf hin, dass man sich früher immer ein Haushaltsgerät von seinen Nachbarn ausleihen konnte, dass man um Lebensmittel, die man selbst vergessen hatte zu kaufen oder gar um einen kleinen Gefallen bitten konnte. Jeder habe im Rahmen seiner Möglichkeiten oder Fähigkeiten stets gerne geholfen. Liudmila Ivanovna lebte selbst in einer Gemeinschaft, die sich aus Mitgliedern einer bestimmten Gesellschaftsschicht bzw. Menschen mit dem gleichen Beruf zusammensetzte, und sie bestätigt die Vermutung, dass die Bewohner der Mikrorayons in Smolensk zunehmend nostalgisch werden. Die Menschen hätten sich vor der Perestroika insgesamt wohler gefühlt, denn jeder verdiente „gleich viel, hatte die gleichen Ausgaben und teilte die gleichen Freuden und Sorgen". Aber sie räumt auch ein, dass nachbarschaftliche Beziehungen oft oberflächlich blieben.

Seit Mitte der neunziger Jahre verlassen immer mehr Menschen die Mikrorayons und ziehen in luxuriöse Neubauwohnungen oder -häuser, die meist näher am Stadtzentrum gelegen sind. Heutzutage ist man nicht mehr mit jemandem benachbart, weil man den gleichen Beruf ausübt oder weil man der gleichen sozialen Schicht angehört, sondern weil man über ein ähnliches Einkommen verfügt. Die neuen Wohnparks werden des öfteren in der Nähe der Mikrorayons gebaut. Die anhaltenden Veränderungen führen zu einer sozialen Segregation. Der schnelle Wechsel der Mieter in den neuen Wohnungen sowie das Unvermögen mancher Bewohner, die *Chruschtschowkas* zu verlassen, treibt diesen Prozess nicht nur innerhalb eines Wohnblocks, sondern sogar innerhalb eines Hauses voran.

Liudmila Ivanovna weist auch auf das veränderte Verhalten von weiterhin in Mikrorayons wohnenden ehemaligen Nachbarn und Freunden ihr gegenüber hin, nachdem sie selbst in eine neue „bürgerliche" Wohnung gezogen ist. Die Bewohner der *Chruschtschowka*, die ihrer Anlage gegenüberliegen, mögen sie nicht, ohne sie überhaupt zu kennen. Sie lehnen die neuen Wohnungen ab, denn diese machen den Transformationsprozess, dem man sich in den letzten Jahren stellen musste, nur zu deutlich. Viele Bewohner des Mikrorayons werden deshalb nostalgisch: Sie erinnern sich gerne an die Zeit, als es zumindest so schien, als wären alle Menschen gleich. Dazu kommt, dass dieser luxuriösen Wohnanlage ein wunderschöner, kleiner Park geopfert wurde. Dieser verschönerte den geschmacklosen Mikrorayon, und man erfreute sich insbesondere an den hübschen Blumen im Park. Man war zufrieden und stolz, in diesem Mikrorayon zu leben. Aber das Bauunternehmen hat alle Bäume gefällt. Es ist den Bewohnern der neuen, komfortablen Wohnanlage nicht verborgen geblieben, dass der Bau ihres neuen Zuhauses die Lebensqualität der Bewohner des Mikrorayons gemindert hat, ihr Wohnpark sozialen Wettbewerb fördert und Misstrauen sät. Gleichzeitig sind sie jedoch froh, dass sie ihre Wohnsituation dank ihres höheren Einkommens verbessern konnten.

Die Interviews, die mit den Bewohnern der Mikrorayons in Smolensk geführt wurden, machen deutlich, dass Nachbarn vor Beginn der Perestroika mehr miteinander kommunizierten. Es ist richtig, dass sie ihr neugewonnenes Privileg der Privatsphäre genießen. Liudmila Ivanovna erklärt warum: „Wenn man in einer Gemeinschaftswohnung oder *kommunalka* wohnt, muss man sich seinem sozialen Umfeld und dessen Regeln anpassen, denn sonst begibt man sich in eine Außenseiterposition oder wird gar von der Gemeinschaft ausgeschlossen. Aber jeder Mensch braucht wenigstens ein bisschen Privatsphäre. Natürlich denkt jeder anders über dieses Thema. Aber als ich noch auf kleinem Raum lebte, war ich oft froh, wenn ich mal die Wohnung für mich allein hatte. Man fühlt sich nicht wohl, wenn man nie allein sein kann. Seit ich in meine neue Wohnung gezogen bin, hat sich das Problem für mich gelöst. Ich habe mein eigenes Zimmer und mein Mann hat seines. Wir streiten uns jetzt auch weniger. In der alten Wohnung gerieten wir viel öfter aneinander. In der neuen Wohnung haben wir beide genug Platz."

Nadezhda Igorevna, eine Frau Ende 60 und auch Lehrerin in Smolensk, vermisst ihre alten Nachbarn: „Meine meisten Freunde sich nach Moskau gezogen, ein paar sind gestorben und einige wenige wohnen noch hier… Früher kannte ich fast jeden, der hier wohnte, aber von den Neuankömmlingen kenne ich fast niemanden."

ly built luxury apartments or houses located closer to the city center. Today people are no longer neighbours because they work in the same field or come from similar backgrounds but because they earn similar wages or salaries. The new housing developments are sometimes built in the vicinity of microrayons. Social segregation is a by-product of the ongoing process of transformation. The frequent turnover of tenants in the new apartments as well as the inability of some people to leave the *khrushchevkas* fosters not only segregation between people living in different blocks but also within one and the same apartment block.

According to Liudmila Ivanovna, the attitude of her old neighbours and friends who still live in microrayons has changed towards her after she moved into a new, "bourgeois" apartment. The residents of the *khrushchovka* located opposite her housing development resent her without even knowing her. The antagonism is caused by the fact that the new apartments highlight the changes that have affected people's lives and they make the residents of microrayons feel nostalgic about the past when everybody at least pretended to be equal. In addition, this particular luxury housing development was built on a site that used to be a gorgeous little park. It beautified the tasteless *khrushchovka* and people enjoyed especially the wonderful flowers. They were happy and proud to live here. But the construction company cut down all the trees. The residents of the new, comfortable apartments sense that their new home robbed the microrayon of some of its more human qualities, encourages social competition and nurtures distrust. At the same time, they are happy that their living conditions improved as they became more affluent.

The interviews with some of the residents living in one of Smolensk's microrayons verify that communication between neighbours was much more intense before Perestroika. To be sure, people greatly enjoy the new privilege of privacy. Liudmila Ivanovna explains why: "When you live in a dorm or *kommunalka* you have to adapt to a very specific social environment and its rules because otherwise you will be marginalised or even excluded from the community. But everybody needs at least some private living space. Of course everybody has a different view of this. While living in a small space I used to think: Thank God nobody but me will be home today. If several private spaces overlap constantly you do not feel very comfortable. My new apartment has solved the problem for me. I have a room to myself and so does my husband. We quarrel less these days. While we still lived in the old apartment we used to argue much more. The new apartment grants both of us enough private space."

Another interviewee, Nadezhda Igorevna, a woman in her late sixties and also a teacher in Smolensk, misses her old community: "Most of my friends moved to Moscow, some died but some still live here (...) I used to know almost everyone living here but I know hardly any of the newcomers."

Many people still living in microrayons do so because they have been unable to realise their dream of a private living space. At the same time they, as well as other residents of Smolensk that were interviewed for this project, wish they had as much contact with their new neighbours as they did with their old ones. They feel that genuine human interaction ceased and that compassion no longer exists. The shift from a society of equal workers to a society of unequal consumers affected people's ability to communicate with each other. Not only the level but also the intensity of interaction between members of different social groups has changed for the worse.

The privatisation of property set in after the collapse of the Soviet Union and even though this process was slow and difficult people were able to purchase property. They could buy their microrayon apartment, invest money in a newly built apartment or build their own, single-family house, which – unlike the *dacha* (summer house) – would be their primary residence. Traditional *dachas* had no running water, gas or electricity and they were typically located in areas that were difficult to reach from the city center. Some of the new single-family houses are actually villas built by new rich Russians and their ostentatious style is a visual marker of the widening gap between the rich and the poor. These new houses are mostly located outside the city limits and tall fences surround them. At last, gated communities have arrived in post-Socialist Russia.

The constant changes and migration have left people without a sense of stability. Traditional concepts of communal living are no longer valid and microrayons are undergoing change, which has the effect that people's attitude towards the private sphere is becoming increasingly ambivalent. As they witness the rapid construction of single-family houses that are gated off from the mass housing districts, they long for security and the bygone community spirit. In the past it would have

Viele derjenigen, die noch in *Chruschtschowkas* wohnen, würden auch lieber in den eigenen vier Wänden wohnen. Wie auch andere, mit denen im Rahmen dieses Projekts gesprochen wurde, wünschen sie sich eben soviel Kontakt zu ihren neuen Nachbarn, wie sie ihn zu den alten hatten.

Es kommt ihnen vor, als würden sie mit niemandem mehr kommunizieren, und jegliches Mitgefühl für den Nachbarn sei verloren gegangen. Die Arbeitergesellschaft ist einer Konsumgesellschaft gewichen, und seitdem man nicht mehr sozial gleichgestellt ist, hat sich das Verhalten der Menschen ihren Nachbarn gegenüber geändert. Menschen, die unterschiedlichen sozialen Schichten angehören, kommunizieren heute seltener miteinander und wenn, dann weitaus oberflächlicher.Mit dem Verfall der Sowjetunion begann die Privatisierung von Eigentum, und obwohl dieser Prozess langsam voranschritt und nicht einfach war, konnten die Menschen dennoch Eigentum erwerben. Sie konnten ihre Wohnung im Mikrorayon kaufen, ihr Geld in eine Neubauwohnung investieren oder ihr eigenes Einfamilienhaus bauen, welches anders als die *Datscha* oder das Sommerhaus zu ihrem Hauptwohnsitz wurde. Herkömmliche *Datschas* hatten kein fließend Wasser, kein Gas und keinen Strom und da sie oft weit vom Stadtzentrum entfernt lagen, waren sie schwierig zu erreichen. Einige der neuen Einfamilienhäuser sind eher Villen und wurden von neureichen Russen gebaut. Ihr protziger Stil verdeutlicht, dass die Schere zwischen Arm und Reich immer weiter auseinanderklafft. Die neuen Häuser liegen meist außerhalb der Stadt hinter hohen Zäunen. Jetzt gibt es auch im postsozialistischen Russland *gated communities*.

Die vielen Veränderungen, aber auch das Phänomen der Migration verunsichern die Menschen zunehmend. Traditionelle, kollektive Wohnmodelle haben ihre Gültigkeit verloren, was sich auch in den Mikrorayons bemerkbar macht. Dort ist die Einstellung der Menschen zur Privatsphäre zunehmend ambivalent. Sie sehen, wie Einfamilienhäuser, die von den Wohnvierteln für die Massen abgeschottet sind, wie Pilze aus dem Boden schießen, und reagieren darauf, indem sie sich nach Sicherheit und dem Gemeinschaftssinn der Vergangenheit sehnen. Früher war es leichter zu erfassen, was die Menschen über kollektive Wohnmodelle und die Privatsphäre dachten. Heute ist es viel schwieriger, die kollektiven Wünsche und Träume der Menschen festzulegen. Der Verfall der Sowjetunion erlaubte es den Menschen, nicht länger an die kommunistische Ideologie zu glauben und sie mussten auch nicht mehr die Meinungen des Kollektivs teilen. Die Doktrin, dass das, was gut für das Kollektiv ist, auch für das Individuum gut ist, verlor seine Gültigkeit. Folglich wurde das eigene Leben wichtiger. Jeder, der für dieses Projekt befragt wurde, dachte anders über das Private und die Gemeinschaft. Alle waren sich jedoch einig darüber, man könne sein Leben durch einen höheren Lebensstandard verbessern. Dies ist jedoch nur möglich, wenn man umzieht und die alten Nachbarn hinter sich lässt. Manche glauben, sie müssten Beziehungen zu Mitgliedern höherer sozialer Schichten aufbauen und aufrechterhalten, wenn sich der Wunsch nach finanzieller Sicherheit und mehr Sozialprestige (z.B. ein Einfamilienhaus oder eine luxuriöse Wohnung) erfüllen soll. Der Traum von einer finanziell abgesicherten Zukunft, aber auch die Möglichkeit frei zu wählen, zu wem man Kontakt sucht, wird eines Tages vielleicht der Nostalgie weichen.

In den Wohnblöcken der Mikrorayons könnten Nachbarn theoretisch weiterhin miteinander kommunizieren, aber die Bewohner leben heute ebenso isoliert, wie die Eigentümer der Einfamilienhäuser. Niemand hält sich mehr in den Gemeinschaftsräumen wie den *bisetkas* oder den Parks auf, und bis jetzt sind alle Bemühungen, diese Orte wiederzubeleben, gescheitert. Heute würde auch niemand mehr auf die Idee kommen, das Treppenhaus zu putzen, etwas, das früher die Menschen zusammengebracht hat.

Der jüngeren Generation, die den Kommunismus und den ideologischen Zwang zum kollektiven Leben nicht miterlebt hat, fällt es leichter, mit den Neuankömmlingen, die von der Innenstadt an den Stadtrand ziehen und aufgrund ihrer schlechten finanziellen Lage ihre hübschen Wohnungen gegen eine *Khrushchovka* im Mikrorayon eintauschen müssen, Kontakte zu knüpfen. Zu den Neuankömmlingen zählen auch jene Migranten, die ursprünglich in russischen Kleinstädten oder anderen postsowjetischen Ländern zu Hause waren und mit der Hoffnung nach Smolensk kamen, eine bessere Arbeit finden zu können. Die ältere Generation jedoch vermisst das Gefühl der Gemeinschaft und die alten Nachbarn sehr.

PRIVATE TRÄUME: DER RÜCKZUG INS EIGENE WOHNZIMMER

Das frühe kommunistische Wohnmodell kann heute eine sozialistische Utopie genannt werden. In den Jahren des gesellschaftlichen Wandels vom

been easier to map and evaluate people's attitude towards collective life and the private space. Today it is more difficult to map people's collective desires and dreams. As the Soviet Union collapsed, people were no longer forced to subscribe to Communist ideology and share the same believes. The doctrine that what is good for the collective is good for the individual was no longer valid. As a result, personal narratives became more important. Everyone interviewed for this project had a different understanding of private space and the community. However, all the interviewees shared the belief that a higher standard of living will improve your life. But this ambition may only be realised if people move into a new home and leave their old neighbourhood community behind. Some people think that the desire for financial security and social prestige (i.e. living in a single-family house or a luxury apartment) requires them to develop and maintain relationships with members of higher social strata. The dream of a financially secure future but also the possibility of being able to choose the people you interact with will perhaps replace people's nostalgia one day.

Microrayons still have spaces that would allow neighbours to interact but today's residents find themselves similarly isolated as the people who moved to single-family houses do. The community spaces such as the *bisetkas* or parks are abandoned and any efforts to revitalise them have failed so far. Today, the mere idea of cleaning common spaces together, which used to encourage communication between neighbours, is a bygone utopia. Members of the younger generation, who did not experience Communism and its ideological praxis of communal living, find it easier to communicate with the newcomers, who are moving away from the city center and swap their nice apartments with a microrayon *khrushchovka* because of their poor economic situation. Migrants from smaller Russian cities or other post-Soviet countries, who moved to Smolensk in the hope of finding a better job, are also among the newcomers. However, for the older generation the more communal past and the old neighbours are irreplaceable.

PRIVATE DREAMS: RETREAT TO THE LIVING ROOM

The early Communist idea of living in collective communities might be considered a Socialist utopia. During the years of transition from Socialism to Post-socialism a development that clashes with this utopia has taken place. People feel very nostalgic about communal living and their feelings are partly triggered by the country's current social and economic problems. At the same time a new dream emerged: people want to live alone but they also want to interact with their neighbours. After the collapse of the Soviet Union people had to face a new situation. As a reaction to the changes, and in order to overcome their sense of alienation, people began to nurture a utopia that clashed with the failed Socialist utopia. This explains why complete privacy inside the home became so important for people.

It is important to stress that the class structure of Russian society plays an important role in the realisation of people's dream of privacy as individual ambitions is strongly tied to money. The majority of the country's wealth is owned by a very small number of Russians and the gap between rich and poor continues to widen. The new Russian villas in the more affluent districts like Skhadowka or the derelict blocks of the old microrayons make this gap strikingly visible. These images as well as the interviews are part of a development that might be called a regressive utopia: imagine huge three-story houses surrounded by tall fences and decorated with marble inside. People who do not live in such houses dream of owning them. Of course there are a few exceptions. Such as 12-year-old Vladlen, who has lived in a microrayon his entire life and who would not want to leave his home for any money in the world.

During Soviet times, the standardisation of public housing required the residents of microrayons to internalise their dreams about private space, think positively about the community and behave nicely towards everyone. Their desire for privacy was reflected by the interior décor of their apartments: it reflected their personal taste. People could only realise their fantasies within the relative privacy of their home. By designing them individually and different from the communal spaces of the building, they could nurture the illusion of owning a unique and colorful private place. However, there were few products to choose from and citizens were not encouraged to consume. In addition, consumer goods were standardised, which made it difficult for people to realise their domestic dreams. The residents of Smolensk have become much more consumption-oriented and even the people who cannot afford to live in a single-family house are able to realise their domestic fantasies. As a result,

Sozialismus zum Postsozialismus fand eine gegenläufige Entwicklung statt. Viele Menschen denken heute gerne an das gemeinsame Wohnen zurück, und ihre Nostalgie wird zumindest zum Teil von den gegenwärtigen sozialen und wirtschaftlichen Problemen genährt. Aber gleichzeitig formte sich auch ein neuer Wunsch: alleine zu leben und trotzdem Kontakt mit den Nachbarn zu haben. Als die Sowjetunion zusammenbrach, mussten sich die Menschen mit einer neuen Situation zurechtfinden. Als eine Reaktion auf den Transformationsprozess und um mit dem neuen Gefühl der Einsamkeit fertig zu werden, begannen sie schnell ,von einer neuen Utopie, die der gescheiterten sozialistischen Utopie gegenüberstand, zu träumen. Dies erklärt, wieso es für viele so wichtig wurde, sich in den eigenen vier Wänden von allem zurückziehen zu können.

Es gilt hervorzuheben, dass die Klassenstrukturen der russischen Gesellschaft eine bedeutende Rolle in der Verwirklichung dieses Traumes spielen, denn individuelle Ambitionen lassen sich nur verwirklichen, wenn man dafür Geld hat. In Russland teilt sich eine kleine Minderheit den Reichtum des Landes, und der Unterschied zwischen Arm und Reich ist groß. Die Villen der neureichen Russen in wohlhabenderen Stadtteilen wie Skhadowka und die heruntergekommenen Häuserblocks der alten Mikrorayons machen diesen Unterschied nur zu deutlich. Diese Bilder und die Interviews zeigen eine Entwicklung auf, die sich als regressive Utopie bezeichnen lässt. Man stelle sich ein riesiges, dreistöckiges Haus vor, welches von einem hohen Zaun umgeben und mit Marmor ausgestattet ist. Diejenigen, die sich ein solches Haus nicht leisten können, träumen von ihm. Natürlich gibt es einige Ausnahmen. Zum Beispiel der zwölfjährige Vladlen, der sein Leben lang in einem Mikrorayon gewohnt hat und um keinen Preis woanders wohnen möchte.

Das vorgeschriebene Wohnen in den staatlichen Siedlungen zu Sowjetzeiten hatte zur Folge, dass die Bewohner von Mikrorayons ihre Sehnsucht nach einer Privatsphäre verdrängen mussten. Sie waren gezwungen, das kollektive Wohnmodell gut zu heißen und zu allen ihren Nachbarn stets nett zu sein. Der Wunsch nach Privatsphäre spiegelte sich in der Inneneinrichtung ihrer Wohnungen wider: Hier konnten sie ihrem persönlichen Geschmack Ausdruck verleihen. Die Menschen konnten ihre Phantasien nur innerhalb ihrer eigenen vier Wände ausleben. Sie versuchten, ihre Wohnungen individuell und vor allem anders als die Gemeinschaftsbereiche zu gestalten. So konnten sie sich wenigstens vorstellen, in einem einzigartigen und bunten Heim zu leben. Jedoch war die Auswahl an Einrichtungsgegenständen begrenzt, und man wurde nicht ermutigt, sein Geld für Konsumgüter auszugeben. Darüber hinaus unterschieden sich die meisten Produkte wenig, was es den Leuten nicht leicht machte, ihren Traum zu verwirklichen. Heute sind die Einwohner von Smolensk weitaus konsumorientierter, und sogar die Menschen, die sich kein Einfamilienhaus leisten können, können sich ihren Traum von einem Zuhause erfüllen. Mit dem Ergebnis, dass die Wohnzimmer in den Mikrorayons jetzt sehr farbenfroh sind: Lebendige, bunte Tapeten und Wandmalereien, Teppiche und schwülstige Vorhänge heben sich deutlich vom grauen Äußeren der Mikrorayons ab. Die Zeitschriften und Zeitungen, die ihren Lesern Tipps für ihre Häuser oder *Datschas* geben, verleihen dem Traum von einem besseren Leben ein Gesicht. Russische Zeitschriften wie das Familienmagazin *Gospagyniya* quellen über mit bunten Bildern von handbestickten Kissenbezügen, Gemüse, das für den Winter eingemacht werden soll, Kochtipps für Hausfrauen, exotischen Pflanzen, Perserteppichen und eleganten Schuhen. Ironischerweise nähren diese Bilder nicht nur die individuellen Träume vereinsamter Bürger, sondern sie spiegeln auch die kollektive Mentalität einer neuen russischen Gesellschaft wider.

Daraus lässt sich schließen, dass die Menschen ihre Erfüllung im Privaten suchen. Es scheint, als würden sich die Einwohner von Smolensk kollektiv nach einem Privatleben sehnen, welches sich innerhalb ihrer eigenen vier Wände abspielt.

ANMERKUNGEN

1 Buchli, Victor: *Archaeology of Socialism*. Oxford 2000

living rooms in microrayon apartments are now very colorful and, decorated with lively wallpapers or murals, carpets or baroque curtains, they mark a strong contrast to the external greyness of the microrayon buildings. People's dream of a better life is expressed visually in the magazines and newspapers that tell them what to do with their house or *dacha*. Russian family magazines like *Gospagyniya* contain colorful images of hand-made pillow cases, vegetables ready to be canned for winter, cooking tips for house wives, exotic plants, Persian carpets and fancy shoes. Ironically, the images tap not only into the private dreams of lonely citizens but they also reflect the collective mentality of a new Russian society.

This suggests that people's dreams revolve around the domestic or private sphere. It seems that the residents of Smolensk share a collective desire for a private life that takes place inside their private homes.

NOTES

1 Buchli, Victor: *Archaeology of Socialism*. Oxford 2000

ÖFFENTLICHER RAUM, MINSK – RÄUME DES JUBELS UND DIE ENTSTEHUNG NEUER ÖFFENTLICHKEITEN

KAI VÖCKLER

In Minsk scheint die Zeit stillzustehen. In die Hauptstadt von Belarus (Weißrussland) verirren sich kaum Touristen und die obligatorische Durchdringung des Stadtraums mit internationalen Markenketten ist hier noch nicht weit fortgeschritten; selbst Werbetafeln sind nur vereinzelt auszumachen. Anders als zum Beispiel in Warschau oder Moskau, finden sich in Minsk keine neuen Hochhäuser privatisierter Staatsunternehmen und globaler Investoren. Prägend für das Stadtbild ist nach wie vor die in der Nachkriegszeit gebaute zentrale, 48 Meter breite und fast drei Kilometer lange Magistrale mit den sie säumenden Regierungsgebäuden, Geschäften und Bildungseinrichtungen, deren stalinistische Prunkfassaden an den verblichenen Glanz vergangener Zeiten erinnern. Seit kurzem erstrahlen sie wieder in neuem Licht: Sie sind nachts vollständig illuminiert, während andernorts in Belarus die Stadtverwaltungen nach zehn Uhr abends die Straßenbeleuchtung abschalten, um Strom zu sparen.

Gegliedert wird die Magistrale durch drei Plätze, deren Dimensionen etwa dem des Roten Platzes in Moskau entsprechen und, gemessen an der Größe von Minsk, deutlich überproportioniert erscheinen. Der im Westen des Zentrums gelegene Leninplatz (heute: Unabhängigkeitsplatz), der dem in den 1930er Jahren im neokonstruktivistischen Stil von Iossif Langbard entworfenen Regierungsgebäude vorgelagert ist, hat bis heute, nicht zuletzt aufgrund seiner Größe (450 x 150 Meter), keine Fassung gefunden. Während er an Feiertagen Raum für Massenumzüge und Militärparaden bietet, dient er in der restlichen Zeit schlicht als Parkplatz. Auch das ihn umgebende Gebäudeensemble spiegelt die wechselvolle weißrussische Geschichte wider. Neben dem Regierungsgebäude erhebt sich die zu Beginn des 20. Jahrhunderts im Stil der Backsteingotik errichtete katholische Kirche St. Simon und St. Helena, die eigentlich einem Kino hätte weichen sollen, aber aufgrund finanzieller Engpässe bis heute überdauerte; schräg gegenüber prägen die neoklassizistische Weißrussische Staatsuniversität und die Pädagogische Hochschule die Ansicht. Bemerkenswert ist auch die Leninstatue, die bis heute vor dem Regierungsgebäude steht.

Ebenso bedeutsam wie der Leninplatz ist der Zentrale Platz (heute: Oktoberplatz), dessen Mittelpunkt von 1952–1961 eine circa zehn Meter hohe Statue von Stalin bildete. Heute beherrscht diese Stelle der in den 1990er Jahren in einem modernistisch-neoklassizistischen Stil gestaltete Palast der Republik, ein wenig genutztes Gebäude, das explizit an die stalinistische Tradition der Monumentalisierung anknüpft (und im Volks-

PUBLIC SPACES IN MINSK – SETTINGS FOR JUBILATION AND THE EMERGENCE OF NEW KINDS OF PUBLIC

KAI VÖCKLER

In Minsk time seems to stand still. Few tourists find their way to the capital of Belarus (White Russia), and the obligatory saturation of the downtown area with international brand names has not made much progress, apart from the occasional billboard. In contrast to such places as Warsaw or Moscow, Minsk boasts no new skyscrapers put up by privatised state enterprises or global investors. The city continues to be dominated by the central, 48-metre-wide and almost three-kilometre-long main street built in the post-war period and lined by government buildings, shops and educational establishments, whose grandiose Stalinist façades recall the faded glory of times gone by. Recently, they have been shining with a new brilliance, being floodlit all night, while in other cities of Belarus the municipal authorities turn off the street lighting after ten o'clock in the evening to save electricity.

The main street is divided into sections by three squares whose dimensions correspond roughly to those of Red Square in Moscow and seem out of all proportion to a city the size of Minsk. Independence Square (formerly Lenin Square) situated to the west of the centre in front of the government building designed in the 1930s by Iosif Langbard in the neoconstructivist style, has not found its proper role to this day, not least on account of its size (450 by 150 metres). On public holidays it offers space for mass processions and military parades, but for the rest of the time it just serves as a car park. The buildings that surround it also reflect the varied history of Belarus. Next to the government building stands the brick-built, Gothic-style Catholic church of St. Simon and St. Helena dating from the early 20th century, which was actually intended to make way for a cinema, but on account of financial bottlenecks has survived so far. Diagonally opposite the view is dominated by the neo-classicist Belarusian State University and the Belarusian State Pedagogical University. Also noteworthy is the Lenin statue which still is in front of before the government building.

Just as remarkable as Independence Square is October Square (formerly Central Square), whose focal point in the years 1952–1961 was a ten-metre-high statue of Stalin. Today this site is dominated by the Palace of the Republic designed in the 1990s in a modernist/neo-classicist style, a little used building that explicitly harks back to the Stalinist tradition of monumentalism (and is popularly referred to as the "Coffin of the Republic"). The Palace of the Republic has a worthy partner in the neighbouring Museum of the History of the Great Patriotic War, built in the early 1950s in the

mund „Sarg der Republik" heißt). Seinen ebenbürtigen Partner findet der Palast der Republik im benachbarten, Anfang der 1950er Jahre im neoklassizistischen „Zuckerbäckerstil" der Stalin-Ära errichteten Museum des Großen Vaterländischen Krieges. Am Runden Platz (später: Siegesplatz), einem Kreisel, in dessen Mitte ein 40 Meter hoher Obelisk an die im Zweiten Weltkrieg gefallenen Soldaten und Partisanen erinnert, endet die Magistrale. Dieses symbolisch hochbedeutsame städtebauliche und architektonische Ensemble wurde mit Monumenten entsprechend ergänzt. So steht beispielsweise vor dem Haus der Offiziere, erhoben auf ein Podest, ein T34-Panzer, jenes sowjetische Militärfahrzeug also, das nach der Befreiung von der deutschen Besatzung als erstes wieder über die Hauptstraße gefahren war.

Dieses monumentale Zentrum einer prototypischen sozialistischen Stadt nimmt im kollektiven Bewusstsein der weißrussischen Bevölkerung immer noch einen zentralen Platz ein. Daran knüpfen auch die ambitionierten Pläne des Staatspräsidenten Alexander Lukashenko an, der per Dekret Großbauprojekte von nationaler Bedeutung anordnet und die Monumentalisierung des Stadtzentrums fortschreiben will. So wird der Bau einer 80 Millionen Euro teuren Nationalbibliothek in Form eines riesigen Diamanten betrieben, und unterhalb des Unabhängigkeitsplatzes entsteht eine vierstöckige Shopping-Mall, deren Glaskuppel den Blick auf die Leninstatue und die Regierungsgebäude freigibt.

Raumgestaltungen, wie sie sich in den Städten materialisieren, drücken ein bestimmtes Selbstverständnis aus, das einem imaginären Gegenüber mitgeteilt wird. Der Semiologe Roland Barthes hat darauf hingewiesen, dass zwischen Bedeutung und Funktion von physischen Räumen ein Spannungsverhältnis besteht, da die Bedeutung eines Raumes in völligem Gegensatz zu der durch seine Gestaltung intendierten Symbolik stehen kann. Es gibt immer auch verschiedene Lesarten von gleichen Räumen, die unterschiedlich konnotiert sind.[1] Aber warum sind Räume öffentlich? Wegen der dort stattfindenden Aktivitäten oder ihrer Funktion im kollektiven Unbewussten der Stadt? Denn unbestreitbar haben bestimmte Orte eine größere Bedeutung als andere. Barthes weist in diesem Zusammenhang dem Stadtzentrum eine zentrale Rolle in der Anlage der Stadt zu, weniger weil es den Kulminationspunkt einer besonderen Aktivität darstellt, sondern eher eine Art leeres „Foyer" der Vorstellung, die sich die Gesellschaft vom Zentrum bildet – eine leere Stelle, die für die Organisation jedweder Stadt (und ihrer Gesellschaft) zentral ist. Und diese Leerstelle wird besetzt, sie wird Kodierungen und Dekodierungen unterworfen und ist durchzogen von imaginären Bedeutungen. Wie Maurice Halbwachs gezeigt hat, ist das Zentrum ein Ort mit hoher symbolischer Bedeutung für die kollektive Erinnerung. Es ist ein Ort, der einerseits eine materielle Realität besitzt und andererseits ein Symbol ist, also eine geistige Bedeutung hat, die sich in der Vorstellung verschiedener Gruppen mit dieser Realität verbindet.[2]

Wie unterschiedlich die Lesarten des Minsker Zentrums sind, zeigt ein Interview mit der 80-jährigen Lidia Bobrousky und ihrem 24-jährigen Enkel Vladislau.[3] Die Großmutter schätzt die Magistrale samt ihren Prunkbauten und Monumenten und steht den Bestrebungen des Staatspräsidenten, diese zu remonumentalisieren und zu ergänzen, positiv gegenüber: „Ich halte nichts von der Idee, die alten sowjetischen Monumente zu beseitigen. Ich bin sie gewohnt und ich mag sie so gern, dass ich sie sogar heute noch interessant finde (...) Ich glaube, die Architekten sind sehr engagiert, die

neo-classicist "wedding cake" style of the Stalin era. Victory Square (formerly Round Square), a roundabout in the middle of which a 40-metre-high obelisk rises in memory of the soldiers and partisans killed in the Second World War, marks the end of the main street. This highly symbolic complex of urban architecture has been appropriately supplemented by monuments. Mounted on a pedestal in front of the Officers' Club, for example, stands a T 34 tank, which was the first Soviet military vehicle to drive down the main street after the liberation from German occupation.

This monumental centre of a prototypical socialist city still occupies a central place in the collective consciousness of the Belarusian population. This awareness is behind the ambitious plans of President Alexander Lukashenko when he decrees large-scale construction projects of national significance in continuation of the monumentalism of the city centre. Thus work is in progress on an 80-million-euro National Library in the shape of a huge diamond, and beneath Independence Square a four-storey shopping mall is under construction, from whose glass dome it will be possible to see the Lenin statue and the government building.

Spatial designs of the kind that materialise in cities make a certain statement about themselves that is communicated to an imaginary other. The semiologist Roland Barthes pointed out that there is a tension between the significance and function of physical spaces, since the significance of a space may be in complete contradiction to the symbolism intended by its design. Furthermore there are always different ways of interpreting the same spaces when the connotations are different.[1] But why are spaces public? Because of the activities that take place in them or because of their function in the city's collective subconscious? For it is indisputable that some places have more significance than others. In this connection Barthes assigns the city centre a central role in the layout of a city, less because it represents the culminating point of a particular activity, but because it is a kind of empty "foyer" for the notion that society has of the centre – an empty place which is central to the organisation of any city (and its society). And this empty place is occupied, subjected to encryptions and decryptions, and shot through with imaginary meanings. As Maurice Halbwachs has shown, the centre is a place with high symbolic significance for collective remembrance. On the one hand, it is a place which has a material reality. On the other hand, it is a symbol, i.e. it has a spiritual significance that mingles with this reality in the imagination of different groups.[2]

How different the interpretations of central Minsk can be is shown by an interview with the 80-year-old Lidia Bobrousky and her 24-year-old grandson Vladislau.[3] The grandmother appreciates the main street together with its stately buildings and monuments and takes a positive view of the president's efforts to re-monumentalise and add to them: "I don't think it's a good idea to get rid of the old Soviet monuments. I am used to them, in fact I like them so much that even today I find them interesting... I think the architects are working very hard to improve the look of the city... As a result of all the efforts that Lukashenko is making Minsk is becoming more and more beautiful... a shopping mall beneath Independence Square is definitely not a bad idea."[4] Her grandson argues against this in a very critical manner – although he agrees that Minsk now looks much better, he thinks all Soviet monuments should be removed: "I think they should get rid of the Lenin statue. If monuments are to be the only re-

Stadt besser zu machen (...) Als Resultat all der Anstrengungen, die Lukashenko unternimmt, wird Minsk immer schöner (...) Eine Shopping-Mall unterhalb des Unabhängigkeitsplatzes ist bestimmt keine schlechte Idee."[4] Ihr Enkel argumentiert dagegen höchst kritisch – zwar findet er auch, dass Minsk jetzt viel besser aussieht, aber seiner Meinung nach sollten alle sowjetischen Monumente entfernt werden: „Ich denke, die Leninstatue muss beseitigt werden. Denn wenn Denkmale einzig unsere Geschichte spiegeln, dann können wir auch Statuen von Hitler und Trotzki aufstellen. Ich glaube, dass jedes Denkmal, das für Krieg, Mord und andere Greueltaten steht, beseitigt werden muss."[5] Für ihn ist es wichtig, dass die Denkmale tatsächlich etwas mit der weißrussischen Geschichte zu tun haben: „Wir sollten Statuen unserer Leute aufstellen. Puschkin – der war gerade einmal in Belarus. Statuen von russischen Schriftstellern aufzustellen bedeutet, dass wir uns an der russischen Geschichte ausrichten und uns mit ihr identifizieren. Das muss aufhören."[6] Und nicht die Gebäude der sowjetischen Ära sind für ihn von Bedeutung, sondern vielmehr die wenigen Bauwerke des präsowjetischen Minsk, etwa die katholische Backsteinkirche am Unabhängigkeitsplatz. In den Aussagen von Großmutter und Enkel zeigt sich eine unterschiedliche Wahrnehmung, die bezeichnend ist für die Auseinandersetzung der weißrussischen Gesellschaft über ihre Zukunft. Zugleich verweist sie auf die besondere Bedeutung von „Öffentlichkeit" und „öffentlichem Raum" in sozialistischen und postsozialistischen Gesellschaften.

DER SOWJETISCHE ÖFFENTLICHE RAUM

Der öffentliche Raum in der Sowjetzeit unterschied sich, wie Victor Voronkov darlegt, wesentlich von demjenigen westlicher Gesellschaften.[7] Öffentlichkeit wurde vom Staat hergestellt und kontrolliert; es gab schlicht keinen Ort in der Sowjetunion, wo ohne staatliche Kontrolle öffentlich diskutiert werden konnte. Selbst in der Privatsphäre war dies lange Zeit unmöglich, denn während der Phase des stalinistischen Terrors existierte selbst diese für drei Jahrzehnte nicht. Der physische Raum des Privatlebens wurde unter Stalin aufgelöst; die im Zuge der Industrialisierung aus den Dörfern in die Städte strömende Landbevölkerung wurde in den „Kommunalkas", den Gemeinschaftswohnungen, untergebracht. Dabei handelte es sich zumeist um vormalige Wohnungen des gehobenen Bürgertums und des Adels, in denen mehrere Mietparteien zusammenlebten und sich Küche und sanitäre Einrichtungen teilten. In der Enge einer Kommunalka blieb kaum etwas verborgen: Die Schnüffelei reichte bis hin zur staatlich geförderten und öffentlich belobigten Bespitzelung von Familienmitgliedern untereinander. Jede Form des Individualismus galt als schädlich, ein homogenisierter Lebensstil wurde angestrebt, wie es die Parole „Der Sowjetmensch hat nichts vor den Genossen zu verbergen" ausdrückt – der „Andere" war der „Gleiche", der „Neue Mensch". Alles war öffentlich und zugleich der staatlichen Kontrolle ausgesetzt. Private Räume entstanden allmählich wieder ab 1950, als zum Ende der Stalinära mit der Massenproduktion kostengünstiger Wohnungen begonnen wurde. Erst nach dem Tode Stalins, als die Furcht, ermordet oder bestraft zu werden, graduell abnahm und durch die neuen Wohnungsbauten ein Privatleben jenseits staatlicher Kontrolle ermöglicht wurde, konnten sich fern der offiziellen, staatlich inszenierten und regulierten Öffentlichkeit neue Formen von Öffentlichkeit entwickeln. In den Privaträumen entstand ein krypto-

flection of our history we might as well put up statues of Hitler and Trotsky. I think that every monument that stands for war, murder and other atrocities should be got rid of."[5] What is important for him is that the monuments should actually have something to do with Belarusian history: "We should put up statues of our people. Pushkin was only in Belarus once. Putting up statues of Russian writers means that we see ourselves as part of Russian history and identify with it. This has got to stop."[6] It is not the buildings of the Soviet era that are important to him, but the few buildings dating from pre-Soviet Minsk, such as the brick-built Catholic church in Independence Square. The statements of grandmother and grandson reveal differing perceptions that are indicative of the debate going on within Belarusian society about its future. At the same time it points to the special significance of "public" and "public space" in socialist and post-socialist societies.

THE SOVIET PUBLIC SPACE

The public space in the Soviet era differed greatly, as Victor Voronkov shows, from that of western societies.[7] The public sphere was created and controlled by the state. There was no place in the Soviet Union at all where public discussion could take place without state control. For a long time – three decades – it was impossible even in private, especially during the phase of the Stalinist terror. Under Stalin the physical space in which private life takes place was suspended, the rural population that poured into the cities from the villages in the course of industrialisation was accommodated in the *kommunalki*, or communal flats. These were mainly the former apartments of the upper middle class and aristocracy, in which several occupants lived together sharing kitchen and sanitary facilities. In the cramped conditions of a *kommunalka* not much could remain concealed. The system of informing extended to state-promoted and publicly commended spying by family members on each other. Any form of individualism was considered harmful, the aim being a homogenised life style summed up in the slogan "Soviet man has nothing to hide from his comrades" – the "other" was the "equal", the "New Man". Everything was public and subject to state control. Private spaces re-emerged gradually from 1950 onwards, when the mass production of affordable flats was begun at the end of the Stalin era. Only after Stalin's death, as the fear of being imprisoned or executed gradually faded away and the new apartment blocks made possible a private life beyond state control, did new forms of public life have a chance to develop far from the official one stage-managed and regulated by the state. The private space gave rise to a crypto-public space (which Voronkov calls "private-public"), an informal sphere which was kept strictly separate from the official space. Marc Garcelon also stresses that the terms "public" and "private" in the context of the communist countries have a completely different meaning than they do in western societies and instead proposes a distinction between "official" and "social".[8] He sees the public sphere ("officialdom") as the public space controlled and stage-managed by the party and administrative apparatus, which was highly visible and omnipresent yet at the same time far removed from the everyday routine of the Soviet citizen. The social sphere, on the other hand, comprises both life at work and activities in the officially sanctioned associations, both cultural and sporting events (which in the West tend to be defined as public activities), the shadow economy, and the domestic sphere with

öffentlicher Raum (Voronkov nennt ihn „privat-öffentlich"), eine informelle Sphäre, die vom offiziellen Raum strikt abgegrenzt war. Auch Marc Garcelon betont, dass die Begriffe „öffentlich" und „privat" im Kontext der kommunistischen Staaten eine völlig andere Bedeutung als in den westlichen Gesellschaften haben und schlägt stattdessen eine Unterscheidung in „offiziell" und „sozial" vor.[8] Für ihn ist der Bereich des Öffentlichen („officialdom") der vom Partei- und Verwaltungsapparat kontrollierte und inszenierte öffentliche Raum, der spektakulär und omnipräsent und zugleich weit entfernt von der Alltagsroutine des Sowjetbürgers war. Das Soziale umfasst hingegen sowohl das Arbeitsleben als auch die Aktivitäten in den offiziell sanktionierten Verbänden, sowohl Kultur- und Sportereignisse (die im Westen eher als öffentliche Aktivitäten definiert werden), die Schattenökonomie wie auch den häuslichen Bereich mit Familie und Freunden. Die „Kolonisierung" des Öffentlichen durch den Staat, so Garcelon, führte ungewollt zur „Privatisierung" von großen Teilen des sozialen Lebens, in dem Sinne, dass die Bevölkerungsmehrheit sich von der Politik und den damit verbundenen Aktivitäten zurückzog und sich aufs „Durchkommen" konzentrierte – wie Voronkov ausführt, mit fatalen Folgen in der postsozialistischen Ära. Gerade weil es keinen unabhängigen Bereich gab, in dem sich zivilgesellschaftliche Prozesse entfalten konnten, blieben die Regeln der Sowjetzeit gültig: Die formellen Gesetze sind ineffektiv wie früher, alles beruht auf Beziehungen. Dass nach dem Zusammenbruch des Sowjetsystems ein Wandel stattgefunden habe, hält Voronkov für eine Illusion. Diese Illusion beruhe auf einer Vermischung der Sphären des realen Lebens und des „offiziellen" öffentlichen Raums, der durch die postsozialistischen Massenmedien (die die sowjetische Propaganda beerbten) geschaffen wurde: Die Flut von immer neuen Themen, die dort verhandelt wurde, hat erst das Bild des Wandels kreiert.

Um den sowjetischen Kommunikationsraum zu verstehen, so Voronkov, müsse die besondere Struktur der sozialen Beziehungen während der Sowjetzeit in Betracht gezogen werden. Es gab geschriebene und ungeschriebene Regeln, die eine strikt geschiedene Parallelexistenz führten: Die auf Konventionen beruhende informelle Sphäre (in der sich unternehmerische Aktivitäten entfalteten und eine informelle Ökonomie entstand, die auf Beziehungen beruhte) war im Alltagsleben vorherrschend und stand im Widerspruch zu den geschriebenen Gesetzen. Dies stellte eine Bedrohung der Stabilität der sowjetischen Gesellschaft dar, so dass, wie Voronkov argumentiert, die ungeschriebene Regel bestand, in den offiziellen öffentlichen Raum keine Themen zu transportieren, die mit dem wirklichen Leben zu tun haben. Jeder Sowjetbürger kommunizierte in beiden Sphären, in zwei verschiedenen „Sprachen", wobei ihm der Unterschied immer bewusst war.

Die strikte Scheidung in eine informell-semiprivate und eine offiziell-öffentliche Sphäre sieht Erhard Stölting als ein Ergebnis des wechselseitigen Misstrauens, das Staat und Bevölkerung einander entgegenbrachten. Die Revolutionierung der Lebensverhältnisse in der Sowjetunion zielte vor allem auf die Vergesellschaftung des Alltagslebens.[9] Zwei besondere Charakteristika städtischen Lebens sollten aufgelöst werden – einerseits die traditionelle urbane Lebensform, also die bürgerliche Vorstellung von Urbanität als einer „privaten Öffentlichkeit", wo einander fremde Individuen unter Wahrung persönlicher Distanz miteinander leben und kommunizieren, und andererseits das häusliche Leben als der Hort des Intimen, Privaten, Verborgenen. Die Differenz zwischen Privat-

family and friends. The "colonisation" of the public sphere by the state, Garcelon says, led to the "privatisation" of large areas of social life in the sense that the majority of the population withdrew from political and associated activities and concentrated on "getting by", which had fatal consequences, as Voronkov demonstrates, in the post-socialist era. Precisely because there was no independent area in which civil-society processes could develop, the rules of the Soviet era remained in force. The formal laws are just as ineffective as they used to be, everything is based on personal contacts. The belief that a transformation has taken place since the collapse of the Soviet system is held by Voronkov to be an illusion, an illusion based on a fusion of the spheres of real life and the "official" public space created by the post-socialist mass media (which inherited Soviet propaganda techniques). The constant flood of new topics emanating from them created the image of transformation.

According to Voronkov, if we want to understand the Soviet communication structure, we have to look at the special structure of social relationships during the Soviet era. There were written and unwritten rules which had a strictly separate but parallel existence. The convention-based informal sphere (in which entrepreneurial activities developed and an informal economy based on personal contacts arose) predominated in everyday life and was in contradiction to the written laws. This constituted a threat to the stability of Soviet society so that, as Voronkov argues, there was an unwritten rule not to transport into the official public space topics that had anything to do with real life. Every Soviet citizen communicated in both spheres, in two different "languages", although he was always well aware of the difference.

The strict division into an informal/semi-private and an official/public sphere is seen by Erhard Stölting as a result of mutual distrust between state and population. The revolutionising of living conditions in the Soviet Union was aimed above all at the socialising of everyday life.[9] Two particular characteristics of urban life were to be eliminated – one was the traditional urban way of life, i.e. the bourgeois notion of urban living as a "private public sphere", where individuals who do not know one another live side by side and engage in communication while maintaining their personal distance, and the other was domestic life as the sanctuary of intimacy, privacy, seclusion. The difference between the private and public spheres was to be shifted in favour of public spaces. The true home of the "New Man" was the community, so that no withdrawal into the private sphere was necessary. Imposing streets and spacious squares were built to provide a worthy setting for an intense public life. Michail Ryklin interprets these structures by referring to Hegel's *Aesthetics* as a symbolic architecture, which has an inherent significance and is not there to lend form to a significance existing independently of itself. In this it resembles the palatial temples of antiquity, except that it had a quasi-religious function – underpinning the unity of the people with the party and the leader. These "settings for jubilation" which served to glorify the "New Life" were meant to make an active contribution to its emergence.[10]

The physical organisation of the socialist city, as of urban life in general, was meant to arouse collective feelings. The celebration of the collective triumph (which compensated for individual frustration) reached its theatrical peak in the ritual mass events.[11]

The collective role-playing of the mass processions, larger-than-life sporting events and public festivals constituted a special kind of "mass consumption", in which the

sphäre und Öffentlichkeit sollte zugunsten der öffentlichen Räume verschoben werden. Das wahre Zuhause des „Neuen Menschen" war die Gemeinschaft, so dass es des Rückzugs in die Privatsphäre nicht bedurfte. Mit dem Bau imposanter Straßenzüge und weiter Plätze wurde der würdige Rahmen für ein intensives öffentliches Leben geschaffen. Michail Ryklin interpretiert diese Bauten mit Verweis auf Hegels *Ästhetik* als eine symbolische Architektur, die ihre Bedeutung in sich trägt und nicht einer unabhängig von ihr existierenden Bedeutung Form verleiht. Sie gleicht damit den altantiken Tempel-Palästen, die hier eine quasi-religiöse Funktion erhalten – in der Untermauerung der Einheit des Volkes mit Partei und Führer. Diese „Räume des Jubels", die der Lobpreisung des „Neuen Lebens" dienten, sollten selbst aktiv zur Herausbildung desselben beitragen.[10] Die physische Organisation der sozialistischen Stadt, wie auch das städtische Leben im Allgemeinen, sollte kollektive Gefühle erwecken. Die Feier des kollektiven Triumphs (die für die individuelle Frustration entschädigte) fand ihren inszenatorischen Höhepunkt in den rituellen Massenveranstaltungen.[11] Das kollektive Rollenspiel der Massenumzüge, aber auch der überdimensionierten Sportveranstaltungen und der Volksfeste stellten einen „Massenkonsum" besonderer Art dar, in der die festliche Masse sich selbst beobachten konnte – und zugleich beobachtet wurde, von den Organen und Repräsentanten des Staates. Die Verstaatlichung und Kontrolle des öffentlichen Raums wird hier am deutlichsten sichtbar, die inoffizielle Seite einer geselligen Kommunikation hatte in die Parks und in die privaten Küchen auszuweichen. Die monumentalisierte öffentliche Stadt fand ihr Pendant in der minimalen Stadt der Existenzsicherung, den Mikrorayons am Stadtrand.

Der theatralische Aspekt des gesellschaftlichen Lebens in der Sowjetunion wird in der Konzeption der Stadt als monumentaler und didaktischer Bühne (die den neuen Menschen hervorbringen sollte) deutlich, wie Iwailo Ditschew ausführt. Die Stadt wurde zum „Schaufenster des Glücks" aufpoliert, die „universalistische Norm implizierte Einheitlichkeit, Licht, große Kaufhäuser und Kantinen, die Ausstrahlung von Radiosendungen auf jedem Platz, von dankbaren Pionieren bewachte Denkmäler, den Anblick sportlich durchtrainierter Körper, rauchende Fabrikschlote".[12] Es galt Modernität und Kultiviertheit herauszustellen. All das, um die in die Stadt strömende Landbevölkerung zu disziplinieren, verwandtschaftliche wie religiöse oder ethnische Bindungen aufzulösen – obwohl das System unter der Hand genau auf diese Solidaritäten angewiesen war, um den strukturellen Mangel auszugleichen. Eine Form der Modernisierung, die ihre Entsprechung in der Kultur des sozialistischen Realismus findet. Diese Kultur war eine Kultur für den „Neuen Menschen", den es noch nicht gab, aber in Zukunft geben sollte. Sie sollte weniger die Bedürfnisse der Massen befriedigen, sondern sie vielmehr umerziehen. Womit, so Boris Groys, der Effekt einer Identifizierung von Traum und Wirklichkeit, von Gegenwart und Zukunft bewirkt wurde.[13] Davon abgesehen, dass dadurch jedem Einzelnen seine Unvollkommenheit vor Augen geführt wurde, manifestierte sich hier eine abgrundtiefe Kluft zwischen realen Lebensbedingungen und inszenierter Ideologie, deren Ineinssetzung fragwürdig ist. Denn das ließe nur die Schlussfolgerung zu, dass alle Wirklichkeit inszeniert ist. Was bleibt aber von der Bühne Stadt, wenn die ideologische Szenographie zusammenfällt?

festive mass could observe itself while at the same time being observed by the organs and representatives of the state. It was here that state control of the public space was most clearly on display, while unofficial companionship and contacts had to withdraw to the parks and private kitchens. The monumentalised public city had its counterpart in the concrete housing estates (*mikrorayony*) on the outskirts, which provided the minimum necessities for day-to-day existence.

The theatrical aspect of social life in the Soviet Union is clearly seen in the concept of the city as a monumental and didactic stage (meant to produce the new man), as Iwailo Ditschew demonstrates. The city was got up as a "showcase of happiness", the "universalist norm implied unity, light, large department stores and canteens, the loudspeakers blaring radio broadcasts in every square, monuments guarded by grateful Young Pioneers, glimpses of lithe athletic bodies, smoking factory chimneys."[12] The emphasis was on modernity and decent behaviour. All this was needed to discipline the rural population that was pouring into the cities and sever its familial, religious or ethnic ties – although unofficially the system had to rely on precisely those types of solidarity in order to make up for its own structural defects. This was a form of modernisation that found its equivalent in the culture of Socialist Realism. It was a culture for the "New Man" who did not yet exist, but would exist in the future – a culture intended not so much to satisfy the needs of the masses as to re-educate them. In this way, according to Boris Groys, an identification of dream and reality, present and future was effected.[13] Apart from the fact that this made each individual vividly aware of his own imperfection, it opened up a profound chasm between real living conditions and staged ideology, a chasm that one could scarcely hope to bridge unless one were to conclude that all reality is staged. But what happens to the city stage when the ideological stage manager collapses?

THE POST-SOCIALIST PUBLIC SPACE

Ditschew sees the appearance of "normality" and the quality of *kul'turnost'* ("decent behaviour") as key ideological components of the attempt to legitimise urban life under socialism. For him the post-socialist city (he has Sofia in mind) continues to simulate "normality" and "decent behaviour" to the extent that it boasts big-name department store chains and famous brands (McDonald's). This fits in with Groys' thesis that there are parallels between Stalin's Socialist Realism and today's commercial mass culture, both of which arose at the same time. Inherent in both is a desire to become submerged in a mass culture that attains a suggestive presence. Although the culture of the Stalin period was anti-commercial, in its essence and aims it had an avant-garde quality. After all, it virtually anticipated the communist utopia. Now this utopian sphere has been replaced by the promise of globalised mass culture to provide individual happiness. Groys' equating of aesthetics with politics seems questionable, however, as it makes a difference whether a political programme enforced by terror finds an aesthetic apotheosis or whether the law of supply and demand is to be manipulated in favour of demand via simulated lifestyles. Groys sees post-socialist development as a kind of reverse modernisation – away from the postulated post-historical communist utopia and backwards in history to the days of markets and nationalisms (which is why the former Soviet republics immediately had to create a national identity for themselves).[14]

DER POSTSOZIALISTISCHE ÖFFENTLICHE RAUM

Für Ditschew waren der Anschein von „Normalität" und die Eigenschaft der „Kultiviertheit" zentrale Bestandteile der Ideologie zur Legitimation des städtischen Lebens im Sozialismus. Die postsozialistische Stadt simuliert für ihn (mit Blick auf Sofia) weiterhin „Normalität" und „Kultiviertheit" in dem Maße, in dem namhafte Kaufhausketten und berühmte Marken (McDonald's) präsent sind. Das trifft sich mit der These von Groys, dass es Parallelen zwischen dem Stalin'schen sozialistischen Realismus und der heutigen kommerziellen Massenkultur gibt, die beide zum gleichen Zeitpunkt entstanden. In beiden sei das Begehren nach einem Aufgehen in einer Massenkultur eingeschrieben, das eine suggestive Präsenz erreicht – wobei die Kultur der Stalinzeit antikommerziell, in ihren Inhalten und Zielen aber avantgardistisch war: Immerhin wurde durch sie die kommunistische Utopie virtuell vorweggenommen. An die Stelle dieser utopischen Sphäre tritt jetzt das Versprechen der globalisierten Massenkultur auf individuelles Glück. Diese von Groys vorgenommene Gleichsetzung von Ästhetik und Politik scheint jedoch fragwürdig, macht es doch einen Unterschied, ob ein politisches Programm, das mit Terror durchgesetzt wird, eine ästhetische Überhöhung findet oder ob das Gesetz von Angebot und Nachfrage qua simulierter Lebensentwürfe zugunsten der Nachfrage manipuliert werden soll. Groys sieht die postsozialistische Entwicklung als eine Art umgekehrter Modernisierung – weg von der postulierten posthistorischen kommunistischen Utopie zurück in die historische Zeit der Märkte und Nationen (weswegen sich die ehemaligen Sowjetrepubliken sofort eine nationale Identität schaffen mussten).[14]

Auch Gregory Andrusz entdeckt in der postsozialistischen Stadt eine rituelle Anrufung der Vergangenheit, die sich in der fußgängerfreundlichen Umgestaltung von Plätzen und Straßen, in ihrer Ausstattung mit historisierendem Mobiliar zeigt. Diese Räume finden nicht mehr ihre Bestimmung in den Zeremonien sozialistischer Macht, sondern inszenieren den Mythos des harmonischen Gemeinwesens, wo jeder mit jedem frei interagiert und dem Exotischen und Bizarren ob ihrer Nonkonformität applaudiert wird (als Ausdrucksformen, die der sozialistischen Konformität widersprechen).[15] Wie auch für Ditschew sind es für ihn die Räume der Unterhaltung und des Konsums, die die Europäisierung und Verwestlichung symbolisieren und zum Ausdruck bringen sollen, dass die Stadt den höchsten Stand zivilisatorischen Fortschritts erreicht hat. Und ähnlich wie Groys sieht er eine Verschiebung hin zum latent Nationalistischen: War die sozialistische Stadt theoretisch international und im Geiste national, so ist für ihn die postsozialistische Stadt theoretisch kosmopolitisch, geistig lokal und praktisch nationalistisch, was sich in der Ausgrenzung des „Anderen", des Fremden, des Migranten manifestiert.

Problematisch an der Umwandlung des öffentlichen Raumes ist, dass sie mit einer Identitätspolitik einhergeht, die die Herauslösung der postsozialistischen Länder aus der Sowjetunion und ihre Unabhängigkeit auch mit der Etablierung einer durch die Rekonstruktion der historischen Innenstadtstrukturen beschworenen Nationalgeschichte stützen will – mit all den Kämpfen zwischen den unterschiedlichen gesellschaftlichen Gruppen um die richtige Interpretation der Symbole, wie das Beispiel Minsk zeigt. Dabei kommt es zu einer Aufspaltung zwischen einem sich an der Vergangenheit orientierenden gesellschaftlichen Leitbild und der tatsächlich stattfindenden ökonomischen, raumstrukturellen und gesellschaftlichen Umstrukturierung, die in immer stärkerem Maße von supranationalen Kräften bestimmt wird. Was rekonstruiert wird, ist

Gregory Andruzs also discerns in the post-socialist city a ritual invocation of the past as manifested in the pedestrian-friendly conversion of squares and streets and their adornment with historical trappings. These spaces no longer find their role in the ceremonies of socialist power, but embody the myth of communal harmony, where everyone interacts freely with everyone else, and the exotic and bizarre are applauded for their nonconformity (as forms of expression opposed to socialist conformity).[15] As with Ditschew, it is the places of entertainment and consumption that for him symbolise and express Europeanisation and westernisation, showing that the city has achieved the highest state of civilisation and progress. And, like Groys, he detects a shift towards latent nationalism. If the socialist city was international in theory and national at heart, he sees the post-socialist city as cosmopolitan in theory, provincial at heart, and nationalist in practice, as manifested in the exclusion of the "other", the foreigner, the migrant.

The problem with the transformation of public space is that it is coupled with a policy of identity aimed at perpetuating the separation of the post-socialist countries from the Soviet Union and cementing their independence by establishing a national history, partly by reconstructing the historic inner cities. This in turn gives rise to conflicts between the various social groups over the correct interpretation of the symbols, as the example of Minsk shows. This brings about a dichotomy between a social model oriented towards the past and the economic, physical and social restructuring that is actually taking place, which is increasingly determined by supranational forces. What is reconstructed is a spatial vision, but the social structures and urban concepts of which this vision is composed do not exist. The obsessive conjuring up of the historic face of the city and its past significance obscures the real changes taking place in the way the present urban space is used.[16]

Has the Soviet propaganda about the "New Life" in the communist community merely been replaced by the commercial advertising of individual happiness in the consumer society, a happiness rooted in an ethnically based national community? Or is a new patchwork quilt of public constituencies emerging which, each in its own way, use and reinterpret the existing symbols and spaces? An attempt was made to find answers to these questions as illustrated by the example of Minsk.

MINSK – THE IMPLEMENTATION OF THE SOVIET MATRIX

When the German Wehrmacht's Army Group Centre withdrew from Minsk in 1944, over 70 per cent of the city had been destroyed. During the German occupation of 1941–1944 over two million people were killed in Belarus, about one quarter of the total population, including nearly the entire Jewish community.[17] Three-quarters of the urban housing stock in Belarus had been destroyed, while the city of Minsk was a sea of ruins. What then began has gone down in history as the "Minsk phenomenon", and the historian Thomas Bohn has made a study of it.[18] Starting in 1950, Minsk underwent a rapid population growth as a result of accelerated industrialisation. In the post-war period the number of inhabitants rose sixfold, from 273,600 in 1950 to 1,636,900 inhabitants in 1990. Minsk became the Soviet Union's sixth largest city.

Plans for changing the whole face of the city had existed back in the 1930s, but it was not until after the war that a start could be made on the project. The aim was

ein Bild, doch die gesellschaftlichen Strukturen und Urbanitätsvorstellungen, aus denen sich dieses Raumbild zusammensetzt, existieren nicht. Die obsessive Beschwörung des historischen Stadtbilds und seiner vergangenen Bedeutung täuscht über den eigentlichen Wandel in der Raumnutzung hinweg.[16]
Ist die sowjetische Propaganda des „Neuen Lebens" in der kommunistischen Gemeinschaft nur durch die kommerzielle Werbung für ein individuelles Glück im Konsum ersetzt worden, das seine Heimat in einer ethnisch begründeten nationalen Gemeinschaft findet? Oder entsteht ein neues Patchwork von Öffentlichkeiten, die alle auf je eigene Weise die bestehenden Symbole und Räume verwenden und umkodieren? Diesen Fragen wurde am Beispiel von Minsk nachgegangen.

MINSK – DIE IMPLEMENTIERUNG DER SOWJETISCHEN MATRIX

Als sich die Heeresgruppe Mitte der Deutschen Wehrmacht 1944 aus Minsk zurückzog, war die Stadt zu über 70 Prozent zerstört. Während der deutschen Besatzung 1941–1944 waren in Belarus über zwei Millionen Menschen umgekommen, etwa ein Viertel der Gesamtbevölkerung, darunter nahezu der gesamte jüdische Bevölkerungsanteil.[17] Drei Viertel des städtischen Wohnungsbestands von Belarus waren vernichtet, die Stadt Minsk glich einem Trümmerfeld. Was danach begann, ist als das „Minsker Phänomen" in die Annalen eingegangen und von dem Historiker Thomas Bohn erforscht worden.[18] Mit der forcierten Industrialisierung setzte in Minsk ab 1950 ein rasantes Bevölkerungswachstum ein. In der Nachkriegsperiode stieg die Zahl der Einwohner um das Sechsfache, von 273 600 im Jahre 1950 auf 1 636 900 Einwohner im Jahre 1990. Minsk entwickelte sich zur sechstgrößten Stadt der Sowjetunion.
Bereits in den 1930er Jahren existierten Pläne, die Stadt vollständig umzugestalten, aber erst nach Kriegsende konnte mit diesem Vorhaben begonnen werden. Das Ziel war jedoch nicht, die historische – in den Kriegsjahren weitgehend zerstörte – Stadtstruktur wiederherzustellen, sondern eine „sozialistische Stadt" zu errichten. Der von russischen und weißrussischen Architekten und Ingenieuren erstellte Generalplan von 1946 avisierte bis 1960 eine Einwohnerzahl von 450 000. Minsk sollte zum administrativen und industriellen Zentrum und zur Hauptstadt der Weißrussischen Sozialistischen Sowjetrepublik (BSSR) ausgebaut werden. Dabei folgte man den Prinzipien stalinistischen Städtebaus mit seinen geradlinigen Magistralen, einer durch eine großzügige Radialringstruktur vorgegebenen Straßenführung und einem repräsentativen Zentrum mit monumentalen Verwaltungsgebäuden, öffentlichen Plätzen von zeremonialem Charakter sowie Parkanlagen mit sozialistischen Monumenten. Von primärer Bedeutung war die Neugestaltung des Stadtzentrums von Minsk, dessen wichtigste Strukturelemente eine Magistrale und die Fassung der Uferanlage des Flusses Svisloch als Grünzone waren; Magistrale und Fluss kreuzen sich im Innenstadtbereich. Man sah die Chance, die ursprünglich enge Straßenführung mit seinen ungeordnet entstandenen, traditionellen Holzhäusern durch ein geordnetes Ensemble von Repräsentations- und Wohnbauten zu ersetzen, die mit Grünräumen vernetzt sind – ein ambitionierter Aufbauplan, dessen Realisierung sich aufgrund der Kriegsschäden bis in die 1960er Jahre hinzog. Sein Herzstück war die bereits beschriebene Gestaltung des Stadtzentrums, das Minsk heute wie ein „Freilichtmuseum des sozialistischen Realismus" (Thomas Bohn) erscheinen lässt.[19]

not, however, to restore the historical structure of the city – which had been largely destroyed in the war years – but to create a "socialist city". The General Plan drawn up by Russian and Belarusian architects and engineers in 1946 envisaged a population of 450,000 by 1960. Minsk was to be expanded into the administrative centre, industrial heart and political capital of the Belarusian Socialist Soviet Republic (BSSR). The plan followed the principles of Stalinist town planning with its straight arterial roads radiating outwards on a grand scale and a grandiose centre with monumental administrative buildings, public squares of a ceremonial nature, and car parks with socialist monuments. Of primary significance was the redesigning of the city centre of Minsk, whose principal structural elements were a main street and a green zone to be created on the banks of the river Svisloch – main street and river intersected in the middle of the city. The opportunity was seen of replacing the original warren of narrow streets and traditional wooden houses that had sprung up randomly over the years by an orderly ensemble of prestigious buildings and apartment blocks linked by green areas. It was an ambitious construction plan whose implementation – owing to the war damage – was to last into the 1960s. At its heart was the design of the city centre described above, which makes today's Minsk seem like an "open-air museum of Socialist Realism" (Thomas Bohn).[19]

REVISING AND RE-REVISING THE SYMBOLS OF THE SOVIET MATRIX

There can be no doubt that the artistic urban architectural ensemble of the Minsk city centre occupies a central place in the collective subconscious of Belarusian society. After all there are but a few structures – most of them destroyed in the Second World War or neglected in the Soviet era – that testify to another, pre- or non-Soviet identity. And if we assume that this fuels the competing visions of the future of the society, the wrangling over the significance of the formerly Soviet matrix in post-Soviet Belarus becomes understandable.

Belarusian society is deeply split into two factions. If one compares the spoken and written utterances of the two sides, it is hard to believe that they share the same living space.[20] They differ as to the language they prefer (Russian or Belarusian), as to their historical memory (does one identify with the Polish-Lithuanian or Russian-Soviet past?), and as to their vision of the future (does one see the future of Belarus in a union with Russia or in integration with the European Union?). Both these groups use completely different symbols in support of their claims (see also the article by Samuel Johnston in this volume). After independence some of the Soviet symbols were abolished – for example the national flag with the Soviet emblems – but there was no iconoclastic frenzy. The Lenin statue in front of the government building remained in its place as did the bust of Felix Dzierzhinski, the founder of the Cheka (later: KGB), which stands in the main street. In the first years of independence various symbolic revisions took place. The Soviet flag was replaced by a national flag with white-red-white stripes dating from the 15th century which had been the country's official flag for a few months in 1918. Lenin Avenue (Prospekt) was renamed after Frantsisk Skorina, the translator, book printer and reformer, who translated the Bible into Old Belarusian in 1517. However, some of these symbolic revisions were reversed after President Alexander Lukashenko assumed office in 1994. Lukashenko introduced a

UMKODIERUNG UND REKODIERUNG DER SOWJETMATRIX

Unbestreitbar nimmt dieses städtebaulich-architektonisch-künstlerische Ensemble der Minsker Stadtmitte einen zentralen Platz im kollektiven Unbewussten der weißrussischen Gesellschaft ein – gibt es doch nur wenige, zumeist im Zweiten Weltkrieg zerstörte oder aber in der Sowjetzeit vernachlässigte, Zeugnisse einer anderen, vor- oder nichtsowjetischen Identität. Und legt man zugrunde, dass sich daraus das Selbstverständnis über die Zukunft der Gesellschaft speist, wird der Kampf um die Bedeutung der ehemals sowjetischen Matrix im postsowjetischen Belarus verständlich.

Die weißrussische Gesellschaft ist zutiefst in zwei Teile gespalten. Vergleicht man mündliche wie schriftliche Äußerungen der beiden Seiten, glaubt man kaum, dass sie den gleichen Lebensraum teilen.[20] Sie unterscheiden sich durch die Sprache, die sie bevorzugen (Russisch oder Weißrussisch), durch ihr historisches Gedächtnis (bezieht man sich auf die polnisch-litauische oder die russisch-sowjetische Vergangenheit?) und durch ihre Zukunftsvision (sieht man die Zukunft von Belarus in der Union mit Russland oder in einer Integration in die Europäische Union?). Diese beiden Gruppen benutzen völlig verschiedene Symbole, um ihre Ansprüche geltend zu machen (siehe auch den Beitrag von Samuel Johnston in diesem Band). So wurden nach der Unabhängigkeit die sowjetischen Symbole teilweise beseitigt – beispielsweise die Landesfahne mit den sowjetischen Emblemen –, aber ein Bildersturm blieb aus. Die Leninstatue vor dem Regierungsgebäude blieb ebenso stehen wie die Statue von Felix Dzerschinski, des Begründers der Tscheka (später: KGB), die ihren Platz an der Magistrale hat. In den ersten Jahren der Unabhängigkeit fanden verschiedene Umkodierungen statt. So wurde die Sowjetfahne durch eine weiß-rot-weiß-gestreifte Nationalflagge ersetzt, die ursprünglich aus dem 15. Jahrhundert stammt und 1918 für wenige Monate die offizielle Landesfahne war. Auch benannte man den Leninprospekt nach Frantsisk Skorina um, dem Übersetzer, Buchdrucker und Reformator, der 1517 die Bibel ins Altweißrussische übersetzt hatte. Allerdings wurden diese Umkodierungen seit dem Amtsantritt des Präsidenten Aleksander Lukashenko 1994 teilweise wieder rückgängig gemacht. Lukashenko führte beispielsweise eine neue Landesfahne ein, die sich wieder deutlich an die Sowjetsymbolik anlehnt, und benannte den Skorinaprospekt im Mai 2005 in Unabhängigkeitsprospekt um.

Dieser Kampf um die nationalen Symbole ist vor dem Hintergrund der derzeitigen politischen Situation in Belarus zu sehen. Belarus gilt bei Bürgerrechtsorganisationen als einziges unfreies Land in Europa.[21] Und dafür bestehen gute Gründe, wie die Untersuchung von Jacek Gadecki verdeutlicht: Seit dem Machtantritt von Lukashenko ist die Pressefreiheit systematisch beschnitten worden, oppositionelle Blätter sind verboten oder ihre Verbreitung wird verhindert.[22] Das Fernsehen ist monopolisiert und sendet nur Lobeshymnen auf die Regierung. Der Zugang zum Internet ist beschränkt und wird kontrolliert (siehe auch den Beitrag von Barbara Sterk in diesem Band), unliebsame Websites werden von der staatlichen Telefonbehörde abgeschaltet. Andererseits gilt das Internet als der einzige wirklich „freie" Raum für Kommunikation. Demonstrationen dürfen, wenn überhaupt, nur außerhalb des eigentlichen Stadtzentrums stattfinden. Unangemeldete öffentliche Veranstaltungen und das Verteilen von Flugblättern werden innerhalb kürzester Zeit von der Miliz unterbunden, unliebsame Graffitis oder auch die mittlerweile verbotene Landesfahne des unabhängigen Belarus

new national flag, for example, which is clearly reminiscent of Soviet symbolism, and changed the name of Skorina Avenue to Independence Avenue in May 2005.

This struggle over national symbols must be seen against the background of the current political situation in Belarus. Civil rights organisations consider Belarus to be the only unfree country in Europe.[21] And there are good reasons for this, as a study by Jacek Gadecki makes clear. Since Lukashenko came to power, freedom of the press has been systematically curtailed – opposition papers are banned or their distribution prevented.[22] Television is a state monopoly and only broadcasts panegyrics to the government. Access to the Internet is limited and subject to control (see also the article by Barbara Sterk in this volume), while unwelcome Web sites are disconnected by the state telephone authority. On the other hand, the Internet is considered to be the only really "free" space for communication. Demonstrations, if allowed at all, may only take place away from the city centre. Unannounced public events and the distribution of leaflets are quickly nipped in the bud by the Militia (police), and unwelcome graffiti or the now banned national flag of independent Belarus are removed within the space of a few days. Public spaces are subject to a large measure of state control. Public interviews require advance approval. Lukashenko, who has now begun an unconstitutional third term of office, is culpably involved in the murders of journalists, businessmen and opposition politicians proven to have been instigated by government circles.[23] The opportunities of the opposition to publicly present their ideas on the future of Belarus are restricted accordingly.

To stabilise the regime Lukashenko is increasingly drawing upon ideological, political and economic elements of the Soviet system. Since spring 2001, state and society have been brought into line with an official national Belarusian ideology.[24] A portrait of the president hangs in every public building, while in every enterprise – and they are all subject to state control – there is a deputy director for ideological questions. This policy serves no other purpose than the retention of power, as Lukashenko's self-willed ventures into foreign policy make clear. The man who initially propagated a union with Russia and Ukraine in the hope that he himself would become its leader in the post-Yeltsin era is now a resolute champion of Belarusian independence – although the formally existing union with Russia has not been dissolved nor is any attempt made to cultivate the national language.[25] The Russian language is accepted without question (one third of the population describe it – as a result of the russification of the Soviet era – as their native tongue,) and the Soviet heritage is upheld. At the same time Lukashenko recodes the Soviet matrix by going back to the days of Tsarist Russia and developing a crude Slav ideology which declares Minsk to be destined "by the cosmic will to become the universal centre of the Orthodox Slav rebirth", to become a "fourth Rome", as the journalist Sergei Pankovskij explains.[26] This policy meets with support in large sections of the population for several reasons. It is certainly mainly due to the domination of the official ideology in the media, but living conditions in Belarus are noticeably better than in Ukraine and Russia, which is very much the result of the "command economy", a peculiar mix of market economy and state supervision.[27] However, it also largely depends on the supply of low-cost energy from Russia. It also seems questionable how long these comparatively good living conditions can be upheld without a modernisation of industrial production and its in-

werden innerhalb weniger Tage entfernt. Der öffentliche Raum untersteht in hohem Maße staatlicher Kontrolle. Öffentliche Interviews bedürfen der Genehmigung. Lukashenko, der mittlerweile eine verfassungswidrige dritte Amtszeit angetreten hat, ist mitverantwortlich für die Morde an Journalisten, Unternehmern und Oppositionspolitikern, die nachweislich von Regierungskreisen veranlasst wurden.[23] Entsprechend eingeschränkt sind die Möglichkeiten der Opposition, ihre Vorstellungen über die Zukunft von Belarus öffentlich zu machen.

Lukashenko knüpft zur Stabilisierung des Regimes zunehmend an ideologische, politische und wirtschaftliche Elemente des Sowjetsystems an. Seit Frühjahr 2001 werden Staat und Gesellschaft auf entsprechende Richtlinien einer nationalweißrussischen Ideologie verpflichtet.[24] Das Porträt des Präsidenten hängt in jedem öffentlichen Gebäude; in jedem Unternehmen – die alle der staatlichen Kontrolle unterliegen – gibt es einen stellvertretenden Betriebsleiter für ideologische Fragen. Diese Politik folgt keinem anderen Ziel als dem des Machterhalts, wie die eigenwilligen außenpolitischen Bestrebungen Lukashenkos verdeutlichen: Propagierte er zunächst eine Union mit Russland und der Ukraine, in der Hoffnung, in der Ära nach Jelzin selbst zu deren Führer aufzusteigen, so ist er jetzt ein entschiedener Verfechter der weißrussischen Unabhängigkeit – obwohl weder die formal bestehende Union mit Russland aufgelöst noch die Pflege der Landessprache angestrebt wird.[25] Die russische Sprache wird anstandslos akzeptiert (ein Drittel der Bevölkerung bezeichnet sie – auch ein Ergebnis der Russifizierung in der Sowjetzeit – als Muttersprache) und das sowjetische Erbe hochgehalten. Dabei rekodiert er die sowjetische Matrix in die Zeit des russischen Zarenreichs zurück, indem er eine krude slawische Ideologie entwickelt, die Minsk „durch den kosmischen Willen zum universalen Zentrum der orthodoxen slawischen Wiedergeburt" werden lässt, zu einem „vierten Rom", wie der Journalist Sergej Pankovskij ausführt. [26] Diese Politik findet aus mehreren Gründen durchaus Rückhalt in großen Teilen der Bevölkerung. Geschuldet ist dies sicherlich der Dominanz der offiziellen Ideologie in den Medien. Aber die Lebensverhältnisse in Belarus sind deutlich besser als in der Ukraine und in Russland, was durchaus das Ergebnis der „Kommandowirtschaft", der eigenartigen Melange von Marktwirtschaft und Staatsaufsicht, ist.[27] Allerdings hängt diese weitgehend von der kostengünstigen Energieversorgung aus Russland ab. Auch scheint es fragwürdig, wie lange sich diese vergleichsweise guten Lebensverhältnisse ohne Modernisierung der Industrieproduktion und ohne deren Anbindung an die Weltmärkte aufrechterhalten lassen.[28] Der augenblickliche Zustand einer vermeintlich sicheren Existenz deckt sich mit der Erinnerung besonders der älteren Generation an die Sowjetzeit als einer Periode des Wohlstands und der Stabilität, die in den ersten Jahren der Unabhängigkeit der Republik Belarus durch eine Rekordinflation und das deutliche Absacken des Lebensstandards konterkariert wurde – erst mit Lukashenkos staatlicher Kontrolle der Wirtschaft trat Stabilität ein. Und nicht zuletzt ist die neue Ideologie erfolgreich, weil sie, wie Marek J. Karp ausführt, auf einem staatlichen Paternalismus beruht, der nur schwer ohne den prägenden Einfluss der sowjetischen Zeit vorzustellen ist und bis in die Zeit des Feudalismus zurückreicht – in einer postulierten „mystischen Verbindung von Volk und Führer", wie sie in der weit verbreiteten Anrede des Präsidenten als „ba'cka" (Vater) zum Ausdruck kommt.[29]

tegration with world markets.[28] The present state of an apparently secure existence matches the older generation's memories of the Soviet era as a period of prosperity and stability, very much in contrast to the early years of the independent Republic of Belarus, which witnessed a record inflation and a sharp decline in the standard of living. Stability was only restored with Lukashenko's assertion of state control over the economy. Not least among the reasons for the new ideology's success is that, as Marek J. Karp shows, it is based on a state paternalism that is hard to imagine without the pervasive influence of the Soviet period and goes back to the days of feudalism – to a postulated "mystical communion of people and leader", as expressed in the widespread practice of addressing the president as "ba'cka" (father).[29]

INTERPRETATIONS OF MINSK

Against this background the significance of the historical testimonials in the city become readily understandable. The future of Belarusian society is undoubtedly bound up with how it defines its national identity. Its place on the fringes of history has led to changing allegiances. From the 13th to the 18th century, Belarus was first part of the Grand Duchy of Lithuania and then of the Polish-Lithuanian gentry republic, after which it belonged to the Tsarist empire and then to the Soviet Union.[30] These historical fluctuations are reflected in the foreign policy attitudes of the White Russians; the number of advocates of a union with Russia roughly corresponds to the number of advocates of accession to the EU.[31] The past is an ever-present point of reference, a fact that is expressed in the reconstruction of historic buildings. Churches are being restored, the Trinity Suburb (Troitskoye Predmestie) of the 18th/19th centuries had already been rebuilt in the 1980s as a museum village with shops and restaurants. A few years ago a small historical theme park was laid out on the corner of the main street and Lenin Street and enjoys great popularity. Yet the symbolic effect is strangely unfocused, although the exhibits stress the need to preserve the country's own national past. There is an unintended correspondence between this need for historical authenticity and the president's curious Soviet-Belarusian fundamentalism, which largely prevents the city from being plastered with international brand names. Although the occasional ad pops up here and there – for a Siemens mobile phone, for instance – while McDonald's has managed to open a (much frequented) branch on the main street, Lukashenko does not desire the presence of foreign brand symbols in the city – not long ago he had all foreign models removed from the billboards.
A curious mixture of historical, national and Soviet symbols, interspersed with a few international product logos, characterises the city centre. Often the intended symbolism is unclear – what is meant by the erection of a Pushkin statue on the banks of the Svisloch? Does it stand for a bourgeois understanding of culture that draws on Belarusian history or for the ties with Russian culture, or for both? Then there is the improvised monument in memory of Viktor Tsoi, the singer of the Soviet Russian rock group Kino – is that an expression of protest or of a profound attachment to Russian rock culture, or both? By building a shopping mall underneath Independence Square the President intends to create a kind of allegory in stone of "good government" and to bring together the different symbolisms under his supervision. The historic church also fits easily into this ensemble, although it has no other significance as long as

Vor diesem Hintergrund wird die Bedeutung der geschichtlichen Zeugnisse im Stadtraum unmittelbar verständlich. Denn die Zukunft der weißrussischen Gesellschaft ist unzweifelhaft damit verknüpft, wie sie ihre nationale Identität definiert. Nun hat die historische Randlage zu wechselhaften Zugehörigkeiten geführt. Vom 13. bis zum 18. Jahrhundert war Belarus zunächst Teil des Großfürstentums Litauen und anschließend der polnisch-litauischen Adelsrepublik, danach gehörte es zum Zarenreich und zur Sowjetunion.[30] Diese wechselvolle Geschichte spiegelt sich wider in der außenpolitischen Einstellung der Belarussen; die Zahl der Befürworter eines Zusammenschlusses mit Russland entspricht ungefähr der Zahl der Befürworter eines EU-Beitritts.[31] Die Vergangenheit wird zum allgegenwärtigen Fixpunkt, was auch in der Rekonstruktion historischer Bauten zum Ausdruck kommt. Kirchen werden wieder instand gesetzt, die Troizker Vorstadt des 18./19. Jahrhunderts wurde bereits in den 1980er Jahren als Museumsdorf mit Läden und Restaurants wieder aufgebaut; an der Magistrale, an der Ecke zur Leninstraße, legte man vor einigen Jahren einen kleinen historisierenden Park an (der sich großer Beliebtheit erfreut). Allerdings bleibt die symbolische Wirkung eigentümlich unkonturiert, die Gestaltungen bekräftigen aber das Bedürfnis, die eigene nationale Vergangenheit zu bewahren. Ungewollt entspricht diesem Bedürfnis nach historischer Authentizität auch der eigentümliche sowjetisch-weißrussische Fundamentalismus des Präsidenten, der die Überlagerung der Stadt mit den Zeichen der internationalen Markenprodukte weitgehend verhindert. Zwar taucht hier und da auch Werbung auf, beispielsweise für ein Siemens-Mobiltelefon, auch hat es McDonald's geschafft, an der Magistrale eine (stark frequentierte) Filiale zu eröffnen, aber Lukashenko wünscht die Präsenz von ausländischen Markensymbolen im Stadtraum nicht – erst unlängst ließ er alle ausländischen Models von den Werbetafeln entfernen.

Eine eigenartige Mischung von historischen, nationalen und sowjetischen Symbolen, vereinzelt durchsetzt von internationalen Produktsignets, prägt das Stadtzentrum. Oft ist die intendierte Symbolik unklar – wofür steht die Errichtung einer Puschkinstatue in den Uferanlagen des Svisloch? Für ein bürgerliches Kulturverständnis, das an die weißrussische Geschichte anknüpft oder für die Verknüpfung mit der russischen Kultur oder für beides? Das improvisierte Denkmal zur Erinnerung an den Sänger der sowjetrussischen Rockgruppe Kino, Viktor Tsoi – ist es Ausdruck einer Protesthaltung oder der tiefen Verbundenheit mit der russischen Rockkultur oder beides? Mit der Errichtung einer Shopping-Mall unterhalb des Unabhängigkeitsplatzes beabsichtigt der Präsident, so etwas wie eine gebaute Allegorie des „Guten Regiments" zu schaffen und die unterschiedlichen Symbolwelten unter seiner Aufsicht zusammenzuführen. Problemlos fügt sich in dieses Ensemble auch die historische Kirche, der weiter keine Bedeutung zugemessen wird, solange die oberirdische Gestaltung des Platzes die Beziehung von Lenin, Regierung und Einkaufen sinnfällig macht (siehe dazu Samuel Johnstons Beschreibung der einzelnen Entwurfsstadien, für die das städtische Planungsbüro Minsk Projekt verantwortlich ist).

Umfragen unter Studenten verschiedener Fakultäten der Weißrussischen Staatsuniversität, die von Viachaslau Filimonau ausgewertet wurden, ergaben, dass für die akademisch gebildete junge Generation die sowjetischen Symbole und Denkmäler eher Relikte aus grauer Vorzeit darstellen, die man ignoriert.[32] Die bevorzugten öffentlichen

the above-ground design of the square insists on a relationship between Lenin, government and shopping (see Samuel Johnston's description of the individual design stages of the project for which Minsk Project is responsible).
Opinion surveys carried out by Viachaslau Filimonau among students in the various faculties of the Belarusian State University have revealed that for the university-educated young generation the Soviet symbols and monuments tend to be regarded as relics of a dim and distant past and simply ignored.[32] The most appreciated public spaces are the car parks, while the public squares, such as October Square or Independence Square (often referred to as "Dependence Square"), are felt to be alienating and held in low esteem. Historical buildings dating from before the Soviet era are highly prized, however. Here we may observe the efforts of the young generation to create a new vision of the national history.[33] This is seen quite differently by the older generation to whom the Soviet symbols represent a period of prosperity and security for which they feel nostalgic yearnings – yearnings which the president knows how to exploit with his political symbolism.
These different interpretations of Minsk reflect a wide range of attitudes, incorporating desires and yearnings as much as fears and rejection. While the official political symbolism of the Lukashenko regime draws a picture of a space which is outside of history, untouched by the dynamic of a second wave of modernisation and in which time seems to stand still, the young generation strives via the Internet and trips abroad to keep abreast of international developments and speed up social development at home – a contradiction that cannot be sustained in the long run and which will have to be resolved in the next few years. Until that happens, Belarus and the city of Minsk will find themselves in a halfway house, a space with an uncertain future, in which the public is subject to strong state control, which in turn forces the various social groups to withdraw to less controlled spaces. The latter may vary considerably. Traditionally, social encounters take place in the parks or in the "banja" (sauna), although the popular knightly tournaments, in which thousands of actors take part, testify to the yearning for a reformulation of Belarusian identity.[34] Or, as an art student who described himself as an "anarchist" put it more significantly: One simply ignores the real situation, sits under the Dzierzhinsky monument, drinks beer and waits for the Militia. The monumentalised city is becoming a meaningless backdrop waiting to be discovered by tourism. But the negative attitude of the young generation also shows that in Minsk the physical public space, in contrast to the situation in western countries, has a far greater symbolic significance in the collective subconscious, while at the same time the withdrawal to other, less controlled public settings is positively indispensable.
What is remarkable about the situation in Minsk is its undecided nature. The collapse of the USSR did not open the way to a state with a ready-made national identity, nor did the promises of western consumer culture manage to conceal what living conditions were really like. This might ultimately represent an opportunity for Belarusian society. For the different meanings which the historical testimonials and symbols have for people indicate that – if it were freely accessible – the public space could indeed become a space in which the society might come to an agreement about its future.

My thanks to Igor Dukhan, Thomas Bohn and Slava Filimonau for their support.

Räume sind vor allem die Parkanlagen; dagegen werden die öffentlichen Plätze wie der Oktoberplatz oder der Unabhängigkeitsplatz (oftmals „Abhängigkeitsplatz" genannt) als abweisend empfunden und gering geschätzt. Die vor der Sowjetzeit entstandenen historischen Gebäude genießen besondere Wertschätzung. Hieran lässt sich das Bemühen einer jungen Generation ablesen, ein neues nationales Geschichtsbild zu entwerfen. Anders dagegen die ältere Generation, für welche die sowjetischen Symbole eine Zeit des Wohlstands und der Sicherheit repräsentieren, nach der man sich nostalgisch zurücksehnt – Sehnsüchte, die die Symbolpolitik des Präsidenten zu bedienen weiß.
Diese Lesungen der Stadt Minsk formulieren unterschiedlichste Sichtweisen, in die Wünsche und Sehnsüchte gleichermaßen wie Ängste und Abwehr eingeschrieben sind. Während die offizielle Symbolpolitik des Lukashenko-Regimes das Bild eines Raumes außerhalb der Geschichte entwirft, der nicht von der Dynamik einer zweiten Modernisierung erfasst wird und in dem die Zeit stillzustehen scheint, sucht die junge Generation via Internet und Auslandsreisen den Anschluss an eine internationale Entwicklung zu halten und die gesellschaftliche Entwicklung zu beschleunigen – ein Widerspruch, der nicht auf Dauer bestehen kann und sich in den nächsten Jahren wird auflösen müssen. Bis dahin befinden sich Belarus und die Stadt Minsk in einem Schwebezustand, einem Raum mit unbestimmter Zukunft, in dem die Öffentlichkeit einer starken staatlichen Kontrolle unterliegt, was wiederum die verschiedenen gesellschaftlichen Gruppen dazu zwingt, auf weniger kontrollierte Räume auszuweichen.
Diese können sehr unterschiedlich sein. Traditionell trifft man sich in den Parks oder in der „Banja" (Sauna), aber auch die beliebten Ritterfestspiele mit tausenden von Akteuren bezeugen die Sehnsucht nach einer Neuformulierung weißrussischer Identität. Oder, wie es ein sich selbst als „Anarchist" bezeichnender Kunststudent beschreibt: Man ignoriert einfach die reale Situation, sitzt vor der Dzerschinski-Statue, trinkt Bier und wartet auf die Miliz. Die monumentalisierte Stadt wird zur bedeutungslosen Kulisse, die der Entdeckung durch den Tourismus harrt. Aber die ablehnende Haltung einer jungen Generation zeigt auch, dass in Minsk der physische öffentliche Raum im Gegensatz zur Situation in den westlichen Ländern eine weit größere symbolische Bedeutung im kollektiven Unbewussten hat und zugleich das Ausweichen auf andere, weniger kontrollierte Teilöffentlichkeiten geradezu unumgänglich ist.
Bemerkenswert an der Situation in Minsk ist die Unentschiedenheit der Situation – weder konnte nach dem Zusammenbruch der UdSSR vorbehaltlos auf eine nationalstaatliche Identität rekurriert werden, noch wurde durch die Versprechungen der westlichen Konsumkultur die Sicht auf die realen Lebensbedingungen verdeckt. Das könnte tatsächlich sogar eine Chance für die weißrussische Gesellschaft bieten. Denn die unterschiedlichen Bedeutungen, die die geschichtlichen Zeugnisse und Symbole für die Menschen haben, verweisen darauf, dass hier der öffentliche Raum tatsächlich zu einem Raum der Selbstverständigung der Gesellschaft über ihre Zukunft werden könnte – wenn er frei zugänglich wäre.

Ich danke Igor Dukhan, Thomas Bohn und Slava Filimonau für ihre Unterstützung.

NOTES

1 Cf. Barthes, Roland: "Semiologie und Urbanismus" in Carlini, Alessandro/Schneider, Bernhard (eds.): *Konzept 3. Die Stadt als Text*, Tübingen, 1976

2 Cf. Halbwachs, Maurice: *Das kollektive Gedächtnis*, Frankfurt am Main, 1985

3 The interviewer was Vladan Paunovic. Cf. "Family vs. Transition" *in* Stiftung Bauhaus Dessau (ed.): *Dokumentation 2. Trimester Bauhaus Kolleg V.* Dessau, 2004

4 Ibid.

5 Ibid.

6 Ibid.

7 Cf. Voronkov, Victor: "Life & Death of the Public Sphere in the Soviet Union" in Goryucheva, Tatiana/Kluitenberg, Eric (eds.): *Debates & Credits. Media / Art / Public Domain. Kat. De Balie – Centre for Culture and Politics*, Amsterdam, 2002

8 Garcelon, Marc: "The Shadow of the Leviathan: Public and Private in Communist and Post-Communist Society" in Weintraub, Jeff/Kumar, Krishan (eds.): *Public and Private in Thought and Practice. Perspectives on a Grand Dichotomy*, Chicago/London, 1997

9 Cf. Stölting, Erhard: "Stadt und Gesellschaft in Russland" in Berking, Helmuth/Faber, Richard (eds.): *Städte im Globalisierungsdiskurs*, Würzburg, 2002

10 Cf. Ryklin, Michail: *Räume des Jubels. Totalitarismus und Differenz*, Frankfurt am Main, 2003, p. 71ff.

11 Cf. Szilágyi, Ákos: "Paradiesischer Realismus. Totalitäre Staatskunst im 20. Jahrhundert" in György, Péter/Turai, Hedvig (eds.): *Staatskunstwerk. Kultur im Stalinismus*, Budapest, 1992

12 Ditschew, Iwailo: "Ost-Metropolen. Von der Bühne des neuen Lebens zur postlokalen Utopie" in *Lettre International*, Heft 67, 2004

13 Groys, Boris: "Die Massenkultur der Utopie" in Groys, Boris/Hollein, Max (eds.): *Traumfabrik Kommunismus. Die visuelle Kultur der Stalinzeit*, Ostfildern-Ruit, 2003

14 Cf. Siemons, Mark: "Postkommunistische Lage. Lauter Projekte" in *Frankfurter Allgemeine Zeitung*, 16 June 2004

15 Cf. Andruzs, Gregory: Further Thoughts on the Post-Socialist City http://www.anthropolis.de/andrusz_2, 31 July 2001

16 Cf. Bittner, Regina/Vöckler, Kai: "Die postsozialistische Stadt" in *UmBau*, Heft 20, 2003

17 Cf. Piterski, Dmitri: "Gegenwärtige Probleme und einige neue Elemente des städtischen Siedlungssystems Weissrusslands" in Sedlacek, Peter (ed.): *Wirtschaft – Region – Entwicklung*, Jena, 2002

18 Cf. Bohn, Thomas: "Das 'neue' Minsk" in Beyrau, Dietrich/Lindner, Rainer (eds.): *Handbuch der Geschichte Weissrusslands*, Göttingen, 2001; "Das Projekt 'Sozialistische Stadt'" in *Belarus-News*, Heft 15, 2001; "'Bau auf...'. Der Maurer Denis Bulachow" in Satjukow, Silke/Gries, Rainer (eds.): *Sozialistische Helden. Eine Kulturgeschichte von Propagandafiguren in Osteuropa und der DDR*, Berlin, 2002; *Das "Phänomen Minsk". Stadtplanung und Urbanisierung in Weissrussland nach dem Zweiten Weltkrieg* (post-doctoral dissertation), Friedrich Schiller University, Jena, 2004

19 Bohn, Thomas: *"Von der Sowjetunion lernen, heisst siegen lernen." – Potemkin'sche Dörfer und ostdeutsche Stadtplanung in der Nachkriegszeit* (manuscript)

20 Cf. Lalkou, Ihar: National Symbolism in Belarus: The Past and the Present. http://www.belarusguide.com/statehood/Belarusian_symbols

21 Cf. http://www.freedomhouse.org

22 Cf. Gadecki, Jacek: "Public Space in Minsk – Political Activities" in Stiftung Bauhaus Dessau (ed.): *Dokumentation 2. Trimester Bauhaus Kolleg V.* Dessau, 2004

23 The present minister of sport, Yuri Sivakov, is strongly suspected of having founded a death squadron in 1999 in his capacity as interior minister and ordering the murder of the former interior minister and opposition politician, Yuri Zakharenko, the opposition politician, Viktor Gonchar, and the businessman, Anatoly Krasovski. Police Colonel Oleg Alkayev, who kept the gun used to carry out the death sentences, told the *Frankfurter Allgemeine Zeitung* that he had had to issue the gun twice at the bidding of Sivakov. The date coincided with that of the disappearance of Zakharenko, Gonchar and Krasovski. The leader of the death squadron, Brigade Commander Dmitri Pavlichenko, a confidant of Sivakov, is said to have confessed to the murders while being interrogated by the Belarusian Public Prosecutor's Office. Cf. Wehner, Markus: "Mehr als ein politisches Spielchen. Die EU will den Minsker Sportminister nicht in Athen sehen" in *Frankfurter Allgemeine Zeitung*, 9 August 2004

24 Cf. Timmermann, Heinz: "Koloboks Union. Belarus und Russland am Wendepunkt?" in *Osteuropa*, Heft 2, 2004

ANMERKUNGEN

1 Vgl. Barthes, Roland: „Semiologie und Urbanismus". In: Carlini, Alessandro/Schneider, Bernhard (Hg.): *Konzept 3. Die Stadt als Text.* Tübingen 1976

2 Vgl. Halbwachs, Maurice: *Das kollektive Gedächtnis.* Frankfurt am Main 1985

3 Das Interview führte Vladan Paunovic. Vgl. „Family vs. Transition". In: Stiftung Bauhaus Dessau (Hg.): *Dokumentation 2. Trimester Bauhaus Kolleg V.* Dessau 2004

4 Ebd.

5 Ebd.

6 Ebd.

7 Vgl. Voronkov, Victor: „Life & Death of the Public Sphere in the Soviet Union". In: Goryucheva, Tatiana/ Kluitenberg, Eric (Hg.): *Debates & Credits. Media / Art / Public Domain. Kat. De Balie – Centre for Culture and Politics.* Amsterdam 2002

8 Garcelon, Marc: „The Shadow of the Leviathan: Public and Private in Communist and Post-Communist Society". In: Weintraub, Jeff/Kumar, Krishan (Hg.): *Public and Private in Thought and Practice. Perspectives on a Grand Dichotomy.* Chicago/London 1997

9 Vgl. Stölting, Erhard: „Stadt und Gesellschaft in Russland". In: Berking, Helmuth/Faber, Richard (Hg.): *Städte im Globalisierungsdiskurs.* Würzburg 2002

10 Vgl. Ryklin, Michail: *Räume des Jubels. Totalitarismus und Differenz.* Frankfurt am Main 2003, S. 71 ff.

11 Vgl. Szilágyi, Ákos: „Paradiesischer Realismus. Totalitäre Staatskunst im 20. Jahrhundert". In: György, Péter/Turai, Hedvig (Hg.): *Staatskunstwerk. Kultur im Stalinismus.* Budapest 1992

12 Ditschew, Iwailo: „Ost-Metropolen. Von der Bühne des neuen Lebens zur postlokalen Utopie". In: *Lettre International,* Heft 67, 2004

13 Groys, Boris: „Die Massenkultur der Utopie". In: Groys, Boris/Hollein, Max (Hg.): *Traumfabrik Kommunismus. Die visuelle Kultur der Stalinzeit.* Ostfildern-Ruit 2003

14 Vgl. Siemons, Mark: „Postkommunistische Lage. Lauter Projekte". In: *Frankfurter Allgemeine Zeitung,* 16.06.2004

15 Vgl. Andrusz, Gregory: Further Thoughts on the Post-Socialist City. http://www.anthropolis.de/andrusz_2, 31.07.2001

16 Vgl. Bittner, Regina/Vöckler, Kai: „Die postsozialistische Stadt". In: *UmBau,* Heft 20, 2003

17 Vgl. Piterski, Dmitri: „Gegenwärtige Probleme und einige neue Elemente des städtischen Siedlungssystems Weißrusslands". In: Sedlacek, Peter (Hg.): *Wirtschaft – Region – Entwicklung.* Jena 2002

18 Vgl. Bohn, Thomas: „Das ‚neue' Minsk". In: Beyrau, Dietrich/Lindner, Rainer (Hg.): *Handbuch der Geschichte Weißrusslands.* Göttingen 2001; ders.: „Das Projekt ‚Sozialistische Stadt'". In: *Belarus-News,* Heft 15, 2001; ders.: „‚Bau auf…'. Der Maurer Denis Bulachow". In: Satjukow, Silke/Gries, Rainer (Hg.): *Sozialistische Helden. Eine Kulturgeschichte von Propagandafiguren in Osteuropa und der DDR.* Berlin 2002; ders.: *Das „Phänomen Minsk". Stadtplanung und Urbanisierung in Weißrussland nach dem Zweiten Weltkrieg.* Friedrich-Schiller-Universität Jena, Habilitationsschrift 2004

19 Ders.: *„Von der Sowjetunion lernen, heißt siegen lernen." – Potemkin'sche Dörfer und ostdeutsche Stadtplanung in der Nachkriegszeit.* Manuskript

20 Vgl. Lalkou, Ihar: National Symbolism in Belarus: The Past and the Present. http://www.belarusguide.com/statehood/Belarusian_symbols

21 Vgl. http://www.freedomhouse.org

22 Vgl. Gadecki, Jacek: „Public Space in Minsk – Political Activities". In: Stiftung Bauhaus Dessau (Hg.): *Dokumentation 2. Trimester Bauhaus Kolleg V.* Dessau 2004

23 Der derzeitige Sportminister Jurij Sirakow ist dringend verdächtig, in seiner Eigenschaft als Innenminister 1999 eine Todesschwadron gegründet zu haben und die Ermordung des ehemaligen Innenministers und Oppositionspolitikers Jurij Sacharenko, des Oppositionspolitikers Viktor Gontschar und des Geschäftsmanns Anatolij Krasowskij angeordnet zu haben. Vgl. Wehner, Markus: „Mehr als ein politisches Spielchen. Die EU will den Minsker Sportminister nicht in Athen sehen". In: *Frankfurter Allgemeine Zeitung,* 09.08.2004

24 Vgl. Timmermann, Heinz: „Koloboks Union. Belarus und Russland am Wendepunkt?" In: *Osteuropa,* Heft 2, 2004

25 Vgl. Marples, David R.: „Bac'ka Lukashenko. Herrschaft ohne Charisma". In: ebd.

26 Vgl. Pankovskij, Sergej: „Minsk – das vierte Rom?" In: ebd., S. 11

27 Vgl. Hofbauer, Hannes: „Ein Modell aus dem Hause Lukashenko – die verstaatlichte Marktwirtschaft". In: *Freitag,* Heft 5, 2005

28 Vgl. Scharff, Roland (Hg.): *Belarus. Zwischenbilanz einer stornierten Transformation. Osnabrücker Studien, Bd. 18.* Osnabrück 2001

29 Karp, Marek J.: „Bialoruska ucieczka od wolnosci". In: *Gazeta Wyborcza,* 28.07.1997. Zit. n. Marples, a. a. O., S. 24

30 Vgl. Lindner, Rainer: „Am Ende des Lateins? Belarus, die EU und das europäische Erbe." In: *Osteuro-*

25 Cf. Marples, David R.: "Bac'ka Lukashenko. Herrschaft ohne Charisma" in ibid.

26 Cf. Pankovskij, Sergej: "Minsk – das vierte Rom?" in ibid., p. 11

27 Cf. Hofbauer, Hannes: "Ein Modell aus dem Hause Lukashenko – die verstaatlichte Marktwirtschaft" in *Freitag*, Heft 5, 2005

28 Cf. Scharff, Roland (ed.): *Belarus. Zwischenbilanz einer stornierten Transformation. Osnabrücker Studien, Vol. 18.* Osnabrück, 2001

29 Karp, Marek J.: "Białoruska ucieczka od wolno ci" in *Gazeta Wyborcza*, 28 July 1997. Quoted in Marples, loc cit., p. 24.

30 Cf. Lindner, Rainer: "Am Ende des Lateins? Belarus, die EU und das europäische Erbe" in *Osteuropa*, Heft 2, 2004

31 Cf. Manaev, Oleg: "Langer Marsch – bloss wohin? Integrationsvorstellungen im Wandel" in ibid.

32 Filimonau, Viachaslau: "Mentality in Transition" *in* Stiftung Bauhaus Dessau (ed.): *Dokumentation 2. Trimester Bauhaus Kolleg V.* Dessau, 2004

33 In private conversations one often encounters a pronounced patriotism, which has even been strengthened by the enlargement of the European Union which is felt to be an exclusion – and this despite the fact that almost 40 per cent of students would like to leave the country in view of the prevailing conditions.

34 Cf. Jaksic, Ivana/Zajaczkowska, Marzena: "City as a Scenography" *in* Stiftung Bauhaus Dessau (ed.): *Dokumentation 2. Trimester Bauhaus Kolleg V.* Dessau, 2004

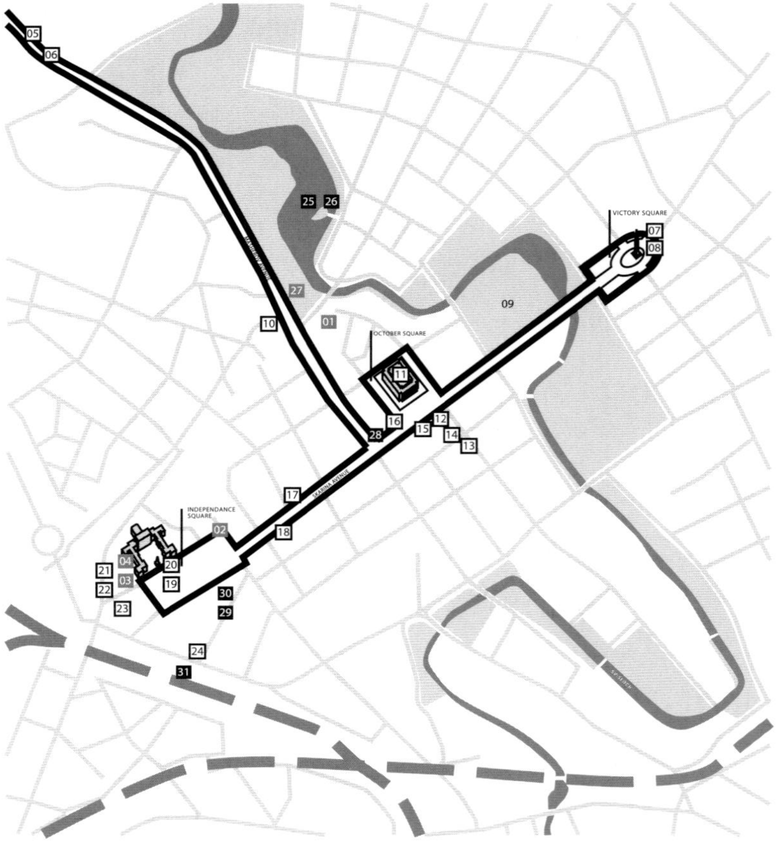

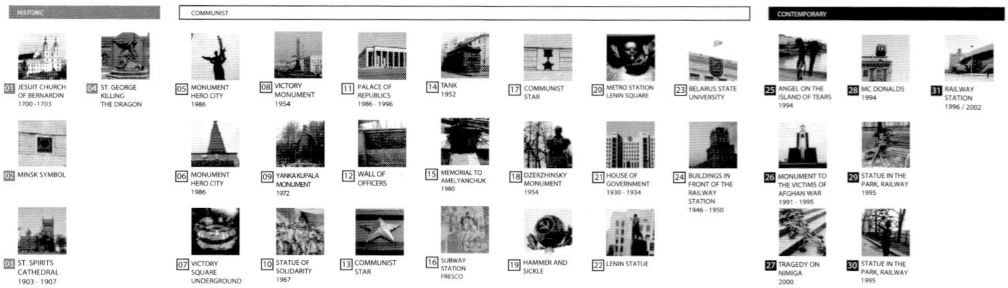

MINSK – MONUMENTE

MINSK – PUBLIC SYMBOLS

Karte Map: Angela Haratyunyan + Ruben Reis Dias

Graphische Überarbeitung Graphical Revision: Rainer Mühr

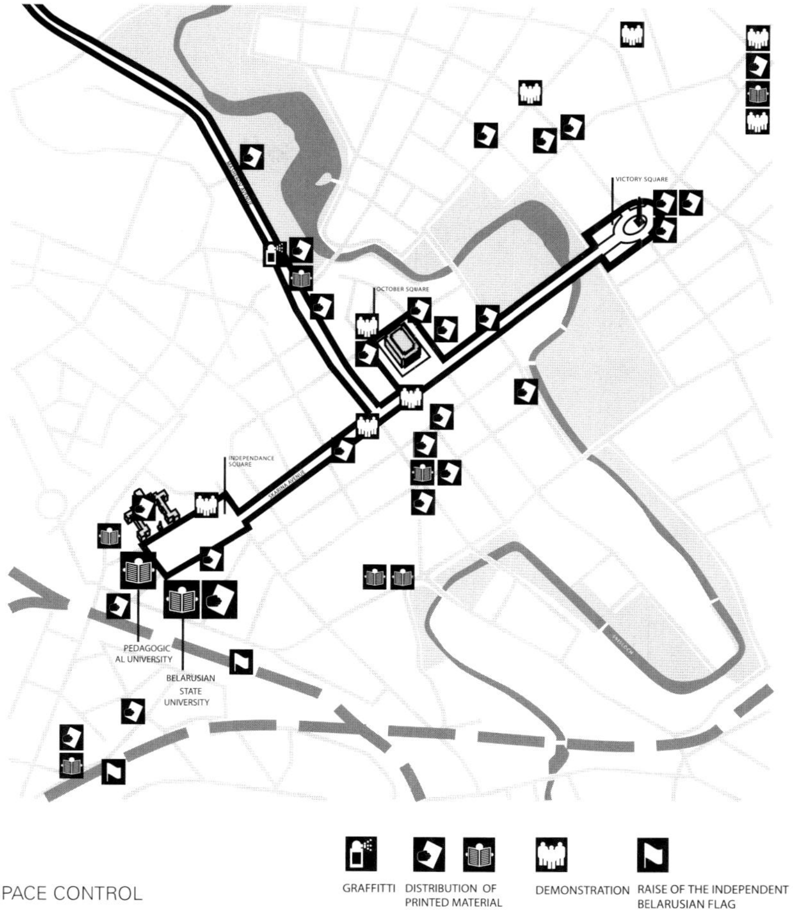

▼ PUBLIC SPACE CONTROL

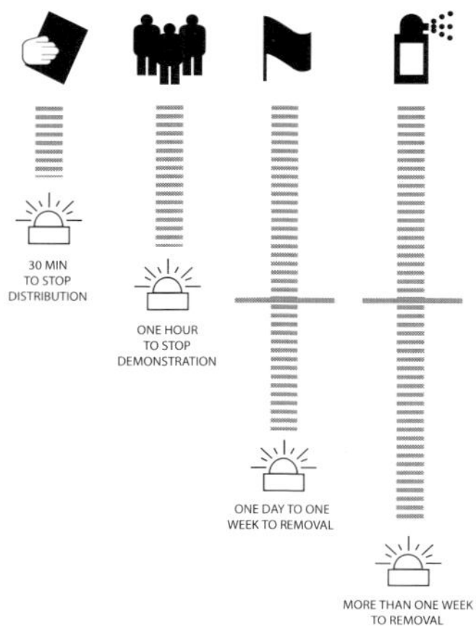

▼ POLITICAL ACTIVITIES OF OPPOSITIONAL ORGANISATIONS 2003/2004

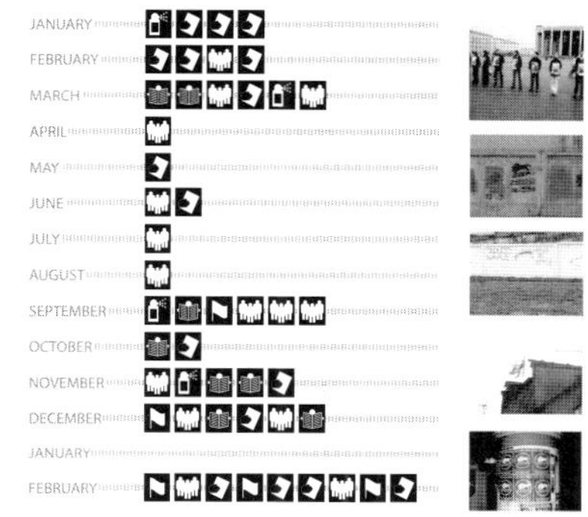

MINSK – AKTIONEN DER OPPOSITIONSBEWEGUNG 2003–2004
MINSK – OPPOSITIONAL ACTIVITIES 2003–2004
Karte Map: Jacek Gadecki
Graphische Überarbeitung Graphical Revision: Rainer Mühr

„EINE GUTE GESELLSCHAFT“

SAMUEL G.R. JOHNSTON

DIE BEDEUTUNG VON SYMBOLEN IN DER WEISSRUSSISCHEN ÖFFENTLICHKEIT

Die Lage einer Nation oder eines Staates spiegelt sich in Symbolen und Orten, er spiegelt sich in der Atmosphäre des öffentlichen Raumes bzw. der öffentlichen Sphäre. Der symbolische Kampf, der an diesen Orten ausgetragen wird, und gleichermaßen der Kampf mittels Symbolen, die Präsenz oder Abwesenheit, das Beibehalten oder Entfernen von Symbolen durch die Behörden oder Minderheitsgruppen, verweisen ebenfalls auf den Stand der Dinge. In dieser Hinsicht befindet sich Minsk seit dem Zusammenbruch der Sowjetunion in einem mehr oder weniger kontinuierlichen Prozess des Wandels. Zur Zeit kämpfen zwei Gruppen, Präsident Alexander Lukashenko und die Opposition, darum, ihre Vorstellungen von einer „guten Gesellschaft“ durchzusetzen.

Das heutige Weißrussland ist ein Phänomen – sowohl was die Bedeutung anbelangt, die den Symbolen von Staat und Öffentlichkeit verliehen wird, als auch den Mangel eben dieser Bedeutungszuschreibung. Der Geist des Sozialismus oder ein gewisser falscher Optimismus hängen noch in der Luft – besonders wenn man die Skarina-Allee hinunterläuft, welche nach den Prinzipien stalinistischer Architektur gebaut wurde. Die breite Allee beginnt am Leninplatz, der heute Unabhängigkeitsplatz heißt. Von dort sollte sie, als eine Metapher kommunistischer Ideologie, die Nation in eine bessere Zukunft führen, vorausgesetzt, die Nation unterwirft sich den Grundsätzen des Sozialismus. Das Stadtbild allein gibt Minsk eine stark neosowjetische Prägung, und Lukashenkos autoritäre Kontrolle über die Politik der Stadt verstärkt diesen Eindruck nur noch.

Abgesehen von der russischen Sprache und dem systematischen Verbot der weißrussischen Sprache an den Schulen, sind es die Flagge und das Wappen des Landes, (die erst nach einem Referendum – das internationale Beobachter für undemokratisch erklärten – das Land repräsentieren) die Lukashenkos pro-russische oder pro-sowjetische Einstellung am deutlichsten zeigen. Wie die folgenden Abbildungen zeigen, ist die Anlehnung an die sowjetische Vergangenheit das wichtigste Designelement der neuen Fahne und des neuen Wappens.

SEIT 1951: DIE SOWJETISCH-WEISSRUSSISCHE STAATSFLAGGE – SEIT 1996: LUKASHENKOS NEOSOWJETISCH-WEISSRUSSISCHE FLAGGE

SINCE 1951: SOVIET-BELARUSIAN NATIONAL FLAG – SINCE 1996: LUKASHENKO'S NEO-SOVIET BELARUSIAN FLAG

Das autoritäre Regime, das heute in Weißrussland an der Macht ist, beruft sich oft auf seine autoritären kommunistischen Vorläufer.

Im Gegensatz dazu orientiert sich die Opposition geistig als auch symbolisch an Weißrusslands europäischer Vergangenheit. Die Opposition bedient sich der Geschichte des Landes – 600 Jahre lang war Weißrussland Teil des Großherzogtums Litva (das heutige Litauen) – und der weißrussischen Sprache, um die Entwicklung einer starken nationalen Identität zu fördern.

Sowohl die weiß-rot-weiße Flagge Weißrusslands, die von 1990 bis 1995 Staatsflagge war, als auch das Staatswappen (die Pahonia) stammen aus dieser Zeit.

Heute versuchen die Behörden mit allen Mitteln, diese beiden Symbole zu unterdrücken. Wer Flagge oder Wappen öffentlich zur Schau stellt, kann damit rechnen, verhaftet zu werden.

"A GOOD SOCIETY"

SAMUEL G. R. JOHNSTON

THE SIGNIFICANCE OF SYMBOLS IN BELARUSIAN PUBLIC SPACE

Symbols, spaces and also the atmosphere of public space or the public sphere reflect the state a society or nation is in. The symbolic battles that take place within these spaces, as well as the presence or absence, the inclusion or removal of symbols by either the authorities or minority groups also mirror its circumstances. In this sense, Minsk has been going through a more or less continuous process of change since the collapse of the Soviet Union. Currently two camps, President Alexander Lukashenko and the opposition, are fighting to assert their ideas of what they think would be a "good society."

Today's Belarus is phenomenal in terms of the meaning or the lack thereof attributed to public and state symbols. The spirit of socialism or a kind of false optimism lingers – especially when you walk down Skarina Avenue, which was built to the standards of Stalinist architecture. The wide avenue begins at Lenin Square (called Independence Square today) and, as a metaphor of Communist ideology, was supposed to lead the nation, provided it subscribed to the fundamentals of Socialism, toward a bright future. The city's physical make-up itself gives the city's public space a strong neo-Soviet touch and Lukashenko's top-down control of local politics further emphasises this link.

Apart from the Russian language and the systematic ban of the Belarusian language from schools, the county's flag and national emblem, which only became official after a referendum that international critics denounced for being undemocratic, indicate Lukashenko's pro Russian or Soviet stance most strongly. As the images below show, the references to the Soviet past are key design elements of both the new flag and the new emblem.

DAS SOWJETISCH-WEISSRUSSISCHE WAPPEN – LUKASHENKOS NEOSOWJETISCH-WEISSRUSSISCHES WAPPEN

SOVIET-BELARUSIAN NATIONAL EMBLEM – LUKASHENKO'S NEO-SOVIET BELARUSIAN EMBLEM

The authoritarian regime of today's Belarus draws frequently on its authoritarian, Communist roots. In contrast, the opposition aligns itself spiritually as well as symbolically with Belarus' European past. The country's history – for 600 years Belarus was part of the Grand Duchy of Litva (today's Lithuania) – as well as the Belarusian language provide the opposition with elements that support the development of a strong national identity.

Both the white-red-white flag of Belarus, which served as the national flag between 1990 and 1995, and the national emblem (the Pahonia) date back to this period.

Today, both flag and emblem are symbols that the authorities strongly try to suppress. Displaying either one in a public space is likely to result in an arrest.

MEETING MINSK PROJECT: PLANNING THE UNDERGROUND SHOPPING MALL AT INDEPENDENCE SQUARE

In addition to fighting over the national symbols, the two opposing camps also struggle to assert their power in Minsk's cityscape. A meeting with

EIN TREFFEN MIT MINSK PROJEKT: DIE PLANUNG EINES EINKAUFSZENTRUMS UNTER DEM UNABHÄNGIGKEITSPLATZ

Die zwei feindlichen Lager kämpfen nicht nur um Symbole, sondern bemühen sich auch, ihre Macht im Stadtbild zu behaupten. Im Folgenden ist ein Treffen mit Minsk Projekt, einem städtischen Planungsbüro für Architektur, Städteplanung, Ingenieurwesen und Landschaftsplanung, das für den Bau einer Shopping-Mall unter dem Unabhängigkeitsplatz (dem Leninplatz) verantwortlich ist, dokumentiert. Es zeigt sich nicht nur deutlich, wie wichtig es für Lukashenko ist, Kontrolle über die öffentliche Sphäre zu haben, sondern verrät auch viel darüber, was für eine Gesellschaft er erschaffen will.

Minsk Projekt trägt die Verantwortung für die Gestaltung aller städtischen Projekte und hat die Aufgabe, alle Arbeiten zu dokumentieren, die an Infrastruktur, Straßen oder Gebäuden ausgeführt werden. Außerdem erstellt es Gestaltungsrichtlinien für Neubauten und Baumaßnahmen an bereits existierenden Gebäuden in der Stadt und es begutachtet alle Anträge betreffs des Baus von Gewerbe- und Wohnanlagen. So erklärt es sich, dass Minsk Projekt Design und Dokumentation des Baus einer 75 000 m^2 großen Shopping-Mall überwacht, die unter dem Unabhängigkeitsplatz realisiert werden soll.

Der Staat gewährt Minsk Projekt eine gewisse kreative Freiheit, was das Design des Projekts betrifft. Aber alle Projekte müssen von Minsks Chefarchitekten, der vom Präsidenten berufen wird, genehmigt werden; und ein Projekt, das so wichtig wie der Unabhängigkeitsplatz ist, wird auch Lukashenkos persönliche Zustimmung erhalten müssen.

Unser hier dokumentiertes Treffen mit Minsk Projekt fand im Büro des Direktors Mikhael Gauhfeld statt. Er trat selbstsicher und souverän auf und präsentierte die Designgrundlagen des Projekts gut. Jedoch schien er sich auch zurückzuhalten. Während der Präsentation fehlte es ihm an Enthusiasmus und er machte nicht den Eindruck, dass er sich für alle Entwürfe begeistern könnte bzw. hinter ihnen stünde.

Während des Treffens wurden die Gestaltungskonzepte für das Einkaufszentrum am Unabhängigkeitsplatz, die auch den eigentlichen Platz über der Mall mit einbeziehen, erklärt. Es war jedoch verboten sich Notizen zu machen oder die Entwürfe zu photographieren, da diese noch nicht endgültig festlagen, d. h. noch nicht genehmigt worden waren. Das Projekt muss einer scharfen politischen Prüfung standhalten, und alle Fragen, die auf den symbolischen Wert der Entwürfe anspielten, wurden diplomatisch beantwortet.

Minsk Projekt stellte zwei Konzepte vor. Für den ersten Entwurf der unterirdischen Shopping-Mall stand offensichtlich das unterirdische Einkaufszentrum Manezh in Moskau Pate. Wie Manezh, sollte auch diese Mall Oberlichter haben, die wie Perlen auf einer Schnur aneinander gereiht sind. Diese Lichterketten hätten eine symbolische Verbindung zwischen den Stadtzentren von Moskau und Minsk geschaffen. Das Projekt wird fast ausschließlich vom Staat finanziert und gehört somit dem Staat. Es wird unter der Erde auf insgesamt 75 000 m^2 Raum geschaffen für Geschäfte, ein Parkhaus und eine Fußgängerzone. Im Ganzen ein Ort von gigantischen Ausmaßen, der die verschiedensten Aktivitäten beherbergen kann. Man kann sich vorstellen, wie die diversen Aktivitäten, die dort stattfinden werden, Dampf erzeugen, der sich zu einer Wolke formiert, die als ein Symbol der Konsumgesellschaft aufsteigt.

Der unterirdische Raum – und insbesondere seine vorgesehene Nutzung – tragen indirekt und unbeabsichtigt dazu bei, dem Platz darüber eine symbolische Bedeutung zu verleihen. Dahingegen wird das Aussehen des Platzes der Unabhängigkeit zu ebener Erde von den Intentionen des Auftraggebers, also des Staates, geprägt werden. Es folgt eine Beschreibung der Designkonzepte für den eigentlichen Platz, die anlässlich des Treffens präsentiert wurden.

Zuerst wurde das Konzept vorgestellt, das ursprünglich dem Chefarchitekten und anderen Funktionären vorgelegt worden war. Es schlug vor, den Platz, der ungefähr 320 x 150 Meter oder 50 000 m^2 misst, in verschiedene Bereiche aufzuteilen. Es wurde beabsichtigt, einen großen, freien Platz zu schaffen, der dem Regierungsgebäude als eine Art Vorplatz gedient hätte. Diese große Fläche hätte das Aussehen des ganzen Platzes geprägt, dem Gebäude einen Rahmen gegeben, und im Grunde genommen diesen Bereich zu einem Teil des Regierungsgebäudes gemacht. Ebenfalls vorgesehen war ein großes, rundes Oberlicht, das fast genau gegenüber der Roten Kirche aus dem Platz geragt hätte. Dieses große Oberlicht hätte einen separaten Bereich auf dem Platz geschaffen und darauf aufmerksam gemacht, dass der Platz eigentlich das Dach des Einkaufszentrums ist. Außerdem war ein Denkmal in der Mitte des Platzes, vor dem Eingang zur Shopping-Mall

Minsk Project, a group of architects, planners, engineers and landscapers responsible for building a shopping mall beneath Independence (Lenin) Square, highlights not only how important it is for Alexander Lukashenko to control public space but also reveals much about what kind of society he intends to create.

Minsk Project is the city's architecture, planning, engineering and landscaping office. The office is in charge of designing all municipal projects and it is also responsible for documenting any work done, for example, to the infrastructure, roads or buildings. It also issues urban design guidelines for both new and existing developments, and assesses all proposals concerning the development of commercial and residential areas. This explains why Minsk Project is in charge of designing and documenting the construction of the 75,000 m^2 shopping mall that is currently being built underneath Independence Square.

The state grants Minsk Project some creative freedom regarding the design of the project. However, all projects must be approved by Minsk's Chief Architect, whom the president appoints, and a project as important as Independence Square must also meet the approval of Lukashenko himself.

The official meeting documented here took place in the office of the Chief of Design, Mikhael Gauhfeld. He seemed confident and in control, and he presented the design fundamentals of the project well. However, he also seemed uneasy; during the presentation he lacked energy and did not make the impression of being passionate about or committed to all of the designs.

The design concepts for the shopping mall at Independence Square, including the outdoor space on street level, were explained during the meeting. Taking photos of the designs or making notes of them was prohibited because they were not finalised, that is approved, yet. The project is subject to much political scrutiny and any questions that touched on the symbolic meaning underlying the designs were answered diplomatically.

Two concepts were presented during the meeting. When Minsk Project developed the first concept it obviously had the Manezh, the underground shopping centre in Moscow, in mind. Like the Manezh, the Minsk mall would have featured skylights that would have been arranged like pearls on a string. These lights would have linked the center of Moscow and the center of Minsk symbolically. The project is almost entirely state-funded and

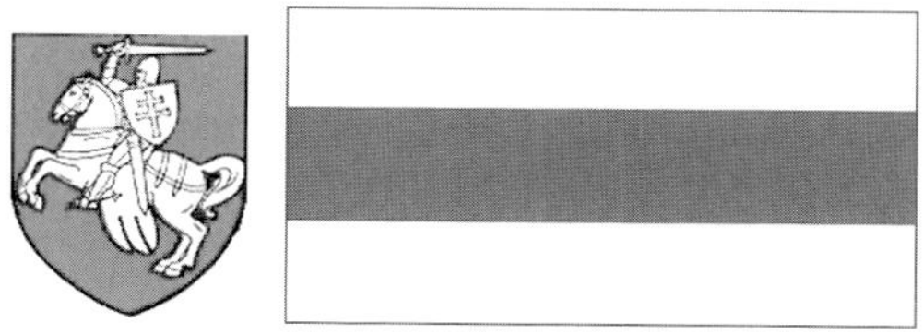

DIE WEISSRUSSISCHE STAATSFLAGGE UND DAS WAPPEN, DATIERT AUS DEM 14. JAHRHUNDERT, WURDEN ZWISCHEN 1990 UND 1995 WIEDER VERWENDET.
THE BELARUSIAN NATIONAL FLAG AND EMBLEM DATE BACK TO THE 14TH CENTURY AND WERE USED BETWEEN 1990 AND 1995.

therefore owned by the state. A total of 75,000 m^2 will be created, providing space below ground for stores, a car park and an area for pedestrians. All in all a gigantic space that can serve as the host for many different activities. It is possible to imagine that the many activities that will take place in this space will generate steam, which forms a cloud symbolising consumerism.

The underground space, especially the way it will be used, contributes to – indirectly and unintentionally – giving the space above ground symbolic meaning. The look of Independence Square on street level, however, will reflect the intentions of the client, that is the state. A description of the designs for the square presented during the meeting follows.

The first concept presented during the meeting was the one originally presented to the Chief Architect and other officials. It proposed that the square, which measures approximately 320 by 150 meters or 50,000 m^2, be divided into sections. It proposed the creation of one large open space that would have served as a kind of courtyard to the House of Government. The large space would define the square, frame the building and essentially make the space part of the House of Government. It also foresaw for a large circular, raised skylight on the square almost opposite the Red Church. This large skylight would have created a space within the square and it would have highlighted that the square actually is the roof of a shopping mall. It also proposed that a monument celebrating Belarus' independence be erected in the center of the square, outside the mall's entrance hall. The highly symbolic monument was supposed to consist of a huge tower that would have featured a viewing platform as well as a large statue of a stork, the symbol of independent Belarus. The design also

geplant, zum Gedenken an die Unabhängigkeit der weißrussischen Republik. Es war ein höchst symbolträchtiges Denkmal geplant, ein gewaltiger Turm mit einer Aussichtsplattform und auch einer großen Storchfigur, dem Symbol des unabhängigen Weißrusslands. Der Entwurf zeigte auch Fußgängerwege, die über den Platz und die Skarina-Allee führen sollten. Sie hätten die in eine Fußgängerzone umgewandelte nördliche Seite der Skarina-Allee mit der Mitte und dem südlichen Ende des Platzes verbunden, dem Teil, der am weitesten vom Lenin-Denkmal und dem Regierungsgebäude entfernt liegt. Schließlich sah der Entwurf vor, die Pädagogische Hochschule von Minsk, die sich auf der westlichen Seite des Platzes gegenüber dem Regierungsgebäude befindet, von Grund auf zu renovieren und als Erweiterung ein hohes, verglastes Bürogebäude auf dem Platz zu errichten.

Das zweite Konzept wurde als eine Verbesserung des ersten Entwurfs präsentiert. Das ursprüngliche Konzept wurde geändert, nachdem der Chefarchitekt und andere Funktionäre (darunter sicherlich auch Lukashenko) konsultiert worden waren. Einige bedeutende Änderungen waren am Entwurf vorgenommen worden. Das Denkmal, das zum Gedenken an die Gründung der weißrussischen Republik im Hauptbereich gegenüber der Kirche errichtet werden sollte, war entfernt worden. Stattdessen sollen eine Reihe kleinerer und unauffälligerer Skulpturen, die die Unabhängigkeit des Landes feiern, aufgestellt werden. Ohne das gewaltige Denkmal können nun andere Denkmäler auf dem Platz, wie etwa das Lenin-Denkmal, an Bedeutung gewinnen. Der Fußweg rund um den Platz wurde mehr oder weniger beibehalten, aber es wurde eine breite Achse hinzugefügt, vom Lenin-Denkmal zum zentralen Oberlicht, die auch eine visuelle Verbindung herstellt. Indem hier absichtlich sowjetische Vergangenheit und weißrussische Zukunft verbunden werden, setzt die Regierung ein klares Zeichen, wie sie die weißrussische Identität definiert. Und zu guter Letzt wurden die Pläne für die Renovierung und Erweiterung der Pädagogischen Hochschule zusammengestrichen. So wird das Regierungsgebäude auch weiterhin den Platz dominieren, was darauf schließen lässt, dass der Staat als eine starke und mächtige Autorität gesehen werden will.

Es ist evident, dass mit jeder Veränderung am Aussehen des Unabhängigkeitsplatzes der Stellenwert bestimmter Symbole steigt oder fällt. Es ist offensichtlich, dass alle Entscheidungen sehr bewusst getroffen wurden. Der neu gestaltete Platz soll ohne Zweifel Lukashenkos Vorstellung von einer weissrussischen Identität widerspiegeln. Die deutliche Anbindung an die sowjetische Vergangenheit (das Lenin-Denkmal), die Verkleinerung des Monuments zum Gedenken an die weissrussische Unabhängigkeit (was einer Ehrerbietung an Russland gleichkommt) und die visuelle Dominanz des Regierungsgebäudes (als Symbol eines starken Staates), all dies trägt dazu bei, den Platz in einen äußerst symbolträchtigen Ort zu verwandeln. In der Gestaltung dieses öffentlichen Ortes zeigt sich Lukashenkos Geschmack; wichtiger ist jedoch, dass er die Ideologie des Präsidenten und seiner Regierung widerspiegelt und ihren Zielsetzungen dient.

Der Kampf mittels Symbolen, der an öffentlichen Orten ausgetragen wird, ist höchst kodiert, und die Wirkung der Symbole hängt vom Kontext und dem ideologischen Standpunkt des Betrachters ab. Dualismus ist ein wesentlicher Teil dieses Kampfes. Während Präsident Lukashenko an Bildern der kommunistischen Vergangenheit festhält, um seine Politik der Russifizierung optisch zu untermauern, orientieren sich die Mitglieder der Opposition an der Unabhängigkeitsbewegung und verwenden Symbole aus der europäischen Vergangenheit des Landes. So gesehen ist das Nebeneinander von Wahrzeichen aus verschiedenen Epochen im Zentrum der weißrussischen Hauptstadt kein Widerspruch.

Gekürzte Fassung der im Rahmen des Bauhaus Kollegs V „Transit Spaces" entstandenen Arbeit.

included pedestrian paths that were to run across the square and Skarina Avenue. They would have linked the pedestrianised north side of Skarina Avenue with the square's center and its southern end, the part of the square that is furthest away from the Lenin Statue and the House of Government. Finally, the plan proposed that Minsk's Pedagogical University, which is located on the western part of the square opposite the House of Government, be fully refurbished and that an addition, a tall glass-covered office block, would be built on the square.

The second concept was presented as an improvement to the first one. The initial design was changed after the Chief Architect and other officials (doubtlessly including Lukashenko) were consulted. A few major changes were made to the design. The monument dedicated to the independence of Belarus, which would have been put up in the main area across the church, was removed. Instead, a number of smaller and less impressive sculptures celebrating Belarus' independence will be erected. Removing the dominant monument will have the effect that other monuments, such as the Lenin Statue, will become more important visually. The circular walkway will more or less remain the same but one wide path, which will link the Lenin Statue and the central skylight visually and physically, was added. This deliberate link of the Soviet past and the Belarusian future is a clear indicator of the administration's understanding of Belarusian national identity. Last not least, the refurbishment of the Pedagogical University as well as the size of the extension building were scaled down. The reason being that the House of Government should remain the dominant building on the square, which implies that the state wants to be seen as a strong and authoritative power.

It is evident that any changes made to the design of Independence Square either increase or reduce the weight of certain symbols. It is also clear that all decisions were made very consciously. Without doubt the newly developed square will reflect Lukashenko's idea of Belarusian national identity. The obvious reference to the Soviet past (the Lenin Statue), downsizing the statue dedicated to Belarusian independence (which implies deference to Russia) and the visual dominance of the House of Government (symbolising a strong state) all contribute to turning this square into a highly symbolic space. The design of this public space is an expression of Lukashenko's taste but more importantly the finished project will reflect the ideology of the president and government officials, and the space will serve the purpose of furthering their objectives.

The symbolic battles that are taking place in public spaces are highly coded and people's perception of symbols depends on the context and the observer's ideological convictions. Dualism is an intrinsic part of this battle. While President Lukashenko adheres to images of the Communist past, which endorse his policy of Russification visually, members of the opposition align themselves with the independence movement and turn to the symbols of Belarus' European past. In this context, symbols of different eras do not conflict with each other but they exist side by side in the center of the Belarusian capital.

This text is a shortened version of the paper presented at the Bauhaus Kolleg V "Transit Spaces".

AKTIVITÄTEN DER POLITISCHEN OPPOSITION IN MINSK: EIN BERICHT

JACEK GADECKI

Am 9. September 2001 fanden in Weißrussland zum zweiten Mal Wahlen statt und es gelang dem amtierenden Präsidenten Alexander Lukashenko abermals, diese für sich zu entscheiden.[1] Internationale Beobachter kritisierten die Wahlen und für eine kurze Zeit prangerte die internationale Gemeinschaft den Missbrauch der Menschenrechte in Weißrussland an. Aber die Ereignisse des 11. September hatten zur Folge, dass das internationale Interesse an Weißrussland schwand und Lukashenko konnte, ohne diplomatische Konsequenzen fürchten zu müssen, Maßnahmen durchsetzen, die den Zweck hatten, sowohl seine Position zu stärken als auch die weißrussische Gesellschaft weiter zu unterdrücken.[2] Er erließ ein Gesetz, das die Meinungsfreiheit des Volkes sowie die Pressefreiheit sehr stark beschnitt und einige Journalisten wurden verhaftet, sogar zu einer Gefängnisstrafe verurteilt, weil sie angeblich den Präsidenten beleidigt hatten. Menschenrechtler sind immer noch entsetzt. Des Weiteren gibt es bis heute keine Erklärung für das Verschwinden zahlreicher bekannter Personen und Hunderte von Menschen wurden in den letzten Jahren verfolgt und inhaftiert, weil sie an friedlichen oppositionellen Aktivitäten teilgenommen hatten. Internationale Berichte kritisieren darüber hinaus das brutale Vorgehen der Behörden gegen Mitglieder oppositioneller Gruppen.

OPPOSITIONELLE AKTIVITÄTEN

Dieser Bericht befasst sich mit der Frage, wie der öffentliche Raum in der Hauptstadt der weißrussischen Republik genutzt wird und konzentriert sich auf die Aktivitäten oppositioneller Gruppen, um eine Antwort zu finden. Um die öffentliche Sphäre in Minsk besser verstehen zu können, ist es sinnvoll, die Beziehung zwischen dem Staat und der oppositionellen Presse näher zu betrachten. In den letzten Jahren mussten die Massenmedien verstärkt gegen Repressalien – insbesondere von Seiten der Legislative – ankämpfen. Seit 2003 wurden an die 20 Zeitungen und Zeitschriften entweder verboten oder erscheinen heute nicht mehr, weil sie auf einem staatlich regulierten Markt nicht wettbewerbsfähig sind. Ungefähr die Hälfte aller unabhängigen Zeitungen oder Zeitschriften meldete Konkurs an.

Der Staat bedient sich verschiedener Methoden, um die unabhängige Presse unter Druck zu setzen:

- Legislative Instrumente: Zum Beispiel darf das Informationsministerium Medienunternehmen abmahnen. Kein Gerichtsbeschluss ist hierfür notwendig. Jede Zeitung und, zum Beispiel, jeder Radiosender, die/der drei Abmahnungen erhält, wird vom Staat geschlossen.
- Wirtschaftlicher Druck: 2002 waren unabhängige Verleger gezwungen, Bieiposzta (dem staatlichen Monopol) 45 bis 60 Prozent mehr an Vertriebs- und Abonnementgebühren zu zahlen als die offizielle Presse.
- Zensur: Seit 1994 ist die Zensur der unabhängigen Presse zunehmend stärker geworden und manch eine Ausgabe einer Zeitung erscheint heute ohne einen einzigen Artikel.
- Prozesse gegen Journalisten und Zeitungen: 2002 verurteilten weißrussische Gerichte eine Rekordzahl von Angeklagten, die angeblich die Ehre des Präsidenten verletzt hatten. Zum Beispiel wurden die Journalisten Pawei Maïejka und Mikoia Markiewicz, die für die Zeitung *Pahonia* arbeiten, zu einem bzw. anderthalb Jahren Gefängnis verurteilt.
- Druck von Seiten der Wirtschaft: Nur ein solcher Fall ist bekannt. Ein weißrussischer Geschäftsmann und gleichzeitig Mitbegründer der *Sobodnyje Nowosti* entzog der Zeitung seine finanzielle Unterstützung, nachdem es zu politischen Unstimmigkeiten zwischen ihm und dem Chefredakteur gekommen war.

OPPOSITIONAL POLITICAL ACTIVITIES IN MINSK: A REPORT

JACEK GADECKI

On September 9 in 2001 elections were held in Belarus for the second time and the country's current President Alexander Lukashenko won them.[1] They were the subject of international criticism and for a short period of time the abuse of human rights in Belarus became a subject of concern to the international community. But the events of 9/11 and their aftermath pushed Belarus out of the international spotlight again and, without fearing diplomatic consequences, Lukashenko seized the opportunity to enforce measures that were supposed to solidify his power and restrict the freedom of Belarusian citizens further.[2] He passed bills that severely restricted the freedom of speech and a number of journalists were arrested, even imprisoned for allegedly slandering the president. Human rights advocates are still in shock. To this day the disappearance of several well-known people remains unaccounted for, and hundreds of people have been persecuted and sentenced to jail because they participated in peaceful oppositional activities. International reports also criticize the brutal treatment of members of oppositional groups by the authorities.

OPPOSITIONAL ACTIVITIES

This analysis of the usage of public space in the capital of the Republic of Belarus focuses on the activities of the oppositional movement. To gain a better understanding of Minsk's public sphere, it is worthwhile to explore the relationship between the state and the oppositional press. Throughout the last few years, the mass media has been the target of repressive legislation and activities. About twenty titles have disappeared from the market since 2003, either because they were banned by the state or because they were not strong enough to survive in a state-controlled market. As a result, about half of the independent newspapers and magazines no longer exist today.

The state resorts to several measures to put pressure on the independent press:

- Legislative instruments: for example, the Ministry of Information may issue warnings to newspapers or magazines. No court orders are needed to do so. Any newspaper or radio station that receives three warnings is shut down by the state.
- Econom c pressure: in 2002 independent newspapers and magazines were forced to pay Bieiposzta (the state monopolist) between 45 and 60 percent more in distribution and subscription fees than the official press.
- Censorsnip: since 1994 censorship of the independent media has become so strict that newspapers sometimes feature no articles at all these days.
- Law suits against journalists and newspapers: in 2002 Belarusian courts enforced a law that is supposed to protect the president against libel a record time. For example, the journalists Pawei Maïejka and Mikoia Markiewicz, who work for the newspaper *Pahonia*, were sentenced to jail for one year and one year and a half respectively.
- Influence on business: only one such case is known. A Belarusian businessman, the cofounder of the newspaper *Sobodnyje Nowosti*, withdrew his financial support form the newspaper because he disagreed with the political views of the chief editor.

DEMONSTRATIONS

To analyze the usage of physical public space in Minsk, this project concentrates on one organization. More specifically, it focuses on one of Belarus' most spectacular and well-documented case of opposition: the "Zubr"-Movement.[3] As will become clear, this young and illegal organization is responsible for many different activities in the capital of Belarus and across the country.

DEMONSTRATIONEN

Um analysieren zu können, wie öffentliche Orte in Minsk genutzt werden, konzentriert sich diese Arbeit auf eine Organisation. Sie untersucht eine der beeindruckendsten und bestdokumentierten oppositionellen Gruppen in Weißrussland, die „Zubr"-Bewegung, und diese Arbeit wird zeigen, dass diese junge und illegale Organisation für viele verschiedene Aktivitäten in der weißrussischen Hauptstadt und im ganzen Lande verantwortlich ist.[3]

„Unsere Verfassung gesteht uns Meinungs- und Pressefreiheit zu und sie sieht vor, dass die Bürger Weißrusslands sich versammeln und frei demonstrieren dürfen. Aber Lukashenkos Regime hat ein Gesetz verabschiedet, das öffentliche Aktivitäten in der Minsker Innenstadt verbietet. Demonstrationen dürfen nur noch außerhalb des Stadtkerns stattfinden. Dies bedeutet, dass uns unsere Meinungsfreiheit de facto entzogen wurde."
(Alexander Otroschenkov von „Zubr")

Zu Beginn der neunziger Jahre, bevor Alexander Lukashenko zum Präsidenten gewählt wurde, durften die Bürger von Minsk überall zusammen kommen und demonstrieren. Im Jahre 1996 änderte sich die Gesetzeslage und es wurde schwieriger für die Bürger, ihr Recht auszuüben. Nach einer „stillen Zeit" in den Jahren 1999 bis 2000 fanden jedoch wieder Großdemonstrationen in der Hauptstadt statt. Oleg Bebenin von Charter 97 erinnert sich, dass „[...] die Menschen auf die Straßen gingen. Ungefähr 10 000 Menschen nahmen an einer Demonstration teil, die wir heute den ‚Marsch der Freiheit' nennen. Ich glaube, dass die Gesetzgebung und alle Maßnahmen der Behörden nur noch ein einziges Ziel haben: sie wollen verhindern, dass die Bürger ungehindert öffentlich demonstrieren und ihren Protest kundtun können. Aber letztendlich kommt es auf das Volk an und das hat sich entschlossen, auf die Straße zu gehen und zu protestieren. In unserem Büro haben wir alle großen Aktivitäten dokumentiert, die seit 2002 stattgefunden haben. Wir haben alle ‚Märsche der Freiheit,' alle so genannten sozialen und ethischen Märsche, die wir organisiert haben, aufgezeichnet."

Seit 1996 darf nicht mehr in der Innenstadt demonstriert werden. Laut Gesetz dürfen Demonstrationen nur an einem Ort – auf dem Bangalor-Platz – stattfinden. Dieser ist ungefähr sechs bis sieben Kilometer von der Skarina-Allee entfernt. Die Opposition glaubt, dass dieses Gesetz verabschiedet wurde, um Aktivisten den Wind aus den Segeln zu nehmen. Die Bürger der Stadt nehmen lieber an legalen Veranstaltungen teil, denn sie fürchten, von den Behörden angehalten oder aufgegriffen zu werden. Alexander Otroschenkov von der „Zubr"-Bewegung meint:

„Der Bangalor-Platz ist zwar nicht weit von der Minsker Innenstadt entfernt, aber die Bürger mögen ihn nicht besonders. Der Platz ist noch nicht mal gepflastert und man geht nur dorthin, wenn man seinen Hund ausführen möchte. Sobald es regnet, verwandelt sich der Platz in eine Schlammwiese. Es hat wenig Sinn, dort Veranstaltungen zu organisieren. Versucht man Leute zu motivieren, an einer Veranstaltung teilzunehmen, die auf dem Bangalo-Platz stattfindet, reagieren sie gereizt. Sie sagen, man sei genauso mies wie Lukashenko. Man kann es ihnen nicht übel nehmen. Lebten wir in einem demokratischen Land, könnten wir, die Bürger von Weißrussland, unsere Meinung in der Innenstadt von Minsk kundtun."

Nichtsdestotrotz fand im Jahre 2003 der „Marsch für ein besseres Leben" in der Minsker Innenstadt statt. Er war der größte Protestakt in der jüngsten Vergangenheit Weißrusslands und Arbeiter aus staatlichen Fabriken, Studenten und Rentner nahmen an dem Marsch teil. Die Demonstration endete jedoch unvorhergesehen am Jakub-Kolas-Platz, da die Miliz sich einer neuen Taktik bediente. Sie sperrte alle um den Platz herum liegenden Straßen ab. Autos blockierten die Straßen und die Demonstranten kamen nicht weiter. Der Platz ist nicht besonders groß und schon bald waren die Menschen zwischen den Autos eingepfercht. So endete die Demonstration vorzeitig. Heute dürfen weder große noch kleine Demonstrationen in der Innenstadt abgehalten werden, da das Gesetz dies verbietet.

DAS VERTEILEN VON ZEITUNGEN UND FLUGBLÄTTERN

„Es bleibt uns nichts anderes übrig, als mit gedruckten Materialien – Zeitungen, Flugblättern und Aufklebern – zu arbeiten. Nur so können wir die Menschen informieren."

Für jede oppositionelle Gruppe, die zur Zeit in Weißrussland agiert, ist die Presse das wichtigste Instrument. Die Presse eignet sich am Besten, um die Bürger über oppositionelle Aktivitäten zu informieren. Während des Präsidentschaftswahlkampfes 2001 wurden täglich eine Million Flugblätter verteilt. So konnten die Bürger zum Beispiel etwas über die Kandidaten der Opposition

"Our constitution grants us freedom of speech as well as the right to assemble and demonstrate peacefully. But this regime passed a law that prohibits any public activities in the center of Minsk. Demonstrations are only permitted far from the city center. This means that we are essentially deprived of the freedom to express ourselves."
(Alexander Otroschenkov, "Zubr" – Movement)
During the first half of the 1990s and before Alexander Lukashenko was elected president, the citizens of Minsk were allowed to assemble and demonstrate everywhere. In 1996 the law changed and it became more difficult for people to exercise their right to protest. After a "period of silence" between 1999 and 2000, massive demonstrations continued to take place in the capital nevertheless. Oleg Bebenin from Charta 97 remembers that "(...)] people were out on the streets. Around 10,000 people participated in a demonstration we now call the March of Freedom. I think today the law and all the measures undertaken by the authorities have only one purpose: to prevent people from demonstrating and protesting. Yet, everything depends on the people and it is their decision to march down the streets and express their dissent. In our office we have records of all mass-scale activities that have taken place since 2002. We have information about all so-called marches of freedom, about all the so-called social and ethical marches that we organized."
Since 1996 it is illegal to organize and hold demonstrations in the city center. There is only one place near the city center where demonstrations are allowed: Bangalor Square. It is located about six or seven kilometers away from Skarina Avenue. Members of the opposition think this law was passed to stop activists. People prefer to go to legal events because they want to avoid being stopped or harassed by the authorities. Alexander Otroschenkov of the "Zubr"-Movement comments on this:
"Bangalor Square is not far away from the center but it is not a very popular destination. The square is not paved and people normally only go there to walk their dogs. When it rains the place is covered in mud. It makes little sense to organize any activities there. When you try to encourage people to go there they take it as an insult. They will respond by telling you that you are as bad as Lukashenko. And I cannot but agree with these people. If we lived in a democratic country we, the citizens of Belarus, would be free to express ourselves in the center of Minsk."
In 2003 the March for a Better Life took place in the city center. It was the biggest act of social protest in recent Belarusian history and workers of state-owned factories, students as well as pensioners participated. Yet, the demonstration came to a sudden end on Jakub Kolas Square because Lukashenko's street militia employed a new tactic: it closed off all the roads that surround the square. As a result cars blocked the streets around Jakub Kolas Square and protesters were unable to move ahead. The square is not very big and soon people were cramped between cars. The demonstration ended prematurely. Today, demonstrations – small or large – no longer take place in the city center because the law prohibits this.

THE DISTRIBUTION OF NEWSPAPERS AND LEAFLETS

"We have to work with print media: newspapers, leaflets and stickers. It is the only weapon we can use to reach people."
The print media is the most important tool for any oppositional group working in Belarus today. It is best suited to inform citizens about any of its activities. During the 2001 presidential election campaign one million leaflets were distributed every day. As a result, people could learn more about, for example, the oppositional candidates or the fact that people were disappearing. Oleg Bebenin remarks:
"We know that print media is all we have. We know that the Solidarity Movement in Poland had secret printing offices. We do not have our own printing offices and therefore we use different printers. We are really careful about using them. We try to distribute our material everywhere. 'Zubr'-activists try to pick busy places. The metro – where people stand in line at the ticket counter and which has many entrances and exits – is one such place. Almost everybody takes the metro: people are either on their way to the city center or traveling from one part of the city to another. We try to staff all stations but sometimes this is difficult. Typically we pick busy stations that are close to the city center. "Zubr"-activists also hand out material at kiosk markets."
Print material is also distributed in residential areas but sometimes this is difficult: "Currently we are unable to produce large quantities. Therefore we put up material at bus stops, supermarkets or kiosk markets. All the places that are frequented by the people living in the areas."

oder das Verschwinden von Menschen erfahren. Oleg Bebenin erklärt:

„Wir wissen, dass wir unsere Inhalte nur durch Zeitungen oder Flugblätter verbreiten können. Wir wissen, dass die polnische Solidaritätsbewegung über geheime Druckereien verfügte. Wir haben keine eigene Druckerei und darum müssen wir verschiedene Druckereien benutzen. Wir sind bei unserer Auswahl sehr vorsichtig. Wir versuchen, unser Material überall zu verteilen. Hierfür suchen die Mitglieder von ‚Zubr' sich meistens belebte Orte aus. Zum Beispiel die U-Bahn, denn hier stehen die Menschen am Schalter in der Schlange, und es gibt viele Ein- und Ausgänge. Fast jeder fährt mit der U-Bahn: Die Menschen sind entweder auf dem Weg in die Innenstadt oder sie fahren von einem Stadtteil in den anderen. Wir würden gerne jede U-Bahnstation bemannen, aber das ist nicht immer leicht. Deshalb suchen wir uns die Stationen aus, wo reger Verkehr herrscht und welche näher zur Innenstadt gelegen sind. „Zubr"-Aktivisten teilen auch auf den Kioskmärkten Material aus."

Zeitungen, Broschüren oder Flugblätter werden auch in Wohngegenden verteilt, aber dies gestaltet sich schwierig: „Im Moment haben wir nicht die Mittel und können keine großen Mengen drucken. Deshalb hängen wir Flugblätter an Bushaltestellen, in Supermärkten und auf Kioskmärkten auf. Orte, die von den Bewohnern der einzelnen Viertel frequentiert werden."

Die „Zubr"-Bewegung hat wenig Geld und es ist schwer für sie, genügend Papier zu kaufen und Aktivitäten zu finanzieren. Deshalb ist die Bewegung sehr auf die kostenlose Nutzung von Druckereien angewiesen. In Minsk können zur Zeit lediglich um die 10 000 Zeitungen täglich gedruckt werden. Und da nur wenige Zeitungen, Broschüren und Flugblätter produziert werden, kann das Potential der „Zubr"-Bewegung nicht voll ausgeschöpft werden. Oft kommen die zahlreichen Freiwilligen nicht zum Einsatz.

DIE FAHNE DER UNABHÄNGIGEN REPUBLIK WEISSRUSSLAND

Die Opposition bedient sich auch des öffentlichen Raumes, indem sie die Fahne der Unabhängigen Weißrussischen Republik an öffentlichen Gebäuden hisst. Dies ist ein sehr symbolischer Akt des Widerstands: die Opposition lehnt die offizielle Fahne ab und erkennt stattdessen nur die weiß-rot-weiße Fahne an, die für das unabhängige Weißrussland steht. Die Fahnen werden vor Ort produziert und schmücken viele Bürogebäude und Wohnhäuser in Minsk. Einmal wurde die Fahne der Unabhängigen Republik Weißrussland an einem Haus gehisst, das dem ehemaligen Sitz des KGB gegenüberliegt.

„Wir machen uns die Elektrizitäts- und Telefonleitungen zu Nutze. Dank ihnen können wir Fahnen hissen und manchmal bleiben diese eine ganze Weile lang an den Leitungen hängen. Manchmal mehrere Wochen lang. Es gibt Leute, die jahrelange Erfahrung im Hissen von Fahnen haben. Unsere Fahne wurde vor zehn Jahren verboten, aber nichtsdestotrotz werden im ganzen Land ständig Fahnen aufgehangen."

POLITISCHES GRAFFITI

Politisches Graffiti ist eine weitere oppositionelle Ausdrucksform, die heute in der Öffentlichkeit von Minsk und Weißrussland praktiziert wird. Politisches Graffiti ist von Ort zu Ort unterschiedlich und wird meistens schnell beseitigt. Manchmal, zum Beispiel während des Wahlkampfes, reagieren die Menschen positiv auf Graffiti. Aber nicht alle Bürger schätzen diese Art des öffentlichen Protests. Oleg Bebenin sagt: „Die meisten Aktivisten, die Graffitis sprühen, sind jung. Graffiti ist ihr Ding. Aber wir müssen auch an die ältere Bevölkerung denken. Es ist sinnvoller, diesen Menschen mit Hilfe von Zeitungen Informationen zukommen zu lassen."

Sogar „Zubr"-Aktivisten wissen, dass „ [...] nicht alle Leute Graffitis mögen. Manche klagen darüber, dass wir Häuser verschandeln. Aus diesem Grund sprühen wir nicht mehr so viel. Graffitis mögen dazu taugen, einen Skandal auszulösen – wie zum Beispiel in Baranowicze. Junge Aktivisten sprühten dort eine ganzen Tag lang Graffitis, denn diese symbolisierten den Kampf, der zwischen ihnen und der städtischen Behörde tobte."

EINE KARTIERUNG OPPOSITIONELLER AKTIVITÄTEN

Alle Aktivitäten, die im Jahre 2003 und in den ersten drei Monaten des Jahres 2004 stattfanden, sind auf S. 445 verzeichnet. Das Ergebnis ist eindeutig: Der Zugang zum öffentlichen Raum in Minsk ist beschränkt.

1. Beschränkter Zugang zu Informationen

Oleg Bebenin sagt: „Unser Pressezentrum ist auf zweierlei Arten von Information, nämlich externe und interne, angewiesen. Wir benutzen das Internet, publizieren Zeitungen und Flugblätter und in-

The "Zubr"-Movement has little money and buying paper or funding activities is difficult. Everything depends on access to printing facilities. Currently the "Zubr"-Movement is only able to print around 10,000 newspapers and flyers in Minsk a day. Because only small batches are produced, the many volunteers of the "Zubr's"-network have no choice but to remain inactive.

RAISING THE FLAG OF INDEPENDENT BELARUS

Another way of using public space is the act of raising the flag of Independent Belarus. It is a highly symbolic act of resistance: the opposition refuses to acknowledge the official flag but instead operates with the white-red-white flag that represents Independent Belarus. The flags are produced locally and, hanging off high residential or commercial buildings, they adorn many places in the city. Once a flag of Independent Belarus was raised opposite the KGB building.

"We make use of the electricity or telephone lines that run between buildings. They allow us to put up flags and the flags might even hang there for quite some time. Sometimes they are up for weeks. Some people have years of experience in raising flags. Our flag has been prohibited for ten years but thousands of flags are being raised across the whole country nonetheless."

POLITICAL GRAFFITI

Political graffiti it is another form of oppositional activity taking place in the public space of Minsk and the Republic of Belarus today. It has a rather local and temporary character to it and at times, for example during election campaigns, people react positively to it. However, not all citizens are keen on this form of public protest. Oleg Bebenin explains: "Mostly young activists engage in this activity. Graffiti is their domain. But we must think about the elderly, too. It is much more efficient to inform them by supplying them with newspapers." Even "Zubr"-activists are aware of the fact that "(...) not all people like graffiti. Sometimes they say that we vandalize houses. This is why we no longer use it much. Graffiti might be useful to cause a scandal – as was the case in Baranowicze. People were spraying graffiti all day because it was the symbol of the war that was going on between young people and the city's administration."

MAPPING OPPOSITIONAL ACTIVITIES

The map on p. 445 documents all activities that took place in 2003 and during the first three months of 2004. The conclusion is evident: access to public space in Minsk is limited.

1. Limited access to information

Oleg Bebenin says: "Our press center relies on two types of information, namely external and internal information. We use the Internet, publish newspapers and spread information across the country. We also do much to inform people abroad about what is going on here. We think that Belarus should be covered by international journalism, which is why we try to maintain our relationships to international journalists, correspondents and press agencies. Unfortunately, most Polish correspondents left the country. Cezary Halinski, a journalist of the *Gazeta Wyborcza*, worked in Minsk for eight years before he left. The correspondent for *PAP (Polska Agencja Prasowa)* left Belarus as well. Only one person from a Polish radio station is still in Minsk. We are trying to prep the station with lots of information. News but also sociological analyses. We also cooperate with many of the large European and American newspapers. This is our job."

2. Limited access to public space

Legally organized mass events staged in the city center of Minsk exist side by side with events on, for example, Bangalor Square. The state tries to control all public activities. The color grey dominates the cityscape of Minsk but the city is clean because it is well maintained. It is also clean because the police have not only an eye on drunks or hooligans but everyone. In addition, the militia heavily patrols the streets and about 6,000 students are currently attending the Militia Academy. The authorities are able to react to civil disobedience very fast and since one military base is conveniently located near Skarina Prospect, the militia can be anywhere within a few minutes. Its structure is very complex and one needs to be a specialist to understand it fully. In case of a demonstration two units are mobilized: the Special Militia Forces (OMON) and the Internal Armed Forces (a small, professional army that is part of the Ministry of Internal Affairs). Almaz is another specialized unit and it is responsible for keeping the opposition in check. The presidential Secret Service also supports the militia.

"There are a lot of units. In our country the army is between 80,000 and 90,000 soldiers strong and between 140,000 and 160,000 people work for the

formieren die Menschen im ganzen Land. Wir sind bemüht, das Ausland darüber zu informieren, was hier passiert. Wir glauben auch, dass Weißrussland von der internationalen Presse mehr Beachtung geschenkt werden sollte und versuchen deshalb unsere Kontakte zu internationalen Journalisten, Korrespondenten und Presseagenturen aufrecht zuerhalten. Leider haben die meisten polnischen Korrespondenten das Land verlassen. Cezary Halinski, ein Journalist der *Gazeta Wyborcza*, hat acht Jahre in Minsk gearbeitet, bevor er ging. Der Korrespondent der *PAP (Polska Agencja Prasowa)* hat Weißrussland ebenfalls verlassen. Es gibt nur noch einen Mitarbeiter eines polnischen Radiosenders, mit dem wir zusammen arbeiten können. Wir sind bemüht, viel Material für diesen Sender vorzubereiten. Nachrichten aber auch soziologische Studien. Wir arbeiten auch eng mit großen europäischen und amerikanischen Zeitungen zusammen. Das ist unsere Aufgabe."

2. Beschränkter Zugang zum öffentlichen Raum

Legale Großveranstaltungen, die in der Innenstadt abgehalten werden, finden in Minsk ebenso statt wie Veranstaltungen auf dem Bangalor-Platz. Öffentliche Aktivitäten können jedoch nur bedingt geschehen, denn der Staat schränkt Veranstalter und Teilnehmer stark ein. Das Stadtbild von Minsk ist überwiegend grau, aber die Stadt ist sauber und gepflegt. Unter anderem ist sie sauber, weil die Polizei nicht nur ein Auge auf Betrunkene und Hooligans, sondern auf jeden Bürger hat. Auch die Miliz patrouilliert die Straßen und zur Zeit besuchen 6000 Studenten die Militärakademie. Die Behörden können schnell auf Demonstrationen oder Protestmärsche reagieren und da eine Militärbasis nahe der Skarina-Allee liegt, kann die Miliz schnell überall hin gelangen. Die Struktur der Miliz ist recht komplex und man muss Experte sein, um sie wirklich zu verstehen. Im Falle einer Demonstration werden zwei Einheiten mobilisiert: die Spezialeinheiten der Miliz (OMON) und eine kleine Berufsarmee, die dem Innenministerium unterstellt ist. Die Almaz, eine weitere Spezialeinheit der Miliz, ist insbesondere für die Opposition zuständig. Auch der Geheimdienst des Präsidenten unterstützt die Miliz in ihrer Tätigkeit.

„Es gibt so viele Einheiten. Die Armee unseres Landes ist 80 000 bis 90 000 Mann stark und zwischen 140 000 und 160 000 Menschen arbeiten für die Truppen des Innenministeriums oder die Miliz. [...] Der Leiter der Sicherheitstruppen sagte einmal in einem Interview, dass seine Leute lediglich fünfzehn Minuten bräuchten, um eine Demonstration aufzulösen. Die Soldaten der Truppen sind starke Kerle, die über Waffen, Hunde und Fahrzeuge verfügen. Der Staat ist zu einer gigantischen, repressiven Maschinerie mutiert und aus diesem Grund reichen Demonstrationen nicht mehr aus. Der Fall Serbien und Milosevic hat dies deutlich gemacht. Er verfügte über eine starke Armee und kämpfte zehn Jahre lang, aber gemeinsam gelang es Opposition, Armee und Polizei, Milosevic zu stürzen. Das Gleiche gilt für Georgien. Wir Weißrussen sind friedliche Menschen und wir sind bereit, uns mit der Regierung an einen Tisch zu setzen und zu reden. Wir sind alle Bürger der gleichen Nation."

SCHLUSSFOLGERUNG

Die Verfassung gesteht den Bürgern Weißrusslands Meinungs- und Pressefreiheit sowie ein Versammlungsrecht zu, aber der Zugang zum öffentlichen Raum in Minsk ist sehr begrenzt. Die Karte zeigt jedoch, dass die Bewohner der Stadt sich nicht aufhalten lassen. Sie demonstrieren weiterhin, sie publizieren und verteilen Informationsmaterial.

Die Karte zeigt auch, wie schwierig es ist, in Minsk öffentlich seine Meinung kundzutun. Öffentlicher Raum existiert dank Demonstrationen und Treffen sowie dem Verteilen von unabhängigen Zeitungen und Flugblättern – allerdings immer nur zeitweise. Ein Anführer der „Zubr"-Bewegung sagte einmal, dass ein Ort, an welchem Menschen zusammenkommen können, ein öffentlicher Raum ist. Politisch gesehen durchläuft der öffentliche Raum in Minsk eine starke Veränderung und im Moment bewegt er sich zwischen Demokratie und Diktatur. Oleg Bebenin von „Charta 97" behauptet, dass „die fortschreitende Einschränkung des Zugangs zum öffentlichen Raum ein großes Problem ist. Dass Oppositionelle verschwinden oder Demonstrationen von den Behörden aufgelöst werden, gibt Einblick in die Ideologie der Regierung oder vielmehr Lukashenkos. Ich möchte hervorheben, dass wir nicht eine zweite Sowjetunion sind. Wir sind kein großes Monster, das lange in Isolation überleben könnte. Weißrussland ist ein kleiner Teil von Europa. Die Leute werden nicht aufgeben, sie werden Bewegungen wie „Solidarität" in Polen, „Charta 77" in der Tschechoslowakei oder die Rosenrevolution in Georgien nicht vergessen. Zu viele Menschen waren schon mal im Ausland. Langsam aber sicher wird das Verlangen nach Freiheit sich durchsetzen. Ansonsten wird dieses Land verrotten, denn Rost zerstört alles."

Internal Armed Forces or the militia. (...)] The head of the Internal Security Forces once said that they only need 15 minutes to break up a demonstration. The soldiers are strong guys equipped with weapons, dogs and vehicles. It is a huge, repressive machinery and this explains why demonstrations alone no longer suffice. We know this from Serbia and Milosevic. He had a strong army and he fought for ten years but together the opposition, the army and the police generals were able to stop Milosevic. The same applies to Georgia. We Belarusians are peaceful people and we are ready to sit down and talk with people from the other camp. We are all members of the same nation."

CONCLUSION

The constitution grants citizens freedom of speech and the right to assemble but access to public space is highly controlled in Minsk. Yet as the map shows, restrictions do no stop citizens and they demonstrate or publish and distribute materials nevertheless.

The map shows that it is difficult to speak of genuine public space. It only ever seems to exist temporarily – thanks to special events like demonstrations, meetings or the distribution of independent newspapers. Public space is, like a "Zubr"-leader once said, a place where it is possible for people to convene. In a political sense public space is in deep transition and currently the country moves back and forth from being a democracy and a dictatorship. According to Oleg Bebenin from Charta 97 "the problem is that public space is becoming increasingly restricted. The disappearance of members of the opposition and the break-up of demonstrations by the authorities are all expressions of the government's or rather Lukashenko's ideology. I would like to stress that we are not another Soviet Union; we are not a great monster that can survive independently for a long time. Belarus constitutes a small part of Europe. It is impossible to wear down the people and to make them forget movements such as Solidarity in Poland, Charta 77 in Czechoslovakia or the Rose Revolution in Georgia. Too many people have traveled abroad. Slowly but surely the desire for freedom will triumph. Otherwise the country will rot because rust destroys everything."

A shorter version of the paper was presented at the Bauhaus Kolleg V "Transit Spaces".

SELECTED BIBLIOGRAPHY:

Amnesty International: Human Rights Watch World Report 2003 – Belarus. http://www.bialorus.pl/index.php?pokaz=human_rights_report_2003_en&&Rozdzial=prawa_czlowieka, 15.06.05.

Preston, Paschal: *Reshaping Communications: Technology, information and Social Change.* London and Thousand Oaks California, 2001.

NOTES

1 Alexander Lukashenko began his political career in 1994 when he began to take on Szuszkiewicz and various civil servants around him. He was able to appear frequently on state-controlled television. Lukashenko seized the opportunity and told Belarusians what they wanted to hear about the issue of corruption among civil servants, conspiracies planned by democrats and traitors who, together with the international press, had brought down the Soviet Union. Postcommunist politicians realized that he was far more popular than then-Prime Minister Kiebicz. Alexander Lukashenko won the elections on June 19, 1994 in the first round by securing 45 percent of the votes for himself. On July 10, 1994 almost 80 per cent of the electors cast their vote for Lukashenko and made him the first president of the Republic of Belarus. Citizens trusted that he would create an honest state, fight for social justice and help the country make the transition to a market economy.

2 Amnesty International: Human Rights Watch World Report 2003– Belarus. http://www.bialorus.pl/index.php?pokaz=human_rights_report_2003_en&&Rozdzial=prawa_czlowieka, 15.06.05.

3 The "Zubr"-Movement was established in 2001 and counts 2,000 members in all of Belarus today. It can be divided into two groups, namely "Zubr"-activists and volunteers. "Zubr"-activists typically participate in all "Zubr"-activities because they pledged allegiance to the Belarusian people and the "Zubr"-Movement.

Diese Arbeit wurde in gekürzter Fassung im Rahmen des Bauhaus Kolleg V „Transit Spaces" präsentiert.

AUSWAHLBIBLIOGRAPHIE

Amnesty International: „Human Rights Watch World Report – Belarus". 2003 http://www.bialorus.pl/index.php?pokaz=human_rights_report_2003_en&&Rozdzial=prawa_czlowieka, 15.06.05.

Preston, Paschal: *Reshaping Communications: Technology, Information and Social Change*. London and Thousand Oaks California 2001

ANMERKUNGEN

1 Alexander Lukashenko begann seine politische Karriere 1994, als er begann gegen Szuszkiewicz und verschiedene Beamte um ihn herum vorzugehen. Er konnte des öfteren im staatlichen Fernsehen auftreten. Lukashenko nutzte diese Chance und erzählte der weißrussischen Bevölkerung, was sie über Korruption unter Beamten, von Demokraten geplanten Verschwörungen und Verrätern, die angeblich gemeinsam mit der internationalen Presse die Sowjetunion zu Fall gebracht hatten, hören wollte. Postkommunistische Politiker merkten schnell, dass Lukashenko beim Volk weitaus mehr Beliebtheit genoss als der damalige Premierminister Kiebicz. Alexander Lukashenko gewann die Wahl am 19. Juni 1994 in der ersten Runde und konnte sich 45 Prozent der Stimmen sichern. Am 10. Juli 1994 stimmten fast 80 Prozent der Wähler für Lukashenko, was ihn zum ersten Präsidenten Weißrusslands machte. Die Bürger erwarteten, dass er den Aufbau eines integren Staates fördern, sich für soziale Gerechtigkeit einsetzen und dem Land auf seinem Weg hin zur Marktwirtschaft helfen würde.

2 Amnesty International (2003): Human Rights Watch World Report – Belarus. http://www.bialorus.pl/index.php?pokaz=human_rights_report_2003_en&&Rozdzial=prawa_czlowieka

3 Die „Zubr"-Bewegung wurde 2001 gegründet und heute zählt sie 2000 Mitglieder in ganz Weißrussland. Die Bewegung kann in zwei Fraktionen unterteilt werden und zwar in „Zubr"-Aktivisten und Freiwillige. Für gewöhnlich nehmen „Zubr"-Aktivisten an allen „Zubr"-Aktivitäten teil, denn sie haben dem weißrussischen Volk und der „Zubr"-Bewegung Treue geschworen.

DIGITALE TECHNOLOGIEN DER KONTROLLE – FALLSTUDIE ZUM VIRTUELLEN ÖFFENTLICHEN RAUM IN WEISSRUSSLAND

BARBARA STERK

EINLEITUNG

Ziel dieser Untersuchung ist die Ermittlung der Besonderheiten des virtuellen öffentlichen Raums in Weißrussland. Dazu sollen zunächst die theoretischen Grundlagen erläutert werden, um ein besseres Verständnis der (nicht-)räumlichen Natur der postmodernen Geographie zu schaffen. Dann werden in der Fallstudie eingehend das befreiende und kontrollierende Potential des Internets und die kulturellen Begriffe untersucht, die mit einem solchen Konzept verknüpft sind. Besonderes Interesses gilt der Funktionsweise des lokalen Segments des weißrussischen virtuellen öffentlichen Raums im Zeitalter der Globalisierung.

CYBERSPACE ALS POSTMODERNE GEOGRAPHIE

Einem häufig geäußerten technisch-kulturell utopischen Argument zufolge zieht die umfassende Verbreitung von Informations- und Kommunikationstechnologien den Triumph des nicht-physischen Cyberspace über den geographischen oder materiellen Raum nach sich. Demzufolge strukturiert nicht länger der Raum die Gesellschaft. Vielmehr wird das Individuum aus dem geographischen Raum in die globale, digitale Welt gerissen. Robin und Webster behaupten, dass in technisch-utopischen Diskursen der physische Raum (oder im weiteren Sinne: die Materialität) sowie die Entfernung negativ belegt zu sein scheinen, weil sie sich mehr auf die Moderne als auf die Spätmoderne beziehen. In diesen Debatten stößt man häufig auf die Beschränkungen der analogen Welt, die der neuen globalen Raumordnung entgegengesetzte Werte vorschlägt.

Mit einem Fokus auf die ökonomischen Auswirkungen der Entwicklung von Informations- und Kommunikationstechnologie gibt Cairncross ein hervorragendes Beispiel für das Werturteil in Bezug auf den Wandel der räumlichen Muster:

„Dass (Informations- und Kommunikations-)Technologien die Welt verändern werden, steht außer Frage. (...) Der Tod der Entfernung befreit uns aus dem Würgegriff der Geographie. (...) Schranken und Grenzen werden verschwinden. (...) Ergebnis dessen ist eine schnellere grenzübergreifende Verbreitung neuer Ideen. Arme Länder werden unmittelbar Zugriff auf Informationen haben, die einst den Industriestaaten vorbehalten waren und deren Grenzen, wenn überhaupt, nur langsam hinter sich ließen."[1]

Besser begründete Theorien gehen von einer Koexistenz von Cyberspace und postmoderner Geographie aus. Solche Argumente gelten sicherlich für den Einfluss der Informations- und Kommunikationstechnologie auf die sozioräumliche Ordnung, gleichzeitig versuchen sie aber, die sich in der Gesellschaft vollziehenden technisch-kulturellen Verschiebungen zu bagatellisieren. Stattdessen legen sie nahe, dass der globale Waren- und Informationsfluss, die „allgegenwärtigen" Kommunikationswerkzeuge wie Mobiltelefone, E-Mail und das Internet zu sich ausbreitenden „vermittelten Erfahrungen" führen, die das Konzept von Raum und Zeit begrifflich neu fassen.

Auf der Basis empirischer Daten aus neueren Untersuchungen im urbanen Raum schlägt Castells eine Differenzierung zwischen einer neuen räumlichen Ordnung vor, die er den „Space of Flows" nennt, und der klassischen räumlichen Erfahrung des „Space of Places".[2] Diese historische Teilung vollziehend, betont er, dass Gesellschaft und Raum nicht getrennt werden können, weil „ (...) räumliche Formen und Prozesse von der Dynamik der sozialen Gesamtstruktur geprägt werden".[3]

Appadurai verweist ferner darauf, dass sich im Zeitalter des desorganisierten Kapitalismus neue, einander überlagernde räumliche und immaterielle Ordnungen zu entwickeln scheinen.[4] Ihm zufolge

DIGITAL TECHNOLOGIES OF CONTROL – CASE STUDY ON THE BELARUSIAN VIRTUAL PUBLIC SPACE

BARBARA STERK

INTRODUCTION

The aim of this study is to map the peculiarities of the virtual public space in Belarus. First we will provide a theoretical framework to ensure a better understanding of the (a)spatial nature of post-modern geography. Then we will go into more detail in our case study on the liberating and controlling potential of the Internet and the cultural notions related to such a concept. We were particularly interested in how the local segment of Belarusian virtual public space operates in the age of globalisation.

CYBERSPACE AS POST-MODERN GEOGRAPHY

One frequently mentioned utopian techno-cultural argument is that the spreading of information and communication technologies results in the triumph of non-physical cyberspace over geographical or material space. According to this argument, society is no longer structured by space; individuals become disembedded from geographic space in the global digital world. Robin and Webster claim that in techno-utopian discourses physical space (or, broadly, materiality) and distance seem to have negative connotations, since they refer more to modernity than to late modernity. In these debates one often encounters the constraints of the analogue world, which suggests opposite values to the new global spatial order.

Concentrating on the economic impacts of ICT development, Cairncross provides a great example of value judgement in terms of the transformation of spatial patterns:

"That [information and communication] technologies will change the world is beyond a doubt. [...] The death of the distance loosens the grip of geography. [...] Barriers and borders will break down. [...] As a result, new ideas will spread faster, leaping borders. Poor countries will have immediate access to information that was once restricted to the industrial world and travelled only slowly, if at all, beyond it." (Cairncross 1997: 2–4)

More grounded theories claim that cyberspace and post-modern geography coexist. Such arguments certainly apply to the impact of ICT on the socio-spatial order, but at the same time they attempt to play down the techno-cultural shifts that take place in society. They claim rather that the global flow of goods and information, the 'omnipresent' communication tools like mobile telephones, e-mail and the Internet result in proliferated 'mediated experiences' which re-conceptualise the notion of time and space.

In presenting some empirical data from contemporary urban studies, for instance, Castells suggests differentiating between a new spatial order, which he calls the 'space of flows', and the classic spatial experience of the 'space of places' (Castells 1996). While creating this historical split, the author emphasises that society and space cannot be divided since 'spatial forms and processes are formed by the dynamics of the overall social structure' (Castells 1996: 441).

Appadurai also points out that some new overlapping spatial and immaterial orders seem to be emerging in the age of disorganised capitalism (Appadurai 1990). He finds five dimensions that differ from the previous social topologies. *Technoscape* is one of these five landscapes of the global flow, by which the author means a complex meta-level referring to the mobility of technology over geographical boundaries.

In pre-modern and modern society, physical space played a huge role in structuring the connection between individuals and information. The very first medium was the telegraph, which allowed messages to travel faster than the messenger (McLuhan: 1964). Later, electronic media further diminished the distance between different geographical loca-

existieren fünf Dimensionen, die sich von den früheren sozialen Topologien unterscheiden. Eine dieser fünf Landschaften des globalen Flusses nennt er *Technoscape*. Damit bezeichnet der Autor eine komplexe Meta-Ebene, die sich auf die Mobilität der Technologie über geographische Grenzen hinweg bezieht.

In der vormodernen und modernen Gesellschaft kam dem physischen Raum eine große Bedeutung bei der Strukturierung der Verbindung zwischen Individuen und Informationen zu. Das erste Medium, das es möglich machte, dass sich Informationen schneller als der Mensch bewegen, war der Telegraph.[5] Durch die elektronischen Medien verkürzten sich später die Entfernungen zwischen geographischen Standorten noch mehr. Nach Meyrowitz ähnelt der moderne Mensch in vielerlei Hinsicht den Nomaden der vormodernen Gesellschaft.[6] So haben beide in erster Linie keinen oder nur einen gering ausgeprägten „Ortssinn" (Sense of Place). Konsumenten von Medien, Internetnutzer und andere „Jäger der Neuzeit" haben unabhängig von ihrem jeweiligen Standort immer Zugriff auf die für sie bedeutsamen Informationen. Weder der Aufenthaltsort der Menschen noch der Herkunftsort der Informationen spielt noch eine große Rolle. Meyrowitz' Konzept aufgreifend lässt sich ergänzend argumentieren, dass es in der entterritorialisierten, postmodernen Geographie noch einige Inseln gibt, auf denen sowohl im Cyberspace als auch im physischen Raum noch ein starker „Ortssinn" herrscht.

FALLSTUDIE

Im Rahmen unserer Untersuchung sollte ermittelt werden, wie die Beschränkung des öffentlichen Raums unter den Bedingungen der Diktatur von den Bürgern Weißrusslands wahrgenommen wird. Hinsichtlich der Überwachung und anderer vom weißrussischen Diktator Alexander Lukashenko und seiner Regierung genutzten Methoden gibt es nur wenig Fakten und Datenmaterial. Deshalb interessierte uns, wie die Nutzer die Kontrolle des Cyberspace beurteilen.

Dazu wurden mit den Teilnehmern halbstrukturierte Tiefeninterviews durchgeführt, die durch die Beobachtung der Teilnehmer ergänzt wurden. Zur Verarbeitung der erfassten Daten wurden so genannte Cognitive Maps und Inhaltsanalysen verwendet.

Insgesamt wurden elf Tiefeninterviews durchgeführt. Die Befragten wurden unter weißrussischen Internetnutzern ausgewählt, die beruflich mit dem Internet zu tun haben. Die Rekrutierung erfolgte per E-Mail, über das Internet und mit Hilfe von Mundpropaganda. Vier der Befragten sind Journalisten, die für oppositionelle News-Portale oder unabhängig arbeiten. Einer ist Leiter der Öffentlichkeitsarbeit einer oppositionellen Bewegung, vier arbeiten als Leiter oder Manager privater Internetfirmen, einer ist Leiter eines staatlichen Internetcafés und einer Systemadministrator einer internationalen Nichtregierungsorganisation. Die Befragten nahmen ihre internetbezogene Tätigkeit zwischen 1996 und 2001 auf. Vor Beginn der Interviews wurde den Teilnehmern die anonyme Behandlung ihrer Angaben zugesichert.

Bevor die Ergebnisse der Untersuchung vorgestellt werden, soll der ökonomische und soziale Hintergrund der Entwicklung des Internet im Land etwas näher beleuchtet werden. 2004 nutzten 13 Prozent der Bevölkerung Weißrusslands das Internet, 5 Prozent regelmäßig jeden Monat. Einige Besonderheiten, die die gesamte Internetwirtschaft des Landes bestimmen, dürfen ebenfalls nicht außer Acht gelassen werden. In diesem Sektor tritt der Staat als Mittler zwischen einer zentral geleiteten und einer Marktwirtschaft auf. Die staatliche Telefongesellschaft Beltelecom verfügt über das landesweite Monopol bei der Bereitstellung des Internetzugangs. Alle anderen staatlichen und privaten Internetanbieter müssen Kanäle und Technik von Beltelecom mieten. Das heißt, dass die Informationen, die von Nutzern oder Anbietern weitergegeben werden, eigentlich über die von der Zentralregierung kontrollierte Telefongesellschaft laufen und deshalb überwacht und gefiltert werden können.

In vielen technisch-kulturellen Diskursen wird die Auffassung vertreten, das Internet sei ein befreiendes Medium.[7] Einige der grundlegenden Merkmale des Internets, darunter seine dezentrale Netzstruktur und die potentielle Anonymität, können eine kollektive und demokratische Teilhabe an einer neuen Art des öffentlichen Raums ermöglichen. Für die weißrussischen Massenmedien ist das Internet von zentraler Bedeutung, da Präsident Lukashenko versucht, alle anderen Medien in Weißrussland zu unterdrücken. Die Mehrzahl der Fernsehsender befindet sich in staatlicher Hand. In den letzten beiden Jahren wurden mehr als zwanzig unabhängige Zeitungen verboten. Neben der Teilnahme an Protestveranstaltungen in den Städten bietet das Internet für die Bürger die einzige Möglichkeit, ihrer Meinung im öffentlichen Raum Ausdruck zu geben.

tions. According to Meyrowitz, modern man in many ways resembles the nomads of pre-modern society (1985). Primarily, both have only little or no 'sense of place'. Media consumers, Internet users and other 'new age hunters' can get almost the same information wherever they are. Neither the location of people nor the original locality of the information plays an important role anymore. We would like to borrow Meyrowitz's notion and argue that de-territorialised, post-modern geography has some isolated islands where people still have a strong 'sense of place' both in cyberspace and physical space.

CASE STUDY

The main aim of our research was to map Belarusian people's notions of the dictatorship's restriction of the virtual public space. Relatively few facts and data exist concerning the surveillance and other methods used by the Belarusian dictator, Aleksandr Lukashenko, and his government. Thus we were interested in what kind of assumptions users have regarding the control of cyberspace.

The two methods we employed were semi-structured, in-depth interviews and participant observation. Cognitive maps and content analysis were used to process the collected data.

A total of 11 in-depth interviews were conducted. The respondents were chosen from among Belarusian users working in Internet-related fields. We found them by means of e-mail, the Internet and with the help of the snowball method. Four of the respondents are journalists working for opposition news portals or independently. One is a press secretary in an opposition movement, four work as directors or managers of private Internet companies, one is the manager of a state-owned Internet cafe and one is a system administrator for an international NGO. The respondents started working with the Internet between 1996 and 2001. Before the interviews were conducted, we assured the respondents that their names would not appear in the study.

Prior to presenting the findings of the research, we need to say something about the economic and social background to the Internet development of the country. In 2004, 13 per cent of the population used the Internet and 5 per cent of users did so regularly each month. Some peculiarities, which determine the country's entire Internet economy, also need to be mentioned. In this sector the state still mediates between a central and a market economy. The state-owned telecommu-

Es gibt jedoch Anzeichen dafür, dass die Regierung neben den anderen Medien auch den Cyberspace reguliert oder dies zumindest versucht.
Der bekannteste Fall von Informationsblockade datiert vom 9. September 2001, dem Tag der Präsidentschaftswahlen. Damals sperrte der größte Internetanbieter des Landes die wichtigsten Sites der Opposition, weil auf ihnen ungefilterte Informationen über die Wahl zu finden waren. Innerhalb von Weißrussland konnten diese Sites nicht mehr aufgerufen werden; sie waren lediglich vom Ausland aus erreichbar. Später entschuldigte sich die Beltelecom unter Verweis auf technische Probleme für diese Vorkommnisse. Dies war offensichtlich nicht der einzige Fall von Informationskontrolle oder Überwachung in Weißrussland. Staatliche Provider entfernen häufig „unsichere" Inhalte von oppositionellen oder privaten Websites. Andere Sites wurden durch so genannte DoS-Attacken[8] regelmäßig lahm gelegt. Infolgedessen hegt der erfahrene Internetnutzer in Weißrussland die Vermutung oder ist der festen Überzeugung, dass seine E-Mail-Korrespondenz überwacht wird.
In aller Welt werden unter Rückgriff auf moderne Informationssysteme Bürger vom Staat überwacht. Darüber hinaus nutzen Regierungen und Behörden des modernen Staates eine verstärkte Paranoia, die Foucault ein „unüberprüfbares Prinzip der Macht"[9] nennt. Die Überwachung des Cyberspace kann transparenter und diskreter als die Überwachung in der realen Welt erfolgen. Deshalb ließe sich argumentieren, dass die Ungewissheit der Überwachten, ob sie beobachtet werden oder nicht, inzwischen der Ungewissheit darüber gewichen ist, ob überhaupt eine Kontrolle stattfindet, weil es im Cyberspace schließlich keine Grenze zwischen dem Inneren und dem Äußeren des Panoptikums gibt.
Dieses Merkmal der elektronischen Überwachung wird in totalitären Regimes offensichtlich häufig ausgenutzt. Giddens, der die Arten von Überwachung und Gewalt in totalitären Systemen untersucht, behauptet, dass die Erfassung von Informationen und der Aktivitäten der Bürger unverzichtbare Elemente der „totalitären Regel"[10] sind. Für ihn sind „(...) in einem Zeitalter, das mehr und mehr von Methoden der elektronischen Speicherung, Erfassung und Verbreitung von Informationen durchdrungen ist, die für die Staatsmacht relevanten Möglichkeiten des Sammelns von Daten nahezu endlos".[11]
Die zunehmenden technischen Möglichkeiten der Überwachung scheinen, in der Terminologie von Lyon, ein „wachsendes Spektrum des Misstrauens"[12] nach sich zu ziehen. Deshalb sind sich die Menschen weniger sicher darüber, was hinsichtlich der Überwachung möglich ist und tatsächlich praktiziert wird. Auch die Weißrussen haben ihre Zweifel. Wir stießen in unseren Untersuchungen diesbezüglich auf unterschiedliche Denkmuster.
Im ersten Teil der Befragung wurden einige allgemeine Fragen zur Kontrolle des Internets gestellt, um den Befragten die Möglichkeit zu geben, ihre Meinung zu äußern, ohne in eine bestimmte Richtung gedrängt zu werden. Später wurden die Fragen dann zielgerichteter. So wurde beispielsweise gefragt, ob ihnen Fälle bekannt seien, in denen Sites blockiert oder E-Mails überwacht wurden.
Alle Befragten, die als Journalisten arbeiten oder in einer oppositionellen Bewegung aktiv sind, berichteten diesbezüglich von eigenen Erlebnissen. Ihre Schilderungen umfassen eigene Erfahrungen und Berichte von Freunden und Bekannten. Einige äußerten auch, dass ihre Website bereits blockiert worden war. Einer der Befragten schilderte, dass ihm vor Gericht E-Mails eines Bekannten vorgelegt wurden. Die folgende Schilderung stammt von einem Mann, der Demonstrationen und andere Veranstaltungen der Opposition organisiert:

> „Wenn wir per E-Mail korrespondierten, stellten wir fest, dass wir nicht die einzigen waren, die Zugang zu diesen Informationen hatten. Die meisten Aktionen [Demonstrationen der Opposition] werden geheim gehalten. Wir verwenden also bei ihrer Vorbereitung keine Telefone und keine E-Mails. Stattdessen treffen wir uns persönlich und mit anderen Aktivisten, um die relevanten Informationen über den Zeitpunkt einer Veranstaltung weiterzugeben. Dabei versuche ich, nach Möglichkeit auf mein Mobiltelefon und E-Mail zu verzichten."
> (Leiter der Öffentlichkeitsarbeit einer politischen Bewegung)

Für einige der Befragten war es offensichtlich wichtig, auf die Tatsache hinzuweisen, dass sie sich der Situation im Land völlig bewusst seien.
Aus den Anzeichen für eine Überwachung können die Befragten zwar nicht schließen, dass tatsächlich eine Überwachung stattfindet bzw. dies von der Regierung ausgeht; häufig wurde aber in den Gesprächen auf „zuverlässige Quellen" verwiesen. Einer der Befragten behauptete, er hätte Beweise dafür, dass eine Kontrolle des Inhalts im Internet stattfinde. Er „könne jedoch nicht mehr sagen".

nications company, Beltelecom, holds a monopoly in the provision of access for the whole country. All the other state-run and private Internet providers have to rent the channels and equipment from Beltelecom. This means that information passed on by users or providers is in effect transmitted by the telecommunications enterprise controlled by the central government and can, therefore, be monitored and restricted.

It is widely accepted in some techno-cultural discourses that the Internet is a liberating medium [see, for instance, Poster (1997) or Robins and Webster (1999)]. Some of the basic characteristics of the Internet, i.e. its decentralised network structure and potential anonymity, can facilitate collective and democratic participation in a new kind of public space. The Internet plays prominent role for the Belarusian mass media, since President Lukashenko attempts to suppress all the other media in Belarus. Most of the television channels are owned by the state. Over the past two years approximately 20 independent newspapers have been shut down. Apart from participating in protest actions in the cities, the only way to express dissent in the public space is by using the Internet. Nevertheless, there have been several instances suggesting that the government is trying to regulate cyberspace as well the other media spaces.

The most famous case of information being withheld occurred on the day of the presidential election on 9 September 2001. The country's main Internet provider blocked the main opposition sites in the country because they were providing real information about the election. This meant that no one could enter these websites from Belarus, only from abroad. Later Beltelecom apologized, referring to technical problems. Obviously, this was not the only case of information control or surveillance in Belarus. State-owned providers often remove 'unsafe' content from opposition or private websites. Other sites have been regularly disabled by so called DoS attacks 1. As a result, advanced Belarusian users appear to be either suspicious or certain that their e-mail is being tracked.

Contemporary information systems have been used widely by states to monitor citizens all over the world. In addition, government agencies of the modern state exploit an intensified paranoia, which Foucault calls an 'unverifiable principle of power' (1975). Since cyber-surveillance can be more transparent and discreet than tracking somebody in the real world, it is possible to argue that the uncertainty surrounding surveillers as to whether they are being watched or not has shifted into an uncertainty as to whether they are being controlled at all, since in cyberspace there is no border between the inside and the outside of the Panopticon.

It seems that this feature of electronic surveillance is greatly exploited in totalitarian regimes. Giddens, who investigates the modes of surveillance and violence in totalitarian systems, states that registering information and the activities of citizens are indispensable elements of 'totalitarian rule'(1985). For him, 'in an age more and more invaded by electronic modes of storage, collation and dissemination of information, the possibilities of accumulating information relevant to the practice of government are almost endless' (Giddens 1985:309).

The spreading technical facilities of surveillance appear to result in a 'broadening spectrum of suspicion', to use Lyon's term. Therefore people are less certain of what can be done and is done in terms of surveillance. Belarusians also have their doubts, and we came across different patterns of thinking in the course of the case study.

In the first part of the in-depth interviews we asked some general questions related to control of the Internet so that the interviewees could express their opinions without being nudged in any particular direction. Later we asked specific questions as to whether they had come across any instances of sites being blocked or e-mails monitored.

All the respondents who work as journalists or come from an opposition background mentioned some cases themselves. They told us about their personal experiences and related stories told to them by their acquaintances. A few of them mentioned that their web sites had been blocked. One respondent also said that his acquaintance's e-mails were presented to him at court. The following example comes from a man who organises opposition demonstrations and other events.

"When we exchanged information via e-mail, we noticed that we were not the only ones who had access to the information. Most of the actions (opposition demonstrations) are kept secret, so we don't use phones or mail when organising them. Instead, we meet personally and with other activists to pass on information about the date of the event. I try not to use my mobile or e-mail for these purposes."
(Press secretary of a political movement)

Andere, die als Betreiber von Internetfirmen ein vorrangig wirtschaftliches Interesse am Web haben, waren sich hinsichtlich der Kontrolle nicht sicher. Auf die Regulierung des Web durch die Regierung angesprochen, neigten sie eher dazu, auf das Monopol des Staates zu verweisen als eine Regulierung des Inhalts zu unterstellen. Einige erwähnten jedoch auch den Fall der Präsidentschaftswahlen als Beweis für Eingriffe seitens des Staates. Generell hielten die Befragten eine Überwachung von Daten für technisch machbar, waren jedoch der Überzeugung, dies sei in Weißrussland nicht der Fall. Die meisten Befragten konnten keine Fälle aus eigenem Erleben nennen.

„Bis jetzt sind mir noch keine derartigen Fälle bekannt, die auf politische Motive zurückzuführen wären. Wahrscheinlich sind als Ursache eher technische Probleme zu suchen."
(Manager einer Internetfirma)

Einige der Befragten legten Wert auf die Aussage, dass die Situation nicht so schlimm sei wie in China:

„Technisch ist es durchaus möglich, Informationen zu blockieren. In Internet-Cafés wurden auch schon Sites gesperrt. Sie galten als ungeeignet für die Öffentlichkeit. Aber mir sind keine politisch motivierten Entscheidungen, zum Beispiel das Sperren von Sites in Internetcafés aus politischen Gründen, bekannt. In dieser Hinsicht unterscheiden wir uns von China."
(Systemadministrator)

„Es gab Befürchtungen, das Internet könne in Weißrussland genau wie in China gefiltert werden. Unser Präsident hat jedoch keine Angst vor dem Internet, weil er weiß, dass es nur von wenigen genutzt wird. Seine Macht stützt sich auf Arbeiter und die Leute auf dem Land. In diesen Bevölkerungsgruppen ist die Nutzung des Internets nicht stark verbreitet."
(Manager eines Internetportals)

Obwohl alle Befragten in internetnahen Bereichen tätig waren, wusste keiner von ihnen genau, welcher Werkzeuge sich das Regime bedient, um den Versammlungsplatz des Cyberspace einzuengen. Deshalb mischen sich Fakten über die staatliche Regulierung und Überwachung im virtuellen öffentlichen Raum häufig mit eigenen Vermutungen und Auffassungen.

In der vorliegenden Studie wurde bereits darauf hingewiesen, dass es mehrere Segmente des virtuellen Versammlungsplatzes gibt, die fragmentiert und vom Hauptinformationsfluss isoliert sind. Es gibt Orte, an denen das universelle Prinzip der Konnektivität kein grundlegendes Merkmal von Kommunikationsnetzen ist, an denen das Internet keine dezentrale und weit verzweigte Form ist, sondern von der politischen Macht strukturiert wird. Ein solches Segment begegnet uns im weißrussischen Cyberspace. Zwar können auch hier die Vorteile des Internets genutzt werden, es gibt jedoch soziale, kulturelle, technische und sprachliche Lücken, die eine andere Nutzung des weißrussischen Cyberspace bedingen.
In einer weiteren Fragerunde verwiesen einige der Befragten auf eine Art „postsozialistischer Haltung" gegenüber neuen Technologien. Einer zitierte die Äußerung eines „berühmten russischen Dissidenten", nach dem es unmöglich sei, Internet und Sowjetmacht zu kombinieren, weil Sozialisten niemals in der Lage seien, die Möglichkeiten eines solchen Mediums zu verinnerlichen. Sie seien an Propaganda und populistische Inhalte gewöhnt, die aus der Vielzahl der Kommunikationskanäle in der Vergangenheit auf sie einströmten. Die vom Internet gebotenen Möglichkeiten unterschieden sich zu stark von den Medien, mit denen frühere Generationen aufwuchsen und sie sozialisiert wurden.
Interessant ist der Blick auf einen Auszug aus der Antwort, in dem es um die kulturelle Kluft zwischen Ost und West geht.

„1996 war ich in Deutschland. Ein Freund zeigte mir das Internet. Ich war beeindruckt. Aber mir erschien es wie ein neues Gerät von Sony für die Leute im Westen. Es ist nur natürlich, dass es zwischen der sowjetischen Kultur und der westlichen Kultur einen großen Unterschied gibt. So hat es beispielsweise zehn Jahre gedauert, bis auch hier der Walkman auftauchte. Das erste Mal habe ich ihn Mitte der 80er gesehen, in Weißrussland fand er erst 1993 oder 1994 Verbreitung. Das Internet bedeutete für mich ebenfalls ein Stück unerreichbaren westlichen Fortschritts."
(Freier Journalist)

Einer der Gründe für kulturelle Unterschiede sind häufig sprachliche Barrieren. Die meisten interessanten Knoten des Internets sind für jene, welche die Sprache dieser Brennpunkte nicht sprechen, kaum zugänglich. Die Lingua franca des Internet ist

Indeed, some of the respondents felt it was important to show that they are totally aware of what is going on in the country. Although they can hardly be sure whether a sign of surveillance really is surveillance or that this sign comes from the government, they often refer to 'reliable sources' in their conversations. One of them said he has proof of content control on the Internet but that 'he cannot say more'.

Others with an economic interest in the web as owners of Internet firms were not so sure about control. When we asked them about the government's regulation on the web, they tended to refer to the state's monopoly rather than content regulation. However, some of them mentioned the case of the presidential election as proof of state intervention. It was generally considered technically possible to track information, but the respondents did not think this would be the case in Belarus. Most of the respondents were not able to supply any personal experience.

"Up to now I haven't come across any such cases based on political motives. They were probably the result of some technological breakdown."
(Manager of an Internet company)

A few of them felt it important to emphasize that the situation is not as bad as in China.

"Technically it is possible to block information and there are sites that have been blocked in Internet cafés. These were considered inappropriate for public usage. But I don't know of any politically oriented decisions, for example the blocking of sites in Internet cafés for political reasons. We are different from China in this respect."
(System administrator)

"There have been some threats that the Internet can be filtered in Belarus just as it can in China. But our president isn't afraid of the Internet because he realises that his people don't use it. His base consists of workers and rural people and they don't make use of the Internet."
(Head of an Internet portal)

To conclude, although all my respondents have worked in Internet-related fields, none of them knew exactly what tools the regime might have used to restrict the agora of cyberspace. Thus, facts about the state's online regulation and surveillance in the virtual public space are often merged with their own assumptions and notions.

We argued above that there are several segments of the virtual agora that are fragmented and isolated from the main flow of information. There are places where the universal principle of connectivity is not a basic characteristic of communication networks, where the Internet does not constitute a decentralised rhizomatic form, but is rather structured by political power. We can find a segment of this kind in Belarusian cyberspace. Although the advantages of the Internet can also be utilised here, there are social, cultural, technical and linguistic gaps that modify the usage of Belarusian cyberspace.

In another set of questions, some of the respondents referred to a kind of 'post-socialist attitude' towards new technologies. One of them quoted a 'famous Russian dissident' who said it is impossible to combine the Internet and Soviet power, since socialist people will never be able to internalise the features of such a medium. They got used to propaganda and populist content, which was fed to them from the plethora of communication channels in the past. The possibilities provided by the Internet are too different from the media which socialised the previous generations.

It is interesting to take a look at one part of a response in which the interviewee talks about the cultural gap between East and West.

"I was in Germany in 1996 and a friend of mine showed me the Internet. It was very cool. But for me it was like a new Sony model for Western people. It's only natural that there should be big differences between Soviet culture and Western culture. For example, it took 10 years before walkmen appeared here. I first saw them in the mid-1980s but they only spread to Belarus in 1993 or 1994. The Internet also meant some kind of unavailable Western progress to me."
(Freelance journalist)

Cultural differences are often fed from linguistic sources, among others. For instance, most nodes of the Internet where things are happening are barely accessible to those who do not speak the language of such spots. The language of the Internet is English, which results in the partial elimination of those who do not live in the Western world.

For the older Belarusian generations English was not a compulsory subject in primary school. So

Englisch. Das schließt einen Teil derer, die nicht in der westlichen Welt leben, von vornherein aus. Für die älteren Generationen in Weißrussland war Englisch in der Grundschule kein Pflichtfach. Der weißrussische Cyberspace ist also nicht nur fragmentiert und wird vom Staat kontrolliert, sondern wird darüber hinaus vom Gebrauch des Russischen statt des Englischen bestimmt. Statt internationaler Websites besuchen die Nutzer häufig russische Seiten. Das Bild, das ihnen von der Welt vermittelt wird, ist deshalb von der russischen Kultur geprägt. Unter Verwendung eines Begriffs aus der Telematik würden wir sagen, dass der weißrussische Nutzer statt zum World Wide Web Zugang zu einem „Local Area Network" hat.

Ein weiterer Grund für die Bevorzugung russischer Sites zum Abrufen von Informationen und Unterhaltung besteht darin, dass nur wenig guter weißrussischer Content existiert. Dies lässt sich der Tatsache zuschreiben, dass es mangels Gewinnaussichten nicht lohnt, neuen Content zu entwickeln. Es gibt nur wenige weißrussische Online-Dienste. Wenn Nutzer nach interessanten Inhalten suchen, sind sie deshalb gezwungen, die Segmente des russischen oder in selteneren Fällen des englischsprachigen Cyberspace aufzusuchen.

An anderer Stelle wurden die Teilnehmer am Interview gefragt, ob ihnen Fälle von Online-Zensur bekannt seien. Sie wurden gebeten, ihnen bekannte Regulierungsmaßnahmen für Online-Content zu nennen. Acht der Befragten erwähnten den berühmten Fall der Präsidentschaftswahlen. Einige hatten lediglich später durch Bekannte davon erfahren, andere, vorrangig Betreiber von Internetseiten der Opposition, hatten die Informationen aus erster Hand:

„Ich werde Ihnen ein Beispiel nennen. Am Tag der Präsidentschaftswahlen von 2001 wurden alle unabhängigen Zeitungen mit Ausnahme von Charter 9713 blockiert. Charter 97 hatte im Vorfeld eine Verteidigungsstrategie entwickelt. Unsere Website war ebenfalls blockiert; wir konnten lediglich einen Link zu Charter 97 anbieten. Eine Woche später wurde unsere Website dann ganz eliminiert. Sie [die Regierung] löschte sie. Wir mussten sie daraufhin komplett neu aufbauen."
(Oppositioneller Journalist)

Da die Regierung versucht, die Redefreiheit im Cyberspace zu unterdrücken, kann das Internet von politischen Aktivisten nicht im gewünschten Maß eingesetzt werden. Um zu verhindern, dass ihre Websites von einem der nationalen Internet-Provider vom Netz genommen wird, hosten sie ihre Websites auf Webservern im Ausland.

Eine verbreitete Vorgehensweise der Kontrolle in totalitären Staaten ist die Überwachung des Privatlebens der Bürger. Im Zuge dessen sammelt man Informationen über die Organisation von Untergrundbewegungen und andere Formen des politischen Widerstands. Außerdem werden Bürger ohne speziellen Grund unter allgemeiner Kontrolle gehalten. Dies ist psychologisch motiviert und hat zum Ziel, dass sich die Menschen einer Selbstzensur unterziehen. Das Schnüffeln in Briefen und Anzapfen von Telefonen war früher mit einem gewissen Aufwand verbunden. Außerdem brauchte man die entsprechende Technik. Die Verfolgung von Daten im Cyberspace ist hingegen relativ einfach, gilt der Computer doch per se als ein Überwachungsapparat, weil das *Auslesen* von Daten aus dem Speicher das gleichzeitige *Schreiben* dieser Daten an einem anderen Ort bedingt.

Hinsichtlich der Überwachung des E-Mail-Verkehrs in Weißrussland herrschen unterschiedliche Auffassungen. Wie im vorigen Fall hatten einige der Befragten davon gehört und andere die Überwachung am eigenen Leib erfahren. Zwei der Befragten waren der Meinung, dass in Weißrussland keine politisch motivierte Überwachung des E-Mail-Verkehrs stattfindet. Jene, die ihre Auffassung auf persönliche Erlebnisse stützten, erwähnten Fälle, in denen sie Termine vereinbart hatten und feststellen mussten, dass andere ebenfalls Zugang zu diesen Informationen hatten. Es herrschte die einhellige Meinung, dass die Kontrolle von E-Mails technisch machbar sei, wenn auch nach Meinung einzelner nur unter Schwierigkeiten. In einem Fall ließen technisches Wissen, digitale urbane Legenden und subjektive Darstellungen eine interessante Geschichte entstehen:

Kennen Sie ein Beispiel für die Überwachung von E-Mails in Weißrussland?

„Wird das, was ich hier sage, an andere weitergegeben? Das macht mir Sorgen."

Nein, wie ich bereits am Anfang sagte, die Angaben werden anonym behandelt.

„Gut, in Weißrussland gibt es keine speziellen Geräte zum Filtern von Informationen aus dem In-

Belarusian cyberspace is not only fragmented and controlled by the state, but also defined by the use of Russian instead of English. Users often visit Russian websites instead of international ones. Therefore the picture of the world that is conveyed to them is determined by Russian culture. Employing a term from telematics terminology, we would argue that Belarusian users have access to a 'Local Area Network' rather than the World Wide Web.

Another reason for choosing Russian sites for information and entertainment is that Belarusian content appears to be very poor. This can be attributed to the fact that it is not profitable to develop and create new content because of the lack of profit. Belarusian online services are limited. Therefore when users try to find some fascinating content, they have to click on the segments of Russian or, more rarely, English cyberspace.

Elsewhere in the course of the interviews we wondered whether the interviewees had heard about some of the incidents of online censorship. When we asked them to tell us about any online content regulation they were aware of, eight of the respondents mentioned the famous case of the presidential election. Some of them had only heard about it later from acquaintances, while others who run oppositional portals experienced it at first hand:

"I will give you an example. On the day of the presidential election in 2001 all the independent newspapers were shut down except Charter 972 because Charter 97 had worked out a defence strategy. Our website was also blocked; we were only able to provide a link to Charter 97. A week later our website was eliminated. They (the government) erased it, so we had to renew our site."
(Opposition journalist)

Since the government tries to suppress freedom of speech in cyberspace, political activists cannot exploit the Internet as a tool as much as they would like to. So to prevent their websites from being shut down by a national Internet provider, they choose international web servers to store their websites instead.

One of the most widespread mechanisms of totalitarian control is the monitoring of people's private lives. The reason for this is to gather information about the organisation of secret movements and other forms of political resistance. It is also necessary to keep citizens under general control for no specific purpose. This serves the psychological purpose of discouraging people from thinking differently. In the past, tracking mail and tapping telephone conversations required extra effort and equipment on the part of surveillers. In contrast, tracking cyberspace data is relatively easy, since the computer can be regarded by its very nature as a piece of surveillance apparatus, since *reading out* the information from the memory means *writing* it somewhere else at the same time.

There are different attitudes to the monitoring of e-mails in Belarus. As with the previous case, some respondents had heard about it while a few had experienced it themselves. In addition, there were two interviewees who did not think that e-mails were tracked for political reasons. Those who referred to personal experiences mentioned cases in which they had made appointments and found out that others had access to the same information. All of them agreed that controlling electronic mails was technically feasible, although some emphasised that it was difficult to do so. There was one case in which technical knowledge, digital urban legend and subjective projections seemed to create an interesting mixture of narratives:

Do you know of any instance of e-mails having been monitored in Belarus?

"Will anybody find out what I say here? I'm worried about that."

No, as I told you at the beginning, no names will be mentioned.

"OK, in Belarus we have no special devices for filtering information from the Internet. So if somebody uses e-mail, I definitely know that it cannot be checked for technical reasons, because this hardware is very, very expensive. Russia has it, but we don't. It's an extremely complex hardware-software system that makes it possible to gather information packages."
(Head of an Internet portal)

The registration and archiving of information is a classic method of surveillance. Registration served as an important deterrent during socialist times and it continues to discourage Belarusian citizens from challenging the status quo. Now, analogue surveillance technology related to cyberspace is

ternet. Ich kann definitiv sagen, dass E-Mails aus technischen Gründen nicht geprüft werden. Die Hardware, die man dafür benötigt, ist extrem teuer. Russland hat sie, wir aber nicht. Es ist ein äußerst komplexes Hardware-Software-System, mit dem sich Informationspakete erfassen lassen."
(Manager eines Internetportals)

Die Registrierung und Archivierung von Informationen ist ebenfalls eine klassische Überwachungsmethode. In der Zeit des Sozialismus diente die Registrierung als wichtiges Abschreckungsmittel, und noch heute nimmt sie den Bürgern Weißrusslands den Mut, den Status quo in Frage zu stellen. Jetzt wird in Weißrussland im Zusammenhang mit dem Cyberspace analoge Überwachungstechnologie eingeführt. 2003 wurde ein Übergangsgesetz verabschiedet, nach dem Besucher in Internetcafés ihren Personalausweis vorweisen müssen, bevor sie die Computer nutzen dürfen. Die Personenangaben des Besuchers wie Name, Anschrift und Geburtsdatum sowie der Code des Computers und die Dauer der Internetnutzung werden von Hand in ein Registrierungsbuch eingetragen *(siehe Abb. S 473)*. Da auf allen Computern Protokolldateien angelegt werden, in denen die von den einzelnen Nutzern besuchten Adressen festgehalten werden, lässt sich ohne großen Aufwand prüfen, wer welche Sites besucht hat.
Unsere Befragten suchen nur selten Internetcafés auf, weil sie durch ihre Arbeit ständig Kontakt mit dem Internet haben. Weil uns aber ihre Meinung zu dieser Art der Registrierung interessierte, fragten wir sie trotzdem, welchen Zweck man damit verfolge. Einige bestritten, dass dieses Gesetz wirklich existiere und bezeichneten dessen Existenz als bloßes Gerücht. Vier der Befragten behaupteten, dass die Registrierung der Verhinderung von Computer-Kriminalität und des Konsums von Pornographie diene. Der Rest – hauptsächlich Mitarbeiter der oppositionellen Portale und Bewegungen – glaubt, dass die Erfassung der Personendaten vor der Nutzung des Internets politische Gründe hat. Zwei kurze Antworten spiegeln eine sehr kritische Sicht auf die Mechanismen der totalitären Macht wider:

Können Sie sich erklären, warum die Leute in Internetcafés ihre Namen angeben müssen?

„Das ist der Alltag in einer Diktatur. Die Menschen müssen vollständig kontrolliert werden. Aus diesem Grund wurde beispielsweise in der Sowjetunion versucht, die Kontrolle sogar auf das Denken der Menschen auszudehnen."
(Oppositioneller Journalist)

„Im Sozialismus geht es um Kontrolle. Und diese Ideologie scheint noch nicht überwunden zu sein."
(Systemadministrator)

SCHLUSSFOLGERUNG

In technisch-kulturellen Studien wird das Internet häufig als ein befreiendes Medium bezeichnet. Deshalb war es interessant zu erfahren, wie Menschen das Potential des Cyberspace in einer Diktatur bewerten. Hintergrund der Studie war die Frage, wie Fakten und individuelle Erfahrungen der Regulierung des virtuellen öffentlichen Raums miteinander in Verbindung stehen. Es wurde zwischen verschiedenen Konzepten der elektronischen Überwachung unterschieden. Die Befragten mit wirtschaftlichem Interesse am Internet schienen hinsichtlich der Online-Zensur optimistischer zu sein. Sie gaben eher der anfälligen Technik die Schuld, als hinter den Fällen von Überwachung politische Motive zu vermuten. Diejenigen, die als freie oder oppositionelle Journalisten tätig sind, berichteten hingegen von persönlichen Erlebnissen im Hinblick auf die Überwachung des Cyberspace. In einigen Fällen waren sie gezwungen, spezielle Strategien zur Abwehr der institutionalisierten Disziplinierungsmechanismen zu entwickeln. Zusammenfassend lässt sich sagen, dass die technischen und politischen Möglichkeiten der Kontrolle offenbar mit kulturellen Vorstellungen von der Überwachung des Cyberspace zusammenfließen. Diese Unsicherheit seitens der Betroffenen schafft eine gute Basis für den nicht verifizierbaren Charakter moderner Technologien der sozialen Kontrolle.
Ferner konnte festgestellt werden, dass es bestimmte kulturelle und sprachliche Dimensionen gibt, die die Nutzung des Internets in Weißrussland strukturieren. Geographische Entfernung und Ordnung spielen in der Kommunikation und der Ausgestaltung der Alltagspraxis nach wie vor eine große Rolle. Es zeigte sich, dass es im totalitären Regime Weißrusslands, in dem der Diktator und seine Regierung versuchen, den Cyberspace zu kontrollieren, hinsichtlich der technischen Vorrichtungen, Möglichkeiten und Grenzen der virtuellen Datensphäre durchaus einen „Ortssinn" (Sense

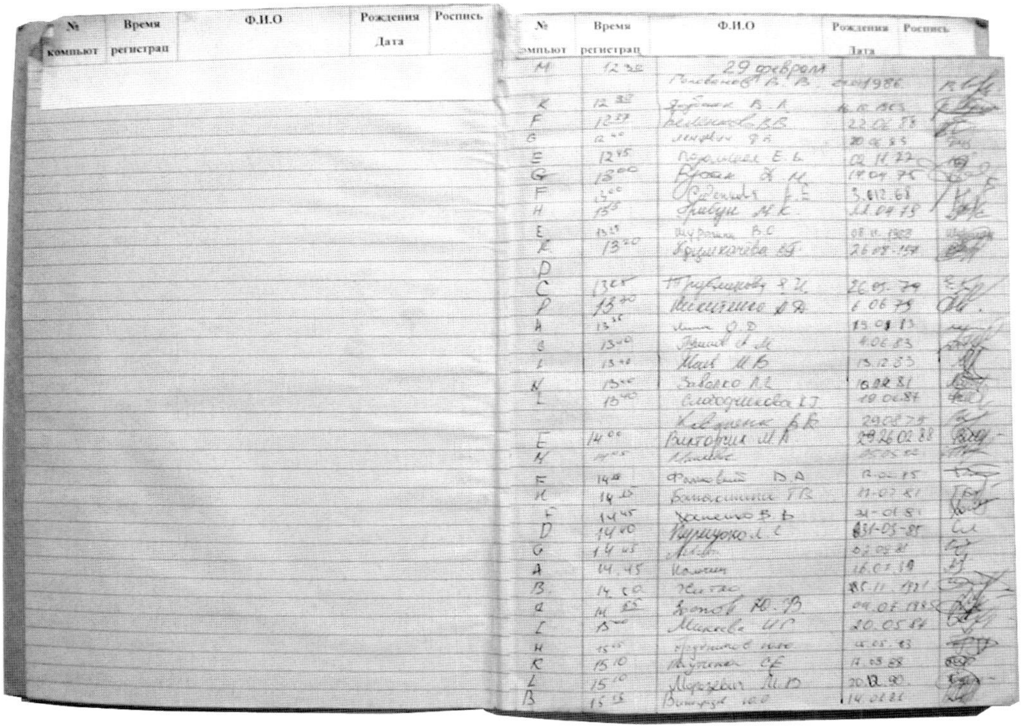

being introduced in Belarus. In 2003, a temporary law was passed requiring visitors to show their identity cards in Internet cafés before being allowed to use the equipment. The visitor's personal information, such as name, address and date of birth as well as the code of the computer and the duration of Internet usage, is written manually into a registration book *(see illustration below)*. Since all the computers save log files of all users and all addresses visited are stored in the system, it is not difficult to check who consults which sites.

Our interviewees rarely visit Internet cafes since their whole work is connected with the Internet. Nevertheless, since we were interested in their opinions on registration of this kind, we asked them what purposes it might serve. Some of them disputed that the legislation actually existed, saying it was no more than a rumour. Four of the respondents claimed that registration was directed against computer crime and pornography. The rest - mainly those from opposition portals and movements – believe that controlling people before they use the Internet is carried out for political reasons. Two short answers reflect a very critical view of the mechanisms of totalitarian power:

Do you have any idea why they ask for people's names in Internet cafes?

"This is how people live in a dictatorship. They have to be totally controlled. That is why in the Soviet Union, for example, they even tried to control people's thoughts."
(Opposition journalist)

"Socialism was about counting and control. And it seems they haven't overcome that ideology yet."
(System administrator)

CONCLUSION

Since the Internet is often referred to as a liberating medium in techno-cultural studies, it was interesting to see how people assess the potential offered by cyberspace in a dictatorship. We wondered how the facts and individual practices related to the regulation of virtual public space. We distinguished different approaches towards electronic surveillance. The interviewees with an economic interest in the Internet seemed to be more optimistic as regards online censorship. They were more likely to put the blame on technological breakdowns rather than as-

of Place) im Meyrowitz'schen Sinne gibt. Diese Studie sollte zeigen, dass die Entterritorialisierung nicht für die abgelegenen Schauplätze der Globalisierung wie Weißrussland gilt.

Ich möchte Maria Ananko, Angela Harutyunyan und Slava Filimonau für ihre Unterstützung danken.

ANMERKUNGEN

1 Cairncross, Frances: *The Death of Distance: How the Communications Revolution Will Change Our Lives.* Boston 1997, S. 2 ff.

2 Castells, Manuel: *The Information Age: Economy, Society and Culture.* Band 1, The Rise of the Network Society. Oxford 1996

3 Ebd., S. 441

4 Vgl. Appadurai, Arjun: „Disjuncture and Difference in the Global Cultural Economy". In: *Theory Culture & Society.* Heft 2–3, 1990, S. 290–306

5 Vgl. McLuhan, Marshall: *Understanding Media.* London 1964

6 Vgl. Meyrowitz, Joshua: „No Sense of Place: the Impact of Electronic Media on Social Behaviour" [1985]. In: Mackay, H./O'Sullivan, T. (Hg.): *The Media Reader: Continuity and Transformation.* London 1999, S. 99–120

7 Vgl. Poster, Mark: *The Second Media Age.* Cambridge 1995; Robins, Kevin/Webster, Frank: *Times of the Technoculture. From the Information Society to the Virtual Life.* London 1999

8 DoS-Attacke steht für Denial-of-Service-Attacke. Bei Angriffen dieser Art wird der Server durch Überschwemmung mit nutzlosem Datenverkehr, beispielsweise einer Unmenge von E-Mails, vorübergehend lahm gelegt.

9 Foucault, Michel: *Überwachen und Strafen. Die Geburt des Gefängnisses.* Frankfurt am Main 1976

10 Giddens, Anthony: *The Nation-state and Violence.* Cambridge 1985

11 Ebd., S. 309

12 Lyon, David: *The Electronic Eye. The Rise of Surveillance Society.* Cambridge 1994

13 „Charter 97" ist eine der wichtigsten oppositionellen Menschenrechtsbewegungen in Weißrussland.

sume there were political reasons behind the cases of surveillance. In contrast, those who work as independent or opposition journalists reported on personal experiences related to cyber-surveillance. In some cases, they were forced to develop individual strategies to counteract the institutionalised mechanisms of discipline. In a nutshell, the technical and political possibilities of control appear to merge with cultural notions of cyber-surveillance. This uncertainty on the part of the subjects provides a good base for the unverifiable nature of contemporary technologies of social control.
We also indicated that there are certain cultural and linguistic dimensions that restructure the use of the Internet in Belarus. Geographical distance and order are still crucial in communication and in shaping everyday practices. We discovered that in the Belarusian totalitarian regime, where the dictator and his government try to control the agora of cyberspace, people do have a 'sense of place' in terms of the facilities, possibilities and limits of the virtual data sphere. This study is intended to illustrate that de-territorialisation does not apply to the remote places of globalisation, such as Belarus.

I would like to thank Maria Ananko, Angela Harutyunyan and Slava Filimonau for the help they provided.

NOTES

1 DoS attack is short for denial-of-service attack. It can disable the server by flooding it with useless traffic, such as a huge amount of e-mails.

2 Charter 97 is one of the main opposition human rights movements in Belarus.

BIBLIOGRAPHY

Appadurai, A.(1990) Difference in the Global Cultural Economy. *Theory Culture & Society* 7 (2-3), pp. 290-306

Cairncross, F.(1997) The Death of Distance: *How the Communication Revolution will change our Lives.* Boston: Harvard Business School Press

Castells, M.(1996) *The Rise of the Network Society. Vol. 1 of The Information Age: Economy, Society and Culture.* Oxford: Blackwell

Foucault,M. (1975(1991)) *Discipline and Punish. The Birth of the Prison.* London: Penguin Books.

Giddens, A.(1985) *The Nation-state and Violence.* Cambridge: Polity Press.

Lyon, D.(1994) *The Electronic Eye. The Rise of Surveillance Society.* Cambridge: Polity Press.

McLuhan, M.(1964) *Understanding Media.* London: Routledge.

Meyrowitz, J.(1999) No Sense of Place: the Impact of Electronic Media on Social Behaviour. In H. Mackay and T. O'Sullivan (ed.) *The Media Reader: Continuity and Transformation.* London:Sage, pp. 99-120

Poster, M.(1995) *The Second Media Age.* Cambridge: Polity Press.

Robins, K. and Webster, F.(1999) *Times of the Technoculture. From the Information Society to the Virtual Life.* London: Routledge.

DANKSAGUNGEN
ACKNOWLEDGEMENTS

Wir möchten uns bei denen bedanken, die uns bei der inhaltlichen Vorbereitung und Durchführung des Programms unterstützt haben:
We would like to thank all the supporters for their contribution to the development and conduction of the program:

Julie Ault, Martin Beck, Wien/New York; Isolde Brade, Dmitrij Piterski, Leibniz-Institut für Länderkunde, Leipzig; Thomas Bohn, Universität Jena; Svetlana Boym, Harvard University; Hinnerk Dedecke + Thilo Fuchs, unit-berlin, Robert Edelman, San Diego; Luis Falcon, Iaac, Barcelona, Francesca Ferguson, urban drift, Berlin; Anselm Franke, Kunstwerke, Berlin; Bart Goldhoorn, Sergej Sitar, Alexej Muratow, PROJECT RUSSIA, Moscow; Arjan Harbers, Architekt, Zürich; Chris Hann, Max Planck Institute for Social Anthropology, Halle; Michael Heimann, groenland.basel.berlin; Hannes Hofbauer, Wien; Till Krause, Galerie für Landschaftskunst, Hamburg; Jo Krausse, Hochschule Anhalt, Dessau; Janina Kopietz-Unger, Instytut Zarzadzania Rozwojem; Christian Kühn, Technische Universität Wien; Neil Leach, Hochschule Anhalt, Dessau; Uwe Rada, tageszeitung, Berlin; Andreas Ruby, Köln/Ithaca; Patricia Ruppert, Geschäftsführung, Weißrussisches Haus, Karlsruhe; Bostjan Vuga, Sadar Vuga Arhitekti, Ljubljana; Axel John Wieder, pro qm, Berlin; Britta Wollenweber, Wostok, Berlin

Unser Dank gilt auch denjenigen, die uns bei unseren Recherchen vor Ort unterstützt haben:
We are also grateful for the supporters of our field research in the various locations:

Herr Retting, Wirtschafts- und Stadtentwicklung, Frankfurt/Oder; Michael Hess, Architect, Poznan; Zuzanna Ziomecka, Warschau; Anda Rottenberg, Warschau; Nicolei Kriwetsci, Head of Administration Zone, FEZ, Brest; Nataly Gurda, Administration FEZ, Brest; Liana Kholodar, Brest State University, Brest; Tatiana Kozik, Cross-Border Info Center, Brest; Alexel Anatolevich, Architect, Brest Town Planning; Keskevich, Chief Architect, Brest Town Planning; Anatoly Nichkasov, Vice-Minister of Architecture and Construction, Belarus; Alexander Chadovich, Chief Architect of the City of Minsk; Igor Dukhan, Chair of Arts, Belarusian State University, Minsk; Peter Stepanovich Peito, Brest Technical University, Brest; Alexander Kratowski, Michail Jewdomikow, Faculty of Geography, University of Smolensk; Pawel Pachomow, Chief Architect of the City of Smolensk; Liudmila Ivanovna, Smolensk; Oleg Kireev, Moskau; Jewgeni Lovchev, Moskau; Alexej Muratov, Sergej Sitar, Bart Goldhoorn, Project Russia, Moskau; Irina Bykhovskaya, Russian State Academy of Physical Culture, Moskau

Wir möchten uns auch bei denjenigen bedanken, welche die unterschiedlichen Ausstellungen ermöglicht haben:
We also express our appreciation to those who have enabled the exhibitions:

Jaroslav Suchan, Piotr Wozniakiewiecz, Ujazdowski Castle – Centre for Contemporary Art Warsaw; Serge Goldberg, Alan Gentil, arc en rêve centre d'architecture Bordeaux; Neil Leach, Architectural Biennial Beijing

AUTORENVERZEICHNIS
LIST OF AUTHORS

Regina Bittner ist Kulturwissenschaftlerin und Leiterin des Bauhaus Kollegs der Stiftung Bauhaus Dessau.
Regina Bittner is a cultural theoretician and senior advisor of the Bauhaus Kolleg, Bauhaus Dessau Foundation.
bittner@bauhaus-dessau.de

Martin Cagno ist Architekt und arbeitet in Barcelona.
Martin Cagno is an architect and works in Barcelona.
mcagno@bofill.com

Anne Deschka ist Theaterwissenschaftlerin und beteiligt sich zur Zeit an einem Aufbaustudium „Cultural & Literary Studies" an der Hong Kong University. Kollegiatin Bauhaus Kolleg V
Anne Deschka is a dramatic advisor and participates at the moment in the postgraduate program "Cultural and literary studies" at the Hong Kong University. Participant of the Bauhaus Kolleg V.
adeschka@yahoo.de

Jacek Gadecki ist Geograph in Krakau. Kollegiat des Bauhaus Kollegs V
Jacek Gadecki is a geographer based in Cracow. Participant of the Bauhaus Kolleg V
jacgadecki@wp.pl

Bart Goldhoorn ist Architekt und Gründer sowie Herausgeber des Architekturmagazins PROJEKT RUSSIA.
Bart Goldhoorn is an architect and founder as well as publisher of the architecture magazin PROJECT RUSSIA. prorus@xs4all.nl

Nina Gribat ist Architektin und Doktorandin an der Universität in Sheffield.
Nina Gribat is an architect and does her PhD at the University of Sheffield.
ninagribat@web.de

Wilfried Hackenbroich ist Architekt und Partner im Büro Hackenbroich Architekten, Berlin. Lehrt am Bauhaus Kolleg, Stiftung Bauhaus Dessau.
Wilfried Hackenbroich is an architect and Partner of Hackenbroich Architekten, Berlin. Adviser of the Bauhaus Kolleg, Bauhaus Dessau Foundation.
wilfried@hackenbroich.com

Angela Harutyunyan ist Kulturwissenschaftlerin und Kuratorin in Eriwan.
Angela Harutyunyan is an art historian based and Curatur in Yerivan.

Linda Hilfling Nielsen ist Filmemacherin und Architektin in Kopenhagen.
Linda Hilfling Nielsen is a filmmaker and architect in Copenhagen.
lindahilfling@yahoo.dk

Samuel G. R. Johnston ist Landschaftsarchitekt in Brisbane. In diesem Jahr macht er seinen Master in Landschaftsarchitektur an der Queensland University of Technology. Kollegiat des Bauhaus Kollegs V
Samuel G. R. Johnston is a practicing landscape architect in Brisbane. He is completing a Master in Landscape Architecture at the Queensland University of Technology. Participant of the Bauhaus Kolleg V.
SJohnston@splat.net.au

Bastian Lange ist Geograph, wissenschaftlicher Mitarbeiter am Leibniz-Institut für Regionalentwicklung und Strukturplanung in Erkner (Berlin), Doktorand an der JWG-Universität Frankfurt/Main sowie freier Wissenschaftlicher Mitarbeiter der Stiftung Bauhaus Dessau.
Bastian Lange is a geographer. He is a research fellow at the Leibniz-Institute for Regional Development and Structural Planning in Erkner (Berlin), PhD at the JWG-University at Frankfurt/Main as well as freelancer for the Bauhaus Dessau Foundation.
Bastian.Lange@Berlin.de

Alena V. Ledeneva ist Hochschullehrerin für Russische Politik und Gesellschaft an der Fakultät für Slawische und Osteuropa-Studien am University College London, UK. Sie ist gegenwärtig Senior Fellow am Davis Center für Russland- und Eurasien-Studien an der Harvard University.
Alena V. Ledeneva is a reader in Russian Politics and Society at the School of Slavonic and East European Studies, University College London, UK, and currently a senior fellow at the Davis Center for Russian and Eurasian Studies, Harvard University.
aledenev@fas.harvard.edu

Joanne Richardson ist Philosophin und Medien-Theoretikerin. Sie arbeitet als Projektkoordinatorin mit neuen Medienzentren in Ungarn, Kroatien und Rumänien und ist Gründerin der D Media Assoziation, Rumänien. Kollegiatin des Bauhaus Kollegs V
Joanne Richardson is a philosopher and media-theorist. She has worked as a project coordinator with new media centers in Hungary, Croatia and Romania and is the founder of the D Media Assoziation, Romania. Participant of the Bauhaus Kolleg V
subsol@mi2.hr

Tim Richardson ist Hochschullehrer für Stadt- und Regionalplanung an der Universität in Sheffield sowie Gastprofessor an der Fakultät für Planung an der Aalborg University, Dänemark.
Tim Richardson is a reader in Town and Regional Planning at the University of Sheffield, and visiting professor at the Department of Development and Planning at Aalborg University, Denmark. tim.richardson@sheffield.ac.uk

Teodor Shanin ist Soziologe und Professor an der Universität in Manchester sowie Rektor der Moscow School of Social and Economic Sciences.
Teodor Shanin is a sociologist and professor at the University in Manchester as well as rector of the Moscow School of Social and Economic Sciences.
teodor_shanin@mail.ru

Silke Steets ist Soziologin und Wissenschaftliche Mitarbeiterin am Institut für Soziologie der TU Darmstadt sowie Mitglied der Künstlergruppe niko.31, Leipzig.
Silke Steets is a sociologist and research fellow at the Institute for Sociology at the Technical University Darmstadt as well as a member of niko 31, a group of artists, based in Leipzig.
steets@niko31.org

Barbara Sterk ist Soziologin und Medienkünstlerin in Budapest. Zur Zeit nimmt sie am Masterstudiengang für Digitale Medien am Goldsmiths College in London teil. Kollegiatin Bauhaus Kolleg V
Barbara Sterk is a sociologist and media artist based in Budapest. She is recently attending the MA on Digital Media at the Goldsmiths College, London. Participant of Bauhaus Kolleg V.
barbara@ipsos-szonda.hu

Elena Trubina ist Philosophin und Kulturanthropologin. Sie lehrt an der Ural State Universität in Jekaterinburg, Russland.
Elena Trubina is a philosopher and cultural anthropologist. She is a professor at the Ural State University Ekaterinburg, Russia.
eletru@hotmail.com

Kai Vöckler ist freischaffender Künstler und Publizist in Berlin. Gründungsmitglied von Archis Interventions. Lehrt am Bauhaus Kolleg, Stiftung Bauhaus Dessau.

Kai Vöckler is a freelance artist and publicist based in Berlin. Founder member of Archis Interventions. Adviser at Bauhaus Kolleg, Bauhaus Dessau Foundation.
kai@voeckler.de

AUSSTELLUNGEN EXHIBITIONS

20.09. – 06.10.2004
„Avantgarde", Architectural Biennial Beijing

17.03. – 29.05.2005
„E-W / N-S 03", arc en rêve centre d'architecture, Bordeaux

17.08. – 02.10.2005
Centre for Contemporary Art, Ujazdowski Castle, Warsaw

WEBSEITEN WEBSITES

www.transitspaces.de
www.bauhaus-dessau.de

BILDNACHWEIS PHOTO CREDITS

A. V. Bokov/D. V. Bush/S. N. Chuklov/I. S. Babak/K. V. Canina/N. Yu. Nikifina (Architekten): 249
Anne Deschka/Akari Nishii: 163, 233, 235, 236, 237, 241
Leonardo Finotti: 41–48, 61, 83, 139, 162, 164–168, 185, 205, 250–259, 265–272, 335, 337, 339, 362–368, 353, 356, 358–359
Nina Gribat/Linda Hifling Nielsen: 91, 93, 95–96, 99–101
Kate Nelson: 253 l.
Joanne Richardson: 343, 345, 347
Silke Steets: 247, 253 r.
Barbara Sterk: 465, 473
Kai Vöckler: 161, 360–361, 354–355, 357, 395, 461